Japanese/Korean
Linguistics
Volume 16

Japanese/Korean Linguistics

Volume 13

edited by

Yukinori Takubo

Tomohide Kinuhata

Szymon Grzelak

Kayo Nagai

Published for the
Stanford Linguistics
Association by

CSLI
PUBLICATIONS
Center for the Study of
Language and Information
Stanford, California

Copyright © 2009
CSLI Publications
Center for the Study of Language and Information
Leland Stanford Junior University
Printed in the United States
13 12 11 10 09   1 2 3 4 5

Library of Congress Cataloging-in-Publication Data

Conference on Japanese/Korean Linguistics (1st : 1989 : University of Southern California)

    Japanese/Korean Linguistics / edited by Hajime Hoji.

    Volume 16 / edited by Yukinori Takubo, Tomohide Kinuhata, Szymon Grzelak and Kayo Nagai.

        p.   cm.

    Includes bibliographical references and index.

    ISBN-13: 978-1-57586-579-9
    ISBN-10:   1-57586-579-3
    ISBN-13: 978-1-57586-578-2 (pbk.)
    ISBN-10:   1-57586-578-5 (pbk.)

1. Japanese language—Congresses. 2. Korean language—Congresses.
3. Japanese language—Grammar, Comparative—Korean—Congresses.
4. Korean language—Grammar, Comparative—Japanese—Congresses.
5. Linguistics—Congresses. I. Hoji, Hajime. II. Stanford Linguistics Association.
III. Center for the Study of Language and Information (U.S.) IV. Title.
503.C6 1989
495.6–dc20
                                        90-2550
                                          CIP

    The acid-free paper used in this book meets the minimum requirements of the American National Standard for Information Sciences—Permanence of Paper for Printed Library Materials, ANSI Z39.48-1984.

    For a list of volumes in this series, along with a cumulative table of contents, please visit
        http://cslipublications.stanford.edu/site/JAKO.html

Contents

Acknowledgments

Part I

Guest Speakers

HIRC, QF and the Definiteness Effect   3
S.-Y. KURODA

On the Chinese Transcriptions of Northeastern Eurasian Languages:
Focusing on Imun [吏文] on the Korean Peninsula and Hanliwen
[漢吏文] in the Yuan Dynasty   25
KWANG CHUNG

Optional A-Scrambling   44
MAMORU SAITO

The Distribution of Subject Properties in Multiple Subject
Constructions   64
JAMES YOON

Part II

Historical Linguistics

Genesis of 'Exemplification' in Japanese   87
TOMOHIDE KINUHATA, MIHO IWATA, TADASHI EGUCHI, SATOSHI KINSUI

A Diachronic Account of the Speaker-Listener Honorific Marker -*sup*-
in Korean   102
CHONGWON PARK, SOOK-KYUNG LEE

Grammaticalization Pathways for Japonic Nominalizers: A View from
the Western Periphery   116
LEON A. SERAFIM, RUMIKO SHINZATO

Diachronic Changes in Korean *Wh*-constructions and
Their Implications for Synchronic Grammar   131
JEONG-ME YOON

Koto and Negative Scope Expansion in Old Japanese   146
JANICK WRONA

Part III

Phonology and Phonetics

The Acquisition of the Constraints on Mimetic Verbs in Japanese
and Korean   163
KIMI AKITA

Language-Specific Production and Perceptual Compensation in V-to-V
Coarticulatory Patterns: Evidence from Korean and Japanese   178
JEONG-IM HAN

Peculiar Accentuation of Prefixes in Pusan Korean
and Its Implications   193
HO-KYUNG JUN

A Phonetic Duration-based Analysis of Loan Adaptation in Korean
and Japanese   202
MIRA OH

Vowel Harmony as an Anti-Faithfulness Effect: Implication from
Nonconcatenative Morphology in Korean Ideophones   217
CHANG-BEOM PARK

Part IV

Discourse/Functional Linguistics

Prompting Japanese Children   235
MATTHEW BURDELSKI

Clause Chaining, Turn Projection and Marking of Participation:
Functions of *TE* in Turn Co-construction in Japanese
Conversation   250
YURIA HASHIMOTO

Roles of Gestures Pointing to the Addressee in Japanese Face-to-face
Interaction: Attaining Cohesion via Metonymy   265
MIKA ISHINO

Intersubjectification and Textual Functions of Japanese *Noda* and
Korean *Kes-ita*   279
JOUNGMIN KIM AND KAORU HORIE

The Asymmetry between the *Iki* (Go)-V and the *Ki* (Come)-V
Constructions   289
NORIKO MATSUMOTO

The Deployment of Korean Negative Interrogatives in Conversational
Discourse: A Sign-based Approach   304
JINI NOH

A Corpus-Based Look at Japanese Giving/Receiving Verbs *ageru*,
kureru, and *morau*   319
TSUYOSHI ONO AND ROSS KREKOSKI

How 'Things' (*mono*) Get Reanalyzed in Japanese Discourse   329
NINA AZUMI YOSHIDA

Part V

Syntax

Right Node Raising as PF Coordination Reduction   347
DUK-HO AN

The Causal *Wh*-phrase *Naze* in Japanese Cleft Constructions   362
TOMOKO KAWAMURA

Processing Left Peripheral NPI in Korean: At the Syntax/Phonology Interface   377
JIEUN KIAER AND RUTH KEMPSON

The Exempt Binding of Local Anaphors: An Empirical Study of the Korean Local Anaphor *Caki-casin*   392
JI-HYE KIM AND JAMES H. YOON

Three Types of Korean Comparatives   407
SO-YOUNG PARK

On the Syntax of External Possession in Korean   422
REIKO VERMEULEN

Shika-NPIs in Tokyo Japanese and the Syntax-Prosody Interface: Focus Intonation Prosody and Prosody-Scope Correspondence   437
HIDEAKI YAMASHITA

Part VI

Formal Semantics and Discourse Analysis

The Korean Double Past form -*essess* and Types of Discourse   455
EUNHEE LEE

Particles: Dynamics vs. Utility   466
ERIC MCCREADY

Perspective, Logophoricity, and Embedded Tense in Japanese   481
DAVID Y. OSHIMA

Tense and Modality in Japanese Causal Expressions   **496**
SANAE TAMURA

Index   **511**

Acknowledgements

This volume contains papers presented at the sixteenth Japanese/Korean Linguistics Conference held at Kyoto University, October 7-9, 2006. It was the first in the history of JK conferences to be held outside of the United States. 151 abstracts were submitted, out of which 32 were accepted, in addition to the four invited presentations. The two keynote lectures were delivered by Kwang Chung (Professor Emeritus, Korea University) and Shigeyuki Kuroda (Professor Emeritus, University of California, San Diego), and the other invited speakers were Mamoru Saito (Nanzan University) and James Yoon (University of Illinois, Urbana-Champaign).

All the submitted abstracts were reviewed by five or more reviewers. We are grateful to all the reviewers for generously offering their time to make the screening process fair and rigorous. Papers selected encompass a variety of areas such as phonetics, phonology, morphology, syntax, semantics, pragmatics, discourse analysis, historical linguistics, sociolinguistics, and psycholinguistics. Presenters came from all over North America, Korea, Japan and Europe. There were more than 130 participants.

The JK 16 was financially supported by the grant from Kyoto University Foundation. The Graduate School of Letters, Kyoto University generously let us use the facilities for the conference and the banquet. We are truly grateful for their support.

I would like to express my deepest gratitude to my co-organizers of the conference, Kayo Nagai, Tomohide Kinuhata, and Szymon Grzelak, for contributing to all aspects of conference organization. As co-editors of this volume, they also were instrumental in all the stages of the editorial process.

The student volunteers from the Department of Linguistics at Kyoto University also helped us greatly in the organization of the conference. Without their help, the conference could never have proceeded as smoothly as it did.

We would also like to extend our appreciation to Dikran Karagueuzian, the Editor of CSLI publications, and Lauri Kanerva, for their advice on and support of the editorial process.

Yukinori Takubo
Department of Linguistics
Graduate School of Letters
Kyoto University

Part I

Guest Speakers

HIRC, QF and the Definiteness Effect

S.-Y. KURODA
University of California, San Diego
International Institute for Advanced Studies, Kyoto

1. Background

The definiteness effect of the English *there* construction is well known.

(1) Definiteness effect. Post-copula DPs in *there* sentences are indefinite.

This generalization is illustrated by the contrast between a and b, and between c and d in (2):

(2)
  a. There are three apples that I bought at the market on the table.
  b. *There are the three apples that I bought at the market on the table
  c. There are lots of apples that I bought at the market on the table
  d. *There are most of/all the apples that I bought yesterday on the table

In the generalization stated in (1) the term 'indefinite' is used informally without any formal definition in mind. Let us define a technical term using this observation in background:

(3) Definition 1. Existential determiner (English)
     The determiners that can modify post copula DPs in *there* sentences are by definition EXISTENTIAL.

3

We have some examples of existential and non-existential determiners in English in (4) and (5):

(4) Existential determiners: *three, a lot of, some, many, no,*...
(5) Non-existential determiners: *the, the three, all, most,*....

Edward Keenan gave a formal characterization of existential determiners:

(6) Determiners are existential iff they are *intersective*. (Keenan 1987)

The definition of *intersective* is given as follows in (7):

(7) Definition 2. Intersective determiners
A determiner D is INTERSECTIVE iff $D(A)(P) = D(A \cap P)(E)$.

The formula in this definition means this: take A as a common noun like *student* and P as one place predicate like *be diligent*. Let D be the determiner *three*. Then, D(A) in the left hand side reads 'three students'; combine it with P *be diligent*, then, we read D(A)(P) as 'three students are diligent'. In the right hand side, $A \cap P$ stands for 'students who are diligent', and the symbol E is the predicate *exist* and stands for anything that exists. Thus, the right hand side reads 'three students who are diligent exist' or 'three diligent students exist'. Definition 2 then says that the determiner *three* is by definition intersective if and only if the equivalence (8) holds:

(8) Informal illustration of *intersective*:
a [Three (students)] are diligent $<=>$ [Three (diligent students)] exist
b. [Every (student)] is diligent $<\ne>$ [every (diligent student)] exists

Indeed, the equivalence (8) holds, hence *three* is an intersective determiner. In contrast, the determiner *every* is not intersective, since the corresponding equivalence does not hold as shown in (8). If the left hand side is true, the right hand side is also true, but even if the left hand side is not true, the right hand side is still true, thus the equivalence fails.

Keenan thus has given a formal account of the definiteness effect. Assertion (6) may be reformulated as follows:

(9) A *there* sentence is well-formed iff the post-copula DP has an intersective determiner.

About the definiteness effect, Keenan in fact obtained a much more general result than (9): a formal characterization of the type of noun phrases, simple as well as complex, that can occupy the post-copula position of the *there* construction. Assertion (9) concerns with simple DPs and is only a part, but the basic part, of Keenan's account of the definiteness effect. For our present purposes (9) suffices.

A mathematical theory of determiners, whose scope goes much beyond the definiteness issue, has been developed by Keenan in last 15 years or so. It has revealed much interesting formal properties of determiners in general and of intersective determiners in particular. What strikes me as remarkable of this theory is that not only does it provide empirically adequate accounts to generalizations obtained in natural language studies, but also it concerns a highly interesting and significant structure of its own right as an object of mathematics. I believe Keenan's work is one of the greatest achievements in formal linguistics in recent years. See Keenan (1987, 2002) among others.

It is significant that there is a grammatical effect in natural language, the definiteness effect, that relates grammar to mathematics: the *there* construction, so to speak, embodies a concept rooted in mathematics such as intersective determiner. But the definiteness effect, as we have introduced above, is defined in terms of the *there* construction, an English particular structure. Is this state of affairs to be understood as a peculiar feature of English, and perhaps of some other few languages where we can find a direct counterpart to the *there* construction? I would rather like to test the hypothesis that it is a common feature of natural languages, sanctioned by universal grammar, that they contain a construction which embodies intersective determiners, that is, which is licensed by intersective determiners.

And we might let ourselves drift in more fanciful imagination and suppose that human language has ways to have contacts with mathematical reality, as it does with mental and physical reality. Universal grammar might also be determined by how it interacts with this reality. We might hypothesize that along with A-P (Articulatory-Perceptual) and C-P (Conceptual-Intentional) Interface Conditions there could be another type of interface conditions, say, F-M (formal-mathematical) Interface Conditions, that mediate between language and mathematical reality. The definiteness effect in the usual sense defined in terms of English grammar must then be interpreted as an instance of an F-M interface condition that is actualized in English, and we might expect that a definiteness effect in a certain generalized sense be formulated in terms of universal grammar free of reference to constructions in some particular languages. Whether and/or how we can understand mathematical reality intelligibly would be, and would remain as, one of the most puzzling problems. Nonetheless, we might put the above thought in a form of a thesis:

(10) Thesis of mathematico-linguistic Platonism:
Human language interfaces with Mathematical Reality. A definiteness effect formulated in a certain generalized and universal form is an instance of a Formal-Mathematical Interface Condition in universal grammar.

This thesis could be interpreted as taking a position for linguistic Platonism, but it should not be meant as taking a simplistic form of realism according to which E-languages in Chomsky's sense are entitled to existence in Platonic reality.

Be that as it may, we must now set out to search for an English-independent definition of "existential sentences" where the "definiteness effect" holds in analogy to (9). But before doing so, let us first look back to English and introduce a couple of terms in preparation for our exploration outside English.

2. Sentence types in English

2.1. The plain sentence S

First of all, for now we restrict our consideration to sentences with a one-place (one-argument) predicate.

(11) PLAIN SENTENCE:

Let D be a determiner, A a common noun and P a one-place predicate; we call a sentence of the following form a plain sentence:

Syntax: $S = [[D \ A]_{DP} \ P]_{CP}$
Semantics: $<S> = [D(A)](P)$

(12) Examples of plain sentences:
   a.   Three students are diligent
   b.   Most students are diligent

2.2. The there transform ^{t}S

Next, let us agree to call sentences of the following form *there* transforms:

(13) *There* transforms:

Syntax: $^{t}S = [\text{there be } [D[A \ [\text{that } P]_{CP}] \ ]_{DP}]$
Semantics: $<^{t}S> = [D(A \cap P)](E)$

To relate *there* transforms to plain sentences, we have the following statement:

(14) A plain sentence S and its *there* transform ^{t}S are equivalent (^{t}S paraphrases S) if and only if D is intersective.

Indeed, if D is not intersective, a *there* transform is ungrammatical, according to assertion (9), hence the equivalence fails. On the other hand, if D is intersective, the plain sentence is equivalent to the corresponding *there* transform. These facts are exemplified by (15) and (16) below:

(15) most (of the) students are diligent $<\neq>$ *there are most (of the) students who are diligent

(16) three students are working <=> there are 3 students who are working
three students are available <=> there are three students available
three students are diligent <=> there are three students who are diligent
three students are tall <=> there are three students who are tall

Some of the sentences like those on the left hand side of <=> with individual level predicates may be judged awkward in English, but for the sake of space I ignore this aspect of complication and assume that they are grammatical without further comment.

Let us summarize: The initial definiteness effect, informally formulated, states that the D in the *there* transform defined in (13) must be indefinite, but Keenan asserts that *indefinite* can be replaced by a formally defined term *intersective*. Statement (14), then, says something very close to the original definiteness effect. However, it is, on the one hand, stronger than the definiteness effect: if D is intersective, (14) not only implies that the *there* transform is grammatical but also states that it is equivalent to the plain sentence. On the other hand, (14) is weaker than the definiteness effect in another respect, because it does not say that the *there* transform is ungrammatical if D is not intersective; it only states that the *there* transform cannot be equivalent to the plain sentence.

2.3. The existential transform ^S

Let us go back to the syntax of the *there* transform in (13); the existential predicate *(there) is/are* precedes the post-copula noun phrase. If we put the existential predicate after the noun phrase, we get sentence forms with the canonical word order without expletive *there* as exemplified below in (17):

(17) most (of the) diligent students are

(18) three students who are working are

These forms are hardly acceptable in English, but we could substitute *exist* for *are*. Then, we would get better acceptability:

(19) most (of the) diligent students exist

(20) three students who are working exist

Let us agree to call the sentence form illustrated by (17)-(20) the existential transform of S, with the notation ^S:

(21) EXISTENTIAL TRANSFORMS:
     Syntax: $^\wedge S = D(A \cap P)be/exist$
     Semantics: $<^\wedge S> = [D(A \cap P)](E)$

The semantics of the existential transform is the same as that of the *there* transform: $<^\wedge S> = <^t S>$. Hence, if D is intersective, by the definition of *intersective,* ^S paraphrases 'S, and hence it does S, too. On the other hand, if D is not intersective, 'S is not grammatical, and it is senseless to ask if ^S paraphrases 'S or not. But we can, and must ask if ^S paraphrases S or not; as a matter of fact, ^S does not paraphrase S: (19) does not imply (12). Thus, we can make the same statement for ^S as for 'S:

(22) The Plain Sentence S and its existential transform ^S are equivalent (^S paraphrases S) if and only if D is intersective.

3. In search of an English-independent definition of the definiteness effect

We are now in a position to leave English behind. First of all, let us agree that the concept *plain sentence* can be used beyond English intact. Now, we wish to extend the idea of the *definiteness effect* beyond English and we do this by turning statement (14) into a definition:

(23) Definition 3. The generalized definiteness effect
A construction with a one-place predicate has the DEFINITENESS EFFECT if it satisfies the following condition: it paraphrases the corresponding plain sentence if and only if the determiner D associated with the subject is intersective.

And on the basis of this definition, let us define *existential sentence*:

(24) Definition 4. Existential sentence
A sentence consisting of a determiner D, a common noun A and a one-place predicate P is EXISTENTIAL if it has the definiteness effect.

According to this definition, both the *there* transform and the existential transform are existential sentences in English. Note, however, that the above two definitions do not imply that an existential sentence is ungrammatical if D is not intersective, as is the case with the *there* transform.

4. Sentence types and determiners in Japanese

We are now going to examine Japanese sentences. But before doing so, let me make one disclaimer. Certain determiners are subject to partitive and non-partitive interpretations. For example, consider the following three sentence forms with the determiner *san-nin* 'three persons':

(25) a. san-nin no   gakusei ga   asoko de   hataraite-iru
       three-CLS GEN student NOM there at   working are
    b. gakusei ga san-nin   asoko de   hataraite-iru
    c. gakusei ga   asoko de san-nin hataraite-iru
       'three (of the) students are working there'

In (25) the determiner *san-nin* is inside a DP, while it floats in (25) and (25). In all of these forms this determiner can be interpreted either as a partitive or not a partitive, as the translations indicate, perhaps with different degrees of preference to one or the other interpretation. Whether we should take these sentences as ambiguous between these two readings or simply as vague about these readings is a moot question. For the sake of space, let us ignore this issue and agree to disregard partitive readings in the examples that follow.

4.1. The plain sentence

The definition of plain sentence is the same as before, which I repeat:

(26) PLAIN SENTENCE
    Syntax: $S = [[D\ A\ (ga)]_{DP}\ P]_{CP}$
    Semantics: $<S> = [D(A)](P)$

Examples follow.

(27) a. san-nin no   gakusei ga   kinben-da
      three-CLS GEN students NOM diligent-are
      'three (of the) students are diligent'
    b. hotondo no gakusei ga   kinben-da
      almost GEN student NOM diligent-are
      'most (of the) students are diligent'
    c. san-nin no   gakusei ga   hataraite-iru
      three-CLS GEN students NOM working-are
      'three (of the) students are working'
    d. hotondo no gakusei ga   hataraite-iru
      almost GEN student NOM working-are
      'most (of the) students are working'

Sentences with individual level predicates and indefinite subjects like (27) may sound awkward, but again for the sake of space, I ignore this issue here without further comment.

4.2. The Q-float plain sentence

In Japanese most determiners, in particular, numerals, can float. We have Q-float plain sentences:

(28) Q-FLOAT PLAIN SENTENCE
    Syntax: ${}^{f}S = [[A\text{-}ga]_{DP}\ [D\ P]]_{CP}$
    Semantics: $<{}^{f}S> = <S> = [(DA)](P)$

I assume without argument here that the "floating" determiner in a Q-float plain sentence is an adverb adjoined to the verb phrase. The semantics of the Q-float plain sentence is the same as that of the plain sentence. Q-float keeps meaning invariant.

(29) a. san-nin no gakusei ga kinben-da (= (27))
      <=> gakusei ga san-nin kinben-da
      'students are, three of them, all diligent'
b. hotondo no gakusei ga kinben-da (= (27))
      <=> gakusei ga hotondo kinbenda
      'students are, most of them, diligent'

We conclude:

(30) ^{f}S paraphrases S.

(31) The Q-float Plain Sentence does not have the definiteness effect.

4.3. The existential transform

4.3.1. The HE (head-external) existential transform $^\wedge$S

Now observe the following examples. Sentences that follow <=> or <≠> are the plain sentences corresponding to those that precede them and illustrate HE existential transforms. Inserting *koko ni/de* 'here' may help process these examples, but *here* must be understood as referring to the entire model/universe, not to a particular location in the model, one place 'here' as opposed to another place 'there'.

(32) a. san-nin no kinben-na gakusei ga (koko-ni) iru
      <=> san-nin no gakusei ga kinben da
  three-CLS GEN diligent-be student NOM (here-at) are
  'three students that are diligent are (here)'
      <=> three students are diligent
b hotondo no kinben-na gakusei(-tati) ga (koko-ni) iru
      <≠> hotondo no gakusei(-tati) ga kinben da
  almost GEN diligent-are student(PL) NOM (here-at) are
  'most of the diligent students are (here)'
      <≠> 'most of the students are diligent'

These examples illustrate the fact that the construction *....ga aru/iru* shows the definiteness effect, that is to say, if D is not intersective, $^\wedge$S does not paraphrase S; indeed, $^\wedge$S (may not be ill-formed but) is a tautology or contradiction, modulo existential presupposition, and may sound odd. If D is intersective, $^\wedge$S is well-formed and paraphrases S. Hence this construction is existential. We agree to call this construction the HEAD EXTERNAL (HE) EXISTENTIAL TRANSFORM: in the construction the subject of the main verb *aru/iru* is modified by the head external relative clause derived from the corresponding plain sentence:

(33) HE EXISTENTIAL TRANSFORM

Syntax: $^\wedge$S = [[D [[e][$^\wedge$P]$_{CP}$A]$_{D'}$]$_{DP}$ (ga) aru/iru]$_{CP}$, where [[e]$^\wedge$P]$_{CP}$ is a head-external relative clause, whose head is A and [e] is an empty subject coindexed with A.

Semantics: $<^\wedge$S$>$ = [D[[P]A]]]aru/iru = D(A $\cap$ P)(E)

The determiner D modifies the complex noun phrase, not just common noun A. It follows that the HE existential transform $^\wedge$S is equivalent to the plain sentence S iff D is intersective, since the condition D(A)(P) = D(A $\cap$ P)(E) is exactly the one that defines the intersective determiner. Thus, we have the following observation:

(34) The HE existential transform has the definiteness effect:

Put it another way, according to our definition of *existential sentence*:

(35) The HE existential transform is an existential sentence.

4.3.2. The HI (Head Internal) existential transform

Next, let us substitute head internal relative clauses for head external relative clauses in existential transforms. Again, the sentences that follow <=> are the plain sentences that correspond to those forms that precede them. In this case, existential transforms are equivalent to the corresponding plain sentences whether the determiners contained in them are intersective or not:

(36) a. san-nin no   gakusei ga   kinben-na no   ga   iru
three-CLS GEN students NOM diligent-are COMP NOM are
    <=> san-nin no gakusei ga kinben-da
'Three students that are diligent are/exist'
    <=> 'three students are diligent'

b. san-nin no   gakusei ga   hataraite-iru no   ga   iru
three-CLS GEN students NOM working-are COMP NOM are
    <=> san-nin no   gakusei ga hataraite-iru
'three students that are working are/exist'
    <=> 'three students are working'

c. hotondo no gakusei ga   hataraite-iru no   ga (koko-ni) iru
most   GEN student NOM working-are COMP NOM (here-at) are
    <=> hotondo no gakusei ga hataraite-iru
'most of the students, who are working, are/exist (here)'
    <=> 'most of the students are working'

Let us call the construction illustrated by these examples the HI (Head Internal) existential transform:

(37) HEAD INTERNAL EXISTENTIAL TRANSFORM
Syntax: $\oplus S = [[[DA]_{DP}P]_{CP}]_{DP}$ ga aru/iru,
where $[[[DA]_{DP}P]_{CP}]_{DP}$ is a head-internal relative clause with DA being its semantic head.
Semantics: $<\oplus S> = [[DA]_{DP}P]_{CP}$ & pro_e ga aru/iru,
where pro_e is an e-type pronoun coindexed with $[DA]_{DP}$.

Whether the determiner is intersective or not, the HI existential transform paraphrases the associated plain sentence; thus, it does not have the definiteness effect and is not an existential sentence. We have the following observation:

(38) The HI existential transform is not existential.

4.3.4. The HI (head internal) existential transform with a FQ
Let us now consider the following examples.

(39) a. gakusei ga   kinben-na no   ga   san-nin   iru
student NOM diligent-be COMP NOM three-CLS are
      <=> san-nin no gakusei ga kinben-da
'Students who are diligent are/exist three in number'
      <=> 'three students are diligent'
  b. gakusei ga   hataraite-iru no ga   san-nin   iru
students NOM work-are COMP NOM three-CLS are
      <=> san-nin no gakusei ga hataraite-iru
'students who are working are/exist three in number'
      <=> 'three students are working'
  c. gakusei ga   hataraite-iru no   ga   hotondo (koko-ni) iru
student NOM working-are COMP NOM most   (here)   are
      <≠> hotondo no gakusei ga hataraite-iru
'students who are working are/exist (here), most of them'
(= 'most of the students who are working are/exist (here)')
      <≠> 'most of the students are working'

These examples are similar to HI existential transforms in that the subjects are HIRCs, but the determiners are outside of HIRC and are adjoined to the matrix existential verb. At the first sight D might appear to float from (that is, be associated with) the embedded subject, but it does not. Instead, it is associated with the matrix subject, which is a HIRC. This difference is crucial; it means that D must be associated with the E-type pronoun pro in the semantics given above for the HI existential transform. Thus, we have the following syntax and semantics for the HI existential transform with a FQ:

(40) HEAD INTERNAL EXISTENTIAL TRANSFORM WITH a FQ

Syntax: $^f\oplus S = [[[A]_{DP}P]_{CP}]_{DP}$ ga D aru/iru,
where $[[A]_{DP}P]_{CP}]_{DP}$ is a HIRC with A its semantic head.

Semantics: $<^f\oplus S> = [[A]_{DP}P]_{CP}$ & $D(pro_e)(be)$,
where pro_e is an e-type pronoun coindexed with $[A]_{DP}$.

Note that the E-type pronoun pro_e here does not have the same denotation as A, but rather it denotes those A's that satisfy the condition defined by the HIRC. Take (39) above, for example. The semantics of this sentence would look like as follows:

(41) students are working and [most of them] are (here).

Here *them* is meant to refer, not to 'students' but 'those students who are working'. Hence meaning is not kept invariant unless the determiner is intersective. We can confirm this situation from the above examples and we have the following observation:

(42) $^f\oplus S$ has the definiteness effect.

(43) $^f\oplus S$ is an existential sentence.

5. Summary

Let us summarize the observations we had above.

(44) Sentence types (English):
Plain sentence: $S = [[D\ A]_{DP}\ P]_{CP}$
There transform: $^tS = [there\ be\ [D[A\ [that\ P]_{CP}]\ ]_{DP}]$
Existential transform: $^\wedge S = [[D[A\ [that\ P]_{CP}]]\ be/exist\ ]_{DP}]$

(45) Sentence types (Japanese):
Plain sentence: $S = [[D\ A\ (ga)]_{DP}\ P]_{CP}$
Q floatplain sentence: $^fS = [[A\text{-}ga]_{DP}\ [D\ P]_{CP}$
HE Existential transform: $^\wedge S = [[D\ [[e][^\wedge P]_{CP}A]_{D'}]_{DP}(ga)\ aru/iru]_{CP}$
HI Existential transform : $\oplus S = [[[DA]_{DP}P]_{CP}]_{DP}\ ga\ aru/iru$
HI Exstntl transform with a FQ: $^f\oplus S = [[[A]_{DP}P]_{CP}]_{DP}\ ga\ D\ aru/iru$

In the following tables (46) and (47) <=> and <≠> mean that the forms in the first column are equivalent to and not equivalent to S, respectively.

(46) The definiteness effect (English):

Determiner	Intersective	Non-intrsctv	Def Effect
S			
^tS	<=>	*	+DF
$^\wedge S$	<=>	<≠>	+DF

(47) The definiteness effect (Japanese):

Determiner S	Intersective	Non-intrsctv	Def Effect
^{f}S	$\Longleftrightarrow$	$\Longleftrightarrow$	- DF
$^\wedge$S	$\Longleftrightarrow$	$<\neq>$	+DF
$\oplus$S	$\Longleftrightarrow$	$\Longleftrightarrow$	-DF
$^f\oplus$S	$\Longleftrightarrow$	$<\neq>$	+DF

Let us conclude. To begin with, the HE existential transform exists both in English and in Japanese, with the definiteness effect. The English *there* transform is peculiar in that it has a stronger form of the definiteness effect. Not only is it the case that the *there* transform is equivalent to the plain sentence if and only if D is intersective, but also it is well-formed only if D is intersective. This is the original, stronger form of the definiteness effect.

English, on the other hand, lacks HIRC as well as a general form of quantifier float. HIRC keeps the function of determiners invariant, and hence yields an existential transform without the definiteness effect, i.e., $\oplus$S, in Japanese. I am here using the term "existential transform" for $\oplus$S, but this sentence is not "existential" in the sense I defined this term in (24).

Now, note the difference between the HI existential transform $\oplus$S and the HI existential transform with a QF, i.e., $^f\oplus$S. The latter form has the definiteness effect. This form is of a particular interest for us, since it leads us to the extension of the theory of determiners I am going to pursue in the next section. I withhold further comment on this form here. For now, let me continue by making a comment on the term *quantifier float*.

I employ here the term *quantifier float* as a descriptive term, informally referring to a phenomenon, not to any exactly defined grammatical process. A number of delicate issues are involved with this phenomenon: the distinction between partitive and non-partitive readings of determiners mentioned above at the beginning of section 4; the distinction between genuinely adverbial "floating" quantifiers and in some sense genuinely floating "floating" quantifiers. Besides, there is an issue of quantifiers that only look like "floating." A comprehensive treatment of the phenomenon of "quantifier float" is thus beyond the scope of this paper. However, although I have not worked out any detail, my feeling is that only intersective determiners should be taken as capable of being genuinely adverbial. If this hypothesis holds and if we agree to understand floating quantifiers in the definitions of all the constructions prefixed with a superscript *f* in the above table as genuinely adverbial, then $^f\oplus$S, and even ^{f}S, too, should turn out to have the definiteness effect in the *strong* form, i.e., they are *grammatical* if and only if D is intersective, just like the English *there* transform. We could claim, then, that it would bring Japanese to the same status as English with respect to the fact that the mathematical concept of *intersective* is embodied in sentence structures of natural language, by the *there* transform in English, and the constructions with "floating" *adverbial* quantifiers in Japanese.

But I have to leave these matters aside for now. We do not make any distinction among "floating" determiners as to whether they are in fact floating and originate in an argument position in some sense or genuinely adverbial. This supposition suffices for our claim that $^{f}\oplus S$ satisfies the definiteness effect in the generalized sense defined in (23). I would now like to proceed to another claim concerning HIRC, and demonstrate that it can contribute to providing empirical motivation for a significant generalization of Keenan's mathematical theory to a new direction.

6. Binary determiners (Determiners in 2-dimensional spaces)

I now wish to extend our study to sentences with transitive predicates. Observe the following examples in (48). (48) is a *plain* sentence S with a transitive verb, *oi-atumete-iru* 'to chase and gather, herd' with both the subject and the object accompanied by intersective determiners. A sentence with multiple determiners is in general subject to more than one interpretation, but in what follow we are interested only in the group reading. The choice of the predicate *oi-atumete-iru* 'herd' is thus deliberate; the semantics of the predicate excludes distributive readings. We also exclude possible partitive readings of indefinite determiners; *go-hiki no inu*, for example, is to be interpreted as 'five dogs,' excluding the possible reading 'five of the'.

Since the verb has two arguments, we can derive two HERC from S, with the subject and the object, respectively, as heads. So, we can construct two HE EXISTENTIAL TRANSFORMS, $^{\wedge 1}S$ and $^{\wedge 2}S$, as shown in (48) and (48c). (48) may sound somewhat, or maybe considerably, awkward, as two quantifiers in the plain sentence S are forced to float, but I would take it acceptable. (48) illustrates a structure impossible in English: $\oplus S$, a HI EXISTENTIAL TRANSFORM. Finally, we have (48), $^{f}\oplus S$ a HI EXISTENTIAL TRANSFORM WITH FLOATING QUANTIFIERS, an example instrumental to my argument below, where both determiners associated with the two arguments of the original plain sentence are floating outside the HIRC. Again, this sentence is unusual, but I would accept it and would take it grammatical. Note that the HIRCs in (48) and (48f) are both meant to have split heads, *go hiki no inu* and *sanzyu-too no usi*, as indicated by the translation given to (48) and (48f).

(48) a. S go-hiki no inu ga sanzyut-too no usi o oi-atumete-iru
    five-CLF GEM dog NOM 30-CLF GEN cow ACC chase-gather-are
    'five dogs are herding thirty cows'

b. $^{\wedge 1}$S sanzyut-too no usi o oi-atumete-iru   go-hiki no inu ga   iru
   30-CLF   GEN cow ACC chase-gather-are 5-CLF GEN dog NOM are
   'there are five dogs that are herding thirty cows'

c. $^{\wedge 2}$S go-hiki no inu ga   oi-atumete-iru] sanzyut-too no usi ga   iru
   5-CLF GEN dog NOM chase-gather-are 30-CLF GEN cow NOM are
   'there are thirty cows that five dogs are herding'

d. fS inu   ga   usi o   go-hiki ga sanzyut-too o   oi-atumete-iru
   dogs NOM cow ACC 5-CLF NOM thirty-CLF ACC chase-gather-are
   'dogs are herding cows, five and thirty in number, rspctvely'

e. ⊕S go-hiki no inu ga sanzyut-too no usi o oi-atumete-iru no ga iru
   5-CL GEN dog NM 30-CF GN cow AC chase-gather-are CMP NM are
   '5 dogs are herding thirty cows and they all exist'

f. ^{f}⊕S inu ga   usi o oi-atumete-iru no ga 5-hiki to sanzyut-too iru
   dog NM cow AC herding-are CMP NM 5-CLF and thirty-CLF be
   'dogs are herding cows, and there are, 5 and 30, respectively'

(49) below displays the same set of examples with non-intersective determiners, *daibubun* 'most' and *zenbu* 'all', substituting for intersective determiners *go-hiki* and *zyut-too*, respectively.

(49) Examples with non-intersective determiners:
a. S   daibubun no inu ga   zenbu no usi o   oi-atumete-iru
   most   GEN dog NOM all   GEN cow ACC herd-are
   'most of the dogs are herding all of the cows'

b. $^{\wedge 1}$S zenbu no usi o   oi-atumete-iru daibubun no inu ga   iru
   all   GEN cow ACC herd-are   most   GEN dog NOM are
   'most of the dogs that are herding all of the cows exist'

c. $^{\wedge 2}$S daibubun no inu ga   oi-atumete-iru zenbu no usi ga   iru
   most   GEN dog NOM herd-are   all   GEN cow NOM are
   'all the cows that most of the dogs are herding exist'

d. ^{f}S inu ga   usi o   daibubun ga zenbu o   oi-atumete-iru
   dog NOM cow ACC most   NOM all ACC herding-are
   'dogs, most of them, are herding cows, all of them'

e. ⊕S daibubun no inu ga   zenbu no usi o oi-atumete-iru no ga iru
   most   GEN dog NOM all GEN cow ACC herding-are CMP NOM are
   'most of the dogs are herding all of the cows and they both exist'

f. ^{f}⊕S inu ga   usi o   oi-atumete-iru no ga   daibubun to zenbu iru
   dog NOM cow ACC herding-are CMP NOM most   and all   are
   'dogs are herding cows and most of the dogs and all of the cows exist'

Let us extend the definition (23) of *definiteness effect* to these sentence constructions with transitive verbs as follows:

(50) Definition 3'. The generalized definiteness effect

A construction with a two-place predicate has the DEFINITENESS EFFECT if it satisfies the following condition: it paraphrases the corresponding plain sentence if and only if the determiners D associated with the subject and the object are both intersective.

Then, we get the following result concerning the definiteness effect.

(51) Summary. Japanese transitive sentence constructions 1:

D S	Intersective	Non-intersective	Definiteness Effect
fS	$<=>$	$<=>$	-DF
$^{\wedge 1}S$	$<=>$	$<\neq>$	+DF
$^{\wedge 2}S$	$<=>$	$<\neq>$	+DF
$\oplus S$	$<=>$	$<=>$	- DF
$^{f}\oplus S$	$<=>$	$<\neq>$	+DF

If we compare this result about the transitive constructions, (51), with the earlier result about the intransitive constructions, (47), we attained basically the same result, provided that we ignore the superscripted prefixes [1] and [2]. Thus, if we extend the definition (24) of *existential sentence* directly to transitive sentences at this point, we get two sets of existential sentences, and would get the impression that we are in the same situation as with the intransitive sentences, as shown in (52) below.

But it is yet premature for us to draw such a conclusion. With transitive sentences, we have two arguments as independent parameters. We can, and we must, substitute a non-intersective determiner for an intersective one for one argument, leaving the other determiner invariant, and try to see what effects we get. We obtain the set of sentences in (53) below by substituting a non-intersective determiner for an intersective one in subject position.

(52) Summary. Japanese transitive sentence constructions 2:

D S	Intersective	Non-intersective	Definiteness Effect
^{f}S	$<=>$	$<=>$	-DF
$^{\wedge 1}S$	$<=>$	$<\neq>$	+DF
$^{\wedge 2}S$	$<=>$	$<\neq>$	+DF
$\oplus S$	$<=>$	$<=>$	- DF
$^{f}\oplus S$	$<=>$	$<\neq>$	+DF

(53) Examples with partially intersective determiners:

a. S daibubun no inu ga sanzyut-too no usi o   oi-atumete-iru
     most   GEN dog NOM thirty-CLF GEN cow ACC herding-are
     'most of the dogs are herding thirty cows'

b. $^{\wedge^{1}}$S sanzyut-too no usi o   oi-atumete-iru daibubun no inu ga iru
     thirty-CLF GEN cow ACC herding-are   most GEN dog NOM are
     'most of the dogs that are herding thirty cows exist'

c. $^{\wedge^{2}}$S daibubun no inu ga oi-atumete-iru sanzyut-too no usi ga   iru
     most   GEN dog NOM herding-are thirty-CLF GEN cow NOM are
     'there are thirty cows that most of the dogs are herding'

d. ^{f}S inu ga   usi o   daibubun ga sanzyut-too o oi-atumete-iru
     dog NOM cow ACC most   NOM thirty-CLF ACC herding-are
     'dogs, most of them, are herding cows, thirty of them'

e. $\oplus$S daibubun no inu ga   30-too no usi o oi-atumete-iru no ga iru
     most   GEN dog NOM 30-CLF GEN cow ACC herd-are CMP NOM be
     'most of the dogs are herding thirty cows and they both exist'

f. $^{f}\oplus$S inu ga   usi o oi-atumete iru no ga daibubun to sanzyut-too iru
     dog NOM cow ACC herding-are CMP NOM most and thirty-CLF are
     'dogs are herding cows and most of the dogs and 30 of the cows
     exist'

With sentences like those in (53) we get the result summarized in the following table (54). The heading "intersective" at the second column means that both arguments are associated with intersective determiners; the heading at the third column "∂^{2}-intersective" means that the second argument, i.e., object position, is associated with an intersective determiner; An entry <=> in the third column means that an intersective determiner in object position entails that the sentence form in the first column of the same row is equivalent to, that is, paraphrases, the plain sentence form S; and an entry <≠> in the same column means that we have no such entailment. Notice that we have now no definiteness effect for $^{\wedge^{2}}$S.

(54) Summary. Japanese transitive sentence constructions 3:

D S	Intersective	∂^{2}-intersective	Definiteness Effect
$^{\wedge^{1}}$S	<=>	<≠>	+DF
$^{\wedge^{2}}$S	<=>	<=>	- DF
$\oplus$S	<=>	<=>	- DF
^{f}S	<=>	<=>	- DF
$^{f}\oplus$S	<=>	<≠>	+DF

By substituting a non-intersective determiner for an intersective one at object position, instead of subject position, we get a similar result, symmetric with respect to the permutation of superscripts [1] and [2]. Combining this predicted result with (54) above, we can now draw the following final conclusion for the transitive structure as below in table (58). We redefine the term EXISTENTIAL, its derivatives and DEFINITENESS EFFECT as follows:

(55) Definition 5. Existential sentence
   A construction built on a transitive predicate is EXISTENTIAL by definition in case it is equivalent to the plain sentence iff both determiners associated with the subject and object are intersective.

(56) Definition 6. Partial existential sentence
   A construction built on a transitive predicate is PARTIALLY EXISTENTIAL by definition in case it is equivalent to the plain sentence iff the determiner associated with one of its argument is intersective; more specifically, it is ∂^1 existential (∂^2 existential) if it is equivalent to the plain sentence in case its subject (object) has an intersective determiner.

(57) Definition 7: Definiteness effect
   A sentence construction with a transitive predicate has the DEFINITENESS EFFECT (and is EXISTENTIAL by definition) if it satisfies the following condition: it is equivalent to the corresponding plain sentence iff both determiners that are associated with the subject and the object are intersective.

(58) Japanese transitive sentence constructions 3

D	Intrsctv	∂^1-Intrsctv	∂^2-Intrsctv	non-Intrsctv	Existentiality
S	<=>	<=>	<=>	<=>	non-existential
$^{\wedge 1}$S	<=>	<=>	<≠>	<≠>	∂^1-existential
$^{\wedge 2}$S	<=>	<≠>	<=>	<≠>	∂^2-existential
$\oplus$S	<=>	<=>	<=>	<=>	non-existential
^{f}S	<=>	<=>	<=>	<=>	non-existential
$^f\oplus$S	<=>	<≠>	<≠>	<≠>	existential

According to (58), only the HI existential transform with FQs, $^f\oplus$S, has the definiteness effect and is existential:

(59) The HI existential transform with FQs, $^f\oplus$S, has the definiteness effect and by definition is existential.

7. An extension of Keenan's mathematical theory of determiners to higher dimensions

To conclude this paper, I would like to discuss very briefly how our findings about Japanese determiners relate to Keenan's mathematical theory of determiners.

In Keenan's theory, a determiner is a function that maps common nouns to functions from the set of one-place predicates to the truth values {0, 1}:

(60)   D: A → (P → {0,1}) (i.e., an entity of type <<e, t>, <<e, t>, t>>)

I already mentioned that Keenan characterizes existential determiners as intersective, where an INTERSECTIVE DETERMINER is defined by the following condition:

(61)   D(A)(P) = D(A∩P)(E).

Now, the attentive reader will have noticed that I am inconsistent in the way I have represented the semantics of sentence constructions with a one place predicate in section 4 above. For S, ^{f}S, ^S and $^{f∧}$S, their semantics are given according to Keenan's theory, but not for the HI existential transform without and with a FQ (i.e., ⊕S and ^{f}⊕S), for a good reason: the semantics of these forms does not conform to the form of a function mapping D to a function mapping predicates P to truth values:

(62)   D(A): P → {0,1}.

For example, take (36)b, which I repeat:

(63)   san-nin no gakusei ga hataraite-iru no ga iru (= (36)b)
        'three students that are working are/exist'

Here, the main predicate is *iru* 'exist', but it is not clear how the determiner *san-nin* relates to the main predicate *exist*. And I am not claiming that we should, or we can, put the meaning of this sentence in a form that conforms to Keenan's theory. However, I would like to claim that if we float the determiner out of the HI relative clause and get the HI existential transform with a FQ (i.e., ^{f}⊕S), then we can interpret its semantics in terms of Keenan's theory. Let us take (39), which I also repeat here:

(64)   gakusei ga hataraite-iru no ga san-nin iru   (= (39))
        'students who are working are/exist three in number'
Let us engage ourselves in maneuvering the formalism of this expression. We may take the determiner *san-nin* 'three-CLF' as a VP adverbial adjoined to the main verb *iru*. Let us move this adverbial to the left:

(65)   (san-nin)(gakusei ga hataraite-iru no)(iru)

Now, we have a form that looks closer to D(X)(E), where D = *san-nin* and E = *iru*. In order to interpret (65) in terms of the form D(X)(P), we must take *gakusei ga hataraite-iru no* as a representation of an argument. This HIRC has the same denotation as the noun phrase with a HERC *hataraite-iru gakusei*. Hence, *gakusei ga hataraite-iru no* taken as a representation of an argument can be coded in the same way as we code *hataraite-iru ga-kusei,* i.e., X = A ∩ P, where A = *gakusei* and P = *hataraite-iru.* We can conclude, then, that the HI existential transform with a FQ (64) has the same representation as the corresponding HI existential transform:

(66)   san-nin no hataraite-iru gakusei ga iru,

namely,

(67) $D(A \cap P)(E)$.

After this preparation, we are now in a position to shift our attention back to the transitive case. Take a pair of determiners D = (D_1, D_2), a pair of common nouns A = (A_1, A_2) and a two-place predicate P, and consider the transitive sentence S = $P(D_1A_1, D_2A_2)$, where D_1A_1 and D_2A_2 are the two arguments of P with the group reading given to the pair (D_1, D_2). D can be taken as a function that maps pairs of common nouns A = (A_1, A_2) to functions that map two place predicates P to truth values:

(68) $D: A \rightarrow (P \rightarrow \{0,1\})$.

We can represent the semantics of S exactly in the same form as that given to the one-place plain sentence:

(69) $D(A)(P) = (D_1, D_2) (A_1, A_2)(P)$.

For example, we can represent (48) as in (70):

(70) $D(A)(P) = (5, 30)(inu, usi)(oi\text{-}atumete\text{-}iru)$.

Let us now look at the HI existential transform with a transitive predicate. Consider (48), which I repeat:

(71)   inu ga usi o oi-atumete-iru no ga 5-hiki to 30-too iru. (= (48))
        'dogs are herding cows, and they exist, 5 and 30 in number'

Let us move the determiners to the left as we did in (65):

(72)   (5-hiki to 30-too)(inu ga usi o oi-atumete-iru no ga)(iru)

We have a binary determiner *(5, 30)*, a two dimensional argument *inu ga usi o oi-atumete-iru no* and the existential predicate *iru*. But what is this argument *inu ga usi o oi-atumete-iru no*? We must consider a two-dimensional argument, but not a simple pair $(A_1, A_2) = (dog, cow)$ of dogs and cows without restriction, but the pair of those dogs and those cows that satisfy the relation P = *X herds Y*. In order to get the set of pairs of A_1 *dog* and A_2 *cow* that satisfy this relation, first, take the intersection $(A_1 \times A_2) \cap P$; we get those dogs and those cows that satisfy this condition by projecting this intersection onto the first and the second axes, respectively. We get (73) as a representation of a two-dimensional argument:

(73) $(prj_1[(A_1 \times A_2) \cap P], prj_2[(A_1 \times A_2) \cap P])$.

Thus, the semantics of $^f \oplus S$ can be given as follows:

(74) $<^f \oplus S> = (D_1, D_2)(prj_1[(A_1 \times A_2) \cap P], prj_2[(A_1 \times A_2) \cap P])(E)$.

Now, define the INTERSECTION Int of a binary argument $A = (A_1, A_2)$ and a two-place predicate P as in (75) below, and extend the concept of *intersective determiner* to 2-dimensional spaces as in (76).

(75) Definition 9. A Int P = $((prj_1[(A_1 \times A_2) \cap P], prj_2[(A_1 \times A_2) \cap P])$.

(76) Definition 10. Intersective binary determiner
A binary D is INTERSECTIVE iff it satisfies the following condition:
D(A)(P) = D(A Int P)(E).

From these definitions follows the proposition (77) and a corollary (78):

(77) If D_1 and D_2 are both intersective determiners, then the binary determiner $D = (D_1, D_2)$ is intersective.

(78) If a construction with a binary determiner D shows the definiteness effect, as defined in (57), D is intersective.

To prove (77), first of all, let us recall that a two-dimensional determiner $D = (D_1, D_2)$ is given a group reading. Hence we have the following equivalences:

D(A)(P) = (D_1, D_2) $(A_1, A_2)(P) = 1$
   $\iff D_1(A_1)(prj_1[(A_1 \times A_2) \cap P]) = 1$ and $D_2(A_2)(prj_2[(A_1 \times A_2) \cap P]) = 1$;
D(A Int P)(E) = 1
   $\iff D_1(prj_1[(A_1 \times A_2) \cap P])(prj_1[prj_1[(A_1 \times A_2) \cap P] \times prj_2[(A_1 \times A_2) \cap P]] \cap E)$
      $= D_1(prj_1[(A_1 \times A_2) \cap P])(prj_1[(A_1 \times A_2) \cap P]) = 1$ and
   $D_2(prj_2[(A_1 \times A_2) \cap P])(prj_2[prj_1[(A_1 \times A_2) \cap P] \times prj_2[(A_1 \times A_2) \cap P]] \cap E)$
      $= D_2(prj_2[(A_1 \times A_2) \cap P])(prj_2[(A_1 \times A_2) \cap P]) = 1$.
Now, if D_1 is intersective, we have

$D_1(A_1)(prj_1[(A_1 \times A_2) \cap P]) = D_1(A_1 \cap prj_1[(A_1 \times A_2) \cap P])(E)$
   $= D_1(prj_1[(A_1 \times A_2) \cap P])(E)$;
$D_1(prj_1[(A_1 \times A_2) \cap P])(prj_1[(A_1 \times A_2) \cap P])$
   $= D_1(prj_1[(A_1 \times A_2) \cap P] \cap prj_1[(A_1 \times A_2) \cap P])(E)$
   $= D_1(prj_1[(A_1 \times A_2) \cap P])(E)$.

Similarly, if D_2 is intersective, we have

$D_2(A_1)(prj_2[(A_1 \times A_2) \cap P]) = D_2(prj_2[(A_1 \times A_2) \cap P])(E)$

$$D_2(prj_2[(A_1 \times A_2) \cap P])(prj_2[(A_1 \times A_2) \cap P])$$
$$= D_2(prj_2[(A_1 \times A_2) \cap P])(E).$$

Hence, if D_1 and D_2 are both intersective, $D(A)(P) = D(A \text{ Int } P)(E)$, that is, $D = (D_1, D_2)$ is intersective. Q.E.D.

8. Summary and Conclusion

I have redefined the DEFINITENESS EFFECT and correlatively the EXISTENTIAL SENTENCE in terms of equivalence to the PLAIN SENTENCE form. I have drawn the conclusion that Japanese grammar exhibits the definiteness effect in a construction based on HIRC and Quantifier Float, two grammatical processes characteristic of Japanese syntax, the construction I have called the HI EXISTENTIAL TRANSFORM WITH a FQ. Furthermore, I have shown that this conception concerning the definiteness effect and existential sentences can be extended to transitive sentence structures and would serve as an empirical basis and motivation for extending Keenan's mathematical theory of determiners to two-dimensional spaces.

In the above determiners for two-dimensional spaces are restricted to binary determiners defined as pairs of determiners in the usual sense interpreted by group reading. But we can define a general concept of determiner for binary arguments directly by the formula (68), and extend the concept of intersective determiner defined by (76) to apply to it. Furthermore, once extended to two-dimensional spaces, Keenan's theory can be generalized to n-dimensional spaces. In the general n-dimensional theory, relevant mathematical concepts defined in the original theory can sometimes be extended or reformulated in more than one way. For example, the concept of INTERSECTIVE defined in (76) is only one of a number of possible natural generalizations of the original definition to the n-dimensional case; the one defined here concerns the group reading of multiply quantified sentences. The concept of a partially intersective determiner can also be generalized to n-dimensional spaces, and it is shown that the concept of a conservative determiner, which is believed to characterize determiners in natural language (Barwise and Cooper 1981), can be interpreted as a limit case of partially intersective determiners. For further details, I have to refer the reader to Kuroda (2008). In this paper, for the sake of space, I also had to limit myself to a minimal amount of data and empirical arguments for the claims made above for Japanese.

References

Barwise, J. and R. Cooper. 1981. Generalized quantifiers and natural language. *Linguistics & Philosophy* 4: 159-219.

Keenan, E. L. 1981. A boolean approach to semantics. *Formal Methods in the Study of Language*, eds. J. Groenendijk, T. Janssen and M. Stokhof, 343-379. Amsterdam: Mathematisch Centrum.

Keenan, E. L. 1987. A semantic definition of "indefinite NP". *The representation of (in)definiteness*, eds. E. Reuland and A. ter Meulen Cambridge, 286-319. Mass: MIT Press.

Keenan, E. L. 2002. Some properties of natural language quantifiers. *Linguistics and Philosophy* 25: 627–654.

Kuroda, S.-Y. 2004. Intersective determiners. ms.

Kuroda, S.-Y. 2008. HIRC, QF and the mathematics of determiners. San Diego Linguistics Papers, Issue. 3.

On the Chinese Transcriptions of Northeastern Eurasian Languages: Focusing on Imun [吏文] on the Korean Peninsula and Hanliwen [漢吏文] in the Yuan Dynasty

KWANG CHUNG
Catholic University of Korea

1. Introduction

Many civilizations in Northeastern Eurasia, especially those neighboring China, have lived under the influence of Chinese culture and further accommodated it for several thousand years. These civilizations suffered from continuous Chinese invasions and the subsequent enormous inflow of Chinese culture that took place. Even though sometimes these civilizations actually conquered China and assumed political control, their own cultures were assimilated to or absorbed into the powerful Chinese culture. [1] The Korean Peninsula, which is located in the eastern part of Eurasia and neighbors China, was in this exact situation.

China is a country occupying a huge territory in eastern Eurasia. Although this area was the habitat of many different civilizations, China built a unified country on this territory a long time ago and formed its peculiar mixture of culture by accommodating the cultures of the other civilizations and blending them with its own. China innovated its own culture by this process of accom-

---

[1] For example, after conquering China, the Mongolians founded the Yuan [元] dynasty and the Manchurians founded the Ch'ing [清] dynasty. In both instances, they governed China for a long period and enforced their own culture on the Chinese, but the Chinese culture absorbed only some parts of their culture and the traditional Chinese culture remained intact. However, the Mongolian and Manchurian cultures assimilated into the Chinese culture, and furthermore, in the case of the latter, they assimilated into the Chinese culture even in their mother land.

modation, and as a result, the Chinese culture of the ancient period became globalized. Thus, in the eastern part of Eurasia, Chinese culture surpassed other cultures in the ancient period.

The influence of Chinese culture compelled other civilizations to borrow and use the Chinese writing system called 漢字, Chinese characters, to transcribe their own languages. These characters are ideograms and were developed to transcribe Chinese, which is an isolating language. The use of Chinese characters did not cause any problem when it came to transcribing the languages of civilizations in China that were also of the isolating type. Furthermore, since Chinese characters were ideograms, the transcriptions of many languages could be unified even though they may have had a different phonemic system. We use the generic term 漢文, Chinese writing, to refer these transcriptions using Chinese characters.

2. Chinese language (漢語) and Chinese composition (漢文)

漢文, Chinese composition, refers to the transcription of the Chinese language using ideograms called 漢字, Chinese characters. Following linguistic classification, 漢語, Chinese language, is a spoken language and Chinese composition is a written language. For all natural languages, it is naturally assumed that a spoken language comes first, and a written language to record it follows. When a spoken language is recorded with a writing system, the transcription commonly shows inconsistencies with the spoken language because of several limitations inherent to writing. Furthermore, since a written language undergoes its own internal changes, further differences also develop with the spoken language over long periods of time. After being born as a written language to record spoken Chinese, Chinese composition also underwent such changes.

One thing to note here is that it is hard to define the identity of Chinese. First, since Chinese underwent historical changes for several thousand years, it has a very different linguistic shape depending on each historical period. Secondly, Chinese has many regional dialects. In fact, the differences between many of these strains of Chinese go above and beyond regional dialect. Furthermore, the official language used in the Zhōngyuán [中原] area was replaced by the language of the ruling race of China or to the regional dialect of a political center at certain times. Thus, the definition of Chinese composition as the written language recording Chinese with Chinese characters is necessarily vague.

When we talk about 漢文, Chinese composition, this usually refers to Gǔwén [古文] of the pre-Qín [先秦] period. In general, the Chinese writing of early Confucian scriptures including *Sìshū Sānjīng* [四書三經] is referred to as an archaic style, Gǔwén and this written language was based on the language of Luòyàng [洛陽] the capital city of Dōng Zhōu [東周 (East Zhōu)]. [2] The official language of the Zhōu [周] period, which was called Yāyàn [雅言] had been the language of scholarity and literature until pre-Qìn and it was the administrative language of the Zhōu dynasty. Gǔwén was formed as a written language with a simple and suggestible style for documentation and communication. [3]

However, Gǔwén [古文] changed in accordance with the passing of different eras. During the period of Chūnqiu Zhànguó [春秋戰國時代] the language of each country changed independently, and after the unification of the Qìn [秦] dynasty, the language used in Chàngān [長安] emerged as a new official language. This new language, which is usually called Tōngyǔ [通語] challenged the authority of Yāyàn [雅言] that had been the official language of Zhōngyuán [中原] area of China. Gǔwén, which was the language of Confucian scriptures, was used very conservatively (as was common with the scriptures of other religions), so it remained impervious to such changes. Thus, although Tōngyǔ could not replace the language of Confucian scriptures, it progressed to the language of literary works. The newly developed written language based on Tōngyǔ which added fanciness to the simplicity and suggestibility of Gǔwén showed increased fanciness during the Liùzhāo [六朝] period. The Chinese writing of this style is referred to as Biànwén [變文].

Some scholars claim that Biànwén [變文] started from the translation of Buddhist scriptures after the mid-Táng [唐] dynasty. While translating Sanskrit into Chinese, people were influenced by its very different grammar, and Buddhist monks in particular used Tōngyǔ [通語] different from the Yāyàn [雅言] of Gǔwén [古文] in their lecturing. When the Buddhist doctrines were taught among people, mixed forms of verse with melody as well as prose explaining the doctrines were often used. Consistent with this, Biànwén has the characteristics of both verse and prose. Whereas Gǔwén is simple and succinct, and has an isolating grammatical structure, Biànwén is extremely fancy and decorative because it was mainly used in a variety of forms in poetry, essays, novels and the like developed during the Táng, Sòng [宋] and Yuán

---

[2] B. Karlgren (高本漢, 1964) divided changing phases of Chinese language into several periods as Antique Chinese (太古 漢語) in the period before *Shijîng* [詩經], Archaic Chinese (上古 漢語) in the period after Shíjìng until Dōng Hàn [東漢], Ancient Chinese (中古 漢語) from the period of Liù zhāo [六朝] to the end of Táng [唐], Early modern Chinese (近古 漢語) in the period of Sòng dynasty [宋朝] and Old Mandarin (老官話) in the period of Yuan-Ming [元明] dynasty (Jiang: 1994).

[3] The written language of Archaic Chinese, Gǔwén, was formed on the basis of philosophers scholarly works such as *Lànyu* [論語], *Mèngzi* [孟子], *Zhuāngzi* [莊子], *Xúnzi* [荀子] and *Hánfēzi* [韓非子] written in the pre-Qìn period, and it progressed to theses in *Zhìàncè* [治安策] and *Guòzòulùn* [過秦論] written by Guyì [賈誼] and to descriptions in *Chūnqiu Zuoshìchu—'an* [春秋左氏傳] written by Zuoqiūming [左丘明] and in *Shiji* [史記] written by Sīmǎqiān [司馬遷] during the Hàn [漢] dynasty.

[元] dynasties. [4] However, Biànwén also appeared in the Chinese transcriptions of other civilizations in the same era, who tried to transcribe their own language with Chinese characters. The reason for this was because they did not follow the grammar of Gǔwén [古文] to transcribe their own languages. This kind of Biànwén [變文] appeared in the Chinese transcriptions of Northeastern Eurasian Altaic languages. For example, Hóngmài [洪邁, 1123-1201] who went to Huìníng [會寧] (present day Jílín [吉林]) as a diplomatic representative of the Jin [金] dynasty in the period of South Sòng [南宋] reported that when the children of Khitan [契丹] read Chinese poetry (漢詩), they read it in accordance with the word order of Jurchen (女眞語) similar to Korea's Itumun [吏讀文]. According to Hóngmài's anecdote, he could not stop laughing when a viceenvoy Wángbu [王補] who welcomed him read one verse of 'Title of Li's seclusion (題李凝幽居)' written by Gudǎo [賈島] in the Táng [唐] period. The line in question -'鳥宿池中樹 僧敲月下門' was read as '月明裏和尚 門子打 水底裏樹上老鴉坐.' Interestingly, there is a record indicating that Wángbu is a Khitan [契丹人] born in Jinzhōu [錦州] (《夷堅志》「丙志」第 18 '契丹誦詩' 條). [5]

This kind of Khitan's recital poem (契丹誦詩) is of course not classified as Biànwén [變文]. Rather, this is more like Korea's Itumun [吏讀文], so even though it was written in Chinese characters, it might have been read in Jurchen [女眞語]. During that period, China and its neighboring races recorded their various languages with Chinese characters, and there seem to be many types of Biànwén which did not correspond with the sentential structures of Gǔwén.

As mentioned earlier, many Biànwén which were developed after the mid-Táng dynasty deviated slightly from Gǔwén, but their basic grammatical structure is based on the archaic language (上古語) of China, Gǔwén [古

---

[4] About twenty thousand books were discovered in the stone room in the thousand Buddha' cavern (千佛洞 石室) located in Dùnhuáng Gānsùsheng [甘肅省 敦煌] China in 1899 (清 光 25 年). Among them, many copies written in Biànwén are included, which seem to be textbooks for lecturing Buddhist scriptures. These are materials of the so called Dùnhuáng biànwén [敦煌 變文], the latest of which was written between the golden age of Táng [盛唐, the late 8th Century] and AD. 977 [宋 太宗 2 年]. Thus, it seems that Biànwén developed after the mid-Táng dynasty.

[5] While comparing '月明裏和尚門子打 水底裏樹上老鴉坐: while the moon is shining, a Buddhist monk beats a door, and a raven sat on the tree in the bottom of water' with the corresponding Mongolian sentences 'saran-du xoošang egüde toγsixu-du naγur taxi modun-du xeriy-e saγumui', Ching (1997) claimed that even though the expressions written in strange Chinese word order sounded very funny to the diplomatic representative to China, Hóngmài this kind of sentential structure is natural to Khitanes (契丹語), and also, it fits with that of Mongolian. If Korean word order had been identical to that, Korean Itumun (吏讀文) would also have been considered as one of these variant forms of strange Chinese. This aspect results from the difference between Chinese with its isolating grammatical structure and Khitanese writings (契丹文) and Itumun with their agglutinative structures.

文]. However, since the influence of Tōngyǔ [通語] was widespread during the Suí [隋] and Táng [唐] dynasties, a new type of written language was developed based on the spoken language, and it was called Báihuà [白話] or Báihuàwèn [白話文]. This new written style, which is more colloquial, was mainly used for prose, but it also became in part the language of literature. During the Táng and Sòng [宋] dynasties, Confucian scripts written in Gǔwén were annotated with this colloquial written style.⁶

This situation changed substantially during the Yuan [元] dynasty. The rulers of this dynasty used Mongolian, which has an agglutinative grammatical structure, and the language of Beijing [北京] which was very different from the official language of Táng [唐]. Furthermore, Sòng [宋] became a new official language of Yuan. This language was a very different Chinese from the traditional language of Gǔwén and the later language of Biànwén. The spoken language used in the Beijing area during the Yuan dynasty was Hànéryányǔ [漢兒言語] influenced by Mongolian. The written language transcribing this spoken language with Chinese characters was called Hanliwen [漢吏文] by the peoples of Goryeo [高麗人] and Joseon [朝鮮人] who had to learn to use it.

In this paper, I will inquire into the Hanliwen [漢吏文] of the Yuan dynasty, which has yet to receive much scholarly interest. I will also introduce Imun [吏文], which was used from the late Goryeo [高麗] period on the Korean peninsula. Imun is very similar to Hanliwen in the sense that it was used to transcribe the Korean language with Chinese characters in accordance with Korean word order. The study of Korean Imun has been completely neglected, largely because its study specifically requires the comparison with the Hanliwen of the Yuan dynasty. Furthermore, the understanding of Chinese Hanliwen is only possible when we admit the existence of Hànéryányǔ, which was the official language of the Beijing area during the Yuan dynasty. However, the existence of this language has been ignored by China and by the scholarly pursuits of Chinese linguistics.

3. Hanliwen [漢吏文] and Hànéryányǔ [漢兒言語] of the Yuan dynasty

3.1. Hànéryányǔ [漢兒言語]

One of the most notable events in the history of Chinese is that the language recognized as official changed to that of Beijing in the North after the Yuan dynasty was established by Mongolia. When Kubillai Khan [忽必

---

⁶ The beginning of this kind of annotation of the Confucian Scripture goes back to *Shísānjingzòushū* [十三經奏疏] written by Zhèngxuán [鄭玄] in the late Hàn [後漢] period, but the annotation of the Scriptures written in the Tōngyǔ of the Táng-Sòng [唐-宋] period was mainly accomplished by Zhūzi [朱子].

烈汗] founded the capital city in Yenching [燕京] present day Beijing [北京], many different languages were used in that area since the Chinese and many other civilizations around Northeastern Eurasia were competing for governance. After Mongolia exercised dominance over this area around the early 13th century, Chinese which appears to have been mixed with Mongolian became widely used. This language is Hànéryányǔ [漢兒言語], which has been called 'a directly translated style of Mongolian (蒙文直譯體)' or 'an administrative style of Chinese composition (漢文吏牘體)'. [7] This language was markedly different from Yāyàn [雅言] and Tōngyǔ [通語] to the extent that they were not mutually comprehensible.

Kim et al. (2000: 369-370) introduced how this kind of language started to be used by means of citing *The Documents of Ambassador Xǔ's Journey* [許奉使行程録] written by Xǔkángzōng [許亢宗] of the North Sòng [北宋] dynasty, who went to the coronation ceremony of Táizōng [太宗], Jin [金] as a congratulating envoy in 1125 (宣和 7 年). While reporting that 'there is a record saying that when Khitan [契丹] was a strong country, many peoples from different areas migrated into this area, and as a result, many cultures were mingled and they could not communicate with one another. However, by using 'Hànéryányǔ [漢兒言語], they started to communicate' (〈 三朝北盟 會編 〉 Vol.20), he pointed out that many peoples who moved into this area communicated with one another using Hànéryányǔ. In fact, many civilizations who gathered around the Beijing area from Northeastern Eurasia used Hànéryányǔas a kind of Koinē, [8] and this was a very different Chinese from Tōngyǔ, which was based on the language used around Chángān [長安] the former official language of Zhōngyuán [中原].

---

[7] Hànéryányǔ which was first introduced to the world by the current author, was the colloquial common language of the Beijing area in the Yuan dynasty. During the period of the Yuan dynasty, Goryeo set up 'the School of Spoken Chinese (漢語都監)' in which this language was taught (Chung 1988), and *Lao Qida* [老乞大] and *PōTōngshi* [朴通事] which were the textbooks for this language were edited. Recently, *Lao Qida* which is assumed to have been published during the Taejong [太宗] period of Joseon was discovered, and the current author proposed that this book was the textbook for learning Hànéryányǔ, and that it was the original copy (Chung 2002a, 2004a). The discovery of the *Original Lao Qida* [原本老乞大] and the claim that it is the textbook for Hànéryányǔ might have come as a great shock to many scholars in China and Japan studying the history of Chinese. In a series of papers (Chung 1999, 2000, 2003b, 2004a), I made repeated claims for the existence of the Hànéryányu of the Yuan dynasty and its textbook, which was already mentioned by Choi Sejin [崔世珍] during the period of Jungjong [中宗] of Joseon. Nowadays, this claim seems to be accepted as truth by many scholars studying the history of Chinese (Kim et al. 2000). Chung (1999) was presented in Tokyo in Japanese, Chung (2000) was presented in Seoul in Korean, Chung (2003b) was presented at ICKL in Turkey, and Chung (2004a) was presented in Beijing in Chinese.

[8] Koinē(κοινη) was the common language of the Greek empire which conquered the Mediterranean area after the period of Alexander the Great, and it is based on the Attica dialect. Since then, the term, Koinē has been used to refer to the common language of an empire.

Hànéryányǔ [漢兒言語] was not a language the same as those previously mentioned in the discussion of 'Khitan's reading poem (契丹誦詩)', that follows Mongolian word order and uses Mongolian case markers and endings. But in Chung (2004a), I treat it as a kind of creole and Kim et al.(2000) also refer to it as 'broken Chinese used as a savage's language (胡言漢語)'. [9] During the Yuan dynasty, this language was used as the official language in the negotiation between Goryeo [高麗] and China. Thus, after the foundation of Yuan, Goryeo sets up the ' the School of Spoken Chinese (漢語都監)' especially to teach this language. [10]

Although Mongolia ruled the country during Yuan dynasty, this was achieved by means of supervising the Chinese ruling class, the Han race (漢人) who in turn controlled the common Chinese people. [11] Therefore, the Chinese needed to write reports for the Mongolian supervisors, and the written language used in those reports was not Gǔwén [古文] but a newly formed written language based on Hànéryányǔ [漢兒言語]. This newly formed written language has been called 'an administrative style of Chinese composition (漢文吏牘體), or 'the directly translated style of Mongolian (蒙文直譯體)', and is described by Kim et al. (2000: 372) as follows.

> Even though the royalty of Jin [金] could speak some spoken Chinese (漢語), the royalty or nobility of Mongolia in general did not know Chinese, and indeed they never even considered learning it. Thus, there was a need to record important matters such as the orders of Khan [汗] in Mongolian, which was Khan's language. It seems that for such purposes, 'Hànéryányǔ' was the most simple and accurate means of transcription. If formal Chinese or Chinese classics (古文 or 白話文 etc.) was used to translate it, semantic translation processes would

---

[9] While referring to 'savage's language of Chinese', Kim et al. (2000: 370-371) wrote that 'when people of South Sòng use the terms 'Hànrén [漢人]' or 'Hàner [漢兒]', these always refer to Chinese people under the governance of the northern Jin dynasty. Thus, 'Hànyǔ [漢語]' also refers to the Chinese used in the north. However, it seems that the language sounded strange to people of South Sòng. In *Xiàngshānyǔlù* [象山語錄, 卷下] written by Lùjiuyuān [陸九淵, 1139-93] who was a famous philosopher of South Sòng and in the article of Rev. Huángbòzhiyîn [黄檗志因禪師] in *Wǔdēnghuìyuán* [五灯會元] (vol. 16) which is a collection of biographies of Buddhist Zen monks, the term 胡言漢語 was used to refer to funny and strange speaking styles.'

[10] I refer readers to Chung (1987, 1990) and Park Yong-un (2005) for the foundation and management of 'the School of Spoken Chinese (漢語都監)' and 'the School of Administrative Chinese Composition (吏學都監)' in the Goryeo Dynasty.

[11] During the Yuan dynasty, Mongolian officials were dispatched to each ministry in order to supervise Chinese officials. For example, there is a record of '中書省 奏過事内件' in *Yuándiǎnzhāng* [元典章, 1320], saying that even though Mongolian officials called Zhálūhuāchì [札魯花赤], Shoulingguàn [首領官], Liùbùguàn [六部官] and Bidūchìrén [必闍赤人] were supposed to supervise Chinese officials in the Ministry of the Capital City (大都省), they were lazy at showing up for work, so the king issued a royal order urging them to go to the office early and to leave work late. Here, the term 'Zhálūhuāchì [札魯花赤]' refers to 'Mongolian Government Official, Duànshìguān [斷事官]'.

be required and as a result, that would inevitably result in the meaning being distorted. Furthermore, the people who needed to read it were 'Chinese people' such as Khitan [契丹人], Jurchen [女眞人] etc. using Hànéryányŭ. Thus, 'Hànéryányŭ' changed from a spoken language to a written language. The Chinese writing, known as 'the directly translated style of Mongolian refers to this.

[Translation author's own]

However, such claims are seriously flawed in that they ignore the fact that the written language reflected Hànéryányŭ, which really existed as a colloquial language during that time. In a series of papers (1999, 2000, 2003b, 2004a), I argued that a variety of Chinese which mixed Hànéryányŭ with Mongolian really existed as a kind of Koinē, and that 'the directly translated style (蒙文直譯體)' is the documentation of this colloquial language. I also claimed that the administrative style (漢文吏牘體) refers to a literary style of the written language mainly used in judicature and administration, which was newly formed based on spoken Chinese at that time.

The second Khan [汗] of the Mongolian empire, Ogotai [窩闊大], gave a royal order [12] that the sons and siblings of Mongolian secretaries learn Hànéryányŭ [漢兒言語] and its documents, and that the sons and siblings of Chinese public servants learn Mongolian. The purpose of the order was to facilitate communication between Chinese and Mongolian officials in the use of translations and written language forms.

3.2. Hanliwen [漢吏文] and Hànwénlidútǐ [漢文吏牘體]

Tanaka (1965) classifies the written style language which is based on Hànéryányŭ [漢兒言語], a spoken language of Yuan dynasty, into 'the direct translated style (蒙文直譯體)' and 'the administrative style (漢文吏牘體)'. He claims in the beginning of his paper that;

> The style of documents included in the *Yuándiǎnzhāng* [元典章] that is *The Documents of National Systems and Holy Governments of the Great Yuan Dynasty* (大元聖政國朝典章) in full name, can be mainly divided into two types: the administrative style and the direct translated style. The former is the literary style for judicial documents which were completed by secretaries working in the legal system and administration. In contrast, the latter refers to a literary style that was used by translators in converting Mongolian judicial documents into Chinese, and it originated in the special situation of the

---

[12] This royal order of Ogotai Khan is recorded in *Xījīnzhì* [析津志] (〈析津志輯佚〉, 北京古籍出版, 1983) which is a geography of Beijing, and issued in 1233 (元 太宗 5 年). He ordered the founding of a school called 'Sìjiàodú [四教讀]' in Yenching, 燕京 (the capital city of Yuan), in which 18 siblings of Mongolian Bidūchì [必闍赤] and 22 siblings of Chinese people were going to live together, and to teach 'the missives written by Hànéryányŭ [漢兒言語] to Mongolian siblings and Mongolian and archery to Chinese siblings. It seems that the term ' Hànéryányŭ ' refers to a colloquial language of Chinese at that time and 'wènshū [文書]' refers to a written language called Hanliwen [漢吏文]. Refer to Kim et al. (2000).

Yuan dynasty in which China was governed by Mongolian. The direct translated style was nothing but a temporary name, and it also referred to a type of
Chinese writing which used Chinese characters. Unfortunately, the sentences
of *Yuándiǎnzhāng* are thought of as very abstruse since the two literary styles
are different from normal Chinese writings, and as a result, in spite of a wealth
of historical records, we could not make full use of them.

(Tanaka 1965: 47, Translation author's own)

Even though claims have been made that the administrative style (漢文
吏牘體) originated from North Sòng (北宋) and that the directly translated
style (蒙文直譯體) was born during the Yuan dynasty, I believe that the latter is actually the direct transcription of Hànéryányǔ [漢兒言語], a spoken
language of the Beijing area during the Yuan dynasty, and the former refers
to a form of written language developed from the latter. Although Kōjirō
Yoshikawa (1953) was not aware of the existence of Hànéryányǔ he accurately described the situation of that period while mentioning the literary style
of *Yuándiǎnzhāng* [元典章], the representative work of lidúwén, 吏牘文 in the
Yuan dynasty:

> ... かくきわめて僅かではあるが、あたかも元曲の白のごとく、口語の直寫
> を志した部分が存在する。なぜこれらの部分だけ口語を直寫しようとする
> のか。それは恐らく、いかなる言語に誘導されての犯罪であるかが、量刑
> に關係するからであり、その必要にそなえる爲であろうと思われるが、要
> するに吏牘の文が、必要に應じてはいかなる言語をも受容し得る態度にあ
> ることを、別の面から示すものである。
>
> ... [in 元典章] Even though they are few, some parts do exist that transcribe
> the spoken language, including the case of 'bài [白]' of 'Dramas of the Yuan
> dynasty (元曲)'. [13] It can be assumed that since what language was used to
> induce a crime was relevant to the verdict, the actual spoken language needed
> to be used in preparation for such cases. In short, this displays the attitude that
> the sentences written in lidú [吏牘] can accommodate any kind of language for
> any purpose.   (Translation author's own)

This statement indicates that when the Lidúwén of Yuan was used in legal
documents, spoken languages were transcribed as they were, regardless of
what languages were used, in order to fully grasp the truth from a criminal's
confession or from an accusation at trial. [14] The spoken language mentioned

---

[13] Yoshikawa (1953) claimed that in *Yuándiǎnzhāng* most of the records in which writers tried
to record the conversations between people involved as they were can be found in the Ministry
of Justice section (刑部) but some of them appeared in the Ministry of Tax section (戶部).

[14] Yoshikawa (1953) presented some examples of cases in which the colloquial language is
recorded as it was in *Yuándiǎnzhāng* [元典章], and one of them is as follows. In *Yuándiǎnzhāng*
(「殺親屬」第 5), it is recorded that according to the interrogation of a criminal who killed his
wife, on June 12th 1312 (皇慶 元年), Huòniúér [霍牛兒] who moved to Chízhōu county [池州
路] in Dōngliú province [東流縣] because of a famine fought with Yuéxiin [岳仙] who was his
begging partner and Huòniúér was beaten by him. Seeing this, his wife said '你喫人打罵. 做不得

here refers to Hànéryányǔ [漢兒言語], which was used in the Beijing area as Koinē, and this spoken language was temporarily referred to as the direct translated style (蒙文直譯體) in the Lidúwén [吏牘文] of the Yuan dynasty. However, scholars of later generations have interpreted these temporary terms used by Yoshikawa and Tanaka as if those literary styles really existed. This misheld belief results from their ignorance as to the existence of Hànéryányǔ.

What I want to argue here is that the administrative style (漢文吏牘 體) which was used for judicature and administration in the Yuan dynasty should be considered as 'Hanliwén [漢吏文]'. That is to say that even though Japanese scholars have claimed that 'the administrative style' and 'the direct translated style (蒙文直譯體)' are kinds of Chinese Biànwén [變文], they really refer to transcriptions of the spoken language in the Liwén [吏文] of the Yuan dynasty. In particular, the Chinese Liwén which was developed from the Yuan dynasty, that is 'the administrative style', has been called 'Hanliwen' to distinguish it from the Korean Imun [吏文] used on the Korean peninsular during the Joseon [朝鮮] dynasty. [15]

Until now, the fact that the written style language of Lidútî [吏牘體] in Yuan had a different literary style from Gǔwén [古文], namely Hanliwen [漢 吏文], has been overlooked. However, one of the facts indicating that Hanliwen really existed is that the Translation Service Examination of Chinese (漢吏科) existed until the early Joseon dynasty, which was an exam system testing Hanliwen. The article of Sejong's Authentic Records (世宗實錄, vol. 47, Sejong 12th 庚戌 Mar.) recorded the guideline for tests, the purpose of which was to recruit government officials issued by Sangjeongso [詳定所] and this includes precise testing methods of Hanrikwa [漢吏科]. According to the guidelines, the texts required for the testing of Translation Service Ex-

---

男子漢. 我每日做別人飯食. 被人欺負.: You are beaten by others and blamed. You are not qual-ified as a man. Since everyday I beg others for food, they call me an idiot', so he killed his wife. The sentences in this record are written in a colloquial style of writing, so it is different from Gǔuwén [古文] as well as the formal style of an administrative style (漢文吏牘體). Actually, the style of those sentences is identical with that of the *Original Laochita* [原本老乞大] which the author introduced as the data of Hànéryányǔ [漢兒言語]. The direct translated style (蒙文直譯 體) refers to Hànéryányǔ, which was used in the Beijing area as an actual colloquial language. Refer to Chung (2004a).

[15] According to an article in 'The Preface of Direct Translated Tóngzixí (直解童子習序)' of Seong Sammun [成三問] Hanliwen was taught in Seungmunwon [承文院] in order to write diplomatic documents in the early Joseon period, and Sayeokwon [司譯院] took charge of inter-pretation by learning a colloquial language, namely Hànéryányǔ. According to the introduction of this article, saying that '... 自我祖宗事大至誠 置承文院掌吏文 司譯院掌譯語 專其業而久 其任... : ... Since the time of our ancestors, we have taken diplomacy very seriously, so Seung-munwon was founded to take charge of Liwen and Sayeokwon was founded to take charge of the interpretation of languages. Thus, the work became easier and the positions remained for a long time... (Translation author's own)', Sayeokwon took charge of interpretation by learning a col-loquial language, and in Seungmunwon, people learned Liwen that is Hanliwen. The translation of the excerpt is based on Hong (1946).

amination of Chinese (漢吏學) included '*Shū* [書], *Shī* [詩], *Sìshū* [四書], *Luzhāi'axué* [魯齋大學], *Zhìjiéxiǎoxué* [直解小學], *Chéngzāixiàojing* [成齋 孝經], *Sǎowēitōngjiàn* [少微通鑑], *Qiànhòuhàn* [前後漢], *Lixuézhinàn* [吏 學指南], *Zhōngyizhiyan* [忠義直言], *Tòngzixi* [童子習], *Dàyuàntōngzhi* [大 元通制], *Zhizhèngtiàogè* [至正條格], *Yùzhidàgào* [御製大誥], *Piao Tongshi* [朴通事], *Lao Qida* [老乞大], the *Register of diplomatic records* (事大文書 謄録), and other composition (製述 奏本, 啓本, 咨文)', and these texts must have constituted the materials used for teaching Hanliwen.

Among those texts, '*Shū* [書], *Shī* [詩], *Sìshū* [四書]' are written in the Gǔwén [古文] of the pre-Qin [先秦] period, and Piao Tongshi [朴通事] and *Lao Qida* [老乞大] must have been the textbooks for learning Hànéryányǔ [漢兒言語]. The rest of them must have been the textbooks used for learning Hanliwen [漢吏文]. I will briefly describe each of these textbooks.

First of all, *Lǔzhāidàxué* [魯齋大學] refers to *Dàxuézhixiè* [大學直解] which is the third volume of *Lǔzhāiyíshū* edited by Xuhéng [許衡] in Yuan, and this seems to be a translated version of *Dàxué* [大學] in Hànéryányǔ. *Chéngzhāixiàojing* [成齋孝經] refers to *Xiàojingzhixiè* [孝經直解] written by Beitíngchéngzhāi [北庭成齋] of the Yuan dynasty. [16] *Dàyuàntōngzhi* [大元 通制] is a book containing comprehensive records of the judicial system of the Yuan dynasty from the foundation of the dynasty to during Yányòu (延 祐年間, 1314-1320). In 1312 (皇慶 1 年), Rénzōng [仁宗] ordered Āsǎn [阿 散] to edit a book collecting judicial cases taking place from the foundation of Yuan, and this book was completed in 1323 (至治 3 年). This is the only systematic code of law completed during the Yuan dynasty.

Zhizhèngtiàogè [至正條格] is the edited version of *Dàyuàntōngzhi* [大元 通制] which was complied during 1346 (至正 6 年) in the Yuan dynasty. Tàizu [太祖] of the Ming [明] dynasty distributed '*Yùzhidàgào* [御製大誥] 74 articles in October 1385 (洪武 18 年), which was a book of law based on criminal cases committed by officials and people, and this was used for correcting the bad customs of the Yuan dynasty. In the following year, 'The Sequel of *Yùzhidàgào* (御製大誥續編)' 87 articles (vol. 1) and 'The third of

---

16 *Chéngzhāixiàojing* is mentioned in ASK(1986: 484) as 'The book written by Chénqióng [陳 瑃] of Ming [明]. It was written to educate children (Translation author's own)'. Therefore, it was claimed in footnote 3 of Chung et al. (2002a: 18) that '*Chéngzhāixiàojing* is the translation of *Zhixièxiǎoxué* [直解孝經] of the Yuan dynasty into the Beijing language of that time achieved by Chénqióng (his pen name (號) is Chéngzhāi [成齋]) of the Ming dynasty. ... Refer to ASK (1986)". However, that claim was found to be incorrect. In fact, *Zhixièxiàojing* was written by Beitíng Chéngzhāi [北庭成齋 (小雲石 海涯, 自號 酸齋, 一名 成齋) in the Yuan dynasty, and according to *Xiàojingzhixiè* [孝經直解] which was handed down in Japan, the title is '新刊全相 成齋孝經直解'. At the end of book, it is recorded as '北庭成齋直説孝經 終', and at the end of the introduction, it is written as '小雲石海涯 北庭成齋自敍'. This represents a mistake made in several papers by the author, that was caused by citing ASK (1986). I sincerely apologize to readers for this.

Yùzhidàgào (御製大誥三)' 47 articles (vol. 1) were published for the same purpose. *Yùzhidàgào* is used as a collective term referring to all of them.

The Register of diplomatic records (事大文書謄錄) is a collection of documents detailing communications between Seungmunwon [承文院] of the Joseon [朝鮮] dynasty and the Chinese royal court (朝廷). According to the articles of *Sejong's Authentic Record* (〈世宗實錄〉, vol. 51, 世宗 13 年 1 月 丙戌, 同 vol. 121, 世宗 30 年 8 月 丙辰) and *Tanjong's Authentic Record*,(〈端宗實錄〉, vol. 13, 端宗 3 年 1 月 丁卯), these were transcribed once every five years and printed once every ten years for publication (Chung et al. 2002).

Thus, '*Luzhāidàxué* [魯齋大學], *Zhìjiéxi—vaoxué* [直解小學], *Chéngzhāi xiàojing* [成齋孝經], *Shǎowēitōngjiàn* [少微通鑑], *Qiànhòuhān* [前後漢]' are translations of scriptures and history books including '*Dàxué* [大學], *Xiǎoxué* [小學], *Xiàojing* [孝經], *Tōngjiàn* [通鑑], *Qiànhānshū* [前漢書] and *Hòuhānshū* [後漢書]' into Hànéryányǔ [漢兒言語]. '*Lìxuézhǐnàn* (吏學 指南), *Zhōngyizhiyan* [忠義直言], *Dàyuàntōngzhi* [大元通制], *Zhizhèng-tiàogè* [至正條格] and *Yùzhidàgào* [御製大誥]' are written in Hanliwen, which was the new written language of the Yuan dynasty known as the administrative style (漢文吏牘體). Among these, '*Lìxuézhǐnàn* [吏學指南] was a reference book for learning Hanliwen (漢吏文). [17] In addition, '*Zhōngyizhiyan* [忠義直言], *Dàyuàntōngzhi* [大元通制], *Zhizhèngtiàogè* [至正條格], *Yùzhidàgào* [御製大誥]' are books similar to the previously mentioned Yuándiǎn- zhāng [元典章]. In other words, these were books collecting administrative documents such as the laws, the Imperial edicts and memorials to the Throne of the Yuan dynasty. '*Lao Qida* [老乞大] and *Piao Tongshi* [朴通事]' are textbooks for learning the spoken language Hànéryányǔ as I mentioned before.

4. Imun [吏文] and Itumun [吏讀文] of the Korean Peninsular

On the Korean peninsular, Imun [吏文] was developed to be used in official judicial and administrative documents, imitating the Hanliwen [漢吏文] developed during the Yuan dynasty. However, since Imun was mingled with the Itumun of the later period, it became impossible to distinguish between them. Furthermore, after the discovery of *Old Translated Inwanggyeong* [舊譯仁王經] in the mid 70s, which represented important data regarding 釋讀 口訣, the confusion worsened since the difference between 口訣文 and the others was not clear.

---

[17] For *Lixuézhínán*, I refer readers to Chung et al. (2002b). *Lixuézhínán* edited by Xúyuánruì [徐元瑞] in 1301(元 大德 5 年) was republished in Kyeongju [慶州] of Joseon around 1458 (世祖 4 年) (which is in the collection of Kyujanggak [奎章閣]), and the photoprint version of this book is released in Chung et al. (2002b) with detailed explanations and indexes. *Lixuézhínán*, I refer readers to Chung et al (2002b).

I have explained the reasons why Itumun [吏讀文] needs to be distinguished from Imun [吏文]. On the Korean peninsula, a literary style to transcribe official documents was developed in the same way as Chinese Hanliwen [漢吏文]. There has been no research as to when Joseon Imun [18] became the official written language for administrative documents. However, based on the assumption that Joseon Imun was formed under the influence of Hanliwen, it can be assumed that it became the official written language around the late Goryeo dynasty or the early Joseon dynasty.

After Imun [吏文] became the official written language, all administrative documents were considered effective only when they were written in Imun. According to the record '出債成文 ... 諺文及無證筆者 勿許聽理' written in the Ministry of Tax (戶部) of *Sygyojipram* [受教輯録] (1698), bonds were considered void if they were written in the Korean alphabet (諺文), or when there was no witness of the contract, or when it was unclear who wrote it.

We can confirm the fact that Imun [吏文] was distinguished from Itumun [吏讀文] considering the article below, quoted from *Sejo's Authentic Record* [世祖實録].

吏曹啓 吏科及承蔭出身 封贈爵牒等項文牒 皆用吏文 獨於東西班 五品以下 告身 襲用吏讀 甚爲鄙俚 請自今用吏文 從之

The Ministry of Administration (吏曹) reported that 'the officials recruited through the Government Examination for Office (吏科) all used Imun in the documents for bestowing appointment, but the civil and military officials ranked lower than the fifth grade habitually used Itu [吏讀], so it was considered contemptible and vulgar. Thus, we ask them to use Imun from now on." It was granted...   (Translation author's own)

The Imun [吏文] mentioned here refers to the written language used in administrative offices during late Goryeo and early Joseon based on Hanliwen [漢吏文]. Itu [吏讀] refers to the recording of Korean with Chinese characters on the basis of their sound or meaning.

A typical example of Joseon Imun [吏文] appears in *The Great Teacher of Imun* (〈 吏文大師 〉, henceforth '*Isa* [吏師]') edited by Choi Seijin [崔世珍] in the Jungjong [中宗] period. This was nothing but a textbook for Joseon Imun (comparable with Hanliwen [漢吏文]), which was edited by Choi Sejin, an expert in Hanliwen.

Since the Imun [吏文] of the early Joseon period was based on the literary style of Hanliwen [漢吏文], it was different from Itumun [吏讀文]. The Chinese writing which was mainly used in administrative documents and which had peculiar formats and used specific idiomatic expressions shown in *Isa* [吏師] was called Imun. Interestingly, the specific idiomatic expressions used in

---

[18] It is not confirmed yet whether Imun existed in the Goryeo period. Thus, Joseon Imun is tentatively compared with Hanliwen.

Imun were borrowed from Itumun.

Most of the idiomatic expressions introduced in the introductory part of *Isa* [吏師] were written in Itu [吏讀]. For example, '右謹言所志矣段' is an idiomatic expression usually used in the beginning of Soji [所志] (petition or written accusation). This expression is written in accordance with Korean grammatical structure and contains Itu such as 'etan [矣段]', meaning roughly 'what I would like to humbly mention is'. Also, the phrase '右所陳爲白內等: what I would like to say hereafter is' is an idiomatic expression used at the beginning of official documents and contains Itu such as 'hasapnetan (爲白內等)'.

The Chinese writing style which uses an abundance of four letter phrases (四字成句) such as those listed above is a characteristic of Hanliwen [漢吏文], and Joseon Imun [吏文] imitated this style. Yoshikawa (1953) mentioned that a stylistic characteristic of Hànwèn lidù [漢文 吏牘] of Yuándiǎnzhāng [元典章] is 'strain', and pointed out two factors which cause that kind of strain, as below.

a Four letter phrases (四字句) or rhythm based on their modification.

b Frequent use of terms which are peculiar to lidù [吏牘] including certain kinds of colloquial lexical items. [19]

Considering this observation, it seems that Joseon Imun [吏文], in the same way as Hanliwen [漢吏文], also had stylistic rhythm caused by using four letter phrases (四字句) and used colloquial expressions. Furthermore, this writing preserved the authority of official documents and invoked strain by using frequent idiomatic expressions which were only used in Imun. This is due to the fact that Joseon Imun imitated the literary style of Hanliwen.

The format of Imun [吏文] was still maintained until late Joseon, but the use of the writing style of Itu [吏讀] increased. I came across an old document which confirms this claim, the petition for postponement of examination (陳試 所志) written by Hyeon Kegeun [玄啓根] which is included amongst old documents kept by the Hyeon family (川寧 玄氏家), a reputable family of interpreter officials. According to the content of this petition, 所志 written in October 1744, even though Hyeon Kegeun passed a previous interpreter examination, he could not take the second examination (譯科 覆試) which was going to be held the following year because of the death of his father, so

---

[19] Yoshikawa (1953)) summarized the characteristics of Hanliwen including the following; 元典章中の漢文吏牘の文體は、(1) 古文家の文語と文法の基本をおなじくしつつも、古文家の文語のごとく藝術的緊張をめざさない. (2) しかも吏牘の文をしての緊張をめざす. (3) 緊張を作る要素としては (a) 四字句もしくはその變形を基本とするリズム (b) ある種の口語的語彙をふくむ吏牘特有の語の頻用、(4) しかしその緊張は、容易に弛緩をゆるすのであって、往往、更に多くの口語的要素を導入して、緊張をやぶる. (5) さればといつて緊張を全くくずし去ることはない.' These stylistic characteristics can also be applied to Joseon Imun.

he asked for permission to take the exam at a later date. [20]

Original text:

譯科初試舉子喪人玄敬躋[21]

右謹言所志矣段　矣身今甲子式年譯科初試　以漢學舉子入格矣
五月　分遭父喪是如乎　依例陳試　事後考次立旨　成給爲只爲
行下向敎是事

禮曹　處分　手決　依法典

甲子　十月　日　所志[22]

This Imun [吏文] contains the idiomatic expression '右謹言所志 矣段' used at the beginning of all administrative petitions (所志) and also other idiomatic expressions such as '矣身, 是如乎, 立旨, [23] 爲只爲, 行下向 是事' written in Itu [吏讀] or Imun.

Thus, Joseon Imun [吏文] was formed under the influence of Hanliwen [漢 吏文]. Joseon Imun was formed based on Itumun [吏讀文] which progressed from the Hyangchal [鄕札] of Shilla [新羅] in the same way as Hanliwen was formed based on Hànéryányǔ [漢兒言語] which is also known as the so called direct translated style of Mongolian (蒙文直譯體), and it also accommodated the literary style of Hanliwen.

Joseon Imun [吏文] was the only official written language of Joseon until the royal order that Hangeul could be used in official documents was issued. It is frustrating that not many researchers have been interested in the study of Joseon Imun, which was the only official written language for many years.

---

[20] I refer readers to Chung (1990: 210) for explanations of the first examination (初試) and the second examination (覆試) of the government examination for interpreter officials (譯科) and what happened to the Japanese interpreter Hyeon, in applying for this examination and his postponement of the examination because of his father's death.

[21] Hyeon [玄敬躋] is 玄啓根, Hyeon Kyegun's childhood name. (Chung 1990).

[22] Translation:
Hyeon [玄敬躋] who passed the preliminary examination for recruiting interpreters and also a mourner.
What I want to ask for is that even though I took the preliminary examination for recruiting interpreters of the stated examination for Chinese language and passed, I would like to postpone taking the follow up exam based on the precedents because my father passed away in May. Please make an order to issue a document verifying this for me.
The Minister for Examinations (禮曹) handled this and left his signature.
The petition (所志) written in October, 1744(甲子)

[23] '立旨' is an idiomatic expression usually used in documents for slavery or registration of land etc., and it refers to an addition (附記) saying that an administrative office verifies the petition written in 所志. Examples: 本文段 失於火燒是遣 立旨一張乙 代數爲去乎 (the registrational document for land of the Kim family of Andong, 安東 金俊植 宅), 各別 立旨成給爲白只爲 行 下向敎是事 (海南 尹泳善 宅〈 所志 〉). Chang (2001: 432).

5. Conclusion

In this paper, I have discussed the relationship between the Hanliwen [漢吏文] developed after the Yuan dynasty and Imun [吏文] which was the official written language for administrative documents in Joseon. I have claimed that Hanliwen was a written language form based on Hànéryányǔ [漢兒言語] which was a Koinē used by Northern Eurasian races migrating to the Beijing [北京] area during the Yuan dynasty. Hànéryányǔ was a kind of creole composed of a mixture of Chinese with its isolating grammatical structures and languages of other races with their agglutinative grammatical structures. It was mainly used in judicial and administrative documents. Thus, I put emphasis on the fact that Hànéryányǔ was a written language very different from the well known Gǔwén [古文].

I also argued that in the Korean peninsula, Imun [吏文] was born after the late Goryeo dynasty under the influence of the Hanliwen [漢吏文] of the Yuan dynasty and used for the judicial system and administration. Even though Imun was formed based on Chinese and Hanliwen and Itu [吏讀] were used for the transcription of lexical items including some special idiomatic expressions and proper nouns, the distinction between them was clear in the earlier period. However, since Korean Imun accommodated Itumun [吏讀文], which recorded Korean in accordance with Korean word order just like Hànéryányǔ [漢兒言語], which was the basis of Chinese Hanliwen accommodated agglutinative grammatical structures, the distinction between Imun and Itumun became blurred in the later period.

I think the fact that Imun [吏文] followed the Korean word order to such a degree that it is often confused with Itumun [吏讀文] even though it was originally formed based on Chinese Hànéryányǔ [漢兒言語], renders Imun as an important and influential area of Korean study. More interest and more research are surely in demand for Korean Imun.

References

AKS. 1986. *The Translation of the Annotation of 'Gyeonggugdaejeon [經國大典]'.* Seoul: The Academy of Korean Studies-research Center of Liberal Arts. [精文研: 韓沽劻他 〈 經國大典 註釋編 〉, 韓國精神文化研究院 人文研究室]

Chung, K. 1988. *Studies of Japanese Department of Sayeokwon in Joseon Dynasty.* Seoul: Taehaksa [拙著: 〈 司譯院 倭學 研究 〉. 太學社]

Chung, K. 1990. *The Study on the Examination System for Interpreters During the Joseon Dynasty.* Seoul: Institute of Big East Asian Culture, Seonggyungwan University. [拙著:〈 朝鮮譯科試科研究 〉, 大東文化研究院. 成均館大學]

Chung, K. 1999. The Chinese of the Yuan Dynasty and the Old Edition Lao Qida. *Research on the Chinese Linguistics* 19-3: 1-23. Tokyo: Waseda University. [拙稿: 元代漢語の 〈 舊本老乞大 〉〈 中國語學 開篇 〉19-3. 早稻田大學 中國語學科]

Chung, K. 2000. The Old Editions of *Nobakjiplam* [老朴集覽] and *Lao Qida* [老乞

大] and *Piao Tongshi* [朴通事]. *Jindanhakbo*(Jindanhakhoi) 89: 155-188. [拙稿: 〈
老朴集覽 〉과〈 老乞大 〉, 〈 朴通事 〉의 舊本. 〈 震檀學報 〉89 震檀學會]

Chung, K. 2002. The Formation and Change of *LaoQita*. *Pathway into Korean Language and Culture*, ed. G. K. Iverson, 85-102. Seoul: Pagijong Press.

Chung, K. 2003a. The Accommodation of Chinese Characters and the Changes of Korean Transcriptions with Chinese Characters on the Korean Peninsula. *Gugyeolyeongu* 11: 53-86. Gugyeolhakhoe. [拙稿: 韓半島에서 漢字의 受容과 借字表記의 變遷, 〈 口訣研究 〉11. 口訣學會]

Chung, K. 2003b. The Establishment and Changes of 'Nogeoldae [老乞大]'. *Pathways into Korean Language and Culture*, eds. S. Lee, G. Iverson, S. Ahn and Y. Yu, 151-168. Seoul: Pagijong Press.

Chung, K. 2004a. *The Translation and Annotation of 'Original LaoChita [原本老乞大]*. Seoul: Kimyoungsa. [拙著: 〈역주原本老乞大 〉. 김영사]

Chung, K. 2004b. The Textbooks for Chinese and its Education During the Joseon Dynasty with the Case of *Lao Chita*. *The Situations about Teaching Chinese in Foreign Countries* 5: 2-9. Beijing Foreign Language University. [拙稿: 朝鮮時代的漢語 育與 材: 以〈 老乞大 〉爲例. 〈 國外漢語 學動態 〉5. 北京外國語大學]

Chung, K. et al. 2002a. *The Original Lao Qida* (Translation, Original Text and its Photoprint and the Indexes for Pronunciations). Beijing: The Publishing Company of the Education and Study of Foreign Languages. [鄭光主編, 編者 梁伍鎭, 鄭丞惠: 〈 原本老乞大 〉(解題, 原文, 原本影印, 併音索引). 外語教學與研究出版社]

Chung, K. et al. 2002b. *Lìxuézhǐnán* [吏學指南]. Seoul: Taehaksa Press. [정광 외, 정승혜, 양오진 공저, 〈 吏學指南 〉, 태학사]

Chang, S. 2001. *Dictionary for Reading Itu Texts*. Seoul: Hanyang University Press.

Ching, G. 1997. About the Characteristics of Khitane Characters. *The Characters of Asian races*, ed. Gugyeohakhoi [口訣學會], 75-105. Seoul: Taehaksa Press. [清格泰爾: 關於契丹文字的特點〈아시아諸民族의 文字 〉, 口訣學會編. 태학사]

Hong, Q. 1946. *The History of Progress of 'Jeongeum [正音]'*. Seoul: Seoul Newspaper Press. [洪起文: 〈 正音發達史 〉서울新聞社出版局]

Jiang, S. 1994. *The Introduction to the Studies of Modern Chinese*. Beijing: Beijing University Press. [蔣紹愚: 〈 近代漢語研究概況 〉. 北京大學出版社]

Karlgren, B. 1964. *Grammata Serica Recensa*. Stockholm: Museum of Far Eastern Antiquities.

Kim, M. et al. 2000. *Laochita: The Textbook of Chinese Conversations in the Mid-Joseon Dynasty* (Toyoubunko 699). Tokyo: Heibonsya Press. [金文京, 玄幸子, 佐藤晴彦 譯註, 鄭光 解説〈 老乞大: 朝鮮中世の中國語誨化讀本 〉(東洋文庫 699). 平凡社]

Lee, C. 1992. *Itu [吏讀] in the Goryeo Dynasty*. Seoul: Taehaksa Press. [李丞宰: 〈 高麗時代의 吏讀 〉. 太學社]

Miyazaki, I. 1987. *History of Government Examination of China*. Tokyo: Heibonsya. [宮崎市定: 〈 科擧史 〉. 平凡社]

Nagasawa, N. 1933. On the Chéngzhaixiàojingzhìjié Published in the Yuan Dynasty. *Philology* 1-5: 20-38. Japanese School of Philology. (later republished in *The Study of the Editions of the Song and Yuan Dynasties, the Volume 3 of the Collection of the Essays of Nagasawa*) [長澤規矩也: 元刊本成齋孝經に關して. 〈 書誌學 〉1-5.

日本書誌學會. (〈 長澤規矩也著作集 〉3 「宋元版の研究」)

Nam, P. 1980. Gugygeol [口訣] and To [吐]. *Korean Linguistics* 9: 55-74. The School of Korean Linguistics. (later republished in Nam (1999)) [南豊鉉: 口訣과吐. 〈 국어학〉9. 국어학회]

Nam, P. 1999. *The Study of 'Kugyeol' for the History of Korean.* Seoul: Taehaksa Press. [南豊鉉: 〈 國語史를 위한口訣研究 〉. 太學社]

Oda, T. 1953. About the Language of Laochita. *Essays on the Studies of Chinese Linguistics* 1: 1-14. [太田辰夫: 老乞大の言語について. 〈 中國語學研究會論集 〉1]

Oda, T. 1954. About Hànéryányǔ Language. *Kobe Foreign Language University's Collection of Essays* 5-3: 1-29. [太田辰夫: 漢兒言語について 〈 神戸外大論叢 〉5-3]

Oda, T. and H. Sato. 1996. *The Original Edition of 'Xiàojīngzhíjié'.* Tokyo: Kyūkosyoin. [太田辰夫・佐藤晴彦: 〈 元版孝經直解 〉 汲古書院]

Park, Y. 2005. On the Haneotokam[漢語都監] in Koryoe Dynasty. *Korean Repository* 50: 35-58. [朴龍雲: 高麗時代의 漢語都監에 대하여. 〈 韓國學報 〉]

Poppe, N. 1954. *Grammar of Written Mongolian.* Wiesbaden: Otto Harassowitz.

Rin, T. 1987. The Origin of Beijing Mandarin. *Chinese Language and Writings*, 33-50. Beijing: Chinese Language and Writings Publishing Comapany. [林燾: 北京官話溯源. 〈 中國語文 〉. 中國語文雜誌社]

Ryu, L. 1983. *The Study of* Itu *in the Period of Three Kingdoms.* Pyeongyang: Science, Encyclopedia Press. [劉烈: 〈 세나라시기의 리두에 대한 연구〉. 과학, 백과사전출판사]

Tanaka, K. 1962. The Style of the Chinese Literal Translations of the Mongolian in the Yüan-tien-chang. *Tôhôgakuhô* 32: 187-224. (this paper is also included in *The Literary Style of 'Yuándianzhang'*) [田中謙二: 元典章における蒙文直譯體の文章. 〈 東方學報 〉 32. (〈 元典章の文體 〉. 校正本 元典章 刑部 第 1 冊 附録)]

Tanaka, K. 1965. The Organization of the Documents of 'Yuándianzhang'. *The Literary Style of 'Yuándianzhang'*, 47-161. Institute for Reseach in Humanities, Kyoto University. [田中謙二: 元典章文書の構成. 〈 元典章の文體 〉 (校正本 元典章 刑部 第 1 冊 附録)]

Tung, T. 1968. *Chinese Phonology.* Taipei: Guangwénshujú. [董同龢: 〈 漢語音韻學 〉. 廣文書局]

Wang, L. 1958. *Essays on the History of Chinese.* Beijing: Science Publishing Company. [王力: 〈 漢語史稿 〉. 科學出版社]

Wang, L. 1985. *The History of Chinese Phonemes.* Beijing: Social Science Publication Company. [王力: 〈 漢語語音史 〉. 社會科學出版社]

Yoshikawa, K. 1953. The Literary Style of Hànwènlidú Found in 'Yuándianzhang'. *The Literary Style of 'Yuándianzhang'*, 1-45. Institute for Research in Humanities, Kyoto University. [吉川幸次郎: 元典章に見えた漢文吏牘の文體. 〈 元典章の文體 〉 (校定本 元典章 刑部 第 1 冊 附録)]

Yu, Z. 1983. The Postposition 'Xìng [行]' Found in Chinese of the Yuan Dynasty. *The Study on Language and Literature* 1983-3: 56-72. Beijing. [余志鴻: 元代漢語的後置詞 '行'. 〈 語文研究 〉]

Yu, Z. 1992. The Genealogy of Chinese Postpositions in the Yuan Dynasty. *National Language and Literature* 1992-3. Beijing. [余志鴻: 元代漢語的後置詞系統. 〈 民

族語文〉1992-3. ÝÁIÈ]

Zhou, F. 1973. *The Dictionary of Ancient and Present Sounds of Chinese.* Hongkong: Hongkong Chinese Literature University. [周法高:〈漢字古今音彙〉. 香港中文大學]

Optional A-Scrambling*

MAMORU SAITO

Nanzan University

1. Introduction

The non-uniform approach to Japanese scrambling as developed in a series of works by Shigeru Miyagawa (2001, 2003, 2005) has been quite influential. It admits two distinct kinds of scrambling operations. One is A-movement to TP Spec triggered by the EPP-feature on T and the other is A'-adjunction motivated by focusing. The obvious advantage of this approach is that scrambling is assimilated to other widely attested types of movements. There is no need to revise the theory to accommodate scrambling, and there is no need in particular to postulate 'optional movement'.

In this paper, I will develop Miyagawa's analysis of A-scrambling and explore its consequences. The discussion will lead to conclusions that contradict the non-uniform approach. More specifically, I will argue that A-

---

* The material in this paper was presented in syntax seminars at Nanzan University and the University of Connecticut, in colloquia at Keio University and Stony Brook University, and at the 16th Japanese/Korean Linguistics Conference. I would like to thank the audience, especially Jonathan Bobaljik, Tomoko Kawamura, Hisatsugu Kitahara, and Masaki Sano, as well as Hiroshi Aoyagi, Keiko Murasugi, Masashi Nomura, and Koji Sugisaki for helpful comments and suggestions.

scrambling is neither movement to TP Spec nor is triggered by the EPP-feature.

In the following section, I will introduce Miyagawa's core data and his analysis. I will also discuss the binding properties of A-scrambled phrases and present suggestive evidence that their landing site is not TP Spec. In Section 3, I will try to define 'subject' under Miyagawa's analysis and show that this leads to the conclusion that A-scrambling is not triggered by the EPP-feature. Then, in Section 4, I will suggest an alternative analysis for Miyagawa's core data. Section 5 concludes the paper.

2. Miyagawa's Analysis of A-scrambling

2.1. The Core Data

Miyagawa presents the following extremely interesting paradigm as evidence for his non-uniform approach to scrambling:

(1) a. Zen'in-ga   sono tesuto-o   uke -na -katta (yo /to   omo -u)
        all   -NOM that test   -ACC take-Neg-Past   Part that think-Pres
        'All did not take that exam'
        (All > Not, *Not > All)

    b. Sono tesuto-o$_i$ zen'in-ga t_i uke -na -katta (yo /to   omo -u)
        that test   -ACC all   -NOM   take-Neg-Past   Part that think-Pres
        'That exam, all did not take'
        (All > Not, Not > All)

(2) Syukudai -o$_i$ zen'in-ga   [$_{CP}$ sensei -ga t_i das   -u   to]
    homework-ACC all   -NOM   teacher-NOM   assign-Pres that
    omow-ana -katta (yo)
    think -Neg-Past   Part
    'Homework, all did not think that the teacher would assign'
    (All > Not, *Not > All)

In (1a), the quantified NP in the subject position, *zen'in* 'all', takes wide scope over negation, and the sentence expresses total negation. (1b) is derived from (1a) by scrambling the object to the sentence-initial position. In this case, the subject quantified NP is no longer sentence-initial, and it can take narrow scope with respect to negation. The example is ambiguous between total negation and partial negation. This effect is observed only with clause-internal scrambling. Thus, in (2) the subject quantified NP takes scope over negation despite the fact that the embedded object is preposed over it by long-distance scrambling.

Miyagawa argues that (1)-(2) can be readily accounted for under his non-uniform analysis of scrambling. Let us consider the structure in (3).

(3)
```
            TP
          /    \
         α      TP
              /    \
             β      T'
                  /    \
                 vP     T [+EPP]
               /   \   Neg
             NP₁    v'
                  /    \
                 VP     v
               /   \
             NP₂    V
```

(1a), according to Miyagawa, is derived when the subject NP_1 moves to TP Spec (β) in order to check the EPP-feature on T. In this case, the NP asymmetrically c-commands the negation and hence takes wide scope. (1b) can be derived from (1a) by adjoining the object NP_2 to TP (α) by A'-scrambling. Then, the subject takes wide scope over negation just as in the case of (1a). However, given that A-scrambling can be to TP Spec, there is an alternative derivation for (1b). That is, NP_2 can move to TP Spec (β) instead of NP_1 and satisfy the EPP requirement of T. With this derivation, NP_1 remains in vP Spec and hence takes narrow scope with respect to negation. The scope fact in (2) follows because movement to TP Spec cannot take place across a CP boundary, and long-distance scrambling must involve adjunction. The matrix subject must move to TP Spec in order to check the EPP-feature of the matrix T.

The generalization observed with (1)-(2) is not always clear-cut, and there are some loose ends in Miyagawa's analysis. First, the clarity of the contrasts depends on the specific quantified NP, the verb form, and the sentence-ending, as Miyagawa notes. For example, when a sentence of the form in (1a) is embedded in a conditional, a scope ambiguity emerges as (4) shows.

(4) Zen'in-ga   sono tesuto-o   uke -na -katta-ra, raigetu   mata
     all   -NOM that test   -ACC take-Neg-Past -if next month again
     tesuto-o   su -ru
     test   -ACC do-Pres
     'If all do not take the exam, (we will) have another exam next month'
     (All > Not, Not > All)

Miyagawa suggests that tense may be subjunctive in this case, and that this may be the cause of the availability of the narrow scope reading of the subject. On the other hand, potentially problematic examples are found in other contexts as well. Thus, (5) seems totally ambiguous when uttered in the context where students have a choice of taking an exam or handing in a term paper to receive credit for a course.

(5) Zen'in-ga   siken -o   erab -ana -i   to omo -u
    all   -NOM exam-ACC choose-Neg-Pres that think-Pres
    'I think that all will not choose an exam (over a term paper)'
    (All > Not, Not > All)

As far as the analysis is concerned, comparison of (1a) with its English counterpart raises a question. As (6) indicates, a quantified NP in TP Spec can fall within the scope of negation in English.

(6) Everyone had not left the party. There were still some people talking and drinking.

The narrow scope reading of 'everyone' may arise due to its reconstruction to vP Spec or because negation can take TP as its scope. Whichever the reason is, it is puzzling why the same mechanism does not yield ambiguity in the case of Japanese (1a).[1]

Nevertheless, I believe that the contrasts in (1)-(2) obtain in a wide variety of contexts and are definitely worth exploring. In the following subsection, I will consider the effect of scrambling in (1b) and show that it is observed even when the scrambled object clearly does not occupy the TP Spec position.

2.2. The Binding Properties of A-Scrambled Phrases

It was proposed originally by Mahajan (1990) that scrambling is of two types, A and A', because of its effects on the binding relations.[2] Let us consider the following examples:

(7) a. *[Otagai   -no   sensei] -ga   karera-o   hihansi -ta (koto)
       each other-GEN teacher-NOM they   -ACC criticize-Past fact
       '*Lit*. Each other's teachers criticized them'

    b. Karera-o$_i$ [otagai   -no   sensei] -ga t_i hihansi -ta (koto)
       they   -ACC each other-GEN teacher-NOM   criticize-Past fact
       '*Lit*. Them, each other's teachers criticized'

---

[1] See also Yamashita 2001 and Kawamura 2004 for much relevant discussion. They argue that A-scrambling does not observe the locality expected of movement to TP Spec.

[2] Mahajan's proposal is based on Hindi data. See Tada 1993 and Nemoto 1993 for detailed discussion on the Japanese data considered here.

(8) a. *[Otagai   -no   sensei] -ga   [Hanako-ga   karera-o
     each other-GEN teacher-NOM   -NOM they -ACC
     hihansi -ta   to]   it -ta   (koto)
     criticize-Past that say-Past fact
     'Lit. Each other's teachers said that Hanako criticized them'

  b. *Karera-o$_i$ [otagai   -no   sensei] -ga   [Hanako-ga t_i
     they -ACC each other-GEN teacher-NOM   -NOM
     hihansi -ta   to]   it -ta   (koto)
     criticize-Past that say-Past fact
     'Lit. Them, each other's teachers said that Hanako criticized'

(7a) is out because the anaphor *otagai* 'each other' is not bound by its antecedent *karera* 'they'. As shown in (7b), if *karera* is scrambled to a position that c-commands *otagai*, the sentence becomes grammatical. This indicates that a scrambled phrase can serve as an A-binder for an anaphor. This effect, however, is limited to clause-internal scrambling. In (8b), *karera* is scrambled across a CP boundary to a position that c-commands *otagai*, and no improvement is observed. Mahajan concludes then that clause-internal scrambling can be A-movement while long-distance scrambling is necessarily A'-movement.

If there is scrambling with A'-properties, we would expect it to apply not only across a CP boundary but clause-internally as well. This prediction is borne out by examples such as (9).

(9)   Zibun-zisin-o$_i$ Taroo-ga t_i seme -ta   (koto)
      self -self -ACC   -NOM   blame-Past fact
      'Himself, Taroo blamed'

If the landing site of *zibun-zisin-o* 'self-ACC' is an A-position in (9), the example should be in violation of Condition (C) of the binding theory. Thus, it suggests that clause-internal scrambling can be A'-movement.

Miyagawa follows Mahajan and assumes that there are two types of scrambling, A and A'. As noted at the outset of this paper, his proposal is that A-scrambling is movement to TP Spec while A'-scrambling involves adjunction. Now, if we combine his analysis of the paradigm in (1)-(2) and Mahajan's account of the binding facts in (7)-(9), a clear prediction follows. I will illustrate this with the concrete examples in (10)-(11).

(10) a. Zen'in-ga   zibun-zisin-ni   toohyoosi-na -katta (to   omo -u)
        all   -NOM self -self -DAT   vote   -Neg-Past that think-Pres
        'Everyone did not vote for herself/himself'
        (All > Not, *Not > All)

b. Zibun-zisin-ni$_i$ zen'in-ga t_i toohyoosi-na -katta
self -self -DAT all   -NOM vote   -Neg-Past
(to   omo -u)
that think-Pres
'For herself/himself, everyone did not vote'
(All > Not, Not > All)

(11) a. Zen'in-ga   zibun-zisin-o   seme -na -katta (to   omo -u)
all   -NOM self -self -ACC blame-Neg-Past   that think-Pres
'Everyone did not blame herself/himself'
(All > Not, *Not > All)

b. Zibun-zisin-o$_i$ zen'in-ga t_i seme -na -katta (to   omo -u)
self -self -ACC all   -NOM blame-Neg-Past   that think-Pres
'Herself/himself, everyone did not blame'
(All > Not, Not > All)

In (10a), the quantified NP subject *zen'in* 'all' takes wide scope over negation. This is expected under Miyagawa's analysis since the subject is raised to TP Spec exactly as in the case of (1a). (10b) is ambiguous and parallels (1b). If this example is derived from (10a), the subject is in TP Spec and the scrambled phrase is adjoined to TP. In this case, the subject *zen'in* takes scope over negation. On the other hand, according to Miyagawa, the narrow scope reading of *zen'in* obtains when the scrambled phrase is in TP Spec and check the EPP-feature. Then, *zen'in* remains in *v*P Spec and is within the c-command domain of the negation. But note that the scrambled phrase is a reflexive just as in (9). That is, if it is in TP Spec, the example should be in violation of Condition (C) of the Binding theory. It follows that *zen'in* can take narrow scope even when the scrambled phrase is not in TP Spec but is in an A'-position. The examples in (11) raise the same problem.

The ambiguity of (10b) and (11b) suggests that the narrow scope reading of *zen'in* is not made possible because the scrambled phrase checks the EPP-feature on T in its place. It seems then necessary to come up with an alternative analysis for the paradigm in (1)-(2). Before I pursue this, I will raise another issue in the following section with the analysis of A-scrambling as movement to TP Spec. It has to do with the definition of 'subject'.

3. On the Definition of Subject

As is well known, the Japanese reflexives *zibun* 'self' and *zibun-zisin* 'self-self' are subject-oriented. Thus, only *Hanako* qualifies as the antecedent of *zibun* in (12) and (13).

(12) Hanako-ga   Taroo-ni   zibun-no   hon -o   okut-ta
     -NOM   -DAT self -GEN book-ACC send-Past
     'Hanako sent her book to Taroo'

(13) Hanako-ga   Taroo-o   zibun-no   ie   -de sikat -ta
     -NOM   -ACC self -GEN house-at scold-Past
     'Hanako scolded Taroo at her house'

However, as far as I know, the definition of 'subject' in this context is yet to be made precise. There are two obvious candidates, TP Spec and vP Spec. This is so since *Hanako* in (12), for example, is merged at vP Spec and is raised to TP Spec, as illustrated in (14).

(14) [$_{\text{TP}}$ Hanako$_i$-ga [$_{vP}$ t_i [$_{\text{VP}}$ Taroo-ni zibun$_i$-no hon-o okut-]] ta]

Interestingly, Miyagawa's analysis of A-scrambling as movement to TP Spec is compatible only with the definition of 'subject' as vP Spec. A scrambled object never qualifies as the antecedent of *zibun*, as shown in (15), and hence, the analysis makes incorrect predictions if TP Spec is the 'subject' in the relevant sense.

(15) Taroo-o$_i$ Hanako-ga t_i zibun-no   ie   -de sikat -ta
     -ACC   -NOM   self -GEN house-at scold-Past
     'Hanako scolded Taroo at her house'

In this section, I will first examine 'subjecthood' in examples with complex predicates and present evidence that phrases in vP Spec are indeed possible antecedents for *zibun*. This appears to provide support for Miyagawa's analysis. In Section 3.2, however, I will argue that further exploration of the definition of 'subject' leads us to the conclusion that A-scrambling is not triggered by the EPP-feature on T.

3.1. Subject as vP Spec

It has been known that what qualifies as a possible antecedent for *zibun* is the 'surface subject'. Thus, *zibun* can refer to the subjects of passive and unaccusative sentences, as shown in (16)-(17).

(16) Taroo-ga$_i$ karera-niyotte zibun-no zibun-no ie   -de t_i koros-are   -ta
            -NOM they -by   self -GEN house-at   kill -Passive-Past
     (koto)
     fact
     'Taroo was killed by them at his house'

(17) Taroo-ga$_i$ zibun-no   ie   -de t_i sin-da (koto)
          -NOM self -GEN house-at   die-Past fact
     'Taroo died at his house'

If *Taroo* in (16)-(17) moves directly to TP Spec from the internal argument position, these examples suggest that TP Spec is the 'subject position' in the relevant sense.

On the other hand, the examination of complex predicate constructions leads us to a different conclusion. Let us consider the following causative sentence:

(18) Hanako-ga   Taroo-ni   zibun-no   hon -o   sute   -sase -ta
      -NOM   -DAT self -GEN book-ACC discard-make-Past
      'Hanako made Taroo discard her/his book'

It has been widely assumed since Kuroda 1965 that the causative morpheme *-sase* takes a sentential complement. (18) confirms this since both the causer and the causee qualify as the antecedent for *zibun*. That is, causative sentences contain two 'subjects' and hence two sentences.

On the other hand, the embedded "clause" clearly lacks tense and does not seem to be a full-fledged TP. It is thus assumed to be a *v*P in more recent works such as Murasugi and Hashimoto 2004. The structure of (18) would then be as in (19).[3]

(19)

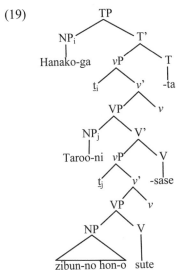

---

3 In (19), the embedded subject *Taroo* moves and merges with a projection of the causative verb *-sase* in order to receive the causee role. (See Saito 2001 for relevant discussion.) But this is not crucial for the discussion here. The argument is unaffected even if *Taroo* stays in the embedded *v*P Spec, or it is merged directly in the matrix VP and controls PRO in the embedded *v*P Spec.

Here, *Taroo*, a possible antecedent for *zibun*, never occupies a TP Spec position. Examples of this kind thus suggest that *v*P Spec, rather than TP Spec, is the 'subject position' in the relevant sense.

Although we apparently have conflicting data on the definition of 'subject', the evidence from the causative construction is more compelling. If 'subject' is defined as TP Spec, it seems impossible to accommodate examples like (18). On the other hand, (16)-(17) are consistent with the definition of 'subject' as *v*P Spec if *Taroo* moves through the *v*P Spec position on the way to TP Spec, as illustrated in (20).

(20)

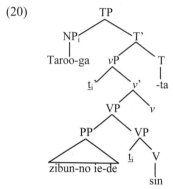

And there is indeed evidence that the subjects of passive and unaccusative sentences move through *v*P Spec. Let us consider the following causative sentence:

(21) Sono isya -wa   Taroo-o   zibun-no ie   -de sin -ase-te
     that doctor-TOP   -ACC self -GEN house-in die-make
     simat-ta
     have -Past
     'The doctor has let Taroo die in his own house'

This sentence can be appropriately uttered when the doctor failed to notice the seriousness of Taroo's illness and has mistakenly let him leave the hospital, indirectly causing him to die at his own house. In this case, *Taroo* is the antecedent for *zibun*.

What is interesting about (21), in comparison with (18), is that the embedded verb *sin* 'die' is unaccusative. This means that *Taroo* is initially merged at the object position of this verb, and then moves to the embedded *v*P Spec so that it qualifies as the antecedent for *zibun*. The derivation is shown in (22).[4]

---

[4] The final verb *simat-ta* in (21) adds perfective meaning to the sentence. It is omitted in the structure in (22).

(22)

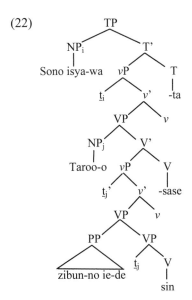

(22) indicates that the object of an unaccusative verb can move through *v*P Spec on the way to a higher position. Then, we would expect this to be the case in (17) as well. That is, the sentence may be derived as in (20), and there is no compelling reason to include TP Spec among the 'subject positions' to accommodate unaccusative sentences. Precisely the same argument can be constructed for the passive (16) on the basis of (23), where the causative *-sase* takes a passive complement:

(23) Taroo-wa   dai-sensei -o   zibun-no   gakusei-tati-niyotte
     -TOP big-teacher-ACC self   -GEN student-PL-by
     suuhais -are   -sase-te oi   -ta
     worship-Passive-make   leave-Past
     'Taroo kept letting the big professor be worshiped by his/her students'

The internal argument of the complement verb *suuhais* 'worship' can be the antecedent of *zibun* in this example.

It was shown in this subsection that *v*P Spec is a plausible candidate for the position of the possible antecedents for the subject-oriented reflexive *zibun*. As noted at the outset of this section, the definition of 'subject position' as TP Spec is incompatible with the EPP analysis of A-scrambling. In this sense, the discussion here provides indirect support for the analysis. However, I will show in the following subsection that a closer examination of the relevant data leads to different conclusions. I will argue in particular that 'subjects' should be defined as those phrases that check the EPP-feature and that A-scrambling is not feature-driven.

3.2. A-Scrambling and the EPP-feature on v

Recall that a scrambled object does not qualify as the antecedent for *zibun*. The relevant example (15) is repeated below as (24).

(24) Taroo-o$_i$ Hanako-ga t_i zibun-no   ie   -de sikat -ta
     -ACC   -NOM   self -GEN house-at scold-Past
     'Hanako scolded Taroo at her house'

If 'subject' is defined as vP Spec, this seems to be expected under the hypothesis that the landing site of A-scrambling is TP Spec. But the situation turns out to be more complex when the precise derivation of (24) is considered.

Note that (24) is a transitive sentence, and hence, its vP should constitute a derivational phase.[5] This implies that the scrambling of *Taroo* should proceed through the edge of vP. If the final landing site is TP Spec, the derivation should be as in (25).

(25)

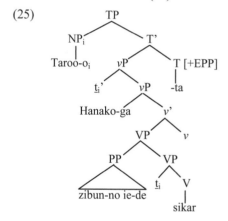

Then, after all, the EPP analysis of A-scrambling makes a false prediction with respect to (24) whether 'subject' is defined as TP Spec or vP Spec.

The problem is clearer when we consider, again, the causative construction. As shown below, a causative sentence counts as simplex for the locality of A-scrambling.

(26) Karera-o$_i$ [otagai   -no   sensei -ga   Taroo-ni t_i
     they -ACC each other-GEN teacher-NOM   -DAT
     home -sase -ta] (koto)
     praise-make-Past fact
     '*Lit.* Each other's teachers made Taroo praise them'

---

[5] I assume, following Chomsky 2000, for example, that C and transitive/unergative v (v^* in Chomsky's terms) project phases.

This is not surprising because scrambling in this case does not cross a CP boundary. And a scrambled phrase cannot be the antecedent for *zibun* in a causative sentence, as shown in (27).

(27) Hanako-o$_i$ [Ziroo-ga Taroo-ni zibun-no ie -de t_i
-ACC -NOM -DAT self -GEN house-at
nagur-ase -ta] (koto)
praise-make-Past fact
'Ziroo made Taroo hit Hanako at his house'

I have been assuming that the causative morpheme *-sase* takes a *v*P complement. If this is correct, the scrambling in (27) must proceed via the edges of two *v*P's; the complement *v*P and the matrix *v*P. Hence, this example is clearly incompatible with the definition of 'subject' as *v*P Spec.

Although (24) and (27) were discussed as problematic examples for the EPP analysis of A-scrambling, the issue they raise is a general one. As discussed in the preceding subsection, when an internal argument of a passive verb or an unaccusative verb moves through *v*P Spec, it qualifies as the antecedent of *zibun*. On the other hand, when an argument is scrambled through *v*P Spec, it does not count as the 'subject'. Then, how can these two cases be distinguished?

It seems to me that Lasnik's (1995) discussion on existential passive sentences provides a hint toward the solution to this problem. Considering the English counterparts of the Italian (28), discussed in Belletti 1988, he presents the contrast in (29).

(28) È stato messo un libro sul tavolo
has been put a book on the table

(29) a. *There has been put a book on the table
b. There has been a book put on the table

(29a), which corresponds to (28), is ungrammatical; the object must be preposed in front of the passive verb as in (29b). In order to account for this short movement, Lasnik suggests that there is a functional head with an EPP-like feature right above the passive verb. If the relevant functional head is *v* and the feature is EPP, the structure of the relevant part of (29b) will be as in (30).

(30)

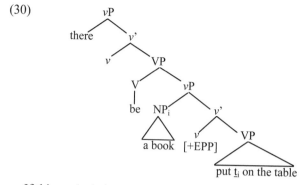

If this analysis is correct, and in particular, if passive and unaccusative *v* has an EPP-feature, a more precise analysis becomes possible for (21) and (23). It was left unaccounted for why *Taroo-o* 'Taroo-ACC' moves though *v*P Spec in (22). The EPP-feature on the embedded *v* provides a reason for this step of the movement. Further, this forces the internal argument to move through *v*P Spec on the way to TP Spec in the simple unaccusative sentence in (17), which is repeated below as (31).

(31) Taroo-ga_i   zibun-no   ie   -de t_i sin-da   (koto)
    -NOM self -GEN house-at   die-Past fact
   'Taroo died at his house'

The precise derivation of this example will be as in (32).

(32)

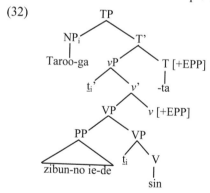

Let us now return to the scrambling example in (24) with this conclusion. The example is repeated below as (33).

(33) Taroo-o_i   Hanako-ga t_i zibun-no   ie   -de sikat -ta
    -ACC   -NOM   self -GEN house-at scold-Past
   'Hanako scolded Taroo at her house'

As noted above, *Taroo-o* moves through the edge of *v*P in this example. If this movement to *v*P Spec is driven by the EPP-feature on *v*, then (33) and (31) will be indistinguishable again. The only way to differentiate these two cases, as far as I can tell, is to say that movement to *v*P Spec is triggered by the EPP-feature in (31) but not in (33) and that only those phrases that satisfy an EPP requirement count as the 'subject'. This correctly accounts for the fact that the subject of an unaccusative/passive verb qualifies as the antecedent of *zibun* while a scrambled object does not. But then, we are led to the conclusion that there is local A-scrambling to the edge of *v*P that has nothing to do with the EPP. This amounts to saying that there is optional A-scrambling. And if scrambling can take place to the edge of *v*P without the aid of an EPP-feature, there does not seem to be reason to suppose that it cannot move a phrase to the edge of TP in the same way. Thus, the examination of the distribution and the interpretation of *zibun*, after all, raises serious doubts for the EPP analysis of A-scrambling.

Given the evidence against the EPP analysis of A-scrambling presented so far, I will suggest an alternative approach to Miyagawa's paradigm (1)-(2) in the following section. In the remainder of this section, I will point out a few consequences of the proposed account for the possible antecedents of *zibun*.

I just argued that possible antecedents for *zibun* are not those phrases in a specific position such as TP Spec or *v*P spec, but those that check the EPP-feature. Thus, phrases in TP Spec and *v*P Spec qualify as 'subjects' as long as they satisfy an EPP requirement of a head. This has a couple of obvious implications. First, let us reconsider the simple causative example in (18), repeated below as (34).

(34) Hanako-ga   Taroo-ni   zibun-no   hon -o   sute   -sase -ta
     -NOM   -DAT self -GEN book-ACC discard-make-Past
     'Hanako made Taroo discard her/his book'

Here the embedded verb *sute* 'discard' is transitive and its external argument *Taroo* is a possible antecedent for *zibun*. Then, a transitive/unergative *v* must also carry an EPP-feature and it must be checked by the external argument.

Second, the EPP-feature of *v* cannot play any part in successive-cyclic operator movement. It is proposed in Chomsky 2000 and 2001, for example, that an EPP-feature can be assigned freely to a transitive/unergative *v* and this makes the initial step of the *Wh*-movement in (35) possible.

(35) $[_{CP}$ What$_i$ did $[_{TP}$ John$_j$ $[_{vP}$ t_i' $[_{vP}$ t_j $[_{VP}$ buy $t_i]]]]]$

But if an EPP-feature can be assigned freely to a transitive/unergative *v*, in addition to the one checked by the external argument, then we lose the account for the fact that a scrambled object does not qualify as the antecedent of *zibun*. This is so because *Hanako* in (27), for example, should be able to check the additional EPP-feature of *v* on its way to the sentence-initial position and be the antecedent for *zibun*. I tentatively suggest that the feature that is assigned freely to *v* is not the EPP-feature but the P-feature, which Chomsky (2000) postulates for the operator movement to an intermediate CP Spec. The P-feature, then, can be assigned to any phase head and attract an operator to its Spec position, while the EPP-feature is inherent in T and *v*.

One example that is still left unaccounted for is the Italian (28), repeated below in (36).

(36) È   stato messo un libro sul tavolo
    has been put   a book on the table

If the passive *v* universally has an EPP-feature, it is not clear why *un libro* 'a book' need not be preposed to the position in front of *messo* 'put' as in its English counterpart (29b). Although I do not have a solution to this problem, I would tentatively assume that the null expletive is initially merged at *v*P Spec and checks the EPP-feature of *v* in (36). English and Italian are then parameterized in the ability of expletives to check the EPP-feature on *v*. Since the expletive *there* is unable to check the EPP-feature of *v*, it is necessary to raise *a book* to *v*P Spec in (29b).[6]

4. Miyagawa's Paradigm and the First-Constituent Effects

Let us finally return to Miyagawa's examples in (1)-(2), repeated below in (37)-(38).

(37) a. Zen'in-ga   sono tesuto-o   uke -na -katta (yo /to omo -u)
      all   -NOM that test -ACC take-Neg-Past Part that think-Pres
      'All did not take that exam'
      (All > Not, *Not > All)

   b. Sono tesuto-o$_i$ zen'in-ga t_i uke -na -katta (yo /to omo -u)
      that test -ACC all   -NOM   take-Neg-Past Part that think-Pres
      'That exam, all did not take'
      (All > Not, Not > All)

---

[6] *There* should be able to check the EPP-feature of unaccusative *v* in English as the following example is grammatical:

(i) There arrived someone

It remains to be seen what property distinguishes English passives on the one hand and Italian passives and English unaccusatives on the other.

(38) Syukudai -o$_i$ zen'in-ga   [$_{CP}$ sensei -ga t_i das   -u   to]
     homework-ACC all   -NOM   teacher-NOM   assign-Pres that
     omow-ana -katta (yo)
     think -Neg-Past Part
     'Homework, all did not think that the teacher would assign'
     (All > Not, *Not > All)

I argued in Section 2 that the narrow scope reading of *zen'in-ga* 'all-NOM' observed in (37b) is possible even when the scrambling exhibits A' properties. In Section 3, I pointed out that the analysis of A-scrambling as an EPP-driven movement to TP Spec faces a problem with the characterization of possible antecedents for *zibun*. I will then suggest an alternative approach to (37)-(38) in this section.

Note first that the effect of scrambling in (37b) is of a familiar kind observed with many other phenomena. That is, scrambling can but need not affect the interpretation of a sentence. Let me illustrate this point with the interpretation of phrases marked by the topic marker -*wa*. As discussed in detail in Kuno 1973, a *wa*-marked phrase can be interpreted as a 'theme' or as a contrastive topic. Thus, (39) is ambiguous.

(39) Taroo-wa   sono hon -o   yon -da
     -TOP that   book-ACC read-Past
     a. 'Speaking of Taroo, he read that book' (thematic)
     b. 'Taroo read that book, but the others did not' (contrastive)

It is also known that although any phrase can be marked by -*wa*, the thematic interpretation is possible only when the phrase is in the sentence-initial position. The object in (40), for example, receives only contrastive interpretation.

(40) Taroo-ga   sono hon -wa   yon -da
     -NOM that   book-TOP read-Past
     'Taroo read that book, but he did not read the others' (contrastive)

Scrambling interacts with these interpretive properties of *wa*-marked phrases in an interesting way. Let us first consider the scrambled version of (39) shown in (41).

(41) Sono hon -o$_i$ Taroo-wa t_i yon -da
     that book-ACC   -TOP   read-Past
     'Taroo' - thematic or contrastive as in (40)

Here, the interpretation of *Taroo-wa* remains ambiguous; in particular it can be interpreted thematically despite the fact that the scrambled object precedes it. This shows that a scrambled phrase need not count in the calculation of the first constituent. At the same time, the following examples indicate that a scrambled phrase can participate in this calculation:

(42) a. Taroo-ga   soko-e it -ta
        -NOM there-to go-Past
        'Taroo sent there'

    b. Taroo-wa soko-e -wa   it -ta
        -TOP there-to-TOP go-Past
        'Taroo' - thematic or contrastive, 'soko-e' - contrastive

    c. Soko-e -wa$_i$ Taroo-wa t_i it -ta
        there-to-TOP   -TOP   go-Past
        'soko-e' - thematic or contrastive, 'Taroo' - contrastive or thematic

(42b) exhibits the expected pattern; only the sentence-initial *wa*-phrase can be interpreted thematically. (42c) is derived from (42b) by scrambling *soko-e-wa* 'there-to-TOP' to the sentence-initial position, and the phrase can be interpreted as a theme, which indicates that a scrambled phrase need not but still can count as the first constituent.

The examples in (37) can be understood in basically the same way. (37a) indicates that a quantified NP in the sentence-initial position takes wide scope over negation. In (37b), the scrambled object can count as sentence-initial. In this case, the subject quantified NP can assume narrow scope with respect to negation. On the other hand, a scrambled phrase need not count in the calculation of the first constituent. If it does not, the subject quantified NP remains the first constituent and takes scope over negation. Thus, (37a-b) and (42b-c) seem to be two instances of the same general phenomenon.

Then what is the position of the first constituent? The English example in (6), repeated below as (43), suggests that negation can take scope over the subject in TP Spec.

(43) Everyone had not left the party. There were still some people talking and drinking.

If this is true in Japanese as well, then the first constituent position must be outside TP as a quantified NP is this position necessarily takes scope over negation. This is in accord with the conclusion drawn from examples like (44) (= (10b)) that the position is an A'-position.

(44) Zibun-zisin-ni$_i$ zen'in-ga t_i toohyoosi-na -katta (to   omo -u)
     self -self -DAT all   -NOM   vote   -Neg-Past that think-Pres
     'For herself/himself, everyone did not vote'
     (All > Not, Not > All)

Recall that if *zibun-zisin-ni* 'self-self-DAT' in this example is in an A-position, the example should be in violation of Condition (C) of the Binding theory.

Based on these considerations, I would like to propose that there is a functional head Th above TP and that the first constituent is attracted to its Spec position. The structure of a Japanese sentence will then be as in (45).

(45)

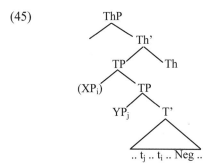

YP is the subject (in TP Spec) and XP is a scrambled phrase. Both can be within the scope of negation, say, because negation takes TP as its scope. However, the functional head Th (for 'theme') attracts the closest phrase to its Spec. If there is no scrambling, the subject is raised to this position and takes scope over negation.

The situation is slightly more complex when scrambling takes place. We have seen that scrambling may or may not affect interpretation. I assume here along the lines of Tada 1993 that this is because scrambling can be undone in LF.[7] If a scrambled phrase stays at the landing site in LF, it can serve as the antecedent of an anaphor as in (46) (= (7b)).

(46) Karera-o$_i$ [otagai -no sensei]-ga t_i hihansi -ta (koto)
     they -ACC each other-GEN teacher-NOM criticize-Past fact
     '*Lit.* Them, each other's teachers criticized'

On the other hand, if scrambling is undone, there is no violation of Condition (C) in (47) (= (9)).

(47) Zibun-zisin-o$_i$ Taroo-ga t_i seme -ta (koto)
     self -self -ACC -NOM blame-Past fact
     'Himself, Taroo blamed'

Finally, the ungrammaticality of (48) (= (8b)) indicates that long-distance scrambling is necessarily undone in LF.

---

[7] This is for ease of exposition. For a more principled interpretive mechanism that has the effect of 'LF undoing', see Saito 2005.

(48) *Karera-o_i   [otagai   -no   sensei]-ga   [Hanako-ga t_i
       they   -ACC   each other-GEN teacher-NOM   -NOM
       hihansi -ta   to]   it -ta   (koto)
       criticize-Past that say-Past fact
       '*Lit.* Them, each other's teachers said that Hanako criticized'

Given this property of scrambling, the scope facts in (37b) and (38) can be correctly captured. (37b) involves clause-internal scrambling. If scrambling is not undone, the scrambled phase is attracted to ThP Spec and the subject *zen'in* 'all' remains in TP Spec. Hence, the narrow scope reading of the subject is possible. On the other hand, if the scrambled phrase moves back to its initial position, the subject *zen'in* moves to ThP Spec and takes scope over negation. (38) is straightforward because long scrambling is always undone. The matrix subject must move to ThP Spec and take wide scope. Note that this account implies that the movement to ThP Spec is covert as it is fed by the LF undoing of scrambling.[8]

The thematic interpretation of *wa*-phrases can be accounted for in the same way. As only the sentence-initial *wa*-phrase can be interpreted as the theme, the following interpretive mechanism can be assumed:

(49) A *wh*-phrase is interpreted as the theme only if it is in ThP Spec.

A clause-internally scrambled phrase may stay at the landing site or move back to its initial position. Hence, in (42c), repeated below as (50), either the scrambled phrase or the subject can be interpreted as the theme.

(50) Soko-e -wa_i   Taroo-wa t_i it -ta
       there-to-TOP   -TOP   go-Past
       'soko-e' - thematic or contrastive, 'Taroo' - contrastive or thematic

Following Heycock 2006, I assume that the thematic interpretation of *wa*-phrases is represented in the information structure. (49), then, should be operative in the mapping from the syntactic structure to the information structure.

5. Conclusion

In this paper, I examined Miyagawa's paradigm in (1)-(2) and proposed an alternative analysis. I argued in the course of the discussion that contrary to his proposals, A-scrambling is neither EPP-driven nor is to TP Spec. On the other hand, the proposed analysis adapts his insights; I have postulated a functional projection above TP and made it play the role Miyagawa at-

---

[8] The analysis, as formulated here, requires that the undoing of scrambling precede movement to ThP Spec in LF. This stipulation in unnecessary under the more principled mechanism for LF undoing alluded to in Fn.7.

tributed to TP. A phrase in the Spec position of this functional projection takes wide scope over negation, and when it is a *wa*-phrase, it can be interpreted thematically. Thus, the projection plays an important role in semantic/discourse interpretation. Although scrambling seems to lack semantic or discourse properties of its own, a phrase scrambled to the sentence-initial position, at least in some cases, qualifies to move to the Spec position of this functional projection. Hence, it can be said that the projection provides a "motivation" for scrambling, allowing it to have semantic and discourse effects.

References

Belletti, A. 1988. The Case of unaccusatives. *Linguistic Inquiry* 19: 1-34.

Chomsky, N. 2000. Minimalist inquiries: The framework. *Step by Step*, eds. R. Martin, et al., 89-155. Cambridge, MA: MIT Press.

Chomsky, N. 2001. Derivation by phase. *Ken Hale*, ed. M. Kenstowicz, 1-52. Cambridge, MA: MIT Press.

Heycock, C. 2006. Japanese -*wa*, -*ga*, and information structure. Unpublished manuscript. University of Edinburgh.

Kawamura, T. 2004. A feature-checking analysis of Japanese scrambling. *Journal of Linguistics* 40: 45-68.

Kuno, S. 1973. *The Structure of the Japanese Language*. Cambridge, MA: MIT Press.

Kuroda, S.-Y. 1965. Causative forms in Japanese. *Foundations of Language* 1: 31-50.

Lasnik, H. 1995. Case and expletives revisited: On greed and other human failings. *Linguistic Inquiry* 26: 615-633.

Mahajan, A. 1990. The A/A-bar distinction and movement theory. Doctoral dissertation, MIT.

Miyagawa, S. 2001. EPP, scrambling, and *wh*-in-situ. *Ken Hale*, ed. M. Kenstowicz, 293-338. Cambridge, MA: MIT Press.

Miyagawa, S. 2003. A-movement scrambling and options without optionality. *Word Order and Scrambling*, ed. S. Karimi, 177-200. Oxford: Blackwell.

Miyagawa, S. 2005. EPP and semantically vacuous scrambling. *The Free Word Order Phenomenon*, eds. J. Sabel and M. Saito, 181-220. Berlin: Mouton de Gruyter.

Murasugi, K. and T. Hashimoto. 2004. Three pieces of acquisition evidence for the *v*-VP frame. *Nanzan Linguistics* 1: 1-19. The Nanzan Center for Linguistics.

Nemoto, N. 1993. Chains and Case positions: A study from scrambling in Japanese. Doctoral dissertation, University of Connecticut.

Saito, M. 2001. Movement and θ-roles: A case study with resultatives. *Proceedings of the Second Tokyo Conference on Psycholinguistics*, ed. Y.Otsu, 35-60. Tokyo: Hituzi Syobo.

Saito, M. 2005. Further notes on the interpretation of scrambling chains. *The Free Word Order Phenomenon*, eds. J. Sabel and M. Saito, 335-376. Berlin: Mouton de Gruyter.

Tada, H. 1993. A/A-bar partition in derivation. Doctoral dissertation, MIT.

Yamashita, H. 2001. EPP and the ordering effects on interpretation: A preliminary study. *Nanzan Studies in Japanese Language Education* 8: 300-308.

The Distribution of Subject Properties in Multiple Subject Constructions[*]

JAMES H. YOON
University of Illinois, Urbana-Champaign

1. Introduction

Grammatical relations (GR) such as subject and object have long been recognized to be indispensable in understanding how grammars of natural languages work, though there seems to be no logical necessity for arguments to be filtered through a layer of grammatical relations (GRs) as they receive morphosyntactic expression. Despite the pervasiveness of GRs, pinning down the properties of GRs has met with repeated challenges.

The goal of this paper is to investigate questions of subjecthood in a well-known construction in the grammar of Japanese and Korean—the

[*] The ideas in this paper were presented at the 2006 Linguistic Society of Korea International Conference (Seoul) and the 16th Japanese/Korean Linguistics Conference (Kyoto, October, 2006). I would like to thank the LSK and Yukinori Takubo, organizer of J/K 16, for their invitation and generosity. The paper has benefited from comments and feedback from the following individuals: Karlos Arregi, Hongbin Im, Ruth Kempson, Ji-Hye Kim, Soowon Kim, Chungmin Lee, Joan Maling, Chongwon Park, Byungsoo Park, Reiko Vermeulen, John Whitman, as well as members of the Korean syntax-semantics group at the University of Illinois— Daeho Chung, Youngju Choi, Juhyeon Hwang, Keunyoung Shin, and Yunchul Yoo.

Multiple Subject Construction (MSC, also called the **Double Subject Construction** or the **Multiple Nominative Construction**). Here are some well-worn examples of MSCs often encountered in the literature:

(1) a. Cheli-ka   meli-ka   pisangha-ta
     C-nom   head-nom   exceptional-decl
     'Cheli is exceptionally smart.'
  b. Nampankwu-ka   mwunmyengkwukka-ka   namca-ka
     southern.hemisphere-nom civilized.country-nom   men-nom
     phyengkyun-swumyeng-i   ccalp-ta
     average-lifespan-nom   short-decl
     'It is the southern hemisphere that it is the civilized countries where it is the men whose lifespan is short.'

The first problem concerning MSCs that this paper addresses is the following: only one of the nom-marked nominals in MSCs seems to be an argument of the predicate. For example, in (1b), the predicate *ccalp-ta* 'be short' is a one-place predicate, but there are four subject-like, nominative-marked, nominals in the sentence. Given the common assumption that subjects are arguments (i.e., the most prominent argument), the appearance of more than one subject-like nominal in MSC is puzzling.

The second problem concerns nominative case-marking. The supposition we made that there may be more than one subject in MSCs was based on nominative case-marking. Since we know that nominative case is neither sufficient nor necessary as a defining property of subjects crosslinguistically, the question arises whether all nominative-marked nominals in MSCs are indeed subjects, and if not, how nominative ends up being expressed on more than one nominal. A related question is whether the function of the particle taken to be a nominative case-marker (*-ka/-i* in Korean) is restricted solely to the case-marking function.

The problem with nominative case-marking is part of a larger problem concerning the distribution of subject properties in MSCs. How are subject properties besides nominative case-marking distributed among the subject-like nominals in MSCs? And why are they distributed the way they are? This constitutes the third problem addressed in this paper. To summarize, the following questions concerning subjecthood arise in the study of MSCs:

(2) Subjecthood in MSCs:
  a. What semantic-thematic mechanisms license the nom-marked NPs that do not appear to be selected by the predicate?
  b. Is nominative a property diagnosing subjects? If so, how can an apparent subject coding property be distributed among several nominals in a sentence?

    c. How are the other subject properties distributed (if they are at all) among nominals that share nominative case?

In the vast literature on MSCs, we can discern the following lines of thinking regarding the first two issues identified above. In one line of thinking, it is maintained that the there is only one subject in an MSC and that the additional nominative-marked nominals are not subjects, but topics and/or foci. Those who adhere to this position write off what looks like nominative case on the non-subject nominals as something other than case (Yoon 1986, J-Y Yoon 1989, Schütze 2001).

A second line of thinking posits that there is more than one subject in MSCs. In this approach, the reason nominative case, a typical subject coding property, is realized more than once is because there is more than one subject in an MSC. This is the line of thinking in traditional accounts of MSCs in East Asian languages and the position taken in Teng (1974), B-S Park (1973), I-H Lee (1987), Heycock (1993), and one that I have defended recently (Yoon 2003, 2004a,b, 2006/to appear).

A third approach posits that there is more than one subject in an MSC, but not at the same level of representation. Treatments of MSCs in the Relational Grammar (RG) framework (C. Youn 1990) are framed in terms of this position. Under this approach, as in the second, nominative is case.

And though not much work has been done on the third issue (2c above) compared to the first two, answers to it depend on whether MSCs are deemed to have more than one subject, and if so, at what level(s) of representation.

My goal in this paper is twofold. In the first part of the paper, I will present arguments in favor of the second type of approach to MSCs. In the second part, I will turn to an examination of the distribution of subject properties in MSCs. I shall demonstrate that the traditionally identified subject properties in Korean are distributed between the higher, or Major, subject and a lower, or Grammatical, subject. The distribution of subject properties in MSCs shows that both are subject-like in important ways, thus supporting the results of the first section. Discussion of the implications of the findings closes the paper.

2. Multiple Subject Construction; not Multiple Nominative Construction

2.1. Initial Nom-marked NPs are not Topics or Foci

Different authors have analyzed all but one nominative-marked NP in MSCs as something other than a subject (Li and Thompson 1976, Yoon 1986, J-Y Yoon 1989, Schütze 2001, C. Youn 1990, Vermeulen 2005). If they are not subjects, what could they be? The most common answer to this question is that the non-subject NPs in MSCs bear the discourse function of focus, but not the grammatical relation of subject. It follows in this approach that the particle -*ka* does not always realize case. However, there are some fundamental difficulties with this type of approach.

The focus analysis is based on the observation that in many contexts, the initial NP in an MSC is interpreted as (exhaustive listing) focus (Kuno 1973). For example, the MSC in (3a) is felicitous only if the initial *ka*-marked NP in (3a) is interpreted as focused, as indicated in the translation. To obtain a non-focused interpretation, the topic-marker (-*nun*) must be used, as we see in (3b). The focus analysis predicts this contrast.

(3) a. Cheli-ka   apeci-ka   hakkyo-ey onul   o-si-ess-ta
        C-nom   father-nom   school-loc today come-hon-pst-decl
        'It is Cheli whose father came to school today.'
        ≠ 'Speaking of Cheli, his father came to school today.'
    b. Cheli-**nun** apeci-ka   hakkyo-ey onul   o-si-ess-ta
        C-top   father-nom   school-loc today come-hon-pst-decl
        'Speaking of Cheli, his father came to school today.'

However, this analysis begins to unravel when we examine additional data. As noted in Yoon (2004b), among others, there are MSCs where the initial NPs either are not or cannot be interpreted as focus. Consider (4a,b) below.

(4) a. pihayngki-**ka** 747-i   ceyil khu-ta
        Airplane-nom   747-nom   most   big-decl
        'As for airplanes, the 747 is biggest.'
        'It is airplanes that the 747 is big.' (pragmatically odd)
    b. pihayngki-**nun** 747-i   ceyil khu-ta
        Airplane-top   747-nom   most   big-decl
        'As for airplanes, the 747 is the biggest.'

Given that the 747 is a type of airplane, the focus interpretation of the initial NP in (4a) is pragmatically odd, since it implies that there are other entities besides airplanes that have the 747 designation. Therefore, the focus analysis predicts this sentence to be rejected by speakers. While a minority of speakers find the sentence odd, choosing (4b) instead (Y-S Kang 1985), most speakers find the sentence acceptable. And speakers who accept it interpret the initial NP as something other than focus.

Another context where the initial NP in an MSC is not (cannot) be interpreted as focus is shown in (5a) below. When the second nominative NP in an MSC is a Wh-phrase, the initial NP can be *ka*-marked.[1] Since the Wh-

---

[1] As far I as I am aware, this is not possible in Japanese.

phrase is in focus, the initial NP cannot be focus. Nonetheless, (5a) is accepted by speakers, including those who find (4a) odd. This is not expected under the focus analysis.

(5) a. pihayngki-**ka** etten kicong-i   ceyil khu-ni?
         airplane-nom   which model-nom most big-inter
         'Which model of airplane is the biggest?'
     b. pihayngki-**nun** etten kicong-i   ceyil khu-ni?
         airplane-top   which model-nom most big-inter
         'Among airplanes, which model is the biggest?'

Similarly, the initial NP in the following MSC need not be interpreted as focus, even though the second NP is not a Wh-phrase.

(6) a. Cheli-**ka** khi-ka   khu-ta
         C-nom   height-nom big-decl
         'Cheli is tall.'
     b. Cheli-**nun** khi-ka   khu-ta
         C-top   height-nom big-decl
         'As for Cheli, he is tall.'

In order to deal with problems such as this, Schütze (2001) claimed that the function of initial NPs in MSCs encompasses both focus and topic. Accordingly, the initial NP in (4-6a) is a topic, while that in (3a) is focus.

Unfortunately, this alternative will not suffice. For example, since there is an undisputed topic-marker -*nun* in (4-6b), just what sort of topic is marked by -*ka* rather than -*nun* in (4-6a)? And why is not the 'topic' -*ka* available in (3a)? If it were, the NP should admit an interpretation as topic, in addition to focus, though we have seen that it does not.

A further argument against the focus analysis of initial NPs comes from the fact that when MSCs like (3a) occur in embedded or non-asserted contexts, no special discourse interpretation is required for the initial NP (Heycock 1994):

(6) a. pihayngki-ka   747-i   khu-ta-nun sasil-ul na-nun   mollassta
         airplane-nom 747-nom big-decl-and fact-acc I-top   not.know
         'I didn't know about the fact that the 747 is big.'
     b. Cheli-ka apeci-ka   hakkyo-ey encey   o-si-ess-ni?
         C-nom   father-nom   school-loc when   come-hon-pst-Q
         'When did Cheli's father come to school?'

What these facts indicate is that the initial NPs MSCs cannot be licensed solely by an information-structural role such as topic or focus, but by something else. Once licensed, they may be interpreted in appropriate contexts as topic or focus.

What could the licensing mechanism in question be? In approaches to MSCs that treat the initial NP as focus/topic, this issue is not addressed systematically. The usual answers that proponents of the topic/focus analysis offer are that the initial nominals are either adjuncts (that have been moved to topic/focus position) or the possessor argument of the subject (that has moved to the initial position). These answers do not suffice, as we shall see. I will argue that they are licensed as subjects.

2.2. Major Subjects and Sentential Predicates

We just saw that the initial NP in MSCs does not have a consistent discourse function, such as topic or focus. We also noted that over and above any discourse function that they may have, we need an account of how they are licensed in the first place. I will argue, following earlier work (Yoon 2003, 2004a, b, 2006/to appear), that the initial NP is licensed as a subject, specifically, a Major Subject. Thus, MSCs have more than one subject—a unique **Grammatical Subject** that is selected by the predicate, which is its most prominent argument, and multiple **Major Subjects** that are in construction with (nested) **Sentential Predicates** (Teng 1974, B-S Park 1973, 1982, I-H Lee 1987, Heycock 1993).

A Major Subject differs from a Grammatical Subject in a number of respects. The obvious difference is that unlike a Grammatical Subject, a Major Subject is not an argument of the predicate. This is because while the predicate in construction with a Grammatical Subject is a thematically unsaturated VP, the predicate of a Major Subject is a thematically saturated sentence that is turned into a predicate, hence, a Sentential Predicate (B-S Park 1982; I-H Lee 1987). A corollary of this fact is that Major Subjects must denote entities on which such predication can be felicitously stated. This rules out expletives or idiom chunks as Major Subjects (Yoon 2003, 2006/to appear). A further property, which Yoon (2004a) calls the 'newsworthiness' condition, is imposed. Namely, the entity chosen as Major Subject must be important enough to predicate something about.

The Sentential Predicate is also restricted, when compared to VP. For a saturated sentence to function felicitously as Sentential Predicate, the sentence must be construable as denoting a characteristic (or characterizing) property of the referent of the Major Subject (Kuno 1973, Y-J Jang 1998). By contrast, predicates in construction with Grammatical Subjects need not denote characteristic properties. Yoon (2003, 2006/to appear) notes that there are additional properties of Major Subjects that can be attributed to the property predication condition. The properties of the Major Subject and Sentential Predicate outlined above are exemplified below.

As noted, not all (referential) Major Subjects are felicitous in MSCs. Consider (7a-c). While (7a, c) are acceptable, (7b) is not. Many account for the contrast between (7a) and (7b) by assuming that the Major Subject in the former is derived by movement from the possessor of the Grammatical Subject. Under this account, (7b) is ruled out since the Major Subject *khi-ka* 'height-nom' has an unbound trace (Akiyama 2004). However, as shown by (7c), this cannot be correct (where MS=Major Subject, GS=Grammatical Subject, SP=Sentential Predicate):

(7) a. Cheli-ka(MS) [$_{SP}$ khi-ka(GS) ceyil khu-ta]
 C-nom   height-nom most tall-decl
 'Cheli is tall.'
 b. *?khi-ka(MS)[$_{SP}$ Cheli-ka(GS) ceyil khu-ta]
 height-nom   C-nom   most tall-decl
 'As for height, Cheli is tall.'
 c. Ku thim-eyse-nun   khi-ka(MS) [$_{SP}$ O'Neal-i ceyil khu-ta]
 That team-loc-top   height-nom   O-nom most tall-decl
 '(In that team), Shaquille O'Neal is the tallest.'

What differentiates (7b) and (7c) is this: while normally people are characterized in terms of height and not vice versa (7a) vs. *(7b), given the right context (a basketball team), height can become 'newsworthy' enough, and when it is, it is felicitous as the Major Subject.

The contrast shown below indicates that not all Sentential Predicates are acceptable in MSCs: universities may be characterized by how many faculty members live close by, but not by whether an average Joe (=Cheli) lives close by. Thus, (8a) is felicitous as an MSC while (8b) is not.

(8) a. Seoul-tayhakkyo-ka(MS) [$_{SP}$ kyoswutul-i kunche-ey santa]
 S-university-nom   faculty-nom nearby-loc live
 'As for/it is SNU (that) faculty members live close by.'
 b. *?Seoul-tayhakkyo-ka(MS) [$_{SP}$ Cheli-ka kunche-ey santa]
 S-university-nom   C-nom   nearby-loc lives
 'As for/it is SNU (that) Cheli lives close by.'

The contrast between (9a,b) and (10a,b) below is amenable to a similar explanation. *Yelum* 'summer' can be expressed either as a (topicalized) temporal adjunct (9a,b) or as the Major Subject (10a,b). However, as (10) shows, not all adjuncts can be turned into Major Subjects (K-S Hong 1997).

(9) a. Yelum-ey-(nun)   maykcwu-ka(GS) choyko-i-ta
 summer-loc-(top) beer-nom   best-cop-decl
 'It is during the summer that beer is best.'
 b. Yelum-ey-(nun)   Cheli-ka(GS) cip-ey   onta
 summer-loc-(top) C-nom   home-loc comes
 'Cheli is coming home this summer.'

(10) a. Yelum-i(MS) [$_{SP}$ maykcwu-ka(GS) choyko-i-ta]
summer-nom beer-nom best-cop-decl
'Summer is the best time to have (a cold) beer.'
b. *?Yelum-i(MS)[$_{SP}$ Cheli-ka(GS) cip-ey onta]
summer-nom C-nom home-loc comes
'As for/it is during the summer (that) Cheli is coming home.'

Why is this so? The reason is that the Sentential Predicate 'Cheli comes home' is not construable easily as expressing a characteristic property of the Major Subject 'summer', while 'beer is good' can. Thus, the Major Subject-Sentential Predicate partition of a sentence cannot be equated with the Modifier-Modifiee partition.

Recall that we have argued in Section 2.1 against taking the Major Subject to be topic or focus. The argument for this conclusion can be strengthened by showing that while the Major Subject-Sentential Predicate articulation of a clause is subject to the interpretive conditions pointed out above, neither the Topic-Comment or Focus-Ground articulations are.[2] For example, the following are felicitous, compared to (10b):

(11) a. Encey Cheli-ka cip-ey o-ni?
When C-nom home-loc come-inter
'When is Cheli coming home?'
b. Yelum-ey(**Focus**) [$_{Ground}$ Cheli-ka cip-ey o-a]
Summer-loc C-nom home-loc come-decl
'(Cheli's coming home) during the summer.'

(12) Yelum-(ey)-n(**Topic**) [$_{Comment}$ Cheli-ka cip-ey o-ko]
Y-(loc)-top C-nom home-loc come-conj
kyewul-(ey)-n(**Topic**) [$_{Comment}$ Yenghi-ka o-n-ta]
winter-(loc)-top Y-nom come-prs-decl
'Cheli is coming home during the summer and Yenghi's coming in the winter.'

2.3. Derivationally Multiple but Stratally Unique Subjects

The position defended in the previous section is not the only one that posits more than one subject in MSCs. In RG, the Stratal Uniqueness Law (SUL) codifies the traditional assumption that a bearer of a given GR is unique, but relativizes uniqueness to a given strata. C. Youn (1990) offers a comprehensive analysis of MSCs that is consistent with SUL.

---

[2] Topics are licensed by an **Aboutness** relation. The Aboutness Condition is looser than the Characteristic/Characterizing Property Condition that Major Subjects are subject to. See Kuroda (1986) for important discussion of this point.

The basic idea in this approach is that MSCs are derived from structures where there is a unique subject (what we are calling GS) through a subject-creating process (Possessor Ascension) which creates a new subject (our MS) and places the erstwhile subject out of commission (*en chômage*, or unemployed). An illustration follows (1=subject, 1-cho=subject chômeur, P=predicate):

(11) *Cheli-ka khi-ka khu-ta* 'Cheli-nom height-nom tall-decl':
    [Cheli-uy   khi]-ka khu-ta   *Stratum n*
        1   P
    → **Possessor Ascension**
    Cheli-ka khi-ka khu-ta   *Stratum n+1*
    1   1-cho   P

This type of analysis appears to kill two birds with one stone. Not only does it leave the stratal uniqueness of subjects (GRs, more generally) unscathed in the face of an apparent counterexample coming from MSCs, it also solves the problem of the semantic-thematic licensing of nominative-marked NPs in MSCs that do not have a direct argument relation to the predicate, without having to resort to the exotic notions of Major Subject and Sentential Predicate. It is no wonder that many researchers are drawn to this class of analysis. H-S Choe (1986) is an early example of this line of thinking for Korean, with Akiyama (2005) being a recent one for Japanese. As attractive as it is, this type of analysis cannot work. Yoon (1986) provided a number of arguments against the derivational analysis of MSCs. I will rehearse them here and add a few more.

The simple reason why MSCs cannot be derived from more basic structures through Possessor Ascension is that there are MSCs where the initial NPs cannot be expressed as a Possessor of a subject. As widely acknowledged in the relevant literature, in addition to the 'Possessor-type' MSCs, there are the so-called 'Adjunct-type' (aka 'Focus-type') MSCs where the initial NP cannot be paraphrased as a possessor of the subject. (12b) below, the putative 'source' of (12a), is not equivalent to (12a).

(12) a. Yelum-i(MS)   maykcwu-ka choyko-i-ta
            Summer-nom   beer-nom   best-cop-decl
            'Summer is the best time for beer.'
      b. *?Yelum-uy maykcwu-ka choyko-i-ta
            summer-gen   beer-nom   best-cop-decl
            'Summer's beer (beer produced during the summer) is the best.'

However, the existence of a second type of MSCs has not resulted in Possessor Ascension analyses being discarded. Instead, it has invited what has become a familiar response: the derivational analysis works only for the

Possessor-type MSCs, but not others. This is the path C. Youn (1990) follows (also Akiyama 2004 for Japanese MSCs). However, this path leads to a dead-end. Even for Possessor-type MSCs, the analysis fails, since constraints on processes that promote a nominal to subject are violated.

Yoon (1986) noted that the derivational analysis of MSCs must severely violate Subjacency given that MSCs such as (13a) are possible. A related problem comes from (13b,c) where we see that the Major Subject can be related to a resumptive pronoun, even within an island, which is something unexpected on a movement analysis.[3]

(13) a. Cheli-ka   ekkay-uy   olunccok-uy   wis-pwupwun-i aphuta-tela
        C-nom   shoulder-gen   rightside-gen top-portion-nom hurts-I.hear
        'I heard that the top part of Cheli's right shoulder hurts.'
    b. ?Yengswu-ka (ku-uy)   hoysa-ka   mangha-lkes   kathta
        Y-nom   (he-gen)   company-nom   go.bankrupt-comp seems
        'It seems that Yengswu's company will soon go bankrupt.'
    c. ?Cheli-ka melcianha [[(ku-lul) koyongha-n] hoysa]-ka   company-nom
        C-nom   soon   he-acc   hire-rel
        mangha-lkes   kathta
        go.bankrupt-comp seems
        'As for Cheli, it seems that the company that hired him will soon go bankrupt.'

Even in MSCs where Possessor Ascension does not incur any violation of known constraints, the movement/ascension analysis falters. This is because the putative input and output structures differ interpretively. We already encountered such data in (12). There are additional examples showing the discrepancy. Yoon (1986) noted that idiomatic interpretations may hold only in MSC but not in the presumed 'source' structure, making the derivational analysis unworkable. This is shown below.

(14) a. Cheli-ka kapangkkun-i   chinkwutul-cwungey kacang   kil-ta
        C-nom   bag.strap-nom   friends-among   most   long-decl
        → ?Among friends, Cheli's shoulder straps are the longest (literal)
        → Cheli is the most highly educated among friends (idiomatic)

---

[3] Vermeulen (2005) notes a similar problem for movement analyses of MSCs. The problem Yoon (1986) noted is for movement accounts of Possessor Ascension. For RG, the problems are different. Advancement to subject is constrained by the Relational Succession Law, by which a constituent that ascends can only take on the GR of the containing constituent. This is violated in (13a). The status of subjacency-like constraints on GR-changing processes is not dealt with in RG.

b. Cheli-uy   kapangkkun-i   chinkwutul-cwungey   kacang   kil-ta
   C-gen   bag.strap-nom   friends-among   most   long-decl
   → literal, *?idiomatic

And even when idiomatic readings are not at stake, a Possessor of a subject cannot always be expressed as the Major Subject, casting doubt on the viability of deriving Major Subjects from Possessors. The following contrasts are illustrative.

(15) a. Cheli-uy   phal-i   sulmyesi   Yenghi-uy heli-lul   kamassta
        C-gen   arm-nom   surreptitiously Y-gen   waist-acc   wrapped
        'Cheli's arms surreptitiously wrapped around Yenghi's waist.'
     b.*?Cheli-ka(MS)   phal-i   sulmyesi   Yenghi-uy heli-lul
        C-nom   arm-nom   surreptitiously Y-gen   waist-acc
        kamassta
        wrapped
        'As for/it is Cheli his (whose) arms surreptitiously wrapped around Yenghi's waist.'

(16) a. Yengswu-uy   etten   chinkwu-ka cwuk-ess-ta (Y-J Jang 1998)
        Y-gen   a.certain friend-nom die-pst-decl
        'A certain friend of Yengswu died.'
     b.*?Yengswu-ka(MS) etten   chinkwu-ka   cwuk-ess-ta
        Yengswu-ka   a.certain friend-nom   die-pst-decl
        'As for/it is Yengswu (that) a certain friend of his died.'

What lies behind the above contrasts are the conditions on Major Subject-Sentential Predicate articulation we noted earlier. Specifically, when Cheli is expressed as the Major Subject, the Sentential Predicate must state a characteristic property of Cheli. However, 'his arm surreptitiously wrapping around Yenghi's waist' is not a plausible characteristic property of Cheli, and that is why (15b) is not felicitous. A similar explanation extends to the contrast between (16a) and (16b). Having an unknown friend die is not sufficient to characterize someone.

We thus claim that there is no difference between the so-called Possessor-type and Adjunct-type MSCs. Both are base-generated, have the same structure, and contain multiple subjects. However, this claim has been contested. C. Youn (1990) took the two types to be generated differently. Vermeulen (2005) also argues that they have different structures and derivations. I argue below that her arguments do not hold up to scrutiny.

Vermeulen's (2005) argument that the types of MSCs are different is based on the claim that the predicates of Possessor-type MSCs and Adjunct-type MSCs cannot be coordinated, because one is a predicate (=VP) while the other is a sentence (Sentential Predicate). However, contrary to her judgment, coordinations of two types of MSCs are acceptable, at least in Korean. The MSCs coordinated in (17) are an Adjunct-type and Possessor-type respectively, as we can see in (18).

(17)　Kyopo-mwunko-ka [[yele　　conglyu-uy chayk-i　　phalli-ko]
　　　 K-bookstore-nom　diverse type-gen　book-nom　sold-conj
　　　 [wichi-to　　acwu　coh-ta]]
　　　 location-also　very　good-decl
　　　 'As for the Kyopo bookstore, many different types of books are
　　　 sold there and its location is also ideal.'

(18) a.　Kyopo-mwunko-ka　yele　　conglyu-uy chayk-i　　phallin-ta
　　　　　K-bookstore　　　　diverse types-gen book-nom　sold
　　　a'. *Kyopo-mwunko-uy　yele　　conglyu-uy chayk-i　　phallinta
　　　　　K-bookstore-gen　　diverse type-gen　book-nom　sold
　　　　　→ **Adjunct-type MSC**
　　　 b.　Kyopo-mwunko-ka　wichi-ka　　　acwu　coh-ta
　　　　　K-bookstore-nom　location-nom　very　good-decl
　　　 b'.　Kyopo-mwunko-uy　wichi-ka　　　acwu　coh-ta
　　　　　K-bookstore-gen　location-nom　very　good-decl
　　　　　→ **Possessor-type MSC**

In fact, the Sentential Predicates of both types of MSCs can be coordinated with VPs as well (cf. Heycock and Doron 2003):

(19) a.　Cheli-ka　[[meli-ka　　coh-ko]　[acwu sengsilha-ta]]
　　　　　C-nom　　head-nom　good-conj very　sincere-decl
　　　　　'Cheli is smart and sincere.'
　　　 b.　Boston-i [[kwankwangkyak-i manhi chac-ko]　[acwu alumtapta]]
　　　　　B-nom　　tourists-nom　　　a.lot　visit-conj　very beautiful
　　　　　'Boston is city that tourists often visit and is very beautiful.'

In (19a), the first conjunct is the Sentential Predicate of a Possessor-type MSC, while the second conjunct is a VP. In (19b), the predicate of the first conjunct is the Sentential Predicate of an Adjunct-type MSC, while the second conjunct is a VP. According to Vermeulen's analysis, these structures should be out, though they seem to be fine.

Another claimed difference between Possessor and Adjunct-type MSCs is that while there may be multiple nom-marked NPs in the former, there are at most two such NPs in the latter (Tateishi 1991, Vermeulen 2005). However, the facts are different in Korean, as we see below:[4]

---

[4] Vermeulen (2005) gives two other arguments intended to show that the two types of MSCs are different. For reasons of space, we will not address them here.

(20) a. Yelum-i   LA-ka   pwulpep-imincatul-i il-ul   manhi
        summer-nom LA-nom   illegal-immigrants   work-acc a.lot
        chac-nun-ta
        seek-prs-decl
        'It is during the summer that it is in LA that illegal immigrants look
        for work a lot.'
      b. Boston-i yelum-i   kwankwangkyaktul-i manhi   pwumpinta
        B-nom   summer-nom tourists-nom   a.lot   bustles
        'Boston during the summer bustles with many tourists.'

Granted, run-of-the-mill MSCs have Major Subjects coindexed with a gap or pronoun within the Sentential Predicate and very often the gap/pronoun is a Possesor within the subject constituent. However, this is neither necessary nor sufficient, as we have seen. MSCs that fail to bind gaps within Sentential Predicates abound, and the existence of a possessor is no guarantee that a felicitous MSC can be constructed.

In the next section, I turn to the issue of subject diagnostics in Korean. We will see that in MSCs, subject diagnostics are distributed between the Grammatical Subject and the Major Subject. We will see, however, that the distribution of subject properties is not random.

3. The Distribution of Subject Properties in Multiple Subject Constructions

3.1. Subjecthood Diagnostics in Korean

The following is a representative list of properties proposed at one time or another as diagnosing subjecthood in Korean.

(21) Proposed subject diagnostics for Korean (Yoon 1986, K-S Hong 1991, C. Youn 1990, etc.):

a. Nominative case-marking
b. Controller of optional plural-marking
c. Controller of subject honorification
d. Target of Subject-to-Object raising
e. Target of Control
f. Controller of PRO in complement (obligatory) control
g. Controller of PRO in adjunct control
h. Controller of coordinate deletion
i. Antecedent of (subject-oriented) anaphors
j. Exhaustive-listing interpretation of -ka/-i.

It should be obvious that MSCs constitute a testing ground for the adequacy of these diagnostics. However, it should also be clear that with MSCs, the answer as to whether something is a genuine subject property depends on one's theory of MSC. If MSCs have a unique subject, the set of subject properties will be quite small. If they have derivationally multiple subjects, subject properties will be larger, and distributed across derivationally distinct subjects. If they have multiple subjects at a single level of representation, subject properties will be distributed across different subjects, but not on a derivational basis.

With the purpose of showing that there is a unique subject in MSCs, Yoon (1986) evaluated some of the diagnostics offered as identifying subjects in Korean and came to the conclusion that of the many properties suggested as diagnosing subjects, only the following are reliable.

(21) Subject diagnostics (Yoon 1986):
  a. Subject honorification
  b. Equi controller in Obligatory Control
  c. Controller of coordinate deletion

Reflexive binding, Subject-to-Object raising (SOR), and exhaustive listing interpretation—which are available to (what we are now calling) Major Subjects and Grammatical Subjects alike—were claimed not to pick out subjects. What about the most obvious subject property, nominative case? Yoon (1986) claimed that it was not a marker of case, but focus, a position articulated further by other researchers, most notably Schütze (2001).

K-S Hong (1991) reduced the list to the first two, claiming that clear non-subjects can control coordinate deletion. She proposed that there are distinct subject-like notions which are responsible for some of the other claimed subject diagnostics. By contrast, researchers in the RG tradition (C.Youn 1990) embraced a larger set of subject properties by relying on the notion of derivational subjecthood. Some of the subject properties rejected by Yoon (1986) and Hong (1991) remain as subject properties in this approach.

Since I am now claiming that there is more than one subject in MSCs and since there are no longer any grounds for thinking of nominative as a marker of focus/topic, the issue of subjecthood in MSCs needs to be revisited. Perhaps the properties written off by Yoon and Hong as not picking out subjects may turn out to be subject properties after all, albeit of Major Subjects. I will argue that this is the case for some of the discarded subject properties. Specifically, following earlier work (Yoon 2003, 2004a, b, 2006/to appear), I will argue for the following:

(22)   Diagnostics for Major Subjects:[5]
        a. Subject-to-Object Raising
        b. Nominative case-marking

(23)   Diagnostics for Grammatical Subjects:
        a. Subject honorification
        b. Equi controller in obligatory control

Yoon (2003, 2006/to appear) argues that while SOR can seemingly target non-subjects, non-subject raising is quite restricted. He interprets this restriction to mean that only those non-subjects that can be expressed as Major Subjects can undergo SOR. If this line of analysis of correct, SOR is in fact a subject diagnostic, contrary to what Yoon (1986) and K-S Hong (1991) surmised. But there is now an interesting twist. Rather than being a diagnostic of Grammatical Subjects, SOR diagnoses Major Subjects. The sentences showing that raised non-subjects are always paraphrasable as Major Subjects are shown below:

(24)   a. na-nun   **Yenghi-lul**$_i$ [ilen os-i   e$_i$ cal   ewullinta-ko]
           I-top   Y-acc   this clothes-nom   well match-comp
           sayngkakhanta
           think
           'I think that Yenghi looks good in this kind of clothing'
        b. Ilen os-i   Yenghi-eykey/*lul cal   ewullinta
           this clothes-nom   Y-dat/*acc   well   match
        c. **Yenghi-ka**$_i$(MS) [ilen   os-i   e$_i$ cal   ewullinta]
           Y-nom   this clothes-nom   well   match
           'It is Yenghi/as for Yenghi (that) this kind of clothing fits well.'

I propose that a second diagnostic of Major Subjects is nominative case. That is, all Major Subjects are nominative-marked. This may seem far-fetched in view of the fact that nominative case-marking is neither necessary nor sufficient for Grammatical Subjects. So how could nominative-marking be a necessary property of Major Subjects?

The argument that nom-marking is necessary on Major Subjects comes from the analysis of nom-stacked nominals as Major Subjects. Yoon (2004a, b) argues that nom-stacked nominals differ from unstacked nominals in requiring that the constituent they are in construction with be interpretable as a Sentential Predicate. Yoon also argues that the positions of nom-stacked and unstacked nominals are different, with the former higher than

---

[5] The statement is to be understood as a conditional. That is, we are claiming that if something is a Major Subject, then it can undergo SOR, not that something undergoes SOR iff it is a Major Subject.

the latter (Schütze 2001, Yoon 2004a, b). Without stacking, we simply have a Modifier-Modifiee partitioning of the clause (or a subject-predicate partition with the inherently case-marked subject in a low subject position). Therefore, in nominative-stacked structures, the only indication that a Major Subject-Sentential Predicate partition exists is nominative-marking. This is what led Yoon to posit nominative as a necessary property of Major Subjects.

As for diagnostics of Grammatical Subjects, I follow K-S Hong (1991) in assuming that subject honorification (extended by metonymic interpretation) is a valid diagnostic. Being the controller in obligatory (subject) control is another valid diagnostic of Grammatical Subjects. Major Subjects cannot figure as the controller in these processes, as we see below.

(25) a. *?Kim-sacangnim-i(MS)   ankyeng-i   kum-i-si-ta
          K-boss-nom   glasses-nom   gold-cop-hon-decl
          'Boss Kim's glasses have rims made of gold.'
      b. Cheli-ka(MS) tongsayng-i$_i$ [e$_i$ yuhak-ul   ka-ko] siphehanta
          C-nom   brother-nom study.abroad-acc go-comp wants
          'Cheli's brother wants to study abroad.'

This naturally leads to the question of why the subject properties are distributed the way they are in MSCs. Many approaches to split subject diagnostics account for the distribution of subject properties by decomposing subjecthood into more elementary notions—typically, the **pivot** and the **most prominent** (core) **argument** (Dixon 1994, Falk 2006).[6] This is a distinction that can be drawn upon to explain the split subject properties.

In a sentence with a single subject in Korean, the subject nominal is both pivot and the most prominent argument.[7] However, in an MSC, the two are split—the subject-as-pivot is the (highest) Major Subject, while subject-as-prominent-argument is the Grammatical Subject. The Major Subject in an MSC can only be a pivot since it is never selected as a direct argument of predicates. We expect properties controlled by the Major Subject to be those of the pivot, while those controlled by the Grammatical Subject to be those of subject-as-prominent-argument.

As Falk (2006) points out, Raising is a property of subject-as-pivot cross-linguistically. Since the Major Subject is a pivot, it is understandable why SOR in Korean targets the Major Subject.

We argued that all Major Subjects are nominative-marked. Nominative is not a reliable property of either type of subject cross-linguistically (Falk

---

[6] The decomposition of subject positions into SpIP and SpvP is one execution of this idea.

[7] For Korean, this is true even for Dative Subject Constructions, since the Dative (prominent argument) also controls pivot properties such as honorification (cf. Yoon 2004b).

2006). Nonetheless, we can hypothesize that the obligatoriness of nominative on Major Subjects is due to its pivot status. Subjects that are prominent arguments (whether or not they are also pivots) do not need recourse to nominative-marking to indicate their subject status (for example, dative subjects), but a pivot subject that is not a prominent argument (that is, the Major Subject) seems to need nominative case-marking.

In addition to these two, there is at least one other respect in which the Major Subject acts as a pivot. Recall that one of the arguments against Vermeulen's (2005) analysis given earlier was based on the fact that the Sentential Predicate of MSCs can be coordinated with VPs. The relevant example is repeated below:

(26) a. Cheli-ka [[meli-ka   coh-ko] [acwu sengsilha-ta]] (=19)
         C-nom   head-nom   good-conj very sincere-decl
         'Cheli is smart and sincere.'
     b. Boston-i [[kwankwangkyak-i manhi chac-ko] [acwu alumtapta]]
         B-nom   tourists-nom   a.lot visit-conj very beautiful
         'Boston is city that tourists often visit and is very beautiful.'

Falk (2006:16) cites 'shared argument in coordinate clauses' as another cross-linguistic diagnostic that is sensitive to subject-as-pivot status. Given this, we can view (26a,b) not as the constituent coordination of VP and SP under a shared subject, but as the coordination of clauses where the null subject pivot of the second clause is controlled by that the Major Subject pivot of the first clause. This is why such coordinations are possible.

As for the Grammatical Subject, it is the subject-as-prominent-argument and hence is expected to control properties sensitive to prominent argument status. Complement subject control in many approaches is based on argument structure (Pollard and Sag 1994). If this type of account is on the right track, we can see why only the Grammatical Subject figures as a controller in obligatory control in MSCs.

This type of explanation can be extended to subject honorification. That is, the controller of subject honorification may be the most prominent argument selected by the predicate. This claim can be tested with derived subjects that are not arguments of the predicates they are in construction with. In the Tough Construction, the raised nominal cannot trigger honorific agreement on the upstairs predicate, confirming this prediction:

(27) *Kim-sensayngnim-i[1]   haksayngtul-eykey-n[2] [PRO[2]
       K-teacher.hon-nom   students-dat-top

      e[1] manna-ki]-ka acwu himtu-**si**-ta
            meet-nml-nom very difficult-hon-decl
      'Professor Kim is difficult for the students to meet.'

Neither are passivized raised (SOR) subjects felicitous as controllers of subject honorification, as we see below:

(28) *Kim-sensayngnim-i[1]   ku   hakkyo-eyse-nun [e[1]   chencayla-ko]
K-teacher.hon-nom   that school-loc-top   genius-comp
sayngkak-toy-**si**-nun   kes   kathta
think-pass-hon-rel   thing seems
'It seems that Professor Kim is considered a genius (by people) in that school.'

In sum, while a more detailed investigation of these conjectures is necessary and a re-examination of other subject diagnostics is needed, we now have an interesting, if tentative, picture of how subject properties are split between the Major and Grammatical Subject and, more importantly, why they are split the way they are. Importantly, the properties controlled by both subjects are subject properties cross-linguistically, and as such, lends support to the hypothesis that MSCs are characterized by the presence of multiple subjects.

4. Conclusion

In this paper, I have revisited the question of the structure and licensing of MSCs. I have argued that MSCs have more than one subject and more than one predicate. I have also examined the distribution of subject properties in Korean. The distribution of subject properties is attributable to the fact that a Major Subject in an MSC is subject-as-pivot, while the Grammatical Subject is subject-as-prominent-argument.

References

Akiyama, M. 2004. Multiple Nominative Constructions in Japanese and Economy. *Linguistic Inquiry* 35: 671-683.
Akiyama, M. 2005. On the General Tendency to Minimize Moved Elements: Multiple Nominative Construction in Japanese and Its Theoretical Implications. *The Linguistic Review* 22: 1-68.
Choe, H-S. 1986. Syntactic adjunction, A-Chains, and the ECP. *Proceedings of the 17th Northeast Linguistic Society*, 100-121.
Diesing, M. 1992. *Indefinites*. Cambridge: MIT Press
Falk, Y. 2006. *Subjects and Universal Grammar*. Cambridge University Press.
Heycock, C. 1993. Syntactic Predication in Japanese. *Journal of East Asian Linguistics* 2:167-211.
Heycock, C. 1994. Focus Projection in Japanese. *Proceedings of the 24th Northeast Linguistic Society*, 157-172.
Heycock, C. and E. Doron 2003. Categorical Subjects. *Gengo Kenkyuu* 123: 95-135.
Hong, K-S. 1991. Argument Selection and Case-Marking in Korean. Ph.D dissertation, Stanford University.

Jang, Y-J. 1998. Multiple Subjects and Characterization. *Discourse and Cognition* 5: 99-116.

Kang, M-Y. 1987. Possessor Raising in Korean. *Harvard Studies in Korean Linguistics-II*, 80-88.

Kang, Y-S. 1985. Korean Syntax and Universal Grammar. Ph.D Dissertation, Harvard University.

Kuno, S. 1973. *The Structure of the Japanese Language*. Cambridge: MIT Press.

Kuroda, S-Y. 1972. The Categorical and the Thetic Judgment. *Foundations of Language* 9: 153-185.

Kuroda, S-Y. 1986. Movement of noun phrases in Japanese. *Issues in Japanese Linguistics*, eds. T. Imai and M. Saito, 229-271. Dordrecht: Foris.

Lee, I-H. 1997. Double Subject Constructions in GPSG. *Harvard Studies in Korean Linguistics II*, 287-296.

Li, C. and S. Thompson 1976. Subject and Topic: A New Typology of Language. *Subject and Topic*, eds. C. Li and S. Thompson, 457-490. New York: Academic Press.

Manning, C. 1996. *Ergativity: Argument Structure and Grammatical Relations*. Stanford: CSLI Publications.

McCloskey, J. 1997. Subjecthood and Subject Positions. *Elements of Syntax*, ed. L. Haegeman, 197-236. Dordrecht: Kluwer Academic Publishers.

Park, B-S. 1973. On the Multiple Subject Constructions in Korean. *Linguistics* 100: 63-76.

Park, B-S. 1982. The Double Subject Constructions Revisited. *Linguistics in the Morning Calm*, ed. The Linguistic Society of Korea, 645-658. Seoul: Hanshin Publishing Company.

Pollard, C. and I. Sag 1994. *Head-driven Phrase Structure Grammar*. Chicago: University of Chicago Press.

Schütze, C. 2001. On Korean 'Case Stacking': The Varied Functions of the Particles *ka* and *lul*. *The Linguistic Review* 18: 193-232.

Tateishi, K. 1991. The Syntax of 'Subjects'. Ph.D dissertation, University of Massachusetts, Amherst.

Teng, S-H. 1974. Double Nominatives in Chinese. *Language* 50: 455-473.

Vermeulen, R. 2005. Possessive and Adjunct Multiple Nominative Constructions in Japanese. *Lingua* 115:1329-1363.

Yoon, J. 1986. Some Queries Concerning the Syntax of Multiple Subject Constructions in Korean. *Studies in the Linguistic Sciences* 16: 215-236. Department of Linguistics, University of Illinois, Urbana-Champaign.

Yoon, J. 2003. Raising Specifiers: A Macroparametric Account of SOR in Some Altaic Languages. Paper presented at the *Workshop on Formal Approaches to Altaic Languages*, MIT, Cambridge, MA.

Yoon, J. 2004a. The Independence of Grammatical Case from Interpretive Factors. Paper presented at the *2004 Linguistic Society of Korean International Conference*, Seoul, Korea.

Yoon, J. 2004b. Non-nominative (Major) Subjects and Case-stacking in Korean. *Non-nominative Subjects, Volume 2*, eds. P. Bhaskararao and K. V. Subbarao, 265-314. Berlin: Mouton de Gruyter.

Yoon, J. 2006/to appear. Raising of Major Arguments in Korean (and Japanese). *New Horizons in the Grammar of Raising and Control*, eds. W. D. Davies and S. Dubinsky. Dordrecht: Springer.

Yoon, J-Y. 1989. On the Multiple *ka* and *lul* Constructions in Korean. *Harvard Studies in Korean Linguistics-III*, 383-394. Seoul: Hanshin Publishing Company.

Youn, C. 1990. A Relational Analysis of Korean Multiple Nominative Constructions. Ph.D dissertation, State University of New York at Buffalo.

Part II

Historical Linguistics

Genesis of 'Exemplification' in Japanese*

TOMOHIDE KINUHATA
Kyoto University

MIHO IWATA
Osaka University

TADASHI EGUCHI
Fukuoka University

SATOSHI KINSUI
Osaka University

1. Introduction

As the following examples show, *nari, tari* and *yara* can function in (Early) Middle Japanese texts as copular verbs (1a), aspectual markers (1b) and question markers (1c) respectively. [1]

(1) a. Tyuunagon, Yukifira -no musume-no   fara-<u>nari.</u>
                    -GEN daughter-GEN womb-Copula
           Tyuunagon is a son of Yukifira's daughter.   *Ise* 10th C.

      b. Sono safa-ni kakitubata ito omosiroku saki-<u>tari.</u>
           that stream-in iris very beautifully bloom-ASP
           'Very beautiful irises bloomed around the stream.'   *Ise* 10th C.

      c. 'Are-fa ikanaru zyaurau   nite-masimasu <u>yaran</u>' to
           that-TOP what   noble.person Copula-HON CJEC Quote.
           'Who is that noble person?'   *K Heike* 14th C.

* We express our gratitude to all the audience in J/K 16th. Our special thanks go to John Whitman and Szymon Grzelak for valuable comments on the substance and the style of the present article.

[1] We use the following abbreviations in glosses. ACC(Accusative), ASP(Aspectual marker), CAU(Causative), CJEC(Conjecture marker), CONC(Concessive particle), COND(Conditional particle), DAT(Dative), DIR(Directive case), EMP(Emphatic particle), FIN(Sentence final particle), GEN(Genitive), HON(Honorific expression), IMP(Imperative), NEG(Negative), NOM(Nominative), PASS(Passive), TOP(Topic particle), VOL(Volitional marker).

However, in Modern Japanese, these expressions occur solely in exemplifications, all having the same function of listing elements partially from a given set. For example 'Tanaka' and 'Yamada' in (2) belong to the set that can be denoted by the following NP 'gakusei'.

(2)   a.   Tanaka-<u>nari</u> Yamada-<u>nari</u> (gakusei)-o   yondek-oi.
               (student)-ACC call-IMP.
               Lit 'Call students such as Tanaka or Yamada.'

    b.   Tanaka-<u>yara</u> Yamada-<u>yara</u> (gakusei)-ga   yatteki-ta.
               (student)-NOM come-Past.
               Lit 'Students such as Tanaka or Yamada came.'

    c.   Amerika-ni it-<u>tari</u> Yōroppa-ni it-<u>tari</u> (ryokō)-o tanoshin-da.
           America-DIR go- Europe-DIR go- (travel)-ACC enjoy-Past.
           Lit 'I enjoyed travels, going to U.S.A and Europe.'

In the present article we will investigate the nature of the historical changes these different lexical items underwent to reach the same stage. We will also demonstrate that the change at issue has both philogenic and ontogenic aspects.

This paper is structured as follows. In section 2, the process of syntactic change is presented, outlining the common characteristics of the development of three expressions. Section 3 goes over the individual aspects of the discussed changes, paying particular attention to the semantics of these items. Section 4 analyzes the motivation of the change and refers to related phenomena found in the history of Japanese. Section 5 concludes the paper and highlights some ramifications of the current analysis.

2. Syntactic Change

Although we noted that *nari*, *tari* and *yara* have different functions in (Early) Middle Japanese, they can all occupy the same syntactic position as sentence final elements as in (1). As far as this article is concerned, acquiring NP status is the goal of the change, which is illustrated in the examples of (2) with case markers directly attached to *nari*, *tari* and *yara*. The objective of this section is to look into the process of transition from sentence final element to NP from a syntactic perspective. We wish to argue that the process of syntactic change took place in the following stages.

(3)   (i) sentence final element > (ii) Element adjoined to the following sentence > (iii) Element adjoined to an NP in the following sentence > (iv) Element constituting an NP

Let us first look at the historical changes of *nari* and *tari*.

Although 'nari' and 'tari' are morphologically classified as adverbial forms ('Renyōkei') and conclusive forms ('Shūshikei') in the conjugational system of Classical Japanese, they did not have adverbial use in the Heian Period and thus had a primarily conclusive function, unless other auxiliaries followed them. The fact that commas do not appear immediately after these forms in the modern interpretations of Heian texts provides some evidence for this.

However, in Middle Japanese examples can be found in which *nari*, as well as *tari*, clauses are adjoined to the following sentence with meanings such as 'causation', 'attendant circumstances' etc. For example:

(4) a. Futakatana sase-ba,   utikabuto-mo   itade-<u>nari</u>, tuini
         two.swords stick-COND inside.helmet-also injured-   finally
         uta-re-ta.
         kill-PASS-Past.
         'When (a servant) attacked him with two swords, at last (Kage-
         tune) was killed, because (he) had gotten injured inside his hel-
         met.'   *A Heike* 1592

     b. Sono sidai mait-te   mausa-mu to   sure-ba   ...yo-fa
         that report go-CONJ tell-VOL   Quote do-COND night-TOP
         fuke-<u>tari</u>, kafa-no   futise-mo   miyewaka-zu.
         get.late- river-GEN surface-even judge-NEG
         'Since the night had deepened, it was difficult to see even the
         surface of the river, when he wanted to report back to his superior.'
                                                            E Heike 14th C.

Each of these examples consists of three clauses. For example in (4a): 'fu-takatana sase-ba,' 'utikabuto-mo itade nari,' and 'tuini uta-re-ta.' The second clause, which includes *nari*, is presented as a reason for the last clause 'tuini uta-re-ta.' The fact that this second clause is adjoined to the following sentence is further supported by the construction it appears in. The first clause 'futakatana sase-ba' functions also as the reason for the last clause and it is evident that the former is adjoined to the latter because of the presence of the suffix 'ba'. Thus, it is natural to consider the clause with *nari* as being par-enthetically adjoined to the following sentence rather than as an independent clause. This argument holds for (4b) as well.

The development of this type of construction is known in the histori-cal studies of Japanese as 'fujūbun shūshi (incomplete conclusiveness)' (see Kyōgoku 1966, Kyō 1993), where it is pointed out that some of the conclu-sive forms from the Heian period lost some of their conclusive functions in Middle Japanese. The class of adjectives is one of the examples.

(5) a. kono kafa-no   utomasiu obosa-ruru koto ito <u>fukasi</u>.
         this river-GEN dislike   think-HON thing very deep
         lit '(Kaoru) deeply dislikes this river.'   *Genji* 10th C.

b. fasi-wo   fika-re-te   kafa-fa fukasi, watasu-ni
    bridge-ACC draw-PASS-CONJ river-TOP deep   carry-DAT
    oyoba-zu-site
    reach-NEG-CONJ
    'Since the bridge was floated and the river was deep, (Kiso) could
    not transport the horses across the river.'   E Heike 14th C.

The observations thus far support our thesis of the syntactic change from (i)
to (ii) in diagram in (3).

The examples where *nari* and *tari* are adjoined to the NP in the following
sentences begin to appear at some time in the 19th century (see Eguchi (1998)
for the characteristics of this construction). [2]

(6) a. Kubidaikin-nari Gesyunin-nari syoti-wo   tuke-nya.
         weregild-   decapitation- excution-ACC attach-must
         'We have to take measures such as weregild or decapitation.'
                                                          hanazome 1832
     b. Kaneuti si-tari kami kit-tari mukō-no   mie-nu
         metal.hit do- hair cut- opposite.site-GEN see-NEG
         tikaigoto-yorimo . . . ,
         vow-than
         'rather than vowing to do things that are unreliable, such as hitting
         the metal or cutting their hair,'   *anakashiko* 1780

'Kubidaikin nari' and 'gesyunin nari' do not have a causal relation with
'syoti-wo tuke-nya nariyasen'; instead they stand in a referential relation,
which we call 'exemplification,' with the NP 'syoti (execution)'. Semantic
changes, discussed in the next section, are involved before *nari* and *tari* enter
into stage (iii).

It was not until the Meiji Period that case markers (or kakari particles) are
directly attached to *nari* and *tari*, as shown in (7), indicating that the category
of the phrase including them is NP.

(7) a. Zibun-no   omou yōni jiken-nari sisō-nari -ga   hakoba-nai.
         onself-GEN think as   event-   thought- -NOM carry-NEG.
         'Events, thoughts etc. didn't go as well as I expected.'
                                                          Kokoro 1914
     b. Sawai-dari nai-tari -wa hito-no   yo-ni   tsukimono-da.
         excited-   cry-   -TOP human-GEN world-in custom-Copula.

---

[2] (6a) and (6b) are from texts published in Edo district, even though the examples before the
18th century is based on Kyoto-Osaka dialect. But we leave the problem of differences between
dialects in this paper. See Iwata (2006a, 2006b) for details.

'It is associated with the human world to be excited, cry and the like.'   *Kusamakura* 1914

The historical data presented so far illustrate the process of syntactic change that took place in (3).

Let us turn to the history of *yara*. *Yara* comes from 'ni-ya-ara-mu', a compositon of the copula *ni-ari*, question marker *ya* and conjecture marker *mu*. Even though the final element *mu* did not have an adverbial form, it is not easy to give concrete evidence from historical materials that the stage (i) precedes (ii). For instance, *Kakuichibon Heike Monogatari*, which is one of the earliest records in which the form 'yara' shows up, has examples like (8) where the clause with *yaran* is interpreted as background information for the following sentence. Also it can be used as a sentence final element, as in (1c).

(8)   Yo-ni-fa   ikanisite more-keru-yaramu, afareni yasasiki
       World-in-TOP how   leak-PAST-CJEC   sad   lovely

       tamesi-ni-zo   fitobito mausi-aferi-keru.
       instance-as-EMP people talk-Habitual-Past
       'How did people come to know, they were talking about the story, seeing it as sad and lovely.'   *K Heike* 14th C.

However, we assume here that the sentence final use is the default, simply because there are more instances of it than of the adjoined use (for example 62 vs. 22 in *Kakuichibon Heike Monogatari*). Admittedly quantitative studies do not necessarily reveal the basic use of a paticular lexical item, but the historical documents afford us no ground for the view that the adjoined use is prevalent.

Apart from the change from (i) to (ii), the syntactic development of *yara* can be attested in the historical data. The examples where phrases with *yara* are adjoined to the NP in the next sentence appear in the 19th century as in (9), followed by the examples of *yara* with directly attached case markers, as in (10).

(9)   Zyōdosyū-yara Hokke-yara Hassyū   Kusyū   iritudou
       Jōdo.sect-   Hokke.sect- eight.sect nine.sect assemble
       'People belonging to various sects, such as the Jōdo and the Hokke assemble.'   *Ukiyoburo* 1809

(10)   Tamoto-kara kaneire-yara tokei-yara -o   muzōsani tsukamidashi-te
       sleeve-from wallet-   watch-   -ACC casually take.out-CONJ
       'He casually took out his wallet, his watch and other things from his kimono sleeves and then ...'   *Seinen* 1911

To summarize, we have examined the syntactic development of *nari*, *tari* and *yara*, which shows they share the pattern of changes in (3). However, this does not mean that we have answered the question of how items which were originally distinct acquired the same status in the end, since, from the syntactic point of view, these expressions have the same function from the beginning. Therefore we have to turn to the investigation of the change of semantic properties.

3. Semantic Change

3.1. *Nari*

As shown in the previous section, *nari* had come to be adjoined to the following sentence by Middle Japanese, still constituting a predicate as a copula verb (see in (4a)). [3] The meaning of *nari* in (6a), however, is to list elements from the set denoted by the following NP, ceasing to function as a predicate of a sentence. The purpose of this subsection is to give a description and an explanation of the semantic change to connect these two meanings. To this end, at least three steps should be supposed.

The first step is the development of the apposition of phrases with *nari*, which is illustrated in (11).

(11) a. Mi-wa hin-<u>nari</u> katawa-<u>nari</u>, . . . burabura iki-temo   kainasi.
    I-TOP poor-   stutterer-   idly   live-CONC worthless
    'Since I am poor and stutter, I am not worth living.'
                                        hangonkō 1708

   b. Muko-<u>nari</u> oi-<u>nari</u>   zihei -ga   koto tanomu
    son.in.law- nephew-   -NOM thing entrust
    'Since he is your son-in-law and your nephew, take care of Jihei'
                                        Tennoamijima 1720

It should be noted that in these examples *nari* functions as a predicate taking an individual as its subject so that, strictly speaking, the semantics of *nari* does not differ from (4a). The apposition of phrases came into existence in the early 18th century as indicated in the each example.

The second step is the change of the meaning denoted by the NP before *nari*. Examine the following examples which appear in the mid 18th century.

(12) a. Omae-<u>nari</u> watasi-<u>nari</u> aiyakedoosi
    you-   me-   parents.of.married.couple
    'You and me are fathers of the married couple.' *Kanatehon* 1748

   b. Imōto-<u>nari</u>   ane-<u>nari</u>   ko-<u>nari</u> ukime-wo   mi-seru
    younger.sister- elder.sister- children- hardship-ACC see-CAU
    'You elder sister, your younger sister and your children will suffer
    . . .'
                                        satonokawazu 1756

---

[3] In the sentence final positon, however, *zya* have been dominantly used instead of *nari* since around the 15th century.

Since the NPs accompanied by *nari* denote individuals, it is difficult to interpret them as predicates. Rather they seem to stand in a subject-predicate relation with the following noun or verb phrase.

We would like to give an argument of how the semantic change from examples like (11) to (12) took place. Let us first assume that the semantics of a nominal predicate is a set of individuals (or 'property' in intensional terms). Then 'hin-nari' and 'katawa-nari' in (11a) each denotes a set of poor individuals or a set of individuals who stutter, and 'Mi,' the speaker in this context, is included in the intersection of this two sets because the speaker has both properties. Given these assumptions, we can reasonably think that the change at issue is due to the reanalysis of the way a set is created.

In general, a set can be expressed in two ways, that is, by exhibiting the properties of the set, i.e. $\{x \mid dog(x)\}$, or by listing the elements in the set, i.e. $\{Shelby, Bucky, Spot\}$. In the same way, *nari* which had been used to exhibit the properties to create a set was reanalyzed as exhibiting the elements to create a set as illustrated in (13).

(13)   a. $\{x \mid hin (poor) \text{-}\underline{nari} (x)\} \cap \{y \mid katawa (stutterer) \text{-}\underline{nari} (y)\}$ (11)

     b. $\{omae (you) \text{-}\underline{nari}, watasi (I) \text{-}\underline{nari}\}$ (12)

While this change seems to be a quantum leap, the function of creating a set and appositon of phrases remain same, which would enable *nari* to underwent the reanalysis from (13a) to (13b).

The last step involves the change where the 'listing' of the elements becomes partial. This presupposes that the way of creating the set in (12) is not 'partial.' We call this type of listing 'total listing' as opposed to 'partial listing.' This is intuitively grasped by the observation of the example (12a). The predicate 'aiyakedosi' is construed as a set of a pair which consists of parents of a certain married couple. Given the assumption that 'omae nari watasi nari' stands in a subject-predicate relation with 'aiyakedousi,' that is the pair 'omae' 'watasi' is in the extension of 'aiyakedousi,' it creates a set by totally listing the elements as represented in (14). [4]

(14) $\{omae, watasi\} \in \{\{x,y\} \mid aiyakedosi (\{x,y\})\}$

On the other hand, all the elements do not have to be listed in the examples such as (6), giving the role of making a set to the following NP. This partial listing type can be seen from around the 19th century.

We have discussed the semantic change of *nari* which is summarized as;

---

[4] Since 'aiyakedousi' refers to the relation between the parent(s) of the hasband and that of the wife, the extension of it includes sets of sets as its member whose combination varies like $\{\{f\}, \{f\}\}, \{\{m\}, \{m\}\}, \{\{f\}, \{m\}\}, \{\{f, m\}, \{f\}\}, \{\{f, m\}, \{m\}\}, \{\{f, m\}, \{f, m\}\}$ where 'f' and 'm' represent 'father' and 'mother' respectively. But we write $\{omae, watasi\}$, instead of using singleton sets as $\{\{omae\}, \{watasi\}\}$ for simplicity.

(15)   intersection of sets > total listing of the elements in the set > partial listing of elements in the set

where 'partial listing' means what we call 'exemplification' in section 1 by definition. [5]

3.2. *tari*

The primary difference between *tari* and *nari* is in the categories of their complements. In Early Middle Japanese, *tari* was combined with verbs as an aspectual marker while *nari* was used with nouns to constitute a nominal predicate as seen in the previous subsection. Since verbs, unlike nouns, express temporal events, it is reasonable to assume that the semantics of *tari* is not just a set of individuals but a set of ordered pairs each consisting of an individual and an interval.

Despite the basic difference, *tari* and *nari* took a similar track of acquiring the apposition of phrases. However, the early attestation of the apposition of verb phrases are better illustrated by the other aspectual markers *nu* and *tu* as in (16), since *tari* replaced *nu* and *tu* in this usage during the Middle Japanese (see Iwata (2006a) for the interaction between these forms).

(16)   a.   Fune-fa   uki-<u>nu</u> sizumi-<u>nu</u> tadayowe-ba
            ship-TOP float- sink-   drift-COND
            'Since the ship drifted, floating up and sinking down,'
                                                              E Heike 14th C.
       b.   Tati-<u>nu</u> wi-<u>nu</u> yubi-wo   sasi-nado katari-wore-ba
            stand- sit-   finger-ACC point-etc. talk-ASP-COND
            'Standing up and sitting down, he talked with pointing ...'
                                                              Ujishūi 13th C.

Provided that 'uki-nu' and 'sizumi-nu' in (16a) each creates a set as assumed above, we can use the same line of thinking with *nari* to interpret the sentence that the subject 'fune', coupled with an interval, is in the intersection of the two sets because this interval contains two states denoted by floating and sinking. [6]

Although the ability to create an intersection is common to the apposition of phrases, *nu* differs from *nari* in that the former can describe all the states of one's body (the ship's body in (16a) and the man's body in (16b)) in the interval under consideration. We regard this as 'total listing' of sets, suggesting that making an intersection of sets, $P \cap Q$, and the listing of sets mean a same

---

[5] Suzuki (1995) and Iwata (2006b) also suppose three steps in the semantic change of *nari* though they give different interpretations from ours to these steps.

[6] Then, to be strict, the interval refered to in the sentence must have two subintervals each corresponding to 'sinking' and 'floating.'

thing with the assumption that the listing at issue is a conjunction operation, $P \wedge Q$.

But why can we not list the sets exhaustively in the case of *nari*? Because the properties of an individual are infinite and thus you cannot enumerate all of them. That is why *nari* evolves into a listing of 'elements,' while *tari* retains the function of listing 'sets' with the help of an interval.

Furthermore we notice that the total listing in (16) is expressed by the lexical properties encoded in 'sinking' and 'floating' in (16a) and 'standing' and 'sitting' in (16b). These antonymous words force us to understand that the ship's body in (16a) is sinking when it isn't floating and vice versa, i.e. the total description of states. We also remark that the apposition phrases of *nu* and *tu* can be seen only with these antonymous words before the 13th century.

In the 15th century, we can find examples where non-antonymous words are used such as (17).

(17) a.　Uttae-<u>tari</u> fikisue-te　　bassi-<u>tari</u> suru-zo
　　　　complain- bring-CONJ punish-　do-FIN
　　　　'They used to do things like complaining to the governor about a criminal, or bringing and punishing him.'　　*Kanjoshō* 15th C.

　　b.　Fooroku-wo toru mono-ga　　ta-wo　　tukut-<u>tari</u> akinai-wo
　　　　pay-ACC　take person-NOM field-ACC make　　akinai-ACC
　　　　si-<u>tari</u> -nado suru
　　　　do-　-etc. do
　　　　'Those who were paid from government used to do things like making fields and going into businesses.'　　*Shikishō* 15th C.

We interpret these examples as 'partial listing' of sets. This leads us to conclude that the following change took place in the semantics of *tari*.

(18)　total listing of the sets > partial listing of sets

Finally, in the syntax, *tari* in (17) functions as a verbal NP. This means that *tari* went through the stage of verbal NP before entering into the stage (iii) in the 19th century. [7] However, in semantic terms, the function of creating a set is consistent during this period. [8]

---

[7] It might be possible for *tari* to undergo the change from verbal NP to NP (with case particles), omitting the stage(iii). We will have to take this possibility into consideration in further research.

[8] Since the exemplification with *tari* tends to be interpreted to mention an event, we assume that an interval should be involved however long the period is. The following example, however, indicates that an individual need not be included as an element in the set formulated with *tari*.

(i)Tanaka -ga　　hon-o　　yon-<u>dari</u> Yamada -ga　　e-o　　　　kai-tari si-teiru
　　　-NOM book-ACC read-　　　　　　-NOM picture-ACC draw-　do-ASP
　　'Tanaka is reading a book, Yamada is drawing a picture and so on.'

3.3. *yara*

From the discussion so far, the semantic change into 'exemplification' involves (a) the acquisition of the apposition of phrases and the transition (b) from making an intersection to total listing of elements (only applied to *nari*) and (c) from total listing to partial listing.

In the 18th century, *yara* acquired the use of apposition, in which verb phrases with *yara* modify the manner of the following predicate as seen in the following examples.

(19) a. Ketumazuku-yara suberu-yara hauhau haidete
   stumble-   slip-   crawl go.out
   'Stumbling and falling, we crawled and went out.'

   yoigōshin 1722

   b. Sugito-ni   hitai   utu-yara ateru-yara yōyōni osihiraki
   ceder.door-DAT forehead bump- hit-   at.least push.open
   'He opened the door which is made of a ceder, by knocking and bumping his forehead against it.'   *nyogonoshima* 1718

Verb phrases, as we argued in the preceding section, can be listed totally if they refer to a specific interval. Though this reasoning applies to the apposition of phrases with *yara* in this period, there is no instance which must be interpreted as total listing. In effect, we cannot find examples of *yara* with antonymous words as is the case with *tari*. This gives us ground to think that *yara* was used as 'partial listing' when it acquired the apposition use.

However, does this mean that the transition from total listing to partial listing is unrelated to the semantic change of *yara*? Readers who recall the origin of *yara* might conjecture that the disjunctive use of question with its negation as in (20) would be the source of the partial listing in (19) for the reason of it listing all the possibilities as to the truth value of the relevant proposition. [9]

(20) Furu-yaran fura-nu-yaran miwake-gatasi
   rain-   rain-NEG-   distinguish-difficult
   lit 'It is difficult to tell whether it will rain or it won't rain.'

   Chūka 16th C.

This line of reasoning faces difficulties both from the theoretical and from the empirical points of view. Theoretically, a set of all possible worlds de-

---

We leave the issue of the semantic type of the elements in the set for further studies. See footnote 11 for a relevant problem.

[9] The repetition of phrases (or clauses) with *yaran* in (20), as well as the one in (21), differs from what we call 'apposition' in this paper. (20) and (21) are examples of embedded questions and 'furu-yaran' and 'fura-nu-yaran' are conjoined as embedded disjuncts as indicated in the translations. See Takamiya (2004) for the birth of embedded questions in Japanese.

noted by the disjunctive sentence 'it will rain or it won't rain' makes little sense. This is because while the total listing of *nari* and that of *tari* describe the relation of individuals and the states of an individual respectively, it is not clear what a set of all possible worlds gives an description of.

Aside from the theoretical defect, it is empirically difficult to show that examples like (20) are the source of (19), because we have examples such as the following alongside the affirmative-negative disjunction.

(21) minami-e ikoo-yara kita-e   ikoo-yara sira-nu-zo
     south-DIR go-   north-DIR go-   know-NEG-FIN
     lit 'I don't know whether he will go to the south or he will go to the
     north.'   *Mōgyūsyō* 16th C.

In this example, *yara* exhibits the possibility without explicating the other candidates (also, see example (8)). If they could be considered as 'partial listing' and there is no evidence of the change from (20) to (21), then the development from total listing to partial listing is not attested in the historical data. [10]

Another question one may raise with respect to the conceptual change given above is how *yara* came to take individuals as its complement as in (2). Although we are yet to be able to give a systematic account to this change, a tentative analysis will be given in 4.1. after providing a supplement of the change.

4. Further issues

4.1. Supplement of the change

In section 2, we showed that the common process from a sentence final element to an NP is observed in the syntactic change of *nari*, *tari* and *yara*. Section 3 examined the process of semantic change for them to acquire the 'partial listing.' Then it is natural to ask about the relevance between the two changes. We would like to answer this question by proposing that the partial listing gives an adverbial and a nominal status to the phrases constituted by these lexical items.

This is illustrated by the fact that adverbial uses, as well as the nominal uses as in (2), is still available in Modern Japanese. *Nari* is used as form such as 'dai-nari shō-nari (more or less)' or 'dō-nari kō-nari (in some way or the other),' and *tari* and *yara* used with VPs.

---

[10] *Yara* in (19) is different from those in (20) and (21) in that while the former expresses the conjunction, the latter disjunction. Then the change from disjunction to conjunction must be involved in the relevant change. Although (21) has only to go through this step to reach the stage of (19), besides the acquisition of the apposition, (20) requires another extra stage such as total listing of conjunction (this is not attested in the historical records) or partial lisitng of disjunction (=(21)) before expressing the parial listing of conjunction as in (19).

(22) a. sono uti-ni-wa   dō-<u>nari</u> kō-<u>nari</u> wake-ga   tati-masyō.
     the period-DAT-TOP how- this- excuse-NOM stand-HON

'In the meantime, ...make excuses in some way or the other.'
                                           Kanjin 1764

  b. hitoride kowagaru-<u>yara</u> omoshirogaru-<u>yara</u> shikirini
     along   fear-   amused-   all.along
     yorokon-dei-ta
     find.pleasure-ASP-Past
     'On his own, (Keitarō) found pleasures all along, being alternately
     amused or afraid.'   *Higansugimade* 1912

The proposal that the partially listed phrases have cross categorial status situates the change of semantics into the process of syntactic change. As described in section 3, semantic change begins after the stage (ii) in syntax because phrases with *nari, tari* and *yara* are adverbially adjoined to the following sentences in this period. By way of gaining the function of partial listing, they enter into the stage (iii) and (iv) in which the phrases with them can be associated with, or occupy the position of, NP.

Let us mention here the problem raised at the end of the last section. We noted there that there remains a problem of how *yara* came to take individuals as its complement. [11] We consider it as a result of the acquisition of nominal status mentioned above, since nouns are interpreted as e or $<e, t>$ in general. But the more explorations should be given to reveal the nature of the relevant change.

4.2. Motivation and related phenomena

The historical change discussed in this literature has the process in which different expressions take part in the same pattern of change to converge into the same function. This implies that the change in question is not entirely incidental and linguists might want to investigate the motivations that drive the change. However, the motivation for the convergence of several items is seldom detected for the reason of the insufficient theoretical considerations on this topic. On the other hand, we might be able to talk about the factors behind the pattern itself. Yet the situation is not so simple here either. That is because there are several changes relevant to the genesis of 'exemplification' and adequate accounts need to explain the heterogeneous and homogeneous aspects of these changes. Hence in the following we will give related phenomena and discuss the way adequate accounts should take to explain the relevant change

---

[11] This problem holds for *tari* since in colloquial Japanese 'Tanaka dat-tari Yamada dat-tari' is often used.

instead of stating the motivation in a haphazard way.

Since Ishigaki's (1955) pioneering work, it has been acknowledged that Japanese has inter-clausal changes. Although his work is solely concerned with the change from a case particle to a connective particle, recent studies have revealed that other changes have common characteristics in this respect (see Kinsui 2007 for overview). Among these studies, the change from connective to focus particles, which is advocated in Kinuhata (2007a), has notable relevance to our change in that both seem to involve a simplification from a biclausal to a monoclausal structure (c.f. Harris & Campbell 1995, ch. 7).

To illustrate the point, let us give you three examples.

(23) a. ware, ... onazi farakara-<u>nari</u>-<u>tomo</u> kanarazu mutubiyori-namasi.
I same siblings-Copula surely get.married-VOL
'Even if we were siblings, I would surely get married to him.'
Genji 10th C.

b. fakanai fude-no ato-wo-<u>naritomo</u> tatematut-te
short pencil-GEN trace-ACC- send-CONJ
'I want to send a short letter.' *A Heike* 1593

c. nikusa-mo nikusi, nabutte-<u>naritomo</u> yara-u
hatefulness-also hateful make.fun.of- do-VOL
'I hate him very much and so I'll make fun of him.' *Toraakira* 1642

It is ascertained from the examples that the two clauses which are connected by *tomo* and constitute the whole sentence of (23a) are merged into a single clause in (23b) and (23c). [12] This inter-clausal change is observed in the formation of 'exemplification' as well, i.e. (ii) > (iii) > (iv) in (3). However, a close look at these examples makes us realize that they have differences in their resulting constructions. In (23b) *naritomo* follows the case markers differing from the syntactic position of *nari, tari* and *yara* as NPs, and further it can focus the verb of the main clause as in (23c). This indicates that we have to take other factors than the simplification of a biclausal structure into consideration in order to account for the issues.

Kinuhata (2007b) attributes the order of particles to the difference of the original construction, claiming that connectives establish a rigid construction between the subordinate clause and the main clause whereas particles that originate in the conclusive forms of the auxiliaries do not. In this rigid construction of connectives, he proposes that the simplification is brought about

---

[12] The merger of the copula verb *nari* and connective particle *tomo* is not directly relevant to the discussion here. See Kinuahta (2007b) for details.

by the syntactic movement as in (24), which results in a construction where case particles precede *naritomo*.

(24) [[NP-wo $_i$] *naritomo* [s ...t$_i$...]]

On the other hand, Kinuhata (2007b) considers the motivation of the change of *yara* as a pragmatic and sematic one. Our proposal in the previous subsection fits this idea in that the 'partial listing' enables the phrase to have an NP function. However, since that proposal is a stipulation and is not explained by other axioms, the discussion comes to a dead end, although we believe it important to spell out the prerequisites for the analysis of the motivation before leaping at the conclusion.

5. Concluding remarks

We argued in this paper that the common process in syntactic change as in (3) is observed in different lexical items and examined the semantic change which involves (a) the acquisition of the apposition and the transition (b) from creating an intersection to total listing of elements (applied to *nari*) and (c) from total listing to partial listing (applied to *nari* and *tari*). In the course of connecting the changes of syntax and semantics, we proposed that the 'partial listing' gives a phrase adverbial and nominal status and discussed its relevance to the motivation of the change.

Before concluding the paper, we would like to briefly comment on the subtypes of 'exemplification' and the implication of this study for the contrastive research. We distinguished two types of changes concerning the simplification of biclausal structure in section 4.2. Even though *Naritomo* came to have a meaning of 'exemplification' as illustrated in (23c), we still maintain that it has different characteristics from *nari*, *tari* and *yara* in its syntactic and semantic behavior: the former cannot have the apposition use and follows the case particle as opposed to the latter and tends to be related with free choice type quatification while the latter existential type. Based on this classification, 'exemplification' in other languages and the formation of them should be investigated. [13]

Texts

Ise monogatari (Nihon Koten Bungaku Zenshū), *Genji Monogatari* (Shinpen Nihon Koten Bungaku Zenshū), *Ujishūi Monogatari* (Nihon Koten Bungaku Taikei), *Engyōbon Heike Monogatari* (Benseisha), *Kakuichibon Heike Monogatari* (Shin

---

[13] For example in Korean *tunci* has same characteristics with items discussed in this paper whereas *lato* with *naritomo*. See also Haspelmath (1997) for the variation of indefinite pronouns in other languages, which is closely related to 'exemplification.' We owe the former to Chungmin Lee and other korean speakers gathered in Omuraya (23/02/2007) and the latter to John Whitman.

Nihon Koten Bungaku Taikei), *Amakusaban Heike Monogatari Taishōhonmon oy-obi Sōsakuin* (Meijishoin), *Kanjoshō* (Zoku Shōmono Shiryōshūsei 4), *Shikishō* (Shōmono Shiryōshūsei 1), *Mōgyūshō* (Shōmono Shiryōshūsei 6), *Chūkajakubokushishō* (Shin Nihon Koten Bungaku Taikei),*ōkura Toraakirabon Kyōgenshū no Kenkyū* (Hyōgensha), *Keisei hangonkō, Heike nyogonoshima, Shinjū Tennoamijima, Shinjū yoigōshin* (Chikamatsu Monzaemon Shū 1-4, Shinpen Nihon Koten Bungaku Zenshū), *Kanatehon Chūsingura* (Jōrurishō, Nihon Koten Bungaku Taikei),*Keisei satonokawazu, anakashiko kuruwabunshō,* (Kabuki Daichō Shūsei 5,11) *Kanjin kanmontekudano hajime* (Kabuki Kyakuhon Shū, Nihon Koten Bungaku Taikei), *Ukiyoburo* (Nihon Koten Bungaku Taikei), *Koinohanazome,* (Ninjōbon Kankōkai),*Seinen, Kusamakura, Kokoro, Higansugimade* (CD-ROM *Meiji no Bungō*)

References

Eguchi, T. 1998. Nihongo no Kansetsu Gimonbun no Bunpōteki Ichizuke nitsuite [On the Grammatical Status of Japanese Indirect Questions]. *Kyūdai Gengogaku Kenkyūshitsu Hōkoku* 19: 5-24. Kyūshū University.

Harris, A. and Campbell, L. 1995. *Historical Syntax in Cross-linguistic Perspective.* Cambridge: Cambridge University Press.

Haspelmath, M. 1997. *Indefinite Pronouns.* New York: Oxford University Press.

Ishigaki, K. 1955. *Joshi no Rekishiteki Kenkyū [Historical Studies of Particles],* Tokyo: Iwanami shoten.

Iwata, M. 2006a. Heiretsu Hyōgen no Shiteki Tenkai [Historical Development of apposition Expression]. *2006nendo Nihongogakkai Shunki Taikai Yōshishū,* 109-116. The Society for Japanese Linguistics.

Iwata, M. 2006b. Heiretsu Keishiki *Nari* no Hensen [Historical Change of apposition Form *Nari*], *Machikaneyama Ronsō Bungakuhen* 40: 75-90, Osaka University.

Kinsui, S. 2007. The Interaction between Argument and Non-argument in the Diachronic Syntax. *Current Issues in the History and Structure of Japanese,* eds. B. Frellesvig et al, 253-261. Tokyo: Kuroshio Publisher.

Kinuhata, T. 2007a. Syntactic Change from Connective to Focus Particles in Japanese. *Japanese / Korean Linguistics* 15, eds. N. McGloin et al., 393-404. Stanford: CSLI.

Kinuhata, T. 2007b. Fukasetsu kara Toritate eno Rekishi Henka no Futatsu no Patān [Two Patterns of the Historical Change from Adjuncts to Focus]. *Nihongo.no Kōzō Henka to Bunpōka,* ed. H. Aoki, 65-91. Tokyo: Hitsuzi syobō.

Kyō, K. 1993. Fujūbun Shūshi no Shiteki Tenkai [Historical development of incomplete conclusiveness]. *Gobun Kenkyū* 75: 1-10. Kyūshū University.

Kyōgoku, K. 1965. Shūshikei niyoru Jōken Hyōgen [Conditional Expressions by Conclusive Forms]. *Seikeidaigaku Bungakubu Kiyō* 1: 29-35. Seikei University.

Suzuki, H. 1995. *Nari* niyoru Heiretsu Hyōgen niokeru Sentaku Yōhōseiritsu no Keii [A Detail Analysis of the Birth of Selective Use Expressed by the Apposition Phrases with *Nari*]. *Kokugogaku* 173: 28-40.

Takamiya, Y. 2004. *Yara(u)* niyoru Kansetsu Gimonbun no Seiritu [Formation of Embedded Question of *Yara(u)*]. *Nihongogaku Bungaku* 15: 17-31. Mie University.

A Diachronic Account of the Speaker-Listener Honorific Marker -*sup*- in Korean

CHONGWON PARK
University of Minnesota Duluth

SOOK-KYUNG LEE
Korea University

1. Overview

Korean exhibits a very complicated honorific system. Though much has been said about the treatment of the honorific affix -*si*- from both synchronic and diachronic perspectives, relatively little attention has been paid to -*sup*-, especially with emphasis on historical analyses. A traditional diachronic treatment of the Korean honorific marker -*sup*- is to claim that the marker was originally used as an object honorific marker based on the relation between a subject and an object. That is, according to this approach, -*sup*- was used when an object needs to be honorified from the subject's point of view as illustrated in (1).

(1) Wang-i   pwuthye-lul   chengho-sop-a
    king-NOM   Buddha-ACC   invite-HON-CON
    'The king invited Buddha'
                                    (15th century, *Welinsekpwo*)

This approach then further states that the marker underwent some syntacto-semantic changes to become a speaker-listener-oriented (S-L) marker by claiming that a new honorific relation had been established between a speaker and a listener in a conversational context. Being assumed as a standard treatment of *-sup-*, this approach raises one empirical question; how can we find any transition stage (which is normally observed in language change in general) between the two uses (from Subject-Object to Speaker-Listener). Theoretically as well, it is hard to find a motivation behind the change of *-sup-*, from an object-oriented honorific marker to an S-L one.

In this paper, different from the traditional treatment of *-sup-*, we report and claim that *-sup-* was used as a Speaker-Object honorific marker in the 15th century as in (2). In (2), *-cop-* (allomorphic variation of *-sop-*) was used even when the subject *wang* 'king' was higher than *tayca* 'crown.prince' in a social status to express the speaker's respect toward *tayca*. Since the 16th century, however, *-sup-* began to be used in a context where a listener was equated with an object as shown in (3). Sentence (3) was thus used only when the object *Tonglay* was the listener. This type of construction began to be attested with extremely high frequency since the 17th century. Due to its high frequency, this specific construction further underwent changes to obsolesce the original usage (object-oriented honorification).

(2) Wang-i   tayca-skuy   mwut-**cop**-osya-toy
    king-NOM   crown.prince-DAT   ask-HON-HON-CON
    'The king asked the crown prince'
    (15th century, *Sekpwosangcel*)

(3) Cengkwan-i   syem-ulosye   wo-l   cek-pwuthe
    Cengkwan-Nom   island-from   come-Adn   time- from

    Tonglay ...   tut-**cop**-kwo
    Tonglay ...   listen-HON-CON
    '**I** (Cengkwan) heard about **you** (Tonglay) when I was coming from the island'
    (17th century, *Chephaysine*)

Given the observation above, we posit three stages for the evolution of the modern usage of *-sup-*. As shown in (5), in Stage I (15th century), *-sop-* was used to establish an honorific relation between a speaker and an object. In a later stage (Stage II, 16th century), *-sop-* began to be used with a contextual restriction where the object was required to be the listener. Because of its high frequency, this use had been standardized by obsolescing the 'equality' requirement between the object and the listener to become a modern usage (Stage III) as in (4).

(4) Onul   nay   ttal-i   hakkyo-eyse   sensayng-nim-ul
       today my daughter-NOM   school-LOC   teacher-HON-ACC
       manna-ss-sup-ni-ta.
       meet- PAST-HON-IND-DCL
       'Today, my daughter met (her) teacher at school'

(5) Stages (➔ means an honorific direction)

         Stage 1: Speaker ➔ Object (15th century)
         Stage 2: Speaker ➔ Indirect Object = Listener (16th century)
         Stage 3: Speaker ➔ ~~Indirect Object~~ = Listener (17th century)

We reach this conclusion by investigating all available historical documents from 15th century to early 20th century in Sejong Corpus containing 16.5 million syllables. More specifically, the documents we instigated include *Welinsekpo, Sekposangcel, Pephwakyengenhay, Samkanhaygsilto* (15th C.); *Penyeknokeltay, Penyekpakthongsa,* and letters (16th C.); *Nokeltayenhay, Cephaysine* (17th C.); *Eceynayhwun, Cephaymonge,* etc. (18th C.); Novels and Bibles (19-20th C.).

2. Organization of this paper

The organization of this paper is as follows. Section 3 briefly introduces previous studies concerning the functions of the honorific marker *-sup/-sop-* (*-sop* is the old form of *-sup*) in Middle Korean.

We then claim that we can explain the given data better by proposing that the *-sup/-sop-* had undergone some changes in function to finally become a Speaker-Listener-oriented honorific marker over time. In Section 4, we raise three questions concerning the functions of *-sop-*. The questions are [1] What was the function of *-sop-* in Middle Korean? [2] When were the changes in function of *-sop-* first attested, and in what fashion? [3] How can we account for the fossilization of *-sop-* in Modern Korean. That is to say, the affix *-sop-* began to undergo obsolescence over time to be found only in fully grammaticalized forms *supnita* and *saoni* in Modern Korean.

We also claim that frequency played a major role in grammaticalizing these forms in the same section. Then, we attempt to analyze our observation in recent theoretical frameworks in Section 5. After very briefly reviewing the two views on grammaticalization, i.e., Heine et al. (1991) and Traugott and Dasher (2002), in section 5, we claim that Traugott and Dasher's Invited Inferencing Theory can nicely account for our observation. Section 6 concludes our paper by summarizing our discussion and claims.

3. Previous Studies

There are two honorific forms that have attracted linguists' interests over the past few decades in Korean from either synchronic or diachronic point of view. The honorific markers in question are *-si-* and *-sop-*. Even though the debate on -*si*- has been settled down in historical linguistics due to the fact that there is no function change in -*si*-, there are still lots of debates on going on -*sop*- (Lee 1974, Ahn 1982, Hong 1998, Park 2000, etc).

The reason why people do not get to the point of agreement appear to be due to the fact that -*sop*- underwent a function change. Because of this change, tracing back the history of this morpheme is not always straightforward. Nonetheless, the previous proposals can be boiled down to two topics. First, they tried to explain the honorification system based on the relation between a subject and an object. Second, their interests were in explaining the -*sop*- honorification based on either 'whether the speaker is humbled' in the -*sop*- honorification or 'whether the speaker honorifies the object'.

In this paper, we claim that the -*sop*- honorification must be understood based on the speaker-listener relationship with emphasis being placed on historical documents. In other words, by modifying previous views, we claim that the honorific marker -*sop*- is used uniformly to honorify the listener, after undergoing some historical changes in its function.

4. The analysis

In this section, we will account for the historical changes (grammaticalization) of -*sop*'s usage. In 4.1, we deal with the change from the Subject-Object honorific marker to the Speaker-Object honorific marker. Then, in Section 4.2, we will examine the details of the grammatical function changes with emphasis on pragmatic motivation. In other words, we claim that the grammaticalization of -*sop*- was motivated pragmatically based on the situations where the form was used. Section 4.3 and 4.4 show what kind of role frequency played in the changes -*sop*- underwent.

4.1. Subject-Object vs. Speaker-Object

The mainstream previous approaches (except for Ahn 1982) assume that -*sop*- is an honorific marker used when the subject is higher in a social position to the object, ignoring the relationship between a listener and a speaker. If this is the case, we cannot clearly explain the change found in 16th century documents where -*sop*- plays a role as an honorific marker to respect the listener. In other words, the sudden change of -*sop*- from an object honorific marker to a listener honorific marker will remain mysterious without positing any transition stage.

As introduced in the overview of this paper, the problem is also confirmed by example (6) below where the speaker is the writer of the text (king Sejo), the subject is the king, and the object is the crown prince. In this case, even though the king is clearly in a higher position than the crown prince, the honorific marker was used. In (6), it is also worth noting that the dative marker *skuy* was attached to *tayca* 'crown.prince' to respect *tayca* not from the king's vantage point but from the speaker's point of view. This shows that the relationship between the subject and the object does not play any role in determining the use of -*sop*-.

(6) Wang-i   tayca-skuy   mwut-**copwo**-sya-toy
     King-NOM   crown.prince-DAT   ask-HON-HON-CONN
     'The king asked the crown princess'

$$\text{(15}^{\text{th}}\text{ century, } Sekpwosangcel \text{ 3:12)}$$

A similar example is illustrated in (7), where the usage of -*sop*- cannot be accounted for by the relationship between the subject and the object. Again, the usage of -*sop*- was determined by the relationship between the speaker and the object.

(7) Senin-i   ku   sto-nim-ol   eyesp-i   neki-e ......
     Senin-NOM   that daughter-ACC poor-AD-AFX   think-CON
     kwasil   pta-a   meki-e   kilu-**sopwo**-ni
     fruit   pick-CON   feed-CON   raise-HON-CO
     'Senin had sympathy for the daughter, so he picked up fruits and fed her
     and raised her'

$$\text{(15}^{\text{th}}\text{ century, } Sekpwosangcel \text{ 11:26)}$$

In addition to these, there are a few more examples similar to those which must be accounted for by emphasizing the relationship between the speaker and the object. We thus claim that in 15th century, the major function of -*sop*- was to honorify the object from the speaker's vantage point. We believe the mistakes found in previous proposals were due to the lack of empirical study dealing with a large amount of data. In 15th century documents, in most cases, the object was *pwuthye* 'Buddha'. Since *pwuthye* 'Buddha' must be higher than anyone else, the honorific marker was used in all the cases.

This usage of -*sop*- caused a lot of confusions in analyzing the honorific system in relation to -*sop*- later in Middle Korean, leading to the conclusion that the use of -*sop*- should be determined solely hinged on the subject-object relation. Our corpus-based study, however, finds several examples that falsify the traditional claim. If our claim is correct, several other factors will also naturally fall out, such as the changes in function of -*sop*-, and current usages of -*sup* (-*sop*-), etc. We will discuss this later in Section 4.3 and 4.4.

4.2. Changes in function

In this section, we explain the changes in the function of the honorific marker –*sop*-. For instance, since 16th century, -*sop*- was frequently used to respect an indirect object (rather than a direct object). In this case, the indirect object often was the same person as the listener. Due to the increase of this usage, -*sop*- began to undergo the function change from the speaker-object marker to the speaker-listener marker.

More specifically, we examined the 16th century documents, *Kim-ssi phyenci, Swohakenhay, Swok-Samkanghayngsildwo,* to illustrate the changes because 16th century is apparently a transition period for this function change. In this period, still the usage of –*sop*- as an object honorific marker was dominant. However, the usage of -*sop*- as a listener honorific marker was also attested with a limited frequency during this period as illustrated in (8). (8) deals with a conversation with a king and his servant. To answer the king's question 'Do all the writings belong to Choi Ho', the servant says 'I did write them with Choi Ho'. Here the allomorph of -*sop*-, -*sao*-, is attached to the verb *ha*- 'do'.

Although it is not completely clear who is actually honorified in this context, based on the general assumptions, we can safely assume that the king is the one who is respected the most, considering the fact that the king should be clearly in a higher position than the servants (Ko Yun and Choi Ho).

(8) (Kwoyun-i)　　　toytapho-ya　　nilwo-tay nay Choi Ho-walwo
　　(Kwoyun-NOM) answer-COM　say-CON　I　Choi HO-COM
　　honkaci-lwo　ho-**sowo**-ni
　　together-ADV do-HON-CON
　　'(Kwoyun) answered by saying that I worked with Choi Ho.'
　　　　　　　　　　　　　　　　　(16th *Penyekswohak* 9:46)

The 16th century document called *Kim-ssi phyenci* 'Kim's letters' contains letters written by a lady who belonged to a noble family. In this document, -*sop* is found six times. Out of six, -*sop* was used as the speaker-listener honorific marker five times. Considering the frequency of the tokens of -*sop*- in 16th century documents, five times seems to be insignificant (6.5%). Nonetheless, considering the fact that this document is one of the few documents that deal with more colloquial and conversational writings, this document should be treated as a good source to sort out the conversational Korean in 16th century. One example from *Kim-ssi phyenci* 'Kim's letters' is demonstrated in (9).

(9) Mwunanho-**op**-kwo　　　yosai-non　　esteho-si-nkwo.
　　Send.regard-HON-CON　recent-TOP　be.how-HON-Q
　　'(I) give my best regards to (my sister) and asks her how she is doing these days'
　　　　　　　　　　　　　　　　　(16th Kim-ssi phyenci)

108/ PARK AND LEE

4.3. Frequency I

We address the frequency issue in this section. We can explain the diachronic change of -sop- by counting the tokens in the corpus. Here we will be interested in three types of forms. First, we will examine the forms which correspond to -supnita in Modern Korean. To do trace the history of -supnita in Modern Korean, we have to consider all possible allomorphs of -sop-, which are -sop-, -zop-, -cop-, -op-, -sowo-, -zowo-, -cowo-, and -owo-.

Although traditionally, -supnita was analyzed as having four morphemes, -sup-, -ni-, -i- and -ta, in Modern Korean, the morphological structure underwent complete obsolescence by making the morphological boundaries of -supnita opaque.

As we claimed, if -sop- underwent a change from a Speaker-Object honorific marker to a Speaker-Listener marker, the frequency of -supnita also should be increased in Modern Korean. The prediction was made based on the fact that the morpheme attached to -sup (-ni-i-ta) was used to highly respect the listener. But if -sop- underwent a function change to be a Speaker-Listener marker, it would combine with -ni-i-ta more frequently because the major function of the two morphemes (-sop-, -ni-i-ta) could be maintained without any conflicts. This prediction is borne out as illustrated in Table 1. The form -sop- and its allomorphs occur 3257 times in 15th century documents, 628 in 16th century documents, 1534 in 17th century, 1178 in 18th century, and 3307 times in 19th century documents. Among these forms, the form -sup-ni-ta and its allomorphic variations occur 38 times in 15th century documents, 32 in 16th century, 184 in 17th century, 114 in 18th century, and 314 times in 19th century documents.

[Table 1] Frequency of the form -sup/sop-ni-i-ta

Century	15th C.	16th C.	17th C.	18th C.	19th C.
Frequency	38	32	184	114	314
Percentage	1.9%	5.0%	13.8%	9.6%	9.4%

As shown in the table above, the frequency of the combination -sup and -ni-i-ta had been increased until 17th century. Even though percentage itself has not been increased after that, the frequency has been maintained around 10 percent. This leads us to two conclusions. First, based on the frequency in 15th century, we can confirm our initial position again by claiming that – sop- was rarely used as a Speaker-Listener maker in 15th century. However, after the transition period (16th century), the usage of the combination began to be increased. Second, the increase of frequency over time can be interpreted as this: the combined form began to be stabilized with the Speaker-Listener marker. One example to show the combination of -sup and -ni-i-ta is illustrated in (10-11).

(10) Cangca-i   stal-i   yelay-skuy   cyes cwuk sswu-e
     Cangca-NOM   daughter-NOM   Buddha-DAT   milk soup cook-CON
     pat-**copo**-ni-i-ta
     give-HON-IND-HON-DCL
     'Cangca's daughter cooked milk soup to give it to Buddha'
                                      (15th century *Sekpwosangcel* 24:36)

(11) Anantaycwung-i   ta salwo-tay nay (cwonghon swoli-lol)
     Anantaycwung-NOM   all say-CON I   (bell.gong sound-ACC)
     tut-cop-now-i-ta.
     hear-HON-IND-HON-DCL.
     'Anantaycwung said that I hear the gonging of the bell'
                                      (15th century *Nengemkyengenhay* 4:125)

Concerning the data given, some people may raise the issue that the 10 percent frequency could be insignificant probabilistically. To answer this possible question, let us consider (10)-(11) again. As shown in (10)-(11), the combination of -*sop/sup*- and -*ni-i-ta* is found even in the 15th century. However, the frequency was extremely low in 15th century. Considering the low frequency in its early stage, we may conclude that the 10 percent frequency in 18th and 19th century is a significant increase.

It is worth noting that, in the examples above, there were clearly two distinct functions for -*cop*- (an allomorph for -*sop*-) and -*i*-; -*cop*- was used to respect the gonging of the bell, whereas -*i*- was used to honor Buddha (the Listener). In this type of context, in most cases, the listener was the same as the object. Since the context where the listener is the same as the object was frequently used, the two different functions carried by -*cop*- and -*i*- began to be collapsed to yield the -*cop-ni-i-ta* form with one function: Listener Honorifier.

Several more examples are illustrated in (12)-(14) to support our view better. All the examples illustrate the case where -*sop*- is combined with -*ni-i-ta*. As shown in these examples, since the 16th century, the combined form -*sop-ni-i-ta* was used as a Listener Honorifier. It was not until 19th century that the Modern Korean form -*sup-ni-ta* was used.

(12) nay nala-ul   wuyho-wa   epeuy-key   kesoli-ni ......
     I   nation-ACC   concern-CON   parent-DAT   disobey-CONN
     syelw-e   ho-op-noy-i-ta.
     sad-CON   do-HON-IND-HON-DCL.
     'I feel sorry because I disobey my parents in favor of my nation'
                                      (16th *Swok-Samkanghayngsildwo* Chwunsin 6)

(13) pwontay   mek-ti   mwosho-op-kesmanon
     Originally eat-CON cannot-HON-CONN
     ta mek-sop-no-i-ta
     all eat-HOP-IND-HON-DCL
     'I couldn't eat it but now I eat it all'

$$(17^{th} \ Chephaysine \ 3:6)$$

(14) Sin-un ......   palwo honkaci-n cwul
     Your.Majesty's.servent-TOP.. just   the.same   thing
     al-as-sop-no-i-ta.
     know-PAST-HON-IND-HON-DCL
     'I thought this is the same (as that one)'

$$(18^{th} \ Chenuyswokam \ 3:18)$$

4.4. Frequency II

The next question we have to consider is how to explain the forms -sa-o-ni and -sop-sosye, which are the forms where -sop- is attached by means of imperative listener honorific markers -o-ni and -so-sosye. Our prediction is that they also must show the same pattern as -sup-ni-ta. Again, if -sop- underwent a change in function to be a listener honorifier, the frequency of its combined forms with -o-ni and -so-sye would have to be increased as well, because both -sop- and -o-ni/-sosye came to share the same function: honorifying the listener.

Our prediction is borne out by our corpus-based study. As illustrated in Table 2 and Table 3, since 17th century, the frequency of the combined forms began to increase dramatically. For example, in Table 2, the frequency of -sa-o-ni in 19th century is 44.5 percent. The actual usage of sop-sosye was first attested in 17th century when -sop- began to be used solely as a listener honorific marker as illustrated in Table 3. Although the frequency is not increased significantly, the -sop-sosye form kept being used continuously. This form later underwent obsolescence in early 20th century, and it is not used in Modern Korean.

[Table 2] Frequency of -sa-o-ni

Century	15C	16C	17C	18C	19C
Frequency	63	23	234	326	1472
Percentage	1.9%	3.6%	15.2%	27.6%	44.5%

[Table 3] Frequency of -sop-sosye

Century	15C	16C	17C	18C	19C
Frequency	0	0	124	60	145
Percentage	0%	0%	8.1%	5.0%	4.3%

In addition to the data we discussed in this section thus far, there is another set of interesting data which are closely related to our discussion. As illustrated in (15) and (16), since 17th century, the -op-swo form began to be used as well. This also shows that -sop- was used with other listener honorific markers after undergoing a function change from an object honorific marker to a listener honorific marker.

(15) I   can-ulan   puti   ta   ca-**op**-swo
     This cup-TOP   please all   eat-HON-IMP
     'Please drink all (of the wine) in this cup'
                                      (17th century *Chephaysine* 3:5)

(16) swul-lan   so-wo-a   sonohoy tyong-tol-ina   mek-i-**op**-syosye.
     liquor-TOP   come-CON   guy   slave-PL-TOP   feed-Ao--HON-IMP.
     '(You should) buy wine to give it to your men-servants'
                                      (17th century Cincwu Ha-ssi Pyenci)

5. Theoretical Applications

In this section, we discuss how we account for our observations made so far in recent theoretical frameworks that deal with grammaicalization. There are three main proposals which have been put forward to account for the phenomenon of grammaricalization: Langacker's (1999a, b) Sujbectification Theory, Heine et al.'s (1991) Metaphorical Extention Theory, and Traugott and Dasher's (2002) Invited Inferencing Theory. Although Langacker's Subjectification Theory provides a view that grammaticalization is immanent in a conceptualizer's constural of a scene encoded in language, his view which is emphasizing concept and equating some grammaticalization as semantic bleaching has been treated as a non-standard approach by many cognitive linguists. Due to the limit of space, we thus exclude Langacker's approach in the current discussion.

5.1. Heine et al.'s Metaphorical Extension

According to Heine et al., grammaticalization is a consequence of human creativity. That is, when speakers develop new expressions for new grammatical concepts, they conceptualize abstract domains of cognition in terms of cognitive domains, and this process involves metaphorical extension. Heine et al.'s well-known hierarchy to introduce the notion of metaphorical extension is illustrated as follows.

(17) Person > Object > Activity > Space > Time > Quality

Clearly, this theory accounts for many language changes catetorized as grammaticalization. For instance, as pointed out by Park and Lee (2006), Korean Dative Markers such as -eykey, -hanthey, -pwokwo, -tele seem to have undergone the metaphorical extension process either Process (Activity) to Space or Space to Time. Nonetheless, it is not clear how we adopt this view in accounting for the emergence of the new honorification system in Korean. If we adopt this view, the burden to explain the development of the Speaker-Listener Marker must be placed on metaphor. However, as we have observed thus far, the emergence of the Speaker-Listener Marker seems to be motivated by pragmatic factors.

5.2. Traugott and Dasher's Invited Inferencing Theory

Invited Inferencing Theory's claim can be summarized as a claim that form-meaning reanalysis that characterizes grammaticalization arises as a result of situated language use. In their theory, they also use the term subjectification, but differently from Langacker (1999a, b). According to Traugott and Dasher, semantic changes in grammaticalization can be nicely understood in terms of shifts from more objective to more subjective meaning, which they call subjectification. More specifically, subjectification involves a shift from a construction encoding speaker-external event to a construction encoding the speaker's perspective in terms of location in space and time, or in terms of the speaker's attitude to what is being said. In this regard, Traugott and Dahser's approach place the burden of explanation of grammaticalization on pragmatics not on metaphors different from Heine et al.

The other term we would like to introduce from Traugott and Dasher is intersubjectification. According to Traugott and Dasher, intersubjectification is a shift from an objective meaning to a meaning that can grammatically encode a relationship between speaker and listener. Given this background, Traugott and Dasher's model is diagramed as follows.

(18)   Traugott and Dasher's model (Traugott and Dasher 2002: 38)

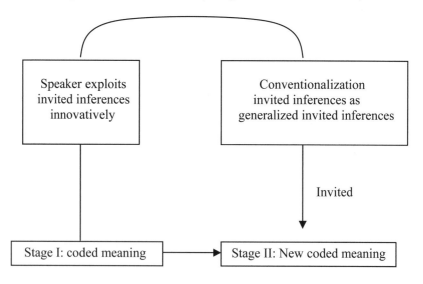

5.3. Invited Inferencing and the Korean honorific marker -sup

Invited Inferencing Theory being introduced briefly, we would like to discuss how we account for our observation in this theory. As observed, the earlier uses of the honorific marker *-sup-* appear to have been participant-external. That is, the honorific marker was used in contexts where the third person was respected. However, when the listener is the same as the object, more subjective participant-internal (Speaker-Listener-oriented) uses began to emerge. Then, the speaker exploited invited inferences innovatively which was followed by conventionalization of invited inferences as generalized invited inferences. That is to day, in this stage, pragmatic meaning has been reanalyzed coded meaning. The process is explained using the same examples we used previously.

In (19), the use of *-cop-* is more objective, establishing a participant-external relationship. The conversation participant, the listener, is excluded here in honorification, by establishing a relationship between the speaker and the object.

(19 = 2) Stage I: More objective, participant external

    Wang-i   tayca-skuy   mwut-**cop**-osya-toy
    king-NOM   crown.prince-DAT ask-HON-HON-CON
    'The king asked the crown prince'

                                    (15th century, *Sekpwosangcel*)

Later, the relationship established by the honorific marker *-op* becomes more subjective by making the listener a conversational participant.

(20 = 9) Stage II: More subjective, Innovative Use, Participant-internal

    Mwunanho-**op**-kwo   yosai-non   esteho-si-nkwo.
    Send.regard-HON-CON   recent-TOP   be.how-HON-Q
    '(I) give my best regards to (my sister) and asks her how she is doing
    these days'

                                    (16th Kim-ssi phyenci)

Finally, the new usage innovated by a speaker was newly encoded in a linguistic system to be a new convention as illustrated in (21).

(21 = 4) Stage III: New coded meaning

    Onul   nay ttal-i   hakkyo-eyse   sensayng-nim-ul
    today my   daughter-NOM   school-LOC   teacher-HON-ACC
    manna-ss-sup-ni-ta.
    meet- PAST-HON-IND-DCL
    'Today, my daughter met (her) teacher at school'

6. Conclusions and summary

In our paper, we showed how -sop- underwent a function change over time. To wrap up, the change is summarized as in (22).

(22)   Stage 1: Speaker → Object (Speaker honorifies Object)
         Stage 2: Speaker → Indirect Object = Listener
         Stage 3: Speaker → ~~Indirect Object~~ = Listener

As shown in (22), different from the mainstream analysis of -sop-, the speaker all the time played the major role in determining the use of the honorific marker -sop-. One question possibly raised here is how to explain sentence (23) where the subject honorifies the object.

(23) (Kyocang-i haksayng-ekey)
     (principal-NOM student-DAT)
     Chelswu-ya,   ney sensayng-nim-kkey   chayk-ul   tuli-ela.
     Chelswu-VOC your teacher-HON.AF-DAT   book-ACC   give-IMP
     '(The principal speaks to a student) Chelswu, (please) give this book to your teacher'

Although this example seems to be an apparent counterexample to our analysis, we can explain the data still from the speaker's point of view. One good analogy to explain the situation is when we talk to children. Often times, when we talk to children, we will kneel or crouch down to look into their eyes and see things from their vantage point. Similarly in (23), the speaker is talking to the listener from his vantage point by using the honorific expression *tuli-ela* 'give' even if the principal is higher than Chelswu's teacher in a social hierarchy. Thus in this example, we can claim that the Speaker-Listener relation is still important in determining the use of -sup-. The only difference in (23) is that the speaker humbles himself to have the same vantage point as the listener.

References

Ahn, B. 1961. Cwucey kyepyangpep-uy cepmisa sop-ey tayhaye [On -sop - the subject honorific marker (written in Korean)]. *Cintanhakpo* 22: 104-126.
Heine, B., Ulrike C. and Friederike H. 1991. *Grammticalization: a Conceptual Framework*. Chicago: University of Chicago Press.
Hong, J. 1998. *Understanding early Modern Korean grammar*. Seoul: Pakiceng.
Huh, W. 1963. *Cwungsey Kwuke Yenkwu* [A research on the Middle Korean]. Cengumsa: Seoul, Korea.
Kim, H. 1947. A research on Korean honorifics (written in Korean). *Hangul* 12: 4: 17-24.
Langacker, R.1999a. *Grammar and Conceptualization*. Berlin: Mouton de Gruyter.
Langacker, R. 1999b. Losing control: grammaticization, subjectification and transparency. *Historical Semantics and Cognition*. eds. A. Blank and P. Koch. Berlin: Mouton de Gruyter, pp. 147-175.

Lee, I. 1974. Some queries on the systematic treatment of Korean honorifics (written in Korean). *Journal of Korean Linguistics* (Kwuehak) 2: 39-63.

Martin, S. E. 1992. *A Reference Grammar of Korean*. Rutland, Vermont & Tokyo, Japan: Charles E. Tuttle Company.

Park, C. and S. Lee. 2006. Grammaticalization and Korean Datives. Paper presented at the 42nd Chicago Linguistic Society. University of Chicago.

Park, J. 2000. A cross-linguistic consideration on the honorifics in Cephaysine. *Korean Linguistics* (Hankwukehak) 12 (written in Korean). 119-146.

Sohn, H. 1999. *The Korean Language*. Cambridge: Cambridge University Press.

Traugott, E. and R. B. Dasher. 2002. *Regularity in Semantic Change*. Cambridge: Cambridge University Press.

Grammaticalization Pathways for Japonic Nominalizers: A View from the Western Periphery

LEON A. SERAFIM
University of Hawai'i

RUMIKO SHINZATO
Georgia Institute of Technology

1. Introduction

Genitives frequently develop into nominalizers in the world's languages (e.g. Yap, et al. 2004). Standard Japanese (genitive **no** > nominalizer **no**), and Toyama and Kōchi (genitive **ga** > nominalizer **ga**) exemplify this development (Yamaguchi 1982; Horie 1998; Hirata 2002; Hikosaka 2005).[1] The path from genitive/pronominal **no** > nominalizer **no** has been well studied and discussed along with such historical changes as the demise of the *shūshi/rentai*[2] distinction, and of *kakari musubi*.[3]

---

[1] We offer thanks to Satoshi Kinsui, Yukinori Takubo, Alexander Vovin, John Whitman, Janick Wrona, and Foong Ha Yap, for their discussion and comments during the writing of this paper. We also wish to thank our native-speaking informants for their judgments. Any remaining weaknesses are of course due to us.

[2] Abbreviations and Conventions: cls: classifier; cop: copula; *fukujoshi*: adverbial particle; gen: genitive; IZ: *izen(kei)*; *izen* 'realis' (paradigm category); *kakari joshi*: focus (= *kakari*)

The nominalizers of the Western-Periphery dialects, namely, Western Ya-maguchi (= WY) **so**, Kyushu (= Ky) **to/tu**, and Okinawan (= Ok) **shi**, however, have received little attention. This paper has three objectives: First, we will argue that these three nominalizers do not trace back to genitives in their origin, but to the noun meaning 'one/thing'. We will explore these nominalizers of nongenitive origin. In doing so, we will necessarily bring into the picture the *shūshi/rentai* distinction, and *kakari musubi*. Second, we will reconstruct a proto-Japonic progenitor for them. Third, we will provide a plausible account for these dialects' not recruiting genitives for their nominalizers.

2. Establishing a Common Origin for the Western Periphery Dialects' Nominalizers

In order to claim a common origin for the three dialects, we will first recon-struct a developmental history of the Okinawan nominalizer **shi**, since Ok preserves written documents dated back to the 16th century, and it is there-fore relatively easier to construct its history. Ok history shows the origin of **shi** as a noun meaning 'one/thing' (Hokama et al. 1995: 350b). The func-tional similarities and phonological correspondences of Ok **shi** and the other two nominalizers to be explored suggest their common origin. Given Ok **shi**'s origin, we hypothesize the other two, also, as having originated in a noun. We also show why Ky **to/tu** does not trace back to a genitive.

2.1. The Development of Ok *shi* (< *si* < **si* < **su* < **sô*)

Based on the oldest record of Ok, the *Omoro Sōshi* (= OS), compiled in the 16th and 17th centuries, it is evident that, for *nonstative* verbs, in any case, the *shūshi/rentai* distinction had come to disappear, just as in MJ (Mamiya 1983, Shinzato 1998). Stative verbs preserved the distinction as ...**ri** = *shūshi* vs. ...**ru** = *rentai*. Unlike MJ, however, Ok had created a New Sys-tem, as in Figure 1, by the time of the OS, with new *shūshi/rentai* forms, through the incorporation of stative extensions, as in Figure 2. This resulted in the reintroduction of the *shūshi/rentai* distinction in all paradigms.

---

particle; *kakari musubi*: focus-particle–verbal-agreement syntax; kp: *kakari* particle; Ky: Kyu-shu; *meirei* 'imperative' (paradigm category); MJ: Middle Japanese; MR: *meirei(kei)*; MZ: *mizen(kei)*; neg: negative; NOk: Modern Okinawan; OJ: Old Japanese; Ok: Okinawan; OS: *Omoro Sōshi*; pass: passive; qt: quotative; *rentai*: adnominal morphology; prt: particle; RT: *rentai(kei)*; *shūshi*: sentence-ending morphology; SS: *shūshi(kei)*; sub: subject; top: topic; WY: Western Yamaguchi.

[3] Yet another origin proposed for the nominalizer **no** in Standard Japanese comes from Frelles-vig (2001), who argues for its origin as the defective copula.

	Old system		New system	
	Rentai (RT)	*Shūshi* (SS)	*Rentai*	*Shūshi*
fall (of rain)	**furu**	**furu**	***furiyoru***	***furiyori***
exist (anim.)	**woru**	**wori**	**woru**	**wori**

Figure 1: Comparison of old/new paradigms – I

		Plain predicates		Progressive → Unmarked Predicates	
		RT	SS	RT	SS
Archaic system	'exist' (anim.)	**worô**	**worî**	-----	-----
	'fall' (of rain)	**purô**	**puru**	-----	-----
Old System		**woru**	**wori**	-----	-----
		furu	**furu**[4]	**furi#woru**	**furi#wori**
New System		**woru**	**wori**	-----	-----
		furu	**furu**	**furiyoru**	**furiyori**
Contem-porary		**wuru**		**wuN**[5]	
		fuyuru		**fuyuN**	

Figure 2: Four-stage development of paradigms' rentai/shūshi forms

The replacement through grammaticalization of the old plain SS/RT forms with the new predicate extensions derived from progressive forms, had three major consequences in the Okinawan syntax. First, it helped to preserve **dö**-type KM[6] (counterpart of OJ **sö/zö**-type KM). Second, it also created a new possibility for a heretofore unused clausal nominalizer ('the one who does X' > 'doing X'), since the reemerged *rentai* form (that is, a form based on the old progressive *rentai* form) only had an adnominal function, not a clausal nominalization function.[7,8] Third, in contrast, the

---

[4] By the time of the Old System, the *shūshi :: rentai* system had merged to one form for both functions, *except for the statives*, upon whose differing *shūshi :: rentai* forms the new progressive construction was built. (Actually, the negative imperative appears to have retained the Archaic system intact, as pointed out by Kinjō (1974 [1944]: 117) as in e.g. **matuna** 'don't wait' < ***matôna.**)

[5] For the changes resulting from the shift of ***ri** to **N**, see Hattori 1977 and Serafim 2008.

[6] Cited in a reconstructed form, for modern Ok **du**. See Serafim & Shinzato 2005.

[7] Interesting in this regard is Wrona's (2005) account of the *rentai* form in OJ. He (2005: 144) states that "the earliest (and only) function of the Adnominal form is to construct relative constructions...." A propos of that, interestingly, the OS form <...ru (=RT) kiyoraya> appears quite frequently (e.g. #50, #59), and refers to the impressiveness of whatever is described in the preceding RT-ending clause. Hokama (2000) translates these examples as if the RT-ending clause were itself a nominalized subject, i.e. as a noun in itself. However, the OS marks subjects overtly with <ka> or <kiya>, and neither of these subject markers appears after the RT form. So, rather than Hokama's interpreta-

new paradigm did very *little* to preserve **sô**-type KM (counterpart of OJ **kösö**-type KM).[9] What happened was a near-merger of *yodan* 'quadrigrade' with *nidan* 'bigrade' verbs in Ok, which blurred the *izen* 'realis' and *meirei* 'imperative' distinction as in Figure 3.

	Archaic system		New system	
	IZ	MR	IZ	MR
'protect'	*maburë	*maburê	<mahure>	<mahure>
'exist'	*kî#öwarë	*kî#öwarê	<tiyoware>	<tiyoware>
(anim.hon.)				

Figure 3: Comparison of old/new paradigms – II

Since such a formal distinction was vital for the *survival* of the **sô**-type KM, one may readily surmise that the IZ::MR merger facilitated the *demise* of **sô**-type KM. The OS texts (16th C) contain about 500 tokens of **sô**-type KM (vis-à-vis 120 for **dö**-type [Mamiya 2005]), but Kumiodori, the theatrical texts (18th C), contain only a few fossilized forms of the **sô**-type. In contrast, **dö**-type KM exists in abundance in Kumiodori, as indeed it does in the contemporary language.

An added push towards the demise of the **sô**-type KM also came from its internal functional changes, most of which parallel what happened in MJ. First, the KP weakened its governing power over the predicate that it binds with, thus being transformed into a *fukujoshi*, or adverbial particle, just like Mod J **koso**.[10] Second, the KP came to focus adverbs (10% in OS), just like MJ. As for OJ, on the other hand, according to Ōno (1993:133), the *Man'-yōshū* lacks this type of new collocation. Third, the *izen* ending governed by the **sô**-type KP had lost its former function as concessive conjunction, and instead expressed mere emphatic assertion in OS (Mamiya 1983: 19, Mamiya 2005: 34), parallel to the pattern in MJ (cf. Ōno 1993; Kobayashi

---

tion, we interpret these <...ru (=RT) kiyoraya> cases as a relative clause construction where the preceding RT-ending clause modifies the nominalized final predicate, <kiyoraya>. Therefore, RT-ending predicates, as far as we know, in and of themselves lack nominalizing function.

[8] OS <koto> has the apocopated form before it, but the single example of <su> has a full RT form. Apocopation, in effect, occurs in two waves, since any type of clause modifying the modern Ok **shi** takes the apocopated form. The form <koto> lacks instances preceded by a full form in the OS, so we do not know whether it had the same functions as in NOk. In any case, OS <su> means 'one', and leaves a trace when raised to head position. We lack any example until the 18th-century documents of <su>'s use as a nominalizer, i.e.,with neither raising nor trace associated with its modifying clause.

[9] For **sô**-type KM, see Serafim & Shinzato 2005.

[10] For instance, several examples show that the **sô**-type KP binds with MZ, RT, and seeming MR. Additional cases occur of **sô**'s use as if a *shūjoshi* or predicator particle.

2003).[11] Fourth, Mamiya (2005: 37) asserts that the two KM originally formed emphatic assertions equally, but with this distinction: **dö**-type KM for more objective description (often with the progressive form 'be doing') as in (1), and **sô**-type KM for more subjective description, often with inferential or volitional auxiliaries, as in (2b). However, as **dö**-type KM gained strength from the new paradigm – the result of the merger of plain and complex predicate paradigms – and as **sô**-type KM went through internal functional change, the functional distinction that had once held between the two types of KM must have become increasingly indistinguishable. Probably due to this functional merger, coupled with phonological similarity, the two fossilized forms of **sô**-type KM and **dö**-type KM (reconstructable as *****dani do** > *****danju** and **dani su** > **dens[h]i**) became synonymous in Kumiodori.[12] The merging functions of the two KM probably gave the needed impetus for **dö**-type KM to win out over **sô**-type.[13,14]

(1) <shiyori   furu   ame   ya   sudemidu   <u>do</u>   furi-yo<u>ru</u>>
     Shuri   fall   rain   TOP   purified water KP   is-fall-ing
     'Speaking of the rain falling in Shuri, it is purified water that falls.'
     (*Omoro Sōshi* 370 [Hokama 2000])

(2) a. <ura   no kazu   kimikimi   <u>siyo</u>   mabu<u>re</u>>
       village-   's no.   priestesses   KP   protect-IZEN
       'It is the priestesses of the inlet's villages who will protect (the ship in its voyage).' (OS 853 [ibid.])

---

[11] Kobayashi (2003: 62) portrays the following sequence:
    A {Ø – *izen*}, B.   ... conditional clause formation
    ↓ insertion of **koso**
    A {**koso** – *izen*}, B.   ... conditional clause formation (concessive)
    ↓ deletion of the apodosis
    A {**koso** – *izen*}, (B). ... finite clause (implication of concession)
    ↓ demise of *izen* function (demise of concessive implication)
    A {**koso** – *izen*}. Ø ... finite clause (simple emphasis)
    Ōnishi (2002: 35) also delineates a similar path of development as: contrastive focus > thematic focus.
[12] Ifa Fuyū assigns (1974: 48, 56), the same gloss *geni koso* 'sure enough' to both **danju** and **dani su**, though their verb endings clearly indicate the *rentai* vs. *izen* distinction.
[13] The Hachijō dialect provides an interesting case, in which the descendant of **kösö** survived and eclipsed **sö/zö/dö**-type KM. The question-forming **ka**-type KM also survived in Hachijō, binding with the inferential auxiliary, just as in Ok. For the latter, see Serafim and Shinzato 2000.
[14] The *Omoro Sōshi* examples in < > are orthographic rather than phonetic representations.

b. <sen-kimi   siyu   siri-yowa-me>
spiritual.power's-priestess KP   protect-EX-INFERENCE.IZ
'None other than the priestess Senkimi will protect you.' (OS 710)[15]

Serafim and Shinzato (2005) claim that the sô-type KP relates to a noun meaning 'people, thing, one'. For instance, in OS, it appeared as a pronominal as in (3), or a classifier for people as in (4).

(3) <ubudama   fa   inoru su   do   yogakeru. >
TOP   pray   person KP   govern
'It is the one/person who prays to Ubudama (life-generating ball) who will govern.' (OS 102 [ibid.])

(4) <momo-so   kirifusete... >
Hundred-CLS   cutting down
'Cutting down a hundred souls...' (OS 103 [ibid.])

The demise of sô-type KM left only pronominal <su> (=[*si]), which required the preceding predicate to end in a *rentai* form, thus allowing the pronominal > nominalizer grammaticalization, and thereby filling in the functional gap – i.e. no nominalizer – created upon the establishment of the new predicate paradigm[16]. In NOk (18C~), <su> is phonetically realized as **shi** (=[ʃi]).[17] Summarizing The foregoing in Figure 4, we have:

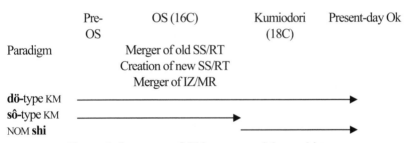

Figure 4. Summary of Okinawan particle-use history

---

[15] These two examples are adapted from Serafim & Shinzato 2005.

[16] Please refer to footnote 7.

[17] The nominalizer **shi** + conjunctive particle **ga**, ~**shiga** is ambiguous. It can mean 'one who does ~', or 'although ~'. The fact that these two meanings have but one form to distinguish them (as in CLAUSE-**no-ga** 'Ving; the one that Vs' vs. CLAUSE-**ga** 'although CLAUSE', in Mod J, where **no** originates from a genitive) stems precisely from the fact that **shi**, far from deriving from a genitive, derives from the defective noun meaning 'one'.

2.2. W.Yamaguchi and Kyushu dialects in comparative perspective with Okinawan

We now turn to WY[18] and Ky dialects. Although the cognation of Ok **shi** and WY **su/so/ho** has attracted very little attention in the mainland circle of linguistics,[19] hints about it appeared as early as 1963 (OGJ 1963: 463a), and later, in 1998 (Nohara: 487-9), and even later, in 2005 (Serafim and Shinzato 2005). Serafim (2003) recently suggested the cognation of Ok **shi**, WY **su/so** and Kyushu **to/tu**. Assuming that these three types of nominalizers are possible cognates, here we will further explore their nominalizer functions in detail. In the following examples, Ky refers to Nagasaki.

(5) Nominalizer-1 (Adj + X; V + X; where X *has* a referent)

WY	**marui so**	'round one' (Nakagawa 1982: 164)
Ky	**chiisaka to**	'small one' (Atago 1999 [1969]: 216)
Ok	**gumasa shi**	'small one'

WY ...**kanten no niru so ga san-bon**
...agar-agar GEN boil NOM SUB three-sticks
'...three sticks of agar-agar that you boil (*lit.,* 'a boil-one of agar-agar, three sticks')' (NHK 1967:243)[20]

Ky **waa-ga kyaata to ba yomi-e-n to ja mon.**
I-SUB wrote NOM OBJ READ-POT-NEG NOM COP SP
'(He) can't read what I wrote.' (Atago ibid: 216)

Ok **'ari ga kachee shee (<shi+ya) churasan.**
he SUB wrote NOM TOP is-beautiful
'What he wrote is beautiful.'

(6) Nominalizer-2 (S + X; where X has *no* referent)

WY **moto-no mici-i de-rare-d-atta cyuu so ga**
original road-to go out-able-not-PAST APPOSITIVE NOM SUB
kicune ga bakasita so de ar-imas-yoo.
fox SUB trick-PAST NOM COP-POLITE-INFERENTIAL
'The fact that I couldn't go back on the road that I had come on is probably that the fox played a trick on me.' (NHK 1967:232)

---

[18] More specifically, Western Yamaguchi and Kokura, Fukuoka along the Kanmon strait area. See Nomura (1988) for details. The Kanmon strait has been regarded as a border to divide the Kyushu and Honshu dialect area. However, based on the comparative study of 88 lexical items, Miyamoto (1978) proposes that the area in question forms a distinct dialect area. This correlates with the isolated occurrence of the **su/so** nominalizers in this area.

[19] For instance, Hikihara (1978: 15) classifies it as *keitō fumei* 'lineage unkown.'

[20] WY examples in (5) and (6) adapted from Serafim & Shinzato 2005.

Ky **aibu to made utsusa-re-t to desu.**
walk NOM even shoot-PASS-PAST NOM COP
'I even had a picture taken of me walking.' (Atago 1999: 216)

Ok **NN-daN shi ga mashi.**
see-not NOM SUB better
'It is better not to look.' (OGJ 1963)

The parallel breaks down, however, when it comes to cleft constructions. WY and Ky developed the 'nominalizer + copula' construction, a rough equivalent of Mod J **no da**, but Okinawan lacks such a construction.

(7) **No da** construction

WY **yomu so desu.**
read NOM COP
'It's that I will read.' (Nakagawa 1982: 164)

Ky **arechi ga ooka to desu.**
barren land SUB a lot NOM cop
'It's that there is lots of barren land.' (Atago 1999: 218; See also the second **to** in example (6) above.)

It has been suggested in several studies that the focus/emphatic function once held by **zo**-type KM transferred to the *no da* construction of Modern Japanese (Funaki 1987; Schaffar 2002). In fact, NOk **du**(< **dö**)-type KM can very easily express the connotation of Japanese *no da*, as shown in (8). This leads to a three-way functional equivalency: J **no da** :: WY/Ky **so/to** + COP :: Ok **du**-type KM.[21]

(8) Japanese **no da** and Okinawan **du**-type KM (cf. example (7) as well)

Ok: **'ichi du su-ru.**
go out KP do-RT
J: iku **n da!**
'Hey, go out, you!'/ 'So, go, already!' / '(It's better) you go.'

Ok: **chimuganasano-o ara-n, chimugurisan di du 'icha-ru.**
cute-COP be-not pitiful QT KP said-RT
J: **kawaii de wa naku, kawaisooda to itta n da.**
cute be-TOP-not pitiful QT said NODA
"Hey, I didn't say 'cute', I said 'pitiful'."

---

[21] Hachijō (Kaneda 2001) has lost **zo**-type KM (the counterpart of Ok **dö**-type KM), and has the **no da** construction, as expected. However, the story has a twist or two, since it preserved **koso**-type KM and a *rentai/shūshi* distinction to a certain extent (the *rentai* form apparently lacks sentence-final emotive function). At any rate, a great deal more elucidation is needed for a comparative analysis with these dialects.

Putting all together, we obtain the following correspondence.

	W. Yamaguchi	Kyushu	Okinawan
Pronominal	**so**	**to**	**shi**
Complementizer	**so**	**to**	**shi**
No-da	**so** + copula	**to** + copula	**du**-type KM

Figure 5: Correspondence of Three Nominalizers

Given the above, the functional similarities of these three nominalizers are striking. Where they differ, we may easily account for the dissimilarities as the result of the loss or persistence of KM. WY and Ky lack KM, whereas Okinawan has it.

2.3. The progenitor of the three nominalizers

The functional parallelism of these three nominalizers leads to a hypothesis that they may come from the same source. In fact, they all appear in the Western periphery dialects in geographical complementary distribution. Adopting Serafim (2003: 472), we propose the following derivations:

(9) Derivation of three nominalizers

Ultimate protoform:	***two** (= ***tô**)
Assibilation:	***two** (= ***tô**) ~ ***swo**
Raising:	***tu** ~ ***two** (= ***tô**) ~ ***su** ~ ***swo** (= ***sô**)
Loss of ***o::*wo** distinction:	**tu** ~ **to** ~ **su** ~ **so**

As for the meaning of ***two**, we assume that it was a noun meaning 'one, thing'. Positing the meaning of ***two** as 'one, thing' is easily substantiated in WY and Ok since both dialects have already had such a meaning documented, and neither has a genitive marker of the same phonetic shape (see immediately below). This ***two** has been claimed of the same origin as ***sô** in the Japanese lineage, leading to OJ, lexicalized – as **su** – into bird and fish names (Serafim and Shinzato 2005, Thorpe 1983), and possibly as part of the negative auxiliary **-azu** < ***-ani#su** (Thorpe 1983).

This hypothesis, however, clashes with a hypothesis tracing back the Ky **tu/to** to the locative-genitive ***tu**, as in Hirata (2002),[22] who analyzes **itutu** 'five' as a double genitive derivative construction as in (10):

(10) **i** 'five' + **tu** 'GEN' + **tu** 'bound pronominal'

He additionally notes the similarity to example (11a), the construction found in Southern Fukuoka. Ōno Sayuri (1983: 58), observes the three varieties of (11b) in Ōita.

---

[22] Another hypothesis traces it back to the quotative complementizer, **to** (Hikosaka 2005).

(11) a. ore 'I' + *ga* 'GEN' + *tu* 'one' (So. Fukuoka, Hirata 2002: 262)

   b. tarō 'Taro (p.n.)' + *ga*   'GEN' +   *tu* 'one'
                        + *no*   'GEN' +   *tu* 'one'
                        + *n*   'GEN' +   *to* 'one' (Ōita)

(12) *watashi 'I' + no   'GEN' +   no 'one' > watashi no 'mine'

Hirata's account is not free from challenges, however. Firstly, while in fact example (10) parallels example (12) (a supposedly underlying Standard Japanese **watashi + no** 'GEN' + **no** 'one', from which the actual string of **watashi no** apparently derived), a contracted form (i.e. **ore** *tu* < **ore** *tu tu*) is lacking. Instead, instances of the genitive + Noun 'one', such as (**ore** +) **ga tu / no tu / n to**, represent the construction. Thus, the parallel between examples (10) and (12) serves only to prove **tu** a *nominalizer*, but *not* a genitive, since just **ga, no,** or **n** serve as the actual genitives in this dialect.

   Secondly, both the nominalizer **-tu** and the nominalizers **-su/-so/-ho** occur in the Western Periphery dialects, in geographical complementary distribution. Given this, if these two types of nominalizers did indeed derive from genitives, we would expect both **-tu** and **-su/-so/-ho** as genitives, in geographical complementary distribution, but that is not the case. Indeed, we lack any sort of evidence of the consonant **-t** of the genitive alternating with **-s**. Thus, it may be more reasonable to connect the Ky nominalizer **-tu** to the nominalizers **-su/-so/-ho**, and to eschew relating any of them to a genitive.

   Thirdly, the other genitives of OJ, **ga** and **nö**, developed a function as nominative case markers at least in subordinate clauses before they developed a nominalizer function. However, Ky **tu** lacks a nominative case marking function, just as Ok **shi** and WY **so** do. Therefore, this fact associates Ky **tu** more closely with the defective noun than with the genitive.

   Fourthly, Vovin (2005: 367f) discusses the OJ numerical classifier **-tu** 'thing', used almost exclusively to count 'nonhumans and nondeities.' Discussing external relationships (2005: 383) he says, 'There are no apparent external etymologies for the classifier **-tu**....' He notes the existence of the classifier corresponding to **-tu** in Ryukyuan, since he ascribes a widespread distribution to the word's *not* being a loan from the Peninsula. On the other hand, he *does* offer an external etymology for **-tu** '(genitive)'[23] (2005: 152-

---

[23] He divides this putative single -tu into a genitive-locative and a defective copula, citing a 2001 article by Bjarke Frellesvig. Most OJ examples instantiate the former. He notes that *Man'yōshū* Azuma-uta examples largely appear in poems indistinguishable from Western OJ (i.e. the Central dialect), rejecting Eastern OJ examples as evidence for a Proto-Japonic *-tu. Vovin further notes this morpheme's absence in Ryukyuan. Then (2005: 157), he cites work by Samuel Martin connecting the Japanese morpheme with the genitive -s in Middle Korean.

158), and he never mentions any etymological link between genitive **-tu** and the classifier **-tu** 'thing'. In short, it appears that the classifier **-tu** and the genitive **-tu** must stem from different sources.

Given this, it is unlikely that Kyushu **to/tu** relates to the OJ locative-genitive **-tu**. Thus, rather than linking **t**-initial nominalizers to the GEN **tu**, we may more soundly connect them to another source, the strong candidate being the noun meaning 'one'.

3. Why so/to? Why not genitives?

Thus, Okinawan, Yamaguchi and Kyushu dialects form a separate class from the rest of Japonic, in that the source of their nominalizers, rather than a genitive, is a noun meaning 'one'. At this point, one may question why these dialects failed to recruit genitives but instead recruited the noun.

In point of fact, the issue is not the *peripheral* dialects, since they simply conserve the old state of affairs. Rather, the *central* dialects have undergone the changes that led to Modern Japanese.

We know that the **s**-initial nominalizer has to have existed in PJ, because it turns up in all dialects, although only as a fossilized form as in **kara-su** 'crow' (< 'black-one'), **ugupi-su** 'bush-warbler-one', **wo-su** 'male-one' in the central dialects.

So, why did the central dialects abandon the **s**-initial-pronominal? We speculate that they abandoned it when whole clans or corporations of refugees fled from the Korean peninsula to Yamato, exerting significant effects upon both high and low levels of pre-OJ language, from as early as the fifth century to as late as the seventh (Inoue 1999). Kansai-area Japanese must then have started using a borrowed noun **-aku** as a nominalizer.[24] By the end of the Nara period, **-aku** had already progressed into lexicalization and disuse; the *rentai* form of predicates now took its place, having expanded from its adnominal/relativizing functions to include nominalization itself (cf. Wrona 2005).

Several linguistic facts line up with this scenario. First, Okinawan has no trace of **-aku**, even in a fossilized form. However, Modern Japanese

---

Vovin believes that an Old-Korean-to-OJ loan ultimately connects the Old Korean and Japanese forms. He tentatively reconstructs Old Korean *-cɨ or *-ci, also speculating that Paekche, a dialect of Old Korean, may have had *-cu, which pre-Old Japanese would have had to borrow as -tu, having no affricates.

[24] Most scholars accept that *ku-gohō* results from adding -aku to the *rentai* form of the verb (Ōno 1953: 50). However, Kiyose 2001 disputes both its origin and its function as a nominalizer. He believes that it is the adverbial-derivation form, formed by adding -"(r)aku to the stem ("Ku-gohō to wa ... gokan ni gobi (bunpō setsubiji) -"(r)aku ga tsuita haseikei de shuju naru fuku-dōshi no naka no hitotsu ...)"; 2001: 246). In this paper we adopt the *teisetsu*, however, i.e. the -aku hypothesis.

(Central dialects) does have fossilized forms, such as **omowaku** 'what I think is'. Second, the **-aku** form and the Okinawan nominalizer **shi** parallel each other *structurally*. (a) Historically, in their participating constructions, both **-aku** and **shi** follow a *rentai* form, and (b) both of them also have undergone grammaticalization, allowing for the elision of a portion of the *rentai* form, **u** in the former, and **ru** in the latter. Third, the **-aku** form lacked an adnominal function, and thus linked to a following nominal with GEN **nö** (Wrona 2005: 144). This entirely parallels Okinawan **shi**.

(13) **tater-<u>aku</u>**   **-no** **taduki-mo** **sir-azu.**
  be-standing-NOM -GEN means-PRT know.NEG
  'standing up I have no way out' (Man'yōshū 13.3272)[25]
  'Tachi-agaru [koto no] sube mo wakarazu.'
  'I don't know even how to stand up.' (*Shōgakukan Man'yōshū*)

(14) **'ama-Nkai surii-<u>shi</u>-nu** **sama-ya** **miimun yan.** (*shi*)
  there-in gather-NOM GEN appearance-TOP spectacle COP
  'ama-Nkai **surii<u>ru</u>** **sama-ya** **miimun yan.** (*rentai*)
  there-in gather-NOM appearance-TOP spectacle COP
  'The procession over there is a spectacle.'[26]

As the adnominal (i.e. relativization) and nominalization functions stayed separate in (pre-)OJ (Wrona 2005), in Okinawan, as well, separate forms presently carry out the two functions: the former, bare *rentai* forms, and the latter, the **shi** nominalizer.[27] Thus it stands to reason that Okinawan **shi** functions like the **-aku** nominalizer.

We speculate as follows: Proto-Japonic (regardless of whether one dialect or many) developed two variants of the original PJ *tô, namely *tô = [two] and *sô = [swo], through irregular assibilation of **t** to following [w]. At this stage, the only nominalizer was one of these forms. Where lexicalization occurred, as in bird and fish names, the variant with **s** was chosen. In the case of numeral generic classifiers, **t** was chosen (e.g. *-tu* as in **pîtö*tu***), and this state of affairs now holds in all dialects.

---

[25] Example from Wrona (2005:144), with slight modification of the translation.
[26] A legitimate question might arise about the differences between the **shi** and *rentai* sentences in Ok. Native informants offer the following accounts:
 Speaker A (80 yrs old, independent scholar of *Omoro Sōshi*, judge of haiku/Ryūka contests)
  Shi= 'future form' *Rentai* = 'present progressive'; seldom uses **shi**.
 Speaker B (65 years old, former high school teacher of Japanese)
  Shi= 'when requested to assemble' *Rentai* = 'assembling of one's own volition'
 Speaker C (Shinzato)
  Shi= gathering completed *Rentai* = gathering in progress.
[27] Preceded by the 'apocopated form,' a shortening of the *rentai* form.

As for the clausal nominalizer, as the dialects developed, they chose either one variant or the other. Currently the **t** variant appears to be limited to Kyushu, whereas the **s** variant is found around the Kanmon Straits between Kyushu and Honshu, and also throughout the Ryukyus. We have already speculated that the **s/t**-initial nominalizers were replaced in the Central dialects because of the ferment caused by events on the Korean Peninsula. Thus we cannot say what the original distribution between **s** and **t** was, but we do believe that this is the Proto-Japonic nominalizer.

4. Conclusion

In our introduction, we stressed that the **t/s** nominalizers have so far eluded investigation in the appropriate detail. In this paper we've pointed out that the **t/s** nominalizers all have the identical origin, and derive from a common progenitor that existed in Proto-Japonic, namely *tô (see the derivation in (9)). Ok **shi**, WY **su/so** and Ky **tu/to** form a natural class, in that they do not trace back to a genitive particle, but rather to a noun meaning 'one'. We also speculated on the reason why the **t/s** nominalizers found themselves relegated to the Western Periphery of the Japonic archipelagos. Political ferment at the center caused abandonment of the **s/t** nominalizers in favor of a new construction with **-aku** (the so-called *ku-gohō*), followed by the spread of the adnominal form to the new function of nominalization, followed in turn by the loss of the distinction between the adnominals and the finite forms, which then allowed the interposition within those dialects of the genitives in nominalizer function. These original genitives follow the path from genitives to nominalizers as predicted in grammaticalization theory (i.e. GENITIVE/Pronominal > COMPLEMENTIZER). The Western Periphery dialects preserved the old nominalizer and took a different path, namely, THING > COMPLEMENTIZER (Heine and Kuteva 2002: 295).

References

Atago, H. Y. 1999 [1976]. Hizen Nagasaki chihō no juntaijoshi 'to' ni tsuite. *Nihon Rettō Hōgen Sōsho 25*, ed. Fumio Inoue, 215-224. Reprinted from *Nagasaki Daigaku Kyōiku Gakubu Jinbun Kagaku Kenkyū Hōkoku* 25. Tokyo: Yumani Shobō.

Frellesvig, B. 2001. A common Korean and Japanese copula. *Journal of East Asian Linguistics* 1: 1-35.

Funaki, S. 1987. Kakari musubi. *Kokubunpō Kōza* 3, ed. Akiho Yamaguchi, 278-306. Tokyo: Meiji Shoin.

Hattori, S. 1977. Ryūkyū hōgen dōshi 'shūshikei' no tsūjiteki henka. *Gengo Kenkyū* 72:19-28.

Heine, B. and T. Kuteva. 2002. *World Lexicon of Grammaticalization*. Cambridge: Cambridge University Press.

Hikihara, S. 1978. Hōgen ni okeru kakujoshi 'ga' 'no': Juntai joshi o chūshin ni. *Dai 27 kai Hōgen Kenkyūkai Kenkyū Happyōkai Happyō Genkōshū*: 13-21.

Hikosaka, Y. 2005. Juntai joshi no yōhō kara mita hōgen chiiki sa. Paper read at 80th meeting of the Nihon Hōgen Kenkyūkai, May 2005, Kōnan University.

Hirata, Y. 2002. Genitive **tu** in OJ and historical changes of genitive particles. *Japanese and Korean Linguistics* 10, eds. Noriko Akatsuka and Susan Strauss, 251-264. Stanford: CSLI.

Hokama, S. ed. & trans. 2000. *Omoro Sōshi*. (Iwanami Bunko 142-1,2.) Tokyo: Iwanami.

Hokama, S. et al. eds. 1995. *Okinawa Kogo Dai-Jiten*. Tokyo: Kadokawa Shoten.

Horie, K. 1998. On the polyfunctionality of the Japanese particle **no**: From the perspectives of ontology and grammaticalization. *Studies in Japanese Grammaticalization* 6, ed. Toshio Ohori, 169-192. Tokyo: Kuroshio Publishers.

Ifa, F. 1974. *Iha Fuyū Zenshū*, eds. S. Hattori et al. Tokyo: Heibonsha.

Inoue, M. 1999. *Kodai no Nihon to Toraijin: Kodaishi ni Miru Kokusai Kankei*. Tokyo: Akashi Shoten.

Kaneda, A. 2001. *Hachijō Hōgen Dōshi no Kiso Kenkyū*. Tokyo: Kasama Shoin.

Kinjō, C. 1974 [1944]. Naha hōgen gaisetsu. *Kinjō Chōei Zenshū*. Naha: Okinawa Taimususha.

Kiyose, G. N. 2001. Jōdaigo 'kagyō engen' mata wa 'ku-gohō' no honshitsu. *Nihongo no Dentō to Gendai*, ed. Nihongo no Dentō to Gendai Kankōkai, 229-249. Tokyo: Izumi Shoin.

Kobayashi, T. 2003. Tsunagu kotoba kara tojiru kotoba e. *Gekkan Gengo,* March: 60-67.

Kokuritsu Kokugo Kenkyūjo, eds. 1963. *Okinawago Jiten*. Tokyo: Ōkurashō Insatsu-kyoku.

Mamiya, A. 1983. *Omoro Sōshi* no kakari musubi ni tsuite. *Okinawa Bunka* 61: 6-18.

Mamiya, A. 2005. *Omoro Sōshi no Gengo*. Tokyo: Kasama Shoin.

Miyamoto, N. 1978. Kanmon Kaikyō shūhen no hōgen-ken ni tsuite. *Dai 27 kai Hōgen Kenkūkai Kenkyū Happyōkai Happyō Genkōshū*: 22-30.

Nakagawa, K. 1982. Yamaguchi-ken no hōgen. *Kōza Hōgengaku* 8, ed. Iitoyo Kiichi, 141-173. Tokyo: Kokusho Kankōkai.

NHK, eds. 1967. *Zenkoku Hōgen Shiryō* 5, *Chūgoku · Shikoku-hen*. Tokyo: Nippon Hōsō Kyōkai.

Nohara, M. 1998. *Shinpen Ryūkyū Hōgen Joshi no Kenkyū*. Okinawa: Okinawagaku Kenkyūjo.

Nomura, K. 1988. Juntaijoshi **so** ni kansuru hōgen chiikiron. *Fukuoka Daigaku Jinbun Ronsō* 19.4: 1-19.

OGJ. See Kokuritsu Kokugo Kenkyūjo, eds.

Ōnishi, T. 2002. Hondo hōgen no kakari musubi dēta ichiran. *Shōmetsu ni Hin-shita Hōgen Gohō no Kinkyū Chōsa Kenkyū (1)*, A4-004, ed. Sanada Shinji, 1-47.

Ōno, S. 1983. Gendai hōgen ni okeru rentai kakujoshi to juntai joshi. *Nihon Gakuhō* 2: 27-66.

Ōno, S. 1953. Nihongo dōshi katsuyōkei no kigen ni tsuite. *Kokugo to Kokubungaku* 30.6: 47-56.

Ōno, S. 1993. *Kakari Musubi no Kenkyū.* Tokyo: Iwanami.

Schaffar, W. 2002. Kakari musubi, **noda**-constructions, and how grammaticalization theory meets formal grammar. *Japanese/Korean Linguistics 10*, eds. Noriko Akatsuka and Susan Strauss, 320-333. Stanford: CSLI.

Serafim, L. A. 2003. When and from where did Japonic language enter the Ryukyus? — A critical comparison of language, archeology, and history. *Nihongo Keitōron no Genzai / Perspectives on the Origins of the Japanese Language*, Nichibunken Sōsho 31, eds. Alexander Vovin & Toshiki Osada, 463-476. Kyoto: Kokusai Nihon Bunka Kenkyū Sentā.

Serafim, L. A. 2008. Progressive stative predicate extensions in Ryukyuan, and their relation to earlier Japonic. *Current Issues in the History and Structure of Japanese*, eds. B. Frellesvig, M. Shibatani, and J. C. Smith, 207-218. Tokyo: Kuroshio Shuppan.

Serafim, L. A., and Rumiko S. 2000. Reconstructing the proto-Japonic *kakari musubi* *-ka ...-(a)m-wo*. *Gengo Kenkyū* 118:81-118.

Serafim, L. A., and Rumiko S. 2005. On the Old Japanese *kakari* (focus) particle k<u>oso</u>: Its origin and structure. *Gengo Kenkyū* 127: 1-49.

Shinzato, R. 1998. Kakari musubi: Its functions and development. *Japanese/Korean Linguistics 8*, ed. D. Silva, 203-216. Stanford: CSLI.

Thorpe, M. L. 1983. *Ryūkyūan Language History.* Unpublished University of Southern California dissertation.

Vovin, A. 2005. *A Descriptive and Comparative Grammar of Western Old Japanese. Part I: Sources, Script and Phonology, Lexicon, Nominals.* Languages of Asia 3. Folkestone, Kent: Global Oriental.

Wrona, J. 2005. Specificational pseudo-clefts in Old Japanese. *Folia Linguistica Historica* XXVI 1-2: 139-157.

Yamaguchi, G. 1982. Fukubun no kōsei: Shiteki kōsatsu. *Kōza Nihongogaku.* ed. Morioka Kenji, 20-42. Tokyo: Meiji Shoin.

Yap, F. H., S. Matthews, & K Horie. 2004. From nominalizer to pragmatic marker: Implications for unidirectionality from a crosslinguistic perspective. *New Reflections on Grammaticalization 2: Unidirectionality in Grammaticalization* [Typological Studies in Language], eds. O. Fischer, M. Norde, & H. Perridon, 137-168. Amsterdam/Philadelphia: John Benjamins.

Diachronic Changes in Korean *Wh*-Constructions and Their Implications for Synchronic Grammar*

JEONG-ME YOON
Myongji University

1. Introduction

In this paper, I will discuss two diachronic changes that took place in Korean wh-constructions. The first change is that wh-words like *nwukwu* changed from exclusively interrogative pronouns to the current use as indeterminate pronouns. Another change I will discuss is the reanalysis of various Q-particles from C to non-C elements. After discussing each change, I will show how the two changes could have been related. My claim is that it is the second change, more specifically, reanalysis of *-nka* from an interrogative C to a delimiter with existential Q-force that triggered the first

* This paper is a modified and shortened version of Yoon (2005). More comprehensive discussion can be found there on some of the issues that could not be included here due to space restrictions.

change. I will also discuss how the diachronic perspective could shed light on the various properties of wh-constructions in the synchronic grammar.

2. Two Diachronic Changes

2.1. First Change: From Interrogative to Indeterminate

2.1.1. Wh-Words in Modern Korean

In the Modern Korean, the Q-forces of wh-words like *nwukwu* 'who' and *mwues* 'what' are determined by the so-called 'Q-particles' they are associated with. In general, the Q-force of these Q-particles are categorized into three different types: Q-particles like *-ni, -kka* have an interrogative Q-force; Q-particles like *-nka* and *-nci* have an existential Q-force; and Q-particles like *-na, -(la)to,* and *-tun* have a free choice/universal-like Q-force, as shown in (1)[1]. In addition, wh-words can also be used alone, without being associated with any Q-particle, in which case they get an existential reading as in (2).

(1) a. Nwukwu-ka o-ess-ni/upnikka?
   who-NOM   come-PST-Qpt
   'Who came?'

   b. [Nwukwu-ka o-na/tun/to] sangkwan eps-ta.
   who-NOM   come-Qpt   not matter-DCL
   'It doesn't matter whoever comes.'

   c. Nwukwu-nka o-ess-ta.
   who-Qpt   come-PST-DCL
   'Somebody came.'

   d. Nwukwu-na/tun/to ha-l swu iss-ta.
   who-Qpt   can do-DCL
   'Everybody/anybody can do it.'

   e. Na-nun eti-ey-na/to/tun ka-l swu iss-ta.
   I-TOP where-to-Qpt   can go-DCL
   'I can go anywhere.'

   f. Na-nun ettehkey-tun mikwuk-ey ka-ko sip-ta.
   I-TOP   how-Qpt   America-to want to go-DCL
   'I want to go to America in any way.'

(2) Nwukwu-ka o-ess-ta.
   who-NOM   come-PST-DCL
   'Somebody came.'

In terms of distribution, these Q-particles can appear in diverse syntactic positions. For instance, Q-particles appear in C-positions in (1a-b), while

---

[1] See Lee et al. (2000) for discussion on the differences in the Q-forces of each Q.

they appear in non-C-positions after categories like NP, PP or AdvP, as in (1c) through (f).

The distribution of wh-words partially overlaps with that of *amwu*, which is a negative polarity word in the Modern Korean. As we see in (3), wh-words can be replaced by *amwu* with almost the same meaning, when it is used associated with Q-particles like *-na/to/tun*.

(3) a. Amwu/nwukwu-ka   o-na/to/tun na-nun sangkwan eps-ta.
    anybody/who-NOM come-Qpt   I-TOP not matter-DCL
    'I don't care whoever comes.'
  b. Ku il-un   amwu/nwukwu-na/to/tun ha-l swu iss-ta.
    that work-TOP anybody/who-Qpt   can do-DCL
    'As for that work, anybody can do it.'

Nwukwu, however, cannot be replaced by *amwu*, when the Qpt involved is interrogative as in (4) or existential as in (5). *Nwukwu* cannot be replaced by *amwu*, either, when it is used as a bare existential pronoun, as in (6).

(4) Nwukwu/*Amwu-ka o-ess-ni?
    who/anybody-NOM come-PST-Qpt
    'Who came?'

(5) Nwukwu/*Amwu-nka o-ess-ta.
    who/anybody-Qpt   come-PST-DCL
    'Somebody came.'

(6) Nwukwu/*Amwu-ka o-ess-ta.
    who/anybody-NOM come-PST-DCL
    'Somebody came.'

2.1.2. Wh-Words in Earlier Korean

The Q-force of wh-words in earlier Korean was different. According to researchers like C-M Suh (1987), C-S Suh (1989, 1990), and Kim (1992), wh-words had been used exclusively as interrogative pronouns until the end of the 19th century. This means that wh-words like *nwukwu* until that time could not be used with non-interrogative Q-particles like *-na/to/tun*. They were not used as bare indefinites, either. Instead, what was used in such contexts was *amwu* (C-M Suh 1987).

What we can conclude from this is that the syntactic distribution of both *nwukwu* and *amwu* underwent some changes. Until the 19th century, their distributions were complementary: *nwukwu* was a purely interrogative pronoun, while *amwu* was used in non-interrogative contexts, either by it-self or in the environment of morphemes like *-na/to/tun*. What the data in the Modern Korean suggest is that the distribution of wh-words, for some reason, had been extended to non-interrogative contexts, i.e., to the places where only *amwu* could be used before.

One question about this change is what triggered it. I will seek an answer for this question in another significant change in Korean wh-constructions, namely, the change in the syntactic and semantic properties of Q-particles. Recognizing this change, however, presupposes an important hypothesis about wh-constructions in Korean, which I will call 'Unified Clausal Approach.'

2.2. Second Change: From C to Delimiter

2.2.1. Unified Clausal Approach

The crux of the Unified Clausal Approach is that all Q-particles in Korean are C-elements, despite that they appear in diverse syntactic positions (C-M Suh 1987, C-S Suh 1990, Chung 1996, Jang 1999, Lee 1999, Yoon 2004, etc.).

The basic arguments for this claim are first, that wh-expressions like *nwukwu-nka* have a copula *-i* inside, and secondly, that Q-particles like *-nka* and *-na/to/tun* are used as conjunctions. Based on these considerations, Suh (1990) proposed that a simple sentence like (1c) has the complex structure as in (7).

(7) [$_{NP}$ [$_{CP1}$ e$_i$ [$_{CP2}$ e$_j$ **nwukwu$_k$-i-nka**] molu-nun] e$_i$] **o-ess-ta.**
　　　　who-be-C$_{interrogative}$　not know-REL come-PST-DCL
　'[(A man$_j$ who I$_i$ do not know) who$_k$ (he$_j$) was] came.' (Suh 1990:251)

What should be noted in this structure is that a hidden predicate *moluta* 'not know' is posited. This is necessary since an interrogative clause should be selected by an interrogative predicate. It is also important since it enables us to 'derive' the existential meaning of *nwukwu-nka*. So, in structure (7), *-nka* is an interrogative C, not an existential Qpt, and its apparent existential Q-force can be derived from the structure: 'a person who I don't know the identity of' can be understood as 'somebody.'

Chung (1996) extended the clausal analysis to universal wh-expressions like *nwukwu-na* and proposed a structure as in (8).

(8) John-un [$_{CP1}$ e$_i$ [$_{CP2}$ e$_j$ **mwues$_k$-i{-na/-tunci}**] Q-Pred-ADV] e$_l$ mek-nun-ta.
　　J-Top　　　　what-be-QE　　　　　　　　　　　　eat-Pres-DE
　'John, (irrespective of/I do not care) what (it) is, eats (it).
　　　　　　　　　　　　　　　　　　　　　　　　　(Chung 1996:215)

Modifying the previous proposals, I proposed the structures (9b) and (10b), for *nwukwu-nka* and *nwukwu-na/to/tun,* respectively (Yoon 2004).[2]

(9) a. Nwukwu-nka o-ess-ta.
'Somebody came.'
b. [e [e nwukwu$_i$-i-nka] mol-ato]] e$_i$ o-ess-ta.
who-be-C$_{interrogative}$ not know-C$_{concessive}$ come-PST-DCL
'Although I don't know who is the person that came, he came.'

(10) a. Nwukwu-na/to/tun phathi-ey ka-l swu iss-ta.
'Anybody can go to the party.'
b. [e nwukwu$_i$-i-na/to/tun] e$_i$ phathi-ey ka-l swu iss-ta..
who-be-C$_{concessive}$ party-to can go-DCL
'Whoever is the person that wants to go to the party, he can go.'

The proposed structures differ from the previous proposals in a few important aspects.

First of all, unlike Suh (1990) and Chung (1996), I am analyzing existential wh-expressions as involving a concessive structure, not as a relative clause structure with a null head noun. As for the FC/universal-like wh-expressions, I am analyzing *-na/to/tun* as concessive/FC conjunctions, not as interrogative C's as in Chung.[3]

Secondly, concerning exactly what are the omitted subjects of the interrogative clause and concessive *na*-clause in (9b) and (10b), I will assume that they involve a kind of cleft structure as shown in (11b-c), which are derived from (11a).[4]

(11) a. Chelswu-ka tosekwan-eyse Yenghi-eykey phyenci-lul ssu-ess-ta.
C-NOM library-in Y-to letter-ACC write-PST-DCL
'Chelswu wrote Yenghi a letter in the library.'

b. [t$_i$ tosekwan-eyse Yenghi-eykey phyenci-lul ssu-un] kes$_i$-un
library-in Y-to letter-ACC write-AND C-TOP

---

[2] Sentence (i) from Chung (1996) shows that omitting the V-C complex of the concessive clause as in (9) is possible.
(i) a. John-un mwues-ul ha-nun-ci/ka ton-ul cal pel-n-ta.
J-TOP what-ACC do-ASP-Q money-ACC well earn-PRS-DCL
'John earns a lot of money, (although I do not know) what (he) is doing.'
b. John$_i$ -un [e$_j$ [e$_i$ mwues-ul ha-nun-ci/ka] mol-ato] ton-ul
J-TOP what-ACC do-ASP-QE not know-though money-ACC
cal pel-n-ta.
well earn-PRS-DCL
[3] See Yoon (2004) for arguments for this modification.
[4] I did not posit the cleft structure in my previous analyses (Yoon 2004, 2005).

Chelswu$_i$-i-ta.
C-be-DCL
'It is Chelswu that wrote a letter to Yenghi in the library.'
c. [Chelswu-ka t$_i$ Yenghi-eykey phyenci-lul ssu-un] kes$_i$-un
   C-NOM   Y-to   letter-ACC write-AND C-TOP
tosekwan-eyse$_i$-i-ta.
library-in-be-DCL
'It is in the library that Chelswu wrote a letter to Yenghi.'

This means that (9a) has a structure like (12) before extensive omission.

(12) [Nay-ka [[t$_i$ o-n]   kes$_i$ -i   **nwukwu$_i$-i-nka**]   mol-ato]
     I-NOM come-ADN C-NOM who-be-C$_{interrogative}$ not know-C$_{concessive}$
ku salam$_i$-i   **o-ess-ta.**
that person-NOM come-PST-DCL
'Although I don't know who is the person that came, he came.'

Positing this kind of cleft structure is based on the following considera-tion. When we think about the interpretation of the empty pronouns posited in (9-10b), they should be interpreted as something like 'the person who came' and 'the person who wants to go to the party,' respectively. The non-simple nature of the posited empty pronouns is more easily seen in sen-tences like (13a-c), where the Qpt is attached to PPs or AdvPs. In these cases, it is clear that what occupies the subject position of -nka/na/to/tun clauses cannot be a simple pronoun: it is because PPs and AdvPs can ap-pear in the complement position of the copula -i only in cleft constructions like (11).[5]

(13) a. Ku-nun nwukwu-eykey-nka kkoch-ul   cwu-ess-ta.
      he-Top who-DAT-Qpt   flower-ACC give-PST-DCL
     'He gave flowers to somebody.'
  b. Na-nun eti-ey-na   ka-l swu iss-ta.
     I-TOP where-to-Qpt can go-DCL
     'I can go anywhere.'
  c. Na-nun ettehkey-tun mikwuk-ey ka-ko sip-ta.
     I-TOP how-Qpt   America-to want to go-DCL
     'I want to go to America in any way.'

As an example, the underlying structure for (13a) should be as follows be-fore omission.

---

[5] In the case of AdvPs, they can appear in the focus position of the cleft construction only somewhat marginally.

(14) **Ku$_i$-nun** [nay-ka   [ku$_i$–ka   t$_j$ kkoch-ul   cwun-kes$_j$]-i **nwukwu-**
he-TOP   I-NOM   he-NOM flowers-ACC give-C-NOM who-
eykey$_j$-i-nka] mol-ato]   ku$_j$-eykey **kkoch-ul   cwu-ess-ta.**
DAT-be-C not know- C$_{concessive}$ he-DAT   flower-ACC give-PST-DCL

2.2.2. Problems and Reanalysis

The UCA as proposed so far has some obvious problems. First of all, the UCA conflicts with the fact that wh-expressions like *nwukwu-nka* are generally perceived by the present-day speakers of Korean as simple, nonclausal arguments or adjuncts of the predicate, not as having the complex clausal structures as proposed in (9)-(10). Thus, in sentences like (15a), *nwukwu-nka* is considered as the NP subject and in (15b), *nwukwu-eykey-na* is considered as the PP adjunct of the sentence.

(15) a. Nwukwu-nka o-ess-ta.
       who-Qpt   come-PST-DCL
       'Somebody came.'
    b. Ku-nun nwukwu-eykey-na chincelha-ta.
       he-TOP who-DAT-Qpt   be nice-DCL
       'He is nice to everybody.'

Accordingly, morphemes like *-nka* and *-na* in (15) are perceived as existential and FC/universal Q-particles, respectively, not as interrogative C and concessive conjunctions.

Secondly, native speakers' perceptions like this are matched by various syntactic properties they show. For example, wh-expressions like *nwukwu-nka, nwukwu-na* show various nominal properties: (16a-b) below show that *nwukwu-nka/na* can be Case-marked; (17a-b) show that they can be used as the complement of a postposition; and (18) shows that they can take a prenominal modifier such as a genitive phrase.

(16) a. Nwukwu-nka-ka o-ess-ta.
       who-Qpt-NOM come-PST-DCL
       'Somebody came.
    b. Ku il-ul   nwukwu-na-ka   ha-l swu iss-ta.
       the work-TOP who-Qpt-NOM can do-DCL
       'Anybody can do the work.'

(17) a. Ku-nun [$_{PP}$ [nwukwu-nka]-lopwuthe] chayk-ul   pilli-ess-ta.
       he-TOP   who-Qpt-from   book-ACC borrow-PST-DCL
       'He borrowed a book from somebody.
    b. ?Ku-nun [$_{PP}$ [nwukwu-na]-lopwuthe] ton-ul   pilli-l swu iss-ta.
       he-TOP   who-Qpt-from   money-ACC can borrow-DCL
       'He can borrow money from anybody.'

(18) [[Wuli-cwung-uy] nwukwu-nka]-ka pemin-i-ta.
   we-among-GEN who-Qpt-NOM   culprit-be-DCL
   'Someone among us is the culprit.'

What these facts suggest is that even if it is historically correct that wh-expressions like *nwukwu-nka* have clausal structures, they cannot be represented as proposed in (9b) and (10b) in the synchronic grammar. Instead, the correct analysis for them is to assume that although they, originally, had clausal structures, they lost their clausal identities and underwent 'reanalysis' to the simpler non-clausal elements (Yoon 2004).

This kind of reanalysis, most of all, could have been made possible thanks to the unique property of Korean, i.e., that Korean allows omission quite freely. Another contributing factor we could think of is the fact that the underlying structures for these wh-expressions involve a cleft construction, which is a focus construction, and that the focused element inside the concessive clause should be equated with some element of the matrix clause. So after the omission, *nwukwunka* in (9b) looks as if it were the subject of the matrix clause, and this could have facilitated reanalysis. As is well-known, reanalysis takes place when there arises a plausible environment for a different structure/meaning through various enabling factors such as inference (Hopper and Traugott 1993). What I am proposing is that this condition for reanalysis was met in structures like (9b) and (10b).

Once the clausal status of wh-expressions is stripped off in certain contexts, other changes, both syntactic and semantic, should follow. Syntactically, Q-particles, which originally are complementizers/conjunctions, should be reanalyzed as something else, i.e., a syntactic element that can attach to various categories such as NP, PP or AdvP. Semantically, the meaning of Q-particles should change, especially in the case of *-nka*. Before reanalysis, *-nka* had an interrogative Q-force, but after the reanalysis, it can no longer have an interrogative meaning but is considered to have an existential Q-force.[6] In the case of *-na/to/tun*, the semantic difference is less noticeable: they were concessive/FC conjunctions before reanalysis but after the reanalysis, they are FC/universal-like Q-particles.

As for the syntactic category to which the Q-particles in non-C positions belong after the reanalysis, I will identify it as 'delimiter,' which independently exists in Korean.[7] This proposal is based on the following facts. Syntactically, delimiters and Q-particles both attach to syntactic categories

---

[6] The more visible meaning change for *-nka* can be attributed to the fact that *nka*-clause, before the reanalysis, is embedded under a question predicate *moluta*. Since *moluta* also undergoes omission, the original interrogative meaning of *-nka* becomes more obscure.

[7] Although the specifics of the proposal are different, Kishimoto (2005) also proposes that Q-particles in Sinhala belong to a delimiter category.

like NP, PP or AdvP, but not to categories like AP or VP. Semantically, they both add certain quantificational meaning to the elements they are attached to. Examples are given in (19).

(19) a. Chelswu-kkaci o-ess-ta.
     C-even   come-PST-DCL
     'Even Chelswu came.'
  b. Na-nun Chelswu-hanthey- kkaci kesismalha-ko sip-ci anh-ta.
     I-TOP   C-to-even   want to lie-not-DCL
     'I don't want to lie even to Chelswu.'
  c. ?Kulehkey- kkaci hayya ha-ess-ni?
     That way-even   shoud do-PST-Q
     'Did you really have to do even in such a way?'

It is also interesting to note that other delimiters like -kkaci and -pakkey are also reanalyzed elements.[8] This renders further support to the delimiter status of Q-particles after the reanalysis.

3. Relating the Two Changes

So far, I have discussed the two changes independently. The two, however, could have been closely related. Specifically, I suggest that the change in the syntactic and semantic properties of -nka triggered the change of wh-phrases from interrogative to indeterminate pronouns. This is for the following reasons.

Once speakers perceive -nka in wh-expressions like nwukwu-nka as an existential delimiter, not as an interrogative C, wh-words like nwukwu can no longer be viewed as exclusively interrogative pronouns. Rather, it now appears that they can be used in both interrogative and non-interrogative contexts and that their Q-forces could vary. When they are associated with an interrogative C, they are interpreted as interrogative pronouns, while when they are associated with an existential delimiter -nka, they get an existential pronoun reading. This change, in turn, could have had the consequence of allowing wh-words like nwukwu to appear in genuinely non-interrogative contexts, where only amwu could appear before, i.e., it allowed wh-words to cooccur with non-interrogative conjunctions/delimiters such as -to/na/ tun. Finally, as the last step of the change, we can hypothesize that nwukwu came to take on the other use of amwu, namely, the function as a bare existential pronoun, while amwu ceased to function as such.

---

[8] See Bak (1997) for discussion on the reanalysis of -pakkey.

4. Implications for Synchronic Grammar

The diachronic perspective gained from studying the two changes allows us to explain various properties of wh-constructions in the synchronic grammar, which, otherwise, would not be easily explained.

4.1. Distribution of Q-Particles

First of all, we can readily explain why Q-particles appear in both C and non-C positions. It is because all Q-particles, historically, are C-elements but that they underwent reanalysis as delimiters in certain environments.

Secondly, we can explain the complementary distribution of interrogative and existential Q-particles, i.e., the fact that existential Q-particles appear only in non-C positions, while interrogative Q-particles appear only in C-positions. It is because -*nka/nci* originally are interrogative C's, and that their existential Q-force is derived only when they head interrogative clauses embedded under a verb like *moluta* 'not know.'

Third, we can also explain why unlike -*nka/nci*, other interrogative C's like -*ni/upnikka* cannot be used as existential Q-particles. It is because they are C's which head 'matrix' questions, and the existential meaning of -*nka/nci* is derived only when the question clause is embedded as a complement of verbs like *moluta*.

Fourth, we can explain the well-formedness of *way-nci* 'for some reason' in contrast to the ill-formedness of **way-na/to/tun* 'for whatever reason.' Wh-words meaning 'why', cross-linguistically, are known to be used only as interrogative pronouns and for this reason, they often have been analyzed as inherently interrogative (Tsai 1994, Cole & Hermon 1998, etc.). Although this would readily explain the ill-formedness of *way-na/to/tun*, the well-formedness of *way-nci* is not explained if -*nci* simply is an existential Q-particle. The diachronic perspective provides an explanation. It is because sentences like (20a) with *way-nci* have a structure as in (20b), where -*nci* is an interrogative C, before reanalysis.[9]

(20) a. Chelswu-nun way-nci sulphu-ta.

    b. Chelswu$_i$-nun [e$_i$ [e$_i$ way kuleha-nci] mol-ato]   sulphu-ta.
      C-TOP   why be so-Qpt not know-although sad-DCL
      'Chelswu is sad although he doesn't know why he is so.'

4.2. Locality of Wh-Words

The diachronic perspective can illuminate various facts about the locality of wh-constructions in Korean.

---

[9] See Yoon (2004) for more discussion on structure (20b).

First, we can explain why the same kind of locality holds between wh-words and Q-particles in both C and non-C positions. As is well-known, strong island effects do not hold between the wh-phrase and interrogative C in Korean, while weak island effects hold between the two. Examples are shown in (21) below.

(21) a. [[Nwukwu-ka ssu-n]   chayk]-i   eps-e-ci-ess-ni?
       who-NOM write-ADN book-NOM disappear-PST-Qpt
       'For which x, y, x a person, y a book x wrote, y disappeared?'
    b. Ne-nun [Yenghi-ka mwues-ul machi-myen] ttena-l ke-ni?
       you-TOP Y-NOM what-ACC finish-if   leave-FUT-Qpt
       'For which x, x a thing, you are going to leave if Yenghi finishes x?'
    c. Ne-nun [Yenghi-ka mwues-ul sa-ess-nunci] al-ko sip-ni?
       You-TOP Y-NOM what-ACC buy-PST-Qpt want to know-Qpt
       (i) 'Do you want to know whether Yenghi bought something?'
  NOT (ii) *'For which x, x a thing, do you want to know whether Yenghi bought x?'

The same kind of locality holds of wh and Q-particles in non-C positions: in (22a), *etten cakka* 'which writer' can be associated with *-tun* over a complex NP island boundary and has the meaning of 'whichever writer,' but the same is not possible in (22b) where a wh-island boundary intervenes.

(22) a. ?[[[Etten cakka-ka   ssu-n]   chayk]-ul   ilk-un]   tokca]-
       which writer-NOM write-ADN book-ACC read-ADN reader-
       tun ta kamtongpat-ess-ta.
       Qpt all be moved-PST-DCL
       'For all x, y, z, x a reader, y a book, z a writer, x was moved if x read y written by z.'
    b. *[[e [Etten cakka-ka   ssu-ess-nunci] molu-nun]   chayk]-itun ta
       which writer-NOM write-PST-Qpt not know-ADN book-Qpt all
       cal phalli-ess-ta.
       well sell-PST-DCL
       (intended meaning) 'For all x, y, x a book, y a writer, x sold well even if people did not know whether y wrote x.'

This can be explained given that Q-particles originally are all C-elements and that the original properties of a construction before reanalysis are generally maintained after the reanalysis (Hopper and Traugott 1993).

Secondly, the diachronic perspective can also provide an explanation for certain subtle but consistent differences in the localities of interrogative and non-interrogative wh-words. First, the locality of non-interrogative wh-words seems to be more local than that of interrogative wh-words in that when the wh-word is associated with a non-interrogative Qpt outside its own clause, the result is somewhat degraded, as in (23). I will call this 'weak clause-boundedness' of non-interrogative *nwukwu,* contrasting it to the strong clause-boundedness of *amwu.*

(23) Na-nun [salamtul-i [?nwukwu/*amwu-ka o-ess-tako] malhaycwu-
I-TOP people-NOM who/amwu-NOM come-PST-C tell-
eto/na/tun] mit-ul swu eps-ess-ta.
Qpt cannot believe-PST-DCL
'I couldn't believe it whoever people told (me) came.'

Another difference between interrogative and non-interrogative wh-words is that the strength of weak island effects for wh-words varies somewhat depending on the kind of Q-particles involved in wh-constructions, as shown in (24): it is almost impossible for the wh-word to be associated with a non-interrogative Qpt over an intervening interrogative Qpt, while the opposite case yields far milder ungrammaticality.

(24) a. *Ku-nun [kica-ka [nwukwu-ka tangsentoy-l-ci] mwul-eto/
he-TOP reporter-NOM who-NOM be elected-FUT-Qpt ask-Qpt
na/tun] taytapha-ci anh-ess-ta.
answer-C not-PST-DCL
'For all x, x a person, he didn't answer even if the reporter asked whether x would be elected.'
b. ?Na-nun [[taum sihap-ey nwukwu-ka naka-to] sangkwan eps-nunci]
I-TOP next game-to who-NOM go out-Qpt not matter-Qpt
al-ko sipta.
want to know-DCL
'I want to know for which x, x a person, it doesn't matter even if x competes in the next game.'

These facts can be explained, if we consider the fact that historically, non-interrogative *nwukwu* derives from *amwu* and that *amwu* has strong clause-bounded locality. More specifically, the weak clause-boundedness of non-interrogaitve wh-words can be explained as the result of a kind of interference effects from *amwu,* i.e., we can say that non-interrogative *nwukwu* inherited the unbounded locality of interrogative *nwukwu* and but its locality was affected by the interference effects from the strong clause-bounded locality of *amwu.* We can also appeal to the weak clause-boundedness of non-interrogative *nwukwu* to explain the severe ungrammaticality of (24a). Given that weak island effects alone are not that strong, the severe ungrammaticality of (24a) suggests that there is some other source of its ungrammaticality, and I suggest that it is the weak clause-boundedness of non-interrogative wh-words.

Third, the current proposal can shed light on why wh-words in the Modern Korean appear to show the properties of both movement and unselective binding. We have already seen that wh-words in Korean show weak island effects, a typical movement property. As for the unselective binding aspect of wh-words, it generally refers to the fact that the Q-forces of wh-words are determined by non-adjacent Q-particles. As a way to handle this state of affairs, Nishigauchi (1986, 1992) assumes that unselective binding of wh-words by Q-particles involves movement, the reason being that the wh-word must be governed by Q.

This approach, however, is problematic given that unselective binding, in general, is not subject to movement localities like Subjacency, as supposed by various researchers (Pesetsky 1987, Watanabe 1992, Tsai 1994, etc.). In fact, Nishigauchi himself discusses another case of unselective binding of wh-phrases which does not involve movement, namely, unselective binding of wh-phrases by quantificational adverbs, as in (25). In the second reading of (25), the Q-force of *dare* is determined by the adverb *taitei* 'most,' and one way to explain is to say that *dare* is unselectively bound by *taitei*.

(25) Dare-ga ki-te-mo, boku-wa taitei   aw-u
    who-N come-Q   I-T   usually   meet
    (i) 'For all x, x a person, if x comes over, I usually meet x.'
    (ii) 'I meet most people who come over.' (Nishigauchi 1986:183)

In short, Nishigauchi is saying that there are two different kinds of unselective binding of wh-phrases, i.e., one that involves movement and the other that does not, and that there is something special about the wh-phrases associated with Q-particles.

The diachronic perspective can shed light on this. As noted, the original properties of a construction before reanalysis generally continue to constrain the use of the reanalyzed forms. Keeping this in mind, let us consider what the syntactic status of wh-words like *nwukwu* had been until the end of the 19th century. Given that they were used exclusively as interrogative pronouns, it is not unreasonable to assume that they were interrogative QPs and as such, they underwent movement to the Spec of interrogative C.

Granting this, the current state of affairs about wh-constructions can be explained by assuming that (i) wh-words are composed of indefinite wh and null Q and the value of null Q changed from interrogative to 'unspecified' as the result of reanalysis; (ii) the original movement property of wh-words was maintained even after the reanalysis. In this approach, the quantificational variability of wh-words can be explained in terms of simple Spec-head agreement, as in (26).[10]

(26) $[_{CP/DIP}$ wh-Q$[_{unspecified}]$ ------- C/Dl $[\alpha Q]$]
    → $[_{CP/DIP}$ [wh-Q$_i$ $[\alpha]$ $[_{C'/DI'}$ .. t$_i$ .. C/Dl $[\alpha Q]$]]

In short, my claim is that all wh-words associated with Q-particles undergo movement and that the appearance of unselective binding, i.e., the quantificational variability of wh-words, is the result of Spec-head agreement.

As for wh-words used as bare existential pronouns, I propose that they are simple indefinite pronouns, not accompanied by Q. Lacking Q, they, naturally, do not move and their Q-force is provided by existential closure (Heim 1982, Diesing 1992). This means that wh-words like *nwukwu* in the Modern Korean are structurally ambiguous.

5. Concluding Remarks

To summarize, in this paper, I have discussed two historical changes that took place in Korean wh-constructions, and shown how the diachronic perspective can shed light on various aspects of wh-constructions in the synchronic grammar. One of the strong advantages of taking the diachronic perspective is that we can provide not only a single unitary analysis of all wh-constructions but also the more principled explanations for the differences among wh-constructions.

References

Bak, S-Y. 1997. *Pakkey*: A case of grammaticalization in Korean. *Korean Journal of Linguistics* 22-1: 57-70, Seoul: Korea.

Chung, D. 1996. *On the representation of Q and Q-dependencies*. Ph. D dissertation, University of Southern California.

Cole, P. & G. Hermon. 1998. The typology of WH movement: WH questions in Malay. *Syntax* 1: 221-258.

Diesing, M. 1992. *Indefinites*. Cambridge: MIT Press.

Heim, I. 1982. The semantics of definite and indefinite noun phrases. Ph.D dissertation, University of Massachusetts, Amherst.

Hopper, P. & E. Traugott. 1993. *Grammaticalization*. Cambridge: Cambridge University Press.

Jang, Y.-J. 1999. Two types of question and existential quantification. *Linguistics* 37-5: 847-869.

Kim, C.-H. 1992. A study on interrogative and indefinite pronouns in Korean (in Korean). Ph.D dissertation, Hanyang University, Seoul: Korea.

---

[10] See Yoon (2006) for more discussion.

Kishimoto, H. 2005. Wh-in-situ and movement in Sinhala questions. *Natural Language & Linguistic Theory* 23: 1-51.

Lee, C., D. Chung & S. Nam. 2000. The semantics of *amu* N-*to/ilato/-ina* in Korean: Arbitrary choice and concession. *Language and Information* 4-2: 107-123, Seoul: Korea.

Lee, S.-W. 2000. On the indefinite use of "WH+(*i*)+*nka*" (in Korean). *Korean Linguistics* 36: 191-219.

Nishigauchi, T. 1986. Quantification in syntax. Ph. D dissertation, University of Massachusetts.

Nishigauchi, T. 1992. Construing wh. *Studies in linguistics & philosophy: logical structure & linguistic structure*. eds. J. Huang & R. May: 197-232. Kluwer Academic Publishers.

Pesetsky, D. 1987. Wh-in-situ: movement and unselective binding. *The Representation of (in)definintess*, eds. E. J. Reuland and A.G.B ter Meulen, 98-129. Cambridge, MA: MIT Press. 98-129.

Suh, C.-M. 1987. *Study of questions in Korean* (in Korean), Tap Publishing Co. Seoul, Korea.

Suh, C.-S. 1989. Interrogatives and indefinite words in Korean: with reference to Japanese. *Harvard Studies in Korean Linguistics* III: 329-340.

Suh, C.-S. 1990. *A Study of Korean grammar* (in Korean), Hankwukmwunhwasa, Seoul: Korea.

Tsai, W.-T. 1994. On economizing the theory of A-bar dependencies. Ph. D. dissertation, MIT.

Watanabe, A. 1992. Subjacency and S-structure movement of wh-in-situ. *Journal of East Asian Linguistics* 1: 255-291.

Yoon, J.-M. 2004. Unified clausal approach to wh-constructions in Korean revisited: An analysis based on reanalysis. *Studies in Generative Grammar* 14-1: 3-39, Seoul: Korea.

Yoon, J.-M. 2005. Two historical changes in wh-constructions in Korean and their implications. *Studies in Generative Grammar* 15-4: 457-488. Seoul: Korea.

Yoon, J.-M. 2006. Selective island effects in Korean wh-constructions: A diachronic approach. *Korean Journal of Linguistics* 31-2: 165-204. Seoul: Korea.

Koto and Negative Scope Expansion in Old Japanese[*]

JANICK WRONA

Kyoto University

1. Introduction

This paper focuses on wide scope, propositional negation in Old Japanese (OJ), but in order to bring out the properties of this type of negation it will be discussed in relation to predicate negation and constituent negation, both of which have narrower scope. It will be argued that in collocation with the negative existential *nasi* 'not exist' *koto* can be used to extend the scope of negation to negate an entire proposition. Of the various types of nominalization in OJ, only *koto* can be used for this function.

The structure of the paper is as follows. In Section 2, I briefly summarize the main functions of *koto* in OJ and in Section 3, I will determine its place in the OJ complement system. Section 4 is the backbone of the paper where I will show that *koto* can be used to extend the scope of the negative

---

[*] I would like to thank Bjarke Frellesvig, Kyung-ae Kim, Hideki Kishimoto, Chungmin Lee, Anna McNay, Masaki Sano, Yukinori Takubo and John Whitman for comments and helpful suggestions. The research reported in this paper was supported by the Japan Society for the Promotion of Science.

operator. I will also show how wide scope negation relates to predicate and constituent negation. In Section 5 it will become apparent that *koto* is used to extend scope in other nonnegative contexts. Before summarizing in Section 7, I will make some brief crosslinguistic remarks in Section 6.

2. Semantic and syntactic properties of *koto* in Old Japanese

Broadly speaking, *koto* can be said to have three sets of meanings in OJ. Each of them is quite abstract, but not equally so. The first set of meanings is related to verbal actions, such as 'word' or 'rumour'. This is illustrated in (1).

(1) [[... imo-*to*   musubi-*te-si*]   **koto**]-*pa* patasa-zu[1]
        wife-COMP   tie-PERF-PST.ADN   **word**-TOP fulfil-NEG
     '(I) have not fulfilled the words which (I) tied with my wife'
     M 3.481

The second set of meanings is related to matters, affairs and facts. This is illustrated in (2).

(2) [[ware-*mo* obo-ni   mi-*si*]   **koto**] kuya*siki*   *wo*
        I-PRT   afar-ADV see-PST.ADN **fact** is regrettable.ADN   CN
     'The fact that (I) only saw (her) from afar is regrettable'
     M 2.217

Finally, *koto* may seem devoid of any lexical meaning in contexts like (3).

(3) [*apu*   **koto**]   *katasi*
        meet.ADN   **COMP**   is difficult
     'it is difficult to meet'
     M 14.3401 (Shinano province)

It is possible that *koto* 'word' is etymologically unrelated to *koto* 'fact, NOMINALIZER', but I argue elsewhere that there is only one polysemous *koto* (Wrona, forthcoming). If one accepts this, it might seem obvious that

---

[1] Phonographically written syllables are *italicized*. Abbreviations: ABL=Ablative; ACC=Accusative; ADN=Adnominal form (連体形); ADV=Adverbial; CN=Conjunction; COMP=Complementizer; CONCL=Conclusive form (終止形); COND=Conditional; CONJ=Conjectural; CONT=Continuative; CTP=Complement-taking predicate DAT=Dative; DEC=Declarative; DIR=Directional; GEN=Genitive; HON=Honorific; HUM=Humble; IMP=Imperative; INF=Infinitive (連用形); INF2=Infinitive2 (ミ語法); KPRT=*Kakari*-particle; LOC=Locative; NEGC=Negative conjectural; NMLZ=Nominalizer; NOM=Nominal form (ク語法); PERF=perfective aspect; PROV=Provisioinal; PRT=Particle; PST=(Direct) Past; PTC=Participle; PROH=Prohibitive; Q=Question particle; STAT=Stative; TOP=Topic.

we are dealing with a grammaticalization path 'word'>'fact'>NOMINALIZER, but there is no empirical evidence for this (cf. Lehmann, 2004: 156).

3. Outline of the Old Japanese complement system

In order to understand the role of *koto* in relation to negation, it is necessary to give a brief outline of the OJ complement system (for details, see Wrona, forthcoming). *Koto* is an integral part of the complement system in Early Middle Japanese, but in Old Japanese its role in the complement system was rather limited. An overview of the Old Japanese complement system is given in Table 1 below.

Table 1: *Overview of the Old Japanese complement system*

Central System	Peripheral System
Nominal complement	Adnominal complement
To-complement	*Koto*-complement
(Relative clauses)	(Paratactic complement)
	(Participial complement)

The names given to the complement types in Table 1 are based on morphological form of the 'complementizer', or the construction used for complementation. So the 'complementizer' of Nominal complements is the Nominal form of predicates (see (4) below for an example). Likewise, the 'complementizer' of Adnominal complements is the Adnominal form of predicates (the *rentaikei* form).

Basically, the complement system in Old Japanese is a two-member system with an opposition between Nominal complements and *to*-complements. Relative clauses perform a limited, but unique role encoding direct perception. The division into a central and a peripheral system is based partly on a diachronic analysis, but it is also a synchronic fact that the central members 1) are more wide-spread and 2) have unique functions within the complement system. In contrast, none of the members of the peripheral system is particularly wide-spread and, more importantly, they do not have a function within the complement system that is not performed by a central member. Finally, the peripheral members all have important functions outside of the complement system.

3.1. Distribution of Nominal and *koto*-complement clauses

There are contexts within the OJ complement system where Nominal complement clauses and *koto*-complement clauses are in synchronic variation. An example is given in (4) and (5).

(4)   Nominal complement clause selected by a commentative predicate
      [...kimi -ga   kiki-*tutu*   *tuge-naku*]-*mo*   *usi*
      you-GEN   hear-CONT   tell-NEG.NOM-PRT   is sad.CONCL
      'It is sad that you (who are in the house) have heard (it), but not told
      (me)'
      M 19.4207

(5)   *koto*-complement clause selected by a commentative predicate
      [...ware-*mo*   kiki-mota*ru*   **koto**]   tomo*si*
      I-PRT   hear-remember.STAT.ADN   COMP   is rare.CONCL
      'it is rare that I (who am here) hear and bear in mind (that...)'
      S 6.6

There is distributional overlap between Nominal complement clauses and
koto-complement clauses in a number of contexts in OJ, and as (4) and (5)
above illustrate, both Nominal complement clauses and *koto*-complement
clauses encode propositions which are presupposed to be true.[2]

3.2. *Koto* and the Nominal form outside of the complement system

There are certain other contexts where *koto*- and Nominal complements are
found.

(6)   [*puyu*   *natu-to*   *waku*   **koto**]-*mo*   **naku**
      winter   summer-ABL   distinguish.ADN   COMP-PRTnot exist.INF
      'It is not the case that (one can) distinguish winter from summer'
      M 17.4003

(7)   [kimi-*ni*   kwopu*raku*]   yamu   toki-*mo*   **nasi**
      you-DAT   love.NOM   stop.ADN   time-PRT   not exist.CONCL
      '(my) love for you never stops' (lit. 'as for the fact that (I) love you
      there is no time at which it stops')
      M 11.2741

This may seem like another context where Nominal complement clauses
and *koto*-complement clauses overlap, but there are reasons to believe that
examples like (6) are different from examples like (7) (and from (4) and
(5)). Firstly, the predicate portion in (7) is different from the one in (6). In
(6) one finds just *naku* 'not exist' whereas (7) has *yamu toki mo nasi* 'does
not stop'. So the Nominal complement in (7) is not selected by the negative
existential predicate alone, but by a construction involving a temporal noun
(*yamu toki* 'stop time' in (7)) and the negative existential (see section 4.2).
Thus the contexts in (6) and (7) are not directly comparable. Secondly, the

---

[2] There are exceptions to this. The *koto*-complement in (3), for instance, is not presupposed to
be true.

bracketed clause in (6) is *not* a complement clause selected by the negative existential *na-* 'not exist'. It is crosslinguistically rare that negative existential predicates act as complement-taking predicates (Noonan, 1985:131). Furthermore, *koto*-clauses can occur not only in collocation with negative existential predicates as in (6), but also with the affirmative counterpart to *na-* 'not exist', *ar-* 'exist' (see Section 4.3). In these contexts, *na-* 'not exist' and *ar-* 'exist' seem more like functional items than full, lexical complement-taking predicates. This is confirmed by the fact that *na-* 'not exist' and *ar-* 'exist' occur in a number of (semi-)grammaticalized contexts like -*subye nasi* 'no means to V'. Another difference is that *koto*-clauses in collocation with *na-* 'not exist' and *ar-* 'exist' are not presupposed to be true (see Section 4.3).

There is therefore good evidence that *koto*-clauses in collocation with a negative existential predicate as in (6) are different from Nominal complements selected by a negative existential predicate (as in (7)), and do not form part of the complement system. So it is clear that even though both *koto*-clauses and Nominal complements occur in contexts with a negative existential predicate, there are important syntactic and semantic differences and they are not in synchronic variation in the same way they were in the complement system.

4. *Koto*, the Nominal form and negation

In order to show how *koto* may expand the scope of negation to create propositional negation in Old Japanese, it is necessary to contrast it with standard (predicate) negation and constituent (narrow) negation.

4.1. Standard (predicate) negation

Standard negation is defined by Payne as "that type of negation that can apply to the most minimal and basic sentences" (Payne, 1985: 198). In Western OJ, standard negation is encoded by means of the negative auxiliary -*(a)z-* ~ -*(a)n-*. This is exemplified in (8).

(8) *oku   tuyu   [simo-ni   ape]-zusite*
     fall.ADN dew   frost-DAT resist-**NEG**.PTC
     '(when autumn comes) the falling dew does not resist the frost'
     M 15.3699

The scope of the negative auxiliary in these two examples can be defined as the VP (or possibly vP), so in (8) negation takes scope over [*simo-ni ape-*] 'resist the frost'. The subject is outside the scope of negation as indicated by the square brackets. Without the interaction of focus with negation, this is the default scope of the negative auxiliary -*(a)z-* ~ -*(a)n-*. One possible formalization of (8) is given in (9):

(9) $\exists x \ (tuyu(x) \land \sim\!apu \ (x,simo))$

4.2. Constituent negation

Constituent negation can be defined as a type of negation where one particular constituent within the potential scope of negation is singled out. In Old Japanese, constituent negation can take the form of a Nominal complement clause in collocation with a negative existential. This is illustrated in (10) - (12) below (see also (7) above for a nontopicalized example).

(10)   [wa-ga   sekwo-*ni*   wa -ga   kwopu*raku*]-*pa*
       I-GEN   girl-DAT   I-GEN   love.NOM-TOP
       yamu   toki   *mo*   **nasi**
       stop.ADN   time   PRT   **not exist**.CONCL
       'my love for my dear girl never stops' (lit. 'time when it stops never exists')
       M 11.2612

(11)   [aki   *tuke-ba*   *momiti*   *tiraku*]-*pa*
       autumn   reach-PROV   autumn leaf   scatter.NOM-TOP
       tune-*wo*   **nami**   *koso*
       forever-ACC   **not exist**.INF2   KPART
       'the scattering of the autmn leaves when autumn comes is because nothing is forever'
       M 19.4161

(12)   apida-mo **nakye**-*mu*.   [Wa-ga kwopwi-*maku*]-*pa*
       lapse-PRT **not exist**-CONJ.CONCL   I-GEN love-CONJ.NOM-TOP
       'It has no lapse, that I love (you)'
       M 4.551

An important characteristic of these constructions is the fact that they always contain a temporal noun, and this is the constituent that the negation takes scope over. In (10) one finds *yamu toki* 'stop time', in (11) *tune* 'forever', and in (12), where the subject complement is right-dislocated, it is *apida* 'interval'. The presence of the temporal noun very clearly distinguishes the constructions in (10) - (12) from wide scope, propositional negation as we will see in the next section. It is strikingly clear that negation in (10) - (12) only takes scope over the temporal noun immediately preceding the negative existential since the Nominal complements (in square brackets) survive negation. The Nominal complements in (10) - (12) are therefore presupposed. This corresponds exactly to other usages of the Nominal form in complement clause constructions as mentioned in Section 3.1. In Wrona (forthcoming) I have suggested that, in fact, it is not the negative existential that constructs with the Nominal complement clause in examples like (10) - (12), but rather the composite predicate N_{TEMP}+na- 'not exist', since the presence of the temporal noun is obligatory. This composite predicate functions as a phasal (or aspectual) complement-taking predicate like *begin, stop, continue* attested in numerous languages (cf. Noonan, 1985: 129). More precisely, N_{TEMP}+na- 'not exist' designates non-completion. So while it is unquestionably a case of constituent negation, the construction as a whole belongs to the system of complementation.

The facts of the scope of negation in the construction dealt with in this section are captured in the formalization of (12) in (13) below.[3] It is clear that the Nominal complement is outside the scope of negation and that negation only includes the temporal noun (*apida* 'interval' in the present case).

(13) $\exists x \, (wa \, ga \, kwopuraku(x) \wedge {\sim}\exists y \, (apida(y)(x)))$

4.3. Wide scope, propositional/event negation.

Propositional negation can be defined as the denial or rejection of a proposition (Dik, 1997; Horn, 2001; Lyons, 1977).[4] I will first deal with the structure and the scope issues, and then turn to the function of propositional/event negation. In Old Japanese, propositional/event negation is expressed by a clause nominalized by *koto* in collocation with the negative existential *na*- 'not exist' (as in (16) below) or with the regularly formed negative of the affirmative existential *ar*- 'exist' (as in (14) below):

(14)   ide ika ni kokodaku kwopu*ru*? [Wagimokwo-ga apa-zi-*to*
        why   this much long.ADN my girl-GEN   meet-NEGC-COMP
        ip-ye*ru*   **koto**]-*mo*   **ara-*naku* ni**
        say-STAT.ADN   COMP-PRT**exist-NEG.NOM**
        'Why do I miss her, this much? It is not the case that my wife, said "I will not meet you (again)"'
        M 12.2889

(15)   wa-ga yuwe-*ni* itaku   *na*-wabwi-*so*.   [Noti tupi-ni
        I-GEN sake-for hard.INF PROH-be depressed-PROH. after never
        apa-zi-*to*   ipi-*si*   **koto**]-*mo*   **ara-*naku* ni**
        meet-NEG-COMP   say-PST.ADN COMP-PRT**exist-NEG.NOM**
        'Please do not be that depressed because of me. It is not the case that (I) have said that we will never meet afterwards'
        M 12.3116

---

[3] I have ignored the right-dislocation of the subject complement in (12).
[4] Horn's term is *metalinguistic negation* and it is broader than Lyon's and Dik's *propositional negation*.

(16) *opu-goto ni*   [*yurusu*   **koto**]   *naku*
      chase-every time let get away.ADN COMP   **not exist.INF**
      'everytime (we) chased (them), there was no letting them get away'
      M 17.4011

(17) [kokoro-*ni-pa*   *yupupu* **koto**]   **naku...**   *suka-naku*
      heart-LOC-TOP   relax.ADN COMP   **not exist.INF** love-NEG.INF
      nomwi   ya kwopwi-watari-na-mu
      PRT   Q love-continue-PERF-CONJ
      'it is not the case that I relax my heart (for you), but will I keep lov-
      ing, or will I stop loving?'
      M 17.4015

(18) [*yuku-sa ku-sa*   *tutumu*   **koto**]   **naku**
      go-NMLZ come- NMLZ   meet obstacle.ADN   COMP notexist.INF
      'Perhaps (your) boat will be fast if it doesn't happen that (you) en -
      counter (any) obstacles coming and going'
      M 20.4514

(19) opo-bune-*wo*   *arumi-ni*   *idasi-imasu*   kimi
      great-boat ACC   wild sea-LOC set out-HON.ADN my lord
      [*tutumu*   **koto**]   **naku**   *paya kapyeri-mase*
      meet obstacle.ADN   COMP **not exist.INF** fast   return-HON.IMP
      'My lord who (is about to) set out on the great boat on the wild sea,
      please return quickly without encountering (any) obstacles'
      M 15.3582

(20) *Katakapi-no kapa-no se   kiywoku   yuku   midu-no*
      Katakai-GEN   river-GEN rapid   is clear.INF   go.ADN   water-GEN
      [*tayuru **koto**]   **naku**   *arigaywopi   mi-mu*
      stop.ADN COMP   **not exist.INF** keep coming.INF see-CONJ
      'Like the water of the rapid of the Katakai river that runs clear, I will
      keep coming [without stopping] to look at (the mountain)'
      M 17.4002 (see also M 17.3985, M 4098)

(see also (6) above). This is a fairly comprehensive list of examples of pro-
positional/event negation in Old Japanese. In (20) the negative existential
predicate *na-* 'not exist' is used, whereas the regularly formed negative of
the affirmative existential predicate *ar-* 'exist' is found in example (14). I
will treat the two types of negative existentials (illustrated in (14) and (20)
above) on par with respect to negation scope in the following.[5]

---

[5] The two types seem to reflect a state of synchronic variation between an older variant where
the negative existential is formed by negating the affirmative existential and an innovative

Recall from section 4.2 that constituent negation in Old Japanese always involved a temporal noun. This is not so with wide scope, propositional/event negation. Take example (17) above. Here there is no temporal noun for the negative existential predicate to construct with between the *koto*-clause and the negative existential predicate. This means that in (17), and in propositional negation in general, negation takes scope over the proposition expressed by the *koto*-clause. Since the proposition expressed in the *koto*-clause is within the scope of negation, it does not survive negation. Thus the proposition in the *koto*-clause is not presupposed according to the standard negation test for semantic presupposition (cf. Levinson, 1983). The non-presupposedness of the propositions expressed by the *koto*-clauses in (14) - (20) is in sharp contrasts to the presuppposedness of proposition expressed by *koto* in the complement system in Old Japanese, as exemplified in (5) above where the *koto*-complement clause was presupposed. Recall that the Nominal complements involved in constituent negation were presupposed just like other Nominal complements selected by complement-taking predicates. This amounts to another important difference between constituent negation and propositional negation. The fact that the proposition expressed by the *koto*-clause is within the scope of negation can be captured in predicate logic as in (21) which is the structure of (17).

(21)   ~∃x (*kokoro ni pa yurupu(x)*)

The differences between constituent negation and propositional negation in Old Japanese are summarized in Table 4.

Table 4:   Summary of the differences between constituent and propositional negation in OJ.

	Constituent negation	Propositional negation
Temporal noun	Always involved	Never involved
Scope of negation	Only over temporal noun	Over the proposition
Presupposition	+ (Nominal complement)	- (*koto*-clause)
CTP reading	Phasal (aspectual) CTP	(not available)

Having established the scope of propositional negation, I now turn to its function. It is necessary in each case in (14) - (20) above to ask why propositional negation is used instead of the default predicate negation negating the VP. Here the concept of proposition denial is important. Geurts (1998) divides denial into four types: proposition, presupposition, implica-

---

variant where the negative existential is distinct from the verbal negator. This is one of three attested types of synchronic variation described in Croft (1991).

ture and form denial. Proposition denial "serve[s] to downright reject a preceding utterance...[proposition denial is] directed at the asserted content of the previous utterance" (Geurts, 1998: 276). Dik, drawing on Lyons (1977: 771), defines propositional negation as follows: "[...] we may deny ... a proposition *p* which in some way is entertained or im   plied in the context..." (Dik, 1997: 176). Dik's definition is interesting because he opens up to the possibility that the denied proposition is not actually uttered, but implied in the context.

This is quite clearly the case with some of the examples in (14) - (20). In (14) the protagonist acts in a way that suggests that he will never see his lover again, but this is denied. Thus he does not deny a previous utterance, but a proposition implied in the context. Essentially the same is the case in (15), except for the fact that it is someone other than the protagonist that is behaving as if he will never see his lover again. In (6), repeated below as (22), the preestablished proposition that it is possible to distinguish between summer and winter is rejected. In this particular poem the poet is talking about the perennial snow on a mountain.

(22)   *[puyu*   *natu-to*   *waku*   *koto]-mo*   ***naku***
       winter   summer-ABL   distinguish.ADN   COMP-PRT**not exist**.INF
       'It is not the case that (one can) distinguish winter from summer'
       M 17.4003

In (17) the protagonist denies the implied proposition that he is falling out of love, but he does not know whether this may happen later. Finally, in (16) the situation is that the poet emphasizes the fact they did not let the birds they were chasing get away. This emphasis is arguably achieved by rejecting an implicit proposition that they did not catch all of the birds they chased.

Not all cases of propositional negation seem to be interpretable as proposition denial. In (18) and (19), it is difficult to get the reading as a rejection of a preestablished proposition. Rather, it seems to be the case that (18) and (19) are negative counterparts of the construction type exemplified below.

(23)   *inoti*   *ara-ba*   *[apu*   *koto]-mo*   *ara-mu*
       life   exist-COND   meet.ADN   COMP-PRT**exist**-CONJ.CONCL
       '(We) will probably meet (again) if (we) are alive'
       M 15.3745

It is possible that (23) has an experiential reading 'it happens that...' as in Modern Japanese. If (18) and (19) are negative counterparts of experientials as in (23), they would mean something like 'it doesn't happen that...'. This seems a particularly appropriate interpretation of examples like (18). It is conceivable that the *koto*-clauses in (18), (19) and (23) are *events* rather than *propositions*, but nonetheless the scope of negation can still be said to be wider than predicate negation and constituent negation. Notice in addition that the event expressed by the *koto*-clause in (23) is within the scope of the (affirmative) predicate of existence *ar*- 'exist'.

The last example to deal with is (20). This type is the only one that finds an equivalent expression with predicate negation. Compare (20) with (24).

(24)   ... *to   ima-no   yo-ni   [taye]-zu   ipi-tutu*
       COMP   now-GEN   generation-DAT   stop-NEG.INF   say-CONT
       'tell the present generation continuously (i.e. without stopping)
       that...'
       M 20.4360

Here we are dealing with two different types of negation of the same verb *taye*- 'stop, break'. One cannot really say that the negation in (20) has wider scope than in (24), since only the verb *taye*- 'stop, break' is within the scope of both. Following the difference argued for in this paper, the difference could be captured by the translation 'there is no stopping' for (20) and 'it doesn't stop' for (24). In spite of the coincidental scope similarity, it is clear that the negation in (20) is marked vis-à-vis the standard negation in (24).

With the exception of (20), there is no question that the negation type dealt with in this section has wide scope. In most cases, negation takes scope over an entire proposition encoded by *koto*, but there were a couple of examples where the negated *koto*-clause seemed to encode an event. In any case the scope of negation is wider than in predicate negation (Section 4.1) and in constituent negation (Section 4.2).

5. *Koto* in other scope-expanding contexts

In the preceding section, *koto* was shown to be the means by which the scope of negation could be expanded to include an entire proposition or, more rarely, an event. In (24) above, *koto* in collocation with the affirmative existential *ar*- 'exist' was suggested to have an experiential reading, but whatever the reading, the affirmative existential took scope over the *koto*-clause. There is yet another context in which *koto* can be said to have this scope expanding function. Observe the following examples.

(25)   [...*opo-miya-no uti-ni   moti-mawiri-ki-te*
       HON-palace-GEN inside-DIR bring-come in(HUM).PTC
       maziwaza se-ru]   koto   mi-tabi   se-ri
       curse   do-STAT.ADN COMP 3-times   do-STAT.CONCL
       '[(he) entered the Imperial Palace bringing (the scull) and did a

curse]ᵢ; thisᵢ he did three times'
S 43.9

(26) [...pito-*wo-ba*   aratamete tate-*mu*]   **koto-*pa***
      person-ACC-TOP do again   instate-CONJ.ADN   **COMP** TOP
      kokoro-*no*   *manima*   *seyo*
      heart-GEN   according **do**.IMP
      'according to your heart, do the fact of instating anew a person...'
      S 45.27

In (25) the frequency adjunct *mi-tabi* 'three times' takes scope over the entire event described in the square brackets, not just the performance of the curse itself, but also the entering into the Imperial Palace bringing a scull. In order to make it clear that the scope of the frequency adjunct extends to the whole event, *koto* is used to nominalize the event. In a similar vein, the manner adjunct *kokoro no manima* 'in accordance with (your) heart' in (26) takes scope over the entire event described in square brackets, not just the instating of a new person, but also preceding events. Thus *koto* is involved in scope expansion not only with respect to negation, but also with adverbial adjuncts. It should be noted that the propositions expressed by the *koto*-clauses in (25) and (26) are not presupposed.

Therefore, there is good evidence that *koto* has carved for itself a specialized function of scope expansion, not just for negation, but for adverbial adjuncts too. Among the nominalizers available in Old Japanese, only *koto* has this function. With respect to negation, Nominal complements are used in contexts with constituent negation. It was argued in Section 4.2 that this construction was part of the complement system and since Nominal complements are one of the core members of the OJ complement system it is not surprising to find Nominal complements with this function. *Koto*, on the other hand, is not an integral member of the complement system in OJ

6. Crosslinguistic similarities

Both Dik (1997: 176) and Horn (2001: 366) make the observation that in general languages do not make a segmental distinction between propositional negation in the sense of denying or rejecting a proposition (section 4.3) and predicate negation (Section 4.1). This is contradicted by a number of papers on languages with such a distinction, but since Geurts' distinction between the four types of denial (see Section 4.3) is generally not observed in these papers, one has to exert caution. For example, Carston & Noh (1996) and Lee (2005) are concerned with metalinguistic negation in Korean, but these papers focus on presupposition, implicature and form denial rather than propositional denial. It is clear, however, that there is at least one device for proposition denial in Korean. In the following example, B denies the proposition in A (taken from Lee (2005: 602)).

(27) A: ku-nun cwuk-ess-ta
         he-TOP die-PST-DEC
         'he died'
     B: ku-nun cwuk-un kes-i-ani-ta
         he-TOP die-ADN NMLZ-NOM-COP.NEG-DEC
         'it is not the case that he died'

B's response is very similar to Old Japanese propositional negation discussed in this paper. It consists of a clause nominalized by means of *kes* 'thing, fact, NOMINALIZER' which is the cognate of Japanese *koto*, and the negative copula *i-ani*.

Other languages with a particular construction for denying propositions are Brazilian Portuguese (Schwenter, 2005), Egyptian Arabic (Mughazy, 2003) and perhaps Turkish (Schaaik, 1994).

7. Conclusion

In this paper, I have argued that one function of *koto* in Old Japanese was to expand the scope of negation to include an entire proposition. This type of negation was called propositional negation. The semantic effect of propositional negation with *koto* is to reject or deny a proposition either explicitly mentioned or implied in the context, or as a negative experiential. It was shown that in some cases the *koto*-clause seemed to encode an event rather than a proposition. Both contrast with two other types of negation, standard (predicate) negation and constituent negation. The scope of negation in these two types is narrower that that of propositional negation. I also showed that *koto*'s use in scope expanding constructions was not limited to negation, but also found with adverbial adjuncts. Finally, I ventured the claim that a distinct construction for propositional negation may not be as rare as previously thought.

Sources:

M=*Man'yôshû* (Takagi, Gomi & Ohno, 1973-1974)
S=*Senmyô* (Kitagawa, 1982)

References

Carston, Robyn & Noh, Eun-Ju (1996). A Truth-Functional Account of Metalinguistic Negation, With Evidence from Korean. *Language Sciences* 18(1-2): 485-504.
Croft, William (1991). The Evolution of Negation. *Journal of Linguistics* 27(1): 1-27.

Dik, Simon C. (1997). *Theory of Functional Grammar. Part 2: Complex and derived constructions.* Berlin: Walter de Gruyter Inc.

Geurts, Bart (1998). The Mechanisms of Denial. *Language* 74(2): 274-307.

Horn, Laurence R. (2001). *A natural history of negation.* Stanford: Center for the Study of Language and Information.

Kitagawa, Kazuhide (Ed.) (1982). *Shoku Nihongi Senmyô.* Tokyo: Yoshikawa Kôbunkan.

Lee, H. K. (2005). Presupposition and implicature under negation. *Journal of Pragmatics* 37(5): 595-609.

Lehmann, Christian (2004). Theory and method in grammaticalization. *Zeitschrift für Germanistische Lingvistik* 32/2: 152-187.

Levinson, Stephen C. (1983). *Pragmatics.* Cambridge: Cambridge University Press.

Lyons, John (1977). *Semantics. Vol. 2.* Cambridge: Cambridge University Press.

Mughazy, M. (2003). Metalinguistic negation and truth functions-the case of Egyptian Arabic. *Journal of Pragmatics* 35(8): 1143-1160.

Noonan, Michael (1985). Complementation. In Shopen, T. (Ed.), *Language typology and syntactic description: Complex constructions* Cambridge: Cambridge University Press. 42-140.

Payne, John R. (1985). Negation. In Shopen, T. (Ed.), *Language typology and syntactic description: Clause Stucture* Cambridge: Cambridge University Press. 197-242.

Schaaik, Gerjan van (1994). Turkish. In Kahrel, P. & van den Berg, R. (Eds.), *Typological studies in negation.* John Benjamins Publishing Company. 35-50.

Schwenter, Scott A. (2005). The pragmatics of negation in Brazilian Portuguese. *Lingua* 115(10): 1427-1456.

Takagi, Ichinosuke, Gomi, Tomohide & Ohno, Susumu (Eds.) (1973-1974). *Man'yôshû. Vol. 1-4.* Tokyo: Iwanami shoten.

Wrona, Janick (forthcoming). *A Study of Old Japanese Syntax: Synchronic and Diachronic Aspects of the Complement System.* London: Global Oriental.

Part III

Phonology and Phonetics

The Acquisition of the Constraints on Mimetic Verbs in Japanese and Korean*

KIMI AKITA
Kobe University

1. Introduction

This paper claims that 1) verb formation of Japanese and Korean sound-symbolic words (or *mimetics*) is constrained by a semantic constraint and a syntactic one, and that 2) the semantic constraint (and possibly the syntactic one) does not exist in (at least Japanese) early child language because of the conditions of its sound-symbolic vocabulary and/or the characteristic way young children look at events. In the former claim, I will propose that the

---

* An earlier version of a part of this paper was presented at the Fifth International Conference on Practical Linguistics of Japanese held at San Francisco State University in March 2006 as well as at the JK 16 conference held at Kyoto University in October 2006. I am grateful to the audiences of both conferences for their insightful comments. My special thanks go to Professors Yo Matsumoto, Natsuko Tsujimura, Kaoru Horie, Alan Hyun-Oak Kim, and Prashant Pardeshi, with all of whom I had constructive discussions on the present topic. Also, the analysis of Korean mimetic verbs was not possible in its current form without the discussions with Youknow Lee. Remaining inadequacies are, of course, my own.

two languages are similar not only in their rich sound-symbolic, phonose-mantic systems (Garrigues 1995; Shibasaki 2002) but also in their *grammars* of sound symbolism. The latter claim is important particularly in that it considers such grammatical matters from a developmental perspective, which has been also rare in the literature.

The specific order of discussions is as follows. In Section 2, the semantic constraint and the syntactic one on Japanese and Korean mimetic verbs will be identified on the basis of various kinds of data. In Section 3, through the observation of some relevant examples, I will frame a hypothesis on the status of these constraints in child language. Finally, Section 4 will examine the hypothesis by thoroughly analyzing one Japanese child's speech data.

This paper adopts the following terminology. First, *mimetic verbs* stand for verb forms of mimetics. The most productive mimetic verb forms are as follows: J. [mimetic + *su-ru* 'do']; K. [mimetic + *ha-ta* 'do, be'] or [mimetic + verbal suffix (*-keli-ta/-tay-ta*)].[1] Second, I employ a tripartite semantic classification of mimetics: *phonomimes* (J. *giongo*; K. *uysenge*) for mimetics of sounds, *phenomimes* (J. *gitaigo*; K. *uythaye*) for mimetics of nonauditory external (i.e. visual and textural) information, and *psychomimes* (J. *gizyoogo*; K. *uycenge*) for mimetics of internal experiences. Finally, I use the notion *iconicity* as a scalar concept that treats the degree of directness of the relationship between form and meaning (cf. Hamano 1998: 9).

2. Constraints on Japanese and Korean Mimetic Verbs

2.1. Semantic Constraint

In Korean and Japanese, some mimetics can form a verb but others cannot. In this subsection, contrary to Tamori and Schourup's assumption that no definite generalization is available for (Japanese) mimetic verb formation (1999: 56), I identify a general semantic constraint on it.

Possibility of verb forms for various subtypes of mimetics in Japanese and Korean is given in (1).[2]

---

[1] Some would say that we should also consider such reduced, suffixed mimetic verb forms as *beto-tuku* (< *betobeto*) 'feel sticky' and *kira-meku* (< *kirakira*) 'glitter' in Japanese. However, since candidate mimetics for these verb forms form a subset of those for the *suru* mimetic verb construction (e.g. *betobeto-suru*, *kirakira-suru*; see Tamori and Schourup 1999: 57), the same constraints (or necessary conditions) as those discussed below are applicable to them. Still, it would be fruitful to question what narrows the candidates for these suffixed verb forms to the subset (see Hamano (1998: 56-57) for a semantic/prosodic explanation for it).

[2] The Japanese/Korean pairings in the lists depict similar but not exactly the same eventualities.

(1) a. Japanese/Korean phonomimes:
       Highly iconic (distinctive sounds):
       *buubuu-suru/*pwungpwung-{hata/kelita} 'zoom-zoom', *byun-
       byun-suru/*ssayngssayng-{hata/kelita} 'whirl', *wanwan-suru
       /??mengmeng-{hata/kelita} 'bowwow'
       Poorly iconic (indistinctive, collective sounds):
       zawazawa-suru/wakulwakul-{hata/kelita} 'hum'

    b. Japanese/Korean phenomimes of walking and running:
       Highly iconic:
       *sutasuta-suru/*chongchong-{hata/kelita} 'walk briskly', *teku-
       teku-suru/*ttwupekttwupek-{hata/kelita} 'trudge', *tobotobo-suru/
       *thepekthepek-{hata/kelita} 'plod'
       Poorly iconic:
       nosonoso-suru/engkumengkum-kelita 'move sluggishly', nyoro-
       nyoro-suru/kkwumthulkkwumthul-{hata/kelita} 'wriggle', tyoro-
       tyoro-suru/chollang-kelita 'run around', urouro-suru/esulleng-
       {hata/kelita} 'loiter', yotayota-suru/pithulpithul-kelita 'totter'

    c. Japanese/Korean psychomimes (poorly iconic):
       bikubiku-suru/humchishumchis-{hata/kelita} 'be scared', dokidoki-
       suru/twukuntwukun-hata 'be excited', hiyat-to-suru/semttuk-hata
       'feel a chill', iraira-suru/ancelpwucel-hata 'be irritated', kura-
       kura-suru/ecilecil-{hata/kelita} 'feel dizzy', mozimozi-
       suru/memwus-{hata/kelita} 'hesitate', tikutiku-
       suru/ttakkumttakkum-hata 'feel prickled'

In both languages, most phonomimes (highly iconically mimicking distinctive sounds) and highly iconic phenomimes cannot form verbs; all psychomimes (which are poorly iconic in nature), poorly iconic phenomimes,
and a few phonomimes (poorly iconically depicting indistinctive, collective
sounds) can.[3,4] (The fact that most phonomimes in Japanese cannot form a
verb has been noted by Nakakita (1991: 255).) This observation leads us to
a generalization like this: Highly iconic mimetics cannot form verbs while
poorly iconic ones can. This generalization is summarized in Figure 1.

---

[3] There are indeed a few Japanese psychomimes that cannot combine with suru (e.g. *gut-to-
suru 'be moved', *pin-to-suru 'be inspired', ??sikkuri-suru 'have a nice fit'). Nevertheless,
even they can form mimetic verbs through combining with the verb kuru 'come' (e.g. gut-to-
kuru, pin-to-kuru, sikkuri-kuru).
[4] Some say that some of the 'ungrammatical' mimetic verbs in (1) are not unacceptable although childish as we will discuss later.

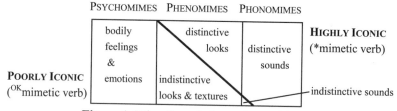

Figure 1. Mimetic verb formation and iconicity

A natural question raised here is how we can measure 'iconicity'. One possible solution is to refer to paralinguistic phenomena (see Kita 1997: 392-399). In the present study, I conducted a simple experiment focusing on the hand gestures accompanying the utterances of phenomimes of walking and running given in (1b). Fifteen native Japanese speakers were asked to make a series of gestures imitating footsteps (i.e. moving their loosely open hands, palms down, up and down one after another in front of their body) while uttering a Japanese phenomime of walking/running repeatedly. As a result, as Table 1 shows, a sharp contrast was obtained between the phenomimes that can form a verb and those that cannot with respect to the numbers of subjects who perfectly synchronized one hand 'step' with the utterance of one mimetic root (e.g. *suta* of *sutasuta*).

Table 1. The results of the gesture experiment (fifteen Japanese speakers)

-*suru*	Mimetic	Synchronized
*	*sutasuta*	10 (66.7%)
	tekuteku	14 (93.3%)
OK	*tyorotyoro*	2 (13.3%)
	urouro	2 (13.3%)

This result suggests that the roots of the mimetics *sutasuta* and *tekuteku* depict a distinct segment of walking, namely one footstep, while the segments of motion depicted by the roots of *tyorotyoro* and *urouro* are unidentifiable. We can thus conclude that the former are highly iconic and the latter poorly iconic. A parallel experiment was conducted for five Korean speakers. Although far from comprehensive or conclusive at the moment, it is expected to reach a similar conclusion in the future.

Concluding the above discussion, the current generalization is valid and the following semantic constraint is obtained:

(2)   *The semantic constraint on Japanese and Korean mimetic verb forms:*
Highly iconic mimetics cannot form verbs.

Finally, I make a brief comment on the reason these mimetic verb forms avoid high iconicity. As to this question, a semantic-integration account is effective. Poorly iconic mimetics are semantically highly integrated with the rest of a sentence they belong to while highly iconic ones are not, for the former are relatively similar to nonmimetic words, which are not iconic at all. The high semantic integration of poorly iconic mimetics allows them to function as a predicate verb (i.e. syntactically perfectly integrated with nonmimetic parts of a sentence), whereas low semantic integration of highly iconic mimetics leads them to be 'quoted' as an adjunct (i.e. syntactically segregated). Thus, the semantic integration at issue can be understood as gradient along the continuum of iconicity (cf. Kita 1997; Tsujimura and Deguchi 2003).[5]

2.2. Syntactic Constraint

This subsection points out the existence of a syntactic constraint on the mimetic verb forms in Japanese and Korean, which has attracted little attention in the literature.

Among all mimetic verbs, only two subtypes of verbs can take accusative-marked NPs. One subtype is what I call 'causative mimetic verbs' ('transitive change-of-state mimetic verbs' in Kageyama, to appear), which are illustrated in (3) and listed in (4). They denote an event in which one moves something, especially one's body part(s).[6]

(3) a. Japanese:
         Ken-ga   te-o   burabura-si-ta.
         Ken-NOM   hand-ACC   MIM-do-PST
         'Ken swung his hands.'
     b. Korean:
         Chelswu-ka   son-ul   huntulhuntul-keli-ess-ta.
         Cheolsu-NOM   hand-ACC   MIM-VBZR-PST-DEC
         'Cheolsu swung his hands.'

---

[5] Some other constructions mimetics can participate in should be also analyzed in relation to the present discussion. For example, Japanese highly iconic mimetics, which cannot form verbs, are the most likely candidates for the prenominal quotative construction [mimetic-*to iu* NP] '(NP) in which someone/something says (the content of the mimetic)' (e.g. *sutasuta-to iu aruki-kata* 'brisk walking'; see Hamano 1998: 15-25, 214). Likewise, in Korean, highly iconic mimetic verbs can appear if used in the constructions in which a mimetic verb modifies the main verb in its nonfinite forms: [mimetic-{*hako/hamie/keliko/kelimie*} (V)] '(V) saying (the content of the mimetic)' (e.g. *pwungpwung-kelimie tallie-kata* 'run away with the sound like *pwungpwung*') (Alan Hyun-Oak Kim, personal communication). In this respect, we can hypothesize that various constructions that are available to mimetics are interrelatedly distributed according to the degrees of iconicity of mimetics.

[6] Abbreviations used in this paper are as below:
    ACC = accusative; DAT = dative; DEC = declarative; FP = final particle; GEN = genitive; IMP = imperative; MIM = mimetic; NMZR = nominalizer; NOM = nominative; NPST = nonpast; PASS = passive; POL = polite; PST = past; QUOT = quotative; TOP = topic; VBZR = verbalizer

(4) Japanese/Korean causative mimetic verbs:
batabata-suru/pwututukpwututuk-{hata/kelita} 'flap one's limbs', *mo-gumogu-suru/wumulwumul-{hata/kelita}* 'chew food with one's mouth closed', *pakupaku-suru/ppakkumppakkum-{hata/kelita}* 'open and close one's mouth repeatedly'

The other subtype is what Kageyama (to appear) classifies as 'verbs of contact and impact', which are illustrated in (5) and listed in (6). They represent an event in which one acts on (e.g. hits, attacks, rubs) something.

(5) a. Japanese:
Mai-ga   doa-o   tonton-si-ta.
Mai-NOM   door-ACC   MIM-do-PST
'Mai knocked on the door.'
b. Korean:
Yengi-ka   mwun-ul   thakthak-{ha/keli}-ess-ta.
Yeongi-NOM   door-ACC   MIM-{do/VBZR}-PST-DEC
'Yeongi knocked on the door.'

(6) Japanese/Korean mimetic verbs of contact and impact:
dondon-suru/khwungkhwung-{hata/kelita} 'pound', *gosigosi-suru/ ppakppak-{hata/kelita}* 'scrub', *huuhuu-suru/hwuhwu-{hata/kelita}* 'blow', *tuntun-suru/khwukkhwuk-{hata/kelita}* 'touch with a stick or finger'

What is important here is that there are so few transitive mimetic verbs in Korean and Japanese.[7] In fact, in Kageyama's (to appear) seven-way classification of Japanese mimetic verbs, only one type (i.e. verbs of contact

---

[7] As Kageyama (to appear) points out about Japanese contact/impact mimetic verbs, the transitivity of the verbs in (3-6) is quite low as shown by the impossibility of passivization in the examples below. This fact supports my claim here that mimetic verbs disfavor high transitivity.
(i)   Causative mimetic verbs:
a. *Ken-no   te-ga   Ken-ni   burabura-s-are-ta. (J)
Ken-GEN hand-NOM Ken-DAT MIM-do-PASS-PST
'Ken's hands were swung by Ken.'
b. *Chelswu-uy   son-i   Chelswu-eykey huntulhuntul-kelye-ci-ess-ta. (K)
Cheolsu-GEN hand-NOM Cheolsu-DAT   MIM-VBZR-PASS-PST-DEC
'Cheolsu's hands were swung by Cheolsu.'
(ii)   Mimetic verbs of contact and impact:
a. *Doa-ga   Mai-ni   tonton-s-are-ta. (J)
door-NOM Mai-DAT MIM-do-PASS-PST
'The door was knocked on by Mai.'
b. *Mwun-i   Yengi-eykey thakthak-kelye-ci-ess-ta. (K)
door-NOM Yeongi-DAT MIM-VBZR-PASS-PST-DEC
'The door was knocked on by Yeongi.'

and impact) is transitive. Thus, we obtain a (weak) syntactic constraint like this:

(7) *The syntactic constraint on Japanese and Korean mimetic verb forms:*
Mimetics which depict a highly transitive event cannot freely form verbs.[8]

This constraint implies that mimetics are in a poor affinity with complicated eventualities that contain two or more participants. This might come from the simplicity and directness of the event depiction of mimetics themselves: They depict the characteristics of sounds, manners, feelings, etc. and can describe causation only so far as it is related to those aspects of events (see also Kageyama and Yumoto 1997: 159).[9]

3. A Hypothesis on Children's Mimetic Verbs

In this section, I form a hypothesis on how the constraints proposed in the previous section are in child language. This objective can be approached through reexamination of the disfavored (or unacceptable) verb forms discussed in Section 2.

First, if we create a verb from a 'highly iconic mimetic' discussed in Section 2.1 (e.g. *byunbyun-suru/ssayngssayng-{hata/kelita}* 'whirl'), the resultant mimetic verb can sound very childish (and colloquial), if not unacceptable. Second, both causative and contact/impact mimetic verbs discussed in Section 2.2 also create a childish tone (cf. Nakakita 1991: 252; Kageyama, to appear; see also footnote 8). To our further interest, these highly childish mimetic verbs are by far less frequently found on the Internet. It thus seems that these mimetic verbs are less productive than the others in adult language.

Significantly, the childishness effect is not generated when these mimetics are used adverbially. In (8a) and (8b), the mimetics *burabura* and

---

[8] There can be an alternative view for the constraints in question: It may be the case that there is only one constraint on mimetic verbs and it has a syntactic and a semantic aspect (Prashant Pardeshi, personal communication). This view might be reasonable when we notice the considerable overlap between the applications of the two constraints. Concretely, many or most of the mimetics that form causative or contact/impact verbs listed in (4) and (6) imitate distinctive sounds (i.e. highly iconic). This overlap would stem from the fact that highly transitive events tend to emit salient sounds (cf. Kageyama, to appear).

[9] One might suspect that there is a phonological restriction on the Japanese mimetic verb form as well, because the quotative particle *to* is obligatory when a mimetic has less than four morae (e.g. *hat*(-to)-suru* 'be startled', *pokan*(-to)-suru* 'be vacant'). This restriction is not placed on the mimetic verb form but on the mimetics themselves however they may be used. These mimetics cannot appear in their bare forms when used adverbially, either (e.g. *hat*(-to) kizuku* 'notice with a startle', *pokan*(-to) kuti-o akeru* 'open one's mouth in a vacant manner') (see Nasu 2002).

huntulhuntul modify the verbs *yurasu* 'swing' and *wumcikita* 'move', respectively, without causing this effect. Likewise, in (9a) and (9b), *tonton* and *thakthak* modify *tataku* 'knock' and *twutulita* 'knock', respectively, without the effect.

(8) Causative mimetic verbs:
To mean 'swing one's hands':
a. Japanese:
te-o burabura-suru (childish) vs.
te-o burabura yurasu (not childish)
b. Korean:
son-ul huntulhuntul-kelita (childish) vs.
son-ul huntulhuntul wumcikita (not childish)

(9) Mimetic verbs of contact and impact:
To mean 'knock on a door':
a. Japanese:
doa-o tonton-suru (childish) vs.
doa-o tonton tataku (not childish)
b. Korean:
mun-ul thakthak-kelita (childish) vs.
mun-ul thakthak twutulita (not childish)

In addition, in Japanese, the effect does not occur if causative mimetic verbs employ the causative morpheme *-(s)ase* (cf. Kageyama, to appear):

(10) Japanese causative mimetic verbs:
To mean 'swing one's hands':
te-o burabura-su-ru (childish) vs.
te-o burabura-s-ase-ru (not childish)

All these facts indicate that it is not the mimetics themselves but the mimetic verb forms that give rise to the childishness effect. Then, where does the effect come from? A promising solution is to suppose that these verbs are perfectly natural and highly productive in child language. The following hypothesis is thus formulated:

(11) *A hypothesis on children's mimetic verbs:*
The semantic and the syntactic constraint on Japanese and Korean mimetic verb formation are *weaker* in their child languages.

4. Mimetic Verbs in a Japanese Child's Speech

To examine the validity of the hypothesis in (11), I collected and analyzed all mimetic verbs in one Japanese child's speech data. The database I used is Noji's (1973-1977) diary record of his monolingual Japanese child named Sumihare, which contains about 40,000 utterances by the boy in his 0;1 through 6;12. The data was originally recorded by stenography on cards. Although this acquisition data is available online through CHILDES, the collection of mimetic verbs from this corpus was made by visually scanning the entire text rather than using a search engine in order not to miss an unconventional mimetic verb form.

As a result, two morphological types of mimetic verbs were obtained with the following frequencies. One type is the normal form consisting of one mimetic and the verb *suru*, and the other is a verb form in which one mimetic is directly accompanied by the past tense morpheme *-ta* (i.e. [mimetic-*ta*]), which I will call 'primitive mimetic verbs'.[10] They form a basis of the discussions in the rest of this paper.

Table 2. Frequencies of mimetic verbs in Sumihare's speech

	Normal	Primitive
Token frequency	225	70
Type frequency	172	70

In what follows, after having a brief look at primitive mimetic verbs in Section 4.1, I will examine the mimetic verbs Sumihare produced in terms of the semantic and the syntactic constraints proposed above in Sections 4.2 and 4.3, respectively.

4.1. Primitive Mimetic Verbs

As Tsujimura (2005) points out, in Sumihare's speech data (as well as in another child's), there is a stage (1;6-2;6) at which a mimetic verb form exemplified in (12) (i.e. primitive mimetic verbs), which is ungrammatical in adult language, is frequently used. The following examples, which are also given in Tsujimura (2005), illustrate this form:

(12) a. Tonton-ta(a). [1;11]
   MIM-PST
   '[I] hit [it].' (after hitting a tile)
 b. Taa-tyan   tabi   pai-ta(a). [1;12]
   Mommy   sock   MIM-PST
   'Mommy, [I] threw [my] sock away.'
 c. O-kaze   byuut-ta. [1;12]
   POL-wind   MIM-PST
   'The wind blew hard.'

---

[10] One may object that this verb form does not have a function equivalent to that of mimetic verbs but rather is a contracted form of (MIM)-*to it-ta* ((MIM)-QUOT say-PST) 'said (the content of the mimetic)'. However, I do not consider this possibility, for there is a case in which this form is used with a psychomime, which is least likely to be compatible with the meaning 'said (the content of the mimetic)' (*Bekkurit-ta* (for *bikkurit-ta*) '[I] was astounded' [2;1]).

Intriguingly, a comprehensive collection of mimetic verbs from Sumi-hare's speech, as graphed below, suggests that the stable use of the 'gram-matical' mimetic verb form (i.e. normal mimetic verbs) follows this stage.

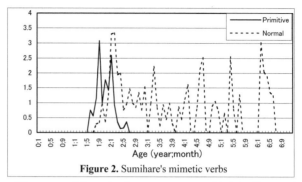

Figure 2. Sumihare's mimetic verbs

Note: 'Frequency' here is the percentage which indicates the propor-tion of the conversation examples containing one or more mimetic verbs uttered by Sumihare out of all examples during each period.

4.2. The Semantic Constraint Examined

In this subsection, I examine Sumihare's mimetic verbs in terms of the se-mantic constraint: Highly iconic mimetics cannot form verbs.

First, as Figure 3 shows, primitive mimetic verbs, which appear at quite an early stage, are predominantly *phonomimic*.[11] In other words, they are highly iconic in most cases and ungrammatical as adults' verbs (see (1a)).

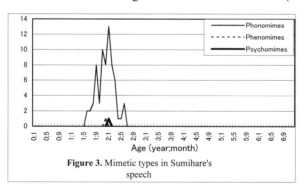

Figure 3. Mimetic types in Sumihare's speech

Here are some examples of phonomimic primitive mimetic verbs:

---

[11] I depended on three mimetic dictionaries, Asano (1978), Chang (1990), and Kakehi et al. (1996), in judging mimetics as a *phono-/pheno-/psycho-mime*.

(13) a. Poosyusyuppoot-ta. [1;8]
    MIM-PST
    '[The locomotive] blew a whistle.'
  b. Razio   tintinpuut-ta. [1;9]
    radio   MIM-PST
    'The radio beeped [a time signal].'
  c. Gotongotont-ta-yo. [2;1]
    MIM-PST-FP
    '[The door] rattled.'
  d. Aka-tyan-ga aat-ta. [2;3]
    baby-NOM   MIM-PST
    'The baby cried.'

Next, as seen in Figure 4, Sumihare's normal mimetic verbs show a similar tendency to his primitive mimetic verbs: Most of them are phonomimic, especially before 3;4.

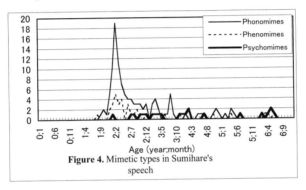

Figure 4. Mimetic types in Sumihare's speech

The following examples illustrate such phonomimic verbs taking the normal mimetic verb form:

(14) a. Mata ton-si-ta-yo. [1;12]
      again MIM-do-PST-FP
      '[I] bumped [against the box] again.'
  b. Kei-tyan an'an-si-ta. [2;2]
    Kei-chan MIM-do-PST
    'Kei-chan cried.'
  c. Sutoon-si-ta. [2;4]
    MIM-do-PST
    '[I] fell off [his back].' (riding on his father's back)
  d. Hikigiiru (for *hikigaeru*) dobun-to-si-ta-n-yo. [2;5]
    toad   MIM-QUOT-do-PST-NMZR-FP
    'A toad dived [into the pond].'

Sumihare's strong preference of phonomimic verbs observed here indicates that, in early Sumihare's Japanese, there is *no* semantic constraint like (2) on the mimetic verb forms.

This conclusion raises a question: Why is there no semantic constraint? There are at least two possible explanations that do not seem to be exclusive to each other. First, it may be because early Sumihare's mimetic vocabulary is semantically homogeneous, nearly all phonomimic, for children acquire phonomimes long before phenomimes and psychomimes (i.e. highly before poorly iconic mimetics) (Herlofsky 1998; Fukuda and Osaka 1999; Tanno 2005: 142). In such vocabulary conditions, a semantic constraint like (2), which crucially refers to the difference in degree of iconicity, is not relevant. From this standpoint, we can conclude that the semantic constraint is acquired along the development of the mimetic vocabulary. Second, it may be because Sumihare looks at various aspects of an event as indivisible (see Tsujimura 2005). For this reason, unlike adults, who prefer the combination of a mimetic adverb and a nonmimetic verb (e.g. *sutasuta aruku* (MIM walk) 'walk briskly'), he prefers conflating manners and sounds into verbs (Natsuko Tsujimura, personal communication).

4.3. The Syntactic Constraint Examined

In this subsection, I examine the same mimetic verbs as those I saw in the previous subsection in terms of the syntactic constraint: Mimetics which depict a highly transitive event cannot freely form verbs. Figure 5 shows the proportion of obviously transitive mimetic verbs (i.e. those found with their object NPs) out of all mimetic verb types Sumihare produced. In this figure, during early periods transitive verbs occupy a large (although not dominant) part of his mimetic verb vocabulary and, significantly, they decrease later.[12]

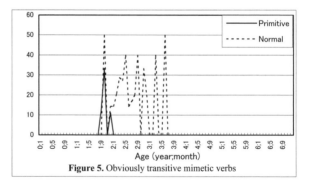

Figure 5. Obviously transitive mimetic verbs

---

[12] Since object NPs can be null in many examples, the actual number of transitive mimetic verbs would be larger.

Here are some examples of transitive mimetic verbs, both primitive and normal, from Sumihare's speech:

(15) a. Ame   pan-ta(a). [1;10]
     candy MIM-PST
     '[You] chopped the candy.'
   b. Nak-u-ko-wa   atti   poi-tyu-ru (for -su-ru) -yo. [2;3]
     cry-NPST-child-TOP over.there MIM-do-NPST   -FP
     '[I will] throw a crybaby [like you] over there.'
   c. Hai (for hae) o-mado-kara   pai-tyu-ru (for -su-ru) -ne. [2;4]
     fly   POL-window-from MIM-do-NPST   -FP
     '[I will] throw the fly out of the window.'
   d. Kore-de tume tyokkintyokkin-si-natyai (for -si-nasai). [2;7]
     this-by nail MIM-do-IMP
     'Clip [your] nails with this (= nail clippers).'

In conclusion, early Sumihare's Japanese is freer from the syntactic constraint on mimetic verbs. However, further research is needed to determine whether such a syntactic constraint *exists* in Japanese speaking infants.

Finally, the holistic-understanding account introduced in Section 4.2 might be also applicable to why child Japanese is different from adult Japanese in terms of this syntactic constraint. It seems that Sumihare looks at an event holistically ('globally' in Tsujimura's terminology) and, as a consequence, can even express causative events synthetically in one verb (cf. the end of Section 2.2).[13]

5. Conclusions and Implications

This paper has reached the following two conclusions. First, Japanese and Korean share semantic and syntactic constraints on their mimetic verb forms: They disfavor highly iconic and highly transitive mimetic verbs. Second, Sumihare's data suggest that early child Japanese does not have the semantic constraint and (perhaps) the syntactic one because almost no degree of iconicity exists in his mimetic vocabulary and/or because children prefer holistic understanding of events.

These achievements have some specific implications for future studies. First, this grammatical study can be a revolution in the histories of mimetic studies in both languages which have had an extreme inclination toward dictionary-oriented description of their phonology, morphology, and phonosemantics.

---

[13] Aspectual properties of Sumihare's mimetic verbs are also worth consideration in relation to the present analysis. As the examples in (12-15) suggest, most of his mimetic verbs are analyzed as an activity verb, retaining the basic (i.e. least extended) meaning of *suru* 'do'.

Second, this paper demonstrated that Japanese and Korean sound-symbolic words can be studied in a parallel manner. Beyond this study, there may be a broader crosslinguistic generalization. As already discussed, in Korean and Japanese, which are two representative languages with a huge sound-symbolic vocabulary of various degrees of iconicity, only poorly iconic mimetics can form verbs. Related phenomena are also observable in other languages like Hungarian. In contrast, Japanese child language, which is similar to English and some other related languages in that it is poor in poorly iconic mimetics, allows (even) highly iconic mimetics to function as predicate verbs. (There is a slight difference even between child Japanese and English. In English, nonce mimetic words like *groahhrrr* and *kerflonk*, which are without doubt regarded as extremely iconic, are unlikely to function as a verb (Tamori and Schourup 1999: 99-100).) The following hypothesis is thus prepared for future research that is based on the iconicity-oriented understanding of the semantic/syntactic integration of sound symbolism in language (see Section 2.1):

(16) *A crosslinguistic hypothesis on the encoding of sound symbolism:*
If one sound-symbolic word can form a verb, then sound-symbolic words of lower iconicity than it can as well.

In this paper, I have demonstrated the possibility of analyzing (Korean and Japanese) sound-symbolic words from a grammatical as well as a crosslinguistic perspective, both of which have not been explored enough before. In addition, the analyses of gestures and acquisition data suggested the significance of studying mimetics from a wider perspective (e.g. psychological, developmental). This study thus tried to put mimetics out of the mainstream of the research on mimetics or sound symbolism in general and function as interfaces with other linguistic or nonlinguistic fields. I hope that greater importance will be attached to this viewpoint in future studies.

References

Asano, T., ed. 1978. *Giongo/gitaigo ziten* [A dictionary of mimetics]. Tokyo: Kadokawa Shoten.

Chang, A. C. 1990. *A Thesaurus of Japanese Mimesis and Onomatopoeia: Usage by Categories.* Tokyo: Taishukan Shoten.

Fukuda, K., and N. Osaka. 1999. Yoozi-no hatuwa-ni mirareru giongo/gitaigo [Mimetics observed in infant speech]. *Kansei-no kotoba-o kenkyuu-suru: Giongo/gitaigo-ni yomu kokoro-no arika* [Studying words of sensitivity: Whereabouts of the mind explored in mimetics], ed. N. Osaka, 155-174. Tokyo: Shinyo-sha.

Garrigues, S. L. 1995. Mimetic Parallels in Korean and Japanese. *Studies in Language* 19: 359-398.

Hamano, S. 1998. *The Sound-Symbolic System of Japanese.* Stanford: CSLI Publications.

Herlofsky, W. J. 1998. The Acquisition of Japanese Iconic Expressions: *Giongo* versus *Gitaigo. Journal of Japanese Linguistics and Education* 5: 1-8. Nagoya Gakuin University.

Kageyama, T. To appear. Explorations into the Conceptual Semantics of Mimetic Verbs. *Proceedings of the 2nd Oxford-Kobe Seminar on Linguistics.*

Kageyama, T., and Y. Yumoto. 1997. *Go-keisei-to gainen-koozoo* [Word formation and conceptual structure]. Tokyo: Kenkyusha.

Kakehi, H., I. Tamori, and L. Schourup. 1996. *Dictionary of Iconic Expressions in Japanese.* Berlin/New York: Mouton de Gruyter.

Kita, S. 1997. Two-Dimensional Semantic Analysis of Japanese Mimetics. *Linguistics* 35: 379-415.

Nakakita, M. 1991. Giongo/gitaigo-to keisiki-doosi *suru*-no ketugoo-ni-tuite [On the combination of mimetic words with the formal verb *suru*]. *Kokubun Meziro* 31: 247-256. Japan Women's University.

Nasu, A. 2002. Nihongo-onomatope-no go-keisei-to inritu-koozoo [Word formation and prosodic structure of Japanese onomatopoeia]. PhD dissertation, University of Tsukuba.

Noji, J. 1973-1977. *Yooziki-no gengo-seikatu-no zittai I-IV* [The real of infant language life I-IV]. Hiroshima/Tokyo: Bunka Hyoron Shuppan.

Shibasaki, R. 2002. On Sound Symbolism in Japanese and Korean. *Japanese/Korean Linguistics* 10: 76-89.

Tamori, I., and L. Schourup. 1999. *Onomatope: Keitai-to imi* [Onomatopoeia: Form and meaning]. Tokyo: Kurosio Publishers.

Tanno, M. 2005. *Onomatope (giongo/gitaigo)-o kangaeru: Nihongo-on'in-no sinrigaku-teki-kenkyuu* [Considering onomatopoeia (mimetics): A psychological study on Japanese phonology]. Kyoto: Airi Publishers.

Tsujimura, N. 2005. Mimetic Verbs and Innovative Verbs in the Acquisition of Japanese. *Proceedings of the Thirty-First Annual Meeting of the Berkeley Linguistics Society,* 371-383.

Tsujimura, N., and M. Deguchi. 2003. Semantic Integration of Mimetics in Japanese. *CLS 39-1: The Main Session: Papers from the Thirty-Ninth Regional Meeting,* 339-351. Chicago Linguistic Society.

Language-Specific Production and Perceptual Compensation in V-to-V Coarticulatory Patterns: Evidence from Korean and Japanese[*]

JEONG-IM HAN
Konkuk University

1. Introduction

Vowel contrast is widely believed to be crucial to the cross-linguistic differences of the vowel-to-vowel (V-to-V) coarticulatory patterns (Manuel 1999, Magen 1984, Choi 1992, 1995, Beddor et al. 2002). Generally languages with a relatively crowded vowel space show weaker V-to-V coarticulatory effects, because speakers try to maintain distinctions among segments, and thus they are sensitive to the acoustic differentiation of the vowels of their language. For example, Manuel and Krakow (1984) conducted a comparative study of V-to-V coarticulation in two Bantu Languages, Shona and Swahili, with the typical five-vowel system, and English with a more

---

[*] I thank Abby Cohn, John Whitman, Jonathan Howell, Haruo Kubozono, and the audience of the 16th Japanese/Korean Linguistics Conference for valuable comments. The present research was supported by the Korea Research Foundation (KRF-2004-D41-A00180).

crowded vowel space. It was shown that the magnitude of the effect was considerably smaller in English than in Shona and Swahili.

On a par with the production patterns, listeners are shown to be sensitive to the coarticulatory information when they recognize words. Even though coarticulation is generally viewed as the primary means by which speakers reduce their articulatory effort, it does not reduce acoustic contrast, negatively affecting the listeners' perception of the speech. Rather, listeners attribute some aspects of the acoustic signal of a target segment to the coarticulatory influence of an upcoming segment, which helps them identify that segment (Alfonso and Baer 1982, van Heuven and Dupuis 1991, Fowler 1984, Whalen 1990, Manuel 1987, Beddor and Krakow 1999). It is of particular interest that listeners not only use coarticulatory information from an adjacent vowel to recognize the target vowel, but they adjust, or 'compensate' for such coarticulatory effects (Fowler 1981, Fowler and Smith 1986, Dahan et al. 2001, Beddor et al. 2001). As listeners anticipate some perceptual reduction or even elimination of the acoustic effects of a coarticulatory context on a target segment, they respond consistently to such effects on the target.

The present study further explores the cross-linguistic pattern of the V-to-V coarticulation. Specifically it will be shown if Korean and Japanese speakers differ in the exhibition of the carryover coarticulatory effects in V-to-V context; and it will be also shown how they use such V-to-V coarticulatory information when they make judgments about the target. Korean and Japanese are chosen for the present study, based on the fact that they differ in terms of the vowel contrast: Korean has been widely known to have seven or eight vowel phonemes, while Japanese has fewer vowels such as five as in (1).

(1) Vowel phonemes of Korean (Shin 2000) and Japanese (Nakajou 1989)

	Korean				Japanese		
front	central	back			front	central	back
i	ɨ	u	high		i		ɯ
ɛ	ʌ	o	mid		e		o
	a		low			a	

Through production and perception experiments, we will test whether Japanese with a less crowded vowel space show larger V-to-V coarticulation than Korean in production (Experiment 1); and whether Japanese listeners show greater compensation effects in perception of the vowel target than Korean listeners when presenting the English non-words with a VCV structure to two language learners (Experiment 2).

2. Experiment 1: Acoustic analysis

2.1. Methods

Three female native speakers of each of Korean and Japanese aged 26 to 40 were recorded. The materials for the acoustic study were two-syllable non-words with the structure of V_1CV_2, where $V_1 = $ [i, o, a], $V_2 = $ [i, o, a]. The C in V_1CV_2 was /p/ in Korean, and /b/ in Japanese, but these two consonants were comparable, because /p/ of Korean becomes voiced in intervocalic context. With these constraints, all possible vowel combinations were created, for a total of nine test words. Each word was recorded in a frame sentence, Korean ____ [saraŋhæjo] ('I love __') and Japanese ____ [sѡkinano] ('I love __').

The stimuli were presented in native language orthography, Hangeul for Korean speakers, and Katakana for Japanese speakers. The recording was done in a sound-attenuated room, and each speaker read fifteen repetitions of the randomized lists of the nine test words embedded in the above frame sentences and the last ten were analyzed among them. Using PRAAT speech analysis software package, ten repetitions for each speaker were digitized at 22,050 Hz and the second formant frequency values of the vowels in the second syllable were measured at ten millisecond intervals.

2.2. Results

To see more clear cases, the following combinations were considered among all possible combination types: /i/ after /i/ vs. /o/, and /a/ after /i/ vs. /a/.

Figure 1 shows the averaged F2 values for three of each of Korean and Japanese speakers from the vowel onset to its onset of steady state when the target vowel is /i/ and the context vowel is /i/ or /o/.

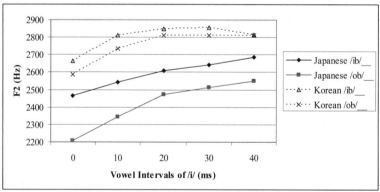

Figure 1. F2 values in Hz for Korean (dashed line) and Japanese (solid line) speakers' production of /i/ from the vowel onset (0 ms) to its onset of steady state (40 ms) when it is preceded by /i/ or /o/.

The vowel /i/ has a high F2, while /o/ has a relatively low F2 and thus the coarticulatory effect of the adjacent vowel /o/ on the target vowel /i/ would be shown as a higher F2. We expect that Japanese speakers will show greater difference in F2 values at the early stage of the second vowel than English, due to their less crowded vowel space. Compare the change in F2 values over time between the case with the same vowels (e.g., /i/ following /ib/) and that with different vowels (e.g., /i/ following /ob/) for each language. As expected, there were substantial coarticulatory effects of the first vowel to the following vowel at vowel onset. Such coarticulatory effects decreased over time for both languages, but the F2 values for the two /i/s were nearly identical for Korean speakers, while they remained distinct until the steady state for Japanese speakers.

The results of the acoustic analyses were separately analyzed using a two-way Analysis of Variance (ANOVA) at vowel onset (0 ms point), and onset of steady state (40 ms point). First, at vowel onset, there were significant coarticulatory effects of vowel type (/i/ vs. /o/) [$F(1,116)=15.5$, $p=.000$], language type (Korean vs. Japanese) [$F(1,116)=45.9$, $p=.000$], and their interaction [$F(1,116)=4.38$, $p=.04$]. Post hoc Tukey tests investigated significant main effects of the V-to-V coarticulation for each vowel type condition: there were significant coarticulatory effects of the preceding vowel quality to the following vowel for Japanese speakers' data, while Korean speakers' data showed no such significant effects at the same position [$p=.000$ for Japanese; $p=.192$ for Korean]. These results show that there were strong carryover F2 effects in Japanese, but not in Korean, quite compatible with the prediction on coarticulation. On the other hand, at the onset of steady state, there were significant coarticulatory effects for vowel type [$F(1,116)=5.39$, $p=.02$], language type [$F(1,116)=47.35$, $p=.000$], but no significant interaction between these two factors [$F(1,116)=1.34$, $p=.25$]. Post hoc Tukey tests reveal that neither Korean nor Japanese showed significant coarticulatory effects in F2 values [$p=.72$ for Japanese; $p=.84$ for Korean]. These results indicate that coarticulatory effects of the preceding vowel to the target vowel in VCV context were not maintained through the vowel steady state.

Figure 2 shows the averaged F2 values in the vowel of /a/ following /a/ vs. /i/. Again the vowel /i/ has a high F2, while /a/ has a low F2, and thus the coarticulatory effect of an adjacent vowel /i/ on the target vowel /a/ will be manifested as a higher F2.

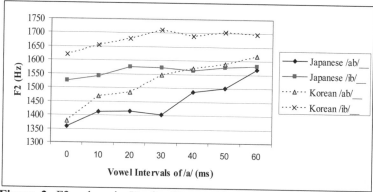

Figure 2. F2 values in Hz for Korean (dashed line) and Japanese (solid line) speakers' production of [a] from the vowel onset (0 ms) to its onset of steady state (60 ms) when it is preceded by /a/ or /i/.

A visual comparison of the second formant frequency changes over time indicates that both Korean and Japanese speakers showed a considerable difference in F2 values at the early stage of the second vowel. At the onset of the vowel, speakers of both languages showed more than 100 Hz difference in F2, suggesting that there were great coarticulatory effects from /i/ to /a/. However, these F2 differences seemed to diminish or disappear at the onset of vowel steady state.

An ANOVA was done to see significant main effects of the V-to-V coarticulation at two points, vowel onset (0ms point) and onset of steady state (60ms point). At vowel onset, there were significant effects of vowel type [$F(1,115)=24.25$, $p=.000$], but not of language type [$F(1,115)=1.89$, $p=.17$] and their interaction [$F(1,115)=.83$, $p=.36$]. Post hoc Tukey tests showed that both Korean and Japanese speakers showed significant coarticulatory effects at the vowel onset [$p=.03$ for Japanese; $p=.000$ for Korean]. Thus it could be said that coarticulatory effects were clearly found at the vowel onset for both languages. On the other hand, at the onset of steady state, there were significant effects on vowel type [$F(1,115)=9.4$, $p=.000$], and language type [$F(1,115)=12.03$, $p=.001$], but not their interaction [$F(1,115)=.41$, $p=.53$]. Post hoc Tukey tests revealed that Korean speakers showed significant coarticulatory effects in F2 values only marginally, but no such effects for Japanese speakers [$p=.32$ for Japanese; $p=.05$ for Korean]. It seems that coarticulatory effects were not clearly shown to maintain through the vowel steady state.

2.3. Discussion

Summarizing the results of Experiment 1, first, at the vowel onset, there were great effects of carryover coarticulation for both languages, namely, the F2 values of the second vowel in VCV context were greatly influenced by the preceding vowel, even though these F2 differences disappeared at the vowel steady state. Second, Japanese and Korean differed in the amount of the acoustic effects of V-to-V coarticulation. If we look at the general pattern of coarticulatory effects over time, the predicted pattern is largely upheld: Japanese speakers showed consistently larger F2 differences than Korean between the target vowel and the context vowel in the relationship between /i/ and /o/, but less between /i/ and /a/. Statistical results showed that language differences were found in the case of /i/ following /i/ or /o/, but only marginally when /o/ follows /i/ or /o/. There were no significant coarticulatory effects in the case where /a/ follows /i/ or /a/.

These results seem to be largely in accord with the previous claim by Manuel (1987, 1999) that languages with a relatively crowded vowel space show weaker V-to-V coarticulatory effects. In Manuel (1987, 1999), Shona and Ndebele with five vowel systems, and Sotho with seven vowels were compared in anticipatory coariculation. The vowels in these three languages were equally crowded with four vowels such as /i, e, o, u/, but they were more crowded in the low and mid vowel region for Sotho (with three vowels) than they were for Shona and Ndebele (with only /a/). Given the fact that the vowel /ɛ/ intervenes between /e/ and /a/, it was expected that /e/ and /a/ were less susceptible to anticipatory coarticulation in Sotho than in the other two languages, and these expectations were generally borne out.

As shown in (1), Korean had greater numbers of vowel phonemes in the high and mid regions than Japanese, while in the low region, both languages have only one vowel, /a/. Due to the crowdedness of vowel space in non-low regions, Korean speakers showed less coarticulatory effects than Japanese from the first vowel to the second vowel in VCV context, when the first vowel is /i/ and the second is /o/. On the other hand, when the target vowel is /a/, Korean speakers as well as Japanese speakers were likely to be free with coarticulation, because they rarely ran a risk of losing contrasts due to coarticulation. Following the hypothesis that speakers are actually sensitive to the specific regions of the vowel space, not overall crowdedness of the vowel space in a language, the results of the acoustic analysis in the present study seem to support the previous claim.

3. Experiment 2: Perception Experiment

3.1. Methods

To prohibit the contextual information of the real words from influencing the listeners' responses, English non-words were provided to each language listener for discrimination. Based on Beddor et al. (2002), disyllables ['CV$_1$CV$_2$] were created whose vowels involved all possible combinations of [i, e, a, o, u] and the consonant was [b] (e.g., ['CiCa], ['CuCe], ['CaCo]). Multiple randomizations of the 25 disyllables embedded in a frame sentence such as 'Say ___ softly' were recorded by a native American English (GAE) speaker (female), who is a trained phonetician, but totally naïve to the purpose of the present study. Three repetitions of the whole 25 disyllables were recorded and a representative sample of test words was selected, based on the acoustic properties of each vowel and consonant, and also the overall intonational pattern of the frame sentences. When she recorded the stimuli, she was asked to produce the vowels in the unstressed position as not reduced to a schwa.

In creating the stimuli for a perception experiment, the ['CV$_1$CV$_2$] disyllables were excised from the frame sentence, and then the target syllables [CV$_2$] were excised from the disyllables with the entire vocalic portion and the preceding stop (closure and the burst plus VOT). These excised syllables were spliced into new contexts ['CV$_1$___] and the resulting cross-spliced disyllables were paired in a 4IAX design to be presented to the listeners. Target vowels in paired disyllables were phonologically identical, only differing in coarticulatory effects. To simplify the tasks, only the pairings whose vowel formant differences were large enough were included in the stimuli types (Beddor et al., 2002). The stimuli for a perception experiment were also based on the pilot testing with the native English speakers who were naïve to the purpose of the present study. Pairings were excluded if native listeners' accuracy fell below 70% correct on control trials. As shown in (2) and (3), experimental stimuli were composed of 10 pairings of coarticulatory effects.

(2) Stimuli types and F1 and F2 differences (Hz) at vowel onset for English vowel pairings

V$_1$	V$_2$	Vowel parings	F1	F2
/i/	/a/	$_i$a-$_a$a	-104	517
	/o/	$_i$o-$_o$o	-7	315
/e/	/a/	$_e$a-$_a$a	-58	302
	/o/	$_e$o-$_o$o	-49	265
/a/	/e/	$_a$e-$_e$e	19	135
	/o/	$_a$o-$_o$o	-8	99
/o/	/a/	$_o$a-$_a$a	-85	176
	/e/	$_o$e-$_e$e	-6	-481
/u/	/a/	$_u$a-$_a$a	-128	232
	/e/	$_u$e-$_e$e	-12	-46

(3) Stimuli for the 4IAX discrimination task

V2	control trial	test trial
$_i$a-$_a$a	bib$_i$a- bib$_i$a / bib$_i$a-bib$_a$a	bab$_i$a-bib$_i$a / bab$_a$a-bib$_i$a
$_i$o-$_o$o	bib$_i$o-bib$_i$o / bib$_i$o-bib$_o$o	bob$_i$o-bib$_i$o / bob$_o$o-bib$_i$o
$_e$a-$_a$a	beb$_e$a-beb$_e$a / beb$_e$a-beb$_a$a	bab$_e$a-beb$_e$a / bab$_a$a-beb$_e$a
$_e$o-$_o$o	beb$_e$o-beb$_e$o / beb$_e$o-beb$_o$o	bob$_e$o-beb$_e$o / bob$_o$o-beb$_e$o
$_a$e-$_e$e	bab$_a$e-bab$_a$e / bab$_a$e-bab$_e$e	beb$_a$e-bab$_a$e / beb$_e$e-bab$_a$e
$_a$o-$_o$o	bab$_a$o-bab$_a$o / bab$_a$o-bab$_o$o	bob$_a$o-bab$_a$o / bob$_o$o-bab$_a$o
$_o$a-$_a$a	bob$_o$a-bob$_o$a / bob$_o$a-bob$_a$a	bab$_o$a-bob$_o$a / bab$_a$a-bob$_o$a
$_o$e-$_e$e	bob$_o$e-bob$_o$e / bob$_o$e-bob$_e$e	beb$_o$e-bob$_o$e / beb$_e$e-bob$_o$
$_u$a-$_a$a	bub$_u$a-bub$_u$a / bub$_u$a-bub$_a$a	bab$_u$a-bub$_u$a / bab$_a$a-bub$_u$a
$_u$e-$_e$e	bub$_u$e-bub$_u$e / bub$_u$e-bub$_e$e	beb$_u$e-bub$_u$e / beb$_e$e-bub$_u$e

In all trial types, the V_2s of one pair were acoustically identical and the V_2s of the other pair were acoustically different, even though all V_2s in a trial were phonologically identical. The control trials were for verifying that the coarticulatory effects were discriminable, and thus it was expected that the listeners performed well on these trials. The test trials examined whether listeners depended their discrimination of vowels on the coarticulatory contexts. For each test trial, the V_2s of the pair with acoustically different vowels were both in coarticulatorily appropriate contexts (e.g., [bab$_a$a-bob$_o$a]), while one of the V_2s of the pair with acoustically identical vowels was in a coarticulatorily inappropriate context (e.g., [bab$_a$a-bob$_i$a]).

Based on the widely accepted view that the introductory level of L2 learners are greatly affected by their own L1, the introductory level of Korean and Japanese learners of English were recruited from various sources. They were either college or graduate students at Cornell University or Tompkins Cortland Community College, or the spouses of the graduate students at Cornell University, all of whom were taking the introductory level of English classes in BOCES, a non-profit institute at Ithaca, New York. All of them had lived in the United States less than two years when they participated in the experiment. Participants were 20 native Korean-speaking subjects (aged 20 through 40) and 22 native Japanese-speaking subjects (aged 23 through 35). The listeners' English proficiency levels in speaking and listening were checked based on the results of the short listening test, comprising of 45 questions. The subjects were paid for their participation.

Randomized test words were presented to the two groups of listeners, Korean and Japanese. Half of the test trials contained coarticulatorily inappropriate V_2s in the first pairs (beb$_u$e-bub$_u$e / beb$_e$e-bub$_u$e) and the other contained them in the second pairs (beb$_e$e-bub$_u$e / beb$_u$e-bub$_u$e). Thus the stimuli listeners heard were 120 trials (10 vowel pairings x 3 tokens (control trial, 2 types of test trials) x 4 repetitions). The perception task was programmed and run on a Dell Dimension 4300 computer with Creative Labs SoundBlaster 5.1, using E-Prime Version 1.0 (Psychological Software Tools 2002). The numbers of correct responses to the stimuli were computed. All subjects were instructed that they were going to hear the English non-word pairs and choose the pair in which the second vowels sounded 'more different'. Each listener heard all test sequences over SONY (MDR-CD160) headphones and responded by pressing one of the two keys arranged horizontally on the number pad in the keyboard, using the fingers of the right hand: they were asked to hit the key '4' when hearing the left pair had the words whose second vowels were more different, and '6' when hearing the right pair had more different vowels. First, they heard 10 practice items, which were followed by a control trial and then test trials. All trials had 0.5s of the within-pair intervals, 1s of the inter-pair intervals, and 3s of the inter-trial intervals. After all trials, they took a short listening test with 45 questions to check their English proficiency. The average scores of the listening test were 35 out of 45 for Korean listeners, and 33 out of 45 for Japanese listeners. Additionally listeners whose accuracy fell below 70% on the control trial were excluded from the analysis. Thus analyses were based on the responses of 19 native Korean listeners and 18 native Japanese listeners.

3.2. Results

Figure 3 gives the pooled responses of the two language listeners to ten vowel pairings in the control condition. Figure 3 shows that both Korean and Japanese listeners performed well, successfully perceiving the coarticulatory effects. Specifically Korean speakers accurately selected the correct response at an average rate of 89.5% correct, and Japanese speakers showed similar results with a slightly higher score (on average, 90.1% correct).

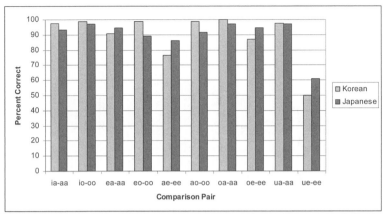

Figure 3. Pooled percent correct responses of the Korean and Japanese listeners to the English 4IAX tests of discrimination of carryover coarticulatory effects at each type of vowel pairings for the control condition.

Apparently these results indicate that discriminating the vowel differences based on F2 values was not inherently difficult for either group of language listeners. An ANOVA showed no main effect of listener language (Korean vs. Japanese) [$F(1,1460)=.215$, $p>.05$], even though it showed a main effect of vowel pairing types [$F(9,1460)=33.06$, $p=.000$], and also significant interaction between the listener language and vowel pairing types [$F(9,1460)=2.48$, $p<.05$].

Based on the results of the previous studies, we expect that even in the control condition, Japanese speakers would show higher scores than Korean speakers, but the differences between these two languages were not significant. These results could be explained by the fact that as Beddor et al. (2002) pointed out, in control condition, context is held constant and compensation is thus not at issue, which made listeners be more accurate on vowel pairs with large and salient acoustic differences. However, these same large differences could mislead listeners if they reflect systematic coarticulatory effects in the listeners' native language. In this respect, the weak coarticulatory effects for the vowel pair 'ue-ee' are worthy to mention here. As shown in (3), the formant frequency differences of the target vowel (V_2) and the context vowel (V_1) in English 'ue-ee' were relatively small as compared to those of other vowel types; provided with relatively small and less salient acoustic differences of the formant values, both Korean and Japanese listeners showed poor discrimination.

The Korean and Japanese listeners' pooled responses to the ten vowel pairings in the experimental condition were shown in Figure 4.

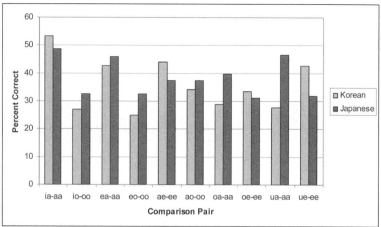

Figure 4. Pooled percent correct responses of the Korean and Japanese listeners to the English 4IAX tests of discrimination of carryover coarticulatory effects at each type of vowel pairings for the experimental condition.

Contrary to the expectation, both listeners in both languages revealed difficulties in discriminating the vowels based on coarticulatory effects. A two-way ANOVA tested for listener language (Korean and Japanese), vowel pairing types, and their interaction. The ANOVA results showed that there was no significant effect of listener language [$F(1, 2940)=.731, p>.05$]. However, there was a main effect of vowel pairing types [$F(9, 2940)=5.831, p<.05$], and also the interaction of the listener language and vowel types [$F(9, 2940)= 2.53, p<.05$].

To see the patterns of the interaction of the listener language and vowel types more specifically, a one-way ANOVA was run for each vowel pairing type separately, and the results are as shown in (4).

(4) Statistical results

ia-aa	$F(1, 294)=1.64, p>.05$	io-oo	$F(1, 294)=.653, p>.05$
ea-aa	$F(1, 294)=.281, p>.05$	eo-oo	$F(1, 294)=1.75, p>.05$
ae-ee	$F(1, 294)=1.95, p>.05$	ao-oo	$F(1, 294)=.346, p>.05$
oa-aa	$F(1, 294)=2.86, p>.05$	oe-ee	$F(1, 294)=.303, p>.05$
ua-aa	$F(1, 294)=10.13, p<.05$	ue-ee	$F(1, 294)=3.71, p<.05$

These results show that only the vowel pairings 'ua-aa' and 'ue-ee' (as represented as the last two column pairs in Figure 4) showed a significant difference, and the other pairs were not shown to be significantly different in responses. However, the results for 'ua-aa' pairing showed that Korean listeners exhibited a higher score, while Japanese listeners showed a higher score in the vowel pair of 'ue-ee'. Thus accommodation for coarticulatory patterns was not seen to be consistent. Namely, Korean and Japanese listeners did not differ consistently in how they responded to the stimuli in the experimental condition.

3.3. Discussion

We expected that Japanese listeners would show more compensatory responses than Korean listeners, making more mistakes consistent with judging vowel similarity on the basis of coarticulatory appropriateness rather than acoustic property of the vowel. This expectation was based on the results of the production study that overall Japanese speakers showed large spatio-temporal effect of carryover V-to-V coarticulation mainly due to less crowded vowel space in Japanese.

However, more compensation for the Japanese listeners was not found. Even though they performed quite successfully in discrimination in the control condition, they showed poor discrimination in the experimental setting. All listeners' scores representing the accuracy in identifying the target vowel based on the coarticulatory context fell below the chance level, except for one vowel pairing for Korean listeners. Thus the listeners participating in the present study, either Japanese or Korean, appeared to have great difficulties to get the information from the context. These results suggest that even though systematic language-specific differences were observed in the carryover V-to-V coarticulatory patterns for Korean and Japanese speakers, these differences were not directly linked to their patterns of perceptual compensation.

4. Conclusion

The present study was designed to test the hypothesis that either production or perception in V-to-V carryover coarticulatory effects is driven by language-specific phonological structure. Contrary to the previous research findings, the results of the present study are indefinite.

First, the results of the acoustic analysis (Experiment 1) provide evidence for the view that the amount and the pattern of V-to-V carryover coarticulation are affected by language-specific phonological structure. Specifically the production of carryover V-to-V coarticulation by Korean and Japanese speakers was shown to be influenced by language-specific vowel contrast. Japanese speakers who have less crowded vowel space in non-low vowel region showed stronger carryover coarticulation effects than Korean in V-to-V context. On the other hand, the vowel in the low region, /a/, which is equally uncrowded in Korean and Japanese, was freely coarticulated in both languages. Thus the results of the production study are largely compatible with the previous claim on language-specific coarticulation.

However, the results of the perception experiment (Experiment 2) indicate that even though listeners seemed to be sensitive to acoustic differences due to coarticulatory effects, they were not shown to be directly affected by their phonological structure in judging the similarity of vowels. Given the fact that Japanese showed less crowded vowel space than Korean, it was expected that when they judged the similarity of the English unstressed vowel, which was preceded by another stressed vowel, Japanese listeners made more mistakes based on coarticulatory context rather than acoustic property. However, both language listeners showed similar responses to the stimuli, and their performance consistently fell below 50% correct. These results suggest that even though systematic language-specific differences were observed in the carryover V-to-V coarticulatory patterns for Korean and Japanese speakers, these differences were not directly linked to their patterns of perceptual compensation.

The results of the present study are contrary to those of the previous studies (Beddor and Krakow 1999, Beddor et al. 2002) where listeners were quite good at using contextual information to identify the target segment. They claim that contextual variability is actually a rich source of information about the target segment, because contextual variability is highly predictable. Bradlow (2002) is also supportive to this approach by showing that even clear speech involves the maintenance of coarticulation, even though her data are only based on production. However, as demonstrated by the present study, the listeners' perception of coarticulated speech was not simply attuned to native language coarticulatory patterns, even though their productions largely showed language-specific patterns. As pointed out by Beddor and Krakow (1999), Beddor et al. (2002) and Pierrehumbert (2003), perceptual compensation is not complete. It seems likely that listeners attribute some acoustic variation to its coarticulatory source, but not all of it. The contextual information from coarticulatory effects facilitates perceptual decisions, but it does not provide all the information listeners could compensate perfectly.

References

Alfonso, P. and T. Baer. 1982. Dynamics of Vowel Articulation. *Language and Speech* 25: 151-173.

Beddor, P. and R. Krakow. 1999. Perception of Coarticulatory Nasalization by Speakers of English and Thai: Evidence for Partial Compensation. *Journal of the Acoustical Society of America* 106: 2868-2887.

Beddor, P., R. Krakow and S. Lindemann. 2001. Patterns of Perceptual Compensation and Their Phonological Consequences. *The Role of Speech Perception in Phonology*, eds. E. Hume & K. Johnson, 55-78. Academic Press.

Beddor, P., J. Harnsberger and S. Lindemann. 2002. Language-Specific Patterns of Vowel-to-Vowel Coarticulation: Acoustic Structures and Their Perceptual Correlates. *Journal of Phonetics* 30: 591-627.

Bradlow, A. R. 2002. Confluent Talker- and Listener-Oriented forces in Clear Speech Production. *Laboratory Phonology* 7, eds. C. Gussenhoven & N. Warner, 241-273. Berlin & New York: Mouton de Gruyter.

Choi, J. 1992. Phonetic Underspecification and Target Interpolation: An Acoustic Study of Marshallese Vowel Allophony. PhD dissertation, UCLA.

Choi, J. 1995. An Acoustic-Phonetic Underspecification Account of Marshallese Vowel Allophony. *Journal of Phonetics* 23: 323-247.

Dahan, E., J. S. Magnuson, M. K. Tanenhause, and E. M. Hogan. 2001. Subcategorical Mismatches and the Time Course of Lexical Access: Evidence for Lexical Competition. *Spoken Word Access Processes, Special Issue of Language and Cognitive Process* 16(5-6), eds. J. M. McQueen & A. Cutler, 507-534. Psychology Press.

Fowler, C. 1981. Production and Perception of Coarticulation Among Stressed and Unstressed Vowels. *Journal of Speech and Hearing Research* 46: 127-139.

Fowler, C. 1984. Segmentation of Coarticulated Speech in Perception. *Perceptual Psychophysics* 36: 259-368.

Fowler, C. and M. Smith. 1986. Speech Perception as Vector Analysis: An Approach to the Problems of Segmentation and Invariance. *Invariance and Variability of Speech Processes*, eds. J. Perkell & D. Klatt, 123-139. Hillsdale, NJ: Erlbaum.

Magen, H. 1984. Vowel-to-Vowel Coarticulation in English and Japanese. *Journal of the Acoustical Society of America* 75, S41.

Magen, H. 1997. The Extent of Vowel-to-Vowel Coarticulation in English. *Journal of Phonetics* 25: 187-205.

Manuel, S. 1987. Acoustic and Perceptual Consequences of Vowel-to-Vowel Coarticulation in Three Bantu Languages. PhD dissertation, Yale University, New Haven, CT.

Manuel, S. 1990. The Role of Contrast in Limiting Vowel-to-Vowel Coarticulation in Different Languages. *Journal of the Acoustical Society of America* 88(3): 1286-1298.

Manuel, S. 1999. Cross-Language Studies: Relating Language-Particular Coarticulation Patterns to Other Language-Particular Facts. *Coarticulation: Theory, Data, and Techniques*, eds. W. Hardcastle & N. Hewlett, 179-198. Cambridge, U.K.: Cambridge University Press.

Manuel, S. and R. Krakow. 1984. Universal and Language Particular Aspects of Vowel-to-Vowel Coarticulation. *Haskins Laboratories Status Reports on Speech Research* SR-77/78: 69-78.

Nakajou, O. 1989. *Nihongo-no Onin-to Akusento* [Phonology and Accentuation of Japanese]. Tokyo: Keisou Shobou.

Pierrehumbert, J. 2003. Phonetic Diversity, Statistical Learning, and Acquisition of Phonology. *Language and Speech* 46(2-3): 115-154.

Shin, J. 2000. *Malsoliuy Ihay [Understanding Speech Sounds]*. Seoul, Korea: Hankwukmwunhwasa.

van Heuven, V. and M. Dupuis. 1991. Perception of Anticipatory VCV-Coarticulation: Effects of Vowel Context and Accent Distribution. *Proceedings of the Twelfth International Congress of Phonetic Sciences* 78-81, Aix-en-Provence, France: Universite de Provence.

Whalen, D. H. 1990. Coarticulation is Largely Planned. *Journal of Phonetics* 18: 3-35.

Peculiar Accentuation of Prefixes in Pusan Korean and Its Implications*

HO-KYUNG JUN

Kyushu University

1. Introduction

It is well known that when two words are combined into a phrase in Japanese, the accent of the first noun is deleted and the one in the second survives as in (1). That is, complex words form one phonological phrase. Accentual patterns of compound and prefixed words in Japanese are shown in (1).

(1)   a.   syákai + séedo → syakáíséedo (*syákaiséedo)
               'society' 'system'   'social system'
    b.   síN + seékátú → siNséekatu (*síNseékátsú)
              'new' 'life'   'new life'

---

* The work in this paper was presented at the Atami Phonology Festa (1st Joint Meeting of PAIK and TCP) in Japan (March 10, 2006) and at the 16th Japanese/Korean Linguistics Conference (October 7-9, 2006). I express my gratitude to Tomoyuki Kubo, Haruo Kubozono and Toshio Matsuura for useful comments and discussion. My deep thanks also go to Kyushu University Linguistics Department and Joan Chen-Main for checking this manuscript. Any remaining errors are my own.

193

However, based on the accentual patterns of certain Japanese prefixes, Poser (1990) argues that these prefixes, which he refers to as 'Aoyagi prefixes', typically belong to a separate minor phrase from the stem to which they attach, as in (2).

(2)   Aoyagi prefixes (Poser 1990).

a.	móto-	'former'	móto-dáiziN	'former minister'
b.	zéN-	'former'	zéN-syusyóó	'former Prime Minister'
c.	hí-	'un-'	hí-goórítékí	'illogical'
d.	kí-	'your'	kí-syokáN	'your letter' (honorific/formal)

Poser argues that the peculiarity of these words in (2) lies in the fact that they exhibit HLH or HLHL tone patterns, which are not possible for single minor phrases. For example, in the case of *móto-dáiziN* in (2a), the fall from *mo* to *to* indicates the presence of an accent on the first syllable. However, the pitch rises again and then falls, indicating the presence of a second accent on *dai*.

In this paper, I claim that some Sino-Korean prefixes and family names in Korean form independent phonological phrases in the same way as Aoyagi prefixes in Japanese. However, these Sino-Korean prefixes and family names in Korean show different behaviors from that of Aoyagi prefixes in Japanese; they are assigned flip-flop tones with respect to the tone that immediately follows. In this case, tone is not specified underlyingly, but is specifed on the basis of the tonal information, i.e., H or L, of the follwing syllable.

The rest of the the paper proceeds as follows. I will briefly take a look at Pusan Korean accentual patterns of native words in section 2. In section 3, typical vs. peculiar accentuation of Sino-Korean prefixes are presented. Finally, in secetion 4, I will show accentual patterns of person names in Pusan Korean, which have the same phonological properties as Pusan Aoyagi prefixes.

2. Pusan Korean accentual patterns in native words

Before examining Pusan Aoyagi prefixes and family names, I will briefly overview accentual patterns of simplex and complex native nouns in this section.

First, let us consider the accentual patterns of simplex nouns. As shown in (3), four patterns are realized in disyllabic and trisyllabic native simplex nouns according to my analysis. The words in isolation are shown in (3a). The words formed by adding by particles such as *-e.nin.* are shown in (3b). The number of accentual patterns in native nouns basically increases as the number of syllables increases. The accentual patterns of native words should be specified in the lexicon.

(3) Simplex nouns

    a. Nouns

Di-syllabic	ká.cí 'branch'	ka.cí 'eggplant'	a.cʰím 'morning'	á.tɨ.l 'son'
Tri-syllabic	mú.cí.ke 'rainbow'	cin.tɨ́.kí 'tick'	so.ná.ki 'shower'	á.ci.me 'aunt'

    b. Nouns + *e.nɨn* ('*-e.nɨn*' is a combination of '*-e*' (dative marker) and '*nɨn*' (topic marker))

Di-syllabic	ká.cí-e.nɨn	ka.cí-é.nɨn	a.cʰí.m-e.nɨn	á.tɨ.l-e.nɨn
Tri-syllabic	mú.cí.ke-e.nɨn	cin.tɨ́.kí-e.nɨn	so.ná.ki-e.nɨn	á.ci.me-e.nɨn

Let us explain how these patterns are classified in (3). In the case of the words in the second column in (3a), A sequence of two high tone is realized on the first and sencond syllables (e.g., *mú.cí.ke* 'rainbow'). In the case of the trisyllabic words in the third column in (3a), a sequence of two high tones is realized on the second and the third syllables (e.g., *cin.tɨ́.kí* 'tick'). In disyllabic words in the same column, high tone is realized on the second syllable in isolation (*ka.cí* 'eggplant'). When particles such as -*e.nɨn* are added as shown in (3b), high tone is realized on the second and third syllables (e.g., *ka.cí-é.nɨn*). In the case of the words in the forth column, high tone is realized on the second syllable (e.g., *so.ná.ki* 'shower'). Finally, in the case of the words in the fifth column in (3a), high tone is realized on the first syllable (e.g., *á.ci.me* 'aunt'). Note that no simplex words show two separate high tones, i.e., *HLH or *HLHL.

Let us move on to the complex nouns. It is important to note that the accentual pattern of one word usually survives while the other is deleted; that is, they form one accentual phrase, as shown in (4).

(4) Complex nouns

    a. kkóc + cíp → kkoc.cíp
        'flower' 'house'   'flower shop'

    b. ə.lin.i + cíp → ə.lin.i.cip
        'child' 'house'   'nursery school'

So far, we have observed that there is only one H or one sequence of H's both in simplex native nouns and in complex native nouns. In other words, neither HLH nor HLHL is possible for a single phonological phrase in Pusan Korean. Given this, I assume that two separate high tones indicate two phonological phrases.

In contrast to the observations above, some Sino-Korean prefixes and family names show peculiar accentual patterns in compounding, which I will present in the next section.

3. Typical vs. Peculiar Accentuation of Sino-Korean Prefixes

Though we will examine a class of exceptions below, Sino-Korean prefixed words and native ones generally show the same accentual patterns, as shown in (5); (i) the accentual patterns are realized as L-HL (e.g., *nìc-yə́.lìm* 'late summer', *ka-mún.sə* 'forged document') or L-HH (*nìc-ká.ìl* 'late autumn', *ka-kən.múl* 'temporary building'), which are the same as the ones observed in native simplex nouns in (3); and (ii) these prefixed words form one phonological phrase, as is the case for compound nouns, as shown in (4).

(5)   Typical accentuation of prefixed words

a.   Native prefixes (-*i/ka* is the nominative marker)

Native prefix		Prefixed word
nìc- 'late'	yə́.lìm-i 'summer'	nìc-yə́.lìm-i 'late summer'
	ka.íl-i 'autumn'	nìc-ká.ìl-i 'late autumn'
hotʰ- 'single layer'	í.pul-i 'bedclothes'	hotʰ-í.pul-i 'sheet'
	cʰi.má-ka 'skirt'	hotʰ-cʰí.má-ka 'unlined skirt'

b.   Sino-Korean prefixes

Sino-Korean prefix		Prefixed word
ka- 'temporary' 仮	mún.sə-ka 'document'	ka-mún.sə-ka 'forged document'
	kən.múl-í 'building'	ka-kən.múl-i 'temporary building'
nan- 'difficulty' 難	kóŋ.sa-ka 'construction'	nan-kóŋ.sa-ka 'difficult construction'
	mun.cé-ká 'problem'	nan-mún.cé-ka 'difficult problem'

In contrast, some Sino-Korean prefixes (henceforth, Pusan Aoyagi prefixes) show peculiar accentuation: (i) the accentual patterns as in (6), such as HLH, are not the same as the ones obsereved in native nouns in (3); (ii) the prefixed words as in (6) form two phonological phrases; and (iii) Pusan Aoyagi prefixes are assigned flip-flop tones with respect to the tone that immediately follows.

(6)   Peculiar Accentuation of Pusan Aoyagi prefixes[1]

Pusan Aoyagi prefixes		Prefixed words
a. pan- 'anti-' 反	mí.kuk-i 'America'	pan-mí.kuk-i 'anti-America'
	koŋ.kún-í 'air force'	pán-koŋ.kún-í 'anti-air force'
b. pəm- 'all' 凡	cí.kú-ka 'earth'	pəm-cí.kú-ka 'worldwide'
	in.lyú-ka 'mankind'	pə́m-in.lyú-ka 'all mankind'
c. kwi- 貴 'your (honorific)'	ín.heŋ-i 'bank'	kwi-ín.heŋ-i 'your bank'
	koŋ.cáŋ-i 'factory'	kwí-koŋ.cáŋ.i 'your company'
d. te- 'against' 対	íl.pón-i 'Japan'	te-íl.pón-i 'against Japan'
	ho.cú-ká 'Austrailia'	té-ho.cú-ká 'against Austrailia'
e. ce- '[prefix for or dinal numbers]' 第	síp.íl-i 'eleven'	ce-síp.íl-i 'eleventh'
	i.síp-í 'twenty'	cé-i.síp-í 'twentieth'

The accentual pattern of the prefixed words highlighted in (6), such as *pán-koŋ.kún-i* 'anti-air force-NOM,' are realized as H-LH, which is not possible for a single phonological phrase in Pusan Korean. This fact indicates that these prefixes form a phonological phrase independently, i.e., (*pán*) (*koŋ.kún*). This is the same behavior triggered by 'Aoyagi prefixes' in Japanese (henceforth, Japanese Aoyagi prefixes). However, note that Pusan

---

[1] List of Pusan Aoyagi prefixes: *pon-* 'this, present', *hyən-* 'current', *ko-* 'late, deceased', *pi-* 'non-', *toŋ* 'above mentioned', *kak-* 'each', *seŋ-* 'unprocessed', *cʰoŋ-* 'entire', *tʰa-* 'different', *cu-* 'main', *pʰi-* '[prefix for passive voice]', *tʰal-* 'out of'

Aoyagi prefixes are realized as either a low tone or a high tone, whereas the tone of Japanese Aoyagi prefixes are not changable. They are assigned flip-flop tones with respect to the tone that immediately follows. i.e., consider *pan.mí.kuk-i* 'anti-America-NOM' vs. *pán-koŋ.kún-i* 'anti-air force-NOM'. *pan* 'anti-' is realized as either a high tone (e.g., *pán-koŋ.kún-i*) or a low tone (e.g., *pan.mí.kuk* 'anti-America') depending on the tone of the immediately following syllable. To account for the phenomenon in (6), I propose (7) and (8) and assume that Pusan Aoyagi prefixes are marked with [+PA].

(7)   Prefix[+PA] Phonological Phrase Formation (PPPF): Form a phonological phrase for a prefix[+PA].

(8)   Flip-flop tone rule for X (Prefix[+PA]), which appears in the enviroment [X [Y Z]]:
       a.   If the tone of Y is high, then assign low tone to X: (L)-(H..)
       b.   If the tone of Y is low, then assign high tone to X: (H)-(L..)

          (X)   (Y...
            | |
        [-α high] [α high]

4. Accentual patterns of person names in Pusan Korean

In this section, I present the observation that family names have the same phonological properties as Pusan Aoyagi prefixes.

Characteristics of person names in Korean are: (i) the family name appears first and the given name second, i.e., *pe-yoŋ.cun*; and (ii) person names usually consist of three syllables, that is, the first one is for family name and the other two are for given name. See below:

(9)   Accentual patterns of full names in Pusan Korean[2]

       a.   L-HH (L)   b.   H-LH (H)
             kim-mín.sú-ka   kím-ce.ú-ká
             kim-ók.cú-ka   kím-mi.kyəŋ-í

       c.   H-LH (L)   d.   L-HL (L)
             kím-ɨn.cín-i   kim-ɨn.cu-ka
             kím-səŋ.kyəŋ-i   kim-səŋ.ho-ka

Four accentual patterns are obsereved in full names. Note that some of the accentual patterns, such as H-LH in (9b-c) are not possible for native words.

---

[2] The data examined consisted of 548 person names. The analysis of accentual patterns is based on my own intuitions.

4.1 Accentual patterns of family names

Family names belong to the same group as Pusan Aoyagi prefixes with respect to their phonological properties: (i) they form independent phonological phrases; and (ii) they are assigned flip-flop tones with respect to the tone of the given name that immediately follows.

(10)   Accentual patterns of given names in Pusan Korean[3]

Patterns / Name	a) HH (L..)	b) LH (HL..)	c) LH (L..)	d) HL (L..)
Name	mín.sú-ka	ce.ú-ká	ín.cín-i	ín.cu-ka
	ók.cú-ka	mi.kyəŋ-í	səŋ.kyə́ŋ-i	sə́ŋ.ho-ka

These four patterns in (10) are the same as the ones observed in native words as in (3).

---

[3] Furthermore, I found that the accentual patterns of given names are predictable from the initial element. Jun (2006) proposes that the accentual pattern of the given name is determined by the accentual pattern of the initial element.

Accentual patterns of initial element	A	B	C	
Given name + nominative marker	mín.ú-ka	ce.ú-ká	ín.cu-ka	
	mín.sə́k-i	ce.tík-í	ín.ok-i	
	mín.cʰə́l-i	ce.cʰə́l-í	ín.sil-i	
	mín.pə́m-i	ce.pə́m-í		in.pə́m-i
	mín.cún-i	ce.ín-í		in.cín-i
	mín.kyə́ŋ-i	ce.hóŋ-í		in.kyə́ŋ-i
Accentual patterns of Given names	A	B	C	D

a. If Given names begin with the same initial element, they fall into the same accentual pattern irrespective the final element, e.g, *mín.ú-ka, mín.sə́k-i, mín.cʰə́l-i, mín.pə́m-i*.
b.When the accentual pattern of the initial element is pattern C, the accentual pattern of the given name falls into either pattern C or D. Pattern C and D show complementary distribution depending on the coda in the final element. I assume that pattern C is specified underlyingly and it surfaces as pattern D when the given name ends in -m, -n, -ŋ, e.g., *ín.ok-i* vs. *in.pə́m-i, in.cín-i, in.kyə́ŋ-i*

(11)   Accentuation of family names in Pusan Korean

Family name		Given name	Full name
kim 金	a)	mín.sú-ka	kim-mín.sú-ka
		ók.cú-ka	kim-ók.cú-ka
	b)	ce.ú-ká	kím-ce.ú-ká
		mi.kyəŋ-í	kím-mi.kyəŋ-í
	c)	ìn.cu-ka	kim-ìn.cu-ka
		sə́ŋ.ho-ka	kim-sə́ŋ.ho-ka
	d)	ìn.cín-i	kím-ìn.cín-i
		səŋ.kyə́ŋ-i	kím-səŋ.kyə́ŋ-i

The accentual patterns of person names highlighted in (11), such as *kím-ce.ú-ka´* are realized as HLH, which is not possible for a single phonological phrase in Pusan Korean. This fact indicates that the family name and the given name each form a phonological phrase independently, i.e., (*kím*)(*ce.ú*) in the same way as words formed with Pusan Aoyagi prefixes. Also, the family name, *kim,* is realized as either a low tone (e.g., *kim-mín.sú-ka*) or a high tone (e.g., *kím-ce.ú-ká*) with respect to the tone of the given name that immediately follows. There are other properties of family names also shared by Pusan Aoyagi prefixes: (i) person names, which consist by the family name and given name, are classified as Sino-Korean, since they can be written in Chinese characters[4]; and (ii) family names behave like bound morphemes, since they are not usually used in isolation. Therefore, I assume that person names have this [X [Y Z]] structure.

5. Conclusion

So far, I have shown that (i) in Pusan Korean, there are two types of elements like Japanese Aoyagi prefixes, i.e., Pusan Aoyagi prefixes and family names; (ii) they are similar to Japanese Aoyagi prefixes in that they form independent phonological phrases; and (iii) however, their accentuation is different from that of Japanese Aoyagi prefixes in that it is dependent on the tone of the immediately following syllable. Consider the following examples, where I compare Pusan Aoyagi prefix, *pan* 'anti' with Japanese Aoyagi prefix, *han* 'anti'. Both *pan* in Korean and *han* in Japanese correspond to the same Chinese character, 反.

---

[4] There are a few names which are not corresponding to the Chinese characters.

(12)   Pusan Aoyagi prefixes vs. Japanese Aoyagi prefixes

        Korean   Japanese

   a. (pán) (koŋkún)   (hán) (rikúgun)
       'anti-air force'   'anti-army'

   b. (pan) (yúkkún)   (hán) (káigun)
       'anti-army'   'anti-navy'

Let us briefly consider the further observation: when two Pusan Aoyagi prefixes are adjacent, as in (13), it is the first prefix that makes its own phonological phrase, not the second or third one, whereas Japanese Aoyagi prefixes always form a phonological phrase.

(13)   Korean   Japanese

   a. (pán) (pan-kóŋkún)   (hán) (hán) (rikúgun)
       'anti-anti-air force'   'anti-anti-army'

   b. (pán) (pan-yúkkún)   (hán) (hán) (káigun)
       'anti-anti-army'   'anti-anti-navy'

On the basis of these facts, I assume that in the case of Pusan Aoyagi prefixes, Prefix[+PA] Phonological Phrase Formation (PPPF) in (7) applies to the prefix which is in the highest node of the morphological structure. However, as for Japanese Aoyagi prefixes, the rule applies iteratively. These facts indicate that Pusan Aoyagi prefixes are highly dependent, not only with the respect to their dependency on the following tone, but also their formation of phonological phrases.

References

Jun, H. 2006. Factors affecting accentual patterns of person names in Pusan Korean. Paper presented at Atami Phonology Festa (1st Joint Meeting of PAIK and TCP), Japan, March 10, 2006.

Poser, W. J. 1990. Word-Internal Phrase Boundary in Japanese. *The Phonology-Syntax Connection*, eds. S. Inknelas and D. Zec, 278-287. Stanford: CSLI.

A Phonetic Duration-based Analysis of Loan Adaptation in Korean and Japanese[*]

MIRA OH
Chonnam National University

1. Introduction

Perceptual similarity plays a crucial role in loanword adaptation in finding the closest match between a source word and a phonotactically permissible output in the native language (Silverman 1992; Kang 2003). It can be determined by the phonetic details which are rarely or never contrastive in phonology of L1 (native language) or L2 (source language). For instance, stress in English affects perceptual similarity in loaning source words in Japanese and Korean although Korean and Japanese lack stress. The examples in (1) illustrate that only stressed lax vowels trigger vowel epenthesis in Korean and gemination in Japanese.

---

[*] I thank the audience at the 16th Japanese and Korean Linguistics conference held at Kyoto University. I would also like to specifically thank Haruo Kubozono and Junko Ito for discussion on various aspects of this paper. The usual disclaimers apply.

(1) a. Vowel epenthesis after word-final English stops in Korean
    i. Vowel epenthesis after a stressed lax vowel
       cut [kʰʌ tʰɨ] ~ [kʰʌ t]
    ii. No vowel epenthesis after an unstressed lax vowel
       gallop [kellʌ p] *[kellʌ pʰɨ]
  b. Gemination in English stop adaptation in Japanese
    i. Gemination after a stressed lax vowel (Shirai 2001)
       kitchen [kitʧ iN] *[kiʧ iN]
    ii. No gemination after an unstressed lax vowel (Kato 2005)
       support [sapo:to] *[sappo:to]

A question arises as to how much phonetic details influence perceptual similarity between languages with the different speech rhythm.[1] We aim to answer the question by examining loan adaptation in Japanese and Korean. (2) summarizes the claims made in this paper.

(2) a. Korean and Japanese speakers perceive the differences between tense and lax vowels, and stressed and unstressed vowels in English as phonetic duration.
  b. The apparently different modes of loan adaptation between Korean and Japanese are determined by output-to-output correspondence between subphonemic durations of vowels and consonants in the source and the native language.
  c. The phonetic duration-based analysis argues for the Phonetic Approach (Silverman 1992; Steriade 2001) as opposed to the Phonological Approach (LaCharité and Paradis 2005) to loan adaptation.
  d. Relative priority among acoustic cues for the purpose of enhancing perceptual similarity can be explained by the constraint ranking within the Optimality Theoretical framework.

This paper is organized as follows: First, we will review the previous studies on loan adaptation and provide a phonetic duration-based account of loan adaptation in Korean and Japanese. We further argue that a faithfulness ranking can be derived from perceptual similarity rankings within the framework of Optimality Theory. Then we will discuss the related issues and conclude the discussion.

---

[1] English is a stress-timed language, while Japanese is a mora-timed language and Korean a syllable-timed language (Pike 1945; Dauer 1983; de Jong 1994).

2. A phonetic duration-based account of loan adaptation

2.1 Loan adaptation in Korean

2.1.1 A vowel duration-based analysis of vowel epenthesis

Kang (2003) makes three observations on the likelihood of vowel insertion after a word-final postvocalic stop by examining a loanword list compiled by the Kwulipkwukeyenkwuwen (National Academy of the Korean Language, 1991) as given in (3).

(3) Vowel insertion is more likely to occur
   a. when the pre-final vowel is tense rather than lax (vowel-tenseness effect).
   b. when the final stop is voiced rather than voiceless (voicing effect).
   c. when the final stop is in the order of coronal> velar> labial (place of articulation effect).

Kang's analysis of vowel epenthesis employs three different factors: phonetic, phonological and morphophonemic constraints in Korean. She attributes the vowel-tenseness effect to a good perceptual approximation to stop release since final stops are more frequently released after a tense vowel than after a lax vowel in English. However, the degree of stop release cannot account for the voicing effect since voiced stops tend to be released as much as voiceless stops in English (Rositzke 1943). Then, she explains the voicing effect in terms of a phonological process of intervocalic voicing of plain stops in Korean and open syllable lengthening of vowels. Finally, she accounts for the higher frequency of vowel insertion after coronal stops relying on morphophonemic restrictions against underlying /t/-final nouns in Korean.[2]

Likewise, Kang's (2003) analysis lacks a uniform account for vowel epenthesis. Moreover, Kang (2003) only considers the relevance of stop release to the higher likelihood of vowel epenthesis after coronal stops without taking any other phonetic details into consideration. Furthermore, she does not provide any criterion as to when the morphophonemic constraint wins over the phonetic constraints in perceptual similarity calculation.

On the other hand, Oh and Kim (2006) observe that the loanwords ending with coronal stops have the larger number of long prefinal vowels than

---

[2] Korean does not allow a /t/-final noun and a loanword ending with a coronal stop is inflected as if it is /s/-final. If English word-final /t/ is adapted as the coda /t/, it would yield a non-uniform paradigm of an alternation between [s] (before a vowel-initial suffix) and [t] (elsewhere), as in cut [kʰʌ t], cut-il [kʰʌ sɨl] (ACC), and cut-e [kʰʌ sɛ] (LOC). In contrast, vowel insertion would keep the uniformity for word-final coronals as in [kʰʌ tʰɨ], [kʰʌ tʰɨ-lɨl], and [kʰʌ tʰɨ-ɛ].

those ending with noncoronal stops in the corpus of NAKL. Thus, they argue that the place of articulation effect can in fact be explained by the phonetic duration-based account. To put it another way, vowel epenthesis more likely occurs when the pre-final vowel is long as shown in Table 1.

Table 1. Frequency of vowel insertion after coronal and noncoronal stops according to pre-final vowel duration (Oh and Kim 2006: 330)

Coronal final stops	LV	SV	Total	t-test
Vowel insertion	152	7	159	1.277589E-22
No vowel insertion	16	26	42	1.305061E-1
Total	168	33	201	
$\chi^2 = 80.05508$, p = 3.64118E-19				
Non-coronal final stops	LV	SV	Total	t-test
Vowel insertion	64	2	66	1.317005E-10
No vowel insertion	57	96	153	1.947748E-3
Total	121	98	219	
$\chi^2 = 66.50157$, p = 3.49614E-16				

In Table 1, LV stands for both phonemically and phonetically long vowels which are determined by phonetic contexts, while SV indicates phonetically short vowels. (4) shows when vowels are considered phonetically long.

(4) Phonetically long vowels (House and Fairbanks 1953; Ladefoged 2001)
a. Tense and diphthongal vowels are longer than lax vowels.
b. Stressed lax vowels are longer than unstressed lax vowels.
c. Vowels before voiced stops are longer than those before voiceless stops.

Table 1 illustrates that both coronal stop-final and noncoronal stop-final loanwords trigger vowel epenthesis as long as the pre-final vowels are phonetically long. The vowel-tenseness effect and the voicing effect can also naturally fall out from the fact that tense vowels are phonemically long and vowels before voiced stops are phonetically long. In English, the durational difference between vowels followed by a voiceless consonant and those followed by a voiced consonant is quite large, about 50-100 ms in a phrase-final syllable (House and Fairbanks 1953; Raogael 1971). Likewise the frequency of vowel insertion is significantly related with the duration of the pre-final vowel. Then, vowel epenthesis after a word-final stop can be uniformly accounted for by the phonetic duration-based analysis.

2.1.2 A VOT-based account of word-initial tensification

The voiced stop in English can be rendered as either a lax or a tense stop in Korean. Oh (2006) makes two observations based on the corpus in NAKL (1991). First, tensification only occurs in the word-initial position. Second, only singleton voiced stops undergo word-initial tensification to the exclusion of word-medial, word-final voiced stops and voiced stops in a cluster. These two points are illustrated in (5).[3]

(5) a. No tense adaptation of word-medial voiced stops (Oh 2006)
candy [kʰendi] * [kʰent'i], Aladdin [alladin] *[allat'in]
  b. No tense adaptation of word-final voiced stops
card [kʰadɨ] *[kʰat'ɨ], gag   [kegɨ] *[kek'ɨ]
  c. No tense adaptation of voiced stops in a cluster
drama [tɨrama] *[t'ɨrama], green [kɨrin] *[k'ɨrin]
  d. Tense adaptation of word-initial voiced stops
box [paks'ɨ] ~ [p'aks'ɨ], jelly [celli]~ [c'elli]

(6) summarizes word-initial strengthening in Korean loanwords.

(6) Summary of the phonology of [+tense] obstruents in Korean loanwords

	Possibility of word-initial strengthening	Examples
Singleton voiced stops	Possible	box [paks'ɨ] ~ [p'aks'ɨ] game [keim] ~ [k'eim]
Voiced stops in a cluster	Impossible	drama [tɨrama] *[t'ɨrama] green [kɨrin] *[k'ɨrin]

Given that loan adaptation is guided by a general model of sound similarity called the P-Map (Steriade 2001), similarity is based on the distance

---

[3] The Korean lexicon as a whole is also affected by word-initial strengthening as given in (i).
(i) Word-initial strengthening in native colloquial Korean
  kwa   [k'wa]   'department'
  sonaki   [s'onagi]   'shower'
We term this process as word-initial strengthening to distinguish it from other types of tensification since it occurs only in the word-initial position. In Korean, such word-initial strengthening is reported to begin from the end of 15th century. Why and where this process occurs is unclear yet despite sporadic sociolinguistic study. The environment of this process is unclear since the similar environments do not guarantee the application as given in (ii).
(ii)a. kwa #il   [kwail] ~ [k'wail]   'departmental duty'
   kwail   [kwail] * [k'wail]   'fruit'
  b. kong-c'a   [koɲc'a] ~ [k'oɲc'a]   'free'
   kong-ca   [koɲja] * [k'oɲja]   'Confucius'

in auditory space that is highly sensitive to the effects of context and sub-phonemic properties on the relative salience of sounds. Under the view that the adapter exercises control over the native grammar to take account of the foreign source, Oh (2006) argues that the rejection of *[t'ɨrama] in favor of [tɨrama] from English 'drama' indicate a dispreference for large durational difference between English stops in a cluster and Korean tense stops. If sounds are judged in terms of their distance in auditory space, then it is conceivable that short closure duration of the English stop in a cluster is considered to be far from the long closure duration of a tense stop in the Korean speaker's P-Map.

However, any acoustic cue during stop closure can hardly be found in the word-initial position. If VOT is instead longer for the voiced stops in a cluster than for the singleton voiced stops, the voiced stops in a cluster are not likely mapped to a tense in Korean since a tense stop in Korean has smaller VOT than a lax stop (Silva 2006).

We conducted a phonetic experiment to test the hypothesis that VOT differences in English are in fact correlated with the variable adaptation of English voiced stops as either a lax or tense in Korean. The data for the production experiment consist of two sets. The one set includes 23 minimal pairs beginning with the singleton voiceless stop, /t/ or /k/, and the voiceless stops followed by /w/; e.g., *tween* vs. *teen*, *queen* vs. *keen*. Three American English speakers (two females and one male) produced 5 repetitions of 46 words; 690 tokens (46 words x 5 repetitions x 3 speakers). The other set consists of 12 minimal pairs between the singleton voiced stops, /b, d, g/, and the voiced stops followed by /l/ or /r/; e.g., *back* vs. *black, dink* vs. *drink*. The set was repeated twice by two English speakers (one female and one male); 96 tokens (24 words x 2 repetitions x 2 speakers). The results are given in Table 2.

Table 2: VOT of English stops (*p<0.01)

Word-initial stop in English	VOT (ms)	t-test
Singleton /t,k/	95.81	1.73E-23*
/t, k/ followed by /w/	110.63	
Singleton /b, d, g/	15.14	0.0017*
/b, d, g/ followed by /l, r/	32	

Table 2 shows that the word-initial stops have longer VOT when followed by another sonorant consonant than word-initial singleton stops in English. It is generally known that the intraoral pressure for voiceless English stops is greater than for voiced stops (Lubker and Parris 1970) accounting for a delay in the onset of phonation. Furthermore, the stops tend to be realized with a greater fricated release when they are followed by closed vowels. Ohala (1983: 204) ascribes this tendency to the fact that the high velocity of the airflow created upon release is maintained longer when a stop is followed by a close vowel as opposed to an open vowel. That account can also hold for the greater VOT of a stop followed by a glide, in that intraoral pressure for a glide is greater than for a vowel. A two-way repeated measures ANOVA on release noise duration (corresponding to VOT in most cases) in the voiced and voiceless stops showed highly significant main effects for the singleton or the cluster.

English voiced stop to tense stop rendition in Korean loanwords testifies that a language specific phonetic detail (i.e., VOT difference) affects a phonological pattern of loanwords (i.e., word-initial strengthening). The long VOT of the English voiced stop in a cluster is considered to be far from the short VOT of the tense stop in the Korean speaker's P-Map. On the other hand, the short VOT of the English singleton voiced stop can be matched to Korean tense stop with short VOT.

2.1. 3 Consonant closure duration identity in English stop adaptation in an sC cluster

Given that loan adaptation is phonetic approximation between source and loan sounds, the voiceless unaspirated stop after /s/ in English, e.g. /t/ in 'star', is expected to be perceived either as tense, [t'], or lax, [t], but not aspirated, [tʰ], at least. However, the examples in (7) illustrate that the post-s stop in English is uniformly adapted into Korean as a voiceless aspirated stop (Oh 1996).

(7) star [sɨtʰa] *[sɨt'a], spy [sɨpʰai] *[sɨp'ai], sky[sɨkʰai] *[sɨk'ai]

Oh (2006) argues that such adaptation results from consonant closure duration identity between the source and loaned sounds. In other words, the post-s stop in English cannot be interpreted as a tense since an intervocalic tense stop is a geminate phonetically in Korean (Han 1992) but the English stop after /s/ is shorter than the singleton stop (Iverson and Salmons 1995). In other words, the sequence of [ɨ] and the tense stop would exhibit a notable durational difference in consonant closure between source and loan sounds. The English stop after /s/ cannot be interpreted as lax either, because intervocalic lax stops would be voiced. This would result in a perceptual mismatch with the English voiceless unaspirated stop. Thus, the unaspirated stop after /s/ can only be rendered as aspirated.

To conclude, vowel epenthesis, word-initial strengthening and stop after /s/ adaptation in Korean loans show that phonetic duration similarity determines loan adaptation.

2.2 Gemination in Japanese

2.2.1 Word-medial gemination

Subphonemic durational identity in loan adaptation is also attested in loan adaptation from English to Japanese. When adapting English stops, Japanese makes use of gemination to enhance perceptual similarity word-medially and word-finally. To begin with, word-medial gemination in English stop adaptation in Japanese is similar to vowel epenthesis in Korean in that stressed and unstressed lax vowels behave differently as given in (8).

(8) Word-internal gemination in Japanese (Shirai 2001; Kato 2005)

    a. Gemination after a stressed lax vowel
        kitchen   [kitʃ iN]   *[kiʃ iN]
        cookie   [kukki:]   *[kuki:]
    b. No gemination after an unstressed lax vowel
        support   [sapo:to]   *[sappo:to]
        economy   [ekonomi:]   *[ekkonomi:]
    c. No gemination after a tense vowel and a diphthong
        beacon   [bi:koN]   *[bi:kkoN]

Word-internal gemination neither occurs after a tense or a diphthong as in (8c) nor after an unstressed lax vowel as in (8b). It only takes place after a stressed lax vowel. To understand such an adaptation mode, phonotactics and phonetics of Japanese geminates are in order. No geminate is allowed after a long vowel due to *Superheavy syllable constraint which does not allow any geminate after a long vowel (Takagi and Mann 1994; Kubozono 1995). Then gemination after a tense vowel and a diphthong will violate *Superheavy syllable constraint. Thus, we have to refer to the output of the source sounds to find the best match. The stressed lax vowel is longer than the unstressed lax vowel in English. That is to say, phonetically short unstressed lax vowels of English do not trigger gemination, while phonetically long stressed lax vowels trigger gemination. The fact can be understood if we relate it to the phonetics in Japanese that vowels are longer before geminates than before singletons (Han 1994, Kawahara 2006). Then, word-medial gemination in Japanese is performed to be faithful to the preceding vowel duration through output-to-output correspondence (Kato 2005). In other words, the stressed lax vowel of English is long enough to be perceived as the vowel before a geminate in Japanese. But the tense vowels and diphthongs in English are too long to be perceived as the vowel before a geminate in Japanese. To summarize, stress in English is perceived by the speakers of Korean and Japanese with the different speech rhythm in terms of the difference in vowel duration (Kato 2005).

Such subphonemic durational identity predicts that the epenthetic vowels which do not have any corresponding source vowels never trigger word-medial gemination as given in the examples in (9).

(9) ski [suki:] *[sukki:], star [suta:] *[sutta:], risk [risuku] *[risukku]

Furthermore, the phonetic vowel duration-based account for gemination nicely explains why gemination does not occur after a rhotacized vowel. Postvocalic coda /r/ in English affects the preceding vowel so heavily that vowel-/r/ combinations are considered simply as /r/-colored vowels or phonetically a vowel-like rhotic glide (Olive et al. 1993: 216). The /r/-colored vowels are longer than the stressed lax vowels and thus cross over the threshold for the vowel length for word-medial gemination. (10) summarizes the environments of word-medial gemination.

(10) Environments for word-medial gemination

Preceding vowel	Gemination	Examples	
Tense vowels and diptongs	Impossible	beacon [bi:koN] icon [aikoN]	*[bi:kkoN] *[aikkoN]
Stressed lax vowels	Possible	kitchen [kitʃ iN] cookie [kukki:]	*[kitʃ iN] *[kuki]
Unstressed lax vowels	Impossible	support [sapo:to] economy[ekonomi:]	*[sappo:to] *[ekkonomi:]
No vowel (epenthesized vowel)	Impossible	ski [suki:] star [suta:]	*[sukki:] *[sutta:]
Lax vowel + r	Impossible	report [repo:to] park [pa:ku]	*[repo:tto] *[pa:kku]

To sum up, word-medial geminaton occurs after the stressed lax vowels since they are long enough to be perceived as the phonetically long vowel preceding a geminate in Japanese. However, it does neither apply after too short vowels such as unstressed lax or epenthesized vowels nor after too long vowels such as tense vowels, diphthongs and rhotacized vowels. Thus, word-medial gemination results from global durational identity between the source sound sequence and the corresponding loaned sound sequence. Likewise, the phonetic details of L1 and L2 can directly influence loan adaptation.

2.2.2 Word-final gemination

Word-final gemination is also employed to enhance perceptual similarity between the source and loaned sounds as given in (11).

(11) Word-final gemination in Japanese
    a. Word-final gemination after a stressed lax vowel
        cut [katto]   *[kato], black [burakku] *[buraku]
    b. Word-final gemination after an unstressed lax vowel
        tulip [ʧ u:rippu] *[ʧ u:ripu]
    c. No word-final gemination after a tense vowel
        keep [ki:pu]   *[ki:ppu]

Word-final gemination does not occur after a tense vowel as given in (11c). However, in contrast to word-medial gemination, English word-final stops undergo gemination regardless of whether the preceding lax vowel is stressed or not. Shirai (2001) and Kato (2005) argue that such word-final gemination be a strategy to remain faithful to the coda of the English source but still conform to the native syllable structure which bars codas unless they are the first half of a geminate. However, such an analysis cannot account for no gemination in a word-final cluster as given in (12).

(12) No gemination in an obstruent cluster (Shirai 2001)[4]
    abstract   [abusutorakuto] *[abusutorakkuto]
    act   [akuto]   *[akkuto]

Each consonant in the word-final cluster is the coda but any consonants in the word-final position do not undergo gemination in (12).

    Word-final gemination testifies that consonant duration also plays a role in perceptual similarity calculation. Word-final consonants are longer than word-medial ones. For instance, English /s/ is longer in the word-final position than in the word-medial position (Klatt 1974). Word-final gemination after an unstressed lax vowel as in (11b) suggests that duration of consonant plays a crucial role in gemination in Japanese. Such sensitivity to consonant duration in gemination is also supported by no word-medial gemination in a cluster as shown in (13).

(13) mixer   [mikisa:] *[mikkisa:] (Shirai 2001)

The first consonant in a cluster is short and thus it cannot be geminated although it is preceded by the stressed lax vowel in (13).[5] Takagi and Mann

---

[4] The following examples in (i) and (ii) illustrate word-final gemination:
  (i) box [bokkusu], tax [takkusu], mix [mikkusu], sex [sekkusu]
  (ii) couple [kappuru], lesson [ressun] (Shirai 2001)
Lovins (1973) attributed stop gemination before [s] to vowel devoicing. However, the examples in (ii) suggest that the word-final cluster gemination has to do with the phonetic duration of the word-final consonant. /š/ and sonorants have such long phonetic duration that they trigger gemination.
[5] The prevocalic long /s/ is adapted as the tense [s'], while short /s/ in a cluster is loaned as the lax [s] in Korean loanwords (Kim and Curtis 2000): e.g., sign [s'ain] vs. style [siᵗʰail].

(1994: 349) report that a voiceless stop after a lax vowel has longer closure duration than that after a tense vowel in English as given in (14).

(14) Vowel and consonant closure duration in the word-final position

Speaker	Lax V duration	Consonant closure duration	Tense V duration	Consonant closure duration
1	146 ms	183ms	181 ms	154 ms
2	145 ms	76 ms	181 ms	68 ms

Stops after lax vowels are longer than those after tense vowels in (14). Different consonant duration differences depending on the preceding vowels also explain gemination exclusively after lax vowels; the longer stop after a lax vowel is perceptually closer to a geminate than the shorter stop after a tense vowel.

Furthermore, the examples in (15) clearly show that gemination in the word-final position is related to consonant closure duration.

(15) No gemination in word-final fricatives
love   [rabu]   *[rabbu]
give   [gibu]   *[gibbu]

Shirai (2001) reports that voiceless obstruents, especially affricates and stops, are highly geminated in Japanese while voiced fricatives systematically fail to geminate. Voiced fricatives have weaker acoustic cues than voiceless counterparts and lack closure duration (Ladefoged 2001). Then no gemination of word-final fricatives can be accounted for by lack of closure duration.

The asymmetry between word-final stops and voiced fricatives with respect to gemination also results from judgment on their distance in auditory space. Word-final gemination shows that consonant closure duration influences gemination more than the duration of the preceding vowel since it occurs even after an unstressed lax vowel. To summarize, both vowel duration and consonant duration play a role in gemination of loanwords in Japanese.

3. Discussion and conclusion

We argued that phonetic vowel duration determined by stress and tenseness in English directly affect loan adaptation in Korean and Japanese. However, the question that immediately arises is how Korean and Japanese speakers perceive stressed vowels when they lack stress. Flege and Bohn (1989) found that Spanish learners of English employ temporal cues in both perception and production although Spanish has no length distinction. It means that L2 learners rely on durational cues regardless of whether length is contrastive in the L1. In the similar vein, loan adapters have knowledge of faithfulness rankings that can go beyond what can be inferred from their native phonology. To put it another way, Japanese and Korean lack stress and do not distinguish between tense and lax vowels but they perceive them in terms of vowel duration.

Loan adaptation in Korean and Japanese provides faithfulness rankings predicted by the P-map hypothesis proposed by Steriade (2001) that can be derived from perceptual similarity rankings. In subsection 2.1.3, we discussed that English stops in a cluster are adapted as aspirated in Korean since the aspirated stops are faithful to the unaspirated stop in English in terms of consonant closure duration at the expense of VOT. Likewise, consonantal duration identity plays a crucial role in loan adaptation. The tableau in (16) illustrates the point.

(16)

Star	Ident [consonant closure duration]	Ident [voice]	Ident [VOT]
☞A. [s ɨ tʰ a]			*
B. [s ɨ t'a]	*!		
C. [s ɨ d a]		*!	

Mapping L2 phonetic categories to L1 contrasts involves a choice among the perceptual dimensions (here voiced, duration, and VOT or aspiration) that provide conflicting information: Korean learners categorize the stop after /s/ in English based on duration and voiced, but disregard VOT or aspiration information. Thus, candidates (16B) and (16C) are ruled out since they violate Ident [consonant closure duration] and Ident [voice], respectively. Candidate (16A) is the optimal output since it satisfies higher ranking Ident [dur] and Ident [voice] at the expense of Ident [VOT]. The L1 adapters' behavior, thus, reflects an implicit ranking among conflicting cues, with voicing and durational cues outranking in this case aspiration information.

Loan adaptation in Japanese also informs a faithfulness ranking. In gemination in Japanese loanwords, both vowel and consonant durations play a crucial role in gemination. Then a question arises regarding which acoustic cue is more influential to find the best match. Two pieces of evidence illustrate that consonant duration identity takes a priority over vowel duration identity in loanword adaptation in Japanese. To begin with, word-final gemination occurs after an unstressed lax vowel in contrast to word-medial gemination. It means that faithfulness to the longer consonant duration outranks faithfulness to the longer vowel duration: Ident [consonant duration] outranks Ident [vowel duration]. Tableau in (17) illustrates the point.

(17)

tulip[+long]	Ident [consonant closure duration]	Ident [vowel duration]
☞A. [tʃ uːrippu]		*
B. [tʃ uːripu]	*!	

Candidate B violates Ident [consonant duration] which outranks Ident [vowel duration] since the English word-final stop is phonetically long but the corresponding sound is a singleton. On the other hand, candidate A satisfies Ident [consonant duration] but violates Ident [vowel duration] since the unstressed lax vowel in English is short but the the corresponding vowel preceding a geminate is long in Japanese. But it is chosen optimal since the Ident [consonant duration] constraint outranks the Ident [vowel duration] constraint.

The second piece of evidence comes from "the prohibition of two geminates" in Japanese (Tsuchida 1995). When both word-medial and word-final geminations are possible, only word-final gemination surfaces in Japanese as given in (18).

(18) Shirai (2001)
    packet [paketto] *[pakketto]
    gossip [gašippu] *[goššippu]

Two geminates are not allowed due to the *Two geminates constraint which asks for no more than one geminate within a morpheme. Word-final gemination over word-medial gemination indicates that the consonant duration effect has a priority over the vowel effect, i.e., stressed lax vowel condition. Tableau in (19) shows the constraint ranking: *Two geminates, Ident [consonant duration] >> Ident [vowel duration].

(19)

packet	*Two geminates	Ident [consonant duration]	Ident [vowel duration]
☞A. [paketto]			*
B.[pakketto]	*!		
C. [pakketo]		*!	

Candidate B is ruled out due to the violation of *Two geminates. Candidate C is ruled out by violating the Ident [consonant duration] constraint since the word-final consonant is not geminated. Candidate A is chosen optimal since it satisfies the higher ranked Ident [consonant duration] constraint at the expense of the Ident [vowel duration] constraint.

Language adaptation is a perceptual process to be achieved by phonetically minimal transformations. There are two approaches for the phonetic information on which initial perception is based. In the Phonetic Approach, the acoustic output of L2 functions as the auditory input to loanwords (Silverman1992; Steriade 2001). On the other hand, the Phonological Approach contends that the borrower operates on the mental representation of an L2 sound or structure, not directly on its surface form (LaCharité and Paradis 2005). In this paper, we have shown that the listener of the native language makes a distinction which does not contrast phonologically both in the donor language and the native language. The crucial role of subphonemic duration of vowels and consonants in loan adaptation in Japanese and Korean argues for the Phonetic Approach as opposed to the Phonological Approach.

References

Dauer, R. M. 1983. Stress-timing and syllable-timing reanalyzed. *Journal of Phonetics* 11: 51-62.

De Jong, K. 1994. Initial tones and prominence in Seoul Korean. *OSU Working Papers in Linguistics* 43: 1-14.

Flege, J. E. and O.-S. Bohn. 1989. The perception of English vowels by native Spanish speakers. *Journal of Acoustical Society of America* 85 (suppl.), S85(A).

Han, J.-I. 1992. On the Korean tense consonants, *Chicago Linguistic Society* 28: 206-223.

Han, M. 1994. Acoustic manifestation of mora timing in Japanese. *Journal of the Acoustic Society of America* 96: 73-82.

House, A. S. and Fairbanks, G. 1953. The influence of consonantal environment upon the secondary acoustical characteristics of vowels. *Journal of Acoustical Society of America* 25: 105-113.

Iverson, G. and Joseph C. Salmons. 1995. Aspiration and laryngeal representation in Germanic. *Phonology* 12: 369-396.

Kang, Y. 2003. Perceptual similarity in loanword adaptation: English postvocalic word-final stops in Korean. *Phonology* 20: 219-273.

Kato, S. 2005. Loanword adaptation in Japanese: consonant gemination of English loanwords, ms.

Kawahara, S. 2006. A faithfulness ranking projected from a perceptibility scale: The case of [+voice] in Japanese. *Language* 82.3: 536-574.

Kim, S. and E. Curtis. 2000. Phonetic duration of English /s/ and its borrowing in Korean. *Japanese/Korean Linguistics* 10.

Klatt, D. H. 1974. The duration of [s] in English words, *Journal of Speech and Hearing Research* 17: 51-63.

Kubozono, H. 1995, Perceptual evidence for the mora in Japanese. Phonology and Phonetic Evidence: *Papers in Laboratory Phonology* IV: 141-156.

Kwulipkwukeyenkwuwen [The National Academy of the Korean Language]. 1991. *Oylaye sayong siltay cosa: 1990 nyendo.* [survey of the state of loanword usage: 1990]. Seoul: Kwulipkwukeyenkwuwen.

LaCharité, D. and C. Paradis. 2005. Category preservation and proximity versus phonetic approximation in loanword adaptation. *Linguistic Inquiry* 36: 223-258.

Ladefoged, Peter. 2001. *A Course in Phonetics*, Heinle and Heinle.

Lubker, J.F. and P.J. Parris. 1970. Simultaneous measurements of intraoral pressure, force of labial contact, and labial electromyographic activity during production of the stop consonant cognates /p/ and /b/. *Journal of Acoustical Society of America* 47: 625-633.

Oh, M. 2006. English Stop Adaptation as Output-to-output Correspondence, *Phonological Studies* 9: 165-172. The Phonological Society of Japan.

Oh, M. and H. Kim. 2006. A phonetic duration-based analysis of vowel epenthesis: English postvocalic word-final stops. *Studies in Phonetics, Phonology and Morphology* 12: 325-338.

Ohala, J. 1983. The origins of sound patterns in vocal tract constraints. In P. MacNeilage. ed., *The Production of Speech*, 189-216, New York: Springer Verlag.

Olive, J., A. Greenwood and J. Coleman. 1993. *Acoustics of American English Speech: A Dynamic Approach.* New York : Springer-Verlag.

Pike, K. L. 1945. *The Intonation of American English.* University of Michigan, Ann Arbor.

Raogael, L. J. 1971. Preceding vowel duration as a cue to the perception of the voicing characteristic of word-final consonants in American English. *The Journal of the Acoustical Society of America* 51: 1296-1303.

Rositzke, H. A. 1943. The articulation of final stops in general American speech. *American Speech* 18: 39-42.

Shirai, S. 2001. Gemination in loans from English to Japanese. *University of British Columbia Working Papers in Linguistics* 8: 155-179.

Silva, D. 2006. Variation in voice onset time for Korean stops. *Korean Linguistics* 13: 1-20.

Silverman, D. 1992. Multiple scansions in Loanword Phonology: Evidence from Cantonese. *Phonology* 9: 289-328. Cambridge: Cambridge University Press.

Steriade, D. 2001. Directional asymmetries in place assimilation: a perceptual account, In E. Hume and K. Johnson. eds., *The Role of Speech Perception in Phonology*, 219-250, New York: Academic Press.

Takagi, N. and V. Mann. 1994. A perceptual basis for the systematic phonological correspondences between Japanese loan words and their English source words. *Journal of Phonetics* 22: 343-356.

Vowel Harmony as an Anti-Faithfulness Effect: Implication from Nonconcatenative Morphology in Korean Ideophones*

CHANG-BEOM PARK
University of Essex

1. Introduction

This paper proposes a new approach to vowel harmony in contemporary Korean ideophones, [1] by employing Anti-Faithfulness (Alderete 1999) within the framework of Optimality Theory (OT; Prince & Smolensky 1993, McCarthy & Prince 1995).

---

* I am very grateful for the continuous support of Iggy Roca, who has provided advice and guidance throughout this work. An earlier version of this paper was presented at the 11th Essex Graduate Conference in Linguistics and LanguE 2006 at the University of Essex, and Linguistics Association of Great Britain (LAGB) Annual Meeting 2006 at the University of Newcastle. I am grateful for the helpful comments and discussions by the audience at the conferences. I also appreciate the valuable feedback I received from anonymous JKL16 reviewers, and JKL16 audience members (particularly Itô Junko, Chungmin Lee, and Alan Kim). All errors and omissions are mine.
[1] I focus on the vowel harmony in ideophones. Other related phenomena like reduplication and consonantal harmony are not discussed in this paper. In addition, vowel harmony in verbal morphology is not treated as well.

1.1. Dark and Light vowels in Korean ideophones

Korean has numerous onomatopoeic and mimetic expressions traditionally called 'ideophones'. Basically, there are two types of ideophones: Dark and Light forms. From the semantic viewpoint, they express a subtle meaning distinction: Dark forms usually have dark, heavy, big, dim, slow, solid, deep meanings, whilst Light forms usually have bright, light, small, clear, fast, fragile, shallow meanings, according to Martin (1962), J-S Lee (1992), H-M Sohn (1999), among others. For example, $p^h u\eta t \partial\eta$ as a Dark form means 'sound of falling plop into the water of heavier or larger objects', whilst its counterpart Light form $p^h o\eta ta\eta$ means 'sound of falling plop into the water of lighter or smaller objects'.

From the phonological viewpoint, there are some interesting aspects. First, each form divides vowels into two groups, namely Dark and Light vowels. Consider the Korean vowel system below:

(1)   Korean vowel system[2]

	[-back]	[+back]	
	[-round]	[+round]	
[+high, -low]	i	ɨ u	Dark vowels
[-high, -low]	e	ə o	Light vowels
[-high, +low]	ɛ	a	

Korean has eight vowels: i, ɨ, u, e, ə, o, ɛ, a. Interestingly, Dark and Light vowels are divided by the line as illustrated in (1): /i, ɨ, u, e, ə/ are regarded as Dark vowels, and /ɛ, a, o/ are Light vowels. Second, Dark and Light vowels cannot normally co-occur in each form. For example, there is no word like *$p^h u\eta ta\eta$ or *$p^h o\eta t\partial\eta$, because they involve Dark vowel u and Light vowel a, or Light vowel o and Dark vowel ∂, in one form, respectively. The following examples illustrate it:[3]

(2) | Dark forms | Light forms | Gloss |
|------------|-------------|-------|
| pʰuŋtəŋ | pʰoŋtaŋ | 'splash' |
| tʰəpək | tʰapak | 'ploddingly' |
| cicəl | cɛcal | 'chattering' |
| t'eŋkəŋ | t'ɛŋkaŋ | 'cling' |
| k'ɨtək | k'atak | 'nodding' |
| pʰəlt'ək | pʰalt'ak | 'jumping' |
| səlle | sallɛ | 'waving' |
| hullətəŋ | hollataŋ | 'inside out' |

---

[2] I regard the underlying vowel inventory in contemporary Korean has eight vowels throughout this paper, following H-S Sohn (1987), J-K Kim (2000), J-H Lee (2003), among others.
[3] Korean data in this paper are mainly from J-S Lee (1992), M-H Cho (1994), J-K Kim (2000), and mine.

For this reason, Korean ideophones are often regarded as involving vowel harmony. Third, every vowel has its counterpart: /i/ in Dark forms contrasts with /ɛ/ in Light forms, and /e/ also contrasts with /ɛ/, likewise /ɨ/ in Dark forms alternates with /a/ in Light forms, /ə/ alternates with /a/, and /u/ with /o/. Therefore, we can assume that it involves vowel-height lowering or raising, as observed in K-O Kim (1977).

1.2. Some issues

Several aspects need to be reconsidered with regard to vowel harmony in Korean ideophones. The first issue concerns the exact features involved. As seen in the previous subsection, contemporary Korean vowels are divided into two classes, namely, Dark vowels (/i, ɨ, u, e, ə/) and Light vowels (/a, o, ɛ/). However, the problem is which harmonic features play a role in the process, because there is no known phonetic features distinguishing Light vowels from Dark ones within the standard feature theory. It means that Dark and Light vowels do not form a natural class.

The second issue is what morphological factor makes the distinction between Dark and Light forms. There seems no apparent affix here, unlike English plural suffix –s. That's why the formation of Korean ideophones is regarded as involving nonconcatenative morphology.

Since McCarthy's (1979) application of autosegmental theory to non-concatenative morphology, vowel harmony in Korean ideophones have been treated in most of the literature as the realization of a feature-sized morpheme in all the vowels of a word. The basic process can be summarized as follows:

(3)   Vowel harmony in Korean ideophones
        Feature-sized morpheme: [+F]

        Underlying form: C V C V C V ...

The figure illustrates the process like this. A phonetic feature can be regarded as morpheme acting like an affix. It is usually called feature-sized morpheme. So, if we assume [+F] as an affix inducing Light form in Korean ideophones, it can be attached to the stem vowels. Once the morphemic floating feature is associated to the first vowel, the feature spreads to all vowels. In this process, the feature-sized morpheme acts as harmonic feature, and the spreading effect represents phonological vowel harmony.

However, this view has some fundamental problems. First of all, there has been little agreement on which features crucially contribute to the morpheme, because the vowels of each form do not form a natural class in the distinctive feature system, as seen already. A number of proposals have been advanced in this connection: abstract underlying vowel system

(McCarthy 1983), arbitrary features (Y-S Kim 1984, S-C Ahn 1985), underspecification (H-S Sohn 1987), latent features (M-H Cho 1994, C-W Chung 2000, J-K Kim 2000), and others. However, they seem to be unsuccessful because they require ad-hoc feature system or mechanism. In addition, the fact that spreading effect occurs only in ideophones can be problem, because feature-spreading is not automatic rule in Korean phonology. Inevitably, this view requires arbitrary rules only applicable to ideophones.

Another issue is found in the so-called neutral vowels which do not participate in the process. Consider the following examples.

(4)   Neutral vowels

Dark forms	Light forms	Gloss
pəŋsil	paŋsil	'smiling'
əkicək	akicak	'waddling'
pisil	pɛsil	'faltering'
pusilək	posilak	'rustling'
t'əlkɨlək	t'alkɨlak	'rattling'
siŋkɨl	sɛŋkɨl	'smiling'
t'eŋkɨləŋ	t'eŋkɨlaŋ	'clanging'
hintɨl	hantɨl	'waving'
nəpʰul	napʰul	'flapping'
k'upuləŋ	k'opulaŋ	'winding'
t'ekul	tɛkul	'rolling'
pit'ul	pɛt'ul	'crookedly'

As shown in the examples, high vowels in non-initial syllables do not alternate. For instance, high vowel /i/ in the second syllable in *pusilək* and *posilak* acts as a neutral vowel to the harmonic process. The question is how such neutral vowels can be formalized. According to Kiparsky (1973), among others, non-participant vowels in any harmonic language cannot be harmonized with their adjacent vowels, because they would create a vowel disallowed on the surface in the given language. For example, in Wolof ATR harmony high vowels after [-ATR] vowels do not participate in the harmonic process: e.g. *tɛːr-uw-ɔːn* *tɛːr-ʊw-ɔːn* 'welcomed', *tɛk-ki-lɛːn* *tɛk-kɪ-lɛːn* 'untie!' (Archangeli & Pulleyblank 1994). Such non-participant vowels depend on the inventory of the given language: no [-ATR] high vowels in Wolof. Thus, high vowels cannot be harmonized. However, the situation in Korean ideophones is different. High vowels in non-initial syllable in Korean ideophones do not participate to the harmonic process, even if they can be harmonized: e.g. *hintɨl - hantɨl* *hantal* 'waving', *pusilək – posilak* *posɛlak* 'rustling'. They should be treated in different way. In this paper, I shall give clear solution to the issues.

2. Analysis

2.1. The direction of word formation

We begin our discussion examining the directionality of the formation, that is, whether Light forms are derived from Dark forms, or vice versa. I shall assume the former: Dark-to-Light formation, for two crucial reasons.

First, the choice of Dark-to-Light directionality in Korean ideophones is rooted in predictability, as already observed in Kim-Renaud (1976). Consider the following examples.

(5)   First vowel alternation from Dark to Light

    a. {ə, ɨ} → a
       tʰəpək → tʰapak 'ploddingly'   k'itək → k'atak 'nodding'

    b. {e, i} → ɛ
       t'eŋkəŋ → t'eŋkaŋ 'cling'   cicəl → cɛcal 'chattering'

    c. u → o
       pʰuŋtəŋ → pʰoŋtaŋ 'splash'   sukun → sokon 'whispering'

The first vowels of the Light forms can be predicted from the Dark ones. In particular, as shown in (5) above, the first vowels of Dark forms consistently lower their vowel-height to the lowest level available in each column of the vowel system: /i, e/ lower to /ɛ/, /ɨ, ə/ to /a/, and /u/ to /o/. We illustrate in the following figure.

(6)   Vowel-height lowering in Dark-to-Light formation

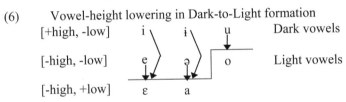

Compare the opposite directionality, from Light to Dark, illustrated in (7) below

(7)   First vowel alternation from Light to Dark

    a. a → {ɨ, ə}
       tʰapak ⇄ tʰəpək 'ploddingly' k'atak ⇄ *k'ətək 'nodding'
          *tʰɨpək   k'itək

    b. ɛ → {i, e}
       t'eŋkaŋ ⇄ t'eŋkəŋ 'cling'   cɛcal ⇄ *cecəl 'chattering'
          *t'iŋkəŋ   cicəl

In (7a), the first vowel /a/ of the Light forms changes to *i* or *ə* in the Dark forms. Likewise, in (7b) the first vowel /ɛ/ of the Light forms raises to *i* or *e*. The problem is that the vowel in the first syllable of the Dark forms is not predictable from the Light forms: there seems to be no phonological clue. This shows that the direction of the formation is from Dark to Light.

Another argument for Dark-to-Light formation is found in the so-called disharmonic forms. There are some exceptional cases in Korean ideophones where Dark (/i, ɨ, u, e, ə/) and Light (/a, ɛ, o/) vowels co-occur in one and the same form. Some such disharmonic forms have a counterpart. Interestingly, this counterpart is always Light, never Dark. The following examples illustrate:

(8)   Disharmonic forms

Disharmonic forms	Light forms		Gloss
t'ukt'ak	t'okt'ak	*t'ukt'ək	'hammering'
kʰuɲc'ak	kʰoɲc'ak	*kʰuɲc'ək	'rhythmic sound'
p'it'ak	p'ət'ak	*p'it'ək	'inclined'
s'akt'u k	s'akt'ok	*s'əkt'uk	'chopping'

Disharmonic forms cannot be derived as Light-to-Dark. In particular, Light forms would be expected to become normal Dark forms without Light vowels (/a, ɛ, o/), instead of disharmonic forms. For example, the Light forms, *t'okt'ak* 'hammering' and *p'ɛt'ak* 'inclined', would yield *t'ukt'ək* and *p'it'ək*, respectively, as usual. It would be extremely hard to find a reason why some Light forms as in (8) should become disharmonic. By contrast, if we adopt Dark-to-Light formation, the process can be captured as vowel-height lowering, as in figure (6) above. For example, *t'ukt'ak* and *p'it'ak* lower consistently to *t'okt'ak* and *p'ɛt'ak*, respectively.

In conclusion, the Light forms of Korean ideophones need viewing as derived from the Dark forms. The Dark forms themselves are not an effect of phonological markedness, but, rather, need listing in the lexicon. In turn, Light forms involve vowel-height lowering in the corresponding Dark forms.

2.2. Anti-faithfulness effect

As we have observed in the previous subsection, Korean ideophones involve vowel-height lowering in the Dark-to-Light formation. The figure (6) above illustrates this. However, the process of vowel-height lowering looks not simple, because unrounded vowels (*i, e, ɨ, ə*) lower to the bottom (*ɛ, a*) in the vowel system, while rounded vowel (*u*) lowers until mid (*o*). I suggest that such an asymmetric vowel-height lowering process can be captured by Anti-faithfulness effect (Alderete 1999, Cf. Kurisu 2001) within the framework of OT. The basic concept of lowering as Anti-faithfulness can be summarized like this:

(9)   The vowel-height lowering as Anti-faithfulness [4]

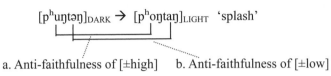

[pʰuntən]DARK → [pʰontaŋ]LIGHT 'splash'

a. Anti-faithfulness of [±high]   b. Anti-faithfulness of [±low]

I propose the two basic Anti-faithfulness constraints ¬MAX[+high] and ¬MAX[-low], in order to account the asymmetric lowering according to the roundness of the vowels in question. The brief process is like this. There is a constraint demanding non-low vowels ([-low]) including high and mid vowels in the base (Dark form) to be lowered to the bottom in the output (Light form), resulting in [+low]. However, certain high vowels could not lower into [+low]. I assume the reason is due to a markedness constraint like *[+low, +round] high-ranked in a given language. If a high vowel is prohibited to be low by the markedness constraint, then nothing will change. Obviously, this is wrong result as shown in (9a): high vowel *u* lowers into *o*. Therefore, we also need another constraint which demands high vowels to be just non-high ([-high]). For further details, at first, let us look at the basic schema of the constraints as follows:

---

[4] In original terms, anti-faithfulness is only implicated in transderivational correspondence. "As with Faithfulness to syllabic positions, Anti-Faithfulness appears to be limited to structures which have an overt surface realization in both members of the pair." (Alderete 1999: 134) This is based on the observation of Anderson & Browne (1973): segmental exchange rules are always morphological (there is no purely phonological mutation. This is also expected property from OT's inherent nature which does not allow input-output exchange mappings or circular chain shifts like /A/ → B and /B/ → A (McCarthy 2002). If we accept the stipulation, the process of Dark-to-Light formation in Korean ideophones would be as follows:

(i) Input: /tʰəpək/   /tʰəpək + Light/   'plodding'
                      | | IO-F
    Output: [tʰəpək]DARK ≠ [tʰapak]LIGHT
                          ¬OO-F

[5] Our Anti-faithfulness version requires the negation narrow scope favoring a total lack of Faithfulness. (Cf. Alderete 1999, Horwood 1999)

(10) a. ¬OO-MAX[-low]^6: Assign one violation-mark for every feature and the value [-low] in the base which have a correspondent in the output. (If any vowels have [-low] in the base, delete the feature or its value in the output.)

    b. ¬OO-MAX[+high]: Assign one violation-mark for every feature and the value [+high] in the base which have a correspondent in the output. (If any vowels have [+high] in the base, delete the feature or its value in the output.)

The constraints have an effect of feature change: [-low] into [+low] and [+high] into [-high], respectively. That is, the constraint (10a) demands that any [-low] vowels in the base change into [+low] vowels in the output, and (10b) demands that any [+high] vowels in the base change into [-high] in the output. This featural change effect is possible from our representational assumption that all vowel features are regarded as binary and fully specified, instead of the private or the underspecified ones. For example, even if the constraint (10a) demands the deletion of [-low], the feature cannot be totally eliminated in the output, since all vowel features should be fully specified everywhere. There would be no vowels absent the feature [±low]. For this reason, the feature still remains and just changes its value into [+low].

Another crucial point in the constraints in (10) is why ¬MAX[-low] is employed instead of others like ¬IDENT(low) or ¬DEP[+low] for example. The reason not using ¬IDENT(low) is rooted on the fact that it requires featural exchange between [+low] and [-low]. Thus, the constraint would be problem to capture the lowering effect in the Dark-to-Light formation, in particular with some disharmonic forms showing absolute lowering as seen in the previous subsection. For example, ¬IDENT(low) saying that every pair of correspondent segments must differ in the feature [±low] would misleadingly change the Dark forms like *t'ukt'ak* 'hammering' into **t'okt'ǝk* as the corresponding Light forms, instead of the real output *t'okt'ak*.

More generally, ¬MAX[F] demands featural distinction between the base and the output, similarly with ¬IDENT(F), but it is also responsible for the directional feature change, unlikely ¬IDENT(F). They have different

---

^{6} Whether MAX or DEP constraints are responsible for the feature change as well as segmental deletion or insertion has been controversial. The negative position is found in some literature: it can predict the unattested result cross-linguistically (de Lacy 2002: 243), "it is unclear how to deal with mismatches between features that stand in correspondence." (Keer 1999: 42), "it demands the preservation in the output of features in the input, but it says nothing about faithfulness to their segmental linkages." (Wolf 2007:324). Thus, MAX(F) might be useful only to the autosegmental floating features as mentioned in de Lcay (2002), Wolf (2007) as well. Nevertheless, I regard it to be responsible for the feature change, especially in our Anti-faithfulness dimension, as stated in the text.

effect with each other as follows:

(11)   The different role of ¬MAX[±F] and ¬IDENT(F)

a. The role of ¬IDENT(F)	[-F] → [+F]	violation if [-F] → [-F]
	[+F] → [-F]	violation if [+F] → [+F]
b. The role of ¬MAX[-F]	[-F] → [+F]	violation if [-F] → [-F]
	[+F] → [±F]	N/A
c. The role of ¬MAX[+F]	[+F] → [-F]	violation if [+F] → [+F]
	[-F] → [±F]	N/A

As shown in (11), ¬IDENT(F) concerns both value of the feature, resulting in the featural exchange, while ¬MAX[-F] or ¬MAX[+F] concerns only one feature value. That is why ¬MAX[-low] is employed for vowel-height lowering in the Dark-to-Light formation of Korean ideophones.

The reason employing ¬MAX[-low] instead of ¬DEP[+low] is just for convenience. Although both constraints have opposite effect for the segments in that ¬MAX would require segmental deletion whereas ¬DEP demands insertion, they seem not to predict different result with each other for the feature values. That is, ¬DEP[+low] requires featural change of [-low] in the input into [+low], but does not concern the feature value [+low] in the input, as the same result of ¬MAX[-low].

As an interim summary, two Anti-faithfulness constraints ¬MAX [+high] and ¬MAX[-low] play a crucial role as a vowel-height lowering in the Dark-to-Light formation of Korean ideophones. They are also responsible for the absolute lowering shown in the disharmonic forms, instead of mere featural exchange.

2.3. Constraints and ranking

Now let us look at how Anti-faithfulness constraints work with the basic patterns in (2) above. We need more specific constraints for this purpose.

(12)   Basic constraints
   a. ¬OO$_{IDP}$-MAX[+high]: In ideophones, assign one violation-mark for every feature and the value [+high] in the base which have a correspondent in the output. (If any vowels have [+high] in the Dark form, delete the feature or its value in the Light form.)
   b. ¬OO$_{IDP}$-MAX[-low]: In ideophones, assign one violation-mark for every feature and the value [-low] in the base which have a correspondent in the output. (If any vowels have [-low] in the Dark form, delete the feature or its value in the Light form.)

    c. OO-IDENT{(back), (round), (low), (high)}: If a pair of words stand in an OO-correspondence relation, all correspondent vowels must be identical for the feature {[±back], [±round], [±low], [±high]}.

    d. *[+rd, +lo]: Rounded low vowels are prohibited.

The constraints (12a,b) represent the main Anti-faithfulness effect for vowel-height lowering as discussed in the above. The faithfulness constraints in (12c) demand the preservation of the features and their values. The markedness constraint (12d) is necessary to prohibit some sounds in a given language. I suppose the ranking of the constraints would be *[+rd, +lo], OO-IDENT(back, round) >> ¬OO$_{IDP}$-MAX[-low], ¬OO$_{IDP}$-MAX [+high] >> OO-IDENT(high), OO-IDENT(low). Since the markedness constraint *[+rd, +lo] is undominated in the ranking, rounded low vowels like /ɔ/ are prohibited in the output of Korean phonology. The ranking also implies that the vowel-height features are preferred to be changed in the Dark-to-Light formation, while others like backness and roundness should be preserved. That is because the constraint OO-IDENT(back, round) out-ranks ¬OOIDP-MAX[-low] and ¬OOIDP-MAX[+high] which dominate their antagonistic faithfulness constraints OO-IDENT(low) and OO-IDENT(high). In other words, the vowel-height difference between the Dark and Light forms is used for the morphological distinct in Korean ideophones.

The following tableau indicates this observation clearly.

(13)   [t'eŋkəŋ]$_{DARK}$ ≠ [t'eŋtaŋ]$_{LIGHT}$ 'cling'

/t'eŋkəŋ + LIGHT/ Base: [t'eŋkəŋ]$_{DARK}$	OO-ID (bk,rd)	¬OO-MAX[-lo]	¬OO-MAX[+hi]	OO-ID (hi,lo)
a. t'eŋkəŋ		**!		
b. ☞ t'ɛŋkaŋ				,**
c. t'aŋkaŋ	*!(bk)			,**

The candidate in (13c), with a change in the feature-value [±back], is crucially ruled out by the undominated constraints OO-IDENT(back, round). In turn, the candidate in (13a) violates ¬OO$_{IDP}$-MAX[-low] twice, since two [-low] features in the base vowels do not change at all. Consequently, the candidate in (13b) is the optimal output, even if it violates low ranked OO-IDENT(low) twice.

    The next tableau clearly captures the asymmetric behaviour of vowel-height lowering between rounded and unrounded vowels: rounded vowels lower down to mid ([-high, -low]), whilst unrounded vowels lower into the bottom ([+low]).

(14)   [pʰuɲtəŋ]ᴅᴀʀᴋ ≠ [pʰoɲtaŋ]ʟɪɢʜᴛ 'splash'

/pʰuɲtəŋ + LIGHT/ Base: [pʰuɲtəŋ]ᴅᴀʀᴋ	*[+lo, +rd]	OO-ID (bk,rd)	¬OO- MAX[-lo]	¬OO- MAX[+hi]	OO-ID (hi,lo)
a. pʰuɲtəŋ			*!*	*!	
b. ☞ pʰoɲtaŋ			*		*,*
c. pʰuɲtaŋ			*!	*!	*
d. pʰoɲtaŋ	*!				*,**

According to the tableau(14), such an asymmetric distribution is due to the undominated markedness constraint *[+lo, +rd]. The candidate in (14d) satisfying all the Anti-faithfulness constraints is crucially ruled out by *[+lo, +rd]. As a result, high rounded vowels are prohibited to be lowered to the bottom.

On the contrary, unrounded vowels are liberal to be lowest one of their vowel height. The next tableau reflects this distribution.

(15)   [k'itək]ᴅᴀʀᴋ ≠ [k'atak]ʟɪɢʜᴛ 'nodding'

/k'itək + LIGHT/ Base: [k'itək]ᴅᴀʀᴋ	*[+lo, +rd]	OO-ID (bk,rd)	¬OO- MAX[-lo]	¬OO- MAX [+hi]	OO-ID (hi,lo)
a. k'ətak			*!		*,*
b. ☞ k'atak					*,**

According to the tableau, the candidate in (15a) crucially violates the constraint ¬OO-MAX[-low], comparing with the winner in (15b). This means that non-low vowels tend to be lowered as possible as they can.

However, this ranking predicts a wrong result with high vowels in non-initial syllables. (⊗ = actual output and ☛ = wrong winner)

(16)   Wrong result: [pusilək]ᴅᴀʀᴋ ≠ [posilak]ʟɪɢʜᴛ 'rustling'

/pusilək + LIGHT/ Base: [pusilək]ᴅᴀʀᴋ	*[+lo, +rd]	OO-ID (bk,rd)	¬OO- MAX[-lo]	¬OO- MAX[+hi]	OO-ID (hi,lo)
a. pusilək			*!**	*!*	
b. ⊗ posilak			*!*	*!	*,*
c. posilək			*!**	*!	*
d. ☛ posɛlak			*		**,**

The candidate in (16d) only violating ¬OOɪᴅᴘ-MAX[-low] once is the winner in this ranking, even if the actual output is (16b). The problem here would be that in the ranking we cannot capture the neutral effect of high vowels in non-initial syllables as given in the examples (4) above. Our present constraints and ranking need to be revised.

In order to capture the neutral effect of high vowels, I amend the constraint and ranking as follows:

(17)   Revised constraint and ranking (Final version)

a. ¬OO$_{IDP}$-MAX[+high]/σ1: In ideophones, assign one violation-mark for [+high] in the initial syllable of the base which have a correspondent in the same syllable position of the output. (If the initial syllable has [+high] in the Dark form and the corresponding feature in the Light form exists in the initial syllable as well, delete the feature or its value.)

b. Ranking: *[+rd, +lo], OO-IDENT(back, round), ¬OO$_{IDP}$-MAX [+high]/σ1 >> OO-IDENT(high) >> ¬OO$_{IDP}$-MAX[-low] >> OO-IDENT(low)

The constraint (17a) involves the concept of positional faithfulness (Beckman 1997) which demands faithfulness between the correspondents within certain prominent positions like the initial syllables, stressed syllables, root, and so on. The basic concept of our positional Anti-faithfulness version is not different from the original one, except for the opposite Anti-faithfulness concept. The reason why the concept of positional faithfulness is employed here is rooted on the observation that non-low vowels (high and mid) in the initial syllable-peak always lower their vowel-height in the Light formation.

Now let us look at how the constraint (17a) predicts the neutral effect of high vowels in non-initial syllables with the revised ranking (17b).

(18)   [pusilək]$_{DARK}$ ≠ [posilak]$_{LIGHT}$ 'rustling'

/pusilək + LIGHT/ Base: [pusilək]$_{DARK}$	*[+lo, +rd]	¬OO-MAX [+hi]/σ1	OO-ID(hi)	¬OO-MAX[-lo]	OO-ID(low)
a. pusilək		*!		***	
b. ☞ posilak			*	**	*
c. posilək			*	***!	
d. posɛlak			**!	*	*

According to the tableau(18), although the optimal output in (18b) violates OO-IDENT(high), its competitors do worse. The candidate in (18a) is crucially ruled out by the undominated positional Anti-faithfulness, because the high vowel *u* in the initial syllable of the base does not lower in the output. The candidate in (18d) violates the faithfulness constraint OO-IDENT(high) twice. The keenest competitor in (18c) is ruled out by ¬OO-

---

[7] One noticeable thing here is that our version concerns the initial syllables in the base as well as in the output. This is only possible from the observation that the Dark-to-Light formation in Korean ideophones is the process in the Output-to-Output dimension, because the syllable structure cannot be concerned in the Input-to-Output dimension cross-linguistically (Clements 1986, Blevins 1995, among others).

MAX[-low], since mid vowel ə does not lower to the bottom as *a*. Accordingly, it is assigned one more violation marks than the winner in (18b) is. This result is due to the tense ranking of OO-IDENT(high) between ¬OO-MAX[+high]/σ1 and ¬OO-MAX[-low], which demands high vowels to be preserved as possible as they can, except in the position of the initial syllables. Thus, the examples lack high vowels in non-initial syllables can also be accounted with our revision (final ranking: (17)).

3. Conclusion

In conclusion, the relationship between the vowels of both Dark and Light forms seems to involve, not mere autosegmental feature-realization, but, rather, an absolute lowering of the Korean vowel height level (as in (6) above). This paper shows that this state of affairs can be captured with the mechanism of Anti-faithfulness, which requires phonological distinction between different members of a paradigm. If our observation is correct, the morpheme that determines Dark and Light forms is implemented as a 'process', rather than a 'thing', in terms of Spencer (1998). Thus, vowel harmony –like phenomenon in contemporary Korean ideophones can be viewed as a by-product of such a morpho-phonological relationship.[8]

References

Ahn, S-C. 1985. The interplay of phonology and morphology in Korean. Ph.D. dissertation, University of Illinois, Urbana-Champaign.

Alderete, J. 1999. Morphologically governed accent in Optimality Theory. PhD dissertation, University of Massachusetts, Amherst.

Anderson, S. and W. Browne. 1973. On Keeping Exchange Rules in Czech. *Papers in Linguistics* VI: 445-82.

Archangeli, D. and D. Pulleyblank. 1994. *Grounded Phonology*. Cambridge: MIT Press.

Beckman, J. 1997. Positional faithfulness, positional neutralisation and Shona vowel harmony. *Phonology* 14: 1-46.

Blevins, J. 1995. The syllable in phonological theory. *The Handbook of Phonological Theory*, ed. J. Goldsmith, 206-44. Cambridge, MA: Blackwell.

Cho, M-H. 1994. Vowel Harmony in Korean: A Grounded Phonology Approach. Ph.D. dissertation, Indiana University, Bloomington.

Chung, C-W. 2000. An optimality-theoretic account of vowel harmony in Korean ideophones. *Studies in Phonetics, Phonology and Morphology* 6-2, 431-450. The Phonology-Morphology Circle of Korea.

---

[8] J-K Kim (2000) and Finley (2006) also drive similar result in that vowel harmony in Korean ideophones is morphological process, instead of phonological one. Nonetheless, they still resort to harmonic features as feature-sized morpheme.

Clements, G. 1986. Syllabification and epenthesis in the Barra dialect of Gaelic. *The phonological Representation of Suprasegmentals*, eds. K Bogers, H Hulst, and M Mous, 317-336. Dordrecht: Foris.

de Lacy, P. 2002. The Formal Expression of Markedness. Ph.D. dissertation, University of Massachusetts, Amherst.

Finley, S. 2006. Morpheme correspondence and vowel harmony in Korean. *Harvard Studies in Korean Linguistics*, XI: 131-144.

Horwood, G. 1999. Anti-faithfulness and subtractive morphology. Unpublished manuscript. New Brunswick, NJ: Rutgers University.

Keer, E. 1999. Geminates, the OCP, and the Nature of CON. Ph.D. dissertation, Rutgers University.

Kim, J-K. 2000. Quantity-Sensitivity and Feature-Sensitivity of Vowels: A Constraint-based Approach to Korean Vowel Phonology. Ph.D. dissertation, Indiana University, Bloomington.

Kim, K-O. 1977. Sound symbolism in Korean. *Journal of Linguistics* 13: 67-75.

Kim, Y-S. 1984. Aspects of Korean Morphology. Ph.D. dissertation, University of Texas, Austin.

Kim-Renaud, Y. 1976. Semantic Features in Phonology: Evidence from Vowel Harmony in Korean. *Chicago Linguistic Society* 12: 397-412.

Kiparsky, P. 1973. Phonological Representations. *Three Dimensions of Linguistic-Theory*, ed. O Fujimura, 1-136. Tokyo: TEC.

Kurisu, K. 2001. The Phonology of Morpheme Realization. Ph.D. dissertation, University of California, Santa Cruz.

Lee, J-S. 1992. Phonology and Sound Symbolism of Korean Ideophones. Ph.D. dissertation, Indiana University, Bloomington.

Lee, J-H. 2003. The Phonology of Loanwords and Lexical Stratification in Korean-with special reference to English Loanwords in Korean. Ph.D. dissertation, University of Essex.

Martin, S. 1962. Phonetic Symbolism in Korean. *American Studies in Altaic Linguistics* 13: 177-189.

McCarthy, J. 1979. Formal Problems in Semitic Phonology and Morphology. Ph.D. dissertation, MIT.

McCarthy, J. 1983. Phonological Features and Morphological Structure. *CLS* 19: 135-161.

McCarthy, J. 2002. *A thematic guide to Optimality Theory*. Cambridge: Cambridge University Press.

McCarthy, J. and A. Prince. 1995. *Faithfulness and Reduplicative Identity*. ms, University of Massachusetts, Amherst and Rutgers University.

Prince, A. and P. Smolensky. 1993. *Optimality Theory: Constraint Interaction in Generative Grammar*. ms. Rutgers University and University of Colorado.

Sohn, H-M. 1999. *The Korean Language*. Cambridge.

Sohn, H-S, 1987. Underspecification in Korean Phonology. Ph.D. dissertation, University of Illinois, Urbana-Champaign.

Spencer, A. 1998. Morphophonological operations. *The Handbook of Morphology*, ed. Spencer and Zwicky, 123-143. Oxford: Blackwell.

Wolf, M. 2007. For an autosegmental theory of mutation. *University of Massachusetts Occasional Papers in Linguistics* 32: *Papers in Optimality Theory III*, 315-404. Amherst: GLSA.

Part IV

Discourse/Functional Linguistics

Prompting Japanese Children[*]

MATTHEW BURDELSKI

Osaka University

1. Introduction

Acquiring the ability to speak as other members of the one or more cultures in which one is raised is an intricate and dynamic process. While much of this ability is gained without direct teaching, caregivers in many societies provide explicit instruction in various ways. In particular, children may be guided what to say through 'prompting routines' (Demuth 1986), a form of 'socialization to use language,' e.g. 'Say "Thank you"' (Schieffelin and Ochs 1986: 163). Prompting socializes children both to language and through language. That is, as children acquire the ability to speak they simultaneously acquire understanding about culture including ways of thinking, feeling, and acting appropriate to membership in a particular social group. While studies in Japan have pointed out that mothers prompt children to use polite expressions (Clancy 1986, Nakamura 2002), there has not been systematic analysis of prompting in relation to its range of functions, and other features including forms, participants and activity settings, which

[*] Fieldwork on which this paper is based was conducted with a Fulbright-Hays Dissertation Grant. I am grateful to Patricia Clancy, Haruko Cook, Chisato Koike, and Tetsuya Sato for comments on an earlier draft, and to the families for their participation in this research project.

235

vary across cultures (Schieffelin 1990: 260). This paper examines prompting of Japanese children. It identifies prompting strategies used and relates these to broader processes of teaching and learning. Finally, it examines the social actions prompted and their relationship to cultural understandings.

2. Data

The data are drawn from a large corpus (126 hours total) of audio-visual recordings of naturally occurring interaction as part of an ethnographic and linguistic study of Japanese children (Burdelski 2006) within the framework of language socialization (Kulick and Schieffelin 2004, Schieffelin and Ochs 1986). Fieldwork was conducted over eighteen months (2004-2005) in the Kansai region, focusing on seven children (four boys, three girls) who were one to two months shy of their second birthday (1;10-1;11) at the beginning of the study. Mothers were primary, full-time caregivers, and fathers were full-time wage earners. Three of these families had an older sibling (4, 5, and 9 years). Recordings were made over a balance of weekdays and weekends, and mornings, afternoons, and evenings in order to obtain a representative sample of children's daily interactions. Sequences in which prompting was used (1117 tokens) were transcribed and coded for linguistic form, social action, participants, and activity.

3. Prompting Strategies

In these data, mothers and fathers, and to a lesser extent older siblings and extended adult family members, prompted children what to say in everyday interaction, as well as in role-play activities. The strategies they used included 'empty slot' (Peters and Boggs 1986: 82), 'leading question' (Ochs 1986: 8), 'performative,' i.e. naming the speech act such as 'apologize,' 'answer,' or 'call out' (Austin, 1962), and 'elicited imitation' (Hood and Schieffelin 1978). Examples are illustrated in (1)-(4). (Transcription conventions and gloss abbreviations appear in the appendix.)

(1) Empty Slot
((Mother and Naoki (2;1) at dining table at beginning of meal))

→　　1　Mother:　*itadaki:?*
　　　　　　　　　partake
　　　　　　　　　'I par-?'

　　　2　　　　　　(0.2)

　　　3　Naoki:　*ma:sh:.*
　　　　　　　　　POL
　　　　　　　　　'-take.'

(2) Leading Question
((Mother, Father, and Masato (2;5) at dining table eating; Masato has finished his noodles and Father has just put some more in front of him.))

→ 1 Father: *age-tara   doo yuu n   yat-ta?*
give-COND how say SE COP-PST
'What do you say when someone gives you something?'

2   (0.5)

3 Masato: *arigatoo.*
thank.you
'Thank you.'

(3) Performative
((Father, Mother, and Takahiro (2;1) at dining table eating; Takahiro had been banging his fork and spoon on his bowl like a drum.))

→ 1 Father: *chanto ayamari[-nasai.]*
properly apologize-IMP
'Properly apologize.'

2 Mother: [*ayamari]-nasai.*
apologize-IMP
'Apologize.'

3   (0.4)

4 Takahiro: °*gomen-nasai.*°
apologize-POL
'°I'm sorry.°'

(4) Elicited Imitation
((Mother, Haruka (2;5), and male playmate (Ken: 3;4) in family living room; Mother has just put a glass of apple juice down in front of Ken.))

→ 1 Mother: *juusu doozo: °tte yut-te.°*
juice here.you.are QT say-TE
'°Say°, "Here's some juice:".'

2 Haruka: *juusu doozo::::::.* ((points towards Ken))
juice here.you.are
'Here's some juice::::::.'

As these excerpts suggest, caregivers use various strategies to guide children to say an intended utterance. Prior research has identified similar strategies including leading questions (e.g. 'What's the magic word?') (Gleason, Perlmann, and Greif 1984) among parents in the U.S., and elicited imitation among Tzotil Mayans (e.g. '"Carry me on your back!", say') (de León 2000). While prompting is widespread, caregivers across communities do not rely on the exact same strategies. In the present data, among all instances of prompting to focal children (1117 tokens), caregivers used elicited imitation (e.g. Say X) more often (95.8%, 1071 tokens) than leading questions (3.0%, 33 tokens), performatives (0.6%, 7 tokens), and empty slot (0.5%, 6 tokens). It should be noted that while prompting was far less frequent with older siblings, when caregivers did prompt these children they also mainly used elicited imitation (97.9%, 46 of 47 tokens).

A crucial insight of the language socialization paradigm is that everyday socializing routines are shaped through historical and socio-cultural processes (Kulick and Schiefflin 2004). From this perspective, Japanese caregiver preference for elicited imitation is linked to ideologies underpinning teaching and learning in Japan. Research on training in music, traditional arts, and craftsmanship has observed an emphasis on teacher/expert modeling and student/novice imitation particularly in the initial stages (e.g. Rohlen and Letendre 1996). Learners are expected to master prescribed 'form' (*kata*) before attempting to develop creativity. In elicited imitation, children are expected to listen to and repeat a model utterance. Repetition is not mindless mimicking, but rather a complex action requiring attention to multiple semiotic resources (Goodwin 2000) including the stream of speech, embodiment, and participants. The utterance to be repeated is often done for a third-party addressee, rather than back to the caregiver, requiring the child to produce the expected utterance for a new addressee. Thus, when children repeat, they not only have to articulate sounds but also have to take into account an array of contextual features. Caregivers guide children's attention towards these features in a variety of ways, which will be pointed out below.

4. Social Actions

Prompting socializes children to perform culturally organized 'social action' (see Atkinson and Heritage 1984) such as greetings, leave-takings, appreciation, requests and offers, asking and answering questions, giving instructions, calling out, reporting, teasing, and criticizing (Demuth 1986, Rabain-Jamin 1998, Schieffelin 1990, Watson-Gegeo and Gegeo 1986). Prompting is often aimed at co-constructing an 'adjacency pair' (Sacks, Schegloff, and Jefferson 1974), contiguous social actions coordinated between different speakers whereby a first-pair part (e.g. a question) makes relevant a particular kind of second-pair part (e.g. an answer). The social actions prompted vary among communities. In the present data, caregivers prompted children to perform the following (Total = 1117 tokens): 1) formulaic expressions (58.6%, 655 tokens), 2) request and response (27.5%,

307 tokens), 3) calling out and response (9.2%, 103 tokens), 4) question-answer (2.1%, 24 tokens), and 5) others (2.5%, 28 tokens). These are shown in Table 1 and examined in the sub-sections below.

Table 1: Prompted social actions

Social Action	Percent	(Tokens)
1. **Formulaic Expressions**	**58.6%**	**(655)**
(a) greeting/parting	25.2%	(286)
(b) offer	11.5%	(128)
(c) appreciation	9.6%	(107)
(d) begin/end meal	6.5%	(73)
(e) apology	5.5%	(61)
2. **Request**	**27.5%**	**(307)**
3. **Calling out**	**9.2%**	**(103)**
4. **Question-answer**	**2.1%**	**(24)**
5. **Others**	**2.5%**	**(28)**
TOTAL	100%	(1117)

4.1. Formulaic Expressions

Caregivers most frequently prompted children to say formulaic expressions, including greeting/parting, offer, appreciation, begin/end meal, and apology. An example of appreciation is shown in (5). The sequence begins when a playmate Taiichi (3;0) hands the focal child Masato (2;1) a toy cellular phone to play with; in response Masato's mother prompts him three times saying, *arigato wa?* 'What about, "Thank you"?', and then prompts him again with an imperative, *Taiichikun ni arigato shina* 'You have to do "Thank you" to Taiichi-*kun*.' Following these prompts, Masato has yet to repeat the expression. The example begins from here.

(5) Formulaic expressions: Appreciation

→ 1 Mother: *sore arigato   tte.* ((pointing towards toy))
               that thank.you QT
               'Say, "Thank you" for that.'

    2   *doozo   shi-te   kure-hatta,*
               here.you.are do-TE gave-PST
               'He gave it to you,'

→ 3   *arigato   tte   iwa-na.*
               thank.you QT   say-IMP
               'you have to say "Thank you."'

4 Masato: *ari::to.* ((turns head and gazes towards Taiichi))
             thank.you
             'Tha::nk <u>you</u>.'

5 Mother: *hai.*
             yes
             'Okay.'

→ 6 Mother-T: *hai, iie dooita[shimashite tte.]*
             yes no you're.welcome QT
             'Okay, say "You're welcome."'

7 Taiichi: [*iie doo   ]itashimashite.* ((bows))
                            no you're.welcome
                            'You're welcome.'

In the entire sequence, Masato's Mother prompts him six times to say
'Thank you.' When he finally repeats the expression to Taiichi (line 4),
Taiichi's Mother (Mother-T) prompts Taiichi to say, 'You're welcome'
(line 6) as a completion of the adjacency pair. Taiichi, who is eleven
months older than Masato, immediately repeats this prompt (in partial overlap before his mother finishes producing it), and also builds upon the action
by bowing (line 7), a non-verbal display of accepting appreciation.

Previous research suggests that prompting socializes children to pragmatic competence, such as to say polite words and phrases including
'Please,' 'Thank you,' 'Excuse me,' and 'I'm sorry' in North American
communities (Becker 1994, Gleason, Perlmann, and Greif 1984, Miller
1982) and 'thank you's, greetings, acknowledgements of being spoken to,
acknowledgements of receipt of gifts, respect to elders, and proper terms of
address' within the Basotho community of South Africa (Demuth 1986: 62).
In Japan there is a wide range of contexts in which speakers are expected to
use formulaic expressions (Clancy 1986: 216). Caregivers instruct young
children to say a dozen or more formulaic expressions, and children gain
increasing competence before the age of three (Yokoyama 1980). In the
present data, these included the following (also see Table 1 above):

(a) greeting: *ohayoo(gozaimasu)* 'Good morning,' *konnichiwa* 'Good af-
     ternoon,' *tadaima* 'I'm home'/*okaeri* 'Welcome back,' *hisashiburi* 'It's
     been a long time,' *genki*? 'Are you well?,' *moshimoshi* 'Hello?,' *irass-
     hai(mase)* 'Welcome'; parting: *ittekimasu* 'I'll go and come back' / *it-
     terasshai* 'You'll go and come back,' *sayoonara* 'Goodbye,' *jaa ne*
     'See you later,' *mata asoboo ne* 'Let's play again,' *mata raishuu ne*
     'See you next week,' *baibai* 'bye-bye';
(b) offer: *doozo* 'Here you are/Please (come in/sit down/have some...),'
     hai 'Here you are';

(c) appreciation: *arigatoo(gozaimashita)* 'Thank you,' *doo itashimashite* 'You're welcome';
(d) begin/end meal or snack: *itadakimasu* 'I partake'; *gochisoosama (deshita)* 'Thank you for the meal'; and
(e) Apology: *gomen ne/gomennasai* 'I'm sorry,' *sumimasen* 'Excuse me/I'm sorry'.

Formulaic expressions include not only verbalization, but also embodiment such as putting the hands together while saying mealtime expressions, and bowing when apologizing and expressing appreciation (as in line 7 above). Caregivers verbally instruct children (e.g. Mother: *otete wa?* 'What about your hands?'), and model these actions; they may also guide young children's bodies such as pressing a hand on a child's head or back to get her to bow (see Hendry 1986: 73). As prompted expressions are often done to third parties, children are required to orient towards a new addressee (as in line 4 above). When children repeat a model utterance without this orientation they may be prompted to redo it (e.g. Mother: *Risachan no kao mite gomen ne iwana* 'You have to look at Risa's face and say "I'm sorry".').

Caregivers prompt children to address formulaic expressions to family members, peers, and others in the community, as well as pets and animals. For instance, while feeding stray cats at a park a father prompted his daughter (Keiko: 1;11) to say, *doozo* 'Here you are,' a polite expression of offering. Another father prompted his son (Naoki: 2;2) to say *ohayoo* 'Good morning' and *konnichiwa* 'Good afternoon' to pigeons when approaching them at the park. Caregivers also prompt children to say expressions to inanimate entities such as toys, religious statues, and natural objects as in (6). While walking back home, Naoki (1;11) picks up a stone and puts it into his mouth. When his mother tells him to take it out, he does so but then throws it down onto the sidewalk. The excerpt begins from here.

(6) Formulaic expressions to inanimate object

    1 Mother: *a sonna   koto shi-tara   akan   wa::::::.*
                  ah like.that thing do-COND no.good PP
                  'Ah if you do like that, it's no good::::::.'

    2 Naoki: ((looking up towards Mother, 0.7))

    3 Mother: *aitata yuu-taharu yo::.*
                  ouch say-ASP   PP
                  'It's saying "Ouch::."'

    4 Naoki: ((looks down towards stone on sidewalk, 0.7))

→   5 Mother: *gomen-nasai tte   Nao-chan.*
                  sorry-POL   QT   Name-DIM
                  'Say, "I'm sorry" (to the stone) Nao.'

     6 Naoki: ((tries to walk away holding his mother's hand, 0.7))

→   7 Mother: *gomen-nasai tte   doo sun no?*
                  sorry-POL   QT   how do Q
                  'How do you do "I'm sorry"?'

     8 Naoki: ((gazes towards stone on ground, 1.0))

→   9 Mother: *ishi   ni   gomen-nasai tte dekiru̱?*
                  stone DAT   sorry-POL   QT able.to.do
                  '<u>Ca</u>n you do "I'm sorry" to the stone?'

    10 Naoki: ((gazes down at sidewalk, but not at stone, 1.0))

Despite his mother's repeated prompts to apologize to the stone, Naoki displays resistance such as looking towards the ground but not at the stone (lines 4 and 10), and pulling her towards home (line 6). In the remainder of this sequence (not shown), though Mother prompts Naoki two more times to apologize, he either ignores her or refuses, and she eventually abandons the sequence.

Prompting children to say formulaic expressions to non-humans (e.g. animals, natural objects) not only teaches language, but also socializes important socio-cultural knowledge. In particular, *omoiyari* (i.e. empathy, compassion, and consideration) is a core cultural value in Japan (Wierzbicka 1991), which is socialized within caregiver-child interaction from a young age (Clancy 1986). When caregivers prompt children to say formulaic expressions to non-humans, as well as point out how these entities might be reacting and feeling (as in line 3 above), they extend the scope of *omoiyari*. This practice is related to raising a child who treats other people, animals, and things with respect and above all does not cause them harm.

4.2. Requests

A request is an utterance designed to get an addressee to do something (e.g. Ervin-Tripp 1982). Caregivers in many communities prompt children to make requests (Demuth 1986, Schieffelin 1990). In the present data caregivers often prompted children to make request for objects. In requesting toys both *kashite* 'Lend it to me' and *choodai* 'May I have it/Give me' are used, while in requesting food *choodai* is used. Caregiver prompts are often responsive to children's verbal and visible actions as in (7). At the beginning of this sequence when Haruka (1;10) reaches towards a toy top that her older sister (9;10) is playing with, the older sister refuses saying, *dame* 'No'.

The excerpt begins as Haruka makes a loud verbalization while reaching towards the toy again.

(7) Requests: *choodai* 'May I have it'

    1 Haruka: *.h A::::::::::::::::::::::* ((reaching towards toy))

    2 Older Sis: ((playing with toy top, 0.4))

→   3 Mother: *Haru choodai tte.*
                      Name give.me QT
                      'Haru, say "May I have it".'

    4   (.)

→   5 Mother: *choodai °tte°.*
                      give.me QT
                      '°Say° "May I have it".'

    6   (0.3)

    7 Haruka: *°(ndai)°.* ((reaching towards toy top))
                      give.me
                      °('May I have it.')°

→   8 Mother: *choodai tte.*
                      give.me QT
                      'Say "May I have it".'

    9 Haruka: *°(n[dai.)°*
                      give.me
                      °('May I have it')°

→ 10 Mother: *[choo[dai.]*
                      give me
                      '"May I have it."'[1]

    11 Older Sis: *[ma:]t-te.* ((playing with toy top))
                      wait-TE
                      'Wa:it.'

→ 12 Mother: *choodai.*
                      give.me
                      '"May I have it."'

[1] In this line, as well as in line 12, there is no explicit directive *tte* 'Say' as in prior uses (lines 3, 5, and 8). Prompting (with an explicit directive) one or more times can provide a frame of interpretation (see Schieffelin 1990: 80), which allows successive prompts (without an explicit directive) to be heard as prompts.

13   *te   dashi-teru   kara age-te.* ((to older sister))
           hand put.out-ASP since give-TE
           'She's holding out her hand, so give it to her.'

14 Older Sis:((blowing on spinning top))

15   *hai.* ((stops spinning top and gives it to Haruka))
           yes
           'Here you are.'

In (7), though Haruka repeats Mother's prompted request, albeit quietly and not fully articulated (lines 7 and 9), Older Sister ignores her requests and then tries to delay (line 11). In response, Mother issues a directive directly to the older sister (line 13) to which the older sister complies (line 15). In the context of requests to older siblings, caregivers often prompted children to make requests on their own and, when the sibling failed to comply, either prompted the older sibling to say *doozo* 'Here you are' or, as in this excerpt, issued a directive to give. In addition to requests for objects, caregivers prompted children to make requests to peers and siblings to play together (e.g. Mother: *Erichan asoboo tte* 'Say [to] Eri [=older sister], "let's play".'). Prompting children to make requests in these ways socializes children to appropriate forms of requests for objects and actions they desire.

In addition to peers and older siblings, parents on occasion prompt young children to make requests to the other parent. The target of these requests was typically a childrearing task or household chore, such as changing the child's diaper (e.g. Haruka (1;10): ((holding out diaper towards Father)) → Father: *okaachan ni kaete choodai tte* 'Say to mommy "Change it for me".'), fixing a toy/object (e.g. Takahiro (1;11): *maachan naoshite* 'Mommy fix it [=broken marker]' → Mother: *maachan naose-nai...papa ni naoshite tte iwanakya* 'Mommy can't fix it...You have to say to papa, "Fix it".'), or making food (e.g. Masato (1;10): ((acting restless just before noon)) → Father: *okaachan tsurutsuru tsukutte tte* 'Say "Mommy make noodles".'). Prompting of these types of requests is often responsive to a child's verbal and/or non-verbal request to the first parent to do something for the child (such as change a diaper or fix a toy). The parent might respond by prompting the child to make the request to the other parent. Prompting children to make these type of requests to the other parent socializes them not only to the forms of requests, but also to the gendered roles of routine activities surrounding particular childrearing tasks and household duties (e.g. mother usually makes lunch, father usually fixes things), and in many families to the sharing of particular activities (e.g. father is currently busy so child should ask mother to change her diaper).

The above discussion pertains to informal requests. Caregivers also on occasion prompt children to say polite requests with the predicate V-*te kudasai* 'Please…'. For instance at the beginning of a visit to their home by two college-aged students, as the students entered the dining room the mother prompted her daughter (Keiko: 1;11), *doozo suwatte kudasai tte* 'Say "Go ahead, please sit down".' In another example, while visiting the home of the paternal grandparents, the mother prompted the focal child (Masato: 2;5) to make a request to the grandmother to relocate her current activity (reading newspaper) from the kitchen to the living room where the child would start playing, *baaba mukoo de mite kudasai tte* 'Say "Granny please look at it over there (=living room)".' Through prompting of informal and polite requests, children learn that language varies in relation to speaker/addressee roles (e.g. host/guest), event, and other features of social context.

4.3. Calling Out

Caregivers in several communities prompt children to call out to others (Schieffelin 1990; Watson-Gegeo and Gegeo 1986). In the present data, caregivers often prompted children to call out to other children within outdoor play. Due to the relatively small living spaces and density in much of Japan, calling out, particularly in a loud voice, is limited inside the home. Children were often prompted outside the home to call out to others using vocatives—siblings with a kinship term (e.g. *oniichan* 'older brother') and playmates with name and diminutive -*chan* (e.g. *Aichan* 'Ai-*chan*'). In (8) Haruka (2;4) is on a swinging tire. When her father takes her off it, he prompts her to call out in a loud voice to her older sister who is playing on the jungle gym bridge, which is about twenty feet away from the tire.

(8) Calling out: vocatives

    1 Father: *na are   ya-ro   ka? Haru.*
                PP that.over.there do-VOL Q   Name
                'Shall we do that over there? Haru.'

    2 Haruka: ((walking towards older sister on jungle gym))

→   3 Father: *ONEE-CHA:N   tte hora.*
                older.sister-DIM QT look
                'Say "OLDER SI:STER," look.'

→   4   *onee-chan   tte.*
                older.sister-DIM QT
                'Say "older sister."'

    5 Haruka: ((begins running towards bridge, 0.6))

6   *ONEE-CHAN.*
                 older.sister-DIM
                 'OLDER SISTER.'

Prompting children to call out in this way engages them in calling out as a form of play, which invites further play. This practice also socializes children to appropriate ways of referring to other persons, which might be different from the way parents refer to them (in the family above, the father typically addresses the older sibling as Eri-*chan* [Name-diminutive]).

In addition to vocatives, caregivers prompted children to call out with other expressions. For instance, in initiating a game of hide-and-seek between her son (Naoki: 2;1) and a playmate, the mother prompted, *ba:: shitemii* 'Do "Peek-a-boo".' In another example, a mother prompted a focal child (Shoota: 1;11) to call out to his older brother who was at the other end of the street, *Takechan o::i tte...Takechan tte* 'Say "Take he::y...Say "Take".' In this example a vocative 'name + diminutive' (instead of a kinship term) is followed by another expression of calling out ('hey'). Caregivers also prompted children to respond to calling out. For instance, at a botanical gardens when a playmate called out to the focal child (Naoki: 2;1) saying *Naochan* 'Nao,' the mother explicitly instructed him how to respond, *Naochan tte yondekuretara HA:::I tte* 'When someone calls out Nao, you say "YE:::S".' Similar to other examples, these here suggest that prompting guides children to initiate and respond to social action that is integral to their interpersonal relationships and everyday activities.

4.4. Question-answer

Question-answer is a common sequence of conversational interaction in general. Prompting is typically aimed at getting children to produce answers to personal information questions from a third person either face-to-face or on the telephone. In particular, in face-to-face encounters unfamiliar adults (e.g. bus driver, store clerk, friend/family of neighbor) and older children might engage young children in conversation; when interaction goes beyond greetings, a typical question asked to children is their age. Young children may hold up one or two fingers to indicate their age, without verbalization. Familiar adults might ask children about past activities such as what they did or ate. In a noteworthy example, when a child's (Masato: 2;5) grandmother asked him what he ate the day before (*Masakun, kinoo nani tabeta::::?*), and the child answered *gohan*, an ambiguous response meaning 'rice/a meal', his mother turned towards him and prompted him to provide more detailed answers: *hambaagu* '(Say) "a hamburger,"' *suupu mo nonda tte* 'Say "I had soup too,"' and *shooboosha atta yo tte* 'Say "It was on a fire engine plate".' The child repeated each of these prompts. This type of prompting socializes children to not only participate in Q-A exchanges, but also design their answers to be specific and relevant.

4.5. Others

Children participate in a range of activities inside and outside the home in which they are prompted to use language for various social actions that do not fit into the first four categories. These include assessments (e.g. Mother: *oishii (no kao) dekiru?* 'Can you do a "It's delicious" (face)?' → Naoki (1;11): *oishi:::* 'It's delicious.') (also Clancy, 1986: 236), informing (e.g. Mother: *koko ni ookii sakana ga iru yo tte, Naoki* 'Naoki, say [to the other boys] "There's a big fish over here [=in the pond]".'), and expressing concern for others (e.g. Mother to focal child (Masato: 2;1): *daijoobu? tte yuutage* 'Say [to the crying girl] "Are you okay?"').

5. Conclusion

This paper has examined prompting within everyday interaction involving Japanese children, family members and others, shedding light on the ways prompting, particularly as elicited imitation, is a key communicative resource through which children acquire language and cultural understanding. The process of acquiring language and culture is gradual and negotiated, and prompting is one of an array of communicative resources including questioning, (other types of) directives, modeling, explanations, reported speech, and assessments that contribute to this process. Prompting in early childhood eventually leads to spontaneous production of the same formulaic expressions and other social actions that help form the foundation for interaction with family and other members of society across the lifespan.

Appendix 1: Transcription conventions

[ ]	overlapping talk
ONEECHAN	capitals indicate increased or loud volume
-	morpheme boundary
:	lengthening (each colon equals approx. 0.1 sec.)
°word°	reduced or low volume
((bows))	nonverbal action or other transcriber comment
.h	inbreath sound
(1.0)/(.)	silence, measured in tenths of a second/less than 0.2
./,/?	falling/continuing/rising intonation contours
word	Emphatic stress
(word)	transcriber uncertain about hearing of word within

Appendix 2: Interlinear gloss abbreviations

ASP	aspect marker	POL	politeness marker
COND	conditional	PST	past tense
COP	copula	Q	question
DAT	dative	QT	quotative
DIM	diminutive	SE	sentence extender
IMP	imperative	TE	*te* directive form
PP	pragmatic particle	VOL	volitional

References

Atkinson, J. M., and Heritage, J. eds. 1984. *Structures of Social Action*. Cambridge: Cambridge University Press.

Austin, J. L. 1962. *How to do Things with Words*. Oxford: Oxford University Press.

Becker, J. A. 1994. Pragmatic Socialization: Parental Input to Preschoolers. *Discourse Processes* 17: 131-148.

Burdelski, M. J. 2006. Language Socialization of Two-year Old Children in Kansai, Japan: The Family and Beyond. Doctoral dissertation, UCLA.

Clancy, P. 1986. The Acquisition of Communicative Style in Japanese. *Language Socialization across Cultures*, eds. B. B. Schieffelin and E. Ochs, 213-250. Cambridge: Cambridge University Press.

de León, L. 2000. The Emergent Participant: Interaction Patterns in the Socialization of Tzotzil (Mayan) Infants. *Journal of Linguistic Anthropology* 8(2): 131-161.

Demuth, K. 1986. Prompting Routines in the Language Socialization of Basotho Children. *Language Socialization across Cultures*, eds. B. B. Schieffelin and E. Ochs, 51-79. Cambridge: Cambridge University Press.

Ervin-Tripp, S. 1982. Ask and it Shall be Given to You: Children's Requests. *Contemporary Perceptions of Language*, ed. H. Byrnes, 235-243. Washington, D.C.: Georgetown University Press.

Gleason, J. B., Perlmann, R. Y., and Grief, E. B. 1984. What's the Magic Word: Learning Language through Politeness Routines. *Discourse Processes* 7: 493-502.

Goodwin, C. 2000. Action and Embodiment within Situated Human Interaction. *Journal of Pragmatics* 32: 1489-1522.

Hendry, J. 1986. *Becoming Japanese: The World of the Pre-school Child*. Honolulu: University of Hawaii Press.

Hood, L., and Schieffelin, B. B. 1978. Elicited Imitation in two Cultural Contexts. *Quarterly Newsletter of the Institute for Comparative Human Development* 2(1): 4-12.

Kulick, D., and Schieffelin, B. B. 2004. Language Socialization. *A Companion to Linguistic Anthropology*, ed. A. Duranti, 349-368. Oxford: Blackwell.

Miller, P. 1982. *Amy, Wendy, and Beth: Learning Language in South Baltimore.* Austin: University of Texas Press.

Nakamura, K. 2002. Polite Language Usage in Mother-infant Interactions: A Look at Language Socialization. *Studies in Language Sciences (2)*, eds. Y. Shirai, H. Kobayashi, S. Miyata, K. Nakamura, et al., 175-191. Kurosio: Tokyo.

Ochs, E. 1986. Introduction. *Language Socialization across Cultures*, ed. B. B. Schieffelin and E. Ochs, 1-13. Cambridge: Cambridge University Press.

Peters, A. M., and Boggs, S. T. 1986. Interactional Routines as Cultural Influences upon Language Acquisition. *Language Socialization across Cultures*, eds. B. B. Schieffelin and E. Ochs, 80-96. Cambridge: Cambridge University Press.

Rabain-Jamin, J. 1998. Polyadic Language Socialization Strategy: The Case of Toddlers in Senegal. *Discourse Processes* 26(1): 43-65.

Rohlen, T. P. and LeTendre, G. eds. 1996. *Teaching and Learning in Japan.* Cambridge: Cambridge University Press.

Sacks, H., Schegloff, E. A, and Jefferson, G. 1974. A Simplest Systematics for the Organization of Turn-Taking for Conversation. *Language* 50: 696-735.

Schieffelin, B. B. 1990. *The Give and Take of Everyday Life: Language Socialization of Kaluli Children.* Cambridge: Cambridge University Press.

Schieffelin, B. B., and Ochs, E. 1986. Language Socialization. *Annual Review of Anthropology*, eds. B. J. Siegel, A. R. Beals and S. A. Tyler, 163-246. Palo Alto: Annual Reviews, Inc.

Watson-Gegeo, K., and Gegeo, D. 1986. Calling Out and Repeating Routines in the Language Socialization of Basotho children. *Language Socialization across Cultures*, eds. B. B. Schieffelin and E. Ochs, 17-50. Cambridge: Cambridge University Press.

Wierzbicka, A. 1991. Japanese Key Words and Core Cultural Values. *Language in Society* 20: 333-385.

Yokoyama, M. 1980. *Jidoo no aisatsu kotoba no shuutoku* [Children's acquisition of *aisatsu* expressions]. *Fukuoka kyooiku daigaku kiyoo* [Bulletin of Fukuoka University of Education] 30(4): 189-194.

Clause Chaining, Turn Projection and Marking of Participation: Functions of *TE* in Turn Co-construction in Japanese Conversation[*]

YURIA HASHIMOTO
University of California, Los Angeles

1. Introduction

The current paper investigates co-construction of turns collaboratively accomplished by participants of Japanese spontaneous conversations. 'Co-construction of turns' refers to a conversational practice by which participants of an ongoing talk collaboratively produce utterances that are designed to syntactically advance the turn initiated by one of the participants (a term modified from Hayashi 2003).[1] The main focus of the paper will be

---

[*]I would like to express my deepest appreciation to my advisors Charles Goodwin, Shoichi Iwasaki and Hongyin Tao for their insightful suggestions. Any errors or misinterpretations are my own.
[1]For Hayashi, co-construction involves a joint 'syntactic completion' of a turn. However, for the current study, the term 'syntactic advancement' would better serve to describe the subject matter, for our primary focus is on the use of middle clauses and its nonfinite ending *te* in turn co-construction, whether the turn gets syntactically completed at its end or not. In fact, some of

on the use and functions of the Japanese conjunctive particle *te* in co-constructed turns.

2. Literature Review

In the field of traditional Japanese linguistics, studies on the Japanese conjunctive particle *te* have, just as morphological studies in general, mostly been limited to the description of its morphosyntactic characteristics observed at the sentence level. It has been assumed that the particle occurs only in a multiclausal sentence as a part of, more specifically as the predicate-ending morpheme of, the preceding clause, just as in the following example:

(1) [gohan wo tabe**te**] [neta]
    meal ACC eat:**TE** sleep:PAST
    '((I)) had a meal **TE** slept'

Te therefore marks the nonfiniteness of the preceding clause to which it is attached in terms of the clause's sentential position, in contrast to the succeeding, final clause of which predicate ends with the finiteness-marking morpheme (e.g. the past marker *ta* in the above example).

It has also long been argued that the events/states described by *te*-conjoined clauses can possess temporal, causal, juxtapositional or other types of relationship with each other, depending not on the meaning of *te* itself but on the semantic types of the *te*-conjoined predicates. Since it does not contribute to the determination of the semantic relationship between the conjoined clauses, *te* had been considered as inherently less specific and thus less 'meaningful' when compared to other conjunctive particles that are semantically more specific: e.g. *tara* 'if,' *temo* 'although/even if' and *kedo* 'but' (Hasegawa 1996).

However, researchers with a functional linguistic perspective have recently made some important findings about the discourse-level function of *te*: rather than merely being a 'not-so-meaningful' particle, it can be systematically deployed by a speaker to develop an iterative chain of clauses, and it can mark topic/subject continuity (Iwasaki 1993) or can be a useful device for storytelling (Iwasaki & Ono 2007).

A number of other significant discussions on the use of *te* and other Japanese conjunctive particles in natural spoken language have been made from a conversational analytic perspective. It has been argued that the syntactic organizations of language, including conjunctive particles and other various unit connectors, generally play a consequential role in the projection

---

the co-constructed turns in my data never reach their syntactic/semantic completion, although they are (inter-)actionally complete.

and construction of conversational turns. More specifically, they can contribute to the projection of multiunit conversational turns that are constructed both by a single speaker and jointly by multiple participants (e.g. Lerner & Takagi 1998, Tanaka 1999, Hayashi & Mori 1998, Hayashi 2003, inter alia). What is meant by 'projection of turns' is the practice of recognition and anticipation by coparticipants of conversation about the possible syntactic shape of unfolding turn and the place of its completion. The occurrence of *te*, for instance, and its inherent 'nonfiniteness' contributes to the participants' projection that the current conversational turn is not yet over, and at least one more clause is further upcoming.

As is briefly reviewed above, the literature on *te*, especially the studies taking a discourse/conversation analytic approach to natural spoken language, have developed insightful arguments on its use and functions in both solely and jointly constructed turns. However, still not enough attention is paid to how exactly the particle can be deployed by the participants in order to accomplish co-construction of turns, in association with other linguistic and nonlinguistic components of interaction. This study attempts to clarify these points by closely examining each example of *te* used in co-constructed turns.

3. Research Questions, Data and Methodology

The specific research questions for the current study are as follows:

(i) How do *te* and its morpho-syntactic and phonological feature(s) contribute to the projection of unfolding turns, and how are they interactionally exploited by the participants in order to accomplish successful co-construction of turns?

(ii) Are other linguistic components surrounding *te* as well as nonverbal bodily conducts also involved in the accomplishment of turn co-construction? If so, how are they deployed by the participants?

(iii) How differently or similarly do different participants contribute to the co-construction of turns when they possess unequal accessibility to the content of unfolding talk?

In order to explore the above questions, examples from two separate sets of spontaneous conversational data are examined. Below is a brief description of the two data sets and their participants:

A. One-hour conversation held between two native speakers of Japanese, both females in their twenties. The two participants are at the same age, attending the same US university as exchange students from Japan.

B. Three-hour lunch table conversation between three native Japanese speakers, two females and one male, each in her/his twenties, thirties and forties. One of the female participants is married to the male participant, with whom she hosted the lunch party. The other female participant was invited as their guest.

4. Analysis

4.1. Morpho-syntactic and phonological resources

Let us first take a look at an example of co-constructed turn in which the conjunctive particle *te* is repeatedly and systematically deployed.

(2) Purikura (from Data A)
((Prior to this segment, the two participants were talking about 'purikura,' small photo stickers that can be taken and printed out using a machine often available at amusement arcades in Japan.))

1	Aya:	tomodachi to au tabi ni
		friend COM meet each.time TMP
		'every time ((I)) saw my friends,
2		purikura toru no ga are datta mo:n.
		purikura take NML SUBJ DEM COP:PAST IP
		taking purikura was *that* thing.'
3	(0.2)	
4	Tomi:	daitai nanka tomodachi to au to:, =
		usually SOF friend COM meet COND
		'usually, like, when ((I/we)) see my friends,'
5	Aya:	=un.
		CONT
		'uh-huh.'
→ 6	Tomi:	ohiru ka-
		lunch or
7	(0.2)	
→ 8		nanka wo tabe ⌐te::,
		something ACC eat:TE

'((we)) eat lunch or- something TE,'

→ 9	Aya:	∟ohiru tabete::,
		lunch eat:TE
		'eat lunch TE,'
→ 10		chotto: omise ⌐nozoite::,
		SOF shop peak:TE
		'take a quick peak at shops TE,'

→ 11　Tomi:　　　　　　　└°nozoite::,
　　　　　　　　　　　　look.into:TE
　　　　　　　　　　　　'peak ((at shops)) TE,'

→ 12　Aya:　　saigo purikura tot ┌te::,
　　　　　　　lastly purikura take:TE
　　　　　　　'lastly ((we)) take purikura TE,'

→ 13　Tomi:　　　　　　　　　　└te::,
　　　　　　　　　　　　TE
　　　　　　　　　　　　'TE,'

14　　　　　　ato:, watashi wa ato >kekko yoku<
　　　　　　　also I TOP also EMPH often
　　　　　　　'also, I also quite often'

15　　　　　　karaoke ni mo itteta.
　　　　　　　karaoke ALL ADD go:ASP:PAST
　　　　　　　'used to go to karaoke.'

16　　Aya:　　a honto.
　　　　　　　oh really
　　　　　　　'oh, really?'

　　The above jointly constructed turn starting from Line 4 through 15 contains as many as 6 instances of *te* conjoining a series of clauses. What is described by the conjoined clauses is a list of events the speakers often used to do with their friends back in Japan.

　　What is most striking about the above example is how smoothly the co-construction in such a significant length is done between the two participants without any recognizable pauses or other kinds of lapse of time between the conjoined clauses, and partially even with a choral production of exactly the same linguistic component(s). How could this be made possible?

　　First, as the literature suggests, the inherent marking by the particle *te* of the nonfiniteness of the current clause does seem to have some significance in the projection of the unfolding turn: The moment *te* is produced, at least one more clause is highly expected to follow. It would also not be impossible for the coparticipants to prospect the conjoining of clauses by *te* to be not only once but further on.

　　However, in this particular example, the inherent morpho-syntactic feature of the particle is not the sole, defining factor for the successful turn co-construction. What should also be definitely taken into account are the phonological characteristics distinct to the tokens of *te* in the above excerpt. Throughout the above co-constructed turn, the particle is constantly articulated with a significant intonation: rising-to-mid pitch and a soundstretch that ends without falling to low (transcribed in the current paper as **te**::,). It has been discussed that a nonfalling or continuous intonation in general can project that the current turn has not reached its completion (Tanaka 1999), and more specifically, a rising-to-mid pitch can be used to mark the continuation of the current turn (Kern 2007). In the data for the current study, similar phonological features are observed with the majority of *te*-tokens in co-constructed turns. Let us compare the following two figures:[2]

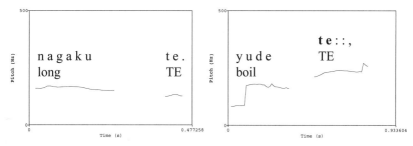

Fig. 1: Pitch contour of TE unstretched, low + falling

Fig. 2: Pitch contour of TE stretched, rising-to-mid + nonfalling

Figure 1 illustrates a pitch contour of *te* articulated without a sound-stretch and with a low and falling intonation. It clearly contrasts with Figure 2, an illustration of the pitch contour of *te* articulated with a soundstretch, high-to-mid and nonfalling intonation. The prosodic contour of the *te*-tokens in Example (2) is highly similar to the one displayed in Figure 2.[3]

As is visible in the transcript, the above described contour is recurrently exploited by the two participants, and its initial exploitation by Speaker T elicits the second use by A, as if imitating T. In addition to the morpho-syntactic continuousness of *te*, this repeated phonological continuousness also seems to greatly enhance the projection that the unfolding turn is yet to reach its completion.[4]

---

[2]The extraction and drawing of the pitch contours were done using a computer-based phonological analyzer called Praat (http://www.fon.hum.uva.nl/praat/).

[3] The pitch contour of the co-constructed turn in Example (2) is not hereby presented, since the recorded sound waves of the overlapped speech by the two participants are not separable, and thus the extracted pitch contour would not properly represent the actual pitch movement of each speaker's utterances. However, when manually audited, it is clear that all of the *te*-tokens in the co-constructed turn share a highly similar prosodic pattern with the one illustrated in Figure 2.

[4]Although it is beyond the scope of the current discussion, let us note that in our data, solely constructed turns frequently contained instances of *te* loaded with the unstretched, low and falling prosodic pattern illustrated in Figure 1, whereas the majority of *te*-tokens occurring in a co-constructed turn had the nonfalling/continuous prosodic pattern shown in Figure 2.

Furthermore, the syntactic recycling of not only *te* itself but also of the whole clausal construction seems to play another important role in the projection of co-construction: A transitive construction consisting of direct object (with/without a preceding adverbial) followed by a verb ending with *te* is the recurring shape of the conjoined clauses through lines 6 through 13. The recurrent use of this construction, together with their semantic components and the relationships of the described events, again strongly projects what syntactic shape the next upcoming fragment of the current turn will take.

It seems that the above morpho-syntactic and phonological characteristics of the linguistic components, including those of the conjunctive particle *te*, recurring throughout the co-constructed turn in Example (2) altogether form a positive circle of enhanced projectability: the more the talk with the same features is repeated, the further the possibility increases for the same features to recur yet another time.

One more important observation to note in the above excerpt is that in Lines 12 and 13, where the listing of events they used to do with friends reaches its final component, the co-construction is accomplished in quite an intriguing way. While Speaker A produces the entire clause *saigo purikura totte*::, 'lastly ((we)) take purikura TE,' Speaker T contributes to the joint production by articulating only a single bit of talk: the particle *te*. It is considered extremely abnormal or even ungrammatical from the traditional linguistic perspective to find this 'bound morpheme' as the one and only linguistic constituent of one's entire utterance. However, being situated in the current specific context of conversational sequence and the activity of turn co-construction, Speaker T's utterance *te*::, is not a flawed but full-fledged talk accepted and understood by the other participant without any troubles.

4.2. Nonlinguistic Conducts

In the previous subsection, it has been observed that various morpho-syntactic and phonological features of talk, including those of the conjunctive particle *te*, can enhance the participants' projection of the unfolding turn and further the successful accomplishment of turn co-construction. Let us now turn to another important kind of resources for turn projection and construction: nonlinguistic bodily conducts. Their significant relevance to turn projection and construction has frequently been discussed (e.g. Emmett 1998, Lerner 2002, Hayashi *et al* 2002, Hayashi 2003). Example (3) (partially repeats (2) in the previous section) illustrates how coparticipants are oriented to and make use of their body behaviors during turn co-construction:

(3)
→ 4   Tomi: daitai nanka tomodachi to au to:, =
                      usually SOF friend COM meet COND
                      'usually, like, when ((I/we)) see my friends,'

5   Aya: =un.
                      CONT
                      'uh-huh.'

6   Tomi: ohiru ka-
                      lunch or

7   (0.2)
→ 8   nanka wo tabe ⌐te::,
                      something ACC eat:TE

                      '((we)) eat lunch or- something TE,'

→ 9   Aya: ⌐ohiru tabete::,
                                  lunch eat:TE
                                  'eat lunch TE,'

Frame 1: Line 4   Frame 2: Lines 8 and 9

→ 10   chotto: omise ⌐nozoite::,
                      SOF shop peak:TE
                      'take a quick peak at shops TE,'

→ 11   Tomi: ⌐°nozoite::,
                                  look.into:TE
                                'peak ((at shops)) TE,'

→ 12   Aya: saigo purikura tot ⌐te::,
                      lastly purikura take:TE
                      'lastly ((we)) take purikura TE,'

→ 13   Tomi: ⌐te::,
                                  TE
                                  'TE,'

Frame 3: Lines 10 and 11   Frame 4: Lines 12 and 13

Each of the above picture frames extracted from the video recording represents the coparticipants' bodily behavior(s) cooccurring with the corresponding line(s) of talk. Frame 1 displays a raised hand position Speaker T takes as she utters the conditional clause at line 4. This hand movement together with the talk establishing background, conditional situation foreshadows a further syntactic-semantic development of the current turn as well as the action that is about to unfold. Speaker T continues at Lines 6 and 8 to provide the succeeding clause which turns out to be an instance of event taking place in the condition set by the previous clause, and the accompanied hand movement, now clearly appearing as 'listing' gesture, enhances the projection that more than a single event are going to be listed in the current turn. T's construction of turn is joined by the other participant, Speaker A, at Line 9 at the beginning of which the both participants give an almost simultaneous eyegaze toward each other. This mutual eyegaze and its place in association with the sequence of talk display the coparticipants' understanding of what action is being achieved by the unfolding turn as well as their entering into the activity of joint turn construction.

The following two frames, Frame 3 and 4, illustrate the participants' continuous bodily engagement in the current turn co-construction. T continues her 'listing' gesture by folding her fingers as they co-construct another two clauses describing another two events to be listed, and both T and A grow a smiling face that is maintained until the end of the co-construction. It is worth noting that the above smiling faces, especially being combined with the 'songlike' prosody loaded on to the recurring particle te, add a playful tone to the participants' ongoing activity. This not only signals the participants' active engagement but also their mutual alignment and its joyful appreciation within the activity of turn co-construction.

The above two subsections have investigated a variety of linguistic and nonlinguistic resources that are deployed by the participants in order to enhance their turn projection and construction, and the observations have given significant implications to the first two of the three research questions raised in Section 3. The most closely observed linguistic resource is the systematic iterative use of the conjunctive particle te, of which inherent marking of the 'nonfiniteness' of the attached clause, as well as a significant 'continuous' prosody loaded onto the particle, can together reinforce the projection and elicit the co-construction of the unfolding turn.

Other linguistic contributions include a recycling of a specific morphosyntactic structure of the previous talk that can display the participants' ongoing projection of emerging turn shape and further increase the possibility of another occurrence of the same structure.

Moreover, it has been illustrated that relevant bodily conducts, e.g. 'listing' gesture, mutual eyegaze and smiling faces can also increase the projection of what is about to be accomplished in the unfolding interaction, and they further display the participants' mutual alignment as well as their orientation to the current activity.

4.3. Turn Co-construction and Unequal Accessibility to the Content of Talk: Marking of Interactional Participation

In this subsection, let us proceed to our third research question: how differently or similarly do different participants contribute to the co-construction of turns when they have unequal degrees of accessibility to the content of unfolding turn, in relation to the participants' previous experience and knowledge relevant to the current talk?

It is a well-observed, overwhelming tendency in conversation that a single speaker takes a turn (Sacks *et al* 1974), and a plausible assumption drawn from this principle is that it should especially be so when a single speaker has an exclusive access to the information of what is going to be told, e.g. when telling a story about which only the teller himself knows. If, on the other hand, there are more than one participant who share a more or less equal access to the content of the talk, the possibility of cotelling should increase. In the data for the current study, that is the case with the majority of the instances of successful turn co-construction using the conjunctive *te*: The participants share the same or same type of past experience closely associated to the content of the currently co-constructed turn, just as in Example (2) = (3) where the two participants both have frequently experienced going out with friends and participating in the series of events listed by the co-constructed turn.

However, interestingly enough, there *are* some cases in which turn co-construction is accomplished among the participants who possess different degrees of accessibility to what is about to get talked. Consider the following excerpt:

(4) Toad (from Data B)[5]

---

[5]In this excerpt, *de*, a phonological/syntactic variant of *te*, appears at Line 27. For the transcriptional and referential convenience, the two variants are represented by the same symbol TE both in the gloss and translation lines.

((The participants have been talking about the dishes they are having as lunch. Right before the current excerpt, Speaker T and Y, the hosts of the party, started to tell S, the guest, how the toads in the soup they prepared were taken care and sold at the supermarket.))

1	Ted:	oretachi no mae de sa:, kawa muite ne?
		we GEN front LOC IP skin peal IP
		'in front of us ((they)) peal the skin, you know?'

2	Yuki:	so::.
		right
		'right.'

3	Ted:	oretachi no ⌈mae de-
		we GEN front LOC
		'in front of us- '

| 4 | Sho: | ⌊konaida katta |
| | | other.day buy:PAST |

| 5 | | ⌈kedo oshietekurenakatta yatsu ⌈desho? |
| | | but tell:AUX:NEG:PAST one COP:MOD |

'the one ((you)) bought the other day but didn't tell me about, right?'

6	Ted:	⌊so: so:.
		right right
		'right, right.'

7	Yuki:	⌊ehehehe, so:.
		right
		'ehehehe, right.'

8	Ted:	koroshite::,
		kill:TE
		'((they)) kill ((them)) TE,'
9	(0.2)	
10	Ted:	(nanka) kawa mui ⌈te sa:,
		'(like) ((they)) peal the skin TE you know,'

11	Yuki:	⌊suisoo ni:, nan(ka) ga::: tte haittete::,
		water.tank LOC SOFT SSW QT enter:ASP:TE
		'in the water tank, ((they)) are like all in TE,
12		nanka kocchi miteru n desu yo:.=
		SOFT here look:ASP SE COP:POL IP
		((they)) are like looking at us, you know.'

13   Ted: =uhuhuhuhu.

14   Yuki: nikot toka ittehehe ⌜hehe.
                MSW SOFT say:TE
                'like smiling.'

15   Ted: ⌞ hhhh
16   (0.5)
17   Sho: u;n.=
                CONT
                'uh-huh.'

18   Yuki: =sore o:,
                that ACC
                'that ((thing)),'

19   (0.2)
20   Yuki: nanka moo
                SOFT EMPH
                'like just,'

21   Sho: un.
                CONT
                'uh-huh.'

22   Yuki: so me no mae de pahpapah ⌜toka itte.
                right eye GEN front LOC MSW SOFT say:TE
                'yeah, in front ((of our eyes)) like 'cut, cut, cut''

23   Sho: ⌞un un un.
                                        CONT CONT CONT
                                        'uh-huh, uh-huh, uh-huh.'

24   (0.5)

25   Yuki: sabaichau.
                take.care:AUX
                '((they)) quickly take care ((of the toads)).'

26   (0.8)

→ 27 Sho: kawa ⌜haide::,
                skin peal:TE
                '((they)) peal the skin TE,'

→ 28 Yuki: ⌞kawa toka ⌜(gari::) toka hai ⌜jyatte::,
                       skin SOFT SSW SOFT peal:AUX:TE
                       '((they)) peal off the skin and the like TE,'

```
29    Ted:                          └un.
                                     CONT
                                     'uh-huh.'

30    Sho:                                          └paatsu ni >ko
                                                    parts ALL this.way
31                    ┌tori< mitaini wakettekureru wake:?
                      chicken like divide:AUX NML

                      '((is it)) that ((they)) divide ((them)) into parts for you
                      like chicken?'
32    Yuki:    └soo soo soo soo, u:n.
               right right right right CONT
               'right, right, right, right, uh-huh.'
```

From Lines 1 to 3 and from 8 through 25 in the above excerpt, the Participants T and Y, the ones who both possess a high accessibility to the content of current talk that is closely related to their shared experience about the toads, take turns to reconstruct the story as the main cotellers. The other participant, S, who at this point have a much lower accessibility to what is being unfold since she does not share the experience, mainly preserve herself to take the recipient role.

However, at Line 27, following a seemingly possible completion of T and Y's co-storytelling, S comes in to provide her understanding of what has been just described, or her own version of the story. This second reconstruction of the story gets assisted at Line 28 by one of the previous main tellers, Y, and the two participants co-construct their turn until Line 21, making systematic use of the conjunctive *te* (and its variant), just as in the previous co-construction example.

The above example illustrates how a participant with a relatively low accessibility to the content of the current turn can still not only display her active participation in the interaction but also linguistically contribute to the co-construction of turn. Such contributions from different kinds of participants formulate a participation framework in which the participants demonstrate actions together, and into and from which the participants make a transition in the course of overall interaction (Goodwin 1984, Rae 2001, Goodwin & Goodwin 2004). While the accomplished action may vary from one instance to another (e.g. joint listing of events by the cotellers in Example (2)=(3) VS the display of understanding by the nonteller and its confirmation by the teller in Example (4)), it is consistently the case that the participants of turn co-construction visibly display their mutual understanding of, and orientation toward, the current participation framework, through various linguistic and nonlinguistic conducts. It is suggested that the systematic recurrent use of the conjunctive particle *te* is one of such indicators the participants signal when both shifting into and further proceeding the current participation framework.

5. Conclusion

In the present paper, a qualitative analysis has been made on turn co-construction in Japanese spontaneous conversations, focusing on the examples of *te*-conjoined clausal turns. It was observed that the turn co-construction is made possible for the coparticipants not only by the morpho-syntactic/phonological characteristics of the particle itself but also through its systematic repetitive use, together with the cooccurring linguistic and nonlinguistic resources that can enhance the projectability of the unfolding turn.

It was further illustrated that different participants with different degrees of accessibility to the content of the current talk can still linguistically contribute to the co-construction of the unfolding turn, and they can also display their involvement in the current participation framework in an equally active way.

For further research, a more systematic observation of diverse examples of turn co-construction is required. For instance, a detailed analysis of different kinds of multiclausal co-construction involving the use of different syntactic connectors other than *te* would bear further important findings. Different or similar ways of contributions to turn co-construction and formulation of participation framework by different parties also needs a closer examination. Continuous investigations on this interesting phenomenon called turn co-construction would contribute to a deeper understanding of the complex, multilayered aspects of conversational and interactional organization that taps into the interface of grammar, its function and social action.

Transcription Conventions

.	falling intonation	-	cutoff
,	continuous intonation	><	rushthrough
?	rising intonation	=	latched utterances
⌐	start of overlap	( )	unclear utterances
∟		(( ))	additional information by the researcher
:	soundstretch	(0.2)	length of silence
°	decrease in volume		

References

Emmett, K. 1998. Projection of Talk Using Language, Intonation, Deictic and Iconic Gestures and Other Body Movements. *Japanese/Korean Linguistics* 8: 17-30. Stanford: CSLI.

Goodwin, C. 1984. Notes on Story Structure and the Organization of Participation. *Structures of social action.* eds. J. M. Atkinson & J. Heritage, 225–246. Cambridge, England: Cambridge University Press.

Goodwin, C. & M. H. Goodwin. 2004. Participation. *A Companion to Linguistic Anthropology.* ed. A. Duranti, 222-244. Malden, MA: Blackwell.

Hasegawa, Y. 1996. The (Non-vacuous) Semantics of TE-linkage in Japanese. *Journal of Pragmatics* 25: 763-790.

Hayashi, M. 2003. *Joint Utterance Construction in Japanese Conversation.* Amsterdam/Philadelphia: John Benjamins.

Hayashi, M. & J. Mori. 1998. Co-construction in Japanese Revisited: We *Do* Finish Each Other's Sentences. *Japanese/Korean Linguistics* 7: 77-93. Stanford: CSLI.

Hayashi, M., J. Mori, and T. Takagi. 2002: Contingent Achievement of Co-tellership in a Japanese Conversation: An Analysis of Talk, Gaze, and Gesture. *The Language of Turn and Sequence,* eds. C. E. Ford, B. A. Fox & S. A. Thompson, 81-122. Oxford: Oxford University Press .

Iwasaki, S. 1993. *Subjectivity in grammar and discourse: Theoretical considerations and a case Study of Japanese spoken discourse.* Amsterdam/Philadelphia: John Benjamins.

Iwasaki, S. & T. Ono. 2007. Sokuji-bun, Hi-sokuji-bun. *Jikan no Naka no Bun to Hatsuwa,* eds. S. Kushida, T. Sadanobu & Y. Den, 135-157. Tokyo: Hitsuji Shobo.

Kern, F. 2007. Prosody as a Resource in Children's Game Explanations: Some Aspects of Turn Construction and Recipiency. *Journal of Pragmatics* 39: 111-133.

Lerner, G. H. 2002. Turn-Sharing: The Choral Co-Production Of Talk in Interaction. *The Language of Turn and Sequence,* eds. C. E. Ford, B. A. Fox & S. A. Thompson, 225-256. Oxford: Oxford University Press.

Lerner, G. H. & T. Takagi. 1998. On the Place of Linguistic Resources in the Organization of Talk-in-interaction: A Co-investigation of English and Japanese Grammatical Practices. *Journal of Pragmatics* 31: 49-75.

Rae, J. 2001. Organizing Participation in Interaction: Doing Participation Framework. *Research on Language and Social Interaction* 34: 253–278.

Sacks, H., E. A. Schegloff, & G. Jefferson. 1974. A Simplest Systematics for the Organization of Turn-taking for Conversation. *Language* 50: 696–735.

Tanaka, H. 1999. *Turn-taking in Japanese Conversation: A Study in Grammar and Interaction.* Amsterdam/Philadelphia: John Benjamins.

Roles of Gestures Pointing to the Addressee in Japanese Face-to-face Interaction: Attaining Cohesion via Metonymy[*]

MIKA ISHINO
University of Chicago

1. Introduction

In face-to-face interaction, not only speech but also gestures co-occurring with speech (henceforth, gestures) play a significant role in incorporating discourse information (McNeill 1992, 2005). This study demonstrates that gestures pointing to the addressee establish cohesion via metonymy in Japanese face-to-face conversation.

2. Previous research

Pointing is the first manual gesture we human beings produce in our life (Lock 1980). Yet, it is not a simple act. It consists of three fundamental components: a point of origin (or 'origo', Bühler 1934), a target, and an iconic line or trajectory connecting the origo to the target (McNeill, Cassell,

[*] This is a part of my doctoral dissertation (Ishino 2007). I would like to thank Amy Franklin and David McNeill for their invaluable comments and suggestions. Needless to say, all remaining errors are mine.

265

and Levy 1993). In the field of gesture study, based on the existence or the presence of their referents, pointing (or deictic) gestures are classified into two types: concrete and abstract deixis (McNeill 1992, McNeill, Cassell, and Levy 1993). Concrete deixis makes a reference to physically present entities and abstract deixis points directed towards a seemingly empty space. The findings of McNeill, Cassell, and Levy (1993) show that abstract deixis provides new references in space. Contrastively, concrete deixis conveys a reference in its generation.

This paper explores concrete deictic gestures in order to demonstrate that some gestures that target persons who are physically present in space, not only refer to the addressee but also establish a cohesive tie by means of metonymy within discourse. According to Halliday and Hasan (1976: 4), cohesion is defined as "relations of meaning that exist within the text, and that defines it as a text." Furthermore, they add that the essence of cohesion is that "one item provides the source for the interpretation of another (ibid. 19)." Halliday and Hasan (ibid.) show that cohesion in speech can be established by: 1) reference, 2) substitution, 3) ellipsis, 4) conjunction, and 5) lexical cohesion (including repetition, synonym, and so on). The deictic gestures that are objects of this paper are concretely deictic but as this paper demonstrates these gestures also reflect abstract thinking. While the deictic gestures concretely point to the persons that are present in actual space, they also reflect metonymy in which the target of the point also stands for the referential contents of the deictic gesture. In that respect, these seemingly concrete pointing gestures have dual statuses: concrete and abstract. Though Bavelas, Chovil, Lawrie and Wade (1992) briefly mention that some interactive gestures have a function of citing what the other person said previously, no study has ever looked deeply into this phenomenon.

Examining pointing gestures in Zincantán, a Tzotzil (Mayan) language, Haviland (2003: 163-164) shows that pointing gestures are not "simple referring devices" but they serve as spoken deictics because pointing gestures do not always co-occur with spoken demonstratives. Ishino (2005) also shows that in Japanese gestures indexing speakers and addressees serve as first and second person pronouns respectively. In sign languages such as American Sign Language and Danish Sign Language, pointing has a function of pronouns (See Engberg-Pedersen 2003, Liddell 2003, among others).

3. Data Collection

The conversational data used in this study is taken from a face-to-face videotaped conversation. The participants in pairs were asked 1) to talk freely on any topic, 2) discuss something that recently made them angry, 3) to talk about the differences between the two idioms of anger; *hara ga tatu* ('for the belly to stand up [with anger]') and *atama ni kuru* ('for anger to come to the head'), or 4) to retell an animated cartoon to the addressee who has not seen it. Deictic gestures indexing addressees are selected for the analysis of their forms, meanings, and functions. Then, these gestures will be further analyzed considering referent. Among those that refer to something that is related to the addressee, conceptual metonymy is inferred from speech-gesture synchrony (Lakoff and Johnson 1980)[1]. Furthermore, I will determine whether or not the second person pronoun or any other linguistic expression referring to the addressee is overtly expressed. In the field of cognitive linguistics, metonymy is defined as:

> A cognitive process in which one conceptual entity, the vehicle, provides mental access to another conceptual entity, the target, within the same idealized cognitive model (Radden and Kövecses 1999).

This paper specifically deals with metonymy in which a person stands for what he or she previously mentioned, or a person stands for something that is related to him or her this is unclear.

4. Data Analysis

4.1. Possessor Stands For Possessed

The two male subjects in the next example had been lived in Southern California for approximately two years at the time of recording. The speaker S was 27 years old and the speaker K was 22 years old. In January, 1997, they were asked to converse freely for about half an hour and talked about their college in Santa Monica, family, and similar issues. The participants interacted on one previous occasion and both attended the college in Santa Monica. Both were speakers of the Japanese Kansai dialect. K is from Wakayama prefecture and S is from Mie prefecture. During their interaction, the speaker S states that he planned on remaining in the United States for five years. Then, the utterance in 2K, the speaker K points to the addressee while asking how many years his visa would be valid for. It is likely that K is thinking that since they have been in the U.S. for the same amount of time, S's visa will be expired within three years. While the gesture points to the addressee, it simultaneously makes a reference to the addressee's visa as inferred from the concurrent speech. Therefore, this deictic gesture is a manifestation of the conceptual metonymy, PERSON STANDS FOR WHAT HE IS ASSOCIATED WITH. Specifically, POSSESSOR STANDS FOR POSSESSED is inferred from the gesture-speech synchrony in Gesture 1. Here, the gesture pointing to the addressee establishes a cohesive linkage between the pointed person and the previous utterance. In response to the utterance in 1S, the speaker K points at the addressee while

---

[1] Conceptual metonymy is the basis of our general metonymic concepts in terms of which we organize our cognition (Lakoff and Johnson 1980). It is usually expressed in terms of A STANDS FOR B.

simultaneously asking how many years his visa would be valid for. The stroke of his pointing gesture synchronizes with the noun *biza* ('visa')[2]. Hence, the gesture-speech synchrony in (1) establishes a cohesive tie between the utterance in 1S and the word *biza* in the utterance in 2K and offers coherence to discourse.

1S: moo/ ato   go nen tat-tara $\emptyset_1$ doo na   n   desu ka nee?/
     more more five year pass-COND   how COP   NL   COP   Q   FP
     'When five more years pass, (I am) wondering how it will be.'

     maa $\emptyset_{it}$ ato   go-ka-nen keekaku na   n desu kedo   ne
     well   more five-CL-year plan   COP NL COP   though FP
     'Well, (it) is another-five-year-plan, you know.'

2K: %laugh [are? $\emptyset_{your}$ **biza** nan   nen?]
            well   visa how.many   year(s)
            'Well, how many year(s) (is your) visa (valid for)?'
                  1

Gesture (1):Pointing<the addressee, the addressee's visa>:RH: An extended index finger with the palm facing down points to the addressee at the right shoulder level.[3]

3S: biza wa
     viza TOP
     'Speaking of visa,'

4K: $\emptyset_{it}$ go nen   yaro
     five year   (I).suppose
     '(It) would be (valid for) five year(s).'

5S: go nen
     five year
     'Five year(s).'

In the pointing gesture in (1), the addressee is pointed at because the topic at hand (i.e., the visa) is in his possession. Japanese is a pro-drop language in which pronouns are usually not expressed when they are recoverable in discourse context. Hence, in the concurrent speech, a possessive pronoun for the visa is not expressed. However, the deictic gesture in (1) serves as a possessive pronoun (Haviland 2003, Ishino 2005). Simultaneously, the deictic gesture in (1) reflects metonymy. Langacker (2000) claims that possessives as well as metonymies are reference point phenomena.

---

[2] One gesture can consist of multiple phases; preparation, pre-stroke hold, stroke, post-stroke hold, retraction. Among them, the stroke phase is the main part of the gesture and conveys semantic or pragmatic information.

[3] <target, referent> indicates the target of the pointing gesture and its referent respectively.

According to Langacker (2000: 173), a referential point is defined as "the ability to invoke the conception of one entity for purposes of establishing mental contact with another, i.e. to single it out for individual conscious awareness." In example (1), the deictic gesture functions as a possessive pronoun while reflecting metonymy. While concretely pointing to the addressee in physical space, the deictic gesture is also abstract. While abstract in content, this gesture differs from the abstract deixis discussed in McNeill, Cassell, and Levy (1993) because its function is not to signal a new discourse topic, rather, it maintains the current discourse topic.

4.2. Narration

The next example is taken from a cartoon narration. In this episode, Sylvester the Cat makes a seesaw-like device to catapult himself up to catch Tweety Bird who is up in a building. Since the narrator M is unclear in his initial description concerning the approximate dimensions of the seesaw, at first the listener L is confused and does not understand what the device looks like even though the narrator says, *siisoo zyootai ni suru no ne* 'The thing is that he turns it into a seesaw.'

6L: aa   aa   aa
    I.see   I.see   I.see
    'I see. I see. I see.'

    nanka $\emptyset_{he}\emptyset_{it}$ GIKKONBATTAN   ni   suru   no   ne?[4]
    well   ONOM (i.e., seesaw) DAT   do   NL   FP
    'Well. (He) turns (it) into (a) seesaw, doesn't he?'

7M: $\emptyset_{that}$ [**soo**   soo   soo]
        right   right   right
    '(That/what you said is) right. Right. Right.'
    2
    Gesture (2):Pointing <addressee, what the addressee mentioned previously>: LH: The palm moves toward the addressee.

Finally, the listener understands it and confirms his understanding as in 6L. In 7M, acknowledging that what the addressee mentioned in 6L is correct, the speaker M utters the demonstrative *soo* meaning right three times.[5] Its first occurrence synchronizes with the deictic gesture in (2). In (2), the speaker M points to the addressee with the left palm. The gesture in (2) together with the speech refers back to the utterance in 6L. Hence, the speech and gesture together establish an anaphoric relation (i.e., cohesion)

---

[4] *GIKKONBATTAN* is used as a noun in this example and is derived from the onomatopoeia that indicates the sound of a seesaw moving up and down.
[5] The demonstrative *soo* in Japanese refers not only to a noun, an adverb, and a verb phrase but also to a clause.

to what the addressee previously mentioned. From the example in (2), the conceptual metonymy, PERSON STANDS FOR WHAT HE MENTIONED PREVIOUSLY is inferred.

4.3. Free discourse between friends

In the next fragment of discourse, the same subjects as in Example 1 begin to talk about how hard it was to get into universities when each of them took the entrance exam in Japan. K says that many of his friends had to take the exams three years in a row even though many new colleges were founded in his time. Then, S says that in his older brother's time, it was the hardest to pass the exam since it was the most competitive year in recent years in Japan. Then, K asks S if S's brother is as old as K is. S answers that he is around 25 years old. Then, he says the following:

8K: a $\emptyset_{that}$ soo?/
     oh   right
     'Oh. (Is that) right?'

$\emptyset_{he}$ wakai ne[e are $\emptyset_{he}$ kekkonsite   ru   tte $\emptyset_{you}\emptyset_{me}$ yuu ta:?]
     young FP well   being.married PRES QT   say PST
     '(He is) young! Well. Have (you) told (me) that (he) is married?'
                          3
Gesture (3):pointing <addressee, what the speaker suspects that the addressee might have said to him>:RH: The extended index finger touching the thumb points at the addressee.

9S: iya: $\emptyset_{he}$ site   nai   desu   yo   sonna zenzen
     no   doing   NEG   COP.P FP   that   absolutely.not
     'No, (he) is not! Absolutely not!'

     kanozyo mo   inai   n zya   nai n   desu ka
     girlfriend even non.existant NL COP.TOP NEG NL COP FP
     '(I am afraid) that (he) doesn't even have a girlfriend!'

The gesture pointing to the addressee in (3) co-occurs with the part of an interjection or a discourse marker (i.e., *are*) and the first part of verbal noun indicating marriage (i.e., *kekkon*) (Schiffrin 1987). The pointing gesture with an extended forefinger is produced precisely when K asks if S previously mentioned S's older brother's marital status. Simultaneously, the pointing gesture refers the speaker as well as to the content previously mentioned. This gesture manifests both deictic reference and metonymy. The conceptual metonymy THE PERSON STANDS FOR WHAT HE HAS MENTIONED is inferred. However, strictly speaking, in this example, the deictic gesture indicates what the speaker suspects that the addressee might have once mentioned. As in example in (2), the generalized conceptual metonymy PRODUCER FOR PRODUCT is inferred as well.

4.4. Conversation about anger between friends 1

In the next example, the participants are two female friends in their thirties discussing something that recently made them angry. The speaker P works at a hospital as an office clerk. She complains about harshness of nurses there. Then, the speaker N talks about her experience with a nurse as a patient.

10N: ano: atasi [maeni $\emptyset_{you}$ **yut-ta**   **kamosire**nai kedo:
     well   I   before   say-PST   might   though
     'Well. Though I might have said (to you) before,'

4

Gesture (4): Pointing <Addressee, what the speaker might have once mentioned to the addressee> and metaphoric:LH: The palm facing up is presented to the addressee at the waist level.

11P: un
     yeah
     'Yeah.'

12N: nanka / $\emptyset_1$ tyotto byooki-si-ta   toki   ni]
     well   little   sick-do-PST   time   LOC
     'Well, when (I) became a little sick,'

13P: un
     yeah
     'Yeah.'

14N: ano: $\emptyset_1$ mainiti tyuusya senna naor-ahen yoona kanzi   yat-te
     well   daily   injection do.must heal-NEG like   situation COP-and
     'Well. (I) was the patient who had to get injected everyday or (I) did not heal.'

Then, the speaker N repeatedly mentions that when she was angry because she was scolded harshly by the nurse. In the utterance in 10N, she says that she might have once said to P before (i.e., *atasi maeni $\emptyset_{you}$ yutta kamosirenai kedo*). On the contrary to the example in (3), here, the deictic gesture in (4) makes a reference to the utterance that the speaker suspects that 'she herself' might have once mentioned to the addressee. The speaker points at the addressee with her left palm facing upward. This gestural deixis simultaneously carries metaphoricity because this gesture also serves as a container for what the speaker might have once mentioned to the addressee. In the gesture in (4), the palm as a container with the speech is presented from the speaker to the addressee.[6] Thus, the origin of the gesture is the speaker and the target is the addressee. Further, this corresponds to

---

[6] This is an example of gestural conduit metaphors (See Reddy 1979).

the subject and the object of the verb (i.e., *yuu* 'to say') in the speech. From the gesture-speech synchrony in (4), the conceptual metaphors MEANINGS ARE OBJECTS IN CONTAINER, LINGUISTIC EXPRESSIONS ARE CONTAINER FOR MEANING OBJECTS, COMMUNICATION IS SENDING MEANING OBJECTS FROM MIND CONTAINER TO ANOTHER MIND CONTAINER ALONG A CONDUIT and the conceptual metonymy PRODUCER STANDS FOR PRODUCT are inferred (Cf. Conceptual metaphors are from Kövecses 2002). This gesture is not necessarily anaphoric to anything earlier in discourse since the utterance might have not been said. However, if it was mentioned, the antecedent or the referent of the deictic gesture is not in the immediate context. Moreover, the post-stroke hold for example (4) is quite long and the form of the gesture as a container is cataphoric to the discourse that follows. In 14N, the speaker N describes that happened when she told the nurse that she was supposed to receive her injection in a particular arm. The nurse scolds her saying that either arm is fine and that if she says such things she will not be able to give a birth to a baby (even if she was not pregnant at that time). In short, while the gesture might have been anaphoric to the utterance, it cataphorically refers to what the speaker is going to say to the addressee. In that respect, the deictic gesture with metaphoricity in example (4) establishes a cohesive link with the speech to follow.

4.5. Conversation about anger between friends 2
    In the next example in (5), two female speakers who are friends are discussing something that recently made them angry. The speaker J has been in Chicago for two years and T has lived in Chicago for three months at the time of recording. J talks about an incident when she made a trip lately. She and her family stayed at a hotel for three days and for the first two days there was always a bottle of water which they assumed was free and drank everyday. On the third day, it was not there. They called the front desk and asked them to bring water to their room. A boy showed up with a bottle. J wanted to confirm that it was free but the boy said to her that it cost her seven dollars. Both being non-native speakers, they had a difficulty in communicating well. So, she thought she would have to pay twenty-one dollars for three bottles of 'plain water.' And it made her angry. Then, in the following fragment, they talk that J and her family would have eaten a delicious meal instead of paying twenty-one dollars for water.

15J: $<$_laughing_ mainiti $\emptyset_{it}$ hurii   da   to: $\emptyset_I$ omotte$>$ %laugh
              everyday   free   COP   QT   thinking
       'Thinking everyday that (it) is free,'

16T: %laughter

17J: %laugh nanka koo   ee
        well   like.this oh.no
'Well. Like this, oh no!'

mikka   de nizyuui{$_1$ti* omizu de   nizyuuiti   doru}
three.days for twenty.one   water for   twenty.one dollar
'Twenty-one for three days, twenty-one dollars for water!'

18T: $\emptyset_{that}$ {$_1$%laughter honto   da:}   motto   hoka{$_2$ni moo}
                   true COP   more   else
                                                   EMPH
'(That) is true. (You could have had) something else.'

19J: {$_2$nan}ka sore   dat-tara /
        well   that   COP-COND
'Well. In that case,'

nanka   i-{$_3$ssyoku-bun   gurai ne?}
something one-CL-portion   about FP
'(We might have had) one portion of something, you know.'

20T: {$_3$oisii   mon / un   un}
        delicious thing   yeah yeah
'Yeah. Yeah. (You could have had) delicious foods.'

21J: $\emptyset_{so}$ [na: **toka**] omo-u   desyoo?
        FP   QT   think-PRES   COP
'(You would) think (so).'
      5
Gesture (5): pointing <addressee, what the addressee has just said>:
LH: The palm with the folded thumb moves toward the addressee.

22T: nanka   zettai   dokka   de   nee
        something absolutely   somewhere LOC FP
'(You) would absolutely be eating something delicious somewhere,'

oisii   no $\emptyset_{you}$ tabete masu yo nee
delicious   NL   eating POL   FP FP
'Right?'

In response to the utterance in 20T, in 21J, without citing what T has just said or intended to convey, J utters *na: toka omou desyoo* (i.e., 'would think that') while pointing to the addressee with her palm with the folded thumb. In 21J, the subject and the object of the verb 'to think' are unexpressed. However, the subject of the verb can be inferred from the target of the deictic gesture (i.e., the addressee) and the direct object (i.e., what the addressee has just mentioned) can be inferred from the gestural form (i.e., the palm). The content of the thought is not expressed in the utterance in 21J probably because the utterances of the two discourse participants overlap with one another intricately. Additionally, in the utterances in (18) – (20), the two discourse participants J and T together express what they might have done. In 21J, the subject and the object of the verb *omou* ('to think') are missing. However, the deictic gesture in (5) indicates that the missing subject is the addressee. Furthermore, the gestural form (i.e., the palm) displays that on the palm what the addressee has just mentioned or intended to convey is conceptualized to be placed. The speech-gesture synchrony in (5) refers back to the utterances in (18) – (20). From gesture-speech synchrony in (5), the conceptual metonymy PRODUCER STANDS FOR PRODUCT is inferred. Furthermore, this is another example of gestural conduit metaphors.

4. 6. Conversation about anger between husband and wife

In the next dyad, a husband and a wife who are happily married and both thirty years old at the time of recording, discuss differences between the two Japanese idioms of anger, *hara ga tatu* (literally, 'for the belly to rise up [with anger],' metaphorically, 'to get angry') and *atama ni kuru* (literally, '[for anger] to come to the head,' metaphorically, 'for anger to rise to the head'). The wife Q tells that when she has made some complaints to the customer service of discount furniture store over the phone and when they do not respond to her sincerely, she feels anger coming to the head in the manner of *KAA::*. Then, the husband R asks her if it is different from anger in which the belly rises up. The wife Q answers that it is different from *hara ga tatu* as in 24Q. Then, R comments that Q easily becomes the state of being *KAA* (i.e., she easily looses her temper) in 27R and 29R. Then, the wife Q points at the husband with her right extended index finger while uttering *dakedo soo dakara* (i.e., 'though, it is so'). The gesture in (6) co-occurs with the informal disjunctive subordinate conjunction *kedo* ('though'). The conjunction *kedo* offers a contrast with the utterance preceding it and here it offers a contrast with the utterance made by the addressee in 25R and 27R. In other words, the conjunction together with the pointing gesture makes a reference to the preceding utterances made by R. Redundant with previous sentence. In 25R and 27R, he says that his wife Q is short-tempered and easily looses her temper. As opposed to that, Q says, anger rising up in the belly stays long. In this way, the disjunctive conjunction together with the pointing gesture establishes a cohesive linkage with the utterances preceding it. The speaker R points at the husband because he is associated with the referential content (i.e., the utterance made by him). Therefore, metonymy reflected in the gesture in (6) provides cohesion in discourse. She continues to say that while anger rising up the belly seems to stay long there, anger coming to the head makes her feel intensive body heat coming to the head instantaneously.

23R: Ø$_{it}$ 'hara-ga-tatu'   to   wa   tigau?
     belly-NOM-rise.up QT   TOP   different
     'Is (it) different from *hara-ga-tatu*?'

24Q: Ø$_{it}$ Ø$_{from-it}$ tigau   //
     different
     '(It) is different (from "*hara-ga-tatu*").'

25R: Ø$_{that}$ a   s{okka:}   Q   wa:
     oh   right   Q   TOP
     'Oh. Is that so? You…'

26Q: {tabun}
     probably
     'Probably.'

27R: KAA-tto   suru   kara   {naa}
     ONOM-ADV   do   because   FP
     'Because you are in the state of being *KAA*. (i.e., "Because you are
     hot-tempered!").'

28Q: {%laughter}

29R: {%laugh} /Ø$_{you}$ iizirii / kire-ya{sui}
                    easily   cut-easy
     '(You) easily loose your temper.'

30Q: {%inhale ha*}

     [Ø$_{that}$ da kedo: soo dakara] 'hara-ga-tatu'   wa motto
             COP though so because   belly-NOM-rise.up TOP more
     'Though it is (so), and then. (I) feel that *hara-ga tatu*,'
                6
     *Gesture (6): pointing <addressee, what the addressee said>: RH: the
     extended index finger points at the addressee*

     nanka rongu taamu na   kanzi   na no yo //
     well   long   term ADJ   feeling COP NL FP
     'takes a long time, you know.'

From gesture-speech synchrony in (6), the conceptual metonymy PERSON
STANDS FOR WHAT HE MENTIONED is inferred.

4.7. Conversation about anger between friends 3

In the next example, after having talked about how harsh her coworker
nurses are and how contradictory they are, the same speaker P as in (4)
utters just the noun phrase marked with the topic marker *okori tai koto wa*
(i.e., 'what (I) want to be angry at') without a predicate in 31P. Then, in
32N, the speaker N adds the predicate to P's speech.

31P: u:n   moo   nee / $\emptyset_\text{I}$ okori   tai   koto   wa
     yeah   EMP FP   get.angry DESI   thing   TOP
     'Yeah. You know. What (I) want to be angry at,'

32N: {[**ippai**]} {%laugh}
     much
     'A lot.'
     7

Gesture (7): pointing <addressee, what the addressee wants to get mad at>:LH: The slightly cupped palm facing upward points to the addressee at left side of the body at a little above the waist level.

As shown, the last half of the utterance in 31P and the utterance in 32N together produce a complete proposition *okori tai koto wa ippai* ('what (I) want to be angry at is much' or 'There is a lot (I)'d like to be angry at'). While adding the noun phrase *ippai*, the speaker N presents the cupped palm facing upward toward the addressee. The form of this gesture in (7) shows metaphoricity as in Gestures (4) and (6) since the palm facing up serves as a container for what the addressee P mentioned in the preceding utterance (i.e., what she wants to be angry at). Additionally, *ippai* in this utterance means 'much' but it literally consists of one (i.e., *iti*) and a numerical classifier indicating a cup (i.e., *-hai*). In that respect, the gesture depicts the original meaning of *ippai* (i.e., one cup) in terms of gesture. At the same time, the gesture in (7) also makes a reference to the addressee's speech content because the palm moves (or is offered) toward her. Hence, the speech in 31 and 32, the gesture in (7), and the referential content of the deictic gesture (i.e., the utterance in 31) complement with one another and provide richer and fuller proposition (namely, 'There is a lot the speaker P would like to be angry at.'). In that respect, the deictic gesture is a part of linguistic system. Additionally, the deictic gesture in (7) unifies the two utterances made by the two discourse participants into one proposition as a whole. Hence, it establishes a cohesive linkage between the two utterances in discourse. In this example, not only metonymy but also metaphor layered in the deictic gesture in (7) contributes to create cohesion in discourse. From the gesture in (7), the conceptual metonymy PRODUCER STANDS FOR PRODUCT (or THE PERSON STANDS FOR WHAT SHE HAS MENTIONED) is inferred because the addressee is pointed at in order to refer back to what she has just mentioned.

5. Conclusion

The aim of this paper has been to show that some gestures pointing to the addressees establish a cohesive tie by means of metonymy. As illustrated in the examples above, gestures pointing to the discourse participants reflect discourse and cognitive information in face-to-face interaction. Furthermore, the data in this paper provide evidence that seemingly concrete pointing gestures are also abstract. They are abstract in the sense that they reflect abstract metonymic thinking while pointing at the persons who are present in physical space. In each example, the addressee is pointed at because he or she is associated with the referential content of the deictic gesture. Unlike abstract deictic gestures discussed in McNeill, Cassell, and Levy (1993), the deictic gestures provided in this paper do not "create a reference in the extra-linguistic context" rather they form cohesive links in discourse. These gestures often maintain discourse topic and unify discourse as a whole by connecting their targets (i.e., the addressee) and the referential contents together within discourse. Furthermore, gestures and concurrent speech in discourse set up cohesion in face-to-face interactions and unify discourse as a whole and so create coherence. Pointing gestures are prevalent and the first manual gesture we human beings make ontogenetically, and seemingly simple in form on the surface (Lock 1980). However, I conclude that they are cognitively complex, part of the linguistic system, and unify discourse as a whole. Most importantly, gestures pointing to the addressee are integral part of cognition and speech since overt linguistic expression such as a demonstrative pronoun is not always realized in Japanese discourse. In that respect, a gesture pointing to the addressee is often the only medium that overtly establishes cohesion within discourse. Though this paper focuses solely on gestures pointing to the addressees, the further research on discourse functions of gestures pointing to the speakers is also anticipated.

Appendix : Transcription Conventions

[ ]	the onset and the end of the gesture movement, respectively
BOLD	the stroke of gesture
UNDERLINE	indicates pre- or post-stroke gestural phase
RH	right hand LH left hand
UNINTEL	unintelligible speech
<$_{laughing}$ speech>	speech uttered while laughing
{$_n$ }	the point where overlapping speech begins and ends, the coindexed numbers indicate that they overlap with one another
:	lengthened syllable ? rising intonation
%	nonspeech sounds / pause
*	self-interruption
Ø$_{you}$	zero anaphor with unexpressed pronoun

References

Bavelas, J. B., N. Chovil, D. A. Lawlie and A. Wade. 1992. Interactive gestures. *Discourse Processes* 15: 469-489.

Bühler, K. 1934. Sprachteorie: *Die Darstellungsfunktion der Sprache*. Jena: Fischer. (Reprinted by Gustav Fischer Verlag, Stuttgart, 1965.)

Engberg-Pedersen, E. 2003. From pointing to reference and predication: Pointing signs, eyegaze, and head and body orientation in Danish Sign Language. *Pointing*. ed. S. Kita, 269-292. Mahwah, NJ: Lawrence Erlbaum Associates, Publications.

Halliday, M.A.K. and R. Hasan. 1976. *Cohesion in English*. London: Lognman.

Haviland, J. B. 2003. How to point in Zinacantán. *Pointing*, ed. S. Kita, 139-169. Mahwah, NJ: Lawrence Erlbaum Associates, Publishers.

Ishino, M. 2005. Pointing in face-to-face interaction. Paper presented at the Second Congress of International Society for Gesture Studies, Lyon, France.

Ishino, M. 2007. Metaphor and metonymy in gesture and discourse. Doctoral dissertation, University of Chicago.

Kövecses, Z. 2002. *Metaphor*. Oxford & New York: Oxford University Press.

Lakoff, G. and M. Johnson. 1980. *Metaphors we live by*. Chicago: University of Chicago Press.

Langacker, R. W. 2000. *Grammar and conceptualization*. Berlin: Mouton de Gruyter.

Liddell, S. 2003. *Grammar, gesture, and meaning in American Sign Language*. Cambridge: Cambridge University Press.

Lock, A. 1980. *The guided reinvention of language*. London: Academic Press.

McNeill, D. 1992. *Hand and mind*. Chicago: University of Chicago Press.

McNeill, D. 2005. *Gesture and thought*. Chicago: University of Chicago Press.

McNeill, D., J. Cassell, and E. Levy. 1993. Abstract deixis. *Semiotica* 95: 5-19.

Radden, G., and Kövesces, Z. 1999. Towards a theory of metonymy. *Metonymy in cognition and language*, eds. G. Radden and U-K. Panther, 17-59. Amsterdam: John Benjamins Publishing Company.

Reddy, M. 1979. The conduit metaphor. *Metaphor and thought*, ed. Ortony, 284-324. Cambridge: Cambridge University Press.

Schiffrin, D. 1987. *Discourse markers*. Cambridge: Cambridge University Press.

Intersubjectification and Textual Functions of Japanese *Noda* and Korean *Kes-ita**

JOUNGMIN KIM
KAORU HORIE
Tohoku University

1. Introduction

Japanese has a variety of nominal predicates e.g. *monoda, kotoda, noda,* and these are known to exhibit various modal-aspectual meanings (Horie 1997, 1998a, b, in press; see also Kim and Horie 2006). Among these nominal predicates, *noda* has been a focus of particularly intense scrutiny by Japanese linguistics (e.g. Tanomura 1990, Maynard 1997, Noda 1997, Kondo 2006, Najima 2007). *Noda* is known to receive contextually variable interpretations as shown in (1)–(2) (examples 1 and 2 are respectively from

* This study was supported in part by a grant from the Tohoku University 21st Century Center of Excellence Program in Humanities (http://www.lbc21.jp/) and a Grant-in-aid for Scientific Research from the Japan Society for the Promotion of Science (#18520290). Our thanks go to Andrew Barke, Alan H. Kim, and Janick Wrona, and the JK 16 editorial board for their constructive feedback.

Noda 1997, 66 and 92; glosses and translations are provided by the current authors):

(1) J. A,   ame-ga   hut-te iru-*nda*.
    A,   rain-NOM   fall-CONT:PRES-NODA
    '(lit.) Ah, it's that (=some evidence suggests) it's raining.'
(2) J. Osoku   nat-te   gomen. Basu-ga   okureta-*nda*.
    Become late be-CONJ   sorry   bus-NOM   was late-NODA
    '(lit.) Sorry for being late. *It's that* (*It is because*) the bus was late.'

Noda thus poses a challenging task to second language (L2) learners, who tend to overuse it when it isn't needed, as in (3). *Noda* in (3) sounds imposing and is not appropriate here. Korean L2 learners are no exception, despite the existence of a nominal predicate *kes-ita*, which is formally similar to *noda* (4).

(3) J. (When asked why one's assignment was submitted late)
    Byooki   datta   *n desu*   kara.
    sickness   was   NODA   because
    'Because I was sick, *you know*.'   (Kondo 2006: 68)
(4) K. Mwulka-ka   caknyen-ey   pihay   olu-n   *kes-ita*.
    price-NOM   last year-compared to   go up-REL:PST   KES-ITA
    '(lit.) It is that prices went up compared to the last year.'

This observation challenges us to investigate how *noda* and *kes-ita* are actually employed in Japanese and Korean texts.

The organization of this paper is as follows. Section 2 provides a brief overview of previous comparative studies on *noda* and *kes-ita*. Section 3 presents a contrastive linguistic analysis of the textual data on *noda* and *kes-ita* we collected. Section 4 addresses the theoretical implications of the contrastive linguistic observations made in section 3 from the perspective of subjectification and intersubjectification (Traugott 2003). Section 5 summarizes the findings and presents possible future directions.

2. Contrastive studies of *noda* and *kes-ita*: The state of the art

Numerous studies on Japanese *noda* have converged on its primary function of providing an explanation based on either linguistically and/or situationally given evidence (e.g. Kuno 1973, Tanomura 1990, Masuoka 1991, Noda 1997). Inspired by these studies, attempts have been made to compare it with its equivalent in other languages like Chinese *de* (Sugimura 1982). However, relatively few contrastive studies between *noda* and its Korean counterpart *kes-ita* have been carried out barring studies such as Horie (2003), Yin (2003), and Yukimatsu (2006).

Horie (2003) and Yin (2003), noting that *noda* and *kes-ita* share the function of 'background explanation', observe some interesting cross-linguistic differences. Horie (2003) draws attention to the fact that the 'evidential' function of *noda*, i.e. that of indexing linguistic or extralinguistic context as factual evidence/ground for a speaker's utterance, may not always be coded by its equivalent *kes-ita* (e.g. *o-n-keya* '*it's that* (rain) came/it rained'). Instead, either an unmarked final predicate form (e.g. *wa-ss-ta* '(rain) came/it rained') or a more explicit causal form (e.g *wa-se kulay* 'it's *because* (rain) came/it rained') may be employed. Such evidential function may not be overtly expressed, or a more overt causal form like *kulay* may be employed.

Yin (2003), a most detailed cross-linguistic study of *noda* and *kes-ita*, points out that, while *noda* can be used in conversation in emotionally neutral or marked contexts (the latter contexts conveying the speaker's surprise, insistence, or complaint), *kes-ita* tends to be employed in emotionally 'marked' contexts in conversation and to convey the speaker's strong opinion.

These studies, while touching on important issues, do not provide a theoretically grounded analysis of the intra-textual functions of *noda* and *kes-ita*. We will build on these cross-linguistic observations and present our analysis and discussion in Sections 3 and 4.

3. Contrasting textual functions of *noda* and *kes-ita*

In order to analyze the use of *noda* and *kes-ita*, we selected two contemporary novels with the same title "What comes after love", i.e. *Aino ato-ni kuru mono* (Japanese Novel, JN) by Hitonari Tsuji and *Salang hwu-ey o-nun kes-tul* (Korean Novel, KN) by Ji-Young Kong. These novels were written by two popular contemporary writers in a corroborative project and published in 2006 (JN) and 2005 (KN) respectively.

For the analytic framework, we adopted Noda (1997)'s classification of the functions of *noda* into (a) the "Event (E)-oriented (taizi-teki)" function, and (b) the "Addressee (A)-oriented (taizin-teki)" function. The "E-oriented function" is identified when *noda* refers to the speaker's attitude/evaluation toward the Event described as in (5)

(5) Sooka,   kono   suitti-wo   osu-*nda*.
    I see   this   switch-ACC push-NODA
    '*(Now I see that)* I should push this switch.'   (Noda 1997:67)

The "A-oriented function" is identified when *noda* is ostensibly targeted toward an addressee as shown in (6).

(6) Boku asita-wa   ko-nai-yo .   Yoozi-ga   aru-*nda*.
    I   tomorrow-TOP come-NEG-SFP business-NOM exist-NODA
    'I will not come tomorrow. It's *that (=because)* I have something to do.'   (Noda 1997:67)

According to Noda (1997: 67), the former (E-oriented *noda*) (5) is used when a speaker, at the time of speech, becomes aware of a state-of-affairs which were not known to her/him until that time. This is, as it were, a self-reflective function and the addressee is not required. On the other hand, the latter (A-oriented *noda*) (6) is used when a speaker conveys the state-of-affairs already known to him/her, to the addressee, who (s/he thinks) has not yet been aware of it. The presence of the addressee is required in the latter case. The presence of the addressee, regardless of whether it is linguistically mentioned or not, is thus a crucial factor in classifying the functions of *noda* into two categories.

Based on the classification above we first counted the tokens of *noda* in JN (including its variants like *nda* and *no*) and *kes-ita* in KN (including its variants *ke-ya*) occurring in the first 500 sentences of each text. We then classified these tokens into "E-oriented" and "A-oriented" tokens as shown in Table 1:

Table 1. Textual functions of *noda* and *kes-ita* in the first 500 sentences of JN and KN

	E(vent)-oriented	A(ddressee)-oriented	Total (%)
Japanese	32 (48.5 %)	34 (51.5 %)	66 (100 %)
Korean	27 (71.1 %)	11 (28.9 %)	38 (100 %)

Our preliminary distributional analysis reveals that the proportion of E-oriented and A-oriented tokens was reversed between the two languages. That is, Japanese had more A-oriented tokens than E-oriented tokens, while the opposite was the case in Korean. Let us look at the example of E-oriented function first (7a-b).

(7a) J. Kanozyo-no hanasu   nihongo-ni-wa   akusento-ga
        she-GEN   speak:REL:PRES Japanese-in-TOP   accent-NOM
        na-katta.   Wazato   isikisite   akusento-wo
        NEG-PST   intentionally   consciously   accent-ACC
        kesi-te iru   *noda*,   toiu   koto-ga
        remove-CONT:PRES   NODA   QT   fact-NOM
        atode   wakaru.
        later   come to know
        'There was no accent with the Japanese she was speaking. I later found *(based on some evidence)* that she got rid of intentionally.'
                                                                        (JN: 9)

(7b) K. Ku-ka   wa-ss-ta.   Ku-ka   cengmallo   nay
        he-NOM   come-PST-DECL   he-NOM   really   my

ap-ey　　　　　nathana-n　　　　　　*kes-ita.*
front-at　　　　appear-REL:PST　　　KES-ITA
'He really presented himself before my very eyes, *as I'm reporting in disbelief.*' (KN: 22)

In (7a), she got rid of her Japanese accent intentionally, and *noda* is used to convey the speaker's realization of the fact at that point in speech. Similarly in (7b), *kes-ita* is used to encode the speaker's sudden awareness of his presence before her very eyes. Both *noda* and *kes-ita* are self-reflective and are not intended for the addressee. Let us next consider the example of A-oriented function (8a-b).

(8a) J. Watasi-wa-ne,　　　anata-to　　kekkonsi-yoo-to　　zutto
　　　 I-TOP-SFP　　　　　 you-with　　marry-will-QT　　　long time
　　　 omot-te ita-*no.*
　　　 think-CONT:PST-NODA
　　　 '*You know*, I have been dreaming of marrying you for a long time'.
　　　 (JN: 19)
(8b) K. Mancye pelye-ss-e.　　Kulayse kunyang　sa-n　　　　*ke-ya.*
　　　 touch　end-PST-SE. so　　　just　　buy-REL:PST　KES-ITA
　　　 '(I) touched (it). So (I) just bought (it), *you see.*' (KN: 6)

No in (8a) is used when the speaker makes a confession that she has wanted to marry him (= the addressee), which wasn't known to him until that point in speech. In a similar fashion, *ke-ya* in (8b) is used to express the reason that the speaker bought it (= the clothes) to her friend (= the addressee), which wasn't revealed until that point in speech. Crucially, in both (8a) and (8b), *noda* and *kes-ita* tokens are intended toward the addressee and require his/her presence.

It is observable that both *noda* and *kes-ita* have two functions, i.e. E-oriented and A-oriented functions, which are distinguishable through contextual analysis. It was found that the proportion of A-oriented tokens and E-oriented tokens was reversed between the two languages, with more A-oriented tokens attested in Japanese. Does this suggest that the A(ddressee)-oriented function is more prominent with Japanese *noda* than with Korean *kes-ita*? We will explore this issue in Section 3.1.

3.1 (Inter)subjective meaning of *noda* and *kes-ita*
In order to ascertain the functional differences between *noda* and *kes-ita*, we conducted another parallel-corpus based study based on a Japanese novel entitled "Madogiwa no Totto Chan" by Tetstuko Kuroyanagi (288 pages) and its Korean translated version "Changka-uy Thotho" (229 pages) translated by Kim Nan-ju, by collecting *noda*-tokens and *kes-ita* tokens. It should be first noted that the number of *noda* tokens in the original Japa-

nese version (219 tokens) was more than twice that of *kes-ita* tokens (71 tokens).

What was more interesting was that, as indicated by Yin (2003), *noda* tended to be translated as *kes-ita* when the former was used to express the speaker's emotivity such as blame, displeasure, and surprise (9a-b) (see Horie, Shimura, and Pardeshi 2006, for an intricate interrelationship between emotivity, language structure and use).

(9a) J. Tukue-de   oto-wo   tate-nai-na- to   omou-to
    desk-INST   sound-ACC make-NEG-SFP-QT   think-as
    kondo-wa   zyugyoo-tyuu   tatte-iru-*ndesu*!
    this time-TOP   class-during   standup-CONT: PRES-NODA
    Zutto!
    continually   (TOTTO: 16)

(9b) K. Eccay   chayksang   soli-lul   nay-ci anhnunda-sip-ese
    somehow   desk   sound-ACC   make-NEG-seem-because
    tolapo-myen   ipen-ey-nun   swuep-cwung-ey
    look back-COND   this time-LOC-TOP   class-during-LOC
    se-iss nun   *ke-ye-yo*!   Kyeysokhayse!
    stand up-CONT:PRES   KES ITA-SE:POL   continually
    'Just as I was thinking (she) does not seem to make sound at the desk, next thing, *(surprisingly)* (she) keeps standing all the time during the class!'

Furthermore, *noda* is generally used in Japanese to mark politeness toward the addressee(s) as in (10a). Such usage of *kes-ita* in Korean does not occur, as demonstrated by the unacceptability of (10b).

(10a) J. Onegai-ga   aru-ndesu-ga...
    favor-NOM   exist-NODA-but
    'Can I ask a favor of you? (lit.) *(It's that)* I have a favor.'

* (10b) K. Pwuthak-i   iss-nun   *kes-i*-ntey-yo...
    favor-NOM   exist-REL:PRES   KES-ITA-but-SE
    'Can I ask a favor of you? (lit.) I have an asking...'

While both *noda* and *kes-ita* can take on subjective meaning (9a, b), *noda* can also take on addressee-oriented meaning with a politeness effect (10a), the latter meaning virtually absent in *kes-ita* (10b).

This contrastive observation accords with the quantitative difference, noted in Table 1, in terms of the reversed proportion of E(vent)-oriented tokens and A(ddressee)-oriented tokens. Event-oriented usage of *noda* and *kes-ita* is subjective in that these forms encode the speaker's (reflective) realization of a state-of-affairs with or without emotive reaction. In contrast, Addressee-oriented usage, prominent with *noda* (see Table 1 and examples

10a), is 'intersubjective' (Traugott 2003) in that the form indexes the speaker's conveyance of his/her realization to his/her addressee, with or without politeness effect. We will address the theoretical implications of this contrast between *noda* and *kes-ita* in Section 4.

4. (Inter)subjectification of *noda* and *kes-ita*

In Section 3, we observed that *noda* and *kes-ita* can serve E(vent)-oriented and A(ddressee)-oriented textual functions, respectively relevant to 'subjective' and 'intersubjective' meanings (e.g. Traugott 2003).

Importantly, we noted some interesting quantitative and qualitative differences between *noda* and *kes-ita*. This section inquires into the nature of the cross-linguistic contrast between *noda* and *kes-ita*.

Recent studies on grammaticalization identify semantic-pragmatic changes referred to as "subjectification" and "Intersubjectification". Subjectification refers to the semantic-pragmatic change in which "meanings tend to become increasingly based in SP/W's (speaker/writer: KH) subjective belief state or attitude toward what is being said and how it is being said" (Traugott 2003: 124). Intersubjectification, in turn, refers to "a mechanism whereby meanings become more centered on the addressee" (Traugott 2003: 129). Crucially, unidirectionality is identified between these two types of change, and subjectification precedes intersubjectification, not vice versa, as proposed in (11):

(11) non-subjective > subjective > intersubjective (p.134)

In terms of subjectification, it is fair to say that both *noda* and *kes-ita* have acquired subjective meaning as markers of a speaker's evidential judgment. However, as pointed out by Yin (2003) *kes-ita* hasn't completely undergone semantic generalization when it is employed in conversation because it tends to be restricted to emotionally marked contexts. Furthermore, in terms of intersubjectification, *noda* appears to have taken on an intersubjective meaning to a greater extent than its Korean counterpart *kes-ita* in view of the fewer attested A-oriented tokens of *kes-ita* (see Table 1) and the virtual absence of the addressee politeness function of *kes-ita* (10b).

Interestingly, this contrast in terms of intersubjectification is also corroborated by the development of pragmatic meaning with other grammatical resources in Japanese and Korean. For instance, Japanese sentence-final particles, e.g. *ne, yone*, are known to index sensitivity to the addressee's territory of information (Kamio 1994) more prominently than their Korean counterparts (H. Lee 1991, Horie and Taira 2002).

In a similar vein, Strauss and Sohn (1998) report that a Japanese completive aspectual *-te simau*, particularly its truncated form *-tyau* has advanced further in terms of addressee-oriented stance-taking meaning (12) than its Korean counterpart *-e pelita*, which lacks such meaning.

(12) Moo   non-*zyat-ta*.   Gomen-ne.
   already   drink-CHAU-PST. sorry-SFP
   'Oh, I started *without you*. Sorry.'(Strauss and Sohn 1998: 229, minor
   modification added)

In fact, as extensively discussed by Horie (2007), the greater prominence of intersubjectification in Japanese as contrasted with Korean is observable in a variety of grammatical constructions (e.g. quotative constructions, modal markers; see Ishihara, Horie, and Pardeshi 2006 for 'double' causative constructions) which are superficially very similar between the two languages in terms of their formal and functional characteristics. This suggests that such a contrast in terms of the greater/lesser degree of prominence in intersubjectification is not accidental, but that it has arguably been nurtured over time through different communicative and cultural practices (cf. Ide 2006, Enfield and Levinson 2006), though it is beyond the scope of this paper.

5. Conclusion

In this paper we have examined the textual functions of the nominal predicates *noda* in Japanese and *kes-ita* Korean. *Kes-ita* was shown to be more restricted to encode subjective (particularly emotive) meaning relative to *noda*. *Noda*, in contrast, exhibits higher sensitivity to the feeling state of an addressee than *kes-ita*. How these cross-linguistic contrasts in the degree of intersubjectification have emerged will need to be investigated from a cultural anthropological point of view.

Abbreviations:

ACC: Accusative	COND:Conditional	CONT: Continue	DECL: Declative
GEN: Genitive	INST: Instrumental	LOC: Locative	NEG: Negative
NOM: Nominative	POL: Polite	PRES: Present	PST: Past
PT: Particle	Q: Question	QT: Quotation	REL: Relative
SE: Sentence Ender	SFP: Sentence Final Particle		TOP: Topic

References

Enfield, Nick J., and Stephen C. Levinson. 2006. (eds.) *Roots of Human Sociality*. London: Berg.

Horie, Kaoru. 1997. Three types of nominalization in Modern Japanese: *No, koto* and zero. *Linguistics* 35-5, 879-894.

Horie, Kaoru. 1998a. Functional duality of case-marking particles in Japanese and its implications for grammaticalization: A contrastive study with Korean. In: Silva, David. (ed.), *Japanese/Korean Linguistics* 8. Stanford: CSLI, 147-159.

Horie, Kaoru. 1998b. On the polyfunctionality of the Japanese particle *no*: From the perspectives of ontology and grammaticalization. In: Ohori, Toshio. (ed.), *Studies in Japanese Grammaticalization: Cognitive and Discourse Perspectives.* Tokyo: Kuroshio, 169-192.

Horie, Kaoru. 2003. Differential manifestations of "modality" between Japanese and Korean: A typological perspective. In: Chiba, Shuji et al. (eds.), *Empirical and Theoretical Investigations into Language.* Tokyo: Kaitakusya, 205-216.

Horie, Kaoru. 2007. Subjectification and intersubjectification: A comparative-typological perspective. *Journal of Historical Pragmatics* 8.2, 311-323.

Horie, Kaoru. In press. In: López-Couso, María José and Elena Seoane (eds.) Grammaticalization of nominalizers in Japanese and its theoretical implications: A contrastive study with Korean. *Rethinking Grammaticalization: New Perspective for the Twenty-first Century.* (Typological Studies in Language Series). Amsterdam: John Benjamins.

Horie, Kaoru, and Kaori, Taira. 2002. Where Korean and Japanese differ: Modality vs. Discourse Modality. In: Akatsuka, Noriko, and Susan Strauss. (eds.), *Japanese/ Korean Linguistics* 10. Stanford: CSLI, 178-191.

Horie, Kaoru, Miya Shimura, and Prashant Pardeshi. 2006. Overt anaphoric expressions, empathy, and the *uchi-soto* distinction. A contrastive perspective. In: Suzuki Satoko. (ed.) 2006. *Emotive Communication in Japanese.* Amsterdam: John Benjamins, 173-190.

Ide, Sachiko. 2006. *Wakimae no Goyooron* ('Pragmatics of *Wakimae*'). Tokyo: Taishukan.

Ishihara, Tsuneyoshi, Kaoru Horie, and Prashant Pardeshi. 2006. What does Korean 'Double Causative' reveal about causation and Korean? A contrastive study with Japanese. In: Vance, Timothy. (ed.), *Japanese/Korean Linguistics* 14. Stanford: CSLI, 321-330.

Kamio, Akio. 1994. The theory of territory of information: The case of Japanese. *Journal of Pragmatics* 21, 67-100.

Kim, Joung-min, and Kaoru, Horie. 2006. Sentence final nominalizaiton in Korean : A contrastive study with Japanese. In: O' Grady, William et al. (eds.), *Inquires into Korean Linguistics* II. Seoul: Thaehaksa, 27-34.

Kondo, Atsuko. 2006. *Noda* ga sihyoosuru hanasite no syukansei ('Speaker's subjectivity Indexed by Noda'). *Gengo* ('Language'). (Taishukan shoten) 35.5, 68-73.

Kuno, Susumu. 1973. *The Structure of the Japanese Structure.* Cambridge, MA: MIT Press.

Lee, Hyo-Sang.1991. *Tense, Aspect, and Modality. A Discourse-Pragmatic Analysis of Verbal Affixes in Korean from a Typological Perspective.* Unpublished doctoral dissertation, UCLA.

Masuoka, Takashi. 1991. *Modariti no Bunpoo* ('The Grammar of Modality'). Tokyo: Kuroshio.

Maynard, Senko K. 1997. *Japanese Communication.* Honolulu: University of Hawaii Press.

Najima, Yoshinao. 2007. *Noda no Imi to Kinoo. Kanrensei Riron no Kanten kara* ('The Meaning and Function of *Noda*. From the Viewpoint of Relevance Theory'). Tokyo: Kuroshio publishers.

Noda, Harumi.1997. *Noda no Kinoo* ('The Function of Noda'). Tokyo: Kuroshio publishers.

Strauss, Susan, and Sung-Ock Sohn 1998. Grammaticalization, aspect, and emotion: The case of Japanese -*te shimau* and Korean -*a/e pelita*. In: Silva, David. (ed.), *Japanese/Korean Linguistics* 8. Stanford: CSLI, 217-230.

Sugimura, Hirobumi. 1982. *Shi...de*: Tyuugokugo no 'noda' no bun (*'Shi...de: Noda* sentence in Chinese'). In: Teramura, Hideo et al. (eds.), *Kooza Nihongogaku* 12. *Gaikokugo to no Taisyoo* Ⅲ. ('Japanese Linguistics Series. A Contrastive Study with Foreign Languages'). Tokyo: Meiji Shoin, 154-172.

Tanomura, Tadaharu. 1990. *Gendai Nihongo no Bunpoo* I: *Noda no Imi to Kinoo* ('Modern Japanese Grammar I: The Meaning and Function of *Noda*'). Osaka: Izumi Shoten.

Traugott, Elizabeth Closs. 2003. From subjectification to intersubjectification. In: Hicky, Raymond. (ed.), *Motives for Language Change*. Cambridge: Cambridge University Press, 124-139.

Yin, Seng-hee. 2003. *Nihongono Noda to Kankokugo no -N kes-ita no Taisyoo Kenkyuu* ('A Contrastive Study of Japanese *Noda* and Korean -*N kes-ita*'). Unpublished doctoral dissertation, Ochanomizu Woman's University.

Yukimatsu, Eri. 2006. *Noda* to *kes-ita* no nikkan taisyoo kenkyuu: Honyaku-wo toosite miru kyootuten-to sooiten ('A contrastive Study of *noda* and *kes-ita*: Similarities and differences through comparison of translations'). In: Ogoshi, Naoki. (ed.), *Nihongo to Tyoosengo no Taisyoo Kenkyuu* ('A Contrastive Study of Japanese and Korean'). Report of the 21st century COE Program Center for Evolutionary Cognitive Sciences, University of Tokyo, 107-158.

Data:

Aino ato-ni kuru mono (2006) by Hitonari Tsuji, Tokyo: Gentosha.

Salang hwu-ey o-nun kes-tul (2005) by Ji-Young Kong, Seoul: Sodam Publishing.

Madogiwa no Totto Chang (1984) by Tetstuko Kuroyanagi, Tokyo: Kodansha.

Changka-uy Thotho (2000) translated by Kim, Nan-ju, Seoul: Prometheus Publishing.

The Asymmetry between the *Iki* (Go)-V and the *Ki* (Come)-V Constructions

NORIKO MATSUMOTO
Doshisha Women's College of Liberal Arts

1. Introduction

Linguistic semantics and grammatical structures are based on conventional imagery, which reflects our ability to construe a conceived situation in alternate ways, and the speaker's role in construing the situations in particular ways is almost always motivated by discoverable aspects of particular usages of grammatical structures. There are many ways of explicating linguistic forms, functions, and meanings. Even when various kinds of phenomena can be subsumed with effort under a highly limited number of rules, this paper, which takes a cognitive linguistic approach to the investigation of linguistic phenomena, cannot accept that such phenomena have thus been explicated. This paper emphasizes that only when linguistic phenomena and human cognition are plausibly connected can such phenomena explicated.

The Japanese deictic verbs, *iku* 'go' and *kuru* 'come', have been a prolific research area for many years. Many approaches to *iku* and *kuru* in the cognitive and the functional paradigms have attached great importance to the meaning(s) of *iku* and/or *kuru*. Although describing the semantic differences between *iku* and *kuru* is of primary importance, this paper will focus specifically on lexical V-V compounds, including *iku* and *kuru*. Many studies on such compounds have paid attention to the meaning(s) of V-*te*(Aspect)-*iku* construction and/or the V-*te*(Aspect)-*kuru* construction. However, this paper will shed light on the *iki*(go)-V and the *ki*(come)-V constructions, to which previous works have paid little attention. Lexical V-V compounds in Japanese can be divided into seven types in terms of the semantic relationships between V1 and V2 (Matsumoto 1996). They are pair compounds, cause compounds, manner compounds, means compounds, compounds exhibiting other relations, compounds with semantically deverbalized V2, and compounds with semantically deverbalized V1. Whereas the *ki*-V construction occurs only in means compounds, the *iki*-V construction occurs in the six types of compounds other than pair compounds. Where does this asymmetry originate in? To answer this question, this paper will explore both the *iki*-V and the *ki*-V constructions through two image schemas, the COMPULSION schema encoded by *iku* and the TERMINATION schema encoded by *kuru* (Radden 1996).

The goal of this paper is to elucidate that the image schematic characterization of *iku* and *kuru* plays a decisive role in determining the meanings of the *iki*-V and the *ki*-V constructions. This paper will proceed as follows. In order to give my cognitive linguistic approach an appropriate context, Section 2 briefly explains what cognitive linguistics is. Section 3 presents two image schemas, the COMPULSION schema encoded by *iku* and the TERMINATION schemas encoded by *kuru*. Section 4 gives a very brief summary of lexical V-V compounds in Japanese. Section 5 explicates the asymmetry between the *iki*-V and the *ki*-V constructions and the distinguishing features of the *iki*-V construction. Section 6 offers some conclusions regarding the two constructions.

2. Cognitive Linguistics

Cognitive linguistics practice can be roughly divided into two main areas of research, cognitive semantics and cognitive grammar. Cognitive semantics is concerned with investigating conceptual structures and conceptualization. In other words, cognitive semantics is concerned with investigating the human mind as well as linguistic semantics. Cognitive semantics is not a single unified framework, but Evans et al. (2007) point out that there are four guiding principles that collectively characterize cognitive semantics: Conceptual structure is embedded; semantic structure is conceptual structure; meaning representation is encyclopedic; and meaning construction is conceptualization. Many significant theories and approaches in cognitive semantics best exemplify the four guiding principles.[1]

In this paper, image schema theory is essential. The theoretical construct of the image schema theory was developed in particular by Johnson (1987), who proposed that one way where embodied experience manifests itself at the cognitive level is in terms of image schemas. As they are dynamic recurring patterning of our mundane bodily experiential interactions, image schemas are embodied. As they can be meaningful for us at a non-propositional level, they derive from and are linked to human preconceptual experience.[2] Image schemas indeed are psychologically real and functional in many aspects of how people process linguistic and nonlinguistic information (Gibbs and Colston 1995). Thus they most transparently reflect the first guiding principle of cognitive semantics which maintains that conceptual structure is embodied.

Cognitive grammar assumes cognitive semantics and is concerned with investigating a model of grammar which is consistent with the assumptions and findings of research in cognitive semantics (see Langacker 1987, 1991, Goldberg 1995, and Croft 2002). In addition to this, there are two guiding principles of cognitive grammar, the symbolic thesis and the usage-based thesis. The symbolic thesis holds that the fundamental unit of grammar is a form-meaning pairing, that is, a symbolic unit. To put it another way, all linguistic forms, from single morphemes to words, phrases, idioms, clauses, and sentences, contribute to and express meaning. This means that meaning must be the primary focus of study in cognitive grammar. The usage-based thesis, which constitutes a nonreductive approach to linguistic structure, is primarily concerned with the characterization of language as it is spoken and understood, as well as with the dynamics of its use. Its goal is to depict the complexity of language use.

---

[1] Some of the significant theories and approaches include image schema theory, encyclopedic semantics approach, categorization and Idealized Cognitive Models (ICMs), cognitive lexical semantics approach, metaphor theory, metonymy theory, Mental Space theory, and conceptual blending theory (see Fillmore 1975, Lakoff and Johnson 1980, Fauconnier 1985, Johnson 1987, Lakoff 1987, Talmy 2000, and Fauconnier and Turner 2002).

[2] Mandler (2004) describes the process of forming image schemas in terms of a redescription of spatial experience. She points out that "one of the foundations of the conceptualizing capacity is the image schema, in which spatial structure is mapped into conceptual structure" (Mandler 1992:591). She further suggests that "basic, recurrent experiences with the world form the bedrock of the child's semantic architecture, which is already established well before the child begins producing language" (Mandler 1992:597).

3. *Iku* and *Kuru* in Japanese and the Image Schemas

Roughly speaking, previous studies on the verbs *iku* and *kuru* are based on two types of properties of motion, deixis and viewpoint. On the basis of deixis, the potential for *iku* and *kuru* to focus on either the starting point or the end point is connected with the deictic grounding of the situation (cf. Fillmore 1971). The different focuses which *iku* and *kuru* impose on a motion event are illustrated in Figure 1.

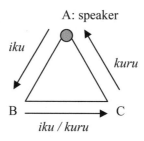

A: speaker

iku

kuru

B ⟶ C

iku / kuru

Figure 1.

Iku from the speaker's place, Point A, to Point B in Figure 1 corresponds to (1), and *kuru* from Point C to Point A to (2). *Iku* and *kuru* from Point B to Point C correspond to (3) and (4).

(1) Watashi wa   ginkoo ni   it-ta.
    I Top   bank Goal   go-Past
    'I went to the bank.'

(2) Sobo ga   boku no   ie ni   ki-ta.
    Grandmother Nom   I Gen   house Goal   come-Past
    'My grandmother came to my house.'

(3) Ani ga   haha no   heya ni   it-ta.
    Brother Nom   mother Gen   room Goal   go-Past
    'My brother went to my mother's room.'

(4) Keikan ga   futari ani no   ie ni   ki-ta.
    Police.officer Nom   two   brother Gen house Goal   come-Past
    'Two police officers came to my brother's house.'

In addition to the actual motion uses, the meanings of *iku* and *kuru* contrast in their non-physical or metaphorical uses. In this sense, *iku* from Point A to Point B corresponds to (5), and *kuru* from Point C to Point A to (6). *Iku* and *kuru* from Point B to Point C correspond to (7) and (8).

(5) Asu   gookaku tsuuchi ga iku-deshou.
   Tomorrow letter.of.acceptance Nom go-Future
   'Tomorrow you will get a letter of acceptance.'
(6) Sakujitsu gookaku tsuuchi ga ki-ta.
   Yesterday letter.of.acceptance Nom come-Past
   'Yesterday I got a letter of acceptance.'
(7) Kooshou wa   umaku it-ta.
   Negotiation Top well   go-Past
   'The negotiation has gone well.'
(8) Kooshou wa   dotanba ni   ki-ta.
   Negotiation Top the.eleventh.hour Goal come-Past
   'The negotiation came to a head.'

Moreover, apart from providing the deictic anchoring of a situation in relation to the speaker or the hearer, *iku* and *kuru* can show a scene from a particular viewpoint, as illustrated in Figure 2 (cf. Clark 1974).

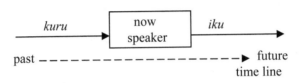

Figure 2.

Kuru in Figure 2 corresponds to (9) and (10), and *iku* to (11) and (12).

(9) Suguni atama ni   pinto ki-ta.
   Soon   Head Goal ping come-Past
   'It clicked right away.'
(10) Kono mise no   seikyuugaku to ki-tara
   This shop Gen price Focus come-Conditional
   shinjirarenai yo.
   unbelievable Sentence final particle
   'I can't believe the prices they charge at this shop.'
(11) Mooichido hajime   kara   iki-mashou
   Again   beginning from Source go- Polite
   'It's back to basics.'
(12) Purasu shikoo de   iki-nasai.
   Plus   thinking Purposive go-Imperative
   'Look at the bright side.'

The notion of viewpoint could be seen as a comprehensive concept which covers both the deictic viewpoint taken by one of the speech act participants and the mental viewpoint taken by the narrator. Nevertheless, it is obvious that the meanings of the deictic verbs *iku* and *kuru* are not simple.

To capture the complexities of *iku* and *kuru*, this paper will propose a schematic characterization of *iku* and *kuru* on the basis of Johnson (1987) and Radden (1996). The schematic characterization is valid for all instances. This paper uses the COMPULSION schema and the TERMINATION schema, as in Figure 3 (see Radden 1996:436-438).

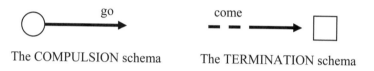

The COMPULSION schema　　The TERMINATION schema

Figure 3.

Such two schemas are called image schema. It should be emphasized here that image schemas are not specific images but are schematic. Both the COMPULSION and the TERMINATION schemas are closely related to the PATH schema (see Johnson 1987:28). The PATH schema is one of the most fundamental image schemas and one of the most common structures that emerge from our constant bodily functioning.[3] As in Figure 4, the PATH schema consists of three elements, a source point A, a terminal point B, and a vector tracing a path between them, and a relation specified as a force vector moving from A to B.

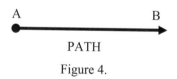

PATH

Figure 4.

Lakoff and Johnson (1999:33) point out that the PATH schema itself is topological in the sense that a path can be expanded, shrunk, or deformed

---

[3] Mandler (1996:373) points out that the first image schema that infants form is the PATH schema, which represents any object moving or any trajectory through space.

and still remains a path. The distinction between the COMPULSION and the TERMINATION schemas depends on what part in the PATH schema is highlighted. The COMPULSION schema focuses on the source part of a movement and is appropriately encoded by *iku*.[4] On the other hand, the TERMINATION schema focuses on the goal part of a movement and is appropriately encoded by *kuru*. Therefore, *iku* and *kuru* are not symmetrical. In Section 5, these two schemas are pivotal to the explanation of the defining characteristics of the *iki*-V and the *ki*-V constructions.

4. Lexical V-V Compounds in Japanese

V-V compounds in Japanese can be divided into two major types, syntactic compound verbs and lexical compound verbs (Kageyama 1993). Syntactic compound verbs are V-V compound verbs which involve some kind of complement structure. In contrast, lexical compound verbs do not involve any complement structure. The two types of V-V compounds also share some common characteristics. Morphologically, V1 is in the Renyookei form, and V2 inflects for tense. The compound constitutes one morphological word, and it satisfies the syntactic criteria for morphological wordhood.[5] This paper will shed light on lexical compound verbs.

This section will demonstrate some semantic characteristics of lexical compound verbs briefly. First, although they have internal relations, lexical compounds as symbolic units, that is, Gestalts, are holistic (see Lakoff 1977).[6] Gestalts have additional properties by virtue of being wholes. In fact, lexical compounds as symbolic units convey additional meanings such as most vivid, lively manner, but the additional meanings are not reducible to each meaning that each verb has. For instance, *iki-ataru* (go-hit, 'come upon') in (13) conveys an implication that the fact that we came upon the accident scene is totally unexpected and so surprising.

(13) Wareware wa   jikogenba ni   iki-atat-ta.
     We Top   accident.scene Goal go-hit-Past.
     'We came upon the accident scene.

Such an implication as the additional meanings does not emerge from the sum of parts, because neither *iku* 'go' itself nor *ataru* 'hit' itself convey the connotation of unexpectedness and of getting g a surprise. Rather, the im-

---

[4] According to Johnson (1987:45-6), compulsion is described as follows: The force comes from somewhere, has a given magnitude, moves along a path, and has a direction.

[5] V1 and V2 cannot be separated from each other by any particles (e.g. *iki wa ataru) and the compound allows Renyookei Nominalization (e.g. *iki-atari* 'encountering by going').

[6] Gestalt means that the whole is different from the sum of all its parts. One Gestalt has qualities that are not present in any of its parts by themselves.

plication emerges from the whole, that is, *iki-ataru* itself. This means that one lexical compound verb semantically constitutes one word.

Second, lexical compounds represent the principle of sequential order as the principle of iconicity. The principle of sequential order is a phenomenon of both temporal events and the linear arrangement of elements in a linguistic construction. The sequence of the two verbs corresponds to the natural temporal order of events, which signifies that V1 precedes V2.

Next, lexical compound verbs can be divided into seven types in terms of the semantic relationship between V1 and V2 (see Matsumoto 1996). The seven types can be divided into two groups. In the first group, V1 and V2 have their full verbal meanings. In pair compounds such as *hikari-kagayaku* (shine-shine, 'shine brightly'), the two component verbs with similar meanings are compounded to indicate the repetitiveness or intensity of the process that the two components express. In cause compounds such as *kuzure-ochiru* (collapse-fall, 'collapse down'), V1 represents the cause by which the process denoted by V2 comes to happen. In manner compounds such as *tachi-narabu* (stand-line.up, 'line up'), V1 represents a manner in which the process denoted by V2 is performed. In means compounds such as *oshi-taosu* (push-topple, 'push down'), V1 is the means by which the process denoted by V2 is performed. There are some compounds exhibiting other relations which are different from the four types indicated above. For instance, V1 cannot represent the result of purpose of V2. An example is *marume-komu* (roll-put.in, 'roll and put in'). In the second group, V1 or V2 loses or bleaches its verbal meaning and is used to add an adverbial meaning to the other verb. There are compounds where V1 loses its verbal meaning, such as *sashi-semaru* (*sasu*-come.close, 'become urgent'). In contrast, there are compounds where V2 loses its verbal meaning and takes on adverbial meaning, such as *shikari-tsukeru* (scold-, 'scold harshly')

5. The *Iki*-V and the *Ki*-V Constructions

In three dictionaries such as *Daijirin* (1995), *Kojien* (1998), and *Nihongo Dai Jiten* (2001), there are 71 entries as instances of the *iki*-V construction and 26 entries as instances of the *ki*-V construction. However, the majority of entries are archaic words. In this paper 14 instances of the *iki*-V construction and 2 instances of the *ki*-V construction are selected as modern words, as in Table 1. In particular, the instances of the *iki*-V construction are so familiar to native speakers of Japanese, and its frequency is high.

Table 1: Instances of the *iki*-V and *ki*-V constructions

	the *iki*-V construction	the *ki*-V construction
pair compounds		
cause compounds	*iki-au* (go-meet) 'go and meet – by chance' *iki-ataru* (go-hit) 'come upon'	
manner compounds	*iki-kau* (go-pass.each.other) 'come and go' *iki-kureru* (go-draw.in) 'get dark on one's way to –'	
means compounds	*iki-awaseru* (go-match) 'happen to go to the same place at the same time' *iki-kakaru* (go-reach) 'pass – by chance' *iki-sugiru* (go-pass) 'go past' *iki-tsuku* (go-arrive) 'arrive at one's destination'	*ki-awaseru* (come-match) 'happen to come to the same place at the same time' *ki-kakaru* (come-reach) 'come in at the right time'
other semantic relations	*iki-chigau* (go-differ) 'go off in different directions'	
compounds with semantically deverbalized V1	*iki-nayamu*(go-suffer) 'come to a dead end' *iki-todoku* (go-reach) 'be in good condition' *iki-wataru* (go-get.across) 'prevail' *iki-zumaru* (go-block.up) 'reach a dead end'	
deverbalized V2	*iki-tsukusu* (go-) 'go everywhere'	

Where does this asymmetry between the *iki*-V and the *ki*-V constructions originate in? The deictic characterization of *iku* and *kuru* is pivotal, because *iku* or *kuru* as V1 cannot be usually replaced with roughly synonymous verbs such as *susumu* 'proceed' and *mukau* 'head for'. For instance, *susumi-au* (proceed-meet), *susumi-awaseru* (proceed-match), *susumi-wataru* (proceed-cross), *susumi-tsukusu* (proceed-), *mukai-ataru* (head.for-hit), *mukai-tsuku* (head.for-arrive), *mukai-chigau* (head.for-differ), *mukai-todoku* (head.for-reach), *mukai-zumaru* (head.for-block.up) are all unacceptable. On the basis of the COMPULSION and the TERMINATION schemas, and the principle of sequential iconicity as mentioned above, Figure 5 and Figure 6 schematically show the *iki*-V and the *ki*-V constructions.

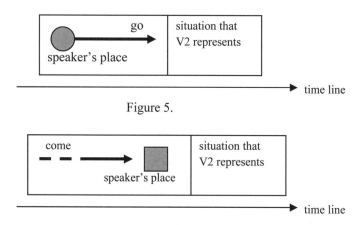

Figure 5.

Figure 6.

Moreover, Table 1 suggests that V2 in the *ki*-V construction is considerably more restricted than V2 in the *iki*-V construction. On the basis of Figure 6, this paper proposes one restriction placed on the *ki*-V construction including V1 *kuru* which focuses on the goal part of movement: The situation that V2 in the *ki*+V construction represents should not occur after the speaker's place in V1 which is equivalent to the goal place. To put it another way, in the *ki*-V construction the TERMINATION schema plays a vital role in determining the meanings of the compounds. In cause compounds and manner compounds, V2 occurs after V1. In compounds where V1 loses its verbal meaning, the speaker's place, that is, the goal place itself is bleached. In such three compounds where V2 cannot be construed explicitly in the *ki*-V construction on the basis of the sequential order, the *ki*+V construction never occurs. However, as V1 in means compounds represents the means by which the process denoted by V2 is performed, a particular part of V1 as the goal place of the verb *kuru*, and the beginning part of V2 in the *ki*-V construction overlap. The *ki*-V construction thus occurs only in means compounds where both V1 and V2 in the *ki*-V construction can be construed explicitly. In contrast, in the *iki*-V construction where the COMPULSION schema functions, it is natural that V1 *iku* which focuses on the source place and V2 which should focus on the goal place co-occur.

This reinforces the fact that the *iki*-V construction occurs in six types of compounds other than pair compounds.[7]

The rest of this section will demonstrate in more detail the asymmetry between the *iki*-V and the *ki*-V constructions and the distinguishing features of the *iki*-V construction. First, the fact that both constructions occur in means compounds, as in (14) and (15), is strongly related to directionality.

(14) Watashitachi ga   jikogenba ni   iki-kakat-ta.
     We Nom   accident.scene Goal go-reach-Past.
     'We passed by the accident scene.'

(15) Kimi ga   heya no   deguchi ni   ki-kakat-ta   toki,
     You Nom   room Gen exit Goal   come-reach-Past when
     'When you came in the room exit at the right time, ...'

In the means compounds, because of the deictic grounding of the situation, each construction gives the speaker's place and directionality clearly. This proves that both the COMPULSION and the TERMINATION schemas function properly. Each construction also conveys the additional meaning by virtue of being the whole. The motion verb *iku* and *kuru* are typically volitional, but *iki-kakaru* and *ki-kakaru* are unvolitional. It should be noted here that the meaning of 'by chance' is due not to V2 *kakaru* itself, but to *iki-kakaru* or *ki-kakaru* itself. Similarly, *iki-awaseru* and *ki-awaseru* as means compounds are closely related to directionality, as in (16) and (17).

(16) Boku ga   Ichiroo ni   iki-awase-ta.
     I Nom   Ichiro Acc   go-match-Past
     'I happened to go to Ichiro.'

(17) Kimi ga   Ichiroo ni   ki-awase-ta
     You Nom   Ichiro Acc   come-match-Past
     'You happened to come to Ichiro.'

The meanings that *iki-awaseru* and *ki-awaseru* convey are more accidental than the ones that *iki-kakaru* and *ki-kakaru* convey. The semantic asymmetry between *iki-awaseru* and *ki-awaseru* exists. *Iki-awaseru* sounds natural, whereas *ki-awaseru* sounds a little old-fashioned. This might indicate that the more accidental situation as a result of the process denoted by the compound verb easily occurs in the source-oriented *iki*-V construction that does not entail the goal place which is equivalent to the accidental situation. (14)-(17) illustrate that the meanings of both the *iki*-V and the *ki*-V con-

---

[7] In compounds where V2 loses its verbal meaning and takes on adverbial meaning, the *ki*-V construction does not occur. In pair compounds, both the *iki*-V and the *ki*-V constructions do not occur. At present there is no convincing explanation of them. These still remain moot questions.

structions are strongly influenced by the deictic verbs *iku* and *kuru*, and that the COMPULSION and the TERMINATION schemas unquestionably play a vital part in determining the meanings of the compounds.

Second, some types of the *iki*-V construction represent both actual and fictive motions, an implicit type of mentally simulated movement (Talmy 2000), but the *ki*-V construction usually represents actual motion. This exemplifies the asymmetry between the *iki*-V and the *ki*-V constructions.[8] *Iki-tsuku* as one means compound expresses not only actual motion, as in (18), but also fictive motion, as in (19).

(18) Boku wa   soko ni   iki-tsui-ta.
     I Top   there Goal   go-arrive-Past.
     'I got there.'
(19) Terebi no   renzokudorama wa   happiiendo ni   iki-tsui-ta.
     TV Gen   series.drama Top   happy.end Goal go-arrive-Past
     'The TV series ended up in the storybook ending.'

In (20)-(23), *iki-ataru* as one cause compound signifies a more complicated shift from actual to fictive motion. Such a shift is an instance of gradient phenomena.

(20) Wareware wa   bouhatei ni   iki-atat-ta.
     We Top   breakwater Goal   go-hit-Past
     'We reached a breakwater by chance.'
(21) Wareware wa   jikogenba ni   iki-atat-ta.
     We Top   accident.scene Goal   go-hit-Past.
     'We came upon the accident scene.'
(22) Kanojo wa   subarashii   kan-gae ni   iki-atat-ta.
     She Top   wonderful   idea Goal   go-hit-Past.
     'She came across the wonderful idea.'
(23) Watashi no   kaisoo wa   wareware no   mura de
     I Gen   reminiscence Top we Gen   village Loc
     okot-ta   jiken ni   iki-ata-ta.
     happen-Past   incident Goal   go-hit-Past
     'My reminiscence reached the incident that happened in our village.'

In (20) and (21), each subject *wareware* 'we' experienced actual motion, reaching a breakwater by chance or coming upon the accident scene. In (22) fictive motion is involved because the subject *kanojo* 'she' does not experience actual motion, reaching a wonderful idea by chance. From (20) and

---

[8] It should be noted that the verb *iku* and *kuru* represent both actual and fictive motion, as in (1)-(10).

(21) to (22), the subject shifts from the agent to the experiencer. As a result, the motion shifts from actual to fictive motion. In (23) where fictive motion is involved likewise, the subject is not the experiencer any more. Both the subject and the goal place are abstract. In (23) fictive motion goes further.

Next, only compounds with semantically deverbalized V1 express state, not activity, as in (24)-(26).

(24) Kooshou ga   iki-nayan-da.
     Negotiation Nom   go-suffer-Past
     'Negotiation have come to a dead end.'

(25) Sooji ga   iki-todo-ite-nai.
     Cleaning Nom   go-reach-Asp-Neg-Present
     'Cleaning is not complete.'

(26) Sora ni   hoshi no   hikari ga   iki-watat-teiru.
     Sky Loc   Star Gen   light Nom   go-get.across-Asp-Present
     'Starlight spreads all over the sky.'

(27) Watashitachi no   kankei wa   iki-zumat-ta.
     We Gen   relationship Top   go-block.up-Past
     'Our relationship broke down.'

The *iki*-V construction including V1 which is indeed semantically deverbalized or bleached still maintains the COMPULSION schema encoded by V1 *iku*. For instance, in (24), *iki-nayamu* implies the additional meaning of the motion verb *iku*. *Iki-nayamu* not only represents a situation from which no more progress is possible, but also implies the laborious process from the beginning of the negotiation to its deadlock.

Finally, in compounds with semantically deverbalized V2, the COMPULSION schema in the *iki*-V construction exists in much the same way as the one encoded by the verb *iku*. In (28), *tsukusu* in *iki-tsukusu* takes on an adverbial meaning 'all over.' In this sense, *tsukusu* cannot signify the situation. *Tsukusu* signifies degree.

(28) Boku wa   Kyooto no   kankoochi o   iki-tsukushi-ta.
     I Top   Kyoto Gen   sightseeing.spots Goal   go-all.over-Past
     'I went to all the sightseeing spots throughout Kyoto.'

As mentioned above, all the examples in this paper reinforce the idea that the COMPULSION and the TERMINATION schemas are valid for all of them, and play a vital role in determining the meanings of the compounds.

6. Concluding Remarks

As Japanese morphology is generally right-headed, many works on lexical compound verbs in Japanese have paid attention to V2. This is why it is natural to expect a lexical compound to inherit the argument structure of V2.

However, this view is of limited importance, as Matsumoto (1996) points out that there are two types of compounds that do not simply inherit the argument structure of V2. For instance, *nage-tsukeru* (throw-, 'throw hard') is a left-headed compound, and *negai-deru* (wish-go.out, 'go forward to ask') is an argument-mixing compound. Nevertheless, previous studies have not added more weight to V1 in lexical compound verbs. This paper will thus venture to focus specifically on both the *iki*-V and the *ki*-V constructions to highlight V1. The meaning-based approach, which this paper maintains, casts doubt on the inheritance view of argument structure and the general right-headedness of Japanese compound verbs. At the same time it could be an alternative approach to lexical compound verbs without regard to the inheritance view of argument structure and the right-headedness.

This paper demonstrates that the *iki*-V and the *ki*-V constructions enhance the understanding of form-meaning pairings that have a cognitive reality, and that image schemas, representing the fundamental, pervasive organizing structures of cognition, play a pivotal part. As the image schemas are dynamic recurring patterns of our mundane bodily experiential interaction, one fascinating aspect is that linguistic phenomena which need to be taken for granted but are in fact unexplained can now be interpreted as manifestations of the image schemas which are embodied. This paper thus assumes that the interpretation of the image schemas has enhanced research. Although the *iki*-V and the *ki*-V constructions have various kinds of internal semantic complexities, the COMPULSION and the TERMINATION schemas are valid for all the instances. Consequently, the two image schemas illustrate that the *iki*-V and the *ki*-V constructions are not symmetrical, and that the schematic characterization of *iku* and *kuru* plays a decisive role in both constructions. Although space constraints do not permit further discussion here, this paper raises a new problem that there might be a possibility that deixis carries very much weight in lexical V-V compounds including *iku* and *kuru* as V1, and thereby opens up avenues for further investigation.

References

Clark, E. 1974. Normal States and Evaluative Viewpoints. *Language* 50:316-331.

Croft, W. 2002. *Radical Construction Grammar: Syntactic Theory in Typological Perspective*. Oxford: Oxford University Press.

Daijirin, 2nd Edition. 1995. Tokyo: Sanseidou.

Evans, V., B. K. Bergen, and J. Zinken. 2007. The Cognitive Linguistics Enterprise: An Overview. *The Cognitive Linguistics Reader*, ed. by V. Evans, B. K. Bergen, and J. Zinken. London: Equinox Publishers.

Fauconnier, G. 1985. *Mental Spaces*. Cambridge: Cambridge University Press.

Fauconnier, G. and M. Turner. 2002. *The Way We Think: Conceptual Blending and the Mind's Hidden Complexities*. New York: Basic Books.

Fillmore, C. J. 1971. *Santa Cruz Lectures on Deixis*. Bloomington, Ind.: Indiana University Linguistic Club.

Fillmore, C. J. 1975. An Alternative to Checklist Theories of Meaning. *Proceedings of the 1st Annual Meeting of the Berkeley Linguistics Society*, 123-131.

Gibbs, R. W. and H. L. Colston. 1995. The Cognitive Psychological Reality of Image Schemas and their Transformations. *Cognitive Linguistics* 6: 347-378.

Goldberg, A.E. 1995. *Constructions: A Construction Grammar Approach to Argument Structure*. Chicago: The University of Chicago Press.

Johnson, M. 1987. *The Body in the Mind: The Bodily Basis of Meaning, Imagination, and Reason*. Chicago: The University of Chicago Press.

Kageyama, T. 1993. *Bunpoo to Gokeisei* [*Grammar and Word Formation*]. Kasukabe: Hitsuzi Shobo.

Kojien, 5th Edition. 1998. Tokyo: Iwanami Shoten.

Lakoff, G. 1977. Linguistic Gestalts. *Proceedings of the 13th Annual Meeting of the Chicago Linguistics Society*, 236-287.

Lakoff, G. 1987. *Women, Fire, and Dangerous Things: What Categories Reveal about the Mind*. Chicago: The University of Chicago Press.

Lakoff, G. and M. Johnson. 1980. *Metaphor We Live By*. Chicago: The University of Chicago Press.

Lakoff, G. and M. Johnson. 1999. *Philosophy in the Flesh: The Embodied Mind and its Challenge to Western Thought*. New York: Basic Books.

Langacker, R.W. 1987. *Foundations of Cognitive Grammar, Vol.I: Theoretical Prerequisites*. Stanford: Stanford University Press.

Langacker, R.W. 1991. *Foundations of Cognitive Grammar, Vol.II: Descriptive Application*. Stanford: Stanford University Press.

Mandler, J. M. 1992. How to Build a Baby II: Conceptual Primitives. *Psychological Review* 99:567-604.

Mandler, J. M. 1996. Preverbal Representation and Language. *Language and Space*, ed. by P. Bloom, M. A. Peterson, L. Nadel, & M. F. Garrett, 365-383. Cambridge, MA: Bradford Books.

Mandler, J. M. 2004. *The Foundations of Mind: Origins of Conceptual Thought*. Oxford: Oxford University Press.

Matsumoto, Y. 1996. *Complex Predicates in Japanese: A Syntactic and Semantic Study of the Notion 'Word.'* Tokyo: Kuroshio Publisher.

Nihongo Dai Jiten, 2nd Edition. 2001. Tokyo: Shougakukan

Radden, G. 1996. Motion Metaphorized: The Case of *Coming* and *Going*. *Cognitive Linguistics in the Redwoods: The Expansion of a New Paradigm in Linguistics*, ed. by E. H. Casad, 423-458. Berlin/New York: Mouton de Gruyter.

Talmy, L. 2000. *Toward a Cognitive Semantics (2 Volumes)*. Cambridge, MA: MIT Press.

The Deployment of Korean Negative Interrogatives in Conversational Discourse: A Sign-based Approach

JINI NOH
University of California, Los Angeles

1. Introduction

It has been widely noted that there are two ways to negate a predicate in Korean: by attaching the negative adverb *an*, 'not', before the main predicate, as in example (1a), or by attaching the suffix *-ci* and the negative predicate *anh-*, 'not do', to the main predicate, as in example (1b). In addition to these traditionally discussed forms of negation, a clause with a predicate can also be negated by nominalizing it with the attributive marker *-(u)n/nun/(u)l*, the general noun *ke*, 'thing, event, fact', and the copula, *ani-*, 'not be,' as in example (1c). (Henceforth, I will refer the three forms of negation as SN, LN, and NN, respectively.)

> (1) *"Aren't you busy recently?"*
>   a. **SN**: Short form negation (pre-verbal negation)
>   yocum **an**   papp-a?
>   recently **SN:not** busy-IE:INT

b. **LN**: Long form negation (post-verbal negation)
yocum   pappu-**ci anh**-a
recently busy-**LN:SUF-not.do**-IE:INT

c. **NN**: Nominalized negation [1]
yocum   pappu-**n ke aniy**-a
recently busy-**NN:ATT-thing-not.be**-IE:INT

As isolated sentences, examples 1a, 1b, and 1c deliver the same referential meaning and can be used interchangeably. Despite the long history of productive discussion that attempts to distinguish the features of SN and LN (Song 1977, 1981; Im 1978, 1987; Lee 1979; Seo 1984; Chang 1987; Lee 2005), previous studies that have not attended to real language use have not reached agreement on the use of SN and LN. In addition, while SN and LN have been extensively studied, NN has not been included as a negation construction in Korean descriptive grammar (Chang 1996; Sohn 1999). However, this study will show that NN should be discussed under the same system with the other two negation constructions, not only because NN employs pragmatic functions which are not predictable from the combination of its components, but also because NN contributes to the construction of a coherent system with the other two negations (Contini-Morava 1995; Kirsner 2000).

There are two main problems in analyzing Korean negation constructions: first, are the three negations really equivalent? Though the negations have been regarded as very nearly synonymous based on their similar syntactic and semantic properties, their pragmatic usage in real discourse, however, reveals striking asymmetrical distributional patterns and distinct preferences of occurrence, particularly in interrogative contexts. Therefore, whether we can still say that the three Korean negations are equivalent or near-synonymous constructions needs to be investigated. The second question is how the functional differences in the usage can be explained. Though discourse analysis of contextual or distributional patterns can describe the phenomena themselves, this is not sufficient to explain *why* Korean speakers use different strategies in deploying different negation constructions.

To investigate the two problems in understanding Korean negations, this study is based on a sign-based approach, the Columbia School theory. This theory views grammar as a tool of human communication that also follows from a 'functional' orientation (cf. Bybee 1998). Communication is achieved by creatively adapting limited sets of linguistic signs to varying contexts. A linguistic sign is defined as the combination of a linguistic sig-

---

[1] NN consists of morphologically analyzable components in modern Korean, which literally means '(it is) not the case that'.

nal (form) and its underlying and invariant meaning[2]. Accordingly, this account of language use relies on the meanings of the signals as well as on the interpretation inferred from contextual information, socio-cultural conventions, and other extralinguistic factors (Contini-Morava 1995; Huffman 2002). To prove that there is a sufficiently objective correlation between meanings and inferred pragmatic functions, quantitative analysis of real discourse should be conducted. This is because if the distribution of linguistic signs can be explained in terms of the contributions of their meanings to pragmatic functions, the hypotheses about the grammatical system is supported empirically (Diver 1995; Reid 1995). For this reason, I will discuss the hypothesized underlying system of verbal negations, particularly negations in interrogative contexts, along with distributional patterns and in-depth analysis[3].

This paper is divided into two parts. First, by analyzing conversational discourse, I present how each negation construction embodies distinctive pragmatic functions. Then, by using the framework of the Columbia School theory, I investigate how the invariant meanings of negations construct or contribute to the inferred pragmatic functions.

2. Conversational functions of negative interrogatives

Negative interrogatives accomplish various conversational functions such as agreement, the assertion of opinion, or the initiation of topics, in addition to information-seeking, which is regarded as an interrogative's inherent function (Heritage 2002).

Based on Heritage's argument and preliminary analysis, I suggest four functions for investigating Korean negations in interrogative contexts: asserting (or suggesting), challenging, confirming, and information seeking. In asserting and suggesting, speakers state their opinions and seek agreement from other interlocutors. Challenging is used by speakers when they are opposed to the previous assertions or suggestions of other interlocutors and want to suggest their own opinion. In confirming, speakers seek to

---

2 As Contini-Morava (1995: 9) notes that "all sign based theories make a distinction between the underlying, abstract, invariant meaning of a sign...and the open-ended set of specific interpretations it can have in particular contexts of use", this paper follows the definition of 'meaning' and 'function (interpretation)' of the Columbia School theory. The pragmatic functions, thus, refer to the strategies which are motivated by the underlying meanings.

3 The data was obtained from the Sejong National Corpus (http://www.sejong.or.kr). From the full corpus, 239,129 words of spontaneous and informal spoken discourse were selected. Negative interrogatives found in the data include 345 tokens of SN, 322 tokens of LN, and 186 tokens of NN.

check their own understanding which is based on previous information[4]. In the last function, information-seeking, speakers expect to receive an answer to their question from other interlocutors. While speaker and addressee share the authorship of the information in confirming, addressees exclusively have the authorship of the information in information seeking.

The following examples illustrate how negative interrogatives are used in real discourse to construct these functions. In example 2, SN is used for information seeking.

(2) Pocket money

01	M;	a:: hyung-un yongton elma pat-ayo?
		How much pocket money do you get (from your parents)?
02	P;	a molla
		I don't know.
03	→M;	|an| pat-ayo?
		|SN| receive-POL:INT
		Don't you get any?
04	P;	silh-e malha-ki silh-e
		I don't want to tell you.

In line 1, speaker M asks speaker P how much pocket money P receives from his parents. With the speaker P's resistance to answering the question in line 2, speaker M urges P to answer by asking in line 3 "don't you get any (pocket money from your parents)?" with SN. Here, M does not have previous knowledge about the answer; the recipient of the question, P, is the person who owns the information. Therefore, in this excerpt, SN can be said to serve the function of information seeking.

On the other hand, based on shared knowledge of the current issue, negations in interrogative contexts can serve to confirm a speaker's conjecture about the answer. In example 3, four participants exchange information about *Na-lae*, who was unable to pass an exam to enter the air force because of his health problems. Speaker A brings up the topic of *Na-lae*'s problem in line 1, and speaker C in line 3 shows interest in the topic by asking the name of the person as a repair initiator. In line 6, Speaker P provides additional information about *Na-lae* by using interrogative NN.

(3) Exam failure

| 01 | A; | Na-lae hyeng ttelecye-ss-taymay |
| | | *I heard Na-lae failed the exam.* |

---

[4] Confirming functions under two presuppositions (cf. Kamio 1997); first, that the speaker possesses his/her own answer to the question which is to be confirmed; second, that addressees have more knowledge on the topic than the speaker and thus have the ability to answer the question.

02	B;	ung.
		Right.
03	C;	nwukwu?
		Who?
04	A;	Na-lae.
		Na-lae.
05	C;	Na-lae,
		Na-lae,

06 → P;   Na-lae heli-ka   an toy-se   ke tteleci-n ke anya?
Na-lae waist-NOM not become-because INS fail-NN:INT
Isn't it true that Na-lae failed because his backbone is not
strong enough?

07	A;	ung.
		Right.

As can be seen in lines 1, 2, 4 and 6, speakers A, B, and P appear to share information about *Na-lae* before the conversation, but they are not sure whether the other interlocutors know the information. Under this circumstance, it might threaten the other interlocutors' face to give specific information on *Na-lae* in the form of assertive statements; to monopolize already shared or known information could make the other interlocutors feel ignored. Speaker P, thus, uses a softening strategy in line 6 by employing the negative interrogative, NN[5]. Since speaker P provides more detailed information in line 6 as the form of negative interrogative, the function of his utterance is not information seeking, but rather to confirm his information by asking other participants about it.

The following example shows how negative interrogatives can embody the function of assertion and contribute to agreement among participants.

(4) My dad

01   A;   emma-ka cincca kekise sal-te-n il nyen-i ceyl silh-ess-tako
kule-telaku,
My mom said that she hated one year when she lived there
02   honcase,
by herself

---

[5] Speaker A in line 1 employs the double reported speech marker *-taymay*, 'I heard that'; this also serves as a softening strategy, because it distributes responsibility for the attached proposition and elicits co-participation (Kim 2003).

03 →   uli appa nemu   ha-ci ahn-nya?
         my dad too.much do-LN-INT:dubious
         Wasn't my dad too mean (to her)?
04   [ettehkey
         How
05 B;   [teyl-ko ka-ya-ci
         He should have brought her.
06 A;   kyelhon-ha-camaca twu tal-man-ey honca kanya.
         (how) could he go alone as soon as they got married
07 B;   kulay teyl-ko ka-ya-ci
         Sure, he should've brought her.

In this segment, speaker A in lines 1 and 2 blames her father, who because of his job left her mother behind just after their marriage, which meant that her mother had to live alone for one year. In line 3, speaker A reveals her negative attitude toward her father's behavior by saying that '*wasn't my father too mean (to my mom)?*'. In this utterance, A, by employing interrogative LN, asserts that her father was too mean to her mother and seeks agreement with her assertion from the other interlocutor B. Aligning to A's attitude B expresses agreement, before A starts to disclose more details in lines 4 and 6. Thus, by virtue of a negative interrogative, A is able to indicate her attitude and at the same time to seek agreement on her evaluation of her father's behavior.

The next example illustrates how speakers M and F arrive at mutual agreement by challenging the other speaker's opinion. They are preparing for their first anniversary and are deciding when to place an order for their rings.

(5) Anniversary
01 M;   um:: kulemyen iltan kihan-ul hanpen cenghay-po-ca
         Then let's decide the dates.
02   o-wol phal-il nal hay-yatoy.
         By May 8th.
03   o-wol phal-il manna-ci?
         We're going to meet on that day, aren't we?
04 F;   ung hey:: kuntey oppa uli-ka sipo-il-i-nikka uli khepulling::
         Yes. But our anniversary is on the 15th, so our rings,
05 M;   o-wol phal-il nal hay-yatoy.
         We should order them on May 8th.
06 F;   o-wol phal-il nal hay-to naw-a? ilcuil-man-ey?
         Do you think it would be enough(time) if we order them on May 8th? Within only one week?

07 →M;   nao-ci anh-nya?
           Come.out-LN-INT:dubious
           Won't they be done by then?
08 →   chungpunhi nao-ci anh-na?
           enough   come.out-LN-INT:dubious
           Isn't it long enough (for them) to get done?
09→ F;   kulay? han yelhul   keli-ci anh-na?
           be.so about ten.days take-LN-INT:dubious
           Is it? Doesn't it take about 10 days?
10   M;   yelhul-ina kelly-e?
           That long?
11 →F;   kule-ci anh-na?
           be.so-LN-INT:dubious
           Doesn't it?
12   M;   iltan o-wol phal-il-kkaci senkullasu.
           at.this.point May 8th-day-by sunglasses
           Then at this point, let's buy sunglasses by May 8th.
13   F;   u:ng.
           Yes.

In lines 1 through 3, and 5, speaker M (male) suggests there should be enough time if they order their rings by 8 May, but in line 6, speaker F (female) shows disagreement because she thinks that one week is not long enough to order their rings. Then speaker M, employing interrogative LN in lines 7 and 8, makes the assertion that one week would be enough. Again, F challenges his assertion by using interrogative LN in lines 9 and 11. Finally, in line 12, they move on to another item they need in preparation for the anniversary, sunglasses. Though the date to order their rings is not finally decided at the end of this excerpt, they can avoid explicit conflict and reach an alternative action by using negative interrogatives, which indirectly imply both the assertion of the speaker's opinion and a challenge to the other speaker's opinion.

This section illustrates that the three forms of negation in interrogative contexts perform a variety of interactional functions. What is called for now is a more comprehensive look at how the negations' underlying meanings are relevant to those functions. The following section will deal with this issue.

3. Correlations between meaning and function

3.1. Hypothesis of the underlying system

Taking the framework of a sign-based theory, I propose the following hypothesis regarding the differences among the three negation constructions. I suggest that an underlying semantic system of the three negations, 'SUBJECTIVITY', motivates the functional differences. 'SUBJECTIVITY' in this study is defined as a system that outlines to what extent the speaker explicitly encodes perspectives and attitudes toward a negated proposition (Traugott 1989; Traugott and Dasher 2002). Each negation construction conveys certain degrees of subjectivity in comparison to the other constructions. Given that marking subjective stance is not decisive but indicates an openness to negotiate with other conversational participants, the more the speaker reveals their stance, the more they are willing to negotiate the issue with other participants.

SUBJECTIVITY
{
an **(SN)** = LOW DEGREE OF SUBJECTIVITY
'SN implies a low degree of subjectivity in expressing the proposition; thereby the speaker indicates a neutral stance toward the proposition.'

ke ani- **(NN)** = HIGHER DEGREE OF SUBJECTIVITY
'NN implies a higher degree of subjectivity in expressing the proposition.'

-ci anh- **(LN)** = THE HIGHEST DEGREE OF SUBJECTIVITY
'LN implies the highest degree of subjectivity in expressing the proposition, and thereby that the speaker is willing to open a negotiation with other participants.'
}

Figure 1. The underlying system of three negations

As shown in Figure 1 above, the semantic substance of three negation constructions is 'SUBJECTIVITY'; according to this semantic property, their invariant meanings are defined as LOW DEGREE OF SUBJECTIVITY, HIGHER DEGREE OF SUBJECTIVITY, and THE HIGHEST DEGREE OF SUBJECTIVITY respectively. By employing SN, the speaker indicates a neutral stance toward the proposition, which tends to be regarded as factual information. NN and LN allow the speaker to show high degrees of subjectivity toward the proposition. LN implies higher subjectivity than NN, which leads to the speaker's willingness to negotiate their stance with other participants. I will investigate the supporting evidence for this hypothesis in the following sections.

3.2. Morphological analysis

Morphological analysis of the three constructions will not only assist in our understanding of why they convey distinct meanings and functions, but also will support the hypothesis of how pragmatic functions are inferred from the invariant meanings.

Noticeably, while LN and NN include complicated structures to negate the attached propositions, SN involves only negative adverb *an*. Given that the adverb *an* does not imply the speaker's epistemic stance other than a negative meaning to the proposition, compared with the other two constructions, SN is morphologically the most neutral construction in relation to the negated proposition.

Conversely, the higher degrees of subjectivity conveyed by NN and LN are partly derived from their morphological components: the general noun *ke* in NN and the committal suffix *-ci* in LN. The general noun *ke* in NN literally means 'thing(s)' and serves as a noun with a very general meaning, referring either to tangible objects or to abstract concepts (Ahn 2001). Based upon the meaning of *ke*, the construction of *ke* and copula *i-*, 'to be' and *an*i-, 'not to be' is used to express a generally accepted truth or rule.

(6) nokcha-nun   samsa   pun   ttukeu-n mul-ey
    green.tea-TOP three.or.four minutes hot-ATT water-LOC
    neh-e   masi-nun   **ke-ya.**
    steep.in-and.then drink-ATT **thing:rule-COP:IE**
    "It is the way of drinking green tea to steep the leaves in hot water
    for three or four minutes and then drink it."

As shown in example 6 above, *ke* implies a generally accepted rule, and accordingly the proposition preceding *ke* indicates the rule, 'how to drink green tea'. Given that the truth or rule expressed by a speaker is based on the speaker's commitment to the proposition, NN, the negation of *ke* and copula *i*, also involves a certain degree of subjectivity (cf. Lee 2002).

In LN, the speaker's strong subjectivity in the attached proposition is explicitly expressed with the suffix *-ci*. Lee (1999) discusses that both examples (7a) and (7b) below delivers the same pragmatic function of showing the speaker's belief and seek agreement on the proposition 'it's cold today'.

(7)   a. onul   chup-**ci anh**-ayo?
       today   be.cold-**ci anh:LN**-POL:INT
    b. onul   chup-**ci**-yo?
       today   be.cold-**ci**-POL:INT
      "It's cold today, isn't it?"

Though this paper argues the pragmatic functions of negative interrogatives can be varied according to their meanings and contextual environments, it can be said that the suffix -ci is relevant to constructing the invariant meaning of LN, in the sense that it implies a high degree of expression of the speaker's perspective.

The difference in the degrees of subjectivity in NN and LN is closely related to the source of the speaker's perspective or attitude; while NN involves generally accepted knowledge within the speech community, LN involves the speaker's personal belief regarding the proposition. Though we generally believe the rules or conventions accepted in our society to some degree, we may have some disagreements with those rules or conventions based upon our own personal beliefs. That is, the degree of speaker's subjectivity is higher in personal beliefs rather than collective truths. This argument is also based on human egocentricity, which is regarded as a fundamental feature of communication (Diver 1995). In this view, greater attention is paid to whatever is more closely associated with the speaker and speakers tend to emphasize their own judgment more than the collectively agreed-upon judgment.

Therefore, the morphological analysis supports the hypothesis proposed in Figure 1; since the structure of SN does not include any marker of the speaker's perspective, it conveys a low degree of subjectivity to the attached proposition. On the other hand, since NN and LN do include markers of speaker's perspective, they convey higher degrees of subjectivity in relation to the attached proposition. Finally, since LN indexes personal beliefs by using the suffix -ci, LN conveys greater subjectivity than NN does.

3.3. Quantitative validation

This section will show that quantitative analysis based on real discourse will support the hypothesis by investigating the correlation between meanings and functions.

3.3.1. Preferences in declarative and interrogative contexts

First, when a speaker displays a higher degree of subjectivity, s/he tends not to be as decisive as when the speaker takes a neutral stance. Given that declarative contexts indicate a more decisive stance than interrogative contexts, constructions expressing higher decisiveness and lower subjectivity may be favored for declarative contexts. On the other hand, constructions conveying the higher subjectivity may be preferred for interrogative contexts.

	SN	NN	LN	Total
Declarative	1285 (78.3%)	250 (15.2%)	154 (9.4%)	1641 (100%)
Interrogative	345 (40.4%)	186 (21.8%)	322 (37.8%)	853 (100%)
Total	1630 (65.4%)	388 (15.5%)	476 (19.1%)	2494 (100%)

Table 1. The distributions in declarative and interrogative contexts

Table 1 illustrates the syntactic environments of the three negations. SN is much more preferred (65.4%) in comparison to NN and LN (15.5% and 19.1% respectively) in general and occurs more frequently in both declarative and interrogative contexts (78.3% and 40.4%) than the other constructions. However, the comparison between the proportions of the negations in relation to total occurrences and in relation to occurrences in interrogative contexts indicates the interesting tendency. See Table 2.

	SN	NN	LN
(1) Interrogative (%)	40.4	21.8	37.8
(2) Total (%)	65.4	15.5	19.1
(1)-(2)	- 25	+ 6.3	+ 18.7

Table 2. The proportions in total and interrogative contexts

SN occurs slightly less in interrogative contexts (40.4%) than in total contexts (65.4%), whereas NN and LN occurs more in interrogative contexts (21.8% and 37.8%) than in total contexts (15.5% and 19.1%). When their occurrence in total and interrogative contexts is compared, thus, the extent to which the three negations occur in interrogative contexts compared to total contexts corresponds to the constructions' degrees of hypothesized subjectivity.

The second analysis will confirm this tendency by showing the tendency of each negation construction to prefer a certain type of sentential context.

	SN	NN	LN
Declarative	1285 (78.8%)	250 (64.4%)	154 (32.4%)
Interrogative	345 (21.2%)	186 (33.6%)	322 (67.6%)
Total	1630 (100%)	388 (100%)	476 (100%)

Table 3. The preferred syntactic contexts of three negations

LN is much more likely to favor the interrogative context (67.6%) than SN and NN (21.2% and 33.6% respectively). This result shows that when LN is employed, it is more likely to serve to display a less decisive and more subjective stance than SN and NN. In order of increasing frequency, negation constructions used in interrogative contexts are SN, NN, and LN, which parallels the degree of the speaker's subjectivity in relation to the proposition from low to high subjectivity.

3.3.2. Functional distributions

The second prediction is associated with the functional distributions of the three negations, which include assertion, challenge, confirmation, and information-seeking. When a speaker expresses a proposition with a high probability of face-threatening effects, I predict that the speaker will display a high degree of subjectivity to provide more possibilities for negotiation with the other participants. In other words, the speaker will tend to choose the more highly subjective stance rather than a decisive or neutral stance to avoid the danger of a face-threatening situation.

Face-threatening effects are determined by the authorship of information (cf. Kamio 1997). In interrogative contexts, the more the speaker claims authorship of the information in the question, the more the situation is likely to be face-threatening. For example, when the speaker makes an assertion or challenges opinions, s/he claims to have more authorship of the attached proposition than the recipient. On the other hand, the more the recipient is given authorship, the less likely the situation is to be face-threatening. Since the recipient has authorship of the answer in seeking information, information-seeking is the least face-threatening activity and involves a lower degree of subjectivity. The following figure illustrates the degrees of subjectivity associated with each function.

← *lower degree of subjectivity   higher degree of subjectivity* →
information-seeking   confirming   asserting   challenging

Figure 2. The degrees of subjectivity and pragmatic functions

To examine the correlation between pragmatic functions and the usage of negations, the distributions of the functions and negative interrogatives were investigated in Table 4 below.

	SN	NN	LN
Information seeking	48 (**76.2**%)	0	2 (3.2%)
Confirming	6 (9.5%)	41 (**65.1**%)	0
Asserting	9 (14.3%)	13 (**20.6**%)	42 (**66.7**%)
Challenging	0	9 (**14.3**%)	15 (**23.8**%)
Other	0	0	4 (6.3%)
Total	63 (100%)	63 (100%)	63(100%)

Table 4. Functional distributions of negations in interrogative contexts[6]

A large majority of LN involves activities with higher degrees of subjectivity (66.7% for assertion and 23.8% for challenging), whereas only 14.3% of SN and 20.6% of NN are used for this purpose. On the other hand, only 3.2 % of LN is employed for information seeking, while the vast majority of SN (76.2%) is used for that function. These results clearly reveal

---

[6] To facilitate analysis of the data, 63 occurrences of each negation construction were randomly selected from the original corpus.

that compared to the other two constructions, interrogative LN is the most likely to be used for pragmatic functions which require a higher degree of subjectivity. It is also very interesting that while SN is not used for challenging, NN and LN are both used for this function. This shows that both NN and LN imply higher subjectivity on the part of the speaker, although the degrees of subjectivity can be different.

3.3.3. Collocations with sentence final suffixes

The third prediction is associated with the degree to which the speaker's stance is implied in deploying negative interrogatives. Korean interrogative suffixes can be largely categorized into three types: neutral suffixes such as -*e/a* which are used in a unmarked way, dubious suffixes which conveys the speaker's doubts or uncertainty such as -*(u)nka, -(u)lkka, -na, -nya*, and the committal suffix -*ci* which conveys the speaker's decisive stance toward the attached proposition (Lee, 1999).

	SN	NN	LN
Neutral suffixes	200 (**58%**)	109(**58.6%**)	92(**28.6%**)
Dubious suffixes	88 (**25.5%**)	73 (**39.2%**)	227 (**70.5%**)
Committal suffixes	38 (**11%**)	2(1.1%)	3(0.9%)
Other	19(5.5%)	2(1.1%)	0(0%)
Total	345(100%)	186(100%)	322(100%)

Table 5. The collocations of negation constructions with suffixes

In Table 5, while only 28.6% of LN is collocated with neutral suffixes, more than half of SN and NN (58% and 58.6%) is collocated with these suffixes; this indicates that SN and NN both imply a more neutral stance than does LN. The use of dubious suffixes more clearly indicates the underlying meanings of the three negation constructions. Given that dubious suffixes imply the speaker's dubious stance toward the attached proposition, which opens up the possibility of negation among participants, the collocations of dubious suffixes with negative interrogatives are relevant to the degrees of subjectivity expressed in the three negation constructions: LN occurs with dubious suffixes the most (70.5%), whereas NN and SN occur with them less frequently (39.2% and 25.5% respectively). The tendency to collocate with dubious suffixes reflects the degrees of subjectivity of the three negative interrogatives proposed in the hypothesis[7].

---

[7] It is noteworthy that in comparison to NN (1.1%) and LN (0.9%), SN prefers the use of committal suffix (11%). This preference can be explained by the definition of subjectivity presented in this paper. Given that subjectivity is operationally defined as a speaker's willingness to open negotiations by revealing a high degree of personal stance, the use of the commit-

4. Final notes

This paper has investigated the hypothesis that the various functions that interrogative negation constructions deliver are not randomly distributed, but rather behave systematically according to their underlying meanings. To prove the correlations between the constructions' invariant meanings and the pragmatic functions, three distributional skewings along with discourse analysis have been presented. Each correlation confirms the hypothesis made on the basis of SUBJECTIVITY meanings. The SUBJECTIVITY system of the three negation constructions is supported because: (a) it hypothesizes that the three constructions are differentiated according to the degrees of the speaker's subjective stance toward the negated proposition, and (b) correlations with syntactic contexts, functional distributions, and sentence-final suffixes demonstrate that a speaker in language use systematically deploys negative interrogatives according to their underlying meanings and corresponding contexts. This paper contributes to the provision of a coherent explanation of language use and the hypothesis proposed here should also be examined in declarative contexts in further studies.

References

Ahn, H. 2001. *Hyŏndae kukŏŭi ŭijonmyŏngsa yŏngu*. Seoul: Yŏkrak.

Bybee, J. 1998. A functional approach to grammar and its evolution. *Evolution of Communication* 2: 249-278.

Chang, K. 1987. Kukŏ pujŏng ŭimunmunkwa jŏnje. *Ŏhakyŏnku* 22 (1): 19-40.

Chang, S. 1996. *Korean*. Amsterdam and Philadelphia: John Benjamins.

Contini-Morava, E. 1995. Introduction: On linguistic sign theory. *Meaning As Explanation: Advances in Linguistic Sign Theory*, ed. E. Contini-Morava and B. Goldberg, 1-42. Berlin: Mouton de Gruyter.

Diver, W. 1995. Theory. *Meaning As Explanation: Advances In Linguistic Sign Theory*, ed. E. Contini-Morava and B. Goldberg, 43-114. Berlin: Mouton De Gruyter.

Heritage, J. 2002. The limits of questioning: negative interrogatives and hostile question content. *Journal of Pragmatics* 34: 1427-1446.

Huffman, A. 2002. Cognitive and Semiotic Modes of Explanation in Functional Grammar. *Signal, Meaning and Message*, ed. W. Reid, R. Otheguy and N. Stern, 311-337. Amsterdam and Philadelphia: John Benjamins.

Im, H. 1978. Pujŏngbŏpŭi nonŭiwa kukŏŭi hyŏnsil. *Kukŏhak* 6: 185-206.

---

tal suffix implying the speaker's strong belief, in relation to a proposition in interrogative contexts indicates a decisive stance. Though the committal suffix denotes the speaker's stance, it is not a negotiable stance but rather a decisive stance, and accordingly it implies a less subjective stance. Therefore, the high collocation of committal suffix with SN supports the underlying meaning of SN, LOW DEGREE OF SUBJECTIVITY.

Im, H. 1987. Kukŏ pujŏngmunŭi t'ongsawa ŭimi. *Kukŏsaenghwal* 10: 72-99.

Kamio, A. 1997. *Territory of information.* Amsterdam: John Benjamins Publishing Company.

Kirsner, R.S. 2000. Empirical pragmatics: Downtoning and predictability in a Dutch final particle. *The Berkeley Conference on Dutch Linguistics 1997,* ed. T. Shannon and J. P. Snapper, 45-62. Lanham, MD: University Press of America.

Lee, H-S. 1999. A discourse-pragmatic analysis of the committal *-ci* in Korean: A synthetic approach to the form-meaning relation. *Journal of Pragmatics* 31: 243-275.

Lee, H. 2005. Presupposition and implicature under negation. *Journal of Pragmatics* 37: 595-609.

Lee, J. 2002. Kusul t'eksŭtŭ hyŏngsŏnge issŏsŏŭi hwaja t'aedo. *Hanguk ŏnŏmunhak* 45: 605-624

Lee, K. 1979. Tu kaji pujŏngmunŭi tongŭisŏng yŏbue taehayŏ. *Kukŏhak 8:* 59-94.

Reid, W. 1995. Quantitative analysis in Columbian School theory. *Meaning As Explanation: Advances In Linguistic Sign Theory,* ed. E. Contini-Morava and B. Goldberg, 115-152. Berlin: Mouton de Gruyter.

Seo, S. 1984. Kukŏ pujŏngmunŭi ŭimi haesŏk wŏnli. *Mal* 9: 41-79.

Sohn, H. 1999. *The Korean Language.* Cambridge: Cambridge University Press.

Song, S. 1977. Pujŏngŭi yangsangŭi pujŏngjŏk yangsang. *Kukŏhak* 5: 45-100.

Song, S. 1981. Hangukmalŭi pujŏngŭi pŏmwi. *Hangŭl* 173 (4): 327-352.

Traugott, E.C. 1989. On the rise of epistemic meanings in English: an example of subjectification in semantic change. *Language* 57: 33-65.

Traugott, E.C. and R.B.Dasher. 2002. *Regularity in Semantic Change.* Cambridge: Cambridge University Press.

A Corpus-Based Look at Japanese Giving/Receiving Verbs ageru, kureru, and morau*

TSUYOSHI ONO
ROSS KREKOSKI
University of Alberta

1. Introduction

Japanese is known for possessing a set of giving/receiving verbs ageru 'give', kureru 'give', and morau 'get', which are generally grouped together in the literature as follows:[1]

(1)   Boku ga tomodati ni hana   o ageta
         I   friend   flowers gave
         'I gave flowers to my friend.'

---

* We would like to thank the Japanese linguistics reading group at the University of Alberta and the audience at the 16th Japanese/Korean conference at Kyoto University for their valuable comments.
[1] *Yaru* is another verb which is often grouped together with these verbs. *Yaru* was excluded from the present study because the number of instances of that form was rather small in our data set.

(2)   Boku wa Mary ni kono hon   o moratta
        I   this   book   received
        'I received from Mary this book.'

(3)   Mary ga boku ni kono hon   o kureta
        I   this   book   gave
        'Mary has given me this book.'   (Kuno 1973: 127-130)

These verbs have traditionally been investigated based on constructed examples with particular attention given to semantic and pragmatic dimensions (Ooe 1975, Kuno 1978, Shibatani 2000, etc.). Studies have centered upon fascinating arrays of examples where notions such as perspective and viewpoint are encoded as part of lexical meanings. Under such a theoretical paradigm, examples such as (2) and (3) are said to describe the same event from two different perspectives. A potential implication arising from such treatment would be that these verbs form a cognitive unit in the mind of speakers.

In this paper, we attempt to go beyond constructed examples, standard data in the field, and make a corpus-based investigation to look at their usage in actual discourse, thereby obtaining a more complete understanding of *ageru*, *kureru*, and *morau*. Specifically, we examine them in three sets of spoken corpora: the Pac Rim/Japanese and the Earthquake corpora, comprised largely of face to face conversational data, and the CALLFRIEND corpus of telephone conversation,[2] altogether totaling approximately 25 hours of talk. Although usage both as main and auxiliary verbs (see (4) below) has been examined, in this paper we present our findings chiefly for the former:[3]

(4)   shashin totte kuremasu   ka?
        photo   take give:POLITE QUES
        'Will you take a photo for (us)?'

Also included in our database are examples such as the following where *ageru* does not literally mean 'give':

(5)   te   agete miru
        hand raise see
        'try raising a hand'

---

[2] The Pac Rim/Japanese corpus was compiled by Tsuyoshi Ono and his associates at UC Santa Barbara and the University of Arizona. The Earthquake corpus was compiled by Shoichi Iwasaki and his associates at UCLA. The CALLFRIEND corpus is available from the Linguistic Data Consortium.

[3] In our preliminary examination, auxiliary usage of these verbs showed dramatically different statistical patterns from main verb use. This should be more closely examined in future studies.

(6)   Ookura de shiki   o ageta
        at wedding   had
        '(She) had a wedding at Ookura'

This methodological decision was partially because we wanted to be maximally inclusive rather than making arbitrary coding decisions based on our interpretation of the semantics of these items. It was also because these uses of *ageru* are lexically related to the 'give' usage of *ageru*; all of these uses are found under one main entry for *ageru* in dictionaries.

In total, we identified 136 examples of *ageru*, *kureru*, and *morau* used as main verbs, and the cross-corpus distributional patterns are focused upon and discussed. Our approach is to observe the behavior of these verbs in spoken language, the primary form of language, and propose hypotheses about what the actual representation of these verbs may be like. In particular, we are interested in finding out if the semantic-based grouping of these verbs as a set based on constructed data is supported by what Japanese speakers do in real life. We carefully reviewed both the transcripts and the recordings of our data. Experience indicates not only that transcripts only represent a tiny fraction of what takes place in actual interaction, but that transcripts do not always accurately depict the actual language used in interactions. In any data-based approach to linguistics, it is our view that it is the important responsibility of the researcher to be intimately aware of the particulars of the data itself. One unanticipated side effect of this was that we found that the quality of transcription for the CALLFRIEND corpus to be somewhat less than ideal, and advocate that the recordings be consulted before the transcriptions are taken at face value.[4] Our database is rather small because we are particularly interested in everyday talk of Japanese, and such data is still not very available. In fact, there is still no sizable corpus of naturally occurring speech of Japanese at the time of writing this paper.[5]

---

[4] Among other reasons, we suspect that prescriptivism on the part of the transcriber(s) of the CALLFRIEND corpus may have resulted in the less than ideal quality of its transcripts. Examples include inserted and omitted particles as well as lexical substitutions and omissions, and even examples of paraphrasing. Please note that we are pointing this out simply to caution analysts of discourse transcripts, especially of CALLFRIEND transcripts, against using transcripts without consulting the original recording. Referring to recordings obviously slows down the research process at a micro level, but in our view that is the minimum requirement in handling this type of data, and, skipping that crucial step actually slows down the progress of the field as a whole in the long run.

[5] In our view, a construction of such a corpus should be every researcher's top research agenda if s/he deems the goal of their research to represent the ability which makes spoken language possible.

2. Overall Distribution

Firstly, a very prominent skew in the frequency of occurrence of the three verbs was discovered. This is shown in the following table:[6]

Table 1 Giving/Receiving Verbs

	ageru	*morau*	*kureru*	Total
N	29	84	23	136

Specifically, *morau* is used much more frequently than the other two verbs (more than 60% of the total number of examples). Fry (2003:62) also finds in the CALLHOME corpus that *morau* is the most frequent.[7] As we saw in Examples (2) and (3), *morau* 'get' and *kureru* 'give' have been said to be used to describe similar situations where a transfer takes place towards the speaker or her/his in-group member (recipient). Please consider:

(7)   panfuretto moratta kara
        pamphlet got   so
        '(I) got a pamphlet so...'

(8)   okane kurereba...
        money give:if
        'If (you) gave (us) money, (we'd move out anytime).'

For *morau*, the subject encodes the recipient, who is the speaker (or her/his in-group member), while for *kureru* it encodes the giver, who is not the speaker (or a member of her or his in-group), as illustrated in the following table:

Table 2 *morau* and *kureru*

	syntactic-semantic configuration
morau	subject = speaker (or her/his in-group) recipient
kureru	subject ≠ speaker (or her/his in-group) recipient

It seems safe to suggest that syntactic subject is the most natural position to encode the speaker. This is clearly supported by Japanese conversation data in Shimojo (2005), where speakers are encoded in the subject position very close to 100 percent of the time (1096 out of 1100 examples).[8] *Kureru* thus involves a inherent conflict in its syntactic-semantic configuration, which accords with Takubo's statement (2000) that *kureru* is a special

---

[6] This table includes 11 cases of *ageru* which does not literally mean 'give', illustrated in examples (5) and (6). If we treat these examples separately, e.g., excluding them, we would have an even a sharper skew.

[7] The CALLHOME corpus is available from the Linguistic Data Consortium.

[8] This figure was obtained based on the information given in Table 3.10 in Shimojo (2005:69)

verb because verbs empathizing with non-subject (i.e., encoding the speaker or her/his in-group member in a non-subject position) are rare in Japanese and not commonly found in other languages.

We would thus like to suggest that *kureru*'s syntactic-semantic configuration is responsible for its less frequent use compared with *morau* (approximately 1 to 4 ratio). *Morau* and *kureru* are often treated as a set in the literature due to their semantic similarities, but this seems to be somewhat unrealistic as they appear to be treated rather differently by speakers.[9]

3. Realis vs. Irrealis

Closely related to the previous point, we also found a skew in the distribution of realis and irrealis[10] in the use of the three verbs: *morau* tends to express realis more (38.6%; 32 out of 83 examples) than *kureu* (8.7%; 2 out of 23 examples) and *ageru* (24.1%; 7 out of 29 examples).[11] Our interpretation is that realized giving/receiving events promote a particular framing of the event. That is, since the transferred material is now with the recipient, the event is viewed from the perspective of the receiving end, resulting a more frequent use of *morau* 'get' over *kureru/ageru* 'give'.[12] This nicely accounts for a much stronger association of realis with *morau* than with *kureru* (38.6% and 8.7%), as illustrated in the following examples:

(9)   Nanno kara denwa moratta no   ne
        from call   got   NOM FP
        '(I) got a call from Nanno.'

(10)   juudoru   kureru tte   iu   kara
        10:dollars give   QUOT say so
        '(They) say thay they will give (you) 10 dollars...'

These verbs both describe a transfer of a material towards the speaker (or her/his in-group member), but *morau* can be said to take the perspective of the recipient by encoding the speaker (or her/his in-group) recipient in the subject position.

---

[9] See Tao (2003) and Ono and Jones (to appear) for similar arguments regarding cognitive sets in the grammar of actual speakers.

[10] Here realis refers to a situation in the utterance which is presented as having taken place.

[11] Excluding instances of *ageru* which don't literally mean 'give', discussed above, would result in a sharper skew where only 16.7% (3 out of 18 examples) of *ageru* is considered as expressing realis.

[12] This interpretation is compatible with DeLancey's (1981) cross-linguistic proposal that perfective aspect is a specification of terminal viewpoint.

4. Clause Structure

Giving/receiving verbs are typically discussed in the literature using constructed examples, which take the form of 'canonical clause' where the verb appears with case-marked subject and object NPs as seen in (1)-(3) above.

Our Japanese conversation data, however, replicates the cross-linguistic findings by Du Bois (2003) that clauses rarely appear in a canonical form in spoken language. Specifically, clauses with overt NP subject and NP object are extremely rare in Japanese. In fact, in our data, there is not even a single canonical clause involving a giving/receiving verb. We did find about 10 examples which assumed some characteristics of a canonical clause where subject and object NPs appear with a giving/receiving verb, as in:

(11)   watashi maaku kara tegami moratta
         I   Mark   from letter got
         'I got a letter from Mark'.

As (11) illustrates, however, even in such examples, one (or more) of the NPs are not canonically case marked: unmarked NPs or NPs marked with a non-case particle such as the so-called topic marker *wa* and *mo* 'also', are common.

Our data thus reveals that an overwhelmingly large majority of Japanese giving/receiving verbs are found in non-canonical clauses, which, at least in the context of giving/receiving verbs may cause some puzzlement as to what specifically 'canonical' refers to. One could perhaps argue that this is due to the phenomena often called 'NP ellipsis' and 'particle ellipsis' which Japanese is known for, and that utterance types found in conversation is a result of canonical clauses at some underlying level interacting with various performance factors. We do not pursue that possibility here specifically because starting out with a canonical form requires one to posit a theoretical entity that does not actually occur in data. Positing 'canonical clause' is redundant in this context and thus makes our theory less elegant.[13] Thus, as a first step to understand the grammar of giving/receiving verbs in Japanese conversation, we will describe these 'non-canonical clause' for the remainder of this paper.

First of all, most of the giving/receiving verbs in our data appear with an explicit NP denoting the object that is transferred (hereafter P), as seen in:

---

[13] It should also be pointed out that canonical clauses might be a form which pertains to written language (see Linell 2005).

(12)   onigiri   o moratta dake desu
        rice.ball   got   only POLITE
        '(I) only got riceballs.'

(13)   nijuudoru gurai agemasu
        20:dollar about give:POLITE
        '(We) will give (you) like 20 dollars.'

The ratio of explicit Ps for these verbs (approx. 85%) is significantly higher than what is reported for verbs in general in Japanese (approx. 50%; Fry 2003 and Shimojo 2005).[14]

Examination of such examples in context shows that explicit Ps are sometimes used to introduce new information into the discourse (Du Bois 2003), as in (14) and (15):

(14)   Talking about a sukiyaki get-together.

        W: sukiyaki wa ashita de=
        '(We) will have sukiyaki tomorrow, and'

        nanka mottekuru no wa kyoo desho?
        '(they) will bring stuff today?'

        H: u=n to omou kedo?
        'yes, (I) think.'

        W: shungiku ageyo
                    give:INTEND
        '(I) will donate crown daisy (sukiyaki ingredient).'

(15)   Trying to select a restaurant for a dinner party. N just came back from one of the candidate restaurants and is talking to Y on the phone (example (7) is also part of this sequence).

        N: shashin deta   panfuretto moratta kara
           photo   appeared pamphlet got   so
        '(I) got a pamphlet with photos so'

        Y: un un
        'mhm mhm'

---

[14] Please note that some may not consider the quantifier *nijuudoru* '20 dollars' in 13) a syntactic object since one cannot mark it with the so-called direct object particle *o*. Further, one could insert another NP such as *orei o* 'gift' in the clause, which would result to mean '(We) will give (you) a gift like 20 dollars.' It is not yet known how to treat such NPs in our attempt to represent the grammar of actual speakers. If one considers examples such as (13) not involving an overt P, the percentage of overt Ps in our data is 66%.

N: ano sore o anata ni okuru kara.
'(I) will send it to you.'

At the same time, there are some clear examples where explicit Ps do not introduce new information. For example, in (16) H talks about an already introduced referent as seen in his use of a demonstrative *kore* 'this':

(16)   Talking about a mattress which H received as a gift.

K: nan no matto na no sore
'What kind of mattress is that?'

H: <u>kore moratta   no   nanka tomodachi ni</u>
   this received FP what   friend   from
'(I) got this, uh from a friend.'

Further, quite a few Ps are found in fixed and semi-fixed expressions such as *ichibetsu kureru* 'have a look', as in (17):

(17)   omizu o ageru 'give water (to plants)/water (plants)'
        shiki o ageru 'have a wedding',
        ten o ageru 'give points'
        denwa morau 'get a phone call'
        onomimono morau 'order a drink'
        kekkon shootaijoo morau 'get a wedding invitation card/
                                 get invited to a wedding'
        kuroobi o morau 'get a blackbelt/blackbelted'

Ps in such examples do not seem to express a referent for which the distinction between newness/giveness is relevant.[15] Further, these examples support recent findings that much of spoken language is fixed, not generative (Erman and Warren 2000; Ono and Jones to appear; Ono and Thompson to appear).

Second, as seen in many examples including (14)-(16) above, we have further found that the subject argument of the verb (hereafter, A) is typically not overtly expressed with giving/receiving verbs; the ratio of explicit mention is less than 10% (13 out of 136), even less than what is reported for verbs in general in the literature (30% overtly expressed; Fry 2003 and Shimojo 2005). It thus appears that Japanese giving/receiving verbs show a strong tendency to be used only with P, suggesting they might be associated with a preferred template [P V].

---

[15] As explicit Ps have been associated with the introduction of new information in the literature (Du Bois 2003), these types of examples would be interesting to investigate in more detail.

Finally, marking of Ps for giving/receiving verbs exhibits a pattern similar to what is reported for verbs in general in the literature (Matsuda 1995; Fujii and Ono 2000; Fry 2003; Shimojo 2005) where non-marking is the majority (57%; 51 out of 89[16]), as illustrated in:

(18)   boonasu moratta atoni
         bonus   got   after
         'After (you) get a bonus, …'

The rest is divided between case particles (29%; 26 out of 89) and non-case particles (13% 12 out of 89) such as *wa, mo,* and *tte*. These figures show that non-marking is the norm for Ps in spoken language and the use of so-called case particles is a marked activity while the use of non-case particles is surprisingly common, calling for a more detailed investigation.

5. Conclusion

To sum up, our corpus-based investigation reveals fascinating new facts that would be inaccessible through the usage of constructed examples, and also raises many more questions about giving/receiving verbs in Japanese. Specifically, we have seen that there are prominent skews both in terms of frequency of these verbs and of their association with the realis mood in conversation data, which correlate with the semantic structures encoded by these verbs. We have also seen that these verbs are found in a particular type of clause structure, rather different from the type which we have been led to believe. These findings should be examined further with a larger amount of discourse data in future studies.

References

DeLancey, Scott. 1981. An interpretation of split ergativity and related patterns. *Language* 57.3: 626-57.

Du Bois, J. W. 2003. Argument Structure: Grammar in Use. *Preferred Argument Strucutre: Grammar as Architecture of Function*, eds. J. W. Du Bois, L. E. Kumpf, and W. J. Ashby, 10-60. Amsterdam: John Benjamins.

Erman, B. and B. Warren. 2000. The idiom principle and the open choice principle. *Text* 20.1: 29-62.

Fry, J. 2003. *Ellipsis and wa-marking in Japnaese Conversation*. New York: Routledge.

Fujii, N. and T. Ono. 2000. The Occurrence and Non-occurrence of the Japanese Direct Object Marker *o* in Conversation. *Studies in Language* 24: 1-39.

---

[16] This figure does not involve Ps which cannot be marked with the direct object marker *o*, discussed in footnote 14. If those Ps are included, the percentage of non marking becomes even higher.

Kuno, S. 1978. *Danwa no Bunpoo*. Tokyo: Taishuukan.

Linell, P. 2005. *The written language bias in linguistics: its nature, origins, and transformation*. Oxford: Routledge.

Matsuda, K. 1995. Variable Zero-marking of (*o*) in Tokyo Japanese. Doctoral dissertation, University of Pennsylvania.

Ono, T. and K. Jones. To appear. Conversation and Grammar: Approaching so-called conditionals in Japanese. *Japanese Applied Linguistics: Discourse and Social Perspectives*, eds. J. Mori and A. S. Ohta. London: Continuum.

Ono, T. and S. A. Thompson. To appear. Fixedness in Japanese adjectives in conversation: Toward a new understanding of a lexical (part-of-speech) category. In Corrigan, Roberta, Edith Moravcsik, Hamid Ouali, and Kathleen Wheatley, eds., Formulaic Language. Amsterdam: Benjamins.

Ooe, S. 1975. *Nichieigo no Hikakukenkyuu*. Tokyo: Nanundoo.

Shibatani, M. 2000. Japanese Benefactive Constructions: Their Cognitive Bases and Autonomy. *Syntactic and Functional Explorations: In Honor of Susumu Kuno*. eds. K. Takami, A. Kamio, and J. Whitman, 185-205. Tokyo: Kurosio.

Shimojo, M. 2005. *Argument Encoding in Japanese Conversation*. Hampshire: Palgrave Macmillan.

Takubo, Y. 2000. Nihongogaku no fookasu: Shiten [Focus in Japanese language study: Viewpoint]. *Bessatsu Kokubungaku* 53: 148-151.

Tao, Hongyin. 2003. A usage-based approach to argument structure: 'remember' and 'forget' in spoken English. *International Journal of Corpus Linguistics* 8.1: 75–95.

How 'Things' (*mono*) Get Reanalyzed in Japanese Discourse*

NINA AZUMI YOSHIDA
University of California, Los Angeles

1. Introduction

This paper examines the grammatical and interactional uses of *mono* in Modern Japanese, and proposes an alternative, unitary analysis to account for the seeming multi-functionalities *mono* has as a marker of speaker modality in Japanese discourse. Numerous studies exist to date on *mono* in Japanese (Teramura 1981, 1984, Agetsuma 1991, Tsubone 1994, Fujii 2000, inter alia) and these have noted its functions of marking for a wide range of the speaker's emotive or subjective affect; however, a vital question that remains unanswered is what particular contribution *mono* itself is making in each instance of such usages.

The present analysis is termed 'unitary' in suggesting that a continuity exists in the semantics born by *mono* in each of its different modal uses, and that these represent inferable extensions of *mono*'s primary meaning that arise as a result of reanalysis when it occurs in certain constructions

---

* I wish to thank Prof. Robert S. Kirsner for his constructive comments on an earlier draft of this paper. I am also grateful to Profs. Yukinori Takubo, Kaoru Horie, and Janick Wrona, whose questions at the JK16 conference helped direct the final version of this paper. All remaining errors are, of course, my own.

which have become grammaticalized in Modern Japanese. The account is moreover 'alternative' in proposing an underlying semantics for *mono* which is variant from those claimed in past studies (e.g. Tsubone 1994, Agetsuma 1991, Fujii 2000). To further illustrate the linguistic phenomenon under examination in this paper, provided in the section to follow is a brief overview of the usages *mono* has in Japanese discourse.

1.1. Lexical and grammatical uses of *mono*

As a lexical item, *mono* has traditionally been categorized as belonging to a relatively small and closed set of nominals called *keisiki meisi* ('formal nouns')[1] and as such, is said to possess a minimal and opaque meaning, much like 'thing(s)' of English. Being a formal or dependent noun, *mono* typically occurs with a modifier, but may appear alone in the limited contexts of fixed or idiomatic expressions. Examples of these uses of *mono* as a bare noun are provided in (1) – (4) below2.

(1) *Iroiro na mono o katta.*
various thing ACC buy:PST
'(I) bought various things'

(2) *Amai mono ga tabetai.*
sweet thing NOM eat:DES:NPST
'(I) want to eat sweet things → (I) want to eat something sweet.'

(3) *Tosiyori wa yoku mono o sitteiru.*
elderly people TOP well thing ACC know:NPST
'The elderly know things well' → 'The elderly are wise.'

(4) *Nihonjin wa hakkiri mono o iwanai.*
Japanese people TOP clearly thing ACC say:NEG:NPST
'Japanese people do not say things clearly' →
'Japanese people do not speak/state(their) opinions clearly.'

In addition to its use as a bare noun, however, *mono* occurs in a number of grammatical constructions that serve to reflect a seemingly wide range of speaker modality or attitudes toward the proposition expressed by the sen-

---

[1] 'Formal nouns', or *keisiki meisi* in Japanese, refer to those morphological items which possess significance as nouns in formal or grammatical terms only. The meanings possessed by such formal nouns are often opaque and lacking in substantial significance.
[2] Abbreviations used in this paper are:
ACC=Accusative; ALL=Allative; ASP =Aspect; CONJ=Conjunctive; COP=Copula; DAT=Dative; DES=Desiderative; GEN=Genitive; NEG=Negative; NOM=Nominative; NPST=Non Past; POL=Polite; PRX=Prefix; PST=Past; QT=Quotative; TE= *Te* Connective; TOP=Topic.

tence[3]. Below is a representative set of examples illustrating the modal functions of *mono*[4].

(5) *Inu   wa   hoeru   mon(o)da.*
   dog TOP bark:NPST *MONO*:COP
   'Dogs naturally bark./It's expected that dogs bark.'

(6) *Mukasi   wa   yoku kono kooen de asonda   mon(o)da.*
   long ago TOP well   this park   at play:PST *MONO*:COP
   'Back then, (I) sure used to play at this park alot'

(7) *Konna   rippa-na   uti   ni itido wa   sumitai   mon(o)da.*
   like.this magnificent house in once TOP live:DES *MONO*:COP
   'If just once, I sure would want to live in a magnificent house like this.'

(8) *Yoku yatta   mon(o)da.*
   well do:PST *MONO*:COP
   'How well (you) did!'/ 'It's amazing (you) did so well.'

(9) *Hito   ni   wa   amari meiwaku o   kakenai   mon(o)da.*
   people DAT TOP much trouble ACC cause:NEG:NPST *MONO*:COP
   'You shouldn't cause people too much trouble.'

(10) *Pari   e   ikeru   mono nara, itte-mitai   desu*[5].
   Paris ALL can go:NPST *MONO* if   go:TE-see:DES COP:POL
   'If (only) I could go to Paris, I would like to go and see (how it is).'

(11) *Mada tiisakatta mono   da kara, yoku   oboete-imasen.*
   still small:PST *MONO* COP so   well   remember:TE-ASP:NEG:POL
   '(I) was still young, so (I) don't remember (it) well.'

(12) *Ore, miito soosu tabenai.   Datte,   kirai da   mon*[6].
   I   meat.sauce eat:NEG:NPST. because hate COP *MONO*
   'I won't the meat sauce. Because, (I) hate (it).'

A number of past studies, citing the occurrence of *mono* usages such as those exemplified in (5)–(12) above, have suggested multiple meanings and functions for the lexeme *mono* (e.g., as a verbal auxiliary in Examples (5)-(8), a connective in examples (9) and (10), an utterance-final particle in Example (11)). However, as aptly stated in Fujii (2000):

---

[3] The term 'sentence', usually employed in specific reference to an established unit of written data, is being employed here generically to refer synonymously to the notion of 'utterance' in spoken data.
[4] Examples 5-9 adapted from Martin (1975: 725-6)
[5] Examples 10 and 11 adapted from Nagara et al. (1987: 112).
[6] Data source: http://plaza.rakuten.co.jp/fourleavespetit/diary/200703250001/

> Crucially, it is not the bare word *MONO* but rather the *MONO* construction as a whole being used in a specific discourse context that evokes specific propositional attitudes. It is thus misleading to treat *MONO* per se as bearing distinct grammatical meanings and functions, [...] (p. 88).

My account takes a position similar to Fujii (2000) in agreeing that it is the occurrence of *mono* within the context of a particular grammatical construction and discourse instance that causes it to be interpreted in association with a certain type of speaker modality. However, it will differ in highlighting the role played by *mono* within these constructions, notably in terms of the semantic contribution this lexical item is making in each grammatical environment involving it. The underlying semantics suggested for *mono* will be arrived at by comparing it against another keisiki meisi ('formal noun') quite similar to *mono* in meaning, namely, *koto*. It is claimed that these two nominals stand in a mutually oppositional, semantic relationship to each other, and that the meaning born by *mono* as a bare noun is more precisely captured when viewed in such contrastive terms. Moreover, it will be hypothesized that the various modal interpretations *mono* receives within a grammatical or discourse context can be accounted for as representing extensions, arrived at by metaphorical or metonymical means, of the underlying semantics proposed.

The next section presents the main grammatical uses of *mono* in Modern Japanese, as viewed in a comparison/contrast fashion with *koto*.

2. Grammatical Uses of *Mono* and *Koto*

2.1. *Mono* and *Koto* as Head Nouns

As previously mentioned, *mono* and *koto* roughly express the meaning 'thing' of English. Reference grammars for students of Japanese commonly explain the choice between them as being governed by the opposing semantic notions of 'concrete' versus 'abstract' (Martin 1975, McGloin 1989), or 'tangible' vs. 'intangible' (Makino and Tsutsui 1986). The following example is an instance where the choice of *mono* or *koto* would render a meaning difference in a pair of otherwise identical sentences[7].

(13) *Kakitai*   *mono*   *ga*   *aru.*
     want to write   MONO   NOM   exist:NPST
     'There is something I want to write.' (e.g. a book, a letter)

(14) *Kakitai*   *koto*   *ga*   *aru.*
     want to write   KOTO   NOM   exist:NPST
     'There is something I want to write (about).' (e.g. a topic or idea)

---

[7] Examples taken from McGloin (1989: 110).

Koto is often preceded or modified by a verb phrase in the non-past or imperfect form to indicate 'the activity of.' *Koto*, together with *no*, is also the most commonly recognized nominalizer in Modern Japanese. When this *koto* is replaced by *mono*, it indicates the object upon which the act takes place or the performer of the act. Examples of such usage, employing a transitive verb, are given in (15a) and (15b):

Verb   Verb +*koto*   Verb + *mono*
(15a)   *<kaku>*   *<kakukoto>*   *<kakumono>*
         'to write' 'writing'   '(some)thing to write on' (paper, desk, etc.)
                                   '(some)thing to write with' (pen, crayon, etc.)
                                   '(some)one who writes'

(15b)   *<tukuru>*   *<tukurukoto>*   *<tukurumono>*
         'to make'   'making' '(some)thing to make'
                         '(some)thing to make (something) with'
                         '(some)one who makes (something)'

2.2. Prenominal/Preadjectival Uses of *Mono*

Mono possesses a grammatical use whose equivalent is not found in the case of *koto*. When *mono* is attached preadjectivally or prenominally, it imparts a sense of indefiniteness or vagueness. It acts to increase the ambiguity or the inability to pinpoint the underlying source of the sensation or phenomenon to which it is prefixed. Examples of this usage of *mono* + adjective and *mono* + noun are provided in (16) and (17), respectively:

(16)(a)   *kanasii* / *mono-ganasii*   'sad' / 'somehow sad'
     (b)   *siduka* / *mono-siduka*   'quiet, serene'/'strangely quiet'

(17)(a)   *oto ga suru*   /   *mono-oto ga suru*
        'hear sounds'   'hear the sounds of something'
     (b)   *kage ni kakureru*   /   *mono-kage ni kakureru*
        'to hide in the shadows'   'to hide in the shadows of something'

2.3. Modal Uses: The Mon(o)da and *Koto*da Construction

The formal nouns *mono* and *koto* are frequently employed as a complementizer in Japanese sentences, the common pattern being that of *mono* or *koto* immediately preceded by a clause in the *rentaikei* /'attributive' form, and followed by the copula *da*, as shown in (18):

(18)   [clause]^{attributive} + *mono/koto* + copula <u>*da*</u>.

The *mon(o)da*[8] construction has been identified by a number of Modern Japanese grammarians (e.g., Martin 1975, Nagara et al 1987, Makino and Tsutsui 1986) as possessing the linguistic capacity to imbue an otherwise neutral or 'objective' statement with various degrees of speaker's subjective or emotive affect, such as conviction toward a natural/general truth (example (5)), nostalgic recollection (example (6)), deep-seated desire (example (7)), amazement (example (8)), or to mark an indirect command (example (9)). In contrast, *kotoda*'s uses are limited to expressions of wonder/mild amazement9 and indirect commands10 (See footnotes 9 and 10 for examples)[11].

It is significant to note that both the *mon(o)da* and *kotoda* constructions bear a striking formal resemblance to the commentary predicate—namely, that of a nominalized predicate occupying the comment position of a topic-comment, or NPA *wa* NPB (*da*)[12] type construction. The current study proposes that this similarity, where the propositional content of this predicate has been made 'nonchallengeable'[13] through its nominalization, and where **mono** and **koto** take on a 'nonreferential'[14] reading—that these are the foremost structural factors contributing to their functional capabilities of marking for speaker modality.

The nominalized predicate takes the propositional contents of what appears, superficially, to be an objectivized event or state, and repackages it as

---

[8] In colloquial or informal discourse contexts, **mono** may be further contracted to **mon**, resulting in the semi-fixed, or 'grammaticalized' form **monda**. The '*o*' of **mono** is enclosed in parentheses to indicate these possible variations..

[9] *Huyu no umi ni otite, yoku sinzoo mahi de sinanakatta* **kotoda.**
winter GEN sea into fall:CONJ well heart.attack from die:NEG:PST *KOTO*:COP
'It's a wonder that (you) fell in to the sea in winter, and didn't die from a cardiac arrest.'

[10] *Yasumi gurai wa benkyoo no koto nado wasurete, zyuubun-ni tanosimu* **kotoda.**
day off at.least TOP studies GEN about such.as forget:CONJ fully enjoy:NPST *KOTO*:COP
'On days off, at least, (you) should forget about such things as studying, and fully enjoy (yourself).'

[11] Examples adapted from Nagara et al. 1987: 29.

[12] The copula *da* is enclosed in parentheses to indicate that it is an optional element in this construction. I will be taking the view that *da* encodes an additional feature here that is compatible with, but not essential to the topic-comment (i.e. A *wa* B) type utterance; namely, that its overt use marks the speaker's explicit assertion of his certainty in his knowledge or his belief in his affirmative judgment about the truth of the sentential content so marked – what Narahara (2002) terms the 'anti-ignorative mode' (Narahara 2002: 163-6).

[13] As initially noted by Givon (1982), the propositional contents of a clause modifying a nominal element have been shown cross-linguistically to be 'nonchallengeable', or shielded from challenge (Givon 1982: 100).

[14] Based on Agetsuma (1991), I will be using the term 'referential' to refer to 'regular' nominalized predicates, where the nominal element serving as the head noun retains its nominal status as the referential object of the *wa*-marked topic, and 'nonreferential' for those which have become formulaic or grammaticalized to the extent that the head noun has lost its nominal status and bears only a modal meaning.

either a *mono* or *koto* in indication of how these contents are to be received. It is this repackaged proposition, made nonchallengeable through its nominalization, and embellished with the speaker's attitudinal stance toward the proposition through his choice of *mono* or *koto*, which is then presented to the hearer when a nonreferential type nominalized predicate like *mon(o)da* or *kotoda*, is uttered.

I further suggest that this attitudinal stance of the speaker—i.e., deontic, epistemic, or evaluative—derives itself from the underlying meanings *mono* and *koto* possess as nominals in this construction. Next, I present what these semantics are, followed up by how these propositional attitudes (Fujii 2000) arise and are inferenced, focusing on the particular case of *mon(o)da*.

3. The Semantics of *Mono* and *Koto*

As previously stated, reference grammars commonly explain the choice between *mono* and *koto* as being regulated by such opposing semantic notions as 'concrete' versus 'abstract' or 'tangible' vs. 'intangible'. Although this simple and seemingly clear-cut rule holds up well in the majority of instances where *mono* and *koto* tend to occur, the distinction becomes difficult to account for when confronted by the acceptability of sentences such as in (19), where the logical referent of *mono* does not appear to possess any obvious features of 'concreteness' or 'tangibility':

(19) *Ano hito wa yasasisa to iu mono/*koto ni kaketeiru.*
that person TOP kindness QT say *MONO* DAT lack:TE-ASP:NPST
'That person is lacking in (the thing called) kindness.'

Teramura (1981) provides the insight that *mono*'s most typical definition is that it signals an object, or a category thereof, possessing some type of 'physical concreteness' which can be perceived by one of the five bodily senses. Additionally, its meaning encompasses those phenomena having 'a reality (capable of being) sensed psychologically' (Teramura 1981: 754).

Based on such past accounts, I propose the following primary meaning for *mono*: *Mono* signals an existence that is 'sensorily' perceptible (i.e., through the bodily senses of sight, smell, sound, taste, and touch—as well as one's inner state experiences, such as pain, hunger, emotions, etc.); hence, *mono* is indicative of a physically perceived, and by token of this notion, an 'unrationalized' phenomenon, an existence that can be directly sensed without the aid or use of one's mind and its rationalizing powers. In contrast, *koto*, refers to an intellectually or cognitively perceived existence; namely, marking an existence as *koto* signals that it will require processing within one's mental faculties and that one's powers of rationalization must be called in to enable this *koto* to become perceptible. These opposing semantics of 'physically sensed/unrationalized' existence versus 'cognitively conceived/rationalized' existence are hypothesized as being the key, definitive features distinguishing *mono* from *koto* in instances when they are to take on a referential reading.

Because *mono*'s semantics denote a phenomenon whose actual existence can be validated by sensorial means alone (i.e. without the need for mental processing), it prototypically indicates a physical/material object. However, because its meaning also signals that whose perceived presence is to remain 'unrationalized', it connotes an existence that 'somehow exists', and by token of this, is unidentified, undifferentiated or un-individuated; namely, a 'generic', 'general', or 'collective' entity. In this respect, *mono* may reference a substance having an (actual or construed) internal homogeneity, such as in the case of abstract nouns (e.g. *yasasisa* 'kindness'), or may potentially reference a person, albeit in a generic, physical sense, and would thus be inappropriate in referring to a uniquely identified individual or one meriting respect or distinction.[15]

Moreover, since *mono*'s meaning typically references a physical object, a proposition presented as a certain type of *mono* may be assumed to occupy a three-dimensional area of space, an assumption that would necessarily be absent in the case of one marked by *koto*.

4. How Speaker Modality Arises in the *Mon(o)da* Construction

4.1. The Topic-Comment [NPA *wa* NPB (*da*)] Construction

It was aforementioned that the *mon(o)da* construction shares a structural likeness to that of a nominalized predicate occupying the comment position of a topic-comment type construction. As noted by Okutsu (1978), one of the intrinsic messages coded by the NP$_A$ *wa* NP$_B$ (*da*), or topic-comment construction is that some sort of relationship exists between the noun phrases 'A' and 'B'; however, the type is not specified. Observe the following pair of examples illustrating this construction type:

(i) *Meerii   wa   gakusei   (da)*   → 'Mary is a student.'
    Mary   TOP   student   COP

(ii) *Boku   wa   unagi   (da)*[16]   → 'I will have the broiled eels.'
     I   TOP   (broiled) eels COP

---

[15] When employed as a bare noun, the Japanese *kanji* orthography allows a distinction to be made between the *mono* meaning 'person' from that of 'physical object', using 者 for the former, and 物 for the latter, respectively. However, as claimed above, *mono* (者) refers to a person, but to one lacking distinction; hence, its common use in the expression used to humbly introduce oneself (e.g., *Yosida to iu mono desu ga./*Lit. 'I am a *mono* (=someone) named Yoshida.')

[16] Example from Okutsu (1978: 8).

In the case of examples like (i) and (ii) above, it is unclear whether the concept expressed by the sentence is simply indicative of a logical, connotative relationship between the *wa*-marked topic 'A' and its comment 'B' (as in example (i)), or whether a full interpretation (i.e., one that is appropriate within the context of the current discourse) involves inferencing an additional unexpressed main idea. For example, if uttered by a male customer in the context of a restaurant, from the minimal pair of concepts 'A' (*boku*/ 'I') and 'B' (*unagi*/ 'eel'), will be inferred the interpretation, 'I will order/eat/have the broiled eels.'

Only after the predicative NP has been supplied can it be interpreted retroactively whether the *wa*-marked NP has been topicalized as an entity to be referenced by the predicative one, or whether it has been topicalized in allusion to some conceptual aspect of it embodied by the commentary predicate itself. In other words, within the NP_A *wa* NP_B *(da)* construction, there are normally no morphological devices or "cues" provided to aid its hearer in interpreting the precise nature of its proposition.

4.2. How the Deontic Stance Arises in the Mon(o)da Construction

On the other hand, I claim that the predicative noun (i.e., *mono*) of a nominalized predicate such as the *mon(o)da* construction--where it takes on a non-referential or extended/secondary meaning--is a morphologically manifested 'cue' whose function it is to direct the hearer on how, or in what manner, a particular topic's comment is to be construed. Due to the underlying semantics of *mono* (as proposed), the speaker's very choice of employing the *mon(o)da* construction to present the proposition is, in itself, reflective of his subjective attitude toward it. Thus, in the absence of further context, native speakers of Japanese might find the following sentence ambiguous with at least two possible readings as given in (20a) and (20b):

(20) *O-toso*   *wa o-syoogatu*   *ni   nomu*
      PFX-spiced.sake TOP PFX-New.Year's.Day DAT drink:NPST
      mono   da
      MONO:COP
(20a) '*Toso*' is (some)thing (that one) drinks on New Year's Day.'
(20b) 'You are supposed to drink *toso* on New Year's Day.'

In the first reading (20a), the head noun *mono* takes on a referential reading, in that it refers semantically to a physical/material object modified by the clause *o-syoogatu ni nomu*/'drink on New Year's Day', which in turn serves to comment on, or define the *wa*-marked topic *o-toso*/'spiced sake'. This results in what may be termed a 'definitional' reading of the topic NP. In the second, however, *mono* is no longer functioning as a nominal with a referent, but simply as a modal marker, in this case, to mark the proposition *o-syoogatsu ni nomu/*'drink on New Year's Day' with the speaker's deontic modality as an indirect command (as in 20b). This then raises the question of what causes these seemingly 'dual' interpretations to arise?

The answer may be found in taking a more careful look at the semantic contribution *mono* is making in this particular example. Interestingly, it has been noted that the *mon(o)da* construction 'always conveys a particular nuance of obligation' (Fujii 2000: 92) and that this is one of the default interpretations of this construction (Fujii 2000: 95). I claim that the potential for a deontic reading lies precisely in *mono*'s underlying semantics of signaling a physically-perceived/unrationalized existence; namely, one that 'somehow exists.' Based on the semantics for *mono* that has been proposed, a more literal English rendering of sentence (20) might read:

'Normally/Generally, *'toso'* is a thing (one) drinks on New Year's Day.'

I suggest that the (purely) deontic reading, as that in (20b), derives as a result of pragmatic implicatures made on the part of the hearer when the *mon(o)da* construction occurs in a particular discourse context[17]. As proposed in Yoshida (2008), the deontic interpretation of a predicate nominalized by *mono* (i.e. the *mon(o)da* construction) emerges (i) when the clause modifying *mono* contains a predicate with nonpast inflection (i.e. future), most typically a verb denoting an agent-controllable action, and (ii) the utterance containing this nominalized predicate is directed toward an overt or implied second-person referent. The fact that the propositional content expressed by the modifying clause has been made nonchallengeable through its nominalization structurally contributes to imbuing this construction with the illocutionary force of a directive. The speaker's choice of marking it with *mono* functions not just to indicate to the hearer that he has an obligation to carry out the designated action, but to direct him to the authoritative 'source' or basis behind why he is obligated to perform it.

I further suggest that the type of authoritative source *mono* references derives itself by extensions metonymically inferred (i.e. PHYSICAL > SOCIAL) of its underlying meaning; namely, a 'physically-perceived existence' is reinterpreted as connoting a 'socially-recognized obligation/necessity.' Moreover, *mono*'s semantics of denoting an existence with a vaguely defined, but constant spatial orientation'shifts' by way of metaphorical extension (i.e. SPACE > TIME) to referencing a basis for an obli-

---

[17] Lyons (1977) points out that when we impose upon someone the obligation to perform (or to refrain from performing) a particular act, we are describing the desirable results that will obtain if the act in question is performed (Lyons 1977: 823). Deontic necessity, moreover, typically proceeds or derives from some source or cause. If we recognize that we are obliged to perform some act, then we usually acknowledge that someone or something is responsible for our obligation (Lyons 1977: 824).

gation with a temporal dimension; hence one whose validity has persisted, unquestioned (i.e. unrationalized), throughout time, such as a social norm, or truth established by consensus or based on common sense.

It is when this nonchallengeable proposition, marked as a social norm/consensual truth with *mono*, is directed toward a second person referent that the deontic reading of a directive surfaces. Pragmatic implicatures come into play, and much like in the case of the topic-comment construction, it is up to the recipient of the utterance (i.e. the hearer) to determine how the relationship between the proposition nominalized by *mono* and the topicalized NP applies to their particular case. In a situation where example (20) is directed toward someone who is drinking *toso*, say, on Christmas, this utterance would be interpreted as a directive stating 'You're (not) supposed to (be) drink(ing) *toso* (now, but) on New Year's Day!' Hence, it is an 'indirect' command in that the speaker is merely stating what the norm or desirable action should be, and it is up to the hearer to then determine how their behavior/actions (as they relate to the current discourse context) deviates from it[18]. Thus, through the speaker's presentation of the propositional contents as a socially-recognized norm, the hearer, as a member or participant of the society (conceptualized by the topic NP), is obliged to conform to it.

A characteristic feature of the *mon(o)da* directive is its inability to take on a second person pronoun as its topic; it always functions to convey an indirect (and not a direct) command. This restriction has been noted in past studies (e.g. Noda 1995, Fujii 2000), but the reason has not been elaborated on. Again, I suggest that the incompatibility of *mono*'s employment in reference to a discourse deictic person derives from its underlying semantics of signaling a physically-perceived/unrationalized existence (i.e. a collective/generic entity with an internal homogeneity), and that this results in its incongruity with a topic indicative of a uniquely identifiable (e.g. second person) referent. Because a social norm is that which applies collectively to a group or community, and not particularly to a specific individual within it, it would logically follow that a propositional content presented as such in the form of *mon(o)da* can only take a general category or set of individuals as its topicalized element.

---

[18] As also claimed in Yoshida (2008) the speaker's ability to cite this social norm, in turn, serves to mark them as standing in a position of higher authority than the hearer, namely, someone who has the authority to acknowledge or identify what constitutes the norm in the community or society they are representing. Thus, by implication, this individual must necessarily be someone of greater superiority in age or experience than the hearer.

4.4. How Epistemic Stance Arises in the Mon(o)da Construction

According to Bybee and Pagliuca (1985), a common tendency regarded as metaphoric of meaning change is the development of meanings related to deontic obligation into that of epistemic possibility and probability. The epistemic sense is a metaphorical extension of obligation being made to apply to the truth of a proposition; namely, that a particular proposition is 'obliged' to be true (Bybee and Pagliuca 1985: 73).

I propose that from *mono*'s underlying semantics of a 'physically-perceived/unrationalized existence', is inferentially derived the epistemic stance that existence implies truth, and a physically-perceived /unrationalized verity is reinterpreted as one that applies generally and (to be) accepted as natural (i.e., uncritically or without question), resulting in *mono*'s secondary meaning of a 'general/natural truth'. A definition is typically that which provides the most commonly recognized description of an entity's qualities or characteristics, namely the one most generally or naturally associated with it. As for the definitional reading of (20), the proposition 'drinks on New Year's Day', made nonchallengeable through its nominalization, is being presented as a generally-known truth regarding the *wa*-marked topic, 'spiced *sake*', and moreover, as one without need of further explication (i.e., unrationalized). This results in the "definitional" interpretation, as given in (20a) above, although somewhat colored with the speaker's subjective affect that this truth is to be accepted 'as is'.

4.5. How the Evaluative Stance Arises in Mon(o)da Constructions

I have proposed that by token of its underlying semantics (i.e. physically-sensed/unrationalized) *mono* potentially references an existence that is unidentified, undifferentiated or un-individuated; namely, a generic, general, or collective entity possessing an internal homogeneity.[19] By token of this meaning, such an entity would necessarily be one lacking in agency; such individual agents would be subsumed and obfuscated within the collective whole. From this, I hypothesize that one of the major functions of presenting a propositional content as a certain type of *mono*, when employed to

---

[19] This meaning is likewise suggested to take effect in appositive constructions involving *mono* (i.e. X *to iu mono*/'the thing called X'), where *mono* functions as a content label noun preceded by the hearsay expression *to iu* (QT + 'say') as in the following example:
   Gakkoo to iu mono wa zyugyoo igai no ba de no zyoohoo kookan, soogoo kooryuu ni mo ookina zyuuyoosei o motte-iru.   (Souce:http://blog.so-net.ne.jp/white-ageha/)
   'Schools, in general, possess a great importance as places for the exchange of information and mutual friendships outside of class.'
Here, by virtue of its re-labeling as a *mono*, *gakkoo*/'school' is being presented as a general, generic, or collective entity with an internal homogeneity; namely, as an 'institution'.

mark the speaker's evaluative stance, is to present it as one which lacks individual (human) agency.

By extension of this meaning, a proposition so marked is also considered one that is 'uncontrollable'. It is this secondary meaning of uncontrollability, coupled with that of temporal persistence (inferred from *mono*'s semantics of spatial persistence by metaphorical extension), which gives rise to the evaluative stance *mono* takes on in examples (6) and (7), where it serves as the head noun of a proposition predicated by a verb in the desiderative (i.e. -*tai* form), or in the past tense indicating a past event or action. The function of *mono* in such instances is to give the effect of emotional and temporal 'depth' to the proposition so marked, resulting in the deepseated desire and nostalgic recollections readings, respectively. An unrationalized sensation is also one that escapes one's mental grasp or comprehension; this is rendered as the evaluative stance of amazement, as in Example (8).

5. *Mono* in clausal-connective constructions

Mono can occur before the conditional and causal connectives *nara* 'if' and *kara* 'because', resulting in the clausal connectives, *mono nara* and *mono da kara*, respectively. Etymologically speaking, *nara* represents an inflected form of the copula *nari*. Moreover, the copula *da* must mediate between *mono* and *kara* in the clausal connective *mono da kara*; thus, these two clausal connectives share the same structural patterning as the *mon(o)da* construction discussed in prior sections, where *mono* functions as the head noun of a proposition made nonchallengeable by nominalization. Likewise in these clausal connective constructions, *mono* serves to mark an otherwise objective propositional content with the speaker's attitudinal stance, as seen in examples (10) and (11). It should be noted that the omission of *mono* in these two examples still results in a grammatical sentence. The addition of *mono* to the conditional clause in (10), however, reveals speaker's additional attitude toward the proposition that they regard the prospects of their being able to go to Paris as unlikely or even impossible, whereas, when *mono (da)* is inserted before causal connective *kara*, the speaker is indicating his lack of control over the situation referred to by the causal clause, thereby appealing to the hearer that their inability to remember was an inevitable result stemming from a situation which they lacked agency over. It is claimed that such evaluative attitudinal stances as 'impossibility' and 'uncontrollability' as evoked by the addition of *mono* in these clausal connectives represent inferable secondary meanings derived from the proposed primary semantics of 'physically perceived/unrationalized existence' which arise as a result of reanalysis, when *mono* takes on a nonreferential reading.

6. Utterance-final *mono*

In the contexts of informal spoken discourse, ***mon(o)*** can occur in utterance-final position with the interactional functions of a pragmatic particle. By the addition of this ***mon(o)***, the speaker expresses the highly subjective attitude that the proposition so marked – typically a reasoning or excuse – should be accepted 'as is', and without further challenge; hence, it has been termed as indicative of 'self-justification' (Fujii 2000). It is significant to note that in this particular usage, ***mon(o)*** is functioning as an independent pragmatic particle that has lost its grammatical status as a nominal. This is evidenced by examples such as (12), where the nominal adjective *kirai/*'hate' takes the finite form *kirai da* instead of its pre-nominal modifier form *kirai na*. This suggests that utterance-final ***mon(o)*** represents a purely grammaticized form, which has undergone both subjectification and pragmatic strengthening, characteristic by-products of the grammaticalization process (Hopper and Traugott 1993). However, despite this formal reanalysis, I claim that the pragmatic effects and attitudinal stance evoked by utterance-final ***mon(o)*** represents an inferable extension of ***mono***'s semantics as a bare noun; namely, a physical entity/truth that 'somehow exists' is inferred as a line of reasoning that 'somehow exists', namely a subjectively based, 'self-justification' reflective of the speaker's lack of control or responsibility over it.

7. Conclusion

In human beings, emotions such as desire and nostalgia tend to make their appearances absent of any solid, 'rational' basis. They exist as natural but somehow inexplicable human traits that can be more easily accepted and apprehended without logical analysis. The deeper the emotion, in fact, the more impervious it is to mental explications.

It has been the aim of this study to demonstrate that a continuity exists in the semantics born by ***mono*** in its uses of marking speaker (deontic, epistemic, and evaluative) modality and that these represent inferable extensions of ***mono***'s primary meaning, as proposed, that arise as a result of reanalysis by metaphorical and metonymical means when this lexical item occurs in certain grammaticalized constructions in Japanese discourse.

References

Agetsuma, Y. 1991. Zissitu meisi "***mono***" to keisikiteki yoohoo to no imiteki tunagari. ('The semantic connection between the substantial and formal uses of *mono*') *Toohoku Daigaku Bungakubu Nihongogakka Ronsyuu* 1: 2-11.

Bybee, J. and W. Pagliuca. 1985. Cross-linguistic comparison and the development of grammatical meaning. *Historical Semantics, Historical Word Formation*, ed. J. Fisiak, 59-83. The Hague: Mouton.

Fujii, S. 2000. Incipient Decategorizaion of *MONO* in Japanese Discourse. *Pragmatic Markers and Propositional Attitude*, eds. G. Andersen and T. Freitheim, 83-118. Amsterdam/Philadelphia: John Benjamins Publishing Company.

Givon, T. 1982. Evidentiality and Epistemic Space. *Studies in Language* 6: 23-49.

Hopper, P. and E. C. Traugott. 1993. *Grammaticalization.* Cambridge: Cambridge University Press.

Lyons, J. 1977. *Semantics: Volume 2*, Cambridge: Cambridge University Press.

Makino, S. and M. Tsutsui. 1986. *A Dictionary Of Basic Japanese Grammar.* Tokyo: The Japan Times.

Martin, S. 1975. *A Reference Grammar of Japanese.* London: Yale University Press.

McGloin, N. H. 1989. *A Student's Guide to Japanese Grammar.* Tokyo: Taisyuukan Publishing Company.

Nagara S., N. Hirota and Y. Nakanishi. 1987. *Japanese for Foreigners: Innovative Workbook in Japanese: Volume 2.* Tokyo: Aratake.

Narahara, T. 2002. *The Japanese Copula: Forms and Functions.* New York: Palgrave Macmillan.

Noda, H. 1995. *Mono*da to *koto*da to noda: meisisei no zyodoosi no tooiteki na yoohoo. *Nihongo ruigi hyoogen no bunpoo,* eds. T. Miyajima and Y. Nitta, 253-262. Tokyo: Kurosio Syuppan.

Okutsu, K. 1978. *"Boku wa unagi da" no bunpoo.* ('The grammar of "*Boku wa unagi da*" [type sentences]') Tokyo: Kurosio Syuppan.

Teramura, H. 1981. *Mono* to *koto.* ('*Mono* and *koto*') *Kokugogaku ronsyuu.* 743-762.

Teramura, H. 1984. *Nihongo no sintakusu to imi* ('Japanese syntax and meaning'), Volume 2. Tokyo: Kurosio Syuppan.

Tsubone, Y. 1994. '*Mono*da' ni kansuru iti koosatu. ('A study of *monoda*') *Nihongo Kyooiku* 84: 65-77.

Yoshida, N. 2008. Nominalized Predicates as Directives in Japanese Discourse. *Japanese Korean Linguistics 13.* Stanford: CSLI Publications.

Part V

Syntax

Right Node Raising as PF Coordination Reduction

DUK-HO AN
University of Connecticut/University of Toronto

1. Introduction

In recent literature on Right Node Raising (RNR), two approaches have been particularly influential: *multi-dominance* (MD) and *deletion* (see Wilder 1999, 2001, Abels 2003, Chung 2004, Park 2005, de Vos and Vincente 2005 for the former; see Wexler and Culicover 1980, Booij 1985, van Oirsouw 1987, Swingle 1993, Wilder 1994, 1997, Hartmann 2000, Mukai 2003, Bošković 1996, 2004, te Velde 2005, Ha 2006, An 2007 for the latter). Under these approaches, an RNR sentence like (1) can be derived as in (2) and (3), respectively.

(1)   Mary suspected and John believed *that Tom was a secret agent*

* I thank Jonathan Bobaljik, Željko Bošković, Toshiko Oda, Mamoru Saito, Susi Wurmbrand, and the audience at the 16th Japanese/Korean Linguistics Conference for helpful comments. All errors are my own.

(2)   Multi-Dominance

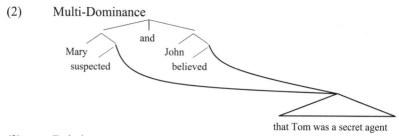

that Tom was a secret agent

(3)   Deletion
[Mary suspected ~~that Tom was a secret agent~~] and
[John believed that Tom was a secret agent]

The difference between the two approaches is clear: under the MD analysis, the RNRed element (henceforth, *the target*) is literally shared via multi-dominance—i.e., the target has more than one mother node that dominates it, while under the deletion analysis, all the conjunct clauses separately involve a full clause, which is subsequently reduced by deletion. Hence, the crucial difference between these approaches is that under the former, there is a single occurrence of the target, while there are multiple occurrences of the target under the latter.

In this paper, I will examine the two approaches based on a set of novel data from Korean and Japanese and argue that the data examined here provide support for the deletion analysis.[1] In so doing, I will also show that the MD system faces the problem of over- and undergeneration. I will also provide evidence that what is involved in deriving RNR is a PF operation.

2. Multiple Traces

The data in (4) and (5) illustrate scrambling in RNR sentences in Korean and Japanese. The point to note is that prior to the application of RNR, the embedded object, indicated by bold letters, is extracted from the embedded clause in each conjunct in a parallel way. After that, the embedded clause, which contains the trace of the scrambled object, is RNRed along with the matrix verb.

(4)   **ppang$_i$-ul** Tomo-ka, kuliko **bap$_j$-ul** Nina-ka,   (K)
        bread-acc T-nom   and   rice-acc   N-nom
        Ana-ka   t   mekess-tako   malhayssta
        A-nom   ate-comp   said
        'Bread, Tomo (said that Ana ate) and rice, Nina said that Ana ate.'

---

[1] Discussing all the relevant properties of the deletion analysis of RNR goes well beyond the scope of this paper. I refer the reader to An 2007 for relevant discussion.

(5) **pan_i-o** Tomo-ga, sosite **gohan_j-o** Nina-ga, (J)
     bread-acc T-nom and rice-acc N-nom
     Ana-ga *t* *tabeta-to* *itta*
     A-nom ate-comp said
     'Bread, Tomo (said that Ana ate) and rice, Nina said that Ana ate.'

If we assume that there is only one occurrence of the target in the structure, as should be the case under the MD analysis, it would be unclear how the distinct objects could be extracted from the unique source, indicated by the trace in (4) and (5). In other words, the problem is that there do not seem to be enough base-positions for the extracted objects under the MD analysis.

Implicit in the discussion above is the assumption that multi-dominance applies to a constituent: here, the relevant constituent may be the category that contains the embedded CP and the matrix verb—something like matrix VP. However, given that RNR may affect non-constituents, as in (6) and (7), we seem to need to allow multiple applications of multi-dominance, where the elements contained in the target are separately multi-dominated.

(6) Aki-nun Ana-ka ppang-ul, kuliko Nina-nun Ana-ka pap-ul, (K)
     A-top A-nom bread-acc and N-top A-nom rice-acc
     mekess-tako kun sori-lo malhayssta
     ate-comp big.voice-with said
     'Aki (said with loud voice that) Ana (ate) bread and Nina said with loud voice that Ana ate rice.'

(7) Aki-wa Ana-ga pan-o, sosite Nina-wa Ana-ga gohan-o (J)
     A-top A-nom bread-acc and N-top A-nom rice-acc
     tabeta-to oo goe-de itta
     ate-comp big.voice-with said
     'Aki (said with loud voice that) Ana (ate) bread and Nina said with loud voice that Ana ate rice.'

Once we allow the option of multiple multi-dominance, the number of possible multi-dominance configurations for an RNR target increases rapidly. For instance, in (4) and (5), we may multi-dominate the embedded CP separately from the matrix verb, which is itself multi-dominated, as shown in (8).[2]

---

[2] Note that for analyses like (8) and (9) to be tenable, it has to be the case that there is no overt V-raising to subsequent functional categories. See however Koizumi 2000 for arguments that verbs overtly raise to higher functional domain in Japanese.

(8)

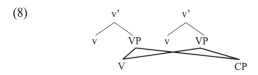

Alternatively, we may apply multi-dominance to all the words in the target individually. In this case, it actually becomes possible to provide separate base-positions for the extracted objects in (4) and (5). (9) illustrates the relevant portion of the structure of (4) and (5) under this view. (I use English words for convenience.)

(9)

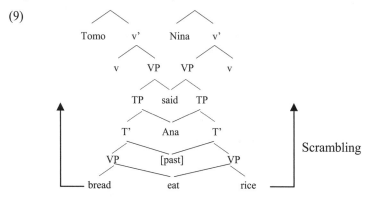

Although (9) provides a technical solution to the problem raised above, it also brings in a different problem—that is, the problem of overgeneration. For instance, it is difficult to see why sentences like (10), whose derivation is illustrated in (11), are disallowed. It is important to note that the relevant portion of the structure in (11)—in particular, the fact that the verb is multi-dominated and that it takes two objects—is identical to that in (9).

(10)   * sakwa-rul   Ana-nun   ppang-ul   mekessta   (K)
          apple-acc   A-top   bread-acc ate
          'Apple, Ana ate bread.'

(11)

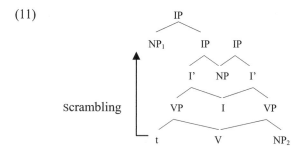

In contrast, sentences like (4) and (5) are readily accounted for under the deletion analysis, if we assume that the relevant deletion operation applies to identical strings in PF—crucially, after scrambling of the embedded objects. Under the usual assumption that traces are eliminated in PF, the two conjuncts will become identical in that component. Hence, deletion will be able to reduce the first conjunct without any problems, as shown in (12).

(12)   ppang$_i$-ul Tomo-ka ~~Ana-ka~~ ~~t$_i$~~ ~~mekesstako~~ ~~malhayssta~~ kuliko
        bread-acc T-nom A-nom ate-comp said and
        bap$_j$-ul Nina-ka *Ana-ka t$_j$ mekess-tako malhayssta*
        rice-acc N-nom A-nom ate-comp said

In this section, I have discussed a problem for the MD analysis that arises due to a discrepancy between the number of elements extracted from inside the target and that of the target itself. I have shown that while a technical solution may be available if we allow multiple multi-dominance, this comes at the cost of overgeneration. The phenomenon examined here provides an argument in favor of the deletion analysis of RNR.

3. Multiple Binders

In this section, I will examine a different type of discrepancy between target-external and target-internal elements. More specifically, I will show that a pronominal contained in an RNR target can be bound by distinct elements outside of the target, allowing a sloppy-identity-like interpretation. This poses a serious problem for the MD analysis since the pronoun stays in situ. Therefore, even the multiple multi-dominance strategy will not help.[3]

(13)   Jeff$_i$-nun Nina-ekey, kuliko Tomo$_j$-nun Lydia-ekey,   (K)
        J-top N-dat and T-top L-dat
        ku$_{i/j}$-uy/caki$_{i/j}$-uy cha-rul pillye cwuessta
        he-gen/self-gen car-acc lent
        'Jeff (lent his car) to Nina and Tomo lent his car to Lydia.'

(14)   Jeff$_i$-wa Nina-ni, sosite Tomo$_j$-wa Lydia-ni,   (J)
        J-top N-dat and T-top L-dat
        kare$_{i/j}$-no/zibun$_{i/j}$-no kuruma-o kasita
        he-gen/self-gen car-acc lent
        'Jeff (lent his car) to Nina and Tomo lent his car to Lydia.'

Here, the pronominal contained in the target can be bound by the different subjects simultaneously, i.e., the sentence allows a sloppy-identity-like interpretation. It is unclear how this can be captured under the MD analysis,

---

[3] In (13) and (14), speakers have different preferences between a pronominal form (*ku, kare*) and a reflexive form (*caki, zibun*). But this does not affect the argument.

since regardless of the mode of multi-dominance employed here, there can be only one occurrence of the pronominal in the structure, although it has to be bound by two distinct antecedents simultaneously.

On the other hand, the deletion analysis provides a rather simple account, as shown in (15).

(15) Jeff-nun   Nina-ekey   ~~ku-uy   cha-rul   pillie ewuessta~~   kuliko
      J-top   N-dat   he-gen   car-acc   lent   and
      Tomo-nun   Lydia-ekey *ku-uy*   *cha-rul*   *pillie cwuessta*
      T-top   L-dat   he-gen   car-acc   lent

4. Multiple Control

In this section, I will examine a case where a PRO subject contained in an RNR target is controlled by the matrix subject of each conjunct at the same time, yielding a sloppy-identity-like interpretation. As discussed in Section 3, the availability of such an interpretation poses a serious problem for the MD analysis. Consider (16) and (17).

(16) Nina$_i$-nun   Jean-ekey,   kuliko   Tomo$_j$-nun   Lydia-ekey,   (K)
      N-top   J-dat   and   T-top   L-dat
      PRO$_{i/j}$ ilchik   tolaokeyss-tako   yaksokhayssta
      early   return-comp   promised
      'Nina (promised) Jean (to come back early) and Tomo promised Lydia to come back early.'

(17) Nina$_i$-wa   Jean-ni,   sosite   Tomo$_j$-wa   Lydia-ni,   (J)
      N-top   J-dat   and   T-top   L-dat
      PRO$_{i/j}$ hayaku   kaeru-to   yakusokusi-ta
      early   return-comp   promised
      'Nina (promised) Jean (to come back early) and Tomo promised Lydia to come back early.'

Here, the target contains a PRO subject, which is controlled by the matrix subject of each conjunct simultaneously, yielding a sloppy-identity-like interpretation. As in Section 3, this is problematic for the MD analysis, since there should be only one occurrence of the PRO in the structure. It is not clear at all how this PRO can be controlled by two distinct elements at the same time.[4]

---

[4] Given the surface form of the sentences, one might suspect that the PRO in (16) and (17) may be outside of the target. That is, what is shared may be smaller than the embedded TP—perhaps, something like vP. If this is correct, then the structure of (16) and (17) would be as in (i).

(i) [$_{TP}$ Subj$_i$ [$_{vP}$ Dat [$_{TP}$ PRO$_i$ [$_{vP}$ ~~Adv Verb~~] ~~Verb~~]] and
     [$_{TP}$ Subj$_j$ [$_{vP}$ Dat [$_{TP}$ PRO$_j$ [$_{vP}$ Adv Verb]] Verb]]

Again, the deletion analysis provides a straightforward account. (18) illustrates the relevant step of the derivation of (16).

(18) Nina$_i$-nun Jean-ekey ~~PRO$_i$ ilchik tolaokeyss-tako yaksokhayssta~~
      N-top   J-dat   early return-comp   promised
      kuliko Tomo$_j$-nun Lydia-ekey *PRO$_j$ ilchik tolaokeyss-tako*
      and   T-top   L-dat   early   return-comp
      yaksokhayssta
      promised

Note incidentally that if we assume that control involves movement (Hornstein 1999, 2001), the data examined here can be considered to pose the same type of problem as that in Section 2. Either way, the data examined in this section are problematic for the MD analysis.

5. Honorification

The discussion so far has relied on the difference between the two approaches in question with respect to the relation between the target and the rest of the conjuncts. In this section, I will examine another aspect of the structural relation between the target and the rest of the conjuncts under the two approaches and show that they make different predictions. Note that under the MD analysis, all the conjuncts lie in the same structural relation with the target, since they literally share the target. Under the deletion analysis, what appears to be shared is in fact part of the second conjunct only. Hence, under the former analysis, the relation is symmetric, while under the latter, it is asymmetric.

In this case, the fact that PRO is controlled by distinct subjects may not be a problem, because we now have two distinct PROs.

However, such a complication can be avoided by burying deeper the nonfinite embedded clause into the target, as in (ii) and (iii). In this case, there is no possibility of putting the PRO subject outside of the target. Hence the argument still holds.

(ii)   Nina-nun cenhwa-ro,   kuliko Tomo-nun imeyil-ro,   (K)
        N-top   telephone-by and   T-top   email-by
        [*(PRO) rwummeyit-ekey [PRO ilchik tolaokeyss-tako] yaksokhayssta*]
        roommate-dat   early   return-comp   promised
        'Nina (promised (her) roommate to come back early) by phone and Tomo promised (his) roommate to come back early by email.'

(iii)   Nina-wa denwa-de,   sosite Tomo-wa email-de,   (J)
        N-top   telephone-by   and   T-top   email-by
        [*(PRO) roommate-ni   [PRO hayaku kaeru-to] yakusokusi-ta*]
        roommate-dat   early   return-comp promised
        'Nina (promised (her) roommate to come back early) by phone and Tomo promised (his) roommate to come back early by email.'

Assuming this, I will examine below subject honorification (SH) in Korean and Japanese, which involves an optional marking of politeness on the predicate when the subject of the sentence is socially superior or respectable to the participants in conversation, as shown in (19). I will show that conjuncts in RNR sentences show an asymmetric behavior with respect to the licensing of SH in the target, consistent with the predictions made by the deletion analysis.[5]

(19)   kyoswunim-un   chayk-ul   sa-(**si**)-ess-ta   (K)
        professor-top   book-acc   buy-hon-past-dec
        'The professor bought a book.'

It should be noted that the nature of honorification has been controversial (Harada 1976, Ura 1996, Namai 2000, Niinuma 2003, Choe 2004, Bobaljik and Yatsushiro 2006). However, it is sufficient for our purposes that this phenomenon is constrained by certain syntactic factors—that is, it is only the local subject that can license honorific marking, as (20) and (21) show.

(20)   [[kyoswunim-uy]   kay-ka]   cicu-(*si)-ess-ta   (K)
        professor-gen   dog-nom   bark-hon-past-dec
        'The professor's dog barked.'

(21)   kyoswunim-un [Ana-ka   chayk-ul   sa-(*si)-ess-tako]   (K)
        professor-top   A-nom   book-acc   buy-hon-past-comp
        malhayssta
        said
        'The professor said that Ana bought a book.'

Assuming this, let us consider the behavior of SH in RNR. In (22)-(25), the predicate contained in the target carries honorific marking. The crucial point is that only one of the subjects—namely, the subject of the second conjunct—is able to license SH here.[6]

(22)   Tomo-nun pap-ul, kuliko **kyoswunim**-un ppang-ul,   (K)
        T-top   rice-acc and   professor-top   bread-acc
        *Nina-ekey cwu-**si**-ess-ta*
        N-dat   give-hon-past-dec
        'Tomo (gave) rice (to Nina) and the professor gave bread to Nina.'

---

[5] SH in Japanese works basically the same. But, for reasons of space, I will not provide Japanese counterparts to (19)-(21).

[6] Van Oirsouw (1987: 234-235) notes a similar case of asymmetric agreement in RNR constructions. For instance, in Hopi and Palestinian Arabic, it is the linearly closest NP to the verb that controls agreement.

(23) * **kyoswunim**-un ppang-ul, kuliko Tomo-nun pap-ul, (K)
professor-top bread-acc and T-top rice-acc
Nina-ekey cwu-si-ess-ta
N-dat give-hon-past-dec

(24) Tomo-wa Jeff-ni, sosite **sensei**-wa Nina-ni, (J)
T-top J-dat and teacher-top N-dat
hon-o o-okurini natta
book-acc hon-send past
'Tomo (sent a book) to Jeff and teacher sent a book to Nina.'

(25) * **sensei**-wa Nina-ni, sosite Tomo-wa Jeff-ni, (J)
teacher-top N-dat and T-top J-dat
hon-o o-okurini natta
book-acc hon-send past

I take this to indicate that conjuncts of an RNR sentence do not have the same structural relation to the target. In fact, only the second conjunct seems to establish a direct relation with the target, which is predicted by the deletion analysis, as shown in (26).[7]

(26) Tomo-nun pap-ul ~~Nina-ekey cwu-ess-ta~~ kuliko
T-top rice-acc N-dat give-past-dec and
kyoswunim-un ppang-ul *Nina-ekey cwu-si-ess-ta*
professor-top bread-acc N-dat give-hon-past-dec

It is not clear at all how the asymmetric behavior of the conjuncts in (22)-(25) can be captured under the MD analysis, since all the conjuncts should lie in the same structural relation with the target. Therefore, the ungrammaticality of (23) and (25) requires additional assumptions under the MD analysis.

6. Linearization

Note that under the MD analysis, a multi-dominated element belongs to all the conjuncts at the same time. This actually causes a contradiction of linear order, since all the elements in the first conjunct, for instance, must precede all the elements in the second conjunct. Consequently, the multi-dominated element must precede itself. Given this, proponents of the MD analysis

---

[7] In (26), the predicates are not completely identical with respect to their morphological form. It is however well-known that certain morphological mismatches do not interfere with deletion (Lasnik 1995, Bošković 1996, 2004).
  (i) a. John will, and Peter was, *sleeping in her office*
    b. John will, and Peter has, *slept in her house* (Bošković 1996: 7)

propose a revision of Kayne's (1994) LCA. The gist of the modifications to the LCA system, adapted from Wilder 1999, 2001, is given below.

(27)   a.   X *c-commands* Y if Y either is or is contained in X's sister.

       b.   A *dominance path* of α is a sequence of categories $<C_1,$ ... , $C_n>$ such that C_1 = the root, $C_n = \alpha$, and for all j $(1 \leq j \leq n)$ C_j immediately dominates C_{j+1}.

       c. α *fully dominates* β iff α is a member of every dominance path of β.

       d. α is a *shared* constituent of X iff X dominates, but not fully dominates α.

       e.   The *image* of a category X, d(X), is the (unordered) set of terminals fully dominated by X.

(28)   (Wilder 2001: 21)

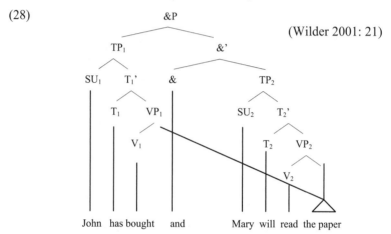

Under the set of assumptions in (27), the multi-dominance structure in (28) can be linearized as in (29).

(29)   a.   Within TP$_1$: John > has > bought > the paper

       b.   Within &': and > Mary > will > read > the paper

       c.   TP$_1$ asymmetrically c-commands elements in &'. Hence, {John, has, bought} > {and, Mary, will, read, the, paper}.

The sum of (29a)-(29c) gives the correct order of the elements in (28): John > has > bought > and > Mary > will > read > the > paper.

    The problem that went unnoticed is a situation where a proper subpart of a left-branch element is multi-dominated along with the right-branch, as in (30). The relevant portion of the structure is given in (31).

(30)   (?) I think Máry's, but he thinks Súsan's, *father is sick*

(31)

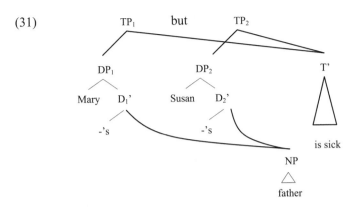

In (31), the shared NP does not c-command out of the DPs—crucially, it does not c-command T'. Being multi-dominated, the NP is not contained in the image of DP₁ and DP₂ either. Hence, we do not have any way to determine the linear order of the elements in NP with respect to the elements contained in T'. Therefore, the structure is unlinearizable.[8]

The deletion analysis accounts for (30) without any additional assumptions, as shown in (32).

(32)   I think Máry's ~~father is sick~~ but he thinks Súsan's *father is sick*

7. Sensitivity to Prosodic Constituency

So far, I have focused on comparing the MD and the deletion analyses and argued that the deletion analysis fares better than the MD analysis. Shifting the focus a little bit, I will argue in this section that RNR is sensitive to the prosodic constituent structure of the sentence, which I argue provides support for the current proposal that RNR involves PF deletion. Let us consider the sentence in (33).[9]

(33)   Mary-nun   wusumyense   cilmwunha-nun   haksayng-ul   (K)
        M-top   with.a.smile ask.a.question-rel   student-acc
        ttari-ess-ta
        hit-past-dec

(33) is ambiguous between (34)a and (34)b, which I call *high* and *low* reading, respectively. Crucially, these interpretations correlate with the position

---

[8] Under the formulation given in (27), elements in T' are actually allowed to precede the NP in question. Under this derivation, the structure may be linearizable, but is still ungrammatical.
[9] For reasons of space, I only provide Korean data here. But, for all the data given below, the same pattern holds in Japanese. For further discussion, I refer the reader to An 2007.

of a pause, as shown in (35). In other words, (33) is disambiguated by the position of a pause.

(34)   a.   With a smile on her face, Mary hit the student who asked a question.   (High reading)
       b.   Mary hit the student who asked a question with a smile on his face.   (Low reading)

(35)   a.   Mary smile # question student hit   (High reading)
       b.   Mary # smile question student hit   (Low reading)

It is worth pointing out that the different prosodic structure of (33) under different interpretations—in particular, the different positions of the pauses in (35)—may be reflecting the difference in syntactic constituent structure. For instance, under the low reading, the *smile*-phrase is presumably adjoined to the object NP and forms a constituent with it, which is consistent with the fact that a pause has to be placed outside of the whole object NP.

Assuming this, consider an RNR version of (33), given in (36).

(36)   Mary-nun   wusumyense,   # kuliko Jane-un   insangss-myense, #
       M-top   with.a.smile   and   J-top   with.a.frown
       cilmwunha-nun   haksayng-ul ttari-ess-ta
       ask.a.question-rel student-acc hit-past-dec
       'With a smile, Mary (hit the student who asked a question) and with a frown, Jane hit the student who asked a question.'

As is well-known, RNR forces a pause to be placed before the target in each conjunct. In the case at hand, the RNR-induced pause appears following the *smile-* and *frown*-phrases. As a result, these conjuncts have the same surface prosodic structure as (35)a. Interestingly, (36) is no longer ambiguous: it only has the high reading. Given this, one may attempt to put a pause before the *smile-* and *frown*-phrases to get a low reading, as in (37). However, as indicated, the result is not grammatical.

(37)   ?*Mary-nun # wusumyense, # kuliko Jane-un # insangssmyense, #
       M-top   with.a.smile   and   J-top   with.a.frown
       cilmwunha-nun   haksayng-ul ttari-ess-ta
       ask.a.question-rel student-acc hit-past-dec
       '(Intended reading) Mary hit the student who asked a question with a smile on his face and Jane hit the student who asked a question with a frown on his face.'

I argue that the contrast between (36) and (37) indicates that the deletion operation in RNR is constrained by prosodic constituent structure, rather than syntactic constituent structure, unlike typical syntactic operations. (38) illustrates what is happening in (37) under the low reading.

(38)   a. *Prosodic constituency under the low reading:*
           [Mary] # [smile question student (][) hit]
        b. *Deletion in (37):*
           * [Mary] # [smile ~~question student (][) hit~~]

Note that deletion affects only a subpart of the prosodic constituent in (38)b.[10] Given the fact that elements affected by RNR do not have to form a syntactic constituent (see (6)/(7), (32), (35)/(36) above)[11], the contrast here would remain a mystery if we do not make reference to the prosodic constituent structure of the sentence, which then clearly suggests that the relevant operation that derives RNR sentences is constrained by factors relevant to PF.

8. Conclusion

In this paper, I have examined the MD analysis and the deletion analysis of RNR based on a set of novel data from Korean and Japanese and argued that the latter analysis fares better. I have also argued that the deletion operation in RNR is constrained by prosodic factors, providing support for the proposal that in RNR sentences, we are dealing with a PF operation.

References

Abels, K. 2003. Right Node Raising: Ellipsis or Across the Board Movement?, *Proceedings of the 34th North East Linguistics Society*, eds. K. Moulton & M. Wolf, 45-59. Amherst: GLSA.

An, D. 2007. *Syntax at the PF interface: Prosodic Mapping, Linear Order, and Deletion.* Ph.D. dissertation. UConn, Storrs.

Bobaljik, J. and K. Yatsushiro. 2006. Problems with honorification-as-agreement in Japanese: A reply to Boeckx & Niinuma. *Natural Language and Linguistic Theory* 24:355-384.

Booij, G.E. 1985. Coordination reduction in complex words: a Case for prosodic phonology, *Advances in nonlinear phonology*, eds. H. Hulst & N. Smith, 143-160. Dordrecht: Foris.

Bošković, Ž. 1996. On right node base-generation. Ms., UConn, Storrs.

Bošković, Ž. 2004. Two notes on right node raising, *UConn Working Papers in Linguistics* 12, eds. M.R. Mondonedo & M.E. Ticio, 13-24. Department of Linguistics, UConn, Storrs.

---

[10] In An 2007, I argue that the PF deletion operation in RNR is based on the intonational phrase structure of the sentence, so that deletion can only affect elements that can stand alone as a separate intonational phrase (see also Swingle 1993).

[11] I refer the reader to An 2007 for further discussion and references to this effect.

Choe, J. 2004. Obligatory honorification and the honorific feature, *Studies in Generative Grammar*, 14.:545-559.

Chung, D. 2004. Multiple dominance analysis of Right Node Raising, *Language Research* 40:791-812.

Ha, S. 2006. Multiple dominance CAN'T, but PF-deletion CAN account for Right Node Raising. Paper presented at the 42nd Annual Meeting of the CLS, April.

Harada, S. I. 1976. Honorifics, *Syntax and semantics 5: Japanese generative grammar*, ed. M. Shibatani, 499-561. New York: Academic Press.

Hartmann, K. 2000. *Right Node Raising and Gapping: Interface conditions on prosodic deletion*. Amsterdam: John Benjamins.

Hornstein, N. 1999. Movement and control, *Linguistic Inquiry* 30:69-96.

Hornstein, N. 2001. *Move! A minimalist theory of construal*. Oxford: Blackwell.

Kayne, R. 1994. *The antisymmetry in syntax*. Cambridge, Mass.: MIT Press.

Koizumi, M. 2000. String vacuous overt verb raising, *Journal of East Asian Linguistics*, 9:277-285.

Lasnik, H. 1995. Verbal morphology: Syntactic Structures meets the Minimalist Program, *Evolution and revolution in linguistic theory*, eds. H. Campos & P. Kempchinsky, 251-275. Washington, DC: Georgetown University Press.

Mukai, E. 2003. On verbless conjunction in Japanese, *Proceedings of the 33rd North East Linguistics Society*, eds. M. Kadowaki & S. Kawahara, 205-224. Amherst, Mass.: GLSA.

Namai, K. 2000. Subject honorification in Japanese, *Linguistic Inquiry* 31:170-176.

Niinuma, F. 2003. *The syntax of honorification*. Ph.D. dissertation. UConn, Storrs.

van Oirsouw, R. R. 1987. *The syntax of coordination*. London: Croom Helm.

Park, M. 2005. When things are coordinated or distributed across coordinate conjuncts. Paper presented at the 7th Seoul International Conference on Generative Grammar. Konkuk University, Seoul.

Swingle, K. 1993. The role of prosody in Right Node Raising, *Syntax at Santa Cruz*, 2:84-111.

Ura, H. 1996. *Multiple feature checking: A theory of grammatical function splitting*. Ph.D. dissertation. MIT.

te Velde, J.R. 2005. Unifying prosody and syntax for right- and left-edge coordinate ellipsis, *Lingua* 115:483-502.

de Vos, M. and L. Vincente. 2005. Coordination under Right Node Raising, *Proceedings of the 24th West Coast Conference on Formal Linguistics*, eds. J. Alderete et al., 97-104. Somerville, Mass.: Cascadilla Proceedings Project.

Wexler, K. and P. Culicover. 1980. *Formal principles of language acquisition*. Cambridge, Mass.: MIT Press.

Wilder, C. 1994. Coordination, ATB and Ellipsis, *Groninger Arbeiten zur Germanistischen Linguistik* 37:291-329.

Wilder, C. 1997. Some properties of ellipsis in coordination, *Studies on universal grammar and typological variation*, eds. A. Alexiadou & T. Alan Hall, 59-107. Amsterdam/Philadelphia: John Benjamins.

Wilder, C. 1999. Right node raising and the LCA, *Proceedings of the 18th West Coast Conference on Formal Linguistics*, eds. A. Carnie, S.F. Bird, J.D. Haugen, & P. Norquest, 586-598. Cascadilla Press.

Wilder, C. 2001. Shared constituent and linearization. Ms. ZAS, Berlin.

The Causal *Wh*-phrase *Naze* in Japanese Cleft Constructions*

TOMOKO KAWAMURA
Stony Brook University

1. Introduction

The Japanese causal *wh*-phrase *naze* 'why' shows an interesting divergence from its fellow wh-words in cleft constructions. As illustrated in (1)-(3), in clefts involving single foci, *wh*-elements behave uniformly. In (1a), an argument is clefted and in (2a), a locative phrase is clefted. (1b) and (2b) show clefts with the corresponding wh-elements. In (3a) a casual *because*-phrase is clefted and (3b) shows the corresponding *wh*-cleft with *naze* (3b).

(1) a. [Taro-ga   Kyoto-de happyosuru no]-wa <u>sono ronbun</u> desu.
Taro-nom Kyoto-in present   C-top   that paper   be
'It is THAT PAPER that Taro will present in Kyoto'
b. [Taro-ga   Kyoto-de happyosuru no]-wa **dono ronbun** desu ka?
Taro-nom Kyoto-in present   C-top   which paper   be Q
'Which paper is it that Taro will present in Kyoto?'

---

* I am indebted to Richard K. Larson for the development of this paper. I appreciate suggestions from Marcel den Dikken, Carlos de Cuba, Dan Finer, Heejeong Ko, and Mamoru Saito. I also would like to thank audience at JK 16th (Kyoto University) for helpful comments.

(2) a. [Taro-ga   sono ronbun-o happyosuru no]-wa <u>Kyoto-de</u> desu.
      Taro-nom that paper-acc present   C-top Kyoto-at be
      'It is AT KYOTO that Taro will present that paper.'
  b. [Taro-ga   sono ronbun-o happyosuru no]-wa **doko-de** desu ka?
     Taro-nom that paper-acc present   C-top where-at be   Q
     'Where is it that Taro will present that paper?'

(3) a. [Taro-ga   sono ronbun-o happyosuru no]-wa <u>komento-ga</u>
      Taro-nom that paper-acc present   C-top   comment-nom
      <u>hitsuyouda kara</u>   desu.
      need   because be
      'It is BECAUSE HE NEEDS COMMENTS that Taro presents that paper.'
  b. [Taro-ga   sono ronbun-o happyosuru no]-wa **naze** desu ka?
     Taro-nom that paper-acc present   C-top why be Q
     'Why is it that Taro presents that paper?'"

Consider now the examples in (4) and (5). (4a,b) illustrates that clefts combining a *wh*- and non-*wh*-element in focus position are typically disallowed in Japanese (4a,b).[1] Interestingly, however, such combination clefts are acceptable in case the *wh*-element is *naze* (5b).

(4) a. *[Taro-ga   happyosuru no]-wa **dono ronbun** Kyoto-de desu ka?
      Taro-nom present   C-top   which paper Kyoto-at be   Q
      (Which paper is it AT KYOTO that Taro will present?)
  b. ?*[Taro-ga   happyosuru no]-wa **dokode** sono ronbun   desu ka?
     Taro-nom present   C-top   where   that paper   be   Q
     (Where is it THAT PAPER that Taro will present?)

(5) a. [Taro-ga Kyoto-de happyosuru no]-wa **naze** sono ronbun desu ka?
     Taro-nom Kyoto-in present   C-top why that paper be Q
     'Why is it THAT PAPER that Taro will present in Kyoto?'
  b. [Taro-ga sono ronbun-o happyosuru no]-wa **naze** <u>Kyoto-de</u> desu ka?
     Taro-nom that paper-acc present   C-top why Kyoto-in be   Q
     'Why is it IN KYOTO that Taro will present that paper?'

Why should this be true? In this paper, I examine combination cleft constructions and show that they have the structure of single clefts, despite surface appearances. I propose that *naze* and the other clefted element form a constituent, a possibility not open to other wh-words. I relate the peculiar behavior of *naze* in Japanese clefts to the special focus sensitive property of *why* in English, first noted by Bromberger (1991).

---

[1] Ji-Yung Kim (p.c.) pointed out that (4b) is slightly better than (4a) with an echo-question reading.

2. Properties of Combination Clefts

At first glance, combination clefts with *naze* in (5b) resemble familiar multiple clefts in Japanese. As (6) and (7) show, Japanese does allow clefts with both single and multiple foci:

(6) [Taro-ga   Kyoto-de happyosuru no]-wa [_{FocP} sono ronbun] desu.
    Taro-nom Kyoto-in present   C-top   that paper be
    'It is THAT PAPER that Taro will present in Kyoto.'   *single cleft*

(7) [Taro-ga   happyosuru no]-wa [_{FocP} Kyoto-de][_{FocP} sono ronbun-o] desu.
    Taro-nom present   C-top   Kyoto-in   that paper-acc be
    'It is IN KYOTO where that paper Taro will present.'   *multiple cleft*

However some important differences emerge between combination and multiple clefts. In multiple clefts, the order of the clefted phrases is free. Both (8a) and (8b) are grammatical and express the same meaning.

(8) a. [Taro-ga   happyosuru no]-wa **[Kyoto-de][sono ronbun-o]** desu.
       Taro-nom present   C-top   Kyoto-in   that paper-acc   be
    b. [Taro-ga   happyosuru no]-wa **[sono ronbun-o] [Kyoto-de]** desu.
       Taro-nom present   C-top   that paper-acc Kyoto-in   be
       'It is THAT PAPER, IN KYOTO that Taro will present.'

In combination clefts, however, the order is fixed: *naze* must precede the non-*wh*-element.

(9) a. [Taro-ga   happyosuru no]-wa **naze   sono ronbun** desu ka?
       Taro-nom present   C-top why   that paper   be   Q
       'Why is it THAT PAPER that Taro will present?'
    b.*[Taro-ga   happyosuru no]-wa **sono ronbun   naze** desu ka?
       Taro-nom present   C-top that paper   why   be   Q

Case-marking patterns also diverge in the two constructions. In single clefts, the case marker on the clefted phrase is optional (10), whereas they are obligatory in multiple clefts (11), as observed by Koizumi (1995).

(10) a. [Taro-ga   happyosuru no]-wa <u>sono ronbun-o</u>   desu.
        Taro-nom present   C-top   that paper-acc be

     b. [Taro-ga   happyosuru no]-wa <u>sono ronbun</u>   desu.
        Taro-nom present   C-top that paper   be
        'It is THAT PAPER that Taro will present.'

(11) a. [Taro-ga   happyosuru no]-wa <u>Kyoto-de</u>   <u>sono ronbun-o</u> desu.
        Taro-nom present   C-top   Kyoto-at   that paper-acc be
        'It is AT KYOTO (and) THAT PAPER that Taro will present.'

   b. *[Taro-ga   happyosuru no]-wa <u>Kyoto-de</u> <u>sono ronbun</u>   desu.
      Taro-nom present   C-top Kyoto-at that paper   be

In combination clefts, the case-marker on the clefted phrase is optional, just like a single cleft.

(12) a. [Taro-ga   happyosuru no]-wa <u>naze</u>   <u>sono ronbun-o</u> desu ka?
       Taro-nom present   C-top why   that paper-acc be   Q
    b. [Taro-ga   happyosuru no]-wa <u>naze</u>   <u>sono ronbun</u>   desu ka?
       Taro-nom present   C-top why   that paper   be   Q
      'Why is it THAT PAPER that Taro will present?'

Furthermore, the two constructions diverge in their meanings. Multiple clefts express pure multiple foci (Ono 2002), but, in the combination clefts, *naze* always associates with the other focused element.

(13) [Taro-ga   happyosuru no]-wa <u>sono ronbun-o</u>   <u>Kyoto-de</u> desu.
     Taro-nom   present   C-top that paper-acc   Kyoto-at be
     'Taro will present THAT PAPER, AT KYOTO.'

(14) [Taro-ga   happyosuru no]-wa <u>naze</u> <u>sono ronbun</u> desu ka?
     Taro-nom present   C-top why that paper be Q
     'Why is it THAT PAPER that Taro will present?'

In (13), both *that paper* and *at Kyoto* are equally focused as new information. In contrast, (14) asks the reason of choosing some particular paper and *naze* associates with the other focused element.

    What these results show is that combination clefts with *naze* do not behave like multiple clefts containing two independent foci. Rather they behave like single clefts: i) order of elements is fixed as we would expect if the focus were a single phrase, ii) case-marking follows the single cleft pattern, and iii) it does not the reading of multiple foci. I propose therefore that in combination clefts, *naze* and the other clefted element form a single constituent which I will label FocP: [$_{FocP}$ *naze* XP].

    According to Herburger (2000), focused elements are interpreted in the scope of the event quantifier, and non-focused elements are interpreted in its restriction, as schematized in (15).

(15) [∃e: X(e)   ]   Y(e)
       RESTRICTION SCOPE
       background   focus

Under this general picture, a single cleft like (16a) is logically represented as in (16b) (ignoring tense.)

(16) a. [Taro-ga   happyosuru no]-wa <u>sono ronbun</u>   desu.
Taro-nom present   C-top that paper   be
'It is THAT PAPER that Taro will present.'
b. [∃e: present (e) & Agent (e, Taro)] **Theme (e, that paper)**
For some presenting event by Taro, its theme is that paper.

In the theory of Generalized Quantifiers (Barwise and Cooper 1981, Keenan and Stavi 1983), quantifiers denote relations between sets which can be regarded as arguments of the quantifier. Larson (1991) develops this idea, arguing that quantifiers also have their own argument structure. He proposes that the notions "restrictions" and "scope" be understood as theta-roles, and argues that the restriction theta-role is assigned to the phrase which merges to the quantifier first (its internal argument), and the scope theta-role is assigned to the phrase which is introduced next (its external argument).

(17)

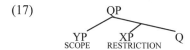

Adopting this structure of quantifiers, I propose that the cleft construction in (16) has the following syntactic structure:

(18)

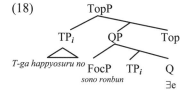

Given that *naze* and the other clefted element form a constituent in combination clefts as in (19a), the sentence has the structure in (19b).

(19) [Taro-ga   happyosuru no]-wa **naze   sono ronbun** desu ka?
Taro-nom present   C-top why   that paper be   Q
'Why is it that paper that Taro will present?'

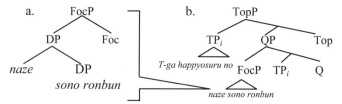

In (19a), *naze* adjoins to the other clefted phrase and the whole constituent appears within a single FocP.

This structure explains why combination clefts behave like single clefts, not like multiple clefts. Recall that combination clefts show fixed order in the clefted phrase. According to Saito and Fukui (1992), right-adjunction is disallowed in all head-final languages, including Japanese. If *naze* adjoins to the other clefted phrase, it must left-adjoin and hence precede the other clefted element. The order of the clefted phrase will not be interchangeable since right-adjunction will be excluded. The second property is optionality of the case marker. In combination clefts, only one FocP is clefted, just like in a single cleft. So, combination clefts should have the same case-marking pattern as single clefts, and whatever explains the optionality of the case marker in single clefts would also explain the optionality of the case-marker in combination clefts. The third and most important property of combination clefts comes from the readings they have. In (19), *naze* does not ask the reason for presenting. Rather, *naze* associates with the focused element and asks for the reason for choosing some particular paper. This reading is parallel to what we find in English focus sensitive *why*-questions. In the following section, I discuss English *why*-questions and show why the causal variable, which corresponds to Japanese *naze*, and other focused element form a constituent for the focus sensitive readings.

3. Focus Sensitive *Why*-questions

3.1. Sensitivity to Focus

Bromberger (1991) observes that focus shift usually does not affect the answer to *wh*-questions (20, 21), but it does in the case of *why*-questions (22).

(20) a. **What** did **ADAM** eat in Eden?   —Apples.
     b. **What** did Adam eat **IN EDEN**?   —Apples.

(21) a. **Where** did **ADAM** eat apples?   —In Eden.
     b. **Where** did Adam eat **APPLES**?   —In Eden.

(22) a. **Why** did **ADAM** eat apples?   —Because he was the one Eve convinced.
     b. **Why** did Adam eat **APPLES**?   —Because it was the only food around.

The sentences in (22) do not ask for the reason for eating: (22a) asks for the reason for Adam being the agent of the eating event and (22b) asks for the reason for choosing apples. So, focus affects the meaning of *why*-questions.

Why-questions are typically answered with a *because*-clause. Davidson (1967) analyzes *(be)cause as* relating two events, as shown below:[2]

(23) John submitted the report [because he failed the exam].

| e_1: submit (John, the report, e_1) |

↑ **cause**

| e_2: fail (John, the exam, e_2) |

[$\exists e_1$: submit (John, the report, e_1)][$\exists e_2$] fail (John, the exam, e_2) & cause (e_2,e_1)

However, there is a traditional puzzle on this event analysis as discussed by Davidson (1967) and Bennett (1988). The asymmetric entailment pattern which is usually observed in sentences with adverbial modifiers disappears with the *because*-clause. The typical entailment relation of the adverbial modification is found in (24). If (24a) is true, then (24b) is always true.

(24) a. John submitted the paper today.
$\exists e$ (submit (John, the paper, e) & At (today, e))
b. John submitted the paper.
$\exists e$ (submit (John, the paper, e))

As seen in their logical representations, this asymmetric entailment relation is explained as a logical consequence of conjunction. The entailment relation is sometimes found in sentences with a *because*-clause. Suppose that only certain people have to submit the paper to get the credit.

(25) a. John submitted the paper today [because he failed the exam].
b. John submitted the paper [because he failed the exam].

When *today* in (25a) is pronounced without stress, (25a) entails (25b). However, when *today* is focused and pronounced with the main stress, then the content of *because*-clause changes and the entailment relation disappears. Suppose that everyone was asked to submit the report by yesterday, but John submitted the report today.

(26) a. John submitted the report **TODAY** [because his computer broke].
b. John submitted the report [because his computer broke].

Unlike in (24) and (25), (26a) does not entail (26b). In (26a), the breaking event of the computer did not cause the submitting event, but it caused the

---

[2] Hooper and Thompson (1973) observe that the *because*-clause expresses the main assertion, as if it is focused, while the main clause expresses the background information. Thus, the *because*-clause should be interpreted in the scope of the event quantifier, and the element in the main clause should be interpreted in the restriction of the event quantifier.

time being today. Thus, three events are involved and the relations among those events are illustrated in (27).

(27) John submitted the report **TODAY** [because his computer broke].

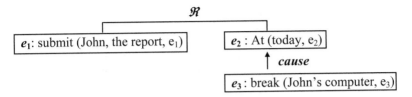

$[\exists e_1$:submit (e_1) & Agent $(e_1,$ John) & Theme $(e_1,$ the report)$]$[$\exists e_2$:$\mathcal{R}(e_2,e_1)]$ **At $(e_2,$ today) & $[\exists e_3]$ break (e_3) & Theme $(e_3,$ John's computer) & <u>cause (e_3,e_2)</u>**

Here, 'being today' is some aspect of the submitting event and these events are correlated with the $\mathcal{R}$-predicate.[3] The *because*-clause provides the cause of e_2, which is 'being today'. Similarly, when the argument is focused, the *because*-clause provides the reason for choosing that particular individual. For example, in (28), the *because*-clause explains the agency of John.

(28) **JOHN** submitted the report [because he was the dean].

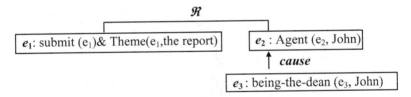

$[\exists e_1$:submit (e_1) & Theme $(e_1,$ the report)$]$[$\exists e_2$:$\mathcal{R}(e_2,e_1)]$ **Agent $(e_2,$ John) & $[\exists e_3]$be-the-dean (e_3) & Theme $(e_3,$ John) & cause (e_3,e_2)**

Here, the *because*-clause explains the agency of John, which is some aspect of the submitting event.

   In the focus sensitive *why*-questions, the content of e_3 is replaced with a predicate variable, which is bound by the *wh*-operator.

---

[3] I am indebted to Richard K. Larson for his suggestion to this solution.

(29) Why did JOHN submit the report?

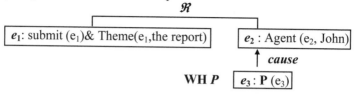

Wh P [$\exists e_1$: submit (e_1) & Theme (e_1, the report)][$\exists e_2$: $\mathscr{R}(e_2, e_1)$]Agent (e_2, John) & [$\exists e_3$]$P(e_3)$ & cause (e_3, e_2)

In this representation, the *wh*-phrase *why* asks for the cause of the agency of John. When the focus position shifts, the description of e_2 changes.

(30) Why did John submit THE REPORT?

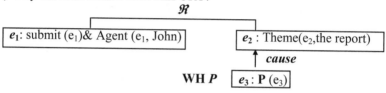

Wh P [$\exists e_1$: submit (e_1) & Agent (e_1, John)] [$\exists e_2$: $\mathscr{R}(e_2, e_1)$] & Theme (e_2, the report) &[$\exists e_3$]$P(e_3)$ & cause (e_3, e_2)

This asks for the property P of the event which made choosing the report as the theme of submitting event. Since focus shift triggers the change of the content of e_2 and focus sensitive *why*-questions ask the cause of e_2, focus shift affects the answer of *why*-questions.

3.2. Syntactic Structure

If the semantic effect is reflected in the syntactic structure, then *because* should correlate two events syntactically. The simple case, *John submitted the report because he failed the exam* is represented as follows:

(31) | e_1: John submitted the report | is because | e_2: he failed the exam |

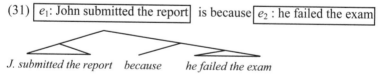

J. submitted the report   because   he failed the exam

Here one constituent expresses the submitting event and another constituent expresses the failing event. These two events are correlated with *because*. When a part of the sentence is focused, *because* semantically connects the event expressed with focus and the event described inside the *because*-clause. For example, in *John submitted the report TODAY [because his computer broke]*, the event of 'being today' is correlated with the event of 'breaking the computer' by *because*. Thus, syntactically, the sentence should have the structure in (32a), with a more detailed version in (32b).

(32) a.

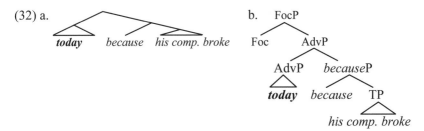

To correlate the causal event and the event expressed with focus, the focus sensitive *because*-phrase should appear inside the FocP, as adjunction to the focused phrase.

In *why*-questions, the content of the *because*-phrase is replaced with the causal variable. The focus sensitive *why*-question *Why did John submit the report TODAY?* is syntactically represented as follows:

(33)

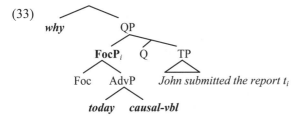

The causal variable adjoins to the adverbial phrase and appears inside FocP together with the focused element.

4. Empirical Consequences

This analysis of focus sensitive *why*-questions predicts several interesting facts cross-linguistically. I first discuss intervention effects and long distance readings of Japanese *naze*-questions, and then discuss Italian *perchè*-questions.

4.1. Intervention Effects and Long Distance Readings

It has been observed that the Japanese Negative Polarity Item (NPI), NP-*shika,* cannot precede a typical *wh*-phrase (Hoji 1985, Ko 2004, and others). In (34a), the NPI *Hanako-shika* follows the *wh*-phrase *nani-o*. In (34b), the NPI *Hanako-shika* precedes *nani-o* and the sentence is out.

(34) a. **Nani-o**   Hanako-shika   yom-anak-atta no?
       what-acc Hanako-only   read-neg-pst   Q
       'What did only Hanako read?'

b. *<u>Hanako-shika</u> **nani-o** yom-anak-atta no?
Hanako-only what-acc read-neg-pst Q

This intervention effect disappears when the *wh*-phrase is *naze* (Miyagawa 1997 and Ko 2004). (35a) and (35b) are both grammatical.

(35) a. **Naze** <u>Hanako-shika</u> sono hon-o yom-anak-atta no?
why Hanako-only that book-acc read-neg-pst Q
b. <u>Hanako-shika</u> **naze** sono hon-o yom-anak-atta no?
Hanako-only why that book-acc read-neg-pst Q
'Why did only Hanako read that book?'

When the object *sono hon-o* is focused and *naze* associates with it as focus sensitive element, *naze* (causal variable) should appear within FocP adjoining to the object DP. Since the causal variable and the argument phrase form a constituent in this reading, we predict that the intervention effect comes back. This prediction is borne out. Under the reading *why that book?*, (36a) is fine, but (36b) is out.

(36) a. [$_{FocP}$ **Naze SONO HON-O**] <u>Hanako-shika</u> yom-anak-atta no?
why that book-acc Hanako-only read-neg-pst Q
'Why that book, did Hanako read?'
b. *<u>Hanako-shika</u> [$_{FocP}$ **naze SONO HON-O**] yom-anak-atta no?
Hanako-only why that book-acc read-neg-pst Q

The ungrammaticality of (36b) supports the analysis that *naze* and the focused element form a constituent.

Another interesting case is found in complex clauses.[4] Long distance scrambling of *naze* is usually disallowed (Saito 1985).

(37) a. Yuri-wa [Taro-ga **naze** sono ronbun-o happyosuru to] omotteiru no?
Yuri-top Taro-nom why that paper-acc present C think Q
'Why does Yuri think [that Taro will present that paper t]?'
b. ***Naze** Yuri-wa [Taro-ga **t** sono ronbun-o happyosuru to]
why Yuri-top Taro-nom that paper-acc present C
omotteiru no?
think Q – no embedded reading

(37b) cannot ask the reason for Taro's presenting the paper. This indicates that the true adjunct *naze* cannot undergo long-distance scrambling. Interestingly however, the sentence improves when the other element of the embedded clause undergoes long-distance scrambling together with *naze*.

---

[4] I appreciate Mamoru Saito for suggesting me to check the correlation of long distance scrambling and the analysis of focus sensitive *naze*-constructions.

(38) **Naze sono ronbun-o** Yuri-wa [Taro-ga t happyosuru to] omotteiru no?
why that paper-acc Yuri-top Taro-nom present C think Q
'Why that paper does Yuri think [that Taro will present t]?'
      – the focus sensitive embedded reading allowed

(38) allows the reading where *naze* asks the reason for choosing that paper as the theme of presenting. *Naze* is considered to be moved from the embedded clause together with *sono ronbun-o*, which is the object of the embedded clause. The grammaticality difference in (37b) and (38) indicates that *naze* must depend on the other element for long-distance scrambling, and it suggests that *naze sono ronbun-o* forms a constituent.

A similar case is observed by Sohn (1994). Scrambling of arguments out of an NP complement is slightly degraded (Saito 1985) as shown in (39a), but scrambling of *naze* out of an NP complement is clearly disallowed (Sohn 1994) as in (39b).

(39) a.?**sono hito-o** John-wa [[Mary-ga t uttaeta to iu] uwasa]-o kiita.
that person-acc John-top Mary-nom sued C say rumor-acc heard
'John heard the rumor that Mary sued that person.'

    b.***Naze** John-wa [[Mary-ga t sono hito-o uttaeta to iu] uwasa]-o
why John-top Mary-nom that person-acc sued C say rumor-acc
kiita no?
heard C
'Why did John hear the rumor [that Mary sued that person t]?'

Sohn observes that when *naze* moves together with an argument in the same clause, the sentence improves, as in (40).

(40) ?(?) **Naze sono hito-o** John-wa [[Mary-ga t uttaeta to iu]
why that person-acc John-top Mary-nom sued C say
uwasa]-o kiita no?
rumor-acc heard Q
'Why that person did John hear [the rumor that Mary sued t]?'

The grammaticality difference between (39b) and (40) again indicates that *naze* in (40) does not move independently. Rather, *naze* forms a constituent with a focused element and the constituent [$_{DP}$ *naze* [$_{DP}$ *sono hito-o*]] undergoes scrambling.[5]

---

[5] Sohn (1994) observes that the sentence is just marginal even when *sono hon-o* precedes *naze*. How this word order is derived is unclear with the current analysis.

4.2. *Wh*-interrogatives in Italian

Italian data also supports the proposed analysis of focus sensitive questions. Calabrese (1984) observes that Italian disallows multiple foci in general.

(41) *__MARIO__ ha scritto una __LETTERA__.
     Mario has written a letter
     'Maria has written a letter.'   (Calabrese 1984)

This suggests that only one FocP is allowed in Italian sentences. Since a *wh*-phrase usually has its own FocP, *wh*-phrases cannot generally co-occur with an independent focused element.

(42) *__Achi__   __QUESTO__ hanno detto?
     to whom this   have said
     'To whom did they say THIS (not something else)?'   (Rizzi 1999)

In the focus sensitive reading, however, the causal-element appears inside the FocP together with the other focused element. Thus, we predict following: 1) The causal *wh*-element (*perchè*) should be able to exceptionally co-occur with a focused element, and 2) The derived sentence should only have the focus sensitive reading. These predictions are borne out. In (42), *perchè* co-occurs with a focused element *questo* and the sentence only allows the focus sensitive reading, asking the reason for choosing "this".

(43) __Perchè QUESTO__ avremmo dovuto dirgli?
     why this   should had   say.him
     'Why should we have said THIS to him?'   (Rizzi 1999)

This shows that the causal *wh*-phrase *perchè* and the focused element share one FocP in the focus sensitive reading.

5. Summary and Further Discussion

In this paper, I have shown that Japanese combination clefts have the property of single clefts and that they are instances of focus sensitive *why*-questions. In focus sensitive *why*-questions, the causal variable forms a constituent with the focused element. This constituency has explained a number of otherwise mysterious cross-linguistic phenomena.

One interesting question remains; Why are causal *wh*-expressions cross-linguistically so special with the focus sensitive property? I do not have a clear answer for this question, but there are other peculiar phenomena which seem to relate to the focus sensitive property of *why*-questions. For example, the bare-binary combination constructions are allowed only with the causal *wh*-phrases (44a, b), and not with the other type of *wh*-

phrase (44c-e). When the bare binary combination construction is allowed, it only has the focus sensitive reading.

(44) a. Why TODAY?   c. *Who TODAY?
     b. How come TODAY?   d. *What TODAY?
                           e. *Where TODAY?

It has been reported by Labov and Labov (1978) and discussed by Kay (1980) that in the process of first language acquisition, all *wh*-words except the causal ones first appear with the bare-binary combination constructions in (44c-e). The causal *wh*-expressions, on the other hand, first appear with a full sentence or a multiple word utterance, and later the bare-binary forms in (44a-b) are developed. Labov and Labov (1978) suggest that the difference between the causal *wh*-expressions and other type of *wh*-expressions comes from the degree of integration with the predicate; Arguments, along with temporal and locative adverbs, require a close relation with the predicate syntactically, while causal phrases do not. This is one possible approach to distinguish the causal expressions from other *wh*-questions, but it does not exclude the other possible analyses. The origin of the peculiarity of causal *wh*-expressions is still an open question and it is left for further research.

References

Barwise, J. and R. Cooper. 1981. Generalized Quantifiers and Natural Language. *Linguistics and Philosophy* 4: 159-219.

Bennett, J. 1988. *Events and their Names.* Indianapolis: Hackett.

Bromberger, S. 1991. *On What We Know We don't Know.* Chicago: The University of Chicago Press.

Calabrese, A. 1984. Multiple Questions and Focus in Italian. *Sentential Complementation,* eds. W. de Geest and Y. Putseys, 67-74. New York: Holt.

Davidson, D. 1967. Causal Relations. *Journal of Philosophy* 64: 691-703.

Herburger, E. 2000. *What Counts: Focus and Quantification.* Cambridge: MIT Press.

Hoji, H. 1985. Logical Form Constraints and Configurational Structures in Japanese. Doctoral dissertation, University of Washington, Seattle, WA.

Hooper, J. B. and S. A. Thompson (1973) On the Applicability of Root Transformations. *Linguistic Inquiry* 4.4:465-497.

Kay, P. 1980. On the Syntax and Semantics of Early Questions. *Linguistic Inquiry* 11: 426-429.

Keenan, E. and Y. Stavi. 1983. A Semantic Characterization of Natural Language Determiners. *Linguistics and Philosophy* 9: 253-326.

Ko, H. 2004. Syntax of *Wh*-in-situ: Merge into [Spec CP] in the Overt Syntax. *Natural Language and Linguistic Theory* 23: 867-916.

Koizumi, M. 1995. Phrase Structure in Minimalist Syntax. Doctoral dissertation. MIT.

Labov, W. and T. Labov. 1978. Learning the Syntax of Questions. *Recent Advances in the Psychology of Language,* eds. R. N. Campbell and P. T. Smith, 1-44. New York, Plenum Press.

Larson, R. K. 1991. The Projection of DP and DegP. Ms. Stony Brook University.

Miyagawa, S. 1997. On the Nature of *Wh*-scope. Ms. MIT.

Ono, H. 2002. Exclamatory Sentences in Japanese: A Preliminary Study. http://www.ling.umd.edu/hajime/papers/OnoTCP02.pdf

Rizzi, L. 1999. On the Position of "Int(errogative)" in Left Periphery of the Clause. Ms. Università di Siena.

Saito, M. 1985. Some Asymmetries in Japanese and their Theoretical Implications. Doctoral dissertation, MIT.

Saito, M. and N. Fukui. 1992. Order in Phrase Structure and Movement. *Linguistic Inquiry* 29: 439-474.

Sohn, K-W. 1994. Adjunction to Argument, Free Ride and a Minimalist Program. *Formal Approaches to Japanese Linguistics* 1, eds. M. Koizumi and H. Ura, 315-334. Cambridge: MIT Working Papers in Linguistics.

Processing Left Peripheral NPI in Korean: At the Syntax/Phonology Interface[*]

JIEUN KIAER
University of Oxford

RUTH KEMPSON
King's College London

1. Introduction

This paper investigates the processing of left-peripheral expressions, in particular, sentence-initial Negative Polarity Items (NPI) dative NPs. *Amwu-hanthey-to* is a strongest NPI and requires its negative licensor(*an-/mot*) to occur in its local structure (Nam 1994) as in (1). Yet, as in (2), *amwu-hanthey/ekey-to* can be licensed within non-local (nonimmediate) structure. When *amwu-hanthey/ekey-to* is interpreted in a nonimmediate clause as in (2), Intonational Phrase (IP) boundary, marked as % immediately follows *amwu-hanthey/ekey-to*.[1]

(1) Amwu-hanthey-to Mina-ka   noymwul-ul **an**-cwuessta-ko
     anyone-DAT-even Mina-NOM bribe-ACC NEG-gave-COMP
     Jiho-nun malhayssta.
     Jiho-TOP said
     'Jiho said that Mina didn't give anyone bribes.'

---

[*] We are grateful to Prof Chungmin Lee, Prof James H. Yoon and the audience at JK 16th for useful comments.

[1] In this paper, we assume the intonational model of Seoul Korean developed by Jun (1993,2000).

(2)   Amwu-hanthey-to% Mina-ka   noymwul-ul cwuessta-ko Jiho-nun
      anyone-DAT-even   Mina-NOM bribe-ACC   gave-COMP Jiho-TOP
      an-malhayssta.
      NEG-said
      'Jiho didn't say to anyone that Mina gave anyone bribes.'

(3)   Amwu-hanthey-to Jiho-nun% Mina-ka   noymwul-ul cwuessta-ko
      anyone-DAT-even Jiho-TOP   Mina-NOM bribe-ACC   gave-COMP
      an-malhayssta.
      NEG-said
      'Jiho didn't say to anyone that Mina gave anyone bribes.'

(4)   Amwu-hanthey-to% Jiho-nun Mina-ka   noymwul-ul
      anyone-DAT-even   Jiho-TOP Mina-NOM bribe-ACC
      an-cwuessta-ko   malhayssta.
      NEG-gave-COMP said
      'Jiho said that Mina didn't give anyone bribes.'

    Whether the embedded clause as a unit is fronted as in (1)-(2) or not, as in (3)-(4), interpretation of a sentence-initial NPI is flexible. In (3), the sentence-initial *amwu-hanthey-to* can be interpreted within the matrix clause together with the following topic-marked NP(=*Jiho-nun*) or it can be interpreted within the embedded clause together with the nominative NP (=*Mina-ka*) as in (4). As in (1)-(2), the interpretation of *amwu-hanthey-to* is strongly influenced by prosodic cues. When *amwu-hanthey-to* is interpreted locally to the following topic-marked NP, IP boundary occurs after the topic marked NP and *an*-NEG appears in the matrix clause. However, when *amwu-hanthey-to* is interpreted nonlocally to the following topic-marked NP but together with the embedded subject, an IP boundary occurs after the dative NP and *an*-NEG appears at the embedded verb. As shown above, left peripheral expressions in Korean are flexibly interpreted when an appropriate intonation is provided. This is in contrast to sentence medial and right peripheral expressions. In particular, the interpretation of right peripheral expressions is restricted. Compared to (5), (6) sounds very odd because the right peripheral NPI should be interpreted within the closest clause only.

(5)   Jiho-nun Mina-ka   noymwul-ul cwuessta-ko **an**-malhaysse.
      Jiho-TOP Mina-NOM bribe-ACC   gave-COMP NEG-said
      amwu-hanthey-to
      anyone-DAT-even
      'Jiho didn't say to anyone that Mina gave anyone bribes.'

(6) ??Jiho-nun Mina-ka   noymwul-ul **an**-cwuessta-ko
     Jiho-TOP Mina-NOM bribe-ACC NEG-gave-COMP
     malhaysse/saynggakhaysse amwu-hanthey-to.
     said/thought   anyone-DAT-even
     'Jiho said/thought that Mina didn't give anyone bribes.'

The apparent asymmetry between left and right peripheral expressions has been ignored in the literature, even though it seems to be universal across the languages that left peripheral expressions can be interpreted more flexibly than right peripheral expressions. It is hard to explain the above structural asymmetry caused by linear order within a transformational grammar formalism. In nontransformational, lexicalist frameworks such as HPSG, LFG or CCG, it may be possible to capture the asymmetry by controlling the lexicon and postulating different lexical entries at different syntactic position (e.g. *+FRONT, +MIDDLE, +END*, See Karamanis (2001) for a similar CCG approach in Greek).

Native speakers' freedom to build a structure at the left periphery is, however, systematically restricted by prosodic cues at the early stage. Hence, they can resolve a sentence initial NPI either locally or nonlocally even when only a partial string is given. This shows native Korean speakers' ability to construct a syntactic structure in an incremental, stepwise way. Particularly, we argue that Korean speakers use case markers and prosodic cues to build their partial structure. Though we certainly need further investigation, the observation at this point can at least challenge the architecture of (universal) grammar in two ways. Grammar formalisms should provide a way to express/explain the syntactic ability in constructing a partially specified structure in a stepwise way, since such ability will form the essence of syntactic structure formation. Furthermore, grammar formalisms should also provide an explanation of how nonsyntactic information such as prosody guides/directs syntactic structure building, rather than syntax determining prosodic structure. The aim of the current proposal is to shed a new light on the role of linear order in the architecture of grammar by taking the challenges from processing and syntax/phonology interfaces seriously. In the next section, we will discuss the two challenges in more detail.

2. Empirical Challenge in Grammar

The motivation for studying language has been to find out the source of syntactic behaviour. Since Chomsky (1965), generative linguists have assumed that linguistic ability is distinct from other cognitive/mental abilities, and requires a methodology in which *competence* models accordingly have to be characterised as entirely independent of any considerations of *performance*.

Nevertheless, there has been increasing realization that such a severe lack of feeding relations between aspects of linguistic performance and articulation of a grammar formalism is, at least, overly restrictive. In particular, Hawkins displayed the extensiveness of correlation between syntactic distributions and performance factors (Hawkins 2004). Phillips (2003) also notes that constituency cannot be established by purely syntactic considerations. In this paper, we argue in line with this research that performance data provide a window onto core grammar, rather than just being regarded as only subsidiary to grammar. Furthermore, more radically, we adopt a newly emerging grammar formalism, Dynamic Syntax, where grammar and parser follow essentially the same mechanisms. In particular, within this framework, on the one hand, the distribution of NPIs in scrambling structures can be explained by projecting structure incrementally along a parsing dynamics, and, on the other hand, by taking information provided by intonation, Korean parsing can be shown to be strictly incremental, with parsers establishing structure appropriately well before the verb is processed.

3. Dynamic Syntax: Grammars with Parsing Dynamics

The motivation of Dynamic Syntax (DS) is to capture how the human parser builds up a syntactic structure incrementally from left to right in real time parsing. The main challenge of this framework is to reflect how human parsers can manipulate partial information at each step of parsing to draw a bigger picture of the meaning of the string as early as possible. The DS framework adopts representationalist assumptions about the nature of mind and assumes that semantic interpretation is given as a structural representation of content, with trees representing predicate-argument structure in which the top node of a tree is decorated with a propositional formula and each dominated node is a subterm of that formula, with type-specifications indicating how the parts combine. The framework assumes furthermore that the human parser displays inferential or anticipatory abilities at each step of parsing until a full proposition is achieved. In DS, the unfolding of a structure, and the making of pro-active guesses for the upcoming structure, are driven by (i) a set of language universal computational actions which induce structural options, (ii) lexical actions of each word, (iii) pragmatic actions (such as substituting a value from context for anaphoric expressions).

3.1. Underspecification of Content and its Update

Because DS is committed to building representations of content rather than structure inhabited by words, it is able to characterize the flexible word order and pro-drop nature of head-final languages (e.g., Korean and Japanese) by assuming that the verb projects a full propositional structure, whose arguments are semantically underspecified (as though projected from anaphoric expressions). Such actions are part of the specification of each verb. For instance, *iki*-'beat' projects the partial tree in Fig 1, with two argument nodes decorated with place-holding metavariables U and V as below (the pointer, $\Diamond$, indicates the node next to be developed).

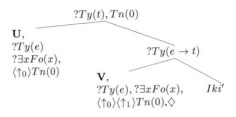

Figure 1. Propositional structure projected by Iki'

The tree gives no indication of order, as this is a representation of content, inhabited by concepts, not by words of the string. $?Ty(t)$ indicates the overall goal of establishing a proposition of $Ty(t)$ with the subgoal of a predicate, $?Ty(e \to t)$. The concept of requirement,$?X$ for any X, is the central concept of the framework: all requirements, whether of content, structure, or type, have to be met by the end of a sequence of parse actions – notice that the argument nodes in Figure 1 equally have a requirement for update of content ($?\exists x Fo(x)$), which can be met either by update from within the structure building process or from context. Thus, by defining words as projecting procedures for building structural representations of content (and not merely some concept-denoting term), an account of pro-drop is naturally made available, and one that is notably more successful than the multiply typed assignment of categories to words as suggested in other constraint-based frameworks (e.g., Combinatory Categorial Grammar).

3.2. Structural Underspecification and Update

Central to this building up of tree structure representations of content is the articulation of different forms of structural underspecification and update within the construction process. Such updates can be motivated or driven by computational, lexical or pragmatic actions. Though such actions may construct 'fixed' tree relations, as in other frameworks, an important property of the tree growth system is that nodes in the partial tree may be introduced without having any particular relation initially fixed; and their syntactic position may be resolved later on in online parsing. This is the basis of long distance dependencylong distance dependency, where the concept of movement is replaced by one of positional underspecification, analogous to anaphora as an alternative form of underspecification.[2] In virtue of having adopted a tree logic for describing the trees, such underspecified relations can be described in terms of $\langle \uparrow * \rangle$, 'X holds at some dominating node'(see the LFG concept of functional uncertainty, Kaplan and Zaenan 1989).[3] The process of seeking a fixed position for the unfixed node is then presumed to take place across an arbitrary sequence of daughter relations. There are three types of Adjunction, reflecting different locality variations in the domain within which update of the underspecified relation is to take place (again analogous to anaphoric expressions). First of all, such underspecifications may require local update within an individual predicate-argument structure: 'Local * Adjunction'. This Local * Adjunction is defined to explain local scrambling in Korean as it can capture flexible ordering of NPs within its local domain, each being taken to decorate some locally underspecified node which is then immediately updated by its attendant case relation (which we return to shortly). Secondly, to model the updating procedure that can be presumed to be construed across the clause boundaries, as displayed by regular instances of long distance dependency-long distance dependency, '* Adjunction' is defined as a process introducing an unfixed node whose hierarchical position in the emergent structure must be resolved within an individual tree structure. Lastly, structural update can take place within some overall construction process, possibly across a sequence of trees. This loosest form of update is termed 'Generalised Adjunction'. Intuitively, what it does is to posit a very weak and arbitrarily dependent relation between two local structures. These processes may, furthermore, feed each other, so a step of *Adjunction may feed a sequence of steps of Local *Adjunction, as we shall see in the analysis of multiple long distance scrambling.

The concept of case in DS interacts with the structural growth process, constraining updates of underspecified structure projected by NPs. For instance, in a local scrambling sequence as in (7), when the parser processes *Mina*, with no other specification, *Mina* may turn out to decorate a subject, an object or a dative. In DS terms, if such a NP is to decorate an unfixed node, it will be decorating a structure whose relative position is merely $\langle \uparrow * \rangle Tn(0)$ ('the root node dominates this node'). However, given that *Mina* is nominative case marked, this requirement can be very much narrowed down, since it

---

[2] To express island constraints, relative clause modification and coordination is associated with the building of paired quasi-independent structures, as the underspecified tree relation in these cases is not to able to be updated across such discrete paired structures (see Kempson et al. 2001, Cann et al. 2005).

[3] The tree itself is described by a modal tree logic (LOFT: Blackburn and Meyer-Viol 1994) in which relations are described between nodes in a tree, with arrow $\langle \uparrow \rangle X$ indicating that X holds at the mother of some current node, $\langle \downarrow \rangle X$ indicating that X holds at its daughter, etc. Two distinct daughter relations are introduced according as $\langle \downarrow_0 \rangle$ the daughter is an argument, $\langle \downarrow_1 \rangle$ the daughter is a functor.

imposes a requirement that the node is immediate daughter of a $Ty(t)$ requiring node: $?\langle\uparrow_0\rangle Ty(t)$. In the case of Local *Adjunction, such a narrowing will indeed determine a fixed result. If accusative case marked, the requirement is that the node be immediate daughter of a predicate requiring node: $?\langle\uparrow_0\rangle Ty(e \to t)$. And so on. Derivations involving Local *Adjunction, the local scrambling phenomenon, that is, follow the pattern displayed in Fig.2 below.

(7)   Jina-lul   Mina-ka   iki-ess-e   [O S V]
        Jina-ACC Mina-NOM beat-PAST,DECL
        'Mina beat Jina'

As Fig 2 displays, each NP is parsed by presuming on a step of Local *Adjunction inducing a weakly specified tree relation; and this relation is enriched into the particular argument node within the emergent structure by the particular case specification. The effect is that argument nodes can be introduced into a structure independent of the projection of the predicate itself, allowing incremental projection of structure from the words, despite the verb not occurring until the end of the string.

(i) Parsing *Jina-lul* :-*lul* updates $\langle\uparrow *\rangle Tn(0)$ into $\langle\uparrow_0\rangle\langle\uparrow_1\rangle\ Tn(0)$ via $?\langle\uparrow_0\rangle Ty(e \to t)$

(ii) Parsing *Mina-ka*:-*ka* updates $\langle\uparrow *\rangle Tn(0)$ into $\langle\uparrow_0\rangle\ Tn(0)$ via $?\langle\uparrow_0\rangle Ty(t)$

Figure 2. Parsing the NP sequences in (7) via Local * Adjunction

3.3. Local and Non-local Update via Adjunction Operations

The availability of the three processes of *Adjunction will of course mean that there will be more than one alternative for any initial step of parsing long distance scrambling construction in Korean, and, as we shall see, the role of intonational break is to eliminate the disjunctions which these alternatives set up. More specifically, the parser will have two choices in parsing a case marked NP as to whether to fix it immediately to its ongoing local structure via Local * Adjunction and immediately enrich it in virtue of case, or to assume through application of * Adjunction that its position will be resolved at some later juncture in the parse process. With no intonational indication to the contrary, the parser will fix the node locally to the ongoing structure via Local * Adjunction as in local scrambling shown in Figure 2. However, if a case marked NP is followed by an intonational break, we take this as indication to the parser that such a sequence of steps of Local *Adjunction is contra-indicated, indicating instead that the expression just parsed is to decorate a node introduced by *Adjunction, forcing the relative independence and later resolution of the underspecified relation. This might seem to immediately lead to an overly flexible system, which contradicts incrementally restricted (from left to right) structure building processes in Korean. Yet, updating structures in Dynamic Syntax is not unrestricted, as we shall now turn to.

4. DS Analysis of left peripheral NPIs

As we have seen, DS assumes that in languages like Korean/Japanese, case-markers are used to construct/guide structure building, not the word-order. So, when native speakers hear *amwu-hanthey-to*, they will anticipate a negative ditransitive verb. This is because *amwu-* is a strongest Negative Polarity Item, which requires a negative licensor like *an-/mot-* and *-hanthey* is a dative case particle, which requires a ditransitive verb (e.g. give). What the case particle does is to narrow down the expectation for the host verb. However, case information cannot tell whether the current expression it to be interpreted locally or nonlocally to the forthcoming sequence. Given that word-order in Korean is flexible and an expressions can be dislocated even across a clause boundary, information via case markers is not enough in capturing native speakers' ability to construct syntactic structure in an incremental way. At this juncture, we can solve the puzzle by considering prosodic information. Prosodic information, namely, Intonational phrase boundary cues guide native speakers whether to build the expression local to the forthcoming structural template or not. Hence, in (8), when there is an Intonational phrase boundary after *amwu-hanthey-to*, native speakers will anticipate negative ditransitive verb in some other local structure, rather than in the same structure with the upcoming material. [4]

(8) Amwu-hanthey-to% Mina-ka   noymwul-ul· · ·
     anyone-DAT-even   Mina-NOM bribe-ACC

Therefore, we assume that when there is no IP boundary after *amwu-hanthey-to*, native speakers choose to fix the partial structure within the immediately following structure, yet, if an IP boundary follow, they will hold such syntactic expectation, hence leaving the syntactic status of the partial structure underspecified. Suppose that a Korean speaker hears *amwu-hanthey-to*. One possible option is to unfold a structural template by using LOCAL * ADJUNCTION as in step (a). In step (b), requirement for the negative trigger is added $(?\langle\uparrow_0\rangle\langle\uparrow_1^*\rangle, Ty(t), NEG)$ and in step (c), requirement for the ditransitive verb is added $(?\langle\uparrow_0\rangle Ty(e \to (e \to t)), \Diamond)$. See Cann et al (2005) and Kiaer (2006) for a more detailed analysis.

(a) Parsing *amwu*   (b) Parsing *amwu-**hanthey**-to*

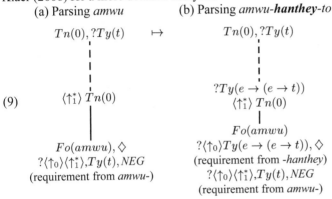

(9)

Another option is to introduce a globally underspecified structure. In this case, $\langle\uparrow_1^*\rangle Tn(0)$ is replaced by $\langle\uparrow^*\rangle Tn(0)$.

---

[4] In languages like Warlpiri, a stacked case-marker plays the same role as Intonational phrase boundaryin Korean. See Nordlinger (1998).

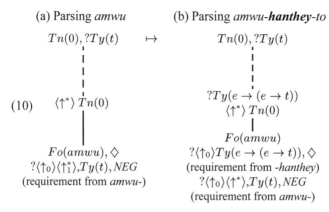

(a) Parsing *amwu*   (b) Parsing *amwu-**hanthey**-to*

In principle, in DS, all the operations are available at every stage of structure building. However, it seems that native speakers of Korean strongly prefer to narrow down/minimise possible parse sequences during their real time understanding by using case information, prosody and contextual information and often routinising the actions of each information.In the following section, we will discuss (i) empirical evidence of step-wise structure building based on syntactic behaviours of left peripheral NPIs and (ii) the implication of such evidence in grammar formalisms and the grammar-processor relation.

5. Evidence for Incremental/Partial Structure Building

5.1. Prosodic Phrasing

The purpose of this test was to see whether Korean speakers use prosodic cues (e.g. IP boundary) when they need to resolve left peripheral expressions in a nonimmediate structure in case when the negative licensor occurs in that structure. The test was a reading aloud test. Ten native Seoul Korean speakers participated in the test. Among them, five of them were instructed to skim the materials ahead of time as in an offline test and other five not to skim the materials ahead as in an online test. Subjects read sixteen target sentences as in (11) and (12), all intermixed with forty eight fillers. The recording took place in a sound-proof booth in the department of linguistics at SOAS.

(11)   NPI Local Condition: NPI resolved in an immediate clause
        Amwu-hanthey-to Mina-ka   noymwul-ul **an-cwuessta-ko**
        anyone-DAT-even Mina-NOM bribe-ACC   NEG-gave-COMP
        Jiho-nun malhayssta.
        Jiho-TOP said
        'Jiho said that Mina didn't give anyone bribes.'

(12)   NPI Non-local Condition: NPI resolved in a nonimmediate clause

Amwu-hanthey-to Mina-ka   noymwul-ul cwuessta-ko Jiho-nun
anyone-DAT-even Mina-NOM bribe-ACC   gave-COMP Jiho-TOP
an-malhayssta.
NEG-said
'Jiho didn't say to anyone that Mina gave bribes.'

We measured[5] the duration of the last syllable -*to*, because an Intonational Phrase(IP) boundary in Korean has the properties of (i) final vowel lengthening; (ii) boundary tones and (iii) optional pause (See Jun 1993). The result shows that subjects both in the skimmed and non-skimmed group preferred to produce the last syllable of the word before the IP boundary significantly longer in a nonlocal condition(ie. NPI to be interpreted in a nonimmediate structure) relative to a local condition (ie. NPI to be interpreted in an immediate structure). The average duration of the last syllable -*to* is as follows. In the skimmed group, the duration of -*to* was on average 90 ms longer in a non-local condition than in a local condition. In the non-skimmed group, the duration of -*to* was on average 83 ms longer in a nonlocal condition than in a local condition. The difference was statistically significant.(In an ANOVA test by both Item and Subject Analysis, $P < 0.001$).

TABLE 1   Duration of the last syllable *to* in *amwu-hanthey-to*

Location of the host verb	Skimmed	Non-Skimmed
Non-Local	371ms	281ms
Local	281ms	198ms

In the following test, based on this production test result, we conducted an auditory fragment completion test.

5.2. Auditory Fragment Completion

The aim of this test is to explore whether not only speakers but also listeners use prosodic cues sensitively for their partial structure formation. Twenty native Korean speakers participated in the test. They heard twenty partial strings such as (13) and (14), ten each, intermixed with forty eight fillers. The material was recorded by a female native Seoul Korean speaker. The whole sentence was recorded and was edited using PRAAT software. The location of the Intonational Phrase(IP) boundary was manipulated as below.

(13)   NPI-DAT % NP-NOM NP-ACC: IP boundary after NP-DAT
      Amwu-hanthey-to %   Jina-ka   Christmas-e   card-lul
      any-DAT-even   pause Jina-NOM Christmas-at card-ACC

(14)   NPI-DAT NP-NOM NP-ACC: NO IP boundary after NP-DAT

---

[5] Thanks to Prof Sun-Ah Jun for suggesting this method.

Amwu-hanthey-to Jina-ka Christmas-e card-lul
any-DAT-even Jina-NOM Christmas-at card-ACC

Subjects were instructed to choose a natural continuation such as (15a,b) after listening to the fragments as in (13) or (14):

(15) a. Verb-COMP Subj Neg-Verb

    ponayssta-ko Mira-ka <u>an-malhaysse</u>
    sent-COMP Mira-NOM NEG-said

  b. Neg-Verb-COMP Subj Verb

    <u>an-ponaysta-ko</u> Mira-ka malhaysse
    NEG-sent-COMP Mira-NOM said

When no IP boundary was given after the NPI dative NP, they strongly preferred to resolve a NPI dative NP within the structure projected by the first upcoming verb. So, they chose a NEG-verb-COMP verb sequence (e.g. NEG-sent-COMP said) as in (15b). However, when the IP boundary was given after a NPI dative NP, they strongly preferred to resolve the NPI dative NP within nonimmediate structure. So, they chose verb-COMP NEG-verb sequence (e.g. sent-COMP NEG-said) as in (15a). 90% of the time, the above correlation was observed. The result of this experiment shows that native Korean speakers can build a partial structure and therefore can decide whether to resolve a left peripheral NPI in an immediate clause or not, even before the actual morphosyntactic trigger(i.e.*an*-NEG) appears.

5.3. Online phrase by phrase Self-Paced Comprehension

In this test, we aimed to investigate how native speakers tend to build a structure in real time, when no prosodic information is given. Twenty two native speakers of Korean participated in the test. Twenty sets of two conditions were used in the test. Experimental items were intermixed with forty eight fillers. The sample set of examples is given in (16). Subscripted numbers refer to a region.

(16) a. Neg-Early Condition: *an*-NEG appears in an embedded verb

    <u>Amwu-hanthey-to$_1$</u> Kiho-ka$_2$ cemsim-e$_3$ bap-ul$_4$
    anyone-DAT-even Kiho-NOM lunch-at meal-ACC
    <u>an-sa-cwuessta-ko$_5$</u> Tongkyu-ka$_6$ malhaysseyo.$_7$
    NEG-bought-COMP Tongkyu-NOM said

    'Tongkyu said that Kiho didn't buy anyone meal at lunch.'

  b. Neg-Late Condition: *an*-NEG appears in a matrix verb

    <u>Amwu-hanthey-to$_1$</u> Kiho-ka$_2$ cemsim-e$_3$ bap-ul$_4$
    anyone-DAT-even Kiho-NOM lunch-at meal-ACC
    sa-cwuessta-ko$_5$ Tongkyu-ka$_6$ <u>an-malhaysseyo.$_7$</u>
    bought-COMP Tongkyu-NOM NEG-said

'Tongkyu didn't say to anyone that Kiho bought (him) a meal at lunch.'

We adopted Just, Carpenter and Wooley (1982)'s methodology. Subjects were timed in a phrase by phrase self-paced noncumulative moving window task.[6] In this test, significant slow-down was observed in the embedded verb region 5 when a negative trigger doesn't appear at that region but in the region of a matrix verb. (The difference was statistically significant. $P<0.001$).

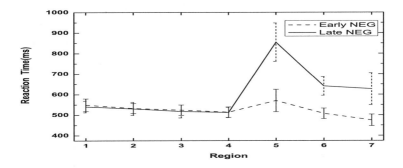

Figure 3. Slow-down at region 5 in Neg-Late condition

Following Miyamoto and Takahashi (2001), we assume that the slow-down at region 5 was caused because the positive verb *sacwuessta-ko* 'bought-COMP' conflicts with native speakers' expectation for a negative licensor. If structure building is nonprocedural, such a delay at region 5 will not be observed as the end of a structure is not yet reached. This also shows that without prosodic disambiguation, and with case information only, native speakers tend to build a partial structure in the same local domain in order to optimise their structure with relatively little effort. This tendency, known as *locality* (ie. build a structure in the same local template) is prevalent across the languages (See Gibson 1998). We also assume that such an option is a default structure building option. The same pattern is observable in the corpus as we shall now turn to.

5.4. Corpus extraction

Balanced, raw 7 million Sejong (written) Corpus was used for our investigation. In this extraction study, we aimed to explore whether the tendency to localise arguments found in real time processing is also observable in a corpus. The result confirmed this. Only 14.7% of the time, sentence initial

---

[6] At first, a dotted line will appear, and then, when the subject presses the space bar, the first word will appear. And then again, when the subject presses the space bar, the second word will appear. The duration of reading time is measured when the space bar is hit.

amwu-hanthey/-ekey-to was interpreted in a nonimmediate clause. In the next section, we will provide a brief sketch of Dynamic Syntax and how case and prosody information are used in building up a partial structure.

6. Conclusion

In this paper, we have challenged what is the basis of syntactic architecture, particularly by looking at Korean. Often, syntactic distributions in head-final languages like Korean/Japanese have been taken to be problematic for attempts to capture the concept of syntactic knowledge in a way that is adequately language general. Yet, the empirical challenges displayed in Korean by incrementality of processing and the feeding relation between phonology and syntax confirms that syntactic structure needs to be modelled in a procedural way following the linear order of a string. With this view, we correctly predict a close relation between the grammar and the parser.

References

Blackburn, P. and W. Meyer-Viol. 1994. Linguistics, logic and finite trees. *Bulletin of Interest Group of Pure and Applied Logics* 2: 2-39.

Cann, R., R. Kempson and R. Marten. 2005. *The Dynamics of Language*. Amsterdam/San Diego: Elsevier.

Chomsky, N. 1965. *Aspects of the theory of syntax*. Cambridge: MIT Press.

Hawkins, J. 2004. *Efficiency and Complexity in Grammars*. Oxford: Oxford University Press.

Jun, S. 1993. The Phonetics and Phonology of Korea Prosody. Doctoral dissertation, The Ohio State University.

Just, M.A., P.A. Carpenter and J.D. Wooley. 1982. Paradigms and Processes in Reading Comprehension. *Journal of Experimental Psychology: General* 111 (2): 228-238.

Kaplan, R. and Zaenen, A. 1989. Long-distance dependencies, constituent structure, and functional uncertainty. *Alternative Conceptions of Phrase Structure*, eds. M. Baltin and A. Kroch, 17-42. Chicago: University of Chicago Press.

Karamanis, N. 2001. A Categorial Grammar for Greek. *Proceedings of the 15th International Symposium on Theoretical and Applied Linguistics*. Aristotle University of Thessaloniki.

Kempson, R., W. Meyer-Viol and D. Gabbay. 2001. *Dynamic Syntax: The Flow of Language Understanding*. Oxford: Blackwell.

Kiaer, J. 2006. Processing and Interfaces in Syntactic Theory: the case of Korean. Doctoral dissertation, University of London.

Miyamoto, E. T. and S. Takahashi. 2002. The processing of wh-phrases and interrogative complementizers in Japanese. *Japanese/Korean Linguistics, 10*, eds. N. M. Akatsuka, and S. Strauss, 62-75. Stanford: CSLI.

Nam, S. 1994. Another Type of Negative Polarity Item. *Dynamics, Polarity, and Quantification*, eds. M. Kanazawa and C. Pinon, 3-15. CSLI, Stanford University.

Nordlinger, R. 1998. *Constructive Case*. Stanford: CSLI.

Phillips, C. 2003. Linear order and constituency. *Linguistic Inquiry* 34: 37-90.

The Exempt Binding of Local Anaphors: An Empirical Study of the Korean Local Anaphor *Caki-casin*

JI-HYE KIM
JAMES H. YOON
University of Illinois at Urbana-Champaign

1. Introduction

Previous investigations of anaphor binding in Korean have focused almost exclusively on the long-distance anaphor (LDA) *caki*, though it is well-known that the language possesses several other anaphors, such as *casin*, *pronoun-casin*, and *caki-casin*. In J-M Yoon (1989), one of the few studies that examined anaphors other than *caki*, it is claimed that morphologically complex anaphors *caki-casin* and *pronoun-casin*, unlike the morphologically simple forms *caki* (and *casin*), are locally bound anaphors. A similar claim was made for Japanese *zibun-zisin* in Katada (1991). B-M Kang's (1998) corpus-based study confirmed the tendency for local binding for *caki-casin*. The studies, except for Kang's, were conducted under the impetus of the LF-movement hypothesis of LDAs (Cole, Hermon, Sung 1990 - CHS), where the claim is made that LDAs are to be analyzed in terms of LF-movement. In CHS, it is further argued that LDAs must be morphologically simple (X^0) anaphors. Complex, or phrasal (XP), anaphors are prevented from exploiting the LF-movement option that yields long-distance binding for simple anaphors.

The typological correlation between simple anaphors and long-distance binding has been verified in a number of languages possessing LDAs. However, the validity of the claim needs to be re-examined. The primary reason is the following. Local anaphors can sometimes be long-distance bound (Pollard and Sag 1992, Reinhart and Reuland 1993). The perspective on anaphor licensing adopted in these works is quite different from the line of research that emanates from what has been dubbed the Standard Binding Theory (Chomsky 1980, 1981). Contrary to Standard Binding Theory, these researchers take the job of licensing of anaphors not to rest entirely with grammar-internal principles. Only certain anaphors need to be licensed grammar-internally, while others need not. Thus, syntactic Binding Theory underdetermines the distribution and interpretive possibilities of anaphors.

Anaphors that need to be licensed grammar-internally are those that have a superior co-argument (for Pollard and Sag 1992) or a Subject/Specifier within a Complete Functional Complex (CFC) in the sense of Chomsky (1986). All other anaphors are licensed by extragrammatical mechanisms. The term **core anaphor** (or **grammatical anaphor**) is used to refer to the former, while the term **exempt anaphor** (or **logophor**) designates the latter. The system of grammar-internal binding principles can correspondingly be termed grammatical binding.

How do we know that a given anaphor is exempt since languages do not have dedicated forms of exempt anaphors? The first indication that an anaphor is exempt is its occurrence in contexts without a minimal Subject (or superior co-argument). However, this is not the only diagnostic property. Exempt anaphors have been found to display a cluster of properties that distinguish them from core anaphors. They include the following:

(1)   a. Exempt anaphors may be unbound (or discourse-bound).
        b. Exempt anaphors do not need c-commanding antecedents.
        c. Exempt anaphors may be long-distance bound.
        d. Exempt anaphors do not show a preference for sloppy readings in VP ellipsis contexts.

Properties (1a-c) can be illustrated with English exempt anaphors. English, a language that is generally thought to lack LDAs, allows its anaphors to be bound long-distance or be discourse-bound, as seen in (2a) and (2b) below. In addition, c-command, which is required in core binding, is not necessary between exempt anaphors and their antecedents (cf. 2c). By contrast, anaphors that cannot be construed as exempt (in virtue of the presence of a locally commanding subject/specifier in the minimal CFC) cannot be licensed in similar contexts. This is seen in (2a'-2c').

(2) a. **Bill** remembered that the Times had printed [a picture of **himself**] in its Sunday edition.
     a'. *__Bill__ remembered that the Times had printed [Mary's picture of **himself**] in its Sunday edition.
     b. [Physicist like **yourself**] are a godsend.
     c. [Incriminating pictures of **himself** published in the Times] have all but eliminated **John's** chances of being promoted.
     c'. *[Mary's pictures of **himself** published in the Times] have all but eliminated **John's** chances of being promoted.

Cole, Hermon, and Huang (2001) propose another diagnostic for core versus exempt anaphors based on sloppy versus strict readings in contexts of VP ellipsis (see also Runner et. al. 2002, Ying 2005).

Unless an explicit context favoring the strict reading is given (say, if the sentence is followed by 'Bill and John are best friends'), the elliptical VP in (3) below is interpreted sloppily, that is, as meaning that Bill defended Bill:

(3) John defended himself against the committee's accusations.
     Bill did so too.

However, even in the absence of a context favoring a strict interpretation, speakers assign a strict interpretation to the missing VP in (4a). (4b) is similar. A strict reading is more likely than the sloppy reading. It is the sloppy readings that require a specific context.

(4) a. John thinks that Susan and himself are to blame for the accident.
        Bill does so, too
     b. John thinks that an article written by himself caused the uproar.
        Bill does so, too.

Assuming this to reflect a general pattern, we can use the lack of preference for strict readings in neutral VP ellipsis contexts as another diagnostic for exempt anaphors.

Now, while exempt anaphors escape the strictures of syntactic conditions that constrain core anaphors, their licensing is nevertheless subject to discourse-pragmatic conditions. Conditions that fall under the rubric of **logophoricity** (Sells 1987, Huang and Liu 2001) are required for an exempt anaphor to be licensed. Sells (1987) also showed that there are logophoric roles that are more canonical than others (see also Huang and Liu 2001). Thus, antecedents of exempt anaphors are optimal if they are logophoric centers.[1]

---

[1] Sells (1987) did not make the core-exempt distinction. We are reinterpreting his conclusions in light of this distinction, following Huang and Liu (2001) who demonstrate convincingly that core anaphors do not require discourse-pragmatic conditions to be licensed.

The contrast shown below can be understood in this light. The structural distance between and relative configurations of the antecedent and anaphor (lack of c-command) are identical in the sentences and yet there are degrees of contrast.

(5) a. [Incriminating pictures of **himself** published in the Times] have been worrying **John** for some time.
   b. [Incriminating pictures of **himself** published in the Times] have all but eliminated **John's** chances of being promoted.
   b. *?[Incriminating pictures of **himself** published in the Times] accidentally fell on **John's** head.

The judgments reflect the ease with which *John* can be identified as a logophoric center. In (5a), *John* is a SELF (and so also a PIVOT), in the sense of Sells (1987), while in (5b) and (5c) it can only be a PIVOT. (5b) is better than (5c) because it is easier to construe this sentence as being reported from the point of view of *John*, compared to the third.

Since properties of exempt/logophoric binding have been investigated primarily for English, and English is a language that lacks genuine LDA's, we might hypothesize that if a language possesses a rich inventory of anaphors, the core-exempt binding distinction may not be manifested in such a language. This is because it is conceivable that some anaphors in the inventory function in contexts of grammatical binding while others are devoted exclusively to contexts of exempt/logophoric binding.

Korean is a language with a rich anaphor inventory. Given the core-exempt distinction in anaphor binding, a number of questions invite themselves about Korean anaphors – What is the division of labor among different anaphors? Since long-distance anaphors have often been characterized as logophors (Sells 1987, Huang & Liu 2001, Iida 1992, Huang, Y 1994, etc), are local anaphors in Korean restricted to contexts of grammatical (core) binding?[2] Or is the core/grammatical vs. exempt/logophoric dichotomy of anaphors orthogonal to the long-distance vs. local property of anaphors? And if local anaphors can be licensed as exempt anaphors, are the conditions similar to those that hold in the licensing of exempt anaphors in languages like English?

As a first step in a crosslinguistic investigation of anaphors within an approach that posits the core-exempt distinction, we wanted to investigate whether anaphors previously claimed to be restricted to local binding in languages with both local and long-distance anaphors can be licensed as exempt anaphors. Since the ability to take long-distance antecedents is one

---

[2] For languages like Korean, long-distance binding means binding in violation of SSC, as it is well-established that TSC is not effective in defining a binding domain. Huang and Liu (2001) show that anaphors violating TSC only are core anaphors in Chinese.

of the claimed diagnostics of such anaphors, we focused our attention primarily on whether native speakers of Korean judge sentences with the long-distance bound local anaphor *caki-casin* to be acceptable and if so, to determine whether they are treating it as core or exempt anaphor.

We proceeded to investigate this question through two experimental studies. The primary rationale for conducting an experimental study came from the recognition that individual judgments about anaphor binding were notoriously unreliable, except for the simplest cases. This is as it should be, since according to the best current understanding, judgments about long-distance bound anaphors often involve making inferences about discourse-pragmatic factors involved in logophoricity. Therefore, along with corpus-based studies such as B-M Kang (1998), carefully designed experimental studies are called for to establish a baseline of judgments about various anaphors in Korean. In addition to employing experimental methods, our research is one of the few (if not the first) that investigates core versus exempt binding for Korean anaphors in a systematic way.

2. Empirical Study

2.1. Research Questions

The specific research questions we addressed in our study are the following:

1) Do Korean native speakers accept long-distance binding of the local anaphor *caki-casin*?

2) If they do, do they treat it as a core or exempt anaphor? The answer to this question devolves to the resolution of the following two sub-questions. One, are long-distance antecedents of *caki-casin* optimal when they carry a typical logophoric role? Two, is there a preference for sloppy or strict reading in contexts of VP-ellipsis?

3) Do grammatical-structural factors (subject vs. non-subject antecedents; c-commanding vs. non-c-commanding antecedents; grammatical relation (subject vs. non-subject)/case-marking of *caki-casin*) affect the acceptability of the long-distance binding of *caki-casin*?

The second question is designed to investigate how speakers who judge sentences with long-distance bound *caki-casin* as grammatical are analyzing the anaphor. That is, if we find that long-distance bound *caki-casin* is sensitive to known logophoric factors, it would indicate that the speakers are treating it as an exempt anaphor. Specifically, since not all logophoric roles are created equal (Sells 1987; Huang and Liu 2001), as some roles (SOURCE) are more canonical than others (PIVOT), we expect differences in judgments depending on the logophoric role of the long-distance antecedent of *caki-casin*.

A second test of core vs. exempt anaphors comes from strict vs. sloppy identity readings in VP-ellipsis contexts. If we should find that speakers accept long-distance bound *caki-casin* but do not show a preference for sloppy readings, we can conclude that they are treating it as an exempt anaphor.

The rationale for the third question is the following: while exempt anaphors are judged not to be constrained by structural factors such as c-command, we nevertheless hypothesize that structural factors such as antecedent type (subject vs. non-subject), structural relations between the antecedent and *caki-casin* (c-command vs. no c-command), and structural distance might be factors that have an effect on long-distance bound exempt *caki-casin*. That is, antecedents of exempt anaphors that c-command them might be more optimal than those that don't. Subject antecedents might be more optimal than non-subject antecedents of exempt anaphors. This does not mean that exempt anaphors are restricted by structural conditions like core anaphors. It simply means that structural prominence of antecedents relative to the anaphor could be a factor that facilitates the contextual identification of a pragmatically salient antecedent for exempt anaphors. We therefore varied the test sentences in terms of certain structural properties.

2.2. Experiment

2.2.1. Hypotheses and Predictions

Regarding the questions identified above, we hypothesized the following:

Hypothesis:
Korean native speakers will accept Korean sentences with long-distance bound *caki-casin* by taking it as an exempt anaphor.

In terms of the results of the experiment, our specific predictions were as follows:

1) The average grammaticality score that the subjects give for each sentence with long-distance bound caki-casin will be closer to the 'grammatical' rather than the 'ungrammatical' end of the grammaticality judgment scale.

2) There should be differences in the degree of grammaticality according to the logophoric roles of the long-distance antecedent of caki-casin.

3) Overall, the subjects' response regarding grammaticality and her/his choice of the strict reading will increase, in the case of LD exempt binding, compared with the case of core binding.

4) Structural properties of antecedents in sentences where caki-casin is long-distance bound should have an effect on the degree of grammaticality.

2.2.2. Method

A. Participants

Forty-six Korean monolingual speakers (ages ranging between 42 and 58) residing in and near Seoul, South Korea participated in the experiment. They all grew up in Korea as monolinguals and have never stayed longer than a month in other countries.

B. Task & Materials

The task used in the experiment was a Grammaticality Judgment Task using the Likert scale coupled with a Preferential Sentence Interpretation Task based on Maling, Jun, and Kim (2000). Each task consisted of two parts: The first part of each question asked the subjects to judge the degree of grammaticality of a sentence where *caki-casin* occurs with a long-distance antecedent. The second part was designed to test the strict vs. sloppy readings of long-distance bound *caki-casin* in the context of VP-ellipsis, as this could not be ascertained from the first part. The test materials consisted of 100 items – 65 target items and 35 distractors.

In order to ensure that the anaphors were exempt anaphors, we constructed sentences where the anaphors did not have a potential antecedent within the minimal CFC. However, since core anaphors in languages like Korean and Chinese can violate TSC, we constructed our test items so that the anaphor (or the NP containing the anaphor) would seek a long-distance antecedent in violation of SSC (cf. 6a-e). The long-distance antecedents carry one of the logophoric roles identified in Sells (1987 – SELF, SOURCE, PIVOT) and balance was maintained between subjects and non-subject antecedents, and between c-commanding and non-commanding antecedents.

Some example sentences used as target items are given below. *Caki-casin* in (6a) is forced to take the matrix Subject *Inphyo* as antecedent, in violation of both TSC and SSC. This is so since the local Subject is inanimate and hence not a likely antecedent of *caki-casin*. Similar properties are observed in (6b), except that the anaphor is further embedded within an NP as Possessor. (6c) has more than one third-person antecedent. However, pragmatically, the most local antecedent in the adjunct clause is not a feasible antecedent. The matrix Subject which comes linearly after the anaphor in turn is the only pragmatically possible antecedent.

(6) a. **Inphyo$_i$-nun**   [kyenchalcheng $_j$-i   **caki-casin$_i$-i**   swumki-n
       Inphyo-top   police-nom   self-nom   hide-rel
       cungkemwul-ul   chacanay-ess- ta]-ko   malhay-ss-ta
       exhibit–acc   find-past-dec-comp   say-past-decl
       'Inphyo said that the Police found out the exhibit he (self) had hidden.'

b. **Sangho**$_i$**–nun** [tongchanghoy   meympe-tul$_j$-i   **caki-casin**$_i$**-uy**
Sanghho-top   alumni.assoc   member-pl-nom   self- gen
kyelhon nalcca-lul imi   palpyohayss-ta]-ko   mit-ko   iss-ta.
wedding date -acc already   announced-decl-comp believe asp-decl
'Sangho believes that the alumni association members already announced his (self's) wedding date.'

c. [Chelswu$_j$-ka   **caki-casin**$_i$**-ul** chata o-ass-ul ttay],   **Yenghi**$_i$**-nun**
Chelswu-nom   self-acc seek-come-rel when Yenghi-top
(*pro* $_j$ -ul)   maywu   pankapkey   mac-a cwu-ess-ta.
very   gladly   greet give-pst-decl.
'When Chelswu came to seek her (= self, Yenghi), Yenghi greeted
(Chelswu) very gladly.'

As you can tell, in terms of logophoric roles, the long-distance antecedent in
(6a) is SOURCE, while that in (6b) is SELF. That in (6c) is PIVOT.

Three other sentence types were added to the target items – Sentences
with multiple potential antecedents (cf. 7a), sentences with less logophoricity (cf. 7b), and sentences with TSC-only violation (cf. 7c). They are shown
below.

(7) a.   Hyori$_i$-ka Ceytong$_j$ -eykey [Cenghyeni$_k$-ka   **caki-casin**$_{i\,j\,k}$**-i** ccik-un
Hyori-nom Ceytong -dat   Cenghyuni-nom self-nom   take-rel
sacin-ul   cohahanta] -ko   malhay-ss-ta
photo-acc   like-comp   say-past-decl
'Hyori$_i$ told Ceytong$_j$ that Cenghyen$_k$ liked the photo that self (i, j, k) took.'

b.   **Minhi**$_i$**-nun** [haksayng$_j$ -tul-i   **caki-casin**$_i$ -ul   chac-ule ka-ss-ul
Minhi-top   student-plural-nom self-acc   seek- to go-pst-rel
ttay],   *e*$_i$ pang-eyse   chak-ul   ilk-o   iss-ess-ta-ko   malhayss-ta.
when   room-loc   book-acc read   be-pst-decl-comp said-decl.
'Minhi said that she had been reading a book when the students had
come to seek her(=self).'

c.   **Jieuni**$_i$ -kaHyunmi-eykey ipen hakki-ey-nun **caki-casin**$_i$ -i kkok
Jieuni-nom Hyunmi-dat   thissemester-loc-top self-nom definitely
iltung-ul   ha-lkela-ko   malhayssta-ko   na-nun   alko   iss-ta.
top-acc   do-asp-comp said-comp   I-top   know is-decl.
'I know that Jieun said to Hyunmi that we would be at the top of
class this semester.'

In (7a), *caki-casin* occurs in sentences with multiple potential antecedents. This type of sentences was designed so that subjects' responses on
these items can be used to ascertain answers to questions about the nature of
exempt binding. That is, if *caki-casin* must be licensed as a local anaphor
when local antecedents are available – that is, if exempt binding is found
only in contexts where core binding fails, as commonly assumed (Huang

and Liu 2001) – subjects should show a strong preference for local binding in this sentence type. However, if core and exempt binding are not in complementary distribution (Pollard and Xue 2001, Iida 1992), subjects might still accept long-distance binding in this sentence type.

The second additional type of sentences (cf. 7a), the sentences with less logophoricity, was designed to compare the effect of logophoricity in the context of LD exempt binding. While all other target items were composed of the sentences where the anaphor is bound by logophoric centers (i.e. SOURCE, SELF and PIVOT), this sentence type contains sentences with less logophoricity effect(cf. 7b)[3].

Finally, (7c) is the example of sentences with TSC-only violation, which is legitimate core binding condition in Korean, but in the similar length compared to the sentences with SSC violations. Along with these three additional types of target items, we also have distractors composed of totally ungrammatical sentences in similar length to provide the reference point for the grammaticality judgment.

An example of a test item translated into English is given below:

(8) Mary-nun [nay-ka *caki-casin*-uy kihoy-lul   ppayssessta-ko]   malhayss-ta
    Mary-top I-nom self-gen   chance-acc took-comp   said-decl.
    'Mary said that I robbed her of her opportunity.'
    Ungrammatical   **Grammatical**
        1   2   3   4   5

Laura-to   kulekey malha-yss-ta.
Laura-too so   say-past-decl.
'Laura said so too.'

Interpretation:
A. Laura-nun [nay-ka Laura-uy kihoy-lul ppayssessta-ko] malha-yss-ta.
(= Laura said that I robbed **Laura** of Laura's opportunity.)
B. Laura-nun [nay-ka Mary-uy kihoy-lul ppayssessta-ko] malha-yss-ta.
(= Laura said that I robbed **Mary** of Mary's opportunity.)
C. None of the above is a possible interpretation.

If our hypotheses are correct, we expect subjects to choose a value close to 'Grammatical' for the first part of the task and the reading indicated in B (= strict reading) for the second task.

---

[3] Since it is difficult to come up with longer than bi-clausal sentences with non-logophoric verbs, in this study, the 'less logophoric' sentences are defined as the sentences where internal and external logophoric roles are conflicted.

C. Procedure

Participants were first asked to fill out a simple one-page questionnaire survey about biographical information such as age, gender and dialect(s). They were then asked to proceed to take the main task. In the main task, participants were required to judge the degree of grammaticality of a given sentence in the Likert scale and then to choose the proper interpretation of an immediately following (underlined) sentence containing VP-ellipsis.

Based on the performance on the Preferential Sentence Interpretation task, participants who showed the pattern of outliers were screened. For example, if subjects judge the test sentence as ungrammatical, their responses on the following sentences with VP ellipsis cannot be considered reliable unless they choose the response 'none of the above is a possible interpretation'. Therefore, responses from subjects who judged the sentences as ungrammatical but nevertheless chose the sloppy or strict reading were set aside.

D. Analysis

The grammaticality score for each sentence was calculated with mean score and standard deviation across subjects. The responses were then grouped according to the sentence types (i.e. by logophoric roles of antecedents – SOURCE, SELF, PIVOT; by antecedent types – subject vs. non-subject antecedent; by c-commanding vs. non-c-commanding antecedents; by logophoric vs. less logophoric context; by TSC only violation vs. TSC & SSC violation etc.) and averaged by sentence types. Repeated Measures Analysis of Variance (ANOVA) and Paired Sample T-test were run to determine the statistical significance of the differences for distinct within-subject factors.

2.2.3. Results

Overall results were as follows:

i) Korean native speakers regarded sentences with LD binding of the local anaphor *caki-casin* as grammatical overall when appropriate logophoric context is given. The participants gave significantly higher grammaticality scores for the sentences with logophoric antecedents than the sentences with less logophoricity (i.e. where external and internal logophoric centers were conflicting, cf. 7b). In addition, the degree of grammaticality for the sentences with LD binding of *caki-casin* (with both TSC and SSC violations) did not differ significantly from those with core binding of *caki-casin* (i.e. TSC-only violation, cf. 7c). This was demonstrated by One way ANOVA ($F_{(42)} = .064$, $p < .802$; NS). The pattern of the results on different type of binding is shown in Table 1 and Figure 1 below.

ii) Regarding the logophoric roles of antecedents, sentences with SOURCE antecedents were assigned the highest grammaticality scores, while those where the antecedent was PIVOT got the lowest grammaticality scores. The degree of grammaticality for the sentences with three logophoric centers are consistent with the canonical hierarchy of the logophoricity suggested by Sells (1987) (SOURCE > SELF > PIVOT). The repeated measures ANOVAs demonstrated that there is a significant main effect by logophoric roles (F(41) = 39.023, p < .0001). The pattern of the results with different logophoric roles is shown below in Table 1 and Figure 2.

iii) Structural differences in sentence type (i.e. subject vs. non-subject antecedent, c-commanding vs. non-c-commanding antecedent, subject vs. non-subject *caki-casin* etc.) have not showed expected results for distinct pairs. As for different grammatical relation of the antecedent, there was no statistically significant difference between the grammaticality score of the sentences with LD subject antecedents and that of sentences with LD non-subject antecedents (F (42) = 2.439, p < .126; NS). With regard to the difference between LD c-commanding vs. non-c-commanding antecedents, sentences with not-c-commanding antecedent got much higher grammaticality scores than those with c-commanding antecedent (F (42) = 23.045, p < .0001). Finally, the result with the different case of *caki-casin* did not show significant difference between subject *caki-casin* (i.e. *caki-casin* bearing nominative case) and non-subject *caki-casin* (i.e. *caki-casin* bearing non-nominative case) (F (42) = 3.235, p < .079; NS). These results are shown in Table 1 below.

Table 1. Grammaticality Scores for Sentences with LD Logophoric Binding

Factors	Logophoric Roles	Grammatical relation	Structural condition	Binding type
	SOURCE	Subject Ant.	C-command	Core (TSC-only violation)
Mean	4.45	4.49	3.61	4.20
S.D.	(0.43)	(0.47)	(0.99)	(0.72)
	SELF	Non-subject	Not-c-command	LD-exempt (TSC & SSC violation)
Mean	4.19	4.35	4.37	4.19
S.D.	(0.54)	(0.59)	(0.72)	(0.46)
	PIVOT			
Mean	3.88			
S.D.	(0.68)			

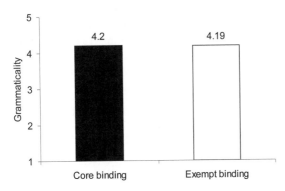

Figure 1. Grammaticality by binding type (LD exempt vs. core binding)

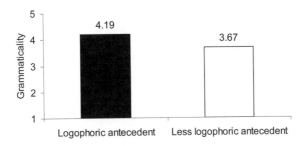

Figure 2-1. Grammaticality of LD binding by Logophoric Roles: Logo-phoric antecedent vs. Less logophoric antecedents

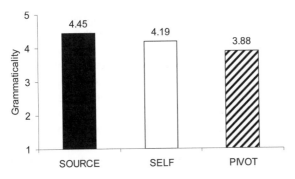

Figure 2-2. Grammaticality of LD binding by Logophoric Roles: Among different Logophoric Roles

iv) Finally, in contexts of VP-ellipsis, speakers showed a fairly strong preference for the strict reading of *caki-casin* in the case of LD exempt binding. The results of Preferential Sentence Interpretation Task demonstrated that the choice of strict reading in VP-ellipsis was dominant in most participants' responses with sentences with long-distance bound *caki-casin* [4]. Overall results are shown below in Table 2 and Figure 3.

Table 2. Strict vs. Sloppy reading Preference in core vs. LD exempt binding

Binding type	Core binding	LD exempt binding
A (sloppy)	39%	**20%**
B (strict)	44%	**57%**
C (neither)	7%	5%
No response	10%	17%

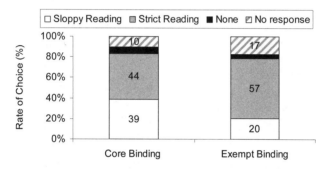

Figure 3. Strict vs. Sloppy Preference in VP-ellipsis

3. Discussion

According to result i), the first prediction of our hypothesis, which stated that sentences with LD bound *caki-casin* with appropriate logophoric conditions would get responses closer to grammatical than ungrammatical, is borne out.

Result ii) seems to support the second prediction that there would be differences in grammaticality according to the distinct logophoric roles of LD antecedents of *caki-casin*. This pattern is even further consistent with what is predicted in Sells (1987).

Result iv) of the present study suggests that majority of the participants who accept LD binding of *caki-casin* treats it as an exempt anaphor, supporting our third prediction. As for the case of core binding, the expected

---

[4] There was a bit of individual variation across speakers in that some participants chose only the sloppy reading throughout all the items or the locally bound interpretation of *caki-casin* even when the phi-feature of the most local antecedent did not match that of the anaphor.

pattern of sloppy reading dominance does not seem to be borne out in that the responses of sloppy reading did not outnumber the choice of strict reading in the cases with core binding. However, this can be explained, because all the sentences with TSC-only violations had longer than bi-clausal structure (to match the length with those with SSC violations), which could increase the possibility of strict reading, even in the context of core binding.

By results iii), our fourth prediction, which expected that the different structural conditions would play a role in deciding different degree of grammaticality, is not borne out.

Finally, the results with multiple potential antecedent filler items (cf. 7a) showed that in the presence of multiple potential LD antecedents, it seems that *caki-casin* demonstrated a strong preference for the most non-local LD antecedent (subject), rather than closer potential antecedents. This can be implied from the fact that the subjects who assigned higher grammaticality score to this type of sentences (45% of all the responses in this sentence type) also demonstrated a preference for the strict reading in VP-ellipsis (92% of all the responses with higher grammaticality score), indicating that LD-bound *caki-casin* is being licensed as an exempt anaphor, even in the presence of local antecedent. Subjects who scored low on these sentences in turn chose none of the reading (i.e. regarding those items as not interpretable) or the sloppy reading (i.e. trying to treat long-distance bound *caki-casin* as a core anaphor, despite the fact that *caki-casin*, unlike *caki*, cannot be a core long-distance anaphor.).

We take the overall results to robustly indicate that *caki-casin* can be LD-bound, and when it is, it behaves as an exempt anaphor. That is, local vs. LD property of anaphors is orthogonal to the core-exempt distinction. Therefore, the existence of LDAs in a language does not rule out exempt local anaphors in the same language, as already shown in Oshima (2006) and Kim and Yoon (2006). Approaches that take LDAs to be exclusively exempt anaphors (Y. Huang 1994) do not fare well in light of these results. Results also bear on the question of whether the domains of core and exempt binding are necessarily disjoint. While Pollard & Sag (1992) assumed that exempt binding (in English) comes in only when core binding is unavailable (regarding which Huang and Liu 2001 agree), the results with multiple potential (local and non-local) antecedents indicate that core and exempt binding may not be mutually exclusive in Korean, similar to the claim made for Chinese *ziji* by Pollard & Xue (2001).

Acknowledgment

This study is a part of a dissertation project supported by National Science Foundation (NSF) dissertation grant (ID# 0616432; PI: Montrul, S., CO-PI: Yoon, J.).

References

Cantrall, W. R. 1969. On the nature of the reflexive in English. PhD dissertation, University of Illinois at Urbana-Champaign.

Chomsky, N. 1980. On binding. *Linguistic Inquiry* 11: 1-46.

Chomsky, N. 1981. *Lectures in Government and Binding*. Dordrecht: Foris.

Chomsky, N. 1986b. *Knowledge of Language: Its Nature, Origina, and Use*, New York: Praeger.

Cole, P., G. Hermon & C.-T. J. Huang. 2001. Introduction: Long-distance reflexives: The State of the Art. *Syntax and Semantics* 33: xiii-xlvii.

Cole, P., G. Hermon & L-M. Sung. 1990. Principles and parameters of long-distance reflexives. *Linguistic Inquiry* 21 (1): 1-22.

Iida, M. 1992. Context and Binding in Japanese. PhD Thesis. Standford University.

Kang, B-M. 1998. Grammar and the use of language: Korean reflexives 'caki, 'casin', and caki-casin'. *Kwuk-e-hak* 31: 165-204.

Katada, F. 1991. The LF representation of anaphors. *Linguistic Inquiry* 22: 287-313.

Kim, J-H. & H-S. J. Yoon. 2006. An Empirical Study of the Long-Distance Binding of the Anaphor *Caki-casin* in Korean. *Harvard Studies in Korean Lingusitics XI*: 493-505. Korea: Hanshin Publishing Company.

Huang, Y. 1994. The syntax and pragmatics of anaphora: a study with special reference to Chinese. *Cambridge studies in linguistics 70*: 299-317. Cambridge, NY: Cambrige University Press.

Huang, C.-T. J. & C.-S. L. Liu. 2001. Logophoricity, attitude, and *ziji* at the interface. *Syntax and Semantics* 33: 141-195.

Maling, J., J-S. Jun & S-W. Kim. 2000. Case-marking on durational adverbials revisited. *Selected Papers from the Twelfth International Conference on Korean Linguistics*, eds. H.-D. Ahn & N. Kim: 323-335. Seoul, Kyungjin Mwunhwasa.

Oshima, D. 2006. On empathic and logophoric binding. *Research on Language and Computation* 5 (1): 19-35.

Pollard, C. J., & I. A. Sag. 1992. Anaphors in English and the scope of Binding Theory. *Linguistic Inquiry* 23: 261-303.

Pollard, C. & P. Xue. 2001. Syntactic and non-syntactic constraints on long-distance reflexives. *Long Distance Reflexives. Syntax and Semantics Series*, eds. P. Cole, G. Hermon and J. Huang: 317-342. Academic Press.

Reinhart, T. & E. Reuland. 1993. Reflexivity. *Linguistic Inquiry* 24 (4): 657-720.

Runner, J. T., R. S.Sussman & M. K. Tanenhaus. 2002. Logophors in Possessed Picture Noun Phrases. *WCCFL 21 Proceedings*, eds. L. Mikkelsen and C. Potts: 401-414. Sommerville, MA: Casadilla Press.

Sells, P. 1987. Aspects of logophoricity. *Linguistic Inquiry* 18 (3): 445-479.

Ying, H.G. 2005. Second language learners' interpretation of reflexive anaphora in VP-ellipsis: A relevance theory perspective. *Language Sciences* 27 (5): 551-570.

Yoon, J-M. 1989. Long-distance Anaphors in Korean and Their Crosslinguistic Implications. In *Papers from the 25th Annual Regional Meetings of the Chicago Linguistic Society*: 479-495, Chicago, IL: The Society.

Three Types of Korean Comparatives*

SO-YOUNG PARK
University of Southern California

1. Introduction

Comparatives in English, descriptively, are divided into two types depending on the category following *than*: phrasal comparatives and clausal comparatives, as exemplified in (1a) and (1b) respectively.

(1) a. Mary is taller than ***John***.   (phrasal comparatives)
   b. Mary is taller than ***John is***.   (clausal comparatives)

Clausal comparatives have been analyzed as follows (Heim 1985); the preposition *than* takes a CP-complement and the Spec of the CP position is occupied by a *wh*-operator which binds a degree variable in the gradable predicate. The gradable predicate inside the *than*-clause is elided under identity with that of the matrix clause by Comparative Deletion (Bresnan 1973).

* Special thanks to Roumyana Pancheva for her numerous discussions and suggestions. Also, many thanks to Joseph Aoun, Jean-Roger Vergnaud, Hagit Borer, Audrey Li, and Hajime Hoji for their comments. I am also grateful to Dongsik Lim, Hyena Byun, Juyoul Kim, and Semoon Hoe for their help with Korean data. Finally, I would like to thank the audience at 2006 J/K for comments and questions, in particular, Chungmin Lee, John Whitman, Toshiko Oda, and James Yoon.

407

When it comes to the syntax of phrasal comparatives, on the other hand, there have been two distinct approaches: the direct phrasal analysis (Hankamer 1973, Napoli 1983) and the reduced clausal analysis (Heim 1985, Hazout 1995, Hackl 2000, etc.), as represented in (2a) and (2b) respectively.

(2) a. Mary is taller [$_{PP}$ than [$_{DP}$ John]]   (direct phrasal)
   b. Mary is taller [$_{PP}$ than [$_{CP}$ wh_1 John ~~is d_1 tall~~]] (reduced clausal)

The direct phrasal analysis contends that *John*, as a DP, originates as the complement of *than* and there is no elliptical clausal structure involved. The reduced clausal analysis, by contrast, argues that phrasal comparatives always have full clausal structures which are masked by PF-deletion.

The direct phrasal analysis has a problem that two distinct *-er*s emerge depending on the structures of *than*'s complement; when *than* take a CP complement, *-er* takes a definite degree *d* as its argument. This meaning of *-er* cannot hold for the *-er* which directly combines with a DP denoting an individual of type *e* (Kennedy 1997). The uniformity of *-er,* on the other hand, can directly follow from the reduced clausal analysis. But this analysis has been posed syntactic challenges regarding Case-dependency or extraction of *than*'s complement (Napoli 1983).

In this paper, I propose three types of Korean comparatives, depending on what the complement of *-pota* 'than' is: a CP, a small clause, and a measure phrase DegP (as also argued in Pancheva (2006) on the basis of Slavic data). The findings require the revision of the direct phrasal analysis as well as the reduced clausal analysis of phrasal comparatives. Also, novel syntactic arguments are provided in support of the presence or the absence of a clausal structure in phrasal comparatives.

In Section 2, I illustrate the typical patterns of Korean comparatives. In Section 3, I propose the analysis of each type of comparatives, and in Section 4, the main claims are recapitulated

2. Data: Korean Comparatives

Korean comparatives can be divided into two types depending on the presence or the absence of the complementizer *-kes*. The comparatives which involve *-kes* have clausal structures, as exemplified in (3) below.

(3) na-nun [Mary-ka [e] ssun ***kes***]-pota te kin nonmwun-ul ssessta.
   I-top Mary-nom wrote comp-than -er long paper-acc wrote
   'I wrote a longer paper than Mary did.'

In the complement clause of *-pota* 'than' in (3), a verb is present but its object is realized as null. I call this type of comparatives *-kes*-comparatives.

Comparatives without *-kes*, on the other hand, correspond to phrasal comparatives, where verbs are missing and only noun phrasal complements appear at surface. But, depending on the presence or the absence of Case marking prior to *-pota*, the phrasal comparatives are further divided into two sub-types: CM (Case-Marked) comparatives and non-CM (non Case-Marked) comparatives, as illustrated in (4) and (5) respectively.

(4) na-nun [Mary-*eykey*]-pota Sue-eykey te   manhun sakwa-lul cwuessta.
    I-top Mary-dat-than   Sue-dat -er many apple-acc gave
    'I gave more apples to Sue than to Mary.'

(5) na-nun [Mary]-pota Sue-lul te   salanghanta.
    I-top Mary-than   Sue-acc -er love
    'I love Sue more than Mary.' / 'I love Sue more than Mary does.'

In the CM-comparative in (4), a dative-marked DP occurs as the complement of *-pota*, while in the non-CM comparative in (5), a bare DP appears as the complement. Non-CM comparative (5) is ambiguous depending on the way in which the complement of *-pota*, *Mary*, is to be interpreted; *Mary* can receive either an object or a subject interpretation.

I will address another type of phrasal comparatives, where a complement of *-pota* consists of a measure phrase, rather than a DP which acts as an event participant, as exemplified in (6) below.

(6) na-nun [170cm]-pota   te   khuta.
    I-top   170cm-than   -er   tall   'I am taller than 170cm.'

Let us call this type of comparatives MP (Measure Phrase) comparatives.

3. The Proposal: Three Types of Comparatives

In what follows, I propose that Korean has three types of comparatives; one type has a degree clause with a CP (i.e. *-kes*-comparatives and CM comparatives), another type has a small clausal structure (i.e. Non-CM comparatives), and the third type has a DegP structure (i.e. MP comparatives).

3.0 Assumptions

There have been two main streams in analyzing the syntax of degree expressions: the classical analysis (Bresnan 1973, Heim 2000) and the Deg-headed analysis (Abney 1987, Kennedy 1999), as shown in (7a) and (7b).

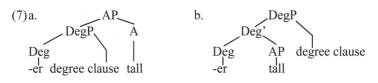

I assume, with the classical analysis given in (7a), the structure in which the Deg Head -*er* and a degree clause form a constituent.[1] In the system of (7a) but not in (7b), the Deg Head and its degree clause can undergo QR together because they form one constituent.

In addition to the assumption of the classical analysis, I introduce the quantity functional projection (#P, Borer 2005) for the locus for gradability. The quantity projection is assumed to serve to introduce a degree argument, severing it from its lexical predicates (Pancheva 2006, Svenonius and Kennedy 2006). I assume the following structure given in (8).

(8) *QR*

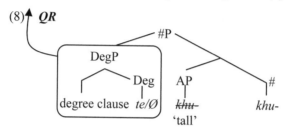

'tall'

In (8), the adjective *khu*- 'tall' of type $<e,t>$ head-raises to the # Head, yielding a gradable predicate of type $<d, <e,t>>$. The DegP undergoes QR, leaving behind a degree variable d^2. Also, I assume the late merger analysis (Bhatt and Pancheva's 2004), whereby a degree clause in Korean is merged late to the comparative quantifier's QR-ed position.

When it comes to elliptical elements, there have been discussions on the question as to what the syntactic status of elliptical elements in the grammar, as one of the phonologically null elements. There are two options; one is to reduce the elliptical elements to one sub-type of traces, which is subject to the conditions on syntactic movement such as the ECP (Empty Category Principle) (Lobeck 1995). The other option is to assimilate the elliptical elements with null pronominals. However, those two options have been rejected (Johnson 2001, Aoun and Li 2006).

I assume a null element, apart from traces as well as pronominals. This null element is semantically empty and exists as a categorially neutral proform in the lexicon, which can be employed in syntactic numeration. Along

---

[1] Refer to Bhatt and Pancheva (2004), for the drawbacks of the Deg-headed analysis. The Deg-Headed analysis cannot account for the facts regarding QR and selection restrictions between -*er* and its argument *than*-clause.

[2] I claim that Korean comparatives involve degree variables, contrary to Japanese comparatives. Beck et al. (2004) argues that Japanese comparatives do not involve degree operator movement. Korean comparatives exhibit negative island effects, scope-interactions with intensional verbs, in contrast to Japanese comparatives reported in Beck et al. (2004), which demonstrate that Korean comparatives involve degree operator movement.

the lines of the syntax-driven approach (Marantz 1997, Borer 2005), I assume that the category of this pro-form is determined by the projection which selects it in the syntax[3]. The semantic content of this pro-form is recovered by making reference to its linguistic antecedent or a contextually salient antecedent at LF (Fiengo and May 1994).

3.1 Type I: -Kes Comparatives and CM Comparatives with CP

Based on the assumptions laid out in Section 3.0, let us get into the first type of comparatives with CP structures. I argue that *-kes* comparatives and CM comparatives have degree clauses with CP structures.

3.1.1 -Kes Comparatives

-Kes comparatives exemplified in (3) have degree clauses with CP structures, as indicated by the complementizer *-kes*. I propose the structure of *-kes* comparatives, as represented in (9) below.

(9) a. na-nun [Mary-ka [e] ssun ***kes***]-pota te kin nonmwun-ul ssessta.
　　 I-top　Mary-nom wrote comp-than -er long paper-acc　　 wrote
　　 'I wrote a longer paper than Mary did.'

b. [$_{VP}$[$_{DegP}$ [Mary-ka [e] ssun　kes]-pota te] [$_{VP}$ te d-kin nonmwun-ul..]]
　　　　　　　Mary-nom wrote cmp-than -er　　 -er long paper-acc
　　　　　　　　　　　(QR of Deg & late merge of its restrictor)

c. [$_{VP}$ [$_{CP}$ Mary-ka [d-kin nonmwun] ssun kes]-pota te
　　　　　Mary-nom　long　paper　　　wrote comp-than -er

　　　[$_{VP}$ te [d-kin nonmwun-ul] ss-]]
　　　　　 -er　long paper-acc　　write
　　　　　　　　　　(copying at LF)

d. ∃ d₁[d₁>ıd₂(Mary wrote a d₂-long paper) and I wrote a d₁-long paper]

The comparative quantifier undergoes QR and adjoins to its scope position followed by late merge of its restrictor, a *-pota*-clause, as shown in (9b). In (9b), we see that inside the degree clause, an empty DP is merged as an object[4]. Next, the reference of the empty DP is recovered by copying the

---

[3] This assumption is tenable, because an elliptical element is always a selected element by a Head (Lobeck 1995, Merchant 2004, Aoun and Li 2006).

[4] I claim that what is elided in *-kes*-comparatives is an object DP, rather than a VP. I will not get into the detailed arguments in this paper, due to the space limit. In Japanese and Korean, lexical verbs are present and their objects are realized as null in the contexts corresponding to English-like VP-ellipsis constructions. The question as to what is missing in these constructions has been discussed, in close relation with the availability of a sloppy reading. The VP-ellipsis account argues that the element which is missing is a VP and a sloppy reading is derived from an elided VP which involves λ-abstraction (Otani and Whitman 1991). However,

corresponding matrix DP, as represented in (9c). Inside the degree clause, degree abstraction is applied and its degree is compared with the degree which has been abstracted from the matrix clause, as represented in (9d).

I analyze a degree clause led by -*kes* as having a CP structure as given in (10a), rather than an NP free relative structure given in (10b). The morpheme -*kes* in degree clauses is, thus, analyzed as a complementizer.

(10) a. [CP   -*kes*]
     b. [NP [CP   ]   -*kes*]

The analysis of a -*kes*-clause as having a free relative structure yields a consequence that the degree clause would involve an individual variable, rather than a degree variable. But, there is evidence in support of the involvement of degree variables in Korean comparatives. Comparative (11), for instance, cannot be interpreted without assuming a degree variable.

(11) John-un [CP nay-ka   mitessten kes]-pota   te sengsilhata.
     John-top   I-nom   believed   comp-than   -er truthful
     'John is more truthful than I believed.'

In (11), we cannot postulate an individual variable which corresponds to the degree clause. Rather, the -*kes*-clause represents the degree of truthfulness.

Also, Korean comparatives exhibit negative island effects, as exemplified in (12) below, which shows that they involve degree variables.

(12) *John-un [amwuto sa-*cianhun* kes]-pota te pissan   chayk-ul
     John-top anybody buy-neg   comp-than-er expensive book-acc
     sassta.
     bought '*John bought a more expensive book than nobody did.'

Negative island effects have been received a syntactic account (Rizzi 1990) or a semantic account (Kroch 1989, Fox and Hackl to appear). But the crucial point here is that Korean comparatives behave like *wh*-movement with respect to negative islands. The unacceptability of (12) can be captured only with the assumption of degree variables; we cannot define a maximal degree d such that nobody bought a d-expensive book (von Stechow 1984). In sum, Korean comparatives necessitate degree variables, and we are left with one option of -*kes*-clauses with having a CP-structure, instead of a free relative structure.

---

this VP-ellipsis account has been falsified (Hoji 1998, Kim 1999). Hoji (1998) argues that sloppy readings in Japanese, addressed in Otani and Whitman (1991), are not genuine sloppy readings but rather sloppy-like readings, which arise from the way that a null argument is recovered. Kim (1999) also argues that null object constructions in Korean do not involve VP-ellipsis, but rather involve ellipsis of an object argument.

I argue that *-kes*-clauses involve degree operator movement, leaving behind a degree variable, as also evidenced from island effects in (13).

(13) a.*John-un [[$_{Complex\ NP}$ ku-ka   mekesstanun cwucang]-ul mitnun kes]
　　　John-top   he-nom ate   claim-acc   believe cmp
　　　-pota te manhun sakwa-lul mekessta.
　　　than   -er many   apple-acc ate
　　　'*John ate more apples than he believed the claim that he ate.'
　　b.* John-un [[$_{Adjunct}$ chayk-ul ilk-konase] sayngkakhankes]-pota   te
　　　John-top   book-acc read-after   thought   comp-than -er
　　　manhun   capci-lul   ilkessta.
　　　many   magazine-acc read
　　　'*John read more magazines than he thought after reading books.'

The island effects can directly follow from syntactic movement, whereby the operator *Op$_i$*, presumably at the Spec of CP position, binds the degree variable *t$_i$*, as schematically represented in (14) for sentence (13a).

(14) [$_{CP}$ ***Op$_i$*** $_{island}$ ku-ka ***t$_i$***-Ø mekesstanun cwucang]-ulmitnun kes]
　　　　　　　　he-nom   ate   claim-acc   believe comp

3.1.2 CM Comparatives

CM comparatives have degree clauses with CP structures. I propose the semantic interpretation and the structure given in (15b) and (15c) below for CM comparative (4).

(15) a.na-nun [Mary-*eykey*]-pota Sue-eykey te   sakwa-lul cwuessta.
　　　I-top   Mary-dat-than   Sue-dat   more apple-acc gave
　　　'I gave more apples to Sue than to Mary.'
　　b.∃ d$_1$[d$_1$>$_{\iota}$d$_2$ (I gave d$_2$-many apples to Mary) and I gave d$_1$-many apples to Sue]

c.

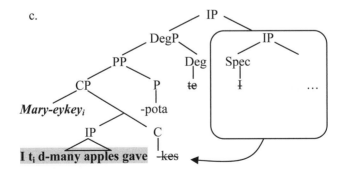

The degree clause has a CP structure and an empty element selected by the C Head turns out to be an IP. The dative-marked argument *Mary-eykey* has undergone movement to the Spec of CP position (or to the Spec of FocusP position, as suggested by Merchant (2004)). Let us suppose that the complementizer -*kes* has cliticized onto the lower I/V Head. As a result, -*kes* should be omitted whenever an empty IP is merged. The semantic content of the empty IP is fixed by copying the matrix IP at LF, avoiding the ACD (Antecedent Contained Deletion). Degree abstraction takes place in the degree clause and the degree is compared with the degree abstracted from the matrix clause, as shown in (15b). CM-comparatives involve clausal structures, which can be supported by the evidence concerning Case connectivity effects (Heim 1985, Hazout 1995).

In (15c), the dative-marked argument undergoes movement, which, in turn, yields a prediction that a locality condition arise (similar facts in sluicing contexts, Fukaya and Hoji 1999). This is borne out to be true, as in (16).

(16) *na-nun [Mary-eykey]-pota [$_{Comp\ NP}$ ku-ka   John-eykey sakwa-lul
     I-top   Mary-dat-than   he-nom John-dat   apple-acc
     cwuesstanun cwucang]-ul te kwutkey   mitnunta.
     gave   claim-acc   -er strongly believe
     'I believe the claim that he gave apples to John more strongly than
     the claim that he gave apples to Mary (intended).'

The dative-marked argument in (16), *Mary-eykey*, cannot be extracted from the complex NP island context. After IP-copying, the LF representation of the degree clause will be like (17) below.

(17) [$_{CP}$ ***Mary-eykey***$_i$ [$_{IP}$ nay-ka [$_{island}$ ku-ka *t*$_i$ sakwa-lul cwuesstanun
     Mary-dat   I-nom   he-nom   apple-acc   gave
     cwucang]-ul d-kwutkey mitnun kes]-pota
     claim-acc   strongly   believe comp-than

3.2 Type II: Non-CM Comparatives with SC

The second type of comparatives has a degree clause with a small clausal structure. Non-CM comparatives fall into this group. I propose the analysis given in (18) for non-CM comparatives as exemplified in (5).

(18) a.na-nun [Mary]-pota Sue-lul   te   salanghanta.
        I-top Mary-than   Sue-acc   -er   love
        'I love Sue more than Mary.'
        'I love Sue more than Mary does.'

     b. [-*er* [λd$_2$ (I love ***Mary*** d$_2$-much) and λd$_1$ I love Sue d$_1$-much]]
        [-*er* [λd$_2$ (***Mary*** love Sue d$_2$-much) and λd$_1$ I love Sue d$_1$-much]]

c.[$_{SC}$] [Mary$_i$] [$_{VP}$ I love t$_i$ d-much]   ]-pota
  [$_{SC}$] [Mary$_i$] [$_{VP}$ t$_i$ love Sue d-much]]-pota
(copying the matrix VP at LF)

Sentence (18a) is ambiguous depending on the way in which the non-Case marked *Mary* is to be interpreted; *Mary* can be interpreted either as an object of my loving or as a subject of loving Sue, as given in (18b). As shown in (18c), the complement of -*pota* 'than' has a small clause structure with an empty VP merged, whose reference is fixed by copying the matrix VP.

Note that in this paper, I propose that non-CM comparatives involve clausal structures, arguing against the direct phrasal analysis of non-CM comparatives. There is evidence in support of this claim. The first piece of evidence comes from Principle C and subject/object asymmetry (Lechner, to appear), as exemplified in (19) below.

(19) a. Mary-nun [ku$_i$]-pota   [John$_i$-uy emma]-lul   te   manhun
      Mary-top   he-than   John-gen mom-acc   -er   many
      salamtul-eykey   sokaysikhiessta.
      people-dat   introduced
      *'Mary introduced John's$_i$ mom to more people than he$_i$ did (subj)
      √'Mary introduced John's$_i$ mom to more people than him$_i$.' (obj)
   b. [John$_i$-uy emma]-pota   [ku$_i$]-ka   Mary-lul   te   manhun
      John-gen mom-than   he-nom   Mary-acc   -er   many
      salamtul-eykey   sokaysikhiessta.
      people-dat   introduced
      √'He$_i$ introduced Mary to more people than John's$_i$ mom did.'(subj)
      *'He$_i$ introduced Mary to more people than John's$_i$ mom.'   (obj)

On the condition that *John* and *ku* 'he' are coindexed, (19a) can only have the reading that *ku*, the complement of -*pota*, is interpreted as an object. (19a) does not allow the reading that *ku* is interpreted as a subject. On the other hand, (19b) only has the reading that *John-uy emma* 'John's mom', the complement of -*pota*, is construed as a subject, instead of an object.

The direct phrasal analysis cannot account for this asymmetry. This fact can be captured only under the assumption that non-CM comparatives involve underlying clausal structures. The degree clause of (19a) can be represented as in (20) below.

(20) a. *[$_{SC}$ [$_{DP}$ *he$_i$*] [$_{VP}$introduce *John's$_i$* mom to d-many people]]-pota
          (*subject interpretation due to Condition C)
   b. √[$_{SC}$ [$_{DP}$ *he$_i$*] [$_{VP}$ Mary introduce t$_i$ to d-many people]]-pota
          (√object interpretation)

(20a) represents the structure of the degree clause when *ku* 'he', the complement of *-pota*, is interpreted as a subject, which should be ruled out due to the violation of Condition C. The configuration in (20b) is legitimate, which correctly predicts the availability of the object interpretation.

The following structures given in (21) stand for those of (19b).

(21) a. √[$_{SC}$ [$_{DP}$ ***John$_i$ mom***] [$_{VP}$introduce him$_i$ to d-many people]]-pota
    (√subject interpretation)

b. *[$_{SC}$ [$_{DP}$ ***John$_i$ mom***][$_{VP}$ ***he$_i$*** introduce *t$_i$* to d-many people]]-pota
    (*object interpretation due to Condition C)

In (21), only (21a), when *John's mom* is interpreted as a subject, is a legitimate configuration. But, (21b) is prohibited. In sum, the asymmetry shown in (19) supports that non-CM comparatives project a clausal structure.

The second piece of evidence concerns the availability of a sloppy identity reading, as exemplified in (22) below.

(22) John-un   [Mary]-pota *caki* atul-ul   te   manhi salanghanta.
    John-top   Mary-than   self   son-acc -er many   love
    'John loves his son$_i$ more than Mary loves his son$_i$.'   (strict)
    'John loves his son$_i$ more than Mary loves her son$_j$.'   (sloppy)

The degree clause in (22) can have either a strict reading or a sloppy reading. Note that the anaphor *caki* 'self', which has been characterized by its subject-oriented property, appears in the matrix clause. The sloppy reading necessitates copying of the matrix VP in which λ-abstraction takes place and *caki* is bound by the new subject *Mary*, which, in turn, suggests that non-CM comparatives involve underlying clausal structures.

I conclude that non-CM comparatives have clausal structures. But non-CM comparatives should be differentiated from CM comparatives with respect to their clausal structures. I proposed that CM comparatives have full CP structures, while non-CM comparatives have small clausal structures. The necessity of this contrast correlates to the well-known observation that small clauses are transparent for Case-licensing from a selecting Head. A non-Case marked arguments of *-pota* 'than' must be in a position which is transparent for Case-assignment by *-pota*. In contrast, a Case-marked argument of *-pota* should be in a position which is opaque to Case-assignment by the postposition, and otherwise they would be doubly Case-marked. In order to satisfy those conditions, I propose that non-CM comparatives have small clausal structures, where a DP can be governed by the postposition *-pota* and get assigned Case by *-pota* without serious interference. But, CM-comparatives involve full CP structures, and thereby the postposition *-pota* assigns Case to the entire CP degree clause and a Case-marked argument is within the CP.

The implementation of small clausal structures yields desirable consequences. First of all, we can obtain the uniformity of a comparative morpheme[5], by positing a clausal structure with degree abstraction out of a DP complement of *-pota*. This position sharply contrasts with Kennedy (1997), which claims that there are two different *-er*s depending on the types of its complement, as represented in (24a) and (24b) respectively.

(23) a. Mary is taller than ***John is***.
　　 b. Mary is taller than ***John***.

(24)

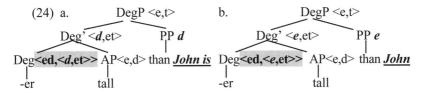

When *than* takes a clausal complement where degree abstraction is applied, as illustrated in (23a) and (24a), the comparative Head *-er* takes the complement of type *d*. On the other hand, when *than* takes a phrasal complement, as shown in (23b) and (24b), *-er* takes a complement of type *e*, because degree abstraction cannot take place with this DP structure. But, given that the comparative quantifier is pronounced the same in English, the claim of two distinct *-er*s seems to be untenable. In my analysis, however, I postulate a clausal source for the phrasal comparative in which degree abstraction is applicable. The computation of *-er* can be achieved in the same fashion we did when *-er* takes a clausal complement. Thus, we can dispense with the need for positing the two different *-er*s.

Also, the following examples, which have been used as arguments in support of the direct phrasal analysis for phrasal comparatives, cannot hold given that they have small clausal structures.

(25) a. John is taller than ***me***
　　 b. *John is taller than ***me*** am.　　　　　　　　　　(Napoli 1983)
(26) a. ***Who*** is John taller than?

---

[5] A degree clause with a CP structure denotes a maximal degree of type *d* (Jacobson 1995, Rullman 1995), where a *wh*-operator binds a degree variable. In contrast, a degree clause with a small clausal structure can be interpreted as a predicate of degrees of type <d,t>. Following Pancheva (2006), I assume that there are two *than*s; one *than* which takes a definite degree and returns a set of degrees of type <d, <d,t>>, and the other *than* which takes a set of degrees and returns a part of it, i.e., a set of degrees of type <<d,t>, <d,t>>. Given this assumption, a uniform meaning of the comparative quantifier of type <<d,t>, <<d,t>,t>> can be achieved, on a par with the quantifiers over individuals of type <<e,t>, <<e,t>,t>>. This system sheds light on the parallelism between the domains of degrees and individuals in the core grammar.

b. *__Who__* is John taller than is? (Hankamer 1973)

(25a) shows that the complement DP is Case-dependent on *than*, while in the clausal version as in (25b) the DP is not Case-dependent. The apparent phrasal complement of *than* in (26a) can be extracted, in contrast to its clausal version in (26b). These examples have posed problems to the reduced clausal analysis. However, insofar as those examples have small clausal structures, such problems disappear; the DP governed by *than* in (25a) can be assigned accusative Case by *than*. The complement *wh*-word in (26a) can be extracted satisfying the ECP (Empty Category Principle).

3.3 Type III: MP Comparatives with DegP

The third type of comparatives has a DegP structure, without involving any extra clausal structure. I argue that MP comparatives, as exemplified in (6), have this structure, as shown in (27) below.

(27) a. na-nun [170cm]-pota te khuta.
  I-top 170cm-than -er tall 'I am taller than 170cm.'
  b. [-*er* [λd₂ (d₂ = 170cm)]] λd₁ I am d₁-much tall
  c.

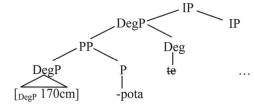

MP comparatives receive the direct phrasal analysis. In terms of semantics, given that a measure phrase denotes a degree (d) or a predicate of degrees (<d, t>) (Schwarzschild 2004), a measure phrase can yield a right interpretation without necessitating the positing of extra clausal structure. In addition to this semantic evidence, there is syntactic evidence as well; MP comparatives, in sharp contrast to CM comparatives, tolerate island effects, as exemplified in (28) below.

(28) a.*na-nun [Mary-eykey]-pota [ku-ka John-eykey sakwa-lul
  I-top Mary-dat-than he-nom John-dat apple-acc
  cwuesstanun cwucang]-ul te kwutkey mitnunta.
  gave claim-acc -er strongly believe
  'I believe the claim that he gave apples to John more strongly than the claim that he gave apples to Mary (intended).'

b.(?)na-nun   [5 kwen]-pota   [Mary-ka   7 kwen   chayk-ul
    I-top   5 cl-than   Mary-nom 7 cl   book-acc
ilkesstanun cwucang]-ul te kwutkey mitnunta.
read   claim-acc   -er strongly believe
'I believe the claim that Mary read 7 books more strongly than
the claim that she read 5 books.'

There is a radical contrast in acceptability between (28a) and (28b). CM comparatives are sensitive to the island effect, because there is a copying process of a clausal structure and degree operator movement involved, as we saw in (17) before. By contrast, under the same condition, the MP comparative, exemplified in (28b), is well-formed. This suggests that MP comparatives involve no copying process and no operator movement, which corroborates the direct phrasal analysis for MP-comparatives.

4. Conclusion

In this paper, I proposed the three types of comparatives depending on the category of the complement following -pota 'than': a CP, a small clause, and a measure phrase DegP. The findings require the revision of the reduced clausal analysis as well as the direct phrasal analysis; there are indeed comparatives which require the presence of clausal structures in spite of the apparent absence of the structures at surface (i.e. CM-comparatives and Non-CM comparatives). On the other hand, some subset of comparatives does not involve clausal structures (i.e. MP comparatives) and further there are various types of comparatives depending on the size of elliptical sites, not just one full clausal type (i.e. Non-CM comparatives).

References

Aoun, J. and Li, A. 2006. Identifying Empty Categories. Ms. USC.

Beck, S. et al. 2004. Parametric Variation in the Semantics of Comparison: Japanese vs. English. *Journal of East Asian Linguistics* 13: 289-344.

Bhatt, R. and Pancheva, R. 2004. Late Merger of Degree Clauses. *Linguistic Inquiry* 35: 1-45.

Borer, H. 2005. *In Name Only*. New York: Oxford University Press.

Bresnan, J. 1973. The Syntax of the Comparative Clause Construction in English. *Linguistic Inquiry* 4: 275-343.

Fiengo, R. and May, R. 1994. *Indices and Identity*. Cambridge: MIT Press.

Fox, D. and Hackl, M. 2006. On the Universal Density of Measurement. *Linguistics and Philosophy* 29: 537-586.

Fukaya, T. and Hoji, H. 1999. Stripping and Sluicing in Japanese and Some Implications. *WCCFL 18 Proceedings* 145-158.

Hackl, M. 2000. Comparative Quantifiers. Doctoral Dissertation. MIT.

Hankamer, J. 1973. Why There are Two *Than*'s in English. *CLS* 9:179-191.

Hazout, I. 1995. Comparative Ellipsis and Logical Form. *Natural Language and Linguistic Theory* 13: 1-37.

Heim, I. 1985. Notes on Comparatives and Related Matters. Ms. University of Texas. Austin.

Hoji, H. 1998. Null Object and Sloppy Identity in Japanese. *Linguistic Inquiry* 29: 127-152.

Jacobson, P. 1995. On the Quantificational Force of English Free Relatives. *Quantification in Natural Language*. ed. E. Bach et al. 451-486. Dordrecht: Kluwer.

Johnson, K. 2001. What VP Ellipsis can Do, and What it can't. *The Handbook of Contemporary Syntactic Theory*, eds. M. Baltin & C. Collins. 439-479. Malden: Blackwell.

Kennedy, C. 1997. Projecting the Adjective: The Syntax and Semantics of Gradability and Comparison. Doctoral dissertation. UCSC.

Kim, S-W. 1999. Sloppy/Strict Identity, Empty Objects, and NP Ellipsis. *Journal of East Asian Linguistics* 8: 255-284.

Kroch, A. 1989. Amount Quantification, Referentiality, and Long wh-Movement. Ms. UPenn.

Lechner, W. to appear. On Binding Scope and Ellipsis Scope. *Ellipsis*, ed. K. Johnson. New York: Oxford University Press.

Lobeck, A. 1995. *Ellipsis*. Oxford: Oxford University Press.

Marantz, A. 1997. No Escape from Syntax. *Proceedings of the 21ˢᵗ Annual Penn Linguistics Colloquium.* 201-224.

Merchant, J. 2004. Fragments and Ellipsis. *Linguistics and Philosophy* 27: 661-738.

Napoli, J. D. 1983. Comparative Ellipsis: a Phrase Structure Account. *LI* 14: 675-694.

Otani, K. and Whitman, J. 1991. V-Raising and VP-Ellipsis. *Linguistic Inquiry* 22: 345-358.

Pancheva, R. 2006. Phrasal and Clausal Comparatives in Slavic. *Proceedings of FASL* 14: 146-167.

Rizzi, L. 1990. *Relativized Minimality*. Cambridge: MIT Press.

Rullman, H. 1995. Maximality in the Semantics of wh-Constructions. Doctoral Dissertation. Umass.

Schwarzschild, R. 2004. Measure Phrases as Modifiers of Adjectives. Recherches Linguistiques de Vincennes 35:207-228.

Von Stechow, A. 1984. Comparing Semantic Theories of Comparison. Journal of Semantics 3: 1-77.

Svenonius, P. and Kennedy, C. 2006. Northern Norweigian Degree Questions and the Syntax of Measurement. *Phases of Interpretation.* ed. M. Frascarelli. 133-161. Berlin: Mouton de Gruyter.

On the Syntax of External Possession in Korean

REIKO VERMEULEN
University College London

1. Introduction

The relation of possession is expressed in great many ways across languages. One typical way is for the possessor to appear in the genitive case inside the nominal projection headed by the modified argument. However, a number of languages also permit the possessor to be realized as a separate constituent at the clausal level, especially if the modified argument is an object. Such externally realized possessors often behave like clausal arguments themselves, giving the appearance that the clause contains one too many argument for the type of predicate that heads the clause. This phenomenon is often referred to as 'external possession' in the literature (Payne & Barshi 1999) and is illustrated by the Korean example below.

(1)   Mary-ka   John-ul   ecey   tali-lul   cha-ss-ta
        Mary-Nom   John-Acc   yesterday   leg-Acc   kick-Past-Decl
        'Mary kicked John's leg yesterday.'

Here, *John*, a possessor of the object *tali* 'leg' bears accusative case and is realized externally to the object. That *John* does indeed occupy a position at the clausal level can be seen from the fact that a clausal adverbial such as *ecey* 'yesterday' can appear between the two accusative phrases. In the literature on Korean, the construction is known variously as the multiple accusative construction, the possessive accusative construction or the inalienable possessive construction.

A well-known property of this construction is that the external possessor is necessarily interpreted as 'affected' by the event described by the verb (Yoon 1989, 1990). This constraint is said to explain the unacceptability of examples such as (2): it is difficult to construe *Mary*, the external possessor of *moksoli* 'voice', as being affected by John hearing her voice.

(2)   *John-i   Mary-lul   moksoli-lul   tul-ess-ta
       John-Nom   Mary-Acc   voice-Acc   hear-Past-Decl
       'John heard Mary's voice.'   (Yeon 1999: 219)

It has recently been proposed that the external possessor is licensed in a specifier position of a designated functional projection, indicated as FP in (3), whose head assigns it an *affect* θ-role (Ko 2005, Tomioka & Sim 2005[1] for Korean, Pylkkänen 2002 for Hebrew, Lee-Schoenfeld 2006 for German). Tomioka & Sim (2005), for example, argue that FP and VP represent separate events, which are subsequently identified. Consequently, the example in (1) means 'Mary affected John by kicking his leg'.

(3)   Distinct Projection Approach

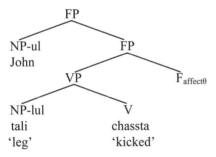

In this paper, I propose that the external possessor is in fact licensed within the VP, as in (4), and argue against the distinct projection approach.

---

[1] Tomioka & Sim (2005), in contrast to the others listed above, argue that the projection represented as FP in (3) is in fact headed by a lexical verb, a phonologically silent verb with the meaning *affect*. Thus, it is a lexical projection, VP, rather than a functional one. However, whether FP in (3) is lexical or functional does not affect the discussion in this paper. The crucial point is that it is a projection distinct from the VP headed by the overt, lexical verb.

(4)   VP approach

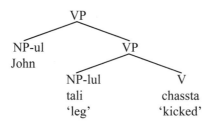

Specifically, I will argue that the external possession construction involves a thematic operation, which I will call 'reassociation'. The operation essentially allows the external possessor to be licensed as an additional argument of the verb (Section 2). The proposal makes some correct predictions regarding the syntactic properties of the construction, which are difficult to capture under the distinct projection approach (Section 3). The proposal also has advantages over other previous analyses which adopt the VP approach, but adopt different types of thematic operations (Section 4). Finally, I argue that the affected interpretation arises due to pragmatics rather than due to a grammatically defined θ-role with the meaning *affect* (Section 5).

The paper concentrates on external possession involving object in Korean. Potential extension of the proposal to other types of constructions, such as external possession involving subject, which is attested in some languages, including Korean, is discussed in the concluding section (Section 6).

2. Reassociation

It is widely assumed that θ-roles are purely syntactic objects and are mapped onto particular semantic representations only at the interface (Grimshaw 1990, Jackendoff 1983, 1990, Zubizarreta 1987, among many others). Thus, in the syntax, verbs such as *kick* simply have two θ-roles in its θ-grid and the θ-roles are associated with their corresponding semantic roles *Agent* and *Patient* only at the interface, as illustrated in (5). More formally, assuming that the verb *kick* has a semantic representation like the one in (6a), the semantic roles refer to parts of this representation which are relevant for interpreting the arguments as Agent and Patient of a kicking event, namely the representations in (6b) and (6c), respectively. An argument that is assigned a particular θ-role usually also replaces the variable in the semantic representation associated with that θ-role.[2] In other words,

---

[2] The proposed analysis does not depend on the neo-Davidsonian approach to semantics. I adopt it here only because it allows simple exposition of which part of semantic information is associated with a θ-role. Moreover, although the representations in (6b) and (6c) are presented as autonomous entities, I will remain agnostic as to their independent existence.

argument-licensing involves two processes: θ-role assignment (syntactic licensing) and replacement of a variable in the associated semantic representation (semantic licensing).

(5) *kick*

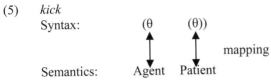

(6) a. *kick*: $\lambda y \lambda x \lambda e$ [kicking (e) & Agent (e, x) & Patient (e, y)]
     b. Agent: $\lambda x \lambda e$ [Agent (e, x)]
     c. Patient: $\lambda y \lambda e$ [Patient (e, y)]

The view that θ-roles and their associated semantic representations exist independently of each other suggests that a single θ-role can, in principle, be associated with more than one semantic representation in the course of a derivation, if an intelligible interpretation can be obtained. More specifically, a derivation such as (7) should be possible. Here, the verb's internal θ-role is associated with one semantic representation, Sem_2, at V, but at VP it is associated with another representation, Sem_3, which is linked to the verb's complement, NP. I argue that such an operation, which I call *reassociation*, is indeed possible and it licenses external possession.[3]

(7) *Reassociation*

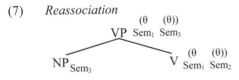

Reassociation is possible only if Sem_3 contains an unbound variable. Otherwise, an argument that may be assigned the verb's θ-role reassociated with Sem_3 cannot be licensed semantically. When does such a situation arise, however? It arises if the NP in the above structure is headed by an argument-taking noun and if that argument is realized as a bound pronoun. A bound pronoun can, of course, function as a syntactic argument and therefore be assigned a θ-role, but it translates as a variable in the semantics, because it depends on another item in the sentence for its interpretation.

The point is illustrated below in (8a) for the case of Korean external possession. The noun's possessor argument is realized as *pro* internally to the nominal projection. It is assigned the noun's θ-role, but in replacing the

---

[3] The θ-Criterion (Chomsky 1981) presumably applies to the combination of a θ-role and its associated semantic representation. As such, reassociation does not cause a violation of the Criterion.

variable in the associated semantic representation *Poss*, shown in (8c), the pronoun, represented as z, leaves an unbound variable in the representation, as in (8d).[4] The absence of the associated θ-role for *Poss* at NP indicates that the θ-role has been assigned.

(8)   a.

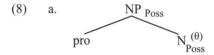

    b. ⟦N⟧: $\lambda y \lambda x$ [n (x) & Possessor (y, x)]
    c. Poss at N: $\lambda y \lambda x$ [Possessor (y, x)]
    d. Poss at NP: $\lambda y \lambda x$ [Possessor (y, x)](z) → λx [Possessor (z, x)]

In the semantics, I argue that reassociation has the effect of introducing a lambda operator into the representation that would otherwise contain an unbound variable, as shown below.

(9)   *Reassociation*: λx [Possessor (z, x)] → $\lambda z \lambda x$ [Possessor (z, x)]

If (8a) appears as an internal argument of the verb, the verb's internal θ-role can undergo reassociation with *Poss* and license an additional internal argument. This additional argument, I argue, is the external possessor, as illustrated in (10).

(10)

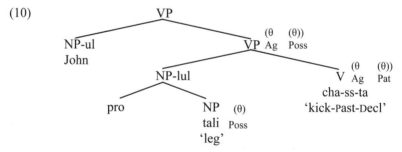

The external possessor *John* is licensed syntactically as a direct object of the verb, as it receives an internal θ-role of a transitive verb, but is interpreted semantically as a possessor of the verb's thematic object, as the associated semantic representation specifies it as such. A slightly more detailed semantic derivation of this structure is provided in the appendix.

The structure in (10) has the effect that *pro* is bound by the external possessor *John*. Thus, as far as the binding is concerned, it is similar to cases where a pronoun is bound by a non-quantificational NP, as in the following example (Reinhart 1983).

---

[4] See Vergnaud & Zubizarreta (1992), Ura (1996), and references therein for the view that a possessee assigns its possessor a θ-role.

(11)   John$_i$ loves his$_i$ mother and Bill$_j$ does [~~love his$_j$ mother~~] too.

Moreover, there is evidence for the existence of *pro* within the NP headed by the possessee argument. As noted by Cho (1992, 1993), a pronoun that is coreferential with the external possessor can be spelled out in this position:[5]

(12) $^?$Mary-ka   John$_i$-ul   [(ku$_i$-uy)   tali]-ul   cha-ss-ta
        Mary-Nom   John-Acc   he-Gen   leg-Acc   kick-Past-Decl
                                                        (Cho 1992: 19)

A final remark on reassociation is that it involves a θ-role of a verb. It therefore seems reasonable to assume that the representation with which the θ-role undergoes reassociation would be linked to an argument of the verb. This seems to be in line with other kinds of thematic operations such as light verb constructions, which typically involve verb's arguments.

3. Predictions

The proposed analysis makes three predictions regarding the syntactic behavior of the construction. The predicted properties are difficult to capture under the distinct projection approach. Firstly, the distinct projection approach, particularly Tomioka & Sim's (2005) implementation, assumes that two events are represented. It should therefore be possible to modify the lower VP in (3) consisting of the lexical verb and it's thematic object with adverbials such as *tasi*, 'again', which is able to target the smallest event unit (von Stechow 1998, Son 2004 and references therein).[6] However, the prediction is not borne out, as illustrated by (13). That such modification does not result in semantic anomaly is shown by the grammaticality of the English translation. By contrast, the VP approach presented here predicts this property, as only one event is involved.

(13)   *Mary-ka   John-ul   tasi   tali-lul   cha-ss-ta
        Mary-Nom   John-Acc   again   leg-Acc   kick-Past-Decl
        Intended: 'Mary affected (annoyed) John by again kicking his leg.'

Secondly, as mentioned above, reassociation involves arguments of the verb. Thus, it should be impossible for the possessee to be contained inside an adjunct, as illustrated below.

---

[5] Kitahara (1993) reports similar examples to those in (12) as ungrammatical. D.-I. Cho (1992, 1993) notes however that the acceptability of the example with an overt *pro* improves if the possessor is scrambled away from the *pro*, and attributes the effect to Avoid Pronoun Principle (Chomsky 1981). My informants agree with Cho's judgments.

[6] Thanks to Satoshi Tomioka for pointing this property of *again* out to me (p.c.).

(14)

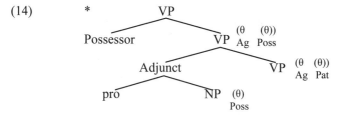

The ungrammaticality of the example in (15a) shows that the prediction is borne out. Here, *cipwung* 'roof' is contained inside an adjunct and its possessor *cip* 'house' cannot be licensed externally. The grammatical example in (15b), where *cipwung* 'roof' is an internal argument of the verb, shows that the relation between *cip* 'house' and *cipwung* 'roof' is a type that can be supported by external possession.

(15) a. *Mary-ka   cip-ul/ey/eyse   cipwung-eyse
          Mary-Nom   house-Acc/Dat/on   roof-on
          John-ul   cha-ss-ta
          John-Acc   kick-Past-Decl
          'Mary kicked John on the roof of the house.'
      b. John-i   cip-ul   cipwung-ul   busu-ess-ta.
          John-Nom   house-Acc   roof-Acc   destroy-Past-Decl
          'John destroyed the roof of the house.'

Unless some independent restrictions are put in place, it is unclear how the above contrast can be accounted for under the distinct projection approach.

Finally, reassociation is potentially a recursive operation: as long as an intelligible interpretation can be obtained from the derivation, there is no restriction on its application. It should therefore be possible for an external possessor itself to be a noun that takes a possessor argument and to license a further external possessor. In other words, more than one external possessor should be permitted within a clause. The example in (16) shows that the prediction is correct (Yoon 1989, inter alia). *John* is the external possessor of *tali*, 'leg', which in turn is the external possessor of *olunccok* 'right side'.

(16) Mary-ka   John-ul   tali-lul   olunccok-ul   cha-ss-ta
      Mary-Nom   John-Acc   leg-Acc   right.side-Acc   kick-Past-Decl
      'Mary kicked the right side of John's leg.'

The above observation is difficult to capture under the distinct projection approach. It would have to assume that the head that licenses an external possessor can be introduced into the structure recursively. However, from a theoretical point of view, this seems an undesirable claim to make, as heads responsible for introducing arguments, be they functional or lexical (see footnote 1), are not usually introduced into the structure recursively.

4. Alternative Approaches in terms of a Thematic Operation

There have been other analyses of external possession in Korean that assume some sort of a thematic operation. Many assimilate their proposed thematic operations to θ-identification (Higginbotham 1985, Speas 1990) or Function Composition (Williams 1994 or in the sense used in Categorial Grammar) with varying effects. In this section, I demonstrate in what ways the present analysis has advantages over them.

J. H.-S. Yoon (1989, 1990) argues that the relevant thematic operation is θ-identification, where the verb's internal θ-role is not assigned to the possessee, but is rather identified with or modified by the θ-role in the possessee's argument structure. Similarly, J.-M. Yoon (1997), who argues that the relevant operation is Function Composition, proposes that the verb does not assign its θ-role to the possessee. The verb simply 'combines' with the possessee, and the possessee's unassigned θ-role is inherited by the argument structure of the verb. In both analyses, one implication is that the possessee is not licensed as an internal argument of the verb and as a consequence, it should not behave like one. However, this prediction is incorrect and there are two pieces of evidence for this.

Firstly, in Korean, nominative and accusative arguments can float quantifiers (Gerdts 1987). It turns out that the external possessor as well as the possessee can host a floating quantifier:

(17) a. Kay-ka   haksayng-ul seys-ul   tali-lul   mul-ess-ta
         dog-Nom   student-Acc three-Acc leg-Acc   bite-Past-Decl
         'The dog bit three students on the leg.'   (O'Grady 1991: 71)
      b. John-un   kemi-lul   tali-lul   seys-ul ppop-ass-ta
         John-Top   spider-Acc   leg-Acc   3-Acc   pull.out-Past-Decl
         'John pulled out three of a spider's legs.'

Secondly, both the external possessor and the possessee can function as the subject of a resultative predicate, a property typical of direct object, and arguably subject, but not of indirect object or non-arguments (Wechsler & Noh 2001 and references cited there). The point is illustrated below for the external possessor in (18a) and for the possessee in (18b).

(18) a. John-un Mary-lul yeppu-key   [meli-lul kkak-(ass)]-ko
         John-Top Mary-Acc pretty-Comp hair-Acc cut-Past –and
         [iphi-ess-ta]]
         dress-Past-Decl
         'John cut Mary's hair and dressed her and as a result she looks pretty.'
      b. Mary-ka   John-ul   tali-lul   mengtul-key cha-ss-ta
         Mary-Nom   John-Acc   leg-Acc   bruised   kick-Past-Decl
         'Mary kicked John's leg until the leg is bruised.'

Mailing & Kim (1992) also propose an analysis in terms of θ-identification, although with a different interpretation from J. H.-S. Yoon (1989, 1990). Crucially, they argue explicitly that the external possessor is not an argument of the verb. However, as we just saw in (17a) and (18a), the external possessor also shows properties associated with direct object.

Cho (1992, 1993) and O'Grady (2002), on the other hand, claim that both the possessee and the external possessor receive a θ-role from the verb, which allows a straight forward account of the observations in (17) and (18). The verb directly assigns a θ-role to the possessee and the unassigned θ-role in the possessee's argument structure is subsequently assigned 'compositionally' by the verb and the possessee together to the external possessor. Although the exact process of compositional θ-role assignment is different for the two authors, the process is unrestricted in both analyses. Consequently, it is unclear how external possession involving an adjunct, which we saw above not to be possible (see (15)), can be ruled out.

5. Affectedness

Recall that the external possessor of an object is interpreted obligatorily as affected by the event described by the verb. The distinct projection approach accounts for this reading by claiming that the external possessor receives a θ-role with the semantic role *affect*. I argue, however, following Shibatani (1994) and Yeon (1999), that the interpretation in fact arises due to pragmatics.

Shibatani claims that cross-linguistically, in constructions with additional arguments, such as external possession, adversative passive constructions (e.g. in Japanese, Korean, Chinese) and ethical dative constructions (e.g. in German, Spanish, Hebrew), the additional arguments must be interpreted as being 'integrated' into the event described by the rest of the clause. They can be integrated most easily if they are interpreted as an inalienable possessor of another argument in the clause and are therefore physically involved in the event. In the absence of such a possessive relation, they may also be integrated by being a participant adversely affected by the event. This claim accounts elegantly for many constructions Shibatani considers in which the additional arguments are interpreted as a possessor, but not affected by the event, or as adversely affected, but not as a possessor.

I agree with Shibatani's claim that the affected reading arises as a result of the external possessor being interpreted as a participant in the event. However, considering that in Korean, the accusative external possessor must be construed both as a possessor of the direct object and as affected, I believe that the possessive interpretation arises by means of reassociation. Moreover, on Shibatani's account, it is not entirely clear why the additional arguments must be interpreted as participants in the event in the first instance. Here, I provide a formal account as to why this is the case.

Recipients of θ-roles in a verb's θ-grid are generally considered to correspond to participants in the eventuality expressed by the verb. The associated semantic representations provide instructions as to how they participate in the eventuality. Thus, in the sentence in (19a), *John's dog* and *Mary's hamster* are understood as participants playing the roles of Agent and Patient in a eating event, respectively, because the verb *eat* has the θ-grid indicated in (19b) and the θ-roles are assigned to these constituents. On the other hand, the possessors *John* and *Mary*, which do not receive θ-roles contained in the verb's θ-grid, are not interpreted as participants of the eating event.

(19) a. John's dog ate Mary's hamster.
      b. ate   (θ   (θ))
              Ag Th

As we saw in Section 2, the external possessor of an object is assigned a θ-role contained in the verb's θ-grid. Consequently, the external possessor must be understood as a participant in the eventuality expressed by the verb. However, the semantic representation linked to the θ-role assigned to the external possessor provides no relevant information concerning participation in the event described by the verb, as it does not have its source in the lexical meaning of the verb. The affected reading arises precisely under such a circumstance due to pragmatics. In the absence of relevant information, if an item is to be interpreted as a participant, it seems only natural that it is somehow affected by the event.

A pragmatic approach to the affected reading like this has advantages over attributing the interpretation to a specific θ-role. Firstly, as noted by Shibatani (1994) and J.-M. Yoon (1997), it explains the widely reported, great variation among speakers on the acceptability of this construction.

Secondly, it also explains the fact that the manner in which the external possessor of an object is affected directly reflects our knowledge of the world. Thus, contrary to what is widely reported in the literature, an accusative external possessor need not be 'adversely' affected. It can be understood as 'positively' affected, as in (20), or be an inanimate item and therefore not be psychologically affected, as in (21).

(20) Uisa-ka   Mary-lul   phal-ul   kochi-ess-ta
      doctor-Nom   Mary-Acc   arm-Acc   cure-Past-Decl
      'The doctor cured Mary's arm.'

(21) Chelswu-ka   sap-ul   caru-lul   cap-ass-ta
      Chelswu-Nom   shovel-Acc   handle-Acc   grab-Past-Decl
      'Chelswu grabbed the handle of the shovel.'

(Tomioka & Sim 2005: 279)

Finally, an accusative external possessor is often reported less accept-able with a stative predicate. Nevertheless, there is a general consensus in the literature that the acceptability improves if the state described is modi-fied in such a way that it becomes easier to construe the external possessor as being a participant in the eventuality (e.g. J. H.-S. Yoon 1989, 1990, J.-M. Yoon 1997, Yeon 1999). This is illustrated by the following examples. The example in (22a) is generally reported as less than perfect. However, as noted by J.-M. Yoon (1997), modification of the eventuality by an adverbial such as *ttwulecikey* 'hard', as in (22b), improves the acceptability. Similarly, in (23a), it is difficult to construe the possessor, *Yenghi*, as being a partici-pant in a state in which someone likes her face. On the other hand, (23b), where the possessee argument has been replaced by *sengkyek* 'personality', is much more acceptable. Considering that liking someone's personality is usually synonymous with liking that person, the possessor of the personal-ity can be readily interpreted as being part of the state in which someone likes that possessor's personality.

(22) a. ??Chelswu-ka   Yenghi-lul   elkul-ul   po-ass-ta
          Chelswu-Nom   Yenghi-Acc   face-Acc   see-Past-Decl
          'Chelswu saw Yenghi's face.'

      b. Chelswu-ka   Yenghi-lul   elkul-ul ttwulecikey   po-ass-ta
          Chelswu-Nom   Yenghi-Acc face-Acc   hard   see-Past-Decl
          'Chelswu looked at Yenghi's face hard [enough to make a hole in it].'
                                        (modified from J.-M. Yoon 1997: 250-52)

(23) a. *Chelswu-ka   Yenghi-lul   elkwul-ul   cohaha-n-ta
          Chelswu-Nom   Yenghi-Acc   face-Acc   like-Pres-Decl
          'Chelswu likes Yenghi's face.'   (J.-M. Yoon 1997: 250)

      b. Nay-ka   Swuni-lul   sengkyek-ul   cohaha-n-ta
          I-Top   Swuni-Acc   personality-Acc like-Pres-Decl
          'I like Swuni's personality.'   (Choo 1994: 129)

Thus, the acceptability of an example containing an accusative external possessor appears to be sensitive to the context, rather than to grammatical notions such as 'stative', which would be expected under the distinct pro-jection approach and has been suggested by Tomioka & Sim (2005).

6. Concluding Remarks

The preceding sections argued that the external possessor of an object is licensed within VP, rather than in the specifier position of a designated pro-jection distinct from VP containing the possessee and the verb. The various syntactic properties of the construction suggest that the claim is on the right track. Moreover, a pragmatic approach to the affected interpretation appears to explain the speaker variation and the sensitivity to the context more naturally than an approach that assumes a grammatically defined *affect* θ-role.

Introduction of a novel thematic operation such as *reassociation* however raises questions regarding its generality. Are there any other phenomena that can be accounted for by this operation? I would like to suggest that the answer is in the affirmative. Firstly, a number of languages exhibit external possession, some involving object, some involving subject (Payne & Barshi 1999). Following Yoon (1989, 1990), I hypothesize that the syntax of external possession is essentially the same cross-linguistically. What regulates the possibility of external possession in each language is the availability of case for the additional argument. In terms of the present proposal, languages may vary with respect to how they realize the possessor argument internally to the possessee NP, namely as *pro* (e.g. Japanese, Korean) or overt pronoun (e.g. Modern Standard Arabic, Hebrew) or they may not realize it at all (e.g. German), but my hypothesis is that the effect is the same: an unbound variable is present in the semantic representation associated with the possessee argument, whose value can be provided by means of reassociation.[7]

Besides external possession, it seems that the proposed operation can be carried over to other types of constructions such as the light verb construction in Italian. As discussed in detail by Samek-Lodovici (2003), Italian has two light verbs which take deverbal nominals as their complements, *fare* and *dare*. The choice between the light verbs is determined by the number of arguments the deverbal nominal has. *Fare*, whose heavy counterpart means 'make', takes nominals with one argument, while *dare*, whose heavy counterpart means 'give', takes nominals with two arguments. An account in terms of reassociation would provide a straightforward explanation for this observation: the number of verb's θ-roles available for reassociation determines the number of semantic arguments of the deverbal nominal that can be realized externally. (see Samek-Lodovici 2003, who proposes a similar operation to *reassociation*, and Vermeulen 2005a: Ch. 6 for further discussion)

Appendix

The semantic derivation of the syntactic structure of external possession presented in this paper, reproduced below, is provided in (25). Much of the semantics of possession I am assuming here is due to Barker (1995).

---

[7]See Vermeulen (2005b) for the lack of affected reading for an external possessor of a subject.

(24)

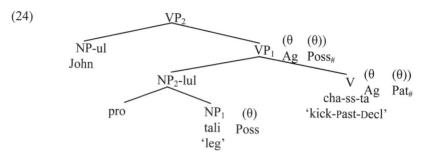

(25)   a. $[\![NP_1]\!]$:

       $\lambda y \lambda x$ [leg (x) & Possessor (y, x)]

     b. $[\![NP_2]\!]$:

       $\lambda y \lambda x$ [leg (x) & Possessor (y, x)](z)   (where z = *pro*)

       $\rightarrow \lambda x$ [leg (x) & Possessor (z, x)] = z's leg

     c. $[\![VP_1]\!]$:

       $\lambda y_2 \lambda x_2 \lambda e$ [kicking (e) & Agent (e, x_2) & Patient (e, y_2)] (z's leg)

       $\rightarrow \lambda x_2 \lambda e$ [kicking (e) & Agent (e, x_2) & Patient (e, z's leg)]

     d.   Re-association:

       $\lambda z \lambda x_2 \lambda e$ [kicking (e) & Agent (e, x_2) & Patient (e, z's leg)]

     e. $[\![VP_2]\!]$:

       $\lambda z \lambda x_2 \lambda e$ [kicking (e) & Agent (e, x_2) & Patient (e, z's leg)] (john)

       $\rightarrow \lambda x_2 \lambda e$ [kicking (e) & Agent (e, x_2) & Patient (e, john's leg)]

Assuming that *tali* 'leg' has the representation in (25a), the presence of *pro* internally to the possessee argument produces a semantic representation appropriate for re-association, one that contains an unbound variable, as in (25b). Obviously, a choice function or an iota operator must be introduced at some stage in this derivation to interpret *tali* 'leg' correctly. However, to facilitate straight forward exposition of the proposed operation, I simply represent the effect of application of such a function by replacing the resultant formula in (25b) by *z's leg*. *Z's leg* then replaces the variable *y* in the semantic representation associated with the verb's argument structure at VP, as in (25c). Re-association applies to this resultant representation, as it contains an unbound variable, *z*, with the effect that a lambda operator is introduced into the representation (25d). With the variable *z* now bound, the external possessor *John* can replace the variable, resulting in its being interpreted as a possessor of *tali* 'leg' (25e).

References

Barker, C. 1995. *Possessive Descriptions*. Stanford: CSLI.

Cho, D.-I. 1992. Multiple Accusative Constructions and Verb Movement. *MIT Working Papers in Linguistics* 16: 11-25.

Cho, D.-I. 1993. Inalienable-type Multiple Accusative Constructions in Korean and Japanese. *Japanese / Korean Linguistics 2*, ed. P. M. Clancy, 319-337. Stanford: CSLI.

Chomsky, N. 1981. *Lectures on Government and Binding*. Dordrecht: Foris.

Choo, M. 1994. A Unified Account of Null Pronouns in Korean. Doctoral dissertation, University of Hawaii.

Gerdts. D. 1987. Surface Case and Acceptable Relations in Korean: Evidence from Quantifier Float. *Studies in Language* 11: 181-197.

Grimshaw, J. 1990. *Argument Structure*. Cambridge MA: MIT Press.

Higginbotham, J. 1985. On Semantics. *Linguistic Inquiry* 16: 547-594.

Jackendoff, R. .1983. *Semantics and Cognition*. Cambridge MA: MIT Press.

Jackendoff, R. 1990. *Semantic Structures*. Cambridge MA: MIT Press.

Kitahara, H. 1993. Inalienable Possession Constructions in Korean: Scrambling, the Proper Binding Condition, and Case-percolation. *Japanese / Korean Linguistics 2*, ed. P. M. Clancy, 394-408. Stanford: CSLI.

Ko, H. 2005. Syntactic Edges and Linearization. Doctoral dissertation, MIT.

Lee-Schoenfeld, V. 2006. German Possessor Datives: Raised and Affected. *Journal of Comparative Germanic Linguistics* 9: 101-142.

Maling J. & S. Kim 1992. Case Assignment in the Inalienable Possession Construction in Korean. *Journal of East Asian Linguistics* 1: 37-68.

O'Grady, W. 1991. *Categories and Case: The Sentence Structure of Korean*. Amsterdam / Philadelphia: John Benjamins.

O'Grady, W. 2002. Korean Case: Extending the Computational Approach. *Korean Linguistics* 11: 29-51.

Payne, D. & I. Barshi 1999. *External Possession*. Amsterdam / Philadelphia: John Benjamins.

Pylkkänen, L. 2002. Introducing Arguments. Doctoral dissertation, MIT.

Reinhart, T. 1983. *Anaphora and Semantic Interpretation*. Chicago: University of Chicago Press.

Samek-Lodovici, V. 2003. The Internal Structure of Arguments: Evidence from Complex Predicate Formation in Italian. *Natural Language and Linguistic Theory* 21: 835-881.

Shibatani, M. 1994. An Integral Approach to Possessor Raising, Ethical Datives, and Adversative Passives. *Proceedings of the 20th Annual Meeting of the Berkeley Linguistics Society*: 461-486.

Son, M.-J. 2004. A Unified Syntactic Account of Morphological Causatives in Korean. *Japanese / Korean Linguistics 13*, eds. M. E. Hudson, P. Sells, and S.-A. Jun. Stanford: CSLI.

Speas, M. 1990. *Phrase Structure in Natural Language*. Dordrecht: Kluwer.

Tomioka, S. & C.-Y. Sim 2005. Event Structure of the Inalienable Possession in Korean. *Proceedings of the 28th Annual Penn Linguistics Colloquium*: 279-292.

Ura 1996. Multiple Feature-Checking: A Theory of Grammatical Function Splitting. Doctoral dissertation, MIT.

Vergnaud, J.-R. & M.-L. Zubizarreta 1992. The definite determiner and the inalienable constructions in French and English. *Linguistic Inquiry* 23, 595-652.

Vermeulen, R. 2005a. The Syntax of External Possession: Its Basis in Theta-theory. Doctoral dissertation, University College London.

Vermeulen, R. 2005b. External Possession in Korean. *UCL Working Papers in Linguistics* 17: 175-213.

Von Stechow, A. 1996. The Different Readings of *wieder* 'again': A structural Account. *Journal of Semantics* 13: 87-138.

Wechsler, S. & B. Noh 2001. On Resultative Predicates and Clauses: Parallels between Korean and English. *Language Science 23*: 391-423.

Williams, E. 1994. *Thematic Structure in Syntax.*, Cambridge, MA.: MIT Press

Yeon, J. 1999. A Cognitive Account of the Constraints on Possessor-ascension Constructions. *Language Research* 35: 211-130.

Yoon, J. H.-S. 1989. The Grammar of Inalienable Possession Constructions in Korean Mandarin and French. *Harvard Studies in Korean Linguistics* III: 357-368.

Yoon, J. H.-S. 1990. Theta Theory and the Grammar of Inalienable Possession Constructions. *Proceedings of NELS* 20: 502-516.

Yoon, J.-M. 1997. The Arguments Structure of Relational Nouns and Inalienable Possessor Constructions in Korean. *Language Research* 33: 231-264.

Zubizarreta, M. L. 1987. *Levels of Representation in the Lexicon and in the Syntax.* Dordrecht: Foris.

Shika-Npls in Tokyo Japanese and the Syntax-Prosody Interface: Focus Intonation Prosody and Prosody-Scope Correspondence[*]

HIDEAKI YAMASHITA
Yokohama National University

1. Introduction: An Interdisciplinary Approach to the Theory of Human Language Grammar

A number of recent works have shown that prosody plays a pivotal role in accounting for the nature of Wh-questions in (Tokyo) Japanese (Deguchi and Kitagawa 2002, Ishihara 2002a, b, 2003, 2004, 2007c, Kitagawa and Deguchi 2002, Kitagawa and Fodor 2003, 2006, Kitagawa 2005, Kuroda 2005; see also Hirotani 2003, et seq., and Sugahara 2003). It is argued that

---

[*] I would like to thank Jun Abe, Hiroshi Aoyagi, Shinichiro Ishihara, Yasuhiko Kato, Shin-Sook Kim, Tomoyuki Kubo, James Mesbur, Asako Uchibori, Akira Watanabe, Keiko Yoshimura, two anonymous *Japanese/Korean Linguistics* 16 abstract reviewers, two anonymous *Workshop on Negation and Polarity* 2007 abstract reviewers, and audiences at *Japanese/Korean Linguistics* 16 (Kyoto University, Oct., 7–9, 2006), WECOL 2006 (California State University, Fresno, Oct., 27–29, 2006), and *International Conference on East Asian Linguistics* (University of Toronto, Nov., 10–12, 2006), and *Workshop on Negation and Polarity* 2007 (University of Tübingen, March 8–10, 2007) for rewarding discussions, comments, and clarifications. The longer version of this paper is available as Yamashita 2006, and in *Proceedings of International Conference on East Asian Linguistics* (which will be published on-line (Spring, 2008) from Toronto Working Papers in Linguistics). All remaining errors are, of course, solely my own.

the licensing and interpretation of Wh-phrases are closely tied to the **Focus Intonation Prosody** (FIP) that Wh-questions exhibit, and there is a close correlation between FIP and the interpretation/scope of Wh-phrases, which is referred to here as the **Prosody-Scope Correspondence** (PSC).[1] This paper argues that the same is true with the licensing and interpretation of *shika*-NPIs in Tokyo Japanese, which require not only syntactic,[2] but also prosodic conditioning (i.e., FIP; Ishihara 2005a, b, 2007a, b), and demonstrate the PSC (Yamashita 2006, 2007a, b; see Sec.2). Our conclusions provide further credence to the 'interdisciplinary' approach to the theory of grammar, in particular along the line of Kitagawa's (2005) research guidelines (1), casting doubt on 'syntax-only' approach(es) (such as Hasegawa's 1994 syntax-only analysis of *shika*-NPIs). For concreteness, I will concentrate on the 'syntax-prosody' interface, but other factors such as processing and pragmatics should also be taken into consideration (which I will leave for future investigation).[3, 4]

(1) *Kitagawa's 2005 Research Guidelines*
     "the study of formal aspects of grammar should be conducted with much more careful attention to a larger context of language such as prosody, processing, and pragmatics than usually done" (Kitagawa 2005: p.303)

---

[1] Due to space limitations, I will not be able to discuss issues regarding prosody and the syntax of Wh-questions in Tokyo Japanese. See Yamashita 2007a: Sec.2, for a brief summary of this issue, and references/works cited therein for much detailed discussions. I should also note here that Kitagawa (2005) argues that not only prosody, but also other factors such as pragmatics and processing must be taken into considerations in investigating Wh-questions in Japanese. See also series of works he is involved with, some of which are referred in Kitagawa 2005.

[2] Since the main purpose of this paper is to show that prosody plays an important role in understanding *shika*-NPI constructions, I will relegate the discussion on the syntactic licensing conditions of *shika*-NPIs in the Appendix. The *shika*-NPI examples used in this paper (except those discussed in the Appendix) satisfy all syntactic conditions, e.g., the *shika*-NPI is c-commanded by a clause-mate negation. All the *shika*-NPIs used in this paper are 'bare' in the sense that there is no Case-marker/postposition on the XP -*shika* attaches to, but the same effect obtains with the *shika*-NPIs with Case-marker/postposition (e.g.,*XP-ni-shika* 'XP-DAT-SHIKA'). I also note here that I won't make any commitment regarding the distinction between 'Negative Polarity Item' and 'Negative Concord Item' (Watanabe 2004). In addition, I won't be concerned with the semantics of *shika*-NPIs (see e.g., Yoshimura 2007, and references cited therein).

[3] Throughout the paper, I only deal with Tokyo Japanese (in a broad sense, which includes the surrounding areas of Tokyo). But see Fn.9, as well as Yamashita 2007a: Note 12, for some possible issues concerning other dialects.

[4] See Poser (1984), Pierrehumbert and Beckman (1988), Kubozono (1993), among others for the basics of the prosody and intonation in Japanese.

2. Prosody and the Syntax of *Shika*-NPI Constructions in Tokyo Japanese

I argue that what has been noted for Wh-questions in Tokyo Japanese is also observed with the *shika*-NPI constructions in Tokyo Japanese, which provides additional evidence for the interdisciplinary approach to the theory of grammar, along the line of Kitagawa's research guidelines in (1).

2.1. The Syntax of *Shika*-NPI Constructions (without Prosody)

Hasegawa (1994: (4c), (16)) observes that otherwise ambiguous (2) becomes unambiguous when *shika*-NPI is scrambled to the vicinity of matrix Neg as in (3) (allowing only the matrix scope interpretation), akin to Takahashi's (1993) observation regarding the Wh-movement effect of long-distance scrambling of Wh-phrase (Takahashi 1993: (4b)), and argues that A'-movement of an NPI to NegP-Spec fixes scope (Hasegawa 1994: (18)).[5, 6]

(2)   Naoya-wa Mari-ni [$_{CC}$ PRO sono ramu-shika   nomiya-de
       N.-TOP   M.-DAT   that rum-SHIKA   bar-LOC
       noma-*na*-i-yooni]   iwa-*nakat*-ta.
       drink-NEG-TNS-C   tell-NEG-TNS

    a.   'Naoya did not tell Mari [$_{CC}$ that she should $_{([Neg])}$ drink
        [$_{NPI}$ only that rum] at the bar].'   (Embedded Scope)

    b.   'It $_{([Neg])}$ was [$_{NPI}$ only that rum] [that Naoya told Mari
        [$_{CC}$ not to drink at the bar]].'   (Matrix Scope)

        (~Hasegawa 1994: (4c/16a))
        (N.B. CC = control complement)

---

[5] All the Japanese examples are transcribed in the modified *Hepburn('Hebon')*-system Romanization (e.g., -*shika*, not -*sika*, which is with *Kunrei*-system Romanization). Most of the examples cited in this paper are modified, but in a way that does not distort the intention of the original data. I use the mark '~' when the cited data are not exactly the same (even if it is a slight modification). The translations are provided to illustrate the rough structures of the examples and are not meant to be 'correct' English translations.

[6] I assume here that *shika*-NPI in (2) stays in-situ inside the embedded clause. 'In-situ' is used here in a broad sense in that *shika*-NPIs are not scrambled out of the clause it is base-generated in. Note that it may be possible to scramble string-vacuously out of the embedded clause to some position in the matrix clause below the matrix indirect object. Such an option may plausibly be blocked by placing an appropriate adverb that modifies only the embedded verb. I won't place any such adverb, so as not to make the sentence complex, but I note here that placing such adverb does not interfere with the interpretation of *shika*-NPIs in any significant way. See also Appendix below for related discussions.

(3)   Sono ramu-shika$_i$ Naoya-wa Mari-ni [$_{CC}$ PRO t$_i$ nomiya-de
       that rum-SHIKA N.-TOP M.-DAT   bar-LOC
       noma-*na*-i-yooni] iwa-*nakat*-ta.
       drink-NEG-TNS-C tell-NEG-TNS
   a. * (Embedded Scope) = (2)a
   b. (Matrix Scope)   = (2)b
       (~Hasegawa 1994: (16b), with her judgment)

The judgment in (2) and (3), especially the crucial contrast regarding the unavailability of the embedded scope reading in (3), however, may not be as clear as Hasegawa observes, especially once FIP is taken into consideration.[7]

2.2. Focus Intonation Prosody and Prosody-Scope Correspondence in *Shika*-NPI Constructions in Tokyo Japanese[8]

2.2.1. Focus Intonation Prosody (FIP)

Ishihara (2005a, b, 2007a, b) has shown (see also Hirotani 2004), by conducting an experimental study, that essentially the same FIP found in Wh-questions is also found in *shika*-NPI constructions, as stated in (4).[9, 10]

---

[7] Hasegawa's (1994) *shika*-NPI examples (*ibid.*: (4c)/(16)) and Takahashi's (1993) Wh-question examples (*ibid.*: (4)) are not completely parallel in that the former involves control complement. This is because cross-clausal licensing of *shika*-NPIs is not possible with finite complement (see Appendix; see also Yamashita 2003a, b) and Wh-island (Tanaka 1997). It is however possible to make more structurally parallel examples using non-control type subjunctive complement (with overt embedded subject) discussed in Uchibori (2000: Ch.5). See Yamashita (2006).

[8] Unfortunately, there is (still) no consensus on the terminologies regarding the prosody/FIP in Japanese. Followings are the partial list of the terminologies used in the recent literature.

(i) FIP = Emphatic Prosody (EPD; Deguchi and Kitagawa 2002, Kitagawa 2005), Focus Intonation (FI; Ishihara 2002a, b, et seq.).

(ii) F_0-boosting = emphatic accent (Deguchi and Kitagawa 2002, Kitagawa 2005), P(rosodic)-focalization (Ishihara 2002a, b, 2003, 2004), F_0-boosting (Ishihara 2005a, b).

(iii) F_0-compression = eradication (Deguchi and Kitagawa 2002), deaccenting (Ishihara 2002a, b), post-focus/FOCUS/focal reduction (PFR; Ishihara 2003, 2004, 2005a, b, Kitagawa 2005), F_0-reduction (Ishihara 2005a, b), post-focal (F_0-)downtrend (Ishihara 2007a, b, c).

(iv) F_0-reset = pitch/F_0-reset (Ishihara 2005a, b, 2007a, b, c).

The terminologies I used in this paper (and Yamashita 2005, et seq.) are based on Ishihara's.

[9] Although *shika*-NPI constructions and Wh-questions in Tokyo Japanese exhibit essentially the same FIP, it does not necessarily mean that this holds for other dialects as well. As Tomoyuki Kubo (p.c., Oct., 2006) pointed out to me, *shika*-NPI constructions in Fukuoka Japanese does not exhibit the same FIP observed for Wh-questions, where deaccenting takes place in the post-focus F_0-compressed materials, a property not observed with FIP of Wh-questions in Tokyo Japanese. See Kubo (1989) and his subsequent works on the FIP of Wh-questions in Fukuoka Japanese.

[10] I will use the following notations in indicating the prosody. **Bold** for F_0-boosting, underline for F_0-compression, and box for F_0-reset. I will also *italicize* and shade the relevant licensing head (e.g., -*na*- 'Neg'). Due to space limitations, I regret that I cannot provide any pitch tracks. See Yamashita (2006).

(4)   **FIP in shika-*NPI* constructions (FIP$_{shika}$)**:
Shika-NPI constructions require
  (i)   **F_0-boosting of XP** -*shika* attaches to,
  (ii) followed by F_0-compression until its licensing *Neg*, and
  (iii) F_0-reset on the material after the licensing Neg, if there is one.[11]
    (~Ishihara 2005b: (2), 2007a: (3), 'NPI-FI Hypothesis')

In this construction, an XP marked with -*shika* gets F_0-boosted and the following sequence up until the licensing negation is F_0-compressed, as indicated in (5). This should be contrasted with (6) where the corresponding XP is not marked by -*shika*. No FIP is detected in this 'normal' declarative sentence with negation, which exhibits 'Normal' Intonation Prosody.

(5)   FIP$_{shika}$ (i) **F_0-boosting** on *(sono) ramu*, and
           FIP$_{shika}$ (ii) F_0-compression until the licensing Neg.
           Mari-ga   **(sono) ramu**-shika nomiya-de noma-*nakat*-ta.
           M.-NOM   (that) rum-SHIKA   bar-LOC   drink-NEG-TNS
           'Mari $_{([Neg])}$ drank [$_{NPI}$ only (that) rum] at the bar.'
           (~Ishihara 2005b: (5B), 2007a: (1), (8B))

(6)   FIP$_{shika}$ (i) NO **F_0-boosting** on *(sono) ramu*, and
           FIP$_{shika}$ (ii) NO F_0-compression until the Neg.
           Mari-ga   (sono) ramu-o   nomiya-de noma-nakat-ta.
           M.-NOM   (that) rum-ACC   bar-LOC   drink-NEG-TNS
           'Mari didn't drink (that) rum at the bar.'
           (~Ishihara 2005b: (5A), 2007a: (8A))

2.2.2. Prosody-Scope Correspondence (PSC)

I argue that, once FIP$_{shika}$ is taken into consideration, (3) is in fact ambiguous and is prosodically disambiguated and such ambiguity shows that PSC is at work for *shika*-NPI construction as well, as stated in (7),[12, 13] making Hasegawa's original observation that (3) lacks the embedded scope reading and 'syntax-only' analysis (that depends on it) quite dubious. Thus, it is not the type of movement (and/or movement to a particular landing site, e.g., NegP-Spec) but the prosody that determines and indicates the scope of *shika*-NPI.

---

[11] Since the F_0-peak on the verbal predicate is in principle subject to a pitch-lowering process (*Downstep*) (see Poser 1984, Selkirk and Tateishi 1991, Kubozono 1993, among others), the effect noted in (iii) may not be easily detected. See Ishihara (2005b: Sec.7.2) for related discussions.

[12] Tips I used when soliciting the judgments using FIP is (i) to put the extra stress on the *shika*-NPIs, and (ii) read/pronounce the F_0-compressed part quicker than usual.

[13] The term 'Prosody-Scope Correspondence' should be distinguished from Hirotani's (2003, et seq.) 'Scope-Prosody Correspondence,' which is a processing principle (see Yamashita 2007a: Note 13). This does not mean, however, that PSC plays no role in the processing of *shika*-NPI constructions. Experimental investigations should verify this, which I leave for future research.

(7) **|PSC in shika-*NPI* constructions (PSC_{shika})|**:
The scope of *shika*-NPIs is determined and indicated by the (post-focus) F_0-compression between *shika*-**NPIs** and the sentential nega-tion morpheme (that (once) c-commanded *shika*-NPIs).

(8) and (9) indicate how the FIP_{shika} disambiguates the embedded and matrix scope reading associated with (2), where *shika*-NPI stays in-situ.

(8) = (2)a; Embedded Scope; FIP_{shika} (i)+(ii) = PSC_{shika}
FIP_{shika} (i) **F_0-boosting** on *sono ramu*, and
FIP_{shika} (ii) F_0-compression until the embedded Neg.
Naoya-wa   Mari-ni [_{CC} PRO **sono ramu**-shika   nomiya-de
N.-TOP   M.-DAT   that rum-SHIKA   bar-LOC
noma-*na*-i-yooni]   iwa-nakat-ta.
drink-NEG-TNS-C   tell-NEG-TNS
'Naoya did not tell Mari [_{CC} that she should _{([Neg])} drink [_{NPI} only that rum] at the bar].'

(9) = (2)b; Matrix Scope; FIP_{shika} (i)+(ii) = PSC_{shika}
FIP_{shika} (i) **F_0-boosting** on *sono ramu*, and
FIP_{shika} (ii) F_0-compression until the matrix Neg.   cf. (8ii)
Naoya-wa   Mari-ni [_{CC} PRO **sono ramu**-shika   nomiya-de
N.-TOP   M.-DAT   that rum-SHIKA   bar-LOC
noma-na-i-yooni]   iwa-*nakat*-ta.
drink-NEG-TNS-C   tell-NEG-TNS
'It _{([Neg])} was [_{NPI} only that rum] [that Naoya told Mari [_{CC} not to drink at the bar]].'

Crucially, the disambiguation strategy by FIP_{shika} is at work for the scrambling example as well, as shown in (10) and (11).

(10) = (3)a; Embedded Scope; FIP_{shika} (i)+(ii) = PSC_{shika}
FIP_{shika} (i) **F_0-boosting** on *sono ramu*, and
FIP_{shika} (ii) F_0-compression until the embedded Neg.
Sono ramu-shika_i Naoya-wa   Mari-ni [_{CC} PRO t_i nomiya-de
that rum-SHIKA   N.-TOP   M.-DAT   bar-LOC
noma-*na*-i-yooni]   iwa-nakat-ta.
drink-NEG-TNS-C   tell-NEG-TNS
'Naoya did not tell Mari [_{CC} that she should _{([Neg])} drink [_{NPI} only that rum] at the bar].'

(11)   = (3)b; Matrix Scope; FIP_{shika} (i)+(ii) = PSC_{shika}
        FIP_{shika} (i)   **F_0-boosting** on *sono ramu*, and
        FIP_{shika} (ii) F_0-compression until the matrix Neg.   cf. (10ii)
        Sono ramu-shika$_i$ Naoya-wa   Mari-ni [$_{CC}$ PRO t$_i$ nomiya-de
        that rum-SHIKA   N.-TOP   M.-DAT   bar-LOC
        noma-na-i-yooni]   iwa-*nakat*-ta.
        drink-NEG-TNS-C   tell-NEG-TNS
        'It $_{([Neg])}$ was [$_{NPI}$ only that rum] [that Naoya told Mari
        [$_{CC}$ not to drink at the bar]].'

What is crucial in the present discussion is that, the availability of embedded scope in (3)a, as indicated by the FIP_{shika} in (10), shows that Hasegawa's (1994) analysis (i.e., *ibid.*: (18), A'-movement of *shika*-NPI to the NegP-Spec fixes its scope), which is based on the absence of such a reading, cannot be maintained.

There are, however, some complications in the examples (8) and (9), and the same holds for (10) and (11). The judgment in (8)–(11) (especially the contrast between (10) and (11)) is not as clear as the FIP and PSC predicts (or as Hasegawa (1994) observes).[14] The embedded scope is the preferred reading for (8)–(9), whereas the matrix scope is the preferred reading for (10)–(11). This is due to the independent factor involving the phonological phrasing in Japanese. The phonological phrasing of the verbal predicates are subject to "downstep," which always induces prosodic effect involving F_0-lowering, that is akin to F_0-compression (Deguchi and Kitagawa 2002: p.74; Ishihara 2002a: Fn.2). Thus to the extent that the embedded and matrix predicates are string-adjacent, it is hard to distinguish whether "F_0-compression/F_0-lowering" is due to FIP or downstep. Hence, the prosody of (8) and (9), and (10) and (11), respectively, are in essence indistinguishable.[15] But the contrast between (10) and (11) (both in terms of FIP and PSC) can be distinguished by, e.g., switching the control complement (CC) and *Mari-ni*. The presence/absence of the F_0-reset on *Mari-ni* (FIP_{shika} (iii) in (4)) enables to distinguish the two.

---

[14] At least, it is less clear when compared with Wh-questions, where a proper attention to FIP clearly dissolves the alleged Wh-movement/island effects. This might be due to the fact that FIP and PSC in *shika*-NPI constructions in Tokyo Japanese are more subtle when compared to that of Wh-questions (see Yamashita 2006; Ishihara 2007b also reports the same effect with respect to the FIP). Despite the complication, it is nonetheless true that when I asked the linguists for the judgment by paying attention to FIP (using the methods mentioned in Fn.12), they were able to disambiguate the interpretations.

[15] I will use the dashed underline to indicate the downstep/F_0-lowering on the verbal predicate, to differentiate it from F_0-compression.

(12)   **Sono ramu**-shika$_i$ Naoya-wa   [$_{CC}$ PRO t$_i$ nomiya-de
                that rum-SHIKA   N.-TOP   bar-LOC
                noma-*na*-i-yooni]$_j$ Mari-ni   t$_j$ iwa-*nakat*-ta.
                drink-NEG-TNS-C M.-DAT   tell-NEG-TNS

      a.   'Naoya did not tell Mari [$_{CC}$ that she should $_{([Neg])}$ drink
               [$_{NPI}$ only that rum] at the bar].'   (Embedded Scope)

      b.   'It $_{([Neg])}$ was [$_{NPI}$ only that rum] [that Naoya told Mari
               [$_{CC}$ not to drink at the bar]].'   (Matrix Scope)

(13)   = (12)a; Embedded Scope;   FIP$_{shika}$ (i)+(ii)+(iii) = PSC$_{shika}$
            FIP$_{shika}$ (i)   **F$_0$-boosting** on *sono ramu*, and
            FIP$_{shika}$ (ii)   F$_0$-compression until the embedded Neg, and
            FIP$_{shika}$ (iii)   F$_0$-reset on *Mari-ni*.
            Sono ramu-shika$_i$ Naoya-wa   [$_{CC}$ PRO t$_i$ nomiya-de
            that rum-SHIKA   N.-TOP   bar-LOC
            noma-*na*-i-yooni]$_j$ Mari-ni   t$_j$ iwa-nakat-ta.
            drink-NEG-TNS-C M.-DAT   tell-NEG-TNS
            'Naoya did not tell Mari [$_{CC}$ that she should $_{([Neg])}$ drink
            [$_{NPI}$ only that rum] at the bar].'

(14)   = (12)b; Matrix Scope;   FIP$_{shika}$ (i)+(ii)+(iii) = PSC$_{shika}$
            FIP$_{shika}$ (i)   **F$_0$-boosting** on *sono ramu*, and
            FIP$_{shika}$ (ii)   F$_0$-compression until the matrix Neg, and   cf. (13ii)
            FIP$_{shika}$ (iii)   NO F$_0$-reset on *Mari-ni*.   cf. (13iii)
            Sono ramu-shika$_i$ Naoya-wa   [$_{CC}$ PRO t$_i$ nomiya-de
            that rum-SHIKA   N.-TOP   bar-LOC
            noma-na-i-yooni]$_j$ Mari-ni   t$_j$ iwa-*nakat*-ta.
            drink-NEG-TNS-C M.-DAT   tell-NEG-TNS
            'It $_{([Neg])}$ was [$_{NPI}$ only that rum] [that Naoya told Mari
            [$_{CC}$ not to drink at the bar]].'

The crucial point here, again, is that the availability of embedded scope in (12)a as indicated by the FIP$_{shika}$ in (13) shows that Hasegawa's (1994) analysis (i.e., *ibid.*: (18), A'-movement of *shika*-NPI to the NegP-Spec fixes its scope), which depends on the now alleged argument on the lack thereof, cannot be maintained.[16] More importantly, the disambiguation strategies for the scope possibilities of *shika*-NPI constructions in Tokyo Japanese exemplify that the prosodic factors (FIP$_{shika}$ and PSC$_{shika}$) are necessary and

---

[16] Unfortunately, the strategy employed to disambiguate the FIP of the scrambled *shika*-NPI is not applicable to the in-situ *shika*-NPI (i.e., the contrast between (8) and (9)). The placement of *Mari-ni* (or any XPs that serve to indicate the F$_0$-reset) between the two predicate forces the embedded scope reading, and prevents the matrix scope reading which is due to an independent syntactic requirement (see Appendix for related discussions).

indispensable for the proper understanding of *shika*-NPIs, on a par with Wh-questions in Japanese as discussed in Deguchi and Kitagawa 2002, Ishihara 2002a, b, 2003, 2004, 2007c, Kitagawa 2005, among others.

To sum up, I have shown that the *shika*-NPI constructions in Tokyo Japanese not only exhibits FIP (Ishihara 2005a, b, 2007a, b, Yamashita 2006; see also Hirotani 2004), but also PSC (Yamashita 2006, 2007a, b).[17]

3. Concluding Remarks

A number of recent works (such as Deguchi and Kitagawa 2002 and Ishihara 2002a, b, 2003, and Kitagawa 2005) which paid close attention to the prosodic properties of Wh-questions in (Tokyo) Japanese revealed that certain apparently syntactic effects observed for this construction are actually prosodic in nature. I have shown in this paper that essentially the same holds for the *shika*-NPI constructions in Tokyo Japanese in that it exhibits both Focus Intonation Prosody (FIP) and Prosody-Scope Correspondence (PSC), akin to what is found in Wh-questions in Tokyo Japanese. I hope to have shown that the prosodic factors (FIP and PSC) are necessary and indispensable for the proper understanding of not only Wh-questions but also *shika*-NPIs construction, calling for the necessity of an interdisciplinary approach to the theory of grammar, which is couched under Kitagawa's research guidelines in (1). As I see it, we must pay serious attention to the prosodic properties when conducting the syntactic analyses, especially of those phenomena involving the so-called "FIP bearing items" (e.g., Wh-phrases and *shika*-NPIs in Tokyo Japanese) which obligatorily exhibit FIP.[18]

Appendix: Syntactic Licensing Conditions on *shika*-NPIs

In this appendix, I will very succinctly go over the necessary syntactic licensing conditions on *shika*-NPIs, making reference to the FIP.[19]

(15) is the top-most priority syntactic conditions that *shika*-NPIs are subject to, which is noted and accepted in the literature (see the works referred in Fn.19).

---

[17] *Shika*-NPIs can be right-dislocated. What is interesting is that contrary to scrambling cases in (10)–(14)), when *shika*-NPIs are right-dislocated, it can only be interpreted as the matrix scope reading. It is also of interest to note that when *shika*-NPIs are right-dislocated, although *shika*-NPIs are F_0-boosted, no other FIP is observed, especially F_0-compression, which prosodically marks the scope, is absent. At the present moment, I have no concrete explanation why the embedded scope reading is not available with right-dislocation.

[18] See Yamashita (2005/in progress, 2007c, d) where it is shown that prosody plays a pivotal role in accounting for the nature of 'split' indeterminate NPI pronouns in (Tokyo) Japanese (e.g., ... *dare* ... V-*mo-si*-Neg, ... *dare* ... *mo* ... V-Neg; see Kuroda (1965: Ch.3, sec.5, pp.93–95, 2005).

[19] See Oyakawa (1975), Muraki (1978), Kato (1985), Aoyagi and Ishii (1994), and references cited therein, for the basics of the syntax of *shika*-NPIs in Japanese.

(15) Syntactic Licensing Conditions on *shika*-NPI:
    (i) **cd(Neg)**:[20]
        Shika-NPIs must once be in the c-command domain of the sentential negation morpheme, and
    (ii) **Clause-mate Condition (CMC):**
        Neg and *shika*-NPIs must be clause-mate.
    (based on Muraki 1978, see also Yamashita 2003a, b)

NPI-licensing is illicit in (16) because it violates cd(Neg). Note here that (16) is still ungrammatical even if the "correct" FIP is assigned/forced.

(16)   * Naoya-wa **Mari-ni-shika** [cc PRO (sono) ramu-o
        N.-TOP   M.-DAT-SHIKA   (that) rum-ACC
        nomiya-de noma-*na*-i-yooni] it-ta.
        bar-LOC   drink-NEG-TNS-C tell-TNS
        'Naoya told [NPI only Mari] [CC not[Neg] to drink (that) rum at the bar].'

Although *shika*-NPIs are (in general) subject to the CMC,[21] *shika*-NPIs contained in the embedded clause can be licensed by the matrix negation when the embedded clause is a 'non-finite' complement (e.g., control complement (CC)), and the embedded and matrix predicates are string-adjacent, as stated in (17) (see e.g., Muraki 1978, Kato 1985, Nemoto 1993, Uchibori 2000).[22]

(17) Syntactic Conditions on Cross-clausal Licensing of *shika*-NPIs:
    (i) **Non-finiteness Condition (NFC):**
        The embedded clause must not be "finite," and
    (ii) **Predicate Restructuring Condition (PRC):**
        The embedded and matrix predicates must be string-adjacent to render predicate restructuring, which makes the bi-clause into mono-clause.
    (based on Muraki 1978, see also Yamashita 2003a, b)

---

[20] I assume the relation between Neg and a *shika*-NPI to be an instance of Agree (Chomsky 2000, 2001), and thus cd(Neg) serves as a prerequisite for Agree; see Yamashita 2003a, b for arguments for this assumption. Once the Agree relation is established between Neg and *shika*-NPI, it is reflected as FIP as stated in (4), and it must be preserved throughout the rest of derivation (the only exception I am aware of is the right-dislocation of *shika*-NPIs (Fn.17)). Note that whether Neg acts as a probe or not is optional since Neg does not require *shika*-NPI in its search domain; rather it is the *shika*-NPI that must be licensed by Neg. Furthermore, Neg can apparently probe bypassing another Neg which is closer to *shika*-NPI, as shown by the availability of the matrix scope interpretation of the in-situ *shika*-NPI in (2).

[21] This is an over-simplification; see the works cited for a fuller description.

[22] See Yamashita 2003a, b for arguments that CMC on NPI-licensing should be eliminated in favor of "phase-mate condition."

For example, cross-clausal NPI-licensing is possible with the 'basic' word order in (18), but not with the 'scrambled' word order in (19) because only the former complies NFC and PRC.[23, 24] Because of the intervening XP (*Mari-ni*), (19) violates PRC and, as a consequence, CMC as well.[25]

(18)   Naoya-wa   Mari-ni [$_{CC}$ PRO   **sono ramu**-shika nomiya-de
            N.-TOP   M.-DAT   that rum-SHIKA   bar-LOC
            nom-u-yooni] iwa-*nakat*-ta.
            drink-TNS-C   tell-NEG-TNS
            'Naoya $_{([Neg])}$ told Mari [$_{CC}$ that she should drink
            [$_{NPI}$ only that rum] at the bar].'
            (~Nemoto 1993: Ch.4, (79), Yamashita 2003b: Part II, (3a))

(19)   * Naoya-wa [$_{CC}$ PRO   **sono ramu**-shika nomiya-de
            N.-TOP   that rum-SHIKA   bar-LOC
            nom-u-yooni]$_j$ Mari-ni   t$_j$ iwa-*nakat*-ta.
            drink-TNS-C   M.-DAT   tell-NEG-TNS
            'Naoya $_{([Neg])}$ told [$_{CC}$ that she should drink [$_{NPI}$ only that rum]
            at the bar]$_j$ Mari t$_j$.'
            (~Yamashita 2003b: Part II, (9a), see also Yoshida 2001: (12b))

Note here that (19) is still ungrammatical even if the "correct" FIP is assigned/forced, just like the case with (16).[26]

    The ungrammatical (19) can be saved by scrambling of *shika*-NPIs out of the embedded complement to some position in the matrix clause. (20) illustrates this with scrambling to the sentence-initial position.

---

[23] Note here that the *shika*-NPI inside the embedded clause and Neg in the matrix clause are able to become clause-mates by virtue of predicate restructuring and thus can satisfy the CMC.

[24] Note that (19) in fact satisfies cd(Neg). Given the discussion in Fn.20 that the relation between Neg and a *shika*-NPI is established via Agree, it seems reasonable to conclude that Agree fails to be established in this example, despite the fact that Neg does c-command *shika*-NPI. See Yamashita (2003b: Part II) for an account that does not utilize PRC.

[25] The ungrammaticality of (16) in fact shows that the priority of cd(Neg) (which is a prerequisite for Agree to take place; see Fn.20) as a licensing condition of *shika*-NPIs. Since the embedded and matrix predicates are string-adjacent, they can undergo predicate restructuring, making the *shika*-NPI and Neg clause-mates. Thus, (16) satisfies CMC, NFC, and PRC. The only condition (16) does not meet is cd(Neg), and hence it should be responsible for the deviance. In fact, cd(Neg) (feeding Agree) is the only syntactic licensing condition on *shika*-NPIs; see Yamashita (2003a,b). (It should be noted here that Muraki (1978) did not take c-command into consideration.)

[26] Few people informed me that (19) is not ungrammatical. It seems to me that they employ string-vacuous scrambling of *shika*-NPI out of the embedded clause to some position in the matrix clause below the matrix indirect object, and as a result of it, meets the CMC. However, even for these type of speakers, (19) becomes ungrammatical once some XP that counts as a base-generated phrase of the embedded complement is placed on top of the *shika*-NPIs.

(20)   **Sono ramu**-shika$_i$ Naoya-wa [$_{CC}$ PRO t$_i$ nomiya-de
that rum-SHIKA N.-TOP   bar-LOC
nom-u-yooni]$_j$ Mari-ni t$_j$ iwa-*nakat*-ta.
drink-TNS-C M.-DAT   tell-NEG-TNS
'[$_{NPI}$ Only that rum]$_i$, Naoya $_{([Neg])}$ told [$_{CC}$ that she should drink t$_i$
at the bar]$_j$ Mari t$_j$.'

(20) becomes grammatical, since as a result of scrambling into the matrix
clause, the CMC is satisfied.[27]
    Finally, consider (21) and (22).

(21)   Naoya-wa Mari-ni [$_{CC}$ PRO **sono ramu**-shika nomiya-de
N.-TOP   M.-DAT   that rum-SHIKA bar-LOC
noma-*na*-i-yooni]   it-ta.
drink-NEG-TNS-C tell-TNS
'Naoya told Mari [$_{CC}$ that she should $_{([Neg])}$ drink
[$_{NPI}$ only that rum] at the bar].'

(22)   **Sono ramu**-shika$_i$ Naoya-wa Mari-ni [$_{CC}$ PRO t$_i$ nomiya-de
that rum-SHIKA N.-TOP   M.-DAT   bar-LOC
noma-*na*-i-yooni]   it-ta.
drink-NEG-TNS-C tell-TNS
'[$_{NPI}$ Only that rum]$_i$, Naoya told Mari [$_{CC}$ that she should $_{([Neg])}$
drink t$_i$ at the bar].'

In (21) and (22), Neg is attached to the embedded predicate, and *shika*-
NPI is base-generated in the embedded clause. The only difference between
the two is that *shika*-NPI is scrambled out of the control complement (CC)
in (22). Although *shika*-NPI in this example is not overtly c-commanded by
the Neg, it can be radically reconstructed to the c-command domain of Neg
(Saito 1989, 2007), thus it satisfies cd(Neg).

References

Aoyagi, H. and T. Ishii. 1994. On NPI Licensing in Japanese. *Japanese/Korean
Linguistics* 4, ed. N. Akatsuka, 295–311. Stanford, Calif.: CSLI.

---

[27] Given the discussion in Fn.24 where the deviance of (19) is attributed to the failure to
establish Agree relation between Neg and an in-situ *shika*-NPI, the grammaticality of (20)
suggests that Agree can be established between Neg and the *shika*-NPI scrambled out of the
control complement. This can be made possible if we assume that, following Yamashita
(2003b: Part II), scrambling in (20) from the in-situ to the surface position passes through
intermediate positions such as the Spec of control complement and matrix VP, and Agree takes
place between Neg and the *shika*-NPI at the point where *shika*-NPI is scrambled to the matrix
VP and Neg is externally merged.

Chomsky, N. 2000. Minimalist inquiries: the framework. *Step by Step: Essays on Minimalist Syntax in Honor of Howard Lasnik*, eds. R. Martin et al., 89–155. Cambridge, Mass: MIT Press.

Chomsky, N. 2001. Derivation by Phase. *Ken Hale: A Life in Language*, ed. M. Kenstowicz, 1–52. Cambridge, Mass.: MIT Press.

Deguchi, M. and Y. Kitagawa. 2002. Prosody in Wh-questions. *NELS* 32, ed. M. Hirotani, 73–92. Amherst, Mass.: GLSA.

Hasegawa, N. 1994. Economy of Derivation and A'-movement in Japanese. *Current Topics in English and Japanese*, ed. M. Nakamura, 1–25. Tokyo: Hituzi Syobo.

Hirotani, M. 2003. Prosodic Effects on the Interpretation of Japanese Wh-questions. *UMOP* 27: *On Semantic Processing*, ed. L. Alonso-Ovalle, 117–137. Amherst, Mass.: GLSA.

Hirotani, M. 2004. Prosodic Scope: Studies on Prosodic Grouping. Paper presented at *Workshop on Prosody, Syntax, and Information Structure*. Indiana University, 4/30–5/1/2004.

Hirotani, M. 2005a. Prosody and LF Interpretation: Processing Japanese Wh-questions. Doctoral dissertation, University of Massachusetts, Amherst.

Hirotani, M. 2005b. Prosodic Processing of Scope Relevant Items in Japanese. Paper presented at *Workshop on Prosody, Syntax, and Information Structure* 2. University of Potsdam, 3/18/2005.

Ishihara, S. 2002a. Invisible but Audible Wh-scope Marking: Wh-constructions and Deaccenting in Japanese. *WCCFL* 21, eds. L. Mikkelsen and C. Potts, 180–193. Somerville, Mass.: Cascadilla Press.

Ishihara, S. 2002b. Syntax-Phonology Interface of Wh-constructions in Japanese. *The Proceedings of the 3rd Tokyo Conference on Psycholinguistics*, ed. Y. Otsu, 165–189. Tokyo: Hituzi Syobo.

Ishihara, S. 2003. Intonation and Interface Conditions. Doctoral dissertation, MIT.

Ishihara, S. 2004. Prosody by Phase: Evidence from Focus Intonation–*Wh*-scope Correspondence in Japanese. *Interdisciplinary Studies on Information Structure 1: Working Papers of SFB632*, eds. S. Ishihara et al., 77–119. Potsdam: University of Potsdam.

Ishihara, S. 2005a. Intonation of Sentences with an NPI. Paper presented at *Workshop on Prosody, Syntax, and Information Structure* 2. University of Potsdam, 3/18/2005.

Ishihara, S. 2005b. *Intonation of Sentences with an NPI: Experiment Overview*. Ms. (3/25/2005), University of Potsdam.

Ishihara, S. 2007a. Intonation of Sentences with an NPI. *Interdisciplinary Studies on Information Structure 9: Working Papers of SFB632 (Proceedings of the 2nd Workshop on Prosody, Syntax, and Information Structure 2 (WPSI 2))*, ed. S. Ishihara., 65–96. Potsdam: University of Potsdam.

Ishihara, S. 2007b. Negative Polarity Items and Focus Intonation in Japanese. Paper presented at *Japanese/Korean Linguistics* 17. UCLA, 11/9/2007.

Ishihara, S. 2007c. Major Phrase, Focus Intonation, Multiple Spell-out (MaP, FI, MSO). *The Linguistics Review* 24(2–3) (Special Issue: Prosodic Phrasing and Tunes): 137–167.

Kato, Y. 1985. Negative Sentences in Japanese. *Sophia Linguistica* 19. Tokyo: Sophia University.

Kitagawa, Y. 2005. Prosody, Syntax and Pragmatics of Wh-questions. *English Linguistics* 22(2): 302–346. Tokyo: Kaitakusha.

Kitagawa, Y. and M. Deguchi. 2002. *Prosody in Syntactic Analyses*. Ms. (Ver.4, June, 2002), Indiana University.

Kitagawa, Y. and J. D. Fodor. 2003. Default Prosody Explains Neglected Syntactic Analyses of Japanese. *Japanese/Korean Linguistics* 12, ed. W. McClure, 267–279. Stanford, Calif.: CSLI.

Kitagawa, Y. and J. D. Fodor. 2006. Prosodic Influence on Syntactic Judgments. *Gradience in Grammar: Generative Perspectives*, eds. G. Fanselow et al., 336–358. Oxford: Oxford University Press.

Kubo, T. 1989. Fukuoka-shi Hougen-no *dare/nani*-tou-no Gimonshi-o Fukumu Bun-no Pitchi Pataan [The Pitch Patterns of Sentences Containing Wh-words such as *dare/nani* in the Fukuoka-city Dialect]. *Kokugogaku* 156: 71–82.

Kubozono, H. 1993. *The Organization of Japanese Prosody*. Tokyo: Kurosio Publishers.

Kuroda, S.-Y.. 1965. Generative Grammatical Studies in the Japanese Language. Doctoral dissertation, MIT.

Kuroda, S.-Y.. 2005. Prosody and the Syntax of Indeterminates. *Syntax and Beyond (Indiana University Working Papers in Linguistics, vol.5)*, eds. D. Roehrs et al., 83–116. Bloomington, Indiana: Indiana University Linguistics Club.

Muraki, M. 1978. The *sika nai* Constructions and Predicate Restructuring. *Problems in Japanese Syntax and Semantics*, eds. J. Hinds and I. Howard, 155–177. Tokyo: Kaitakusha.

Nemoto, N. 1993. Chains and Case Positions: A Study of Scrambling in Japanese. Doctoral dissertation, University of Connecticut.

Oyakawa, T. 1975. On the Japanese *sika nai* Construction. *Gengo Kenkyu* (Journal of the Linguistic Society of Japan) 67, 1–20.

Pierrehumbert, J. and M. Beckman. 1988. *Japanese Tone Structure*. Cambridge, Mass.: MIT Press.

Poser, W. J. 1984. The Phonetics and Phonology of Tone and Intonation in Japanese. Doctoral dissertation, MIT.

Saito, M. 1989. Scrambling as Semantically Vacuous A'-movement. *Alternative Conceptions of Phrase Structure*, eds. M. R. Baltin and A. S. Kroch, 182–200. Chicago: University of Chicago Press.

Saito, M. 2007. Radical Reconstruction and the First-Position Effects. Paper presented at *International Conference of Linguistics in Korea* 2007. Seoul National University, 1/20/2007.

Selkirk, E. and K. Tateishi. 1991. Syntax and Downstep in Japanese. *Interdisciplinary Approaches to Language: Essays in Honor of S.-Y. Kuroda*, eds. C. Georgopoulos and R. Ishihara, 519–543. Dordrecht: Kluwer Academic Press.

Sugahara, M. 2003. Downtrends and Post-FOCUS Intonation in Tokyo Japanese. Doctoral dissertation, University of Massachusetts, Amherst.

Takahashi, D. 1993. Movement of Wh-phrases in Japanese. *Natural Language and Linguistic Theory* 11(4): 655–678.

Tanaka, H. 1997. Invisible Movement in *Sika-Nai* and the Linear Crossing Constraint. *Journal of East Asian Linguistics* 6(2): 143–178.

Uchibori, A. 2000. The Syntax of Subjunctive Complements: Evidence from Japanese. Doctoral dissertation, University of Connecticut.

Watanabe, A. 2004. The Genesis of Negative Concord: Syntax and Morphology of Negative Doubling. *Linguistic Inquiry* 35(4): 559–612.

Yamashita, H. 2003a. On the Distribution and Licensing of Negative Polarity Items in Japanese and the Phase-Impenetrability Condition. *The Proceedings of the 4th Tokyo Conference on Psycholinguistics*, ed. Y. Otsu, 313–337. Tokyo: Hituzi Syobo.

Yamashita, H. 2003b. Phase Theory and the Locality Condition of NPI Licensing in Japanese. Paper presented at *Ling-Lunch*. MIT, 5/8/2003.

Yamashita, H. 2005/in progress. *And Then There Were None Who Believes It (Soshite Dare-mo Shinji-naku-natta/Soshite Dare-ga Shinji-mo shi-naku-natta)* [Tentative/Working Title]. Ms. (12/31/2005), Yokohama National University.

Yamashita, H. 2006. *Prosody and the Syntax of Shika-NPIs in Tokyo Japanese: An Interdisciplinary Approach to the Theory of Grammar.* [Tentative/Working Title]. Ms. (8/31/2006), Yokohama National University (YNU).

Yamashita, H. 2007a. On the Interpretation and Licensing of *Shika*-NPIs in Tokyo Japanese and the Syntax-Prosody Interface. *WECOL* 2006, eds. E. Bainbridge and B. Agbayani, 487–498. Fresno, Calif.: California State University, Fresno.

Yamashita, H. 2007b. Prosody and the Syntax of *Shika*-NPIs in Tokyo Japanese. *Proceedings of the Workshop on Negation and Polarity*, eds. H. Zeijlstra and J.-P. Soehn, 120–126. Tübingen: University of Tübingen.

Yamashita, H. 2007c. *On the So-called "Split Indeterminate NPI Pronouns" in Japanese and Its Implications for the Theory of Grammar.* [Tentative/Working Title; Revised but a shorter version of Yamashita 2005]. Ms. (8/31/2007), YNU.

Yamashita, H. 2007d. Licensing of "Split" Indeterminate NPI pronouns in Japanese and the Syntax-Prosody Interface. Paper presented at *Japanese/Korean Linguistics* 17. UCLA, 11/9/2007.

Yoshida, T. 2001. Review of Tanaka 1999, Conditions on Logical Form Derivations and Representations. *GLOT International* 5(4): 152–157.

Yoshimura, K. 2007. The Semantics of Focus Particle *-shika* 'only' in Japanese. *WECOL* 2006, eds. E. Bainbridge and B. Agbayani, 499–512. Fresno, Calif.: California State University, Fresno.

Part VI

Formal Semantics
and
Discourse Analysis

The Korean Double Past Form -*essess* and Types of Discourse

EUNHEE LEE
University at Buffalo, SUNY

1. Phenomena

The English past -ed and the Korean past -ess both have the potential to move the time forward in narratives, while the English pluperfect (past perfect) had -en and the Korean pluperfect -essess trigger a flashback effect, introducing a background information. (1) is a discourse example extracted from a Korean novel. In (1), the third sentence in the Korean pluperfect (also called the double past, since it is the doubling of the past tense form -ess) describes an event that occurred before the events described by the preceding sentences. As shown in the English example (2), the English pluperfect also induces a flashback effect. In traditional Reichenbachian (1947) analysis, the simple past refers to an event that is included in the contextually given reference time (Rpt), and the past perfect refers to an event that precedes the Rpt. In discourse, the preceding sentences provide a Rpt.

(1)   Yengswuk-uy elkwul-ey cheum-elo huymihan wusum-i   penci
        Yengswuk-PS face -LC first time   faint   smile-NM spread

-**ess**-ta. 'Cal hay-ss-e.   Enni tekpwun-ey'. Tahee-nun apeci
-PST-DC well do-PST-DC sister thanks-to   Tahee-TP father
ceysa   -ka iss-ki ithul   ceney Yengswuk-ul manna
memorial-NM be   two days before Yengswuk-AC meet
ceysa-lul   neknekhi chiluko-to namul
memorial service-AC sufficiently carry out-even remain
ton-ul   cwu-**essess**-ta.[1]
money-AC give-PPF-DC
'For the first time, a faint smile <u>spread</u> over Yengswuk's face.
"Thanks to you, sister, it went well". (Yengswuk <u>said</u>.) Tahee <u>had
met</u> Yengswuk two days before their father's memorial service and
<u>had given</u> her enough money to carry it out'.

(2)   'Happy birthday, Ellie,' he whispered, handing her a gift. 'That's
for you.' Ellie opened it. It was a birthday card, hand-made by her
brother out of cardboard. He <u>had painted</u> a greeting on the front
and inside <u>had drawn</u> a picture of an animal and signed his name.
(In Sunshine or in shadow, Bingham, C, Bantam, London, 1992)

Many researchers have pointed out that the pluperfect form is required
in order to signal a reversed order configuration only in narrative text types
and that a simple past event-event can be interpreted as reversed order in
non-narratives (Caenepeel 1989, 1995; Caenepeel and Moens, 1994). In
other words, the contrast between deictic and non-deictic (or narrative) use
of tense may affect the interpretation of consecutive simple past event sentences. In the non-narrative context of conversations, where the primary
function of tense lies in establishing a relationship between a state of affairs
and its speech point, two simple past events can be interpreted in reverse
order if world knowledge allows for such an interpretation, and the pluperfect will not normally selected to express temporal precedence. In narrative
contexts, on the other hand, the use of the pluperfect is essential for marking anterior time reference: since there is no obvious relationship between
events and the speech time in such texts, greater text-internal restrictions
are imposed on temporal relations, and because of this, two simple past
event-event sentences cannot be interpreted in reverse order in such contexts. Consequently, in narratives we will not find sentences like (3) in an
explanation interpretation.

(3)   Max fell. John pushed him.

---

[1] The abbreviations in the gloss are as follows: PS: possessive, LC: locative, NM: nominative,
PST: past, DC: declarative, TP: topic, AC: accusative, PPF: pluperfect, COND: conditional,
RS: resultative.

Some recent proposals have attempted to explain a reverse order discourse like (3) in terms of world knowledge about causality overriding the principle that events introduce a temporal update (Dahlgren et al., 1989; Lascarides and Asher, 1993). For example, in (3), if a pushing and falling occurred, then one may assume that the pushing caused the falling. However, if we assume that world knowledge alone licenses a reverse order interpretation for simple past sequences, it is not clear why the following discourses sound odd.

(4)   a. ?Everyone laughed. Fred told a joke.
        b. ?The committee applauded. Niegel announced his promotion.

                              (Caenepeel and Moens, 1994:10)

There is a salient causal or scenario-based link between someone telling a joke and people laughing, or between someone's promotion being announced and people applauding, but that does not make these discourses acceptable. In this paper, therefore, I will assume that the contrast between the narrative and the non-narrative discourse types, due to the deictic and anaphoric nature of the tense in each discourse type, plays an important role in determining whether the pluperfect should be used for a temporal precedence relation or not. In narratives, in which tense is anaphoric, the pluperfect is used to encode a reversed order configuration, while in non-narratives, in which tense is deictic, simple past sentences can be interpreted as a reverse order. Given this, (4) is awkward because it is difficult to construct the non-narrative context required for their interpretation (Caenepeel and Moens, 1994:15). Caenepeel (1995:246), in her corpus study, shows that the pluperfect is seldom used in English news reports since they consist of non-narratives. [2]

The Korean -*essess*, by contrast, is freely used in both discourse types, but with different meanings. In narratives, as we observed in (1), -*essess* triggers a flashback effect. In Lee (2007), I have examined 158 narratives consisting of sentences in the -*essess* form. In the majority of the cases (138 out of 158, 87.3%), it is observed that an -*essess* sentence describes a situation occurring before the situation described by the -*ess* sentence preceding it. A similar trend has been observed in Wako et al. (2003). On the other hand, in the face-to-face conversation database used for Oh's (2003) study, the majority of -*essess* utterances signal discontinuity of the effect of a prior situation. (5) contains Oh's example.

---

[2] Caution should be called for, however, in considering different genres as representative of different discourse types because the discourse type can cut across genre lines (Smith, 2003).

(5)   Himtul-myenun mak chwunghyel toy-myense kulayse yak-ul
        be tough-COND wildly eyes became bloodshot so medicine-AC
        ttak nu-myen   na-**ssess**-ketun. Kulentey yopen-cwu-ka toy-nikka
        just put-COND be cured-PPF-DC but this week-NM become-when
        kapcaki nemwu simhay-ci myense ku yak-ul   nuh-etwu
        suddenly too much get worse-while the medicine-AC put-although
        'When I felt tired, my eyes became bloodshot. So I dropped some
        eye lotion into my eyes, and then <u>they got well</u>. But, with the be
        ginning of this week, suddenly they got worse, and even though I
        put the eye lotion into my eyes (they didn't get well)'

Unlike the English pluperfect, -*essess* also appears in isolated sentences, implying that the result state no longer obtains at the utterance time.

(6)   a. Aki-ka   camtul   -**essess**-ta.
        baby-NM fall asleep-PPF-DC
        'The baby fell asleep.' (but is awake now.)
        b. ?* The baby had fallen asleep.

To sum up, I have defined two different discourse types: narrative and non-narrative. Narratives have anaphoric tenses, which are interpreted with respect to verbal context. Non-narratives have deictic tenses, which are related to the speech time. The English pluperfect is only used in narratives because the simple past can supplant it in non-narratives, while the Korean pluperfect is used in both, but with different meanings.

2. Analysis

In this paper, I claim that the English pluperfect is ambiguous between preterit and aspectual meanings (Jespersen, 1924; Comrie, 1976; Ogihara, 1996), while the Korean -essess has only a preterit meaning. Existing analyses of -essess can be divided into two major groups: One group treats it as pluperfect, which corresponds to the English past perfect (Martin, 1954; Sohn, 1995), and the other analyzes it as containing a special aspectual meaning in addition to past, such as discontinuous/ceasing (Kim, 1975; Lee, 1987; Oh, 2003). I argue that -*essess* is a special kind of pluperfect, referring to an event preceding the reference time and lacking the aspectual meaning, requiring "absence of result state" at the given reference time. C. Lee (1987) claims that -*essess* cannot be pluperfect, citing examples like (7). -Essess, unlike the English pluperfect, cannot be used in the main clause in (7).

(7)   #Suni-ka yek-ey tochakhay-(e)ss-ul ttay kicha-nun ttena-(a)ssess-ta.
       Suni-NM station-LC arrive-PST-when train-TP   leave-PPF-DC
       [Intended] 'When Suni arrived at the station, the train had left.'

I argue that *-essess* is unacceptable in sentences like (7) because it lacks an aspectual meaning of resulting states, posessing only preterit meaning, i.e., past in the past. The English past perfect, on the other hand, is ambiguous between preterit and aspectual interpretations. In the English translation of (7), it has an aspectual meaning, referring to a state resulting from an event of the train leaving, i.e., the train's not being at the station at the time when Suni arrived there. The contrast between the two readings of the English perfect is also apparent in discourse (Ogihara, 1996).

(8)   John arrived at the airport at nine. He had left home two hours
       earlier. He had met a friend on his way to the airport.

(9)   John arrived at the airport at nine. Mary had already arrived
       there. He smiled at her.

The first occurrence of the past perfect in (8) induces a flashback effect. The past perfect here introduces a new time located earlier than the time of John's arriving at the airport and asserts that John's leaving home obtains at this time. The second occurrence of the past perfect describes an event that takes place after his leaving home, but before his arrival at the airport. The past perfect in (9) is different: The second sentence describes the "result state" of Mary's arriving at the airport, i.e., Mary's being at the airport. Although it does say that the time of Mary's arrival is located before John's arrival, this is not the main assertion made by the sentence. The assertion is that Mary was already there when John arrived.

Kamp and Reyle (1993:598-599) also maintain that the pluperfect is ambiguous and provide (10) as a clear instance of the aspectual pluperfect.

(10)   Mary was content. The past two days had been strenuous. But now
       she had sent off her proposal.

Due to the presence of the adverb *now*, the second pluperfect in (10) must describe a state holding at the given reference time. The preterit pluperfect, which typically occurs in narrative flashbacks, does not accept the modification of *now*.

(11)   Fred arrived at 10. (*Now) he had got up at 5. He had got dressed
       and had had a leasurely breakfast.

Another important difference between the two types of past perfect is that the preterit pluperfect has the capacity to sustain narrative progression, while the aspectual pluperfect does not. In (8), the second and the third sentences in the pluperfect move the narrative time forward.

In Korean, the resultative form *-a iss* must be used, rather than *-essess*, for a perfect-in-the-past meaning. (12) is the Korean translation of (9).

(12) John-un ahop-si -ey konghang-ey tochakhay-(e)ss-ta.
    John-TP nine -o'clock-at airport -LC arrive -PST-DC
    Mary-nun pelsse konghang-ey tochakhay-**(e) iss**/ *****essess**-ess-ta.
    Mary-TP already airport -LC arrive -RS   -PST-DC
    John-un Mary-lul po-ko uws -ess -ta.
    John-TP Mary-AC see-and smile-PST-DC
    'John arrived at the airport at nine. Mary was already in the state
    of having arrived at the airport. John smiled at Mary.'

Observe that the second sentence in discourse (12) is similar to the example in (7). In (7), the focus is the resulting state of the train's having left, i.e., it was not at the station when Suni arrived there, rather than a previous event of the train leaving. In this context, *-essess* cannot be used due to its absence of result state meaning.

A past time adverbial can modify reference time as well as event time in English (McCoard, 1978; Comrie, 1985).

(13) a. Yesterday, Mary came to John's office at six. But John had already left at six.
    b. Mary came to John's office at seven. John had left at six.

In (13a), John must have left some time before six: 'at six' specifies the reference time. In (13b), 'at six' is the event time, i.e., John's leaving took place at six. In Korean, on the other hand, an adverb modifying an *-essess* clause invariably refers to the event time and never the reference time. For example, (14) cannot mean that Inho was already in the state of having gone to school yesterday, i.e., he went sometime before yesterday.

(14) Inho-nun ecey   Seoul-ey ka-(a)ssess-ta.
    Inho-TP yesterday Seoul-LC go-PPF-DC
    'Inho went to Seoul yesterday.'

Moens (1987) argues that the four types of the perfect distinguished by Comrie (1976) and McCawley (1971) essentially boil down to one core perfect, which expresses a consequent state of some event. If the perfect expresses some consequent state, it can only operate on an event type having the consequent state that follows a culmination as part of its semantic structure. The acceptability of the Korean *-essess* sentence with an activity verb in (15) proves that no consequent state is involved in the Korean pluperfect.

(15)   Inho-nun matang-eyse nol-assess-ta.
        Inho-TP yard-LC   play-PPF-DC
        'Inho played in the yard.'

Based on this semantic difference between the pluperfects in the two languages, let me explain why the Korean pluperfect appears in non-narrative discourses including isolated sentences while the English pluperfects do not. It has been observed in the literature that there is a fundamental processing differences between narrative and non-narrative text types (Caenepeel, 1995; Caenepeel and Sandström, 1992; Caenepeel and Moens, 1994). In the narrative texts, there is no clear relationship between the referential domain of the text and the utterance time. Because of the cutting of the link between the text and the coordinates of its production, the narrative texts do not have a deictic center that links the text to its actual utterance event. The loss of deictic temporal reference is compensated for by the construction of a narrative time line, i.e., an imaginary time line that derives its existence solely from the text. In the absence of an index for speech time, tense will lose the deictic capacity it exhibits in other discourse types and, instead, take on an anaphoric role (Kamp and Rohrer, 1983; Partee, 1984). Since the narrative context is self-contained in the sense that it is independent from the actual speech point, the temporal location of events with respect to each other on the narrative time line becomes the focus for their temporal interpretation, that is, the temporal ordering of events with respect to each other is crucial for an adequate understanding. In non-narratives, on the other hand, the relationship between the discourse and the actual world, as well as the production and its perception, are far less indeterminate than in the case of narratives. Non-narratives are organized with respect to a deictic center (the point of speech), informing the addressee of significant recent events. Therefore, the deictic now of the speaker and addressee and the topical connection between events established from the viewpoint of this deictic center lend coherence to non-narrative discourses.

I argue that, in narratives, where the reference time is in the past and the speech time is bracketed (Caenepeel and Sandstrom 1992; Caenepeel 1995), the pluperfect describes an event preceding the past reference time in both English and Korean. In non-narrative discourse, where the reference time coincides with the speech time, the English pluperfect does not occur because its two functions, i.e., signaling an event preceding the reference time and describing a state holding at that time, are served by the simple past and the present perfect, respectively. By contrast, the Korean pluperfect indicates the discontinuity of the result state, which is not expressed by the simple past. The Korean simple past refers to a past event and pragmatically implicates that the resulting state still obtains at the utterance time (C. Lee, 1987).

(16)   a. Aki-ka   camtul-**ess**-ta.
          baby-NM fall asleep-PST-DC
          'The baby fell asleep (and is still asleep.)'
       b. Aki-ka   camtul-**essess**-ta.
          baby-NM fall asleep-PPF-DC
          'The baby fell sleep (but is awake now.)'

The Korean -*essess* form, therefore, still has a function to serve, namely, expressing the lack of a result state at the reference time (speech time), in non-narrative discourses and isolated sentences.

3. Semantic Representation

The semantics of the pluperfect in both languages is represented by Discourse Representation Theory (DRT, Kamp and Reyle 1993). In DRT, the ambiguity of the English pluperfect is made explicit by different DRS conditions. The pluperfect in an aspectual interpretation is represented as a perfect state which includes the temporal perspective point (TPpt), the point from which the described event is viewed.

(17)   Mary went to the post office. She had written the letter.
        $[n, t_1, e_1, x, y, t_2, s_2, z, u: e_1 \subseteq t_1, t_1 < n$, Mary (x), the post office $(y), e_1: x$ go to y, TPpt: e_1, s_2 O $t_2, t_2 < n, \mathbf{e_1 \subseteq s_2}, z = x$, the letter $(u), e_2 \supset\subset s_2, e_2: z$ write $u]$

In (17), $e_2 \supset\subset s_2$, means e_2 and s_2 abut, i.e., s_2 starts right after e_2 ends. The given TPpt, which is the event e_1 of Mary going to the post office, is included in the perfect state. On the other hand, the preterit pluperfect in (18) does not introduce a perfect state but instead refers to an event which precedes the TPpt.

(18)   Fred arrived at 10. He had got up at 5.
        $[n, e_1, t_1, x, y, e_2, t_2: t_1 < n, e_1 \subseteq t_1$, at $10(t_1)$, Fred $(x), e_1: x$ arrive, TPpt: $e_1, \mathbf{t_2} < \mathbf{e_1}, y = x, e_2 \subseteq t_2$, at $5(t_2), e_2: y$ get up$]$

    Now let me present the DRT representation of discourse containing -*essess*. (19) contains DRS for (16b) and (20) is the DRS for (1).

(19)   *Aki-ka camtul-essess-ta.* 'The baby fell asleep (but is awake now)'
        $[e, s, x, y, t_1;$ baby $(x), e: x$ fall asleep, $e \subseteq t_1$, TPpt: $n, t_1 < n, \neg[s = RS (e), t_1 < s \leq n]]$

(20)   [n, e_1, e_2, e_3, x, y, z, v, t_1, t_2, t_3,;Yengswuk(x), Tahee(y), father(z), memorial service(v), e_1:a faint smile spread over x's face, $e_1 \subseteq t_1$, $t_1 < n$, e_2: x say that thanks to y, v go well, $e_2 \subseteq t_2$, $t_2 < n$, Rpt: e_1, e_1 $< e_2$, e_3: y meet x and give x enough money to carry out v, $e_3 \subseteq t_3$, $t_3 < n$, two days before v(t_3), TPpt: e_2, $e_3 < e_2$]

In (20), the third sentence in the -*essess* form indicates an event of Tahee giving money to Yengswuk that had occurred before the events described by the preceding two sentences. The DRS condition $e_3 < e_2$ specifies this. (21) contains the DRS construction rule for -*essess*.

(21)   DRS construction rule for -*essess*
        Triggering configuration: VP-essess
        Choose TPpt: TPpt:= o
        Introduce into U_K: a new event discourse referent e
                             a new time discourse referent t
        Introduce into Con_K: $e \subseteq t$
                             $e < o$
                             ($\neg$ [s = RS (e), e $\supset \subset$ s, t < s $\leq$ o]])

4. Conclusion

In this paper, I have argued that the English pluperfect is ambiguous between preterit and aspectual meanings, while the Korean pluperfect (double past) has only a preterit meaning, requiring the absence of result state at the reference time. In narratives, where the Rpt is in the past and the speech time is not relevant, the pluperfect in both languages induces a flashback effect. In non-narratives, where the Rpt is the speech time, the English pluperfect does not show up because the presence of the present perfect and the simple past, while the Korean pluperfect odes since it encodes discontinuity. This paper has shown that the preterit and aspectual perfects are semantically distinct, as encoded by different constructions in Korean. It further demonstrated that the knowledge about the discourse structure influences the semantic interpretation of tense.

References

Caenepeel, M. 1989. Aspect, temporal ordering and perspective in narrative fiction. Ph.D. thesis, University of Edinburgh.

Caenepeel, M. 1995. Aspect and text structure. *Linguistics* 33: 213-253.

Caenepeel, M. and M. Moens. 1994. Temporal structure and discourse structure. *Tense and Aspect in Discourse*, eds. C. Vet and C. Vetters, 5-20, Berlin/New York: Mouton de Gruyter.

Caenepeel, M. and G. Sandström. 1992. A discourse-level approach to the past perfect in narrative. *Semantics of Time, Space, Movement and Spatio-temporal Reasoning: Working Papers of the 4th International Workshop*, Place: Chateau de Bonas.

Comrie, B. 1976. *Aspect*. Cambridge: Cambridge University Press.

Comrie, B. 1985. *Tense*. Cambridge: Cambridge University Press.

Dahlgren, K., J. McDowell and E. P. Stabler. 1989. Knowledge representation for commonsense reasoning with text. *Computational Linguistics* 15:149-170.

Jespersen, O. 1924. *The Philosophy of Grammar*. London: George Allen & Unwin.

Kamp, H. and U. Reyle. 1993. *From Discourse to Logic*. Kluwer.

Kamp, H. and C. Rohrer. 1983. Tense in Texts. *Meaning, Use, and Interpretation of Language*, eds. S. Bauerle and A. von Stechow, 250-269. Berlin/New York: de Gruyer,.

Kim, N. 1975. The double past in Korean. *Foundations of Language* 12: 529-536.

Lascarides, A. and N. Asher. 1993. Temporal interpretation, discourse relations and commonsense entailment. *Linguistics and Philosophy* 16: 437-493.

Lee, C. 1987. Temporal expressions in Korean. *The Pragmatic Perspective*, eds. J. Verschueren and M. Bertuccelli-Papi, 405-447. Amsterdam: John Benjamins.

Lee, E. 2007. Dynamic and stative information in temporal reasoning: Interpretation of Korean past markers in narrative discourse. *Journal of East Asian Linguistics* 16:1-25.

Martin, S. 1954. *Korean Morphophonemics*. Linguistic Society of America, Baltimore.

McCawley, J. 1971. Tense and time reference in English. *Studies in Linguistic Semantics*, eds. C. Fillmore and T. Langendoen, 96-113. New York: Holt, Reinhart and Winston.

McCoard, R. 1978. *The English Perfect: Tense-choice and Pragmatic Inferences*. Amsterdam: North-Holland.

Moens, M. 1987. Tense, aspect and temporal reference. Ph.D. thesis, University of Edinburgh.

Oh, S. 2003. The Korean verbal suffix -ess-: a diachronic account of its multiple uses. *Journal of Pragmatics* 35:1181-1222.

Ogihara, T. 1996. *Tense, Attitudes, and Scope*. Dordrecht/Boston: Kluwer Academic Publishers.

Partee, B. 1984. Nominal and temporal anaphora. *Linguistics and Philosophy* 7:243-286.

Reichenbach, H. 1947, *Elements of symbolic logic*. New York: Academic Press.

Smith, C. 2003. *Modes of Discourse*. Cambridge: Cambridge University Press.

Sohn, S. 1995. *Tense and aspect in Korean*. Honolulu: University of Hawaii Press.

Wako, M., K. Horie, and S. Sato. 2003. Reconstructing temporal structure in Korean texts: A comparative study with Japanese. Japanese/Korean Linguistics 11: 203-217. Stanford: CSLI.

Particles: Dynamics vs. Utility[*]

Eric McCready
Aoyama Gakuin University

1. Introduction

This paper is about sentence-final particles in Japanese. I will focus on the particles *yo* and *ne*, as they are perhaps the best understood. Here is an example of the phenomenon under consideration.

(1) ame-ga   futteiru {yo/ne}
     rain-Nom falling YO/NE

     'It's raining, {man/as you know}.'

As the glosses above make clear, the particles have no truth-conditional effects: adding a particle never changes the truth value of a sentence. Despite this lack of truth-conditional content, they are omnipresent in spoken discourse. Nevertheless, they are difficult to paraphrase, and in fact rather unclear in meaning, despite a great deal of research on them (see e.g. Takubo and Kinsui 1997, Noda 2002, among many others).

The goal of the present paper is as follows. The vast majority of work on the particles has been informal in nature. I want to consider two possible formal accounts of their meaning. In many cases, it is hard to see how a given author conceptualizes the particle meanings because of lack of formalization.

[*] Thanks to Nicholas Asher, Chris Davis, Stefan Kaufmann, Kazuo Nakazawa, Yukinori Takubo, Shigeo Tonoike, Henk Zeevat, and the audience at J/K16 for helpful comments.

In the case of particles, the meanings in question are so subtle that it can be difficult to follow explanations couched in ordinary language. I therefore hope that the present project can be of use to researchers in working on accounts of these, and other, particles. The work is also, I think, intrinsically interesting in that each of the approaches I will discuss embodies a particular intuition about what the particles do. This point will become clearer as we consider the formal accounts in question.

For reasons of space, I will not be able to consider the contribution of intonational contours to the interpretation of the particles. As shown by e.g. Moriyama 2001, *yo* and *ne* mean very different things when combined with different kinds of intonation and lengthening. Neither of the accounts discussed in the present paper can therefore be considered to be a full account of particle meanings. This disclaimer aside, I believe that one of the theories I will provide is on the right track. We will see the two theories in section 3, after considering some relevant data in section 2. Section 4 compares the two theories and their predictions. Section 5 discusses why the differences that were found between the theories exist, provides a synthesis of the two based on the conclusions drawn, and indicates some directions for future work.

2. Data on the particles

The core observation to be accounted for, common to nearly all analyses in the literature in one form or another, is that *yo* marks hearer-new information ('tellings') and *ne* marks hearer-old information ('confirmations'). I will discuss the analysis of Takubo and Kinsui 1997, which does not make this assumption, later in the paper.

It is often claimed in the literature that *yo* is used with sentences whose propositional content is not already known to the hearer. The proposal that *yo* marks new information accounts for the infelicity of using *yo* in (2) when the sentence is a reminder.

(2) Kyoo no   miitingu wa   sanzi kara desu (# yo)
     Today GEN meeting TOP 3:00 from COP (YO)
     'Today's meeting starts at 3:00.'   (Suzuki Kose 1997)

Use of *yo* is possible, however, if the hearer seems to have forgotten the meeting time. In the case of (2), for instance, if he doesn't seem to be going anywhere even though it's already 2:55.

Noda (2002) analyzes *yo* as having additional functions in addition to simply marking new information. For Noda, *yo* indicates that the speaker believes that the hearer should recognize, and accept, the propositional content of the sentence. Thus, the content marked by *yo* must not only be new to the hearer, but also believed by the speaker to be of importance to the hearer.

One way to think about how this plays out is by considering (3). In this example, adding *yo* seems to provide emphasis, or add a sense of urgency to the utterance. We might think of this as relating directly to this sense of 'importance,' or in other ways. Again, this will be reflected in the formal analyses I will provide in the next section.

(3)   Taroo-ga   kita   (yo)
       Taro-NOM came (YO)
       'Taro came.'

Yo produces a sense of insistence in both declaratives and imperatives. Let's consider first an imperative case. Here, the *yo*-less version is simply a request for the hearer to buy a new skirt. The version with *yo*, on the other hand, indicates that the speaker is trying to convince the hearer that the buying is something that should happen.

(4)   atarasii sukaato kat-te   (yo)
       new   skirt   buy-IMP (YO)
       '(Come on,) Buy me a new skirt.'   (Kose 1997)

The same happens in declaratives. It's easy to see this in dialogues where dubiety about φ in *yo*'s scope has been expressed. It is rather more natural to use *yo* than not in situations like these if the speaker is actually trying to convince the hearer of the truth of φ. To see this, consider the following dialogue. Here the use of *yo* is more natural than not in A's second utterance, where A is explicitly denying B's denial of A's first utterance. When the particle is not used, there is a nuance that A does not care whether or not B accepts the content; A is simply saying it again, not trying to convince B in any way.

(5)   a.   A: sakki   Jon-ga   kaetta
                just.now John-NOM went.home
                'John just went home.'
       b.   B: uso!
                lie
                'No way!'
       c.   A: kaetta   #(yo)
                went.home (YO)
                'He DID go home!'

There are also situations where *yo* has a modal-like meaning (McCready 2005, 2006); these will not be discussed here. They add another complication to the analysis that—as far as I can see—neither theory I will discuss can derive straightforwardly.

What about *ne*? The basic intuition is that *ne* marks confirmations: sentences the speaker takes to contain non-hearer-new information. Often these are paraphrased in the literature as tag questions:

(6)   Ame-ga   futteiru ne
       rain-Nom falling NE
       'It's raining, isn't it?'

Again I ignore the contribution of intonation, which complicates the picture considerably.

3. Two Formal Accounts

How to think about these facts? At least two options immediately suggest themselves, which turn out to correspond to two different formal accounts.

1. Particles are *instructions*
   ⇒ Dynamic semantic account
2. Particles are *markers of information content*
   ⇒ Utility/relevance-theoretic account

This section is devoted to these two accounts. I will show how each accounts for the facts about *yo* and *ne* discussed in the previous section, or, at least, seems to account for them.

3.1. The Dynamic Account

This account assumes dynamic semantics (see Groenendijk and Stokhof 1991 for the seminal paper). Let me briefly introduce this framework before we get into the meat of the analysis. The basic idea of dynamic semantics is that meanings (particularly sentence meanings) can be identified with the changes they make in the information state of the individual who processes and accepts them, rather than with their truth conditions. Formally, this means that sentence meanings are not propositions, but rather relations between sets of world-assignment pairs; sentence meanings in general serve to filter out pairs that do not verify the sentence content. Some sentences can actually change the context rather than just test it, for instance sentences containing indefinites. Here, the semantics modifies the input set of world-assignment pairs so that it includes at least one pair that verifies the new content. This move allows, for example, binding of variables outside the scope of existentials on standard, static semantic theories: $\exists x[Px \land Qx] \land S(x)$. For our purposes, though, the interest of this theory is that it enables a direct connection between processing and information content.

How can dynamic semantics capture the picture outlined above? Here is one way for *yo* (McCready 2005, 2006, somewhat simplified). We will need one basic concept, what I will call 'strong assertion, ' which I now define.

(7) $\sigma \| sassert\varphi \| \sigma' =$
       $\sigma \| \varphi \| \sigma'$ if $\sigma \| \varphi \| \neq \emptyset$
       $\sigma \| \downarrow \neg\varphi; \varphi \| \sigma'$ else.

That is, update with φ if such an update is admissible (does not result in an empty—crashed—information state)–and, if not, first downdate with the negation of φ and then re-update with φ. Downdate is an operation that removes content from an information state rather than adding it; downdating an information state I with φ (equivalently: updating I with $\downarrow \varphi$) yields $I - \varphi$. Sometimes this operation will require a more complex revision of the information state (belief set), for example when φ is a crucial premise in certain inferences; more details can be found in Gärdenfors 1988.

Armed with this definition, we can proceed to giving a semantics for *yo*, as follows. Here $must_d$ should be read as a deontic necessity modal like *should*.

(8) $[\![yo(\varphi)]\!] =$

    a.   Presupposition: $\mathcal{B}_S \neg \mathcal{B}_H \varphi; \mathcal{B}_S must_d \mathcal{B}_H \varphi$ (i.e. speaker believes hearer doesn't believe φ and speaker believes hearer should come to believe φ)

    b.   Semantics: $\sigma || sassert(\varphi) || \sigma'$ (ie. 'strong-assert' φ)

In words, *yo* states that the proposition in its scope is something the hearer should accept even if doing so requires a revision of her belief-set (Gärdenfors 1988); it also presupposes that the content be both hearer-new and something the hearer should believe. There may be some redundancy here; it could be argued that the second presupposition (that the hearer should believe φ) simply follows from the use of $sassert$ by Gricean reasoning. If the speaker feels strongly enough about the hearer's coming to accept φ that she is willing to force revision, then it follows that φ is something the hearer should believe. Nonetheless, I will keep this explicit here for the present.

This account works very straightforwardly. The presupposition forces hearer-newness, the modal statement accounts for 'relevance', and $sassert$ causes the forceful impression. This seems basically right.

Extending this sort of account, *ne* can be taken to mark information the speaker thinks is hearer-old, as in (9)

(9) $[\![ne(\varphi)]\!] =$

    a.   Presupposition: $\mathcal{B}_S \mathcal{B}_H \varphi$ (i.e. speaker believes it should be the case that the hearer already believes φ)

    b.   Semantics: $\sigma || \varphi || \sigma'$

In the above formula, $ne(\varphi)$ is also taken to assert φ (in order to account for examples like (10)).

(10) a.   A: Asita   Taro kuru no?
               tomorrow Taro come Q

               'Is Taro coming tomorrow?'

    b.   B: Kuru ne
               Come NE

'Yeah, he is.'

This might be a problematic feature. It seems to me though that the question-like aspects of *ne*-sentences actually come from intonation. For the purposes of comparing the two analyses, at least, this point will not cause trouble, so I will maintain this analysis.

3.2. The Relevance Account

The second option involves relevance, as formulated in terms of utility theory.

As Van Rooij (2003a, 2003b, i.a.) shows, one way to define the relevance of a sentence is to understand it with respect to the degree to which it clarifies the answer to the question under discussion (QUD; Roberts 1996). This notion of informativity can then be identified with relevance; it indicates the usefulness of a statement in providing an answer to the question at issue in the discourse, and hence of its relevance in that discourse.

Formalizing this conception of relevance involves making use of ideas from utility theory. The necessary concepts for defining relevance are provided in (11). Here P is a probability function.

(11) a. **Absolute informativity.** $inf(a) = -log_2 P(a)$.
    b. **Entropy.** $E(Q) = \sum_{q \in Q} P(q) \times inf(q)$.
    c. **Informativity value.** $IV(Q, a) = E(Q) - E_a(Q)$.

(11a) gives the 'real' information value of a. This is just the negative log 2 of the probability of a.[1] This means that as the probability of a proposition rises, its absolute informativity decreases. This conception of informativity is standard in utility theory.

To get the definition of informativity we are after, one where informativity is defined with respect to a question under discussion, we need the auxiliary notion in (11b), defined in terms of absolute informativity. This is the entropy of a question, the degree to which its answer is unclear; the closer to equal probability all answers to the question have, the less that's known about the true answer, and the higher the entropy. We can use this in turn to define the informativity value of a proposition (as answer to a question), as in (11c): according to this formula, the informativity value of an answer a is just the difference of the original entropy of Q and the entropy of Q after conditionalizing on a; this is the information added by the answer.

These concepts are applied to *yo* and *ne* in (12). This formulation also makes use of techniques from the semantics of gradable adjectives: context sets a degree above which the proposition can be said to be 'relevant' (cf. Kennedy 2007, though my formulation is somewhat different). This is the

---

[1] Recall that the logarithmic value of a number n for a base is the number that, when applied as an exponent to that base, yields n. For instance, $log_2 \frac{1}{2}$ is -1.

degree d_s in the formulas below. Here I assume that this is simply a point on a real-valued scale (a dense, total linear order), which is also what our formulation of informativity values yields.

(12) Where d_s is a contextually specified relevance threshold:

    a. $[\![yo]\!] = \lambda\varphi.[IV(Q,\varphi) > d_s]$

    b. $[\![ne]\!] = \lambda\varphi.[IV(Q,\varphi) < d_s]$

Thus *yo* just says that a proposition is relevant in the information-theoretic sense, while *ne* says it isn't, for in the one case the informativity value of φ is above d_s, and in the other, it is not. We will take these informativity values to be those of the interpreter, the individual to whom the utterance is addressed. This means that we are taking the hearer's knowledge into account when assessing probabilities and assigning informativity values, not the speaker's. We will play with this assumption a bit later in the paper.

How does this idea account for the facts? Here the computation is pragmatic, rather than semantic, as in the dynamic account: the high relevance of *yo*-marked sentences indicates their hearer-newness and the usefulness of accepting them (to resolve the QUD). Notice that if the hearer already knew the content of the *yo*-marked sentence, it would have a low relevance, for it would not help to resolve the entropy of the question. *Ne* is just the reverse; since the relevance of the content in its scope is low (below d_s), it fails to help resolve the question, and hence must be old information (or else just something irrelevant. I assume this case to be out for Gricean reasons).

4. Comparison

Which way should we go? Which account gives the better predictions? The answer to this question also speaks to the issue of how particle meanings should be conceptualized. Recall that, in a sense, the dynamic account corresponds to a notion of particle meaning on which particles 'issue' instructions on how to process the content in their scope; the relevance account, on the other hand, corresponds to a picture on which particles indicate something about the content in their scope, i.e. that it is relevant, or not. Thus, to the extent that the analyses I have provided are good formalizations of these two intuitions, it becomes possible to compare the two rather directly. This is what we will now do.

Three considerations immediately come to mind when trying to compare the two approaches:

1. Questions and imperatives

2. 'Strength' of utterance

3. Combinations of particles: φ *yo ne*

We will see that the last two are fairly decisive. The first proves to be a bit of a red herring in this context, though it raises interesting and complex issues.

Let's begin with it. What is the issue with questions and imperatives? Just this: *ne* can appear in questions and *yo* in imperatives, but not vice versa. Or so the story usually goes. We will have reason to question the second part of it in a moment.

Can we distinguish the two analyses based on these facts? As it turns out, not really. Both require certain assumptions to be made, but even with them the analyses are not able to fully adequately handle the effects of the particles on sentences that do not make assertions.

Why don't the basic facts differentiate the analyses? Consider first the relevance account. Here *yo* marks highly relevant information, and *ne* marks information that is not highly relevant. Since only the latter can appear in questions, we must assume that questions do not contain much information; since only the former can appear in imperatives, we must assume that imperatives are (potentially) highly informative. This actually accords quite well with intuitions about these clause types.

Now for the dynamic account. Here it is obvious why we cannot use *yo* with questions; questions cannot be asserted and so are not compatible with the *sassert* operator. Imperatives can be analyzed as statements that issue commands, which can then be the object of update (Asher and Lascarides 2004). This makes some sense until we consider the case of *ne*; here we would expect that we couldn't use it in questions either, given that it also involves an update.[2] This points to an issue in the semantics I have given: it can only handle assertions naturally.

The problem is that we have not considered what imperatives and questions *do*. Imperatives ask the hearer to do something; questions ask the hearer to provide some information. Neither of these things involve simple update. They are completely different kinds of speech acts than assertions (cf. Vanderveken 1990). The analysis must be extended to cover them. To see what must be done, consider the effect of *yo* in imperatives. In such examples, *yo* strengthens the request to the hearer. The same is true in questions, if one accepts that *yo* can in fact appear in such examples. It seems that it in fact can, as shown by examples like (13), pointed out to me by Shigeo Tonoike and Kazuo Nakazawa.

(13) doko-ni   iku no yo
      where-Dat go Q YO
      'Where are you going!?' (emphatic)

---

[2] Note that this problem would not arise if *ne* was given a different semantics, e.g. that of a polar question. Doing so would further highlight the problem discussed immediately below in the main text.

Here *yo* makes the request to the hearer for an answer to the question emphatic. What all this indicates is that we need to have a way to make the notion of strength explicit for other speech acts than assertion. I won't try to do this here for reasons of space, as it is a complicated project. Instead, let us now turn to the analysis of utterance strength as the next way to compare the analyses. It will turn out that this is the crucial case.

Recall the intuition that utterances with *yo* are stronger than the corresponding utterance without the particle (e.g. Noda 2002). The notion of relevance does not capture this, for *more relevant* doesn't mean *stronger*. while the dynamic account does. We built strength directly into the semantics by using a downdate operation in our definition of *sassert*. The dynamic account seems to have an advantage here.

Of course this follows from the notion of 'strong assertion,' which isn't used in the relevance account. Some might say that I am not being fair to the relevance story. Let's therefore see what we can do to introduce this notion into a relevance-based account. We might assume a principle along these lines:

(14) Strength for relevance: given a high enough relevance level for φ, accept it at all costs when it's asserted.

This at first glance looks like a good fix, but it is not. The problem is that now *yo* isn't doing anything; a sentence will be relevant with or without marking by a particle. The presence of *yo* is entirely superfluous to the application of this principle. This does not look like the right patch, but there might be one elsewhere.

For instance, we might try this.

(15) Strength with particles: if a speaker marks φ as relevant (using *yo*), accept it at all costs when it's asserted.

We have improved the situation: now *yo* is playing a role. But the principle still seems wrong intuitively, because this principle puts the onus on the hearer to accept the content of *yo*-marked sentences. The problem is that, actually, the hearer has no pragmatic obligation to accept such sentences. Rather, use of *yo* just signals emphasis by the speaker, and thereby that *the speaker* wants the hearer to accept the relevant content. Actually accepting it is not the hearer's responsibility, as the above principle would make it out to be.

We can conclude that this argument favors the dynamic account. This conclusion is strengthened when one takes imperatives and questions into account; if relevance has no way to account for strength in assertions, it certainly won't have any way to do so in questions or imperatives either.

Now we turn to the final point of comparison. Consider cases where *yo* and *ne* both mark utterances as in (16).

(16) Taro-ga   kuru yo ne
      Taro-NOM come YO NE

      'Taro's coming, right?'

If we analyze (16) compositionally as (17), a natural assumption made by many but not all authors, a clear difference emerges.

(17) $ne(yo(come(t)))$

On the dynamic analysis, (16) indicates that the strong assertion made by $yo(\varphi)$ is something the speaker thinks the hearer should already have accepted. This seems right. The relevance analysis, on the other hand, states that the relevance of φ's having high relevance is low, which is in no way the right reading. This actually points up a problem in the way we have formulated the relevance account. On the dynamic analysis, yo and ne introduced presuppositions about new vs. old information. The relevance account as stated makes the analogous relevance-theoretic statements into the main predication of the particle. This all suggests that the statements about relevance should be presuppositional. Making this change will bring the two into alignment, but the relevance account will still fail to account for strength. I will therefore focus on the dynamic account in the following discussion. We will bring relevance back into the picture in the final section.

Now a problem arises. The problem is that the presuppositions of yo and ne are incompatible: one states that φ is new information, and the other that it is not. There are two possibilities for a remedy. The first is that one of the presuppositions is removed or cancelled (cf. Beaver 1997). The story would be that, since the speaker chooses to use both particles together knowing that they are inconsistent, he must have intended that one presupposition disappear. Presuppositions can be cancelled by assertions, as in (18), but I don't know of other cases where they are cancelled by other presuppositions. But that doesn't mean such cases could not exist.

(18)   The king of France isn't bald—-there is no king of France, after all!!

The other possibility is that the presuppositions of ne are satisfied after composition with yo (this idea was suggested to me by Chung-Min Lee). Since before update φ is new information, but after update with $yo(\varphi)$ it is old information, further update with $ne(\varphi)$ will be possible, since the presuppositions of ne are satisfied. Of course, such update will be somewhat irrelevant, since φ is already accepted at this point. But this situation is possible. It further explains why we find the particle sequence *yone* but not the sequence *neyo*: the presuppositions of the latter are unsatisfiable.[3] This is extremely

---

[3] Maintaining the assumption that *ne* is assertive, of course; if it is a question, this explanation is lost.

desirable and intuitive.[4]

For this analysis to work, we must ensure that presuppositions are processed before the next presupposition comes in. There seem to be two ways to do this. The first is to simply resolve the presuppositions at the point at which they enter the composition.[5] With this, the presupposition of *yo* is satisfied when it is computed, and similarly for that of *ne*. This is rather intuitive and I do not see immediate formal difficulties with it.

The second option would involve interpreting the two clauses separately, which in turn requires duplicating φ. In fact, there is a proposal in the literature that lets us do just this. This is the analysis of *conventional implicatures* of Potts (2005). However, this analysis needs a bit of further specification for it to do the job we want it to.

Potts provides a logic for conventionally implicated content that puts it into a separate dimension of meaning. This is done in the logical syntax by separating content into conventionally implicated and at-issue content in the type theory: the first is given types with superscript c and the second types with superscript a. Schematically, when we combine an expression of at-issue type x with a functor y taking at-issue content to conventionally implicated content, we get the pair $\langle x, y(x) \rangle$. The first element of this pair is available for further composition. Effectively we have duplicated the content of x.

This logic will give the desired results, on the assumption that the conventionally implicated content is interpreted before the at-issue content (for otherwise the presupposition of *yo* will be undefined). Further, we must ensure that $yo(\varphi)$ is interpreted before $ne(\varphi)$, for otherwise the presuppositions of *ne* and *yo* will not be satisfied.[6] This might be reasonable; Wang *et al.* (to appear) show that we need to allow various orders of interpretation for at-issue and conventionally implicated content anyway.

Of course, all this depends on whether (17) is the right analysis. If it's not—if *yone* is really grammaticalized as a single particle, as some authors claim—then this argument doesn't let us make any distinctions. But I think the arguments from strength and *yone* together make a good case for pursuing the dynamic path.

The question of interest now is just why the dynamic analysis fares better.

---

[4] Interestingly, it partly corresponds to the analysis of Takubo and Kinsui (1997); for these authors, *yo* and *ne* are operators that manipulate information by moving it between two separate informational domains. The way the analysis derives the infelicity of *neyo* is very much like the one proposed here (as pointed out to me by Yukinori Takubo), although the model is quite different.

[5] Modulo requirements on variable binding and the like; space precludes showing exactly how this could be spelled out. In any case this problem won't be relevant here, since we are dealing only with presuppositions at the level of propositions.

[6] On the Potts analysis, conventionally implicated conditions appear in an unordered set.

What characteristics of this approach allow it to analyze the particles in a way that gives the (apparently) good results it does? There seem to be two parts to this answer, based on the two considerations we saw just above which favored the dynamic account.

The first is the notion of strength. On the dynamic analysis we can easily specify things about the action of the particles, where on the relevance analysis this is quite difficult—which is just to say that the notion of relevance by itself doesn't have anything to say about strength. It seems to me that the main advantage of the dynamic analysis is that it allows us to say things directly about how a particular piece of information—such as that in the scope of a particle—is to be handled. The result is that we can easily give a semantics for the particles that is in a sense 'metasemantic:' without introducing real content of its own, the particle can instead be analyzed as just telling the interpreter what to do with the information in its scope. This in turn speaks for the idea of treating the particles as *instructions*, in the sense that they tell the hearer what to do with information, rather than carrying information themselves.[7]

The second consideration comes from the case of *yone*, where the particles appear together. Here two factors may come into play. The first involves the question of whose information is being manipulated or checked. With the dynamic account, I introduced the $\mathcal{B}$ belief predicate, which was defined for both speaker ($\mathcal{B}_S$) and hearer ($\mathcal{B}_H$). This allowed us to talk about speaker beliefs about hearer beliefs simultaneously. In particular, the dynamic analysis I presented was stated in terms of *speaker beliefs about hearer beliefs*. With the relevance account, we did not have this ability. Perhaps this caused some of the problems.[8]

This discussion suggests that complicating the utility-theoretic model would perhaps solve the problem presented by *yone*. Let us try to do this now. Here is a new definition. $IV_H(Q, \varphi)$ indicates the informativity value of φ with respect to question Q.

(19) Where d_s is a contextually specified relevance threshold:

    a. $[\![yo]\!] = \lambda\varphi.[\mathcal{B}_S IV_H(Q, \varphi) > d_s]$

    b. $[\![ne]\!] = \lambda\varphi.[\mathcal{B}_S IV_H(Q, \varphi) < d_s]$

On the new definition, *yone*φ means: the speaker believes that the proposition that the speaker believes the relevance of φ for the hearer to be high is of low relevance. Or, if we assume that the content of particles is conventionally implicated in Potts's sense, it means that the speaker believes that the infor-

---

[7] Use of the particles does, of course, convey pragmatic information, such as how important the speaker takes the content they modify to be. But this is indirect.

[8] This criticism is due to Stefan Kaufmann.

mativity value of φ with respect to Q for the hearer is both greater than and less than the relevance threshold, which again is inconsistent. Conventional implicature again fails to help. But the first interpretation, while still clearly not the right one, is at least consistent. This avenue does not seem to have been very helpful. Let us turn to the second factor.

What actually seems to have made the difference is the dynamics. Note that if we assume a dynamic semantics, the contradictory interpretation we got from the relevance approach will disappear in just the same way as the problem with presuppositions in the dynamic approach, as discussed above. Again, when $yo(\varphi)$ is processed, the information will be new and thus highly relevant;[9] then update with $ne(\varphi)$, which states that the information is not relevant, will be fine, since the information has now been processed and consequently no longer provides any new content. The options for interpretation are the same as before: assume presupposition resolution occurs at any stage of combinatorics, or assume that particle content is conventionally implicated. Either seems to work fine. What distinguishes between them is that the latter approach forces a number of useless updates (one per particle), which one would expect to be pragmatically marked. Since use of particles is not marked in any way, the first approach should probably be preferred.

5. Conclusion

The dynamic analysis seems preferable to the relevance one, as these analyses were stated here. We proved to need dynamics to make the relevance story turn out consistent, when more than one particle modified a sentence. Still, there seems to be something right about the relevance story as well.

The discussion at the end of the previous section suggests a unification of the two approaches. We can simply omit the presuppositions involving old and new information from the dynamic approach and replace them with the statements about speaker beliefs about hearer informativity values that we used in our second formulation of the relevance account. It may be clear that the function of these statements was essentially to ensure hearer-newness (for *yo*) and hearer-oldness (for *ne*), which, of course, was the reason that adding dynamics enabled us to eliminate the problems with inconsistency that resulted from assuming a static semantics.

Substituting the statements about informativity values for the presuppositions about beliefs results in the following lexical entries for *yo* and *ne*.

(20) $[\![yo(\varphi)]\!] =$
    a.   Presupposition: $\mathcal{B}_S IV_H(Q, \varphi) > d_s$
    b.   Semantics: $\sigma || sassert(\varphi) || \sigma'$

---

[9] Assuming, of course, that the information was new and relevant in the first place.

(21) $[\![ne(\varphi)]\!] =$
   a. Presupposition: $\mathcal{B}_S IV_H(Q, \varphi) < d_s$
   b. Semantics: $\sigma ||\varphi||\sigma'$

The effect is the same as before. However, there are several nice features of this unified analysis. First, we are able to get rid of the awkward modal statement in the original dynamic analysis of *yo* (adopted from McCready 2005, 2006). Recall that we had a presupposition stating that the speaker believes that the hearer should accept the content in the scope of *yo*. Now we can take this to follow directly from the semantics of the relevance statement: given the speaker's belief that something is relevant (for you) in resolving some question under discussion, it would behoove you to come to believe it. This point becomes even more cogent if we assume other definitions of relevance in the literature, on which relevance is defined with respect to changes in perceived expected utilities of actions. If something can be expected to change your knowledge about whether it would be worth performing some action, you certainly ought to give it a fair hearing.

Notice that one might argue that *sassert* has a similar effect, in that it emphasizes the speaker's wish for the hearer to accept the content it modifies. But there is a difference. In the case of *sassert*, the speaker's desires might be entirely selfish. But in the case of relevance, the proposition in question is believed to be relevant (and thus useful) *for the hearer*. For this reason, even a hearer who might be disinclined to accept something strong-asserted from a given speaker would likely be willing to accept, or at least carefully consider, content that the speaker took to be relevant for her.

This observation raises a more general point about the two analyses. Logical dynamics have mostly been used in the literature to model various aspects of information processing, and how new information changes one's knowledge, beliefs, etc. Relevance (and its formalization in terms of utilities) essentially models aspects of how one's choices in dialogue depend on one's existing information and one's preferences in e.g. choosing actions or gaining information. This latter seems to be mainly a pragmatic notion. The extent to which relevance and utilities are appropriate to model particle meanings therefore depends completely on how 'pragmatic' these meanings are. The problem of providing a suitable analysis of particle meanings therefore speaks to a wide range of issues at the semantics-pragmatics interface.

More concretely, this analysis looks quite satisfactory for the assertive case of *yo* (and *ne*). It does not, however, account for situations in which the particles modify questions or imperatives. A second direction for research is the analysis of other particles in Japanese, and of particles in other languages. I have argued elsewhere that sentence-final particles in English such as *man* and *dude* have many semantic similarities to Japanese *yo*, as discussed by Mc-

Cready (2005), but it is not clear how far such similarities extend across other languages. The other particles in Japanese also present many challenges. For example, sentence-final *wa* in standard Japanese contains an emotional component that is not expressed at all in the present semantics, but may admit treatment in terms of expressive content (Potts 2007). Other uses of *wa* in dialects such as that of the Kansai region have a different nature that comes with its own set of problems, as do other dialect particles. All of these issues must be explored if we are to have a real understanding of what particles do and mean in the world's languages.

References

Asher, N. and A. Lascarides. 2004. Imperatives in dialogue. *Perspectives on Dialogue in the New Millennium*, 1-24. Amsterdam: Johns Benjamins.

Beaver, D. 1997. Presupposition. *Handbook of Logic and Language*, 939-1008. Amsterdam/Tokyo : Elsevier.

Gärdenfors, P. 1988. *Knowledge in Flux*. Cambridge, Mass.: MIT Press.

Groenendijk, J. and M. Stokhof. 1991. Dynamic predicate logic. *Linguistics and Philosophy* 14: 39-100.

Kennedy, C. 2007. Vagueness and gradability: The semantics of relative and absolute gradable predicates. *Linguistics and Philosophy* 30: 1-45.

McCready, E. 2005. The Dynamics of Particles. Ph.D. thesis, UTexas-Austin.

McCready, E. 2006. Japanese *yo*: Its semantics and pragmatics. *Sprache und Datenverarbeitung* 30:25-34.

Noda, H. 2002. Syuuzyosi no kinoo [The functions of sentence-final particles]. *Modariti [Modality]*, 261-288. Tokyo: Kurosio Press.

Potts, C. 2005. *The Logic of Conventional Implicatures*. Oxford: Oxford University Press. Revised version of 2003 UCSC dissertation.

Potts, C. 2007. The expressive dimension. *Theoretical Linguistics* 33: 165-197.

Roberts, C. 1996. Information structure: Towards an integrated formal theory of pragmatics. *OSUWPL 49: Papers in Semantics*, 91-136. The Ohio State University Department of Linguistics.

Suzuki Kose, Y. 1997. Japanese Sentence-Final Particles: A Pragmatic Principle Approach. Ph.D. thesis, University of Illinois at Urbana-Champaign.

Takubo, Y. and S. Kinsui. 1997. Discourse management in terms of mental spaces. *Journal of Pragmatics* 28: 741-758.

van Rooij, R. 2003a. Quality and quantity of information exchange. *Journal of Logic, Language and Information* 12: 423-451.

van Rooij, R. 2003b. Questioning to resolve decision problems. *Linguistics and Philosophy* 26: 727-763.

Vanderveken, D. 1990. *Meaning and Speech Acts*. Cambridge: Cambridge University Press.

Wang, L., E. McCready and B. Reese. to appear. Nominal appositives in context. *Proceedings of Western Conference on Linguistics 2004*.

Perspective, Logophoricity, and Embedded Tense in Japanese

DAVID Y. OSHIMA
Ibaraki University

1. Introduction

This paper investigates the following questions regarding the tense system in Japanese:

(i)   Are Japanese tenses (tense forms) indexical? (OR: Do they have an indexical use, at least?)

(ii)   Can tenses occurring in matrix clauses, complement clauses of attitude verbs, and adjunct clauses (e.g. relative clauses) be given a uniform semantic analysis?

(iii)   Sometimes the choice of a tense form is conditioned by the speaker's choice of perspective. Under what conditions, and why?

The organization of the paper is as follows. In Section 2, I review the two major approaches to Japanese tenses in past studies, i.e. the "uniform/non-indexical" approach (e.g. Ogihara 1996) and the "non-uniform/indexical" approach (e.g. Oshima 2006), drawing on data that involve tenses in matrix clauses and in complement clauses (of utterance/attitude predicates).[1] In Section 3, I consider tenses in relative clauses, which are often ambiguous between the so-called independent and relative interpretations, and demonstrate

---

[1] Throughout the paper, by the term "complement clause" I refer to the complement clause of an utterance or attitude predicate.

Это раз

data sets that pose a challenge for the uniform analysis along the lines of Ogihara (1996).

In Section 4, I propose that Japanese tenses are ambiguous between the indexical use and the perspectival use, where the former may be further split into the primary indexical use and the secondary indexical (logophoric) use. I also point out that the proposed indexical/perspectival ambiguity is attested in the domain of pronominal anaphora too, and thus is resonant with Partee's (1973) observation that tenses and pronouns have a number of analogous properties. In Section 5, I discuss properties of the perspectival tense in formal syntactic/semantic terms. In Section 6, I consider tenses in types of adjunct clauses other than relative clauses, such as BEFORE-, AFTER-, and WHEN- clauses, and propose that tenses under BEFORE and AFTER require an exceptional treatment.

2. Tenses in Matrix Environments and Complement Clauses

Japanese has a two-way distinction of tense: present and past. (The present tense is sometimes called the "non-past" tense.) A present tense form on a matrix predicate indicates that the time of the described event is posterior to or includes the speech time (*event time > speech time* or *event time ⊇ speech time*); the "inclusion" interpretation is available only with a stative predicate (Inoue 1989: 177). A past tense form on a matrix predicate, on the other hand, indicates that the time of the described event is prior to the speech time (*event time < speech time*).

(1) a. Ken-wa asita   Mari-ni a-**u**.
         K.-Top tomorrow M.-Dat see-Pres
         'Ken will see Mari tomorrow.'
     b. Ken-wa kinoo   Mari-ni at-**ta**.
         K.-Top yesterday M.-Dat see-Past
         'Ken saw Mari yesterday.'

Data like (1) suggest that Japanese tenses are Kaplanian indexicals on a par with *watashi* 'I', *kyoo* 'today', *koko* 'here', etc., whose meanings are contingent on the (external) context of utterance.

A tense occurring in a complement clause, however, cannot be considered a Kaplanian indexical (a primary indexical; see Schlenker 2003).

(2) (both uttered on Wednesday)
     a. Getuyoobi, Ken-wa [Mari-ga kinyoobi-made-ni ku-**ru**]
         Monday   K.-Top M.-Nom Friday-by   come-Pres
         to   omotte-i-ta.
         Comp believe-Past
         'On Monday, Ken thought that Mari would come by Friday.'

b. Kinyoobi, tabun   Ken-wa [Mari-ga moo   Tokyo-ni
   Friday   probably K.-Top M.-Nom already Tokyo-Dat
   kaet-**ta**]   to   omo-u   daroo.
   return-Past Comp believe-Pres it.is.likely
   'On Friday, Ken will probably think that Mari already returned
   to Tokyo.'

In (2a), if the tense in the complement clause is anchored to the external
"now" (= Wednesday), the complement clause would denote the proposition
that *Mari comes sometime between Wednesday and Friday*. But this is obviously not the proposition that Ken is related to by the "believing" relation; the
object of Ken's original belief must be something like: "Mari comes sometime between *now* and Friday". Similarly, in (2b), if the embedded tense is
anchored to the external utterance time, the complement clause would denote
the proposition that *Mari returns (returned) to Tokyo prior to Wednesday*,
which clearly is not the object of Ken's original belief.

   In the following, I briefly illustrate two competing approaches of Japanese
tenses in matrix clauses and in complement clauses, which I call the "uni-
form/non-indexical" approach and the "non-uniform/indexical" approach.

2.1. The Uniform/Non-indexical Approach

Ogihara (1996) maintains the view that Japanese tenses are not inherently indexical (see also Kusumoto 1999). According to his analysis, a tense form
introduces two temporal arguments, which can be informally called the "reference time" argument and the "event time" argument.

   When a tense form occurs in a matrix environment, the reference time
argument is replaced by the external "now" by a semantic interpretative rule
(truth definition) on the logical translation of the whole sentence; the event
time argument, on the other hand, is existentially bound by the same rule.
The following illustrates a semantic derivational process of a simple tensed
sentence, with relevant syntactic and semantic rules suggested by Ogihara
(1996: 64–66) (here, an intensional logic with time variables is adopted as
the meaning language).

(3)   Ken-ga ki-ta
      K.-Nom come-Past
      'Ken came'

(4)   a. **Relevant Syntactic Rules**:
          S → NP VP T
          VP → V
      b. **Relevant Translation Rules**:
          [$_S$ NP VP T] ↦ **T(NP(VP))**
          [$_{VP}$ V] ↦ **V**

(5) 1. Ken-ga $\mapsto \lambda P_{\langle e,\langle i,t\rangle\rangle}[P(\mathbf{ken})]$
     2. ki- $\mapsto \lambda x[\lambda t_1[\mathbf{come}(x)(t_1)]]$
     3. -ta $\mapsto \lambda\varphi_{\langle i,t\rangle}[\lambda t_2[\lambda t_3[t_3 < t_2 \wedge \varphi(t_3)]]]$
     4. Ken-ga ki-ta $\mapsto \lambda t_2[\lambda t_3[t_3 < t_2 \wedge \mathbf{come}(\mathbf{ken})(t_3)]]$

(6) **Truth Definition**: An IL expression ϕ of type $\langle i, \langle i, t\rangle\rangle$ that serves as a translation of a natural language is true with respect to context c, world w, and assignment g iff $[\![\exists t_0[\phi(c_T)(t_0)]]\!]^{c,w,g} = 1$

(n.b.) $[\![c_T]\!]^{c,w,g}$ = the time of c

When a tense form occurs in a complement clause, on the other hand, its reference time argument is left bound to a lambda operator and is not linked to a particular temporal point. The following illustrates a semantic derivational process for an attitude report sentence (Ogihara assumes that an attitude predicate denotes a relation between an individual and a set of world-time-individual triples).

(7) Mari-wa [Ken-ga ki-ta] to omot-ta
     M.-Top K.-Nom come-Past Comp believe-Past
     'Mari thought that Ken came.'

(8) a. **Relevant Syntactic Rules**:
         CP → S C
         VP → CP V
     b. **Relevant Translation Rules**:
         $[_{CP} S C] \mapsto \mathbf{S}$
         $[_{VP} CP V] \mapsto \mathbf{V}(^\wedge \lambda t_4[\lambda y[\exists t_5[\mathbf{CP}(t_4)(t_5)]]])$

(9) 1. Ken-ga ki-ta (to) $\mapsto \lambda t_1[\lambda t_2[t_2 < t_1 \wedge \mathbf{come}(\mathbf{ken})(t_2)]]$
     2. omot- $\mapsto \lambda\wp_{\langle s,\langle i,\langle e,t\rangle\rangle\rangle}[\lambda x[\lambda t_3[\mathbf{believe}(\wp)(x)(t_3)]]]$
     3. [Ken-ga kita] to omot- $\mapsto \lambda x[\lambda t_3[\mathbf{believe}(^\wedge \lambda t_4[\lambda y[\exists t_5[t_5 < t_4 \wedge \mathbf{come}(t_5, \mathbf{ken})]]])(x)(t_3)]]$
     4. Mari-wa [Ken-ga kita] to omot-ta $\mapsto \lambda t_6[\lambda t_7[t_7 < t_6 \wedge \mathbf{believe}(^\wedge \lambda t_4[\lambda y[\exists t_5[t_5 < t_4 \wedge \mathbf{come}(t_5, \mathbf{ken})]]])(\mathbf{mari})(t_7)]]$

Ogihara's analysis is "uniform" in the sense that it assigns the same lexical meanings to matrix tenses and an embedded tenses.

2.2. The Non-uniform/Indexical Approach

In Oshima (2006), I proposed that (at least certain occurrences of) Japanese tense forms are indexicals, and that they can be used either as primary indexicals (on a par with first person pronouns, etc.), or as secondary indexicals (on a par with logophoric pronouns; see Schlenker 2003, among others). (10) and (11) illustrate a semantic derivation process for (3), where the past tense is used as a primary indexical and is interpreted relative to the external context of utterance; note that the lexical meaning of the tense directly makes reference to the external context, through the special context variable $c*$.[2]

(10) a. **Relevant Syntactic Rules:**
        IV $\rightarrow$ IV$_{\text{stem}}$ T
        S $\rightarrow$ NP IV
    b. **Relevant Translation Rules:**
        $[_{\text{IV}} \text{ IV}_{\text{stem}} \text{ T}] \mapsto \lambda x[\mathbf{T}(\mathbf{IV}_{\text{stem}}(x))]$
        $[_{\text{S}} \text{ NP IV}] \mapsto \exists t_1[\mathbf{NP}(\mathbf{IV}(t_1))]$

(11) 1. ki- $\mapsto \lambda x[\lambda t_1[\mathbf{come}(x)(t_1)]]$
    2. -ta $\mapsto \lambda\varphi_{\langle i,t\rangle}[\lambda t_2[\varphi(t_2) \wedge t_2 < \mathbf{Time}(c*)]]$
    3. ki-ta $\mapsto \lambda y[\lambda t_2[\mathbf{come}\ (y)(t_2) \wedge t_2 < \mathbf{Time}(c*)]]$
    4. Ken-ga $\mapsto \lambda P_{\langle e,\langle i,t\rangle\rangle}[P(\mathbf{ken})]$
    5. Ken-ga ki-ta $\mapsto \exists t_3[\mathbf{come}(\mathbf{ken})(t_3) \wedge t_3 < \mathbf{Time}(c*)]$

(n.b.) a. (i) $[\![c*]\!]^{c,w,g}$ is defined only if $g(c*) = c$. If defined $[\![c*]\!]^{c,w,g}$
            $= g(c*)$.
        (ii) $[\![c_n]\!]^{c,w,g} = g(c_n)$.
    b. $[\![\mathbf{Time}(c)]\!]^{c,w,g} =$ the time of $[\![c]\!]^{c,w,g}$ (where $c = c*$ or c_n)

When tense forms are used as secondary indexicals, they are interpreted with respect to a secondary context associated with a reported attitude, utterance, etc. Following Oshima (2006), here I take the view that propositional attitudes are relations between an agent and a propositional character, i.e., a function from contexts to propositional contents (where a propositional content is understood as a function from worlds to truth values). (12) and (13) illustrate a semantic derivation process for (7), which contains a "logophoric" tense (i.e. a tense as a secondary indexical); "PAV" stands for "propositional attitude verb", and the subscript "log" indicates a logophoric tense.

(12) a. **Relevant Syntactic Rules:**
        CP $\rightarrow$ S C
        S $\rightarrow$ NP CP PAV
    b. **Relevant Translation Rules:**
        $[_{\text{CP}} \text{ S C}] \mapsto \mathbf{S}$
        $[_{\text{S}} \text{ NP CP PAV}] \mapsto \mathbf{NP}(\mathbf{PAV}(\lambda c_1[^\wedge \mathbf{CP}]))$

(13) 1. -ta$_{\text{log}} \mapsto \lambda\varphi_{\langle i,t\rangle}[\lambda t_2[\varphi(t_2) \wedge t_2 < \mathbf{Time}(c_1)]]$
    2. Ken-ga ki-ta$_{\text{log}}$ to $\mapsto \exists t_3[\mathbf{come}(\mathbf{ken})(t_3) \wedge t_3 < \mathbf{Time}(c_1)]$
    3. omot-ta $\mapsto$
        $\lambda\chi_{1\langle c,\langle s,t\rangle\rangle}[\lambda x[\lambda t_4[\mathbf{believe}(\chi_1)(x)(t_4) \wedge t_4 < \mathbf{Time}(c*)]]]$
    4. Mari-wa [Ken-ga ki-ta$_{\text{log}}$] to omot-ta $\mapsto$

---

[2] Here again, an intensional logic equipped with time variables is adopted as the meaning language, for ease of comparison with Ogihara (1996). In Oshima (2006), an extensional logic with world, time, and event variables is adopted as the meaning language.

$$\exists t_5[\textbf{believe}(\lambda c_1[^\wedge \exists t_3[\textbf{come}(\textbf{ken})(t_3) \wedge t_3 < \textbf{Time}(c_1)]])$$
$$(\textbf{mari})(t_5) \wedge t_5 < \textbf{Time}(c*)]$$

The grammar needs further restrictions (which I leave out here) to ensure that the contextual variable introduced by a logophoric tense is properly lambda-bound and that a primary indexical tense does not occur in a complement clause (see Oshima 2006 for a solution).

As long as the types of data discussed so far are concerned, the uniform/non-indexical analysis (along the lines of Ogihara 1996) and the non-uniform/indexical analysis (along the lines of Oshima 2006) make equally adequate empirical predictions. On grounds of conceptual parsimony, however, I believe that the non-uniform/indexical analysis is more advantageous for two reasons: (i) it dispenses with an *ad hoc* interpretative rule along the lines of (6), and (ii) an ambiguity between a primary indexical and a secondary indexical is a commonly attested phenomenon across languages and across various components of the context of utterance (Oshima 2006, 2007b; cf. Schlenker 2003). Besides, it conforms to the "common-sensical" view that tenses are inherently indexical (Perry 1997, among others).

In the following section, I consider additional types of data that involve tenses in relative clauses, and argue that although they provide *prima facie* support for the uniform analysis (and a challenge for the indexicality-based analysis), they bring up a crucial problem for the uniform analysis too (and thus neither Ogihara's nor Oshima's account provides a complete picture of the Japanese tense system).

3. Tenses in Relative Clauses

Tenses occurring in relative clauses are often ambiguous between the so-called "independent" and "relative" interpretations.

(14)   (the "independent" interpretation)

a.   Ken-wa [ima kokuban-no   mae-ni   tatte-i-**ru**]
K.-Top now blackboard-Gen front-Dat stand-Asp-Pres
otoko-to kinoo   kenka-si-ta.
man-with yesterday fight-Past.
'Yesterday Ken had a fight with the man who is now standing in front of the blackboard.'

b.   Ken-wa [sakki   heya-o   dete-it-**ta**] otoko-to
K.-Top a.while.ago room-Acc go.out-Past man-with
kinoo   kenka-si-ta.
yesterday fight-Past.
'Yesterday Ken had a fight with the man who left the room a while ago.'

(15)   (the "relative" interpretation)

a. Ken-wa [soozi-o   site-i-**ru**]   otoko-ni "Ohayoo" to
    K.-Top cleaning-Acc do-Asp-Pres man-Dat *ohayoo*   Comp
    it-ta.
    say-Past
    'Ken said "Good morning" to the man who was cleaning up.'

b. Raisyuu   Ken-wa [yuubinbutu-o azukatte-kure-**ta**] otoko-ni
    next.week K.-Top mail-Acc   keep-Ben-Past   man-Dat
    "Arigatoo" to   i-u-daroo.
    arigatoo   Comp say-Pres-probably
    'Next week, Ken will probably say "Thank you" to the man who
    kept his mail.'

The availability of the relative interpretation is problematic for the indexical-ity-based analysis illustrated above; since the embedded tenses in (15) do not occur under attitude predicates, it predicts that only the independent interpre-tation (i.e., the primary indexical interpretation) is available for them.

Ogihara (1996), on the other hand, proposes a rather simple solution, which appears to give credit to his uniform analysis. He attempts to reduce the independent/relative ambiguity of a tense in a relative clause to a matter of NP-scoping. That is, when an NP modified by a relative clause takes wide semantic scope in relation to the matrix tense, the embedded tense receives the independent interpretation; if an NP with a relative clause stays in the scope of the matrix tense, then the embedded tense receives the relative inter-pretation.[3]

The scope-based analysis, however, has one crucial problem: it fails to ac-count for an important property of tenses in adjunct clauses (on their relative interpretation), i.e., their perspective-sensitivity.

Tenses in adjunct clause can receive the relative interpretation only when the speaker takes the viewpoint (in the sense of Kuno and Kaburaki 1977) of a higher subject's referent, and conversely, when the speaker takes the viewpoint of a higher subject's referent, the relative interpretation of the subordinate tense is forced or favored (cf. Uno and Ikegami 2005; Hirose 2000; Inoue 1989: 175–182). Consider the examples below, which all involve perspective-sensitive expressions ($\sqrt{}$ = "fully acceptable").

---

[3] Although Ogihara does not elaborate on this point, his specific analysis (that utilizes a quanti-fier raising rule à la May) appears to make certain problematic predictions, such as: (i) a tense in a relative clause modifying a subject NP allows only the independent interpretation, and (ii) when a quantificational object NP with a relative clause takes wide (narrow) scope in relation to a quan-tificational subject NP, the embedded tense allows only the independent (relative) interpretation. Neither of these predictions holds (I leave out specific illustrations due to space limitation). It may be possible, however, to solve such technical difficulties with additional syntactic/semantic stipulations.

(16) Hanako-ga heya-ni   haitte-kita-toki,   Taro$_i$-wa
      H.-ga   room-Dat enter-come-when T.-Top
      [{a. **kare**$_i$/b. **zibun**$_i$}-ga suwatte-i-**ru**] isu-no   sita-ni
      {a. he/b. self}-Nom   sit-Asp-Pres chair-Gen underneath-Dat
      hon-o   oi-**ta**.
      book-Acc put-Past
      'When Hanako came into the room, Taro put the book under the chair
      on which he **is** sitting (now).' (a: √; b: ?*)
      'When Hanako came into the room, Taro put the book under the chair
      on which he **was** sitting (then).' (a: (?); b: √)

                                                  (adapted from Hirose 2000)

(17) (Intended: 'Ken verbally abused Yumi, who **was** helping him fix the
      car.')
      a. Ken-wa kuruma-no syuuri-o   tetudatte-**agete**-i-**ta** Yumi-ni
          K.-Top car-Gen   repair-Acc help-Ben-Asp-Past Y.-Dat
          akutai-o   tui-ta.
          bad.mouth-Acc make-Past
      b. Ken-wa kuruma-no syuuri-o   tetudatte-**kurete**-i-**ta** Yumi-ni
          K.-Top car-Gen   repair-Acc help-Ben-Asp-Past Y.-Dat
          akutai-o   tui-ta.
          bad.mouth-Acc make-Past
      c. ?Ken-wa kuruma-no syuuri-o   tetudatte-**agete**-i-**ru** Yumi-ni
          K.-Top car-Gen   repair-Acc help-Ben-Asp-Past Y.-Dat
          akutai-o   tui-ta.
          bad.mouth-Acc make-Past
      d. Ken-wa kuruma-no syuuri-o   tetudatte-**kurete**-i-**ru** Yumi-ni
          K.-Top car-Gen   repair-Acc help-Ben-Asp-Past   Y.-Dat
          akutai-o   tui-ta.
          bad.mouth-Acc make-Past

(18) Ken-wa [**migigawa**-ni oite-a(t)-{a. **ru**/b. **ta**}]   hon-o
      K.-Top right-Dat   put-Asp-{a. Pres/b. Past} book-Acc
      te-ni   tot-ta.
      hand-Dat take-Past
      'Ken took in his hand the book that **was** placed on his right (from his
      viewpoint).' (a: √; b: (?))
      'Ken took in his hand the book that **was** placed to the right (from my
      viewpoint).' (a: ?; b: √)
      'Ken took in his hand the book that **is** (now) placed on his right (from
      his viewpoint).' (a: (?); b: *)
      'Ken took in his hand the book that **is** (now) placed to the right (from

my viewpoint.' (a: $\sqrt{}$; b: *)

In (16), when *zibun* in its perspectival use, which indicates that the speaker takes the point of view of its antecedent's referent (Kuno 1978; Oshima 2007a), is used instead of a regular pronoun, the embedded tense allows the relative interpretation only. In (17), the relative interpretation of the embedded tense is easier to obtain with -*kureru*, which indicates that the speaker takes the beneficiary's perspective, than with -*ageru*, which indicates that the speaker takes the benefactor's perspective or the neutral perspective (see also (25) below) (Kuno and Kaburaki 1977; Oshima 2006).[4] (18) illustrates that the relative interpretation of an embedded tense elicits the "intrinsic frame"-based interpretation, rather than the "relative frame"-based interpretation, of a deictic angular expression (e.g. *migigawa* 'to the right'; see Levinson 2003). As pointed out in Oshima (2007a), the choice between the intrinsic and relative frames too has an intimate correlation with the speaker's perspective: when the speaker takes a particular individual's perspective, the intrinsic frame (whose center is the individual in question) becomes predominant.

Obviously, the illustrated, perspective-related phenomena do not follow from the scope-based analysis (alone).

4. Another Analogy between Pronouns and Tenses

Based on the data discussed in the previous section, I propose that "relatively interpreted" tenses in adjunct clauses constitute a distinct use of tense forms: i.e., the perspectival use. A tense in its perspectival use (i) poses a restriction on the time of an event in relation to that of the event described in a higher clause (typically the matrix clause), and furthermore (ii) indicates that the speaker takes the perspective of the referent of the subject of the higher clause in question (see Section 5 for details). Combined with the non-uniform/indexical analysis illustrated in Section 2, this idea implies that Japanese tenses are ambiguous (or underspecified) between: (i) the primary indexical use, (ii) the secondary indexical use (the logophoric use), and (iii) the perspectival use.[5]

Interestingly, a similar type of ambiguity is attested in the domain of pronominal anaphora too. The pronoun *zibun* in Japanese, for example, is ambiguous between the secondary indexical use and the perspectival use (among others) (Oshima 2004, 2006, 2007a; Kuno 1978).

Parallels between *zibun* and Japanese tenses can be summarized as follows:

---

[4] -*ageru* is a polite form of -*yaru*; the two forms share the same argument-taking pattern and are subject to the same perspective-related constraint.

[5] It may be possible to combine the same idea with the uniform/non-indexical analysis as well; here I do not adopt this option, for the reasons stated in Section 2.2.

(19)   *Zibun* has, besides the reflexive use, a secondary indexical use and a perspectival use. *Zibun* in its perspectival use is bound to a structurally commanding subject, and indicates that the speaker takes the viewpoint of its referent. (Furthermore, *zibun* is used as a primary indexical too in certain speech styles.)

(20)   Japanese tenses have, besides the primary indexical use, a secondary indexical use and a perspectival use. A tense in its perspectival use is linked to the tense of a structurally higher clause, and indicates that the speaker takes the viewpoint of the referent of the subject of the higher clause.

The proposed analysis provides a straightforward account of the fact that in many languages, such as Russian and Imbabura Quechua, tenses in complement clauses allow the (so-called) relative interpretation but tenses in relative clauses do not (Kusumoto 1999; Comrie 1985): tenses in such languages simply lack a perspectival use, while they have a secondary indexical use. The tense systems in such languages can be analogized with the pronominal systems in languages like Icelandic and Mundang, which have "logophors" but lack perspectival pronouns (see Table 1, adapted from Oshima 2007a; cf. Culy 1997).

The logophoric/perspectival ambiguity, thus, can be considered an addition to "analogies between pronouns and tenses (pronominal and temporal anaphora)", which are extensively discussed by authors like Partee (1973) and Kratzer (1998).

TABLE 1 Homophony of locally-bound anaphors, logophors, and perspectival pronouns (adapted from Oshima 2007a)

	reflexive	logophoric	perspectival
Japanese	*zibun*	*zibun*	*zibun*
Icelandic	(*sjálfan*) *sig*	*sig*	(no counterparts)
Ewe, etc.	refl. forms	log. pronouns	log. pronouns
Mundang, etc.	refl. forms	log. pronouns	(no counterparts)

5. Syntactic/Semantic Formulations of the Perspectival Tense

Let us now turn to formal discussions of syntactic/semantic properties of the perspectival tense (in Japanese). The meaning of a perspectival tense has a "semantic" side, i.e., a restriction on the temporal ordering of events, and a "pragmatic" side, i.e., a restriction on the speaker's perspective.

5.1. The Semantic Side

A perspectival tense poses a restriction on the time of the event described by a subordinate predicate in relation to the time of the event described by a higher predicate. The event that serves as the "reference point" for a perspectival tense does not have to be the one described by the matrix predicate, or the one described by the immediately dominating predicate; the following example illustrates this point, where the deeply embedded tense can be interpreted with respect to either the time of the matrix event or the time of the intermediate event (or the utterance time).

(21) 2-nen-mae, Ken-wa [[Kanbozia-de NGO-katudoo-o
      2.years.ago K.-Top   Cambodia-Loc NGO-activity-Acc
      site-i-**ru**] zyosee-ga   kai-ta]   hon-o   yon-da.
      do-Asp-Pres woman-Nom write-Past book-Acc read-Past
      'Two years ago, Ken read a book written by a woman working for an NGO in Cambodia.'

(22) Possible interpretations of (21), where:
      t_0 = the utterance time; t_1 = the time of reading (= two years ago); t_2 = the time of writing; t_3 = the time of being an NGO member
      a. **relative interpretation #1:** $t_2 < t_1 < t_0$ and $t_2 \subseteq t_3$
      b. **relative interpretation #2:** $t_2 < t_1 < t_0$ and $t_1 \subseteq t_3$
      c. **independent interpretation:** $t_2 < t_1 < t_0$ and $t_0 \subseteq t_3$

Even if we put aside the issue of perspective-sensitivity, to give a proper logical representation of a sentence involving a perspectival tense (or a relative tense in the general sense) is not a trivial matter. While sentences like (15) and (21) are relatively unproblematic, as far as I can tell, there is no straightforward way to provide adequate logical translations of sentences like (23), which involve quantification with ALL, MOST, etc., in a static framework (let alone deriving them compositionally).

(23) a. Sotugyoo-su-**ru** dono gakusee-mo Yamada-kyoozyu-ni
          graduate-Pres any student   Y.-professor-Dat
          aisatu-ni-it-ta.
          greet-go-Past
          'Every student who was going to graduate paid a visit to Professor Yamada.'
      b. Hotondo-no sotugyoo-su-**ru** gakusee-ga
          most   graduate-Pres   student-Nom
          Yamada-kyoozyu-ni aisatu-ni-it-ta.
          Y.-professor-Dat   greet-go-Past
          'Most students who were going to graduate paid a visit to Professor Yamada.'

The problem here is that the time (or event) variable introduced by the subordinate predicate cannot be properly linked to the one introduced by the higher predicate. Partee (1989) discusses similar types of difficulties concerning the treatment of temporal bound variables in English sentences like (24), and provides a (somewhat schematic) solution couched in the Discourse Representation Theory framework (cf. Pratt and Francez 2001).

(24) a. Whenever Mary telephoned, Sam was asleep.
      b. When Mary telephoned, Sam was always asleep.

The solution suggested by Partee (1989), which utilizes the concept of (up-datable) "reference time", seems to be applicable to the perspectival tense as well.

5.2. The Pragmatic Side

A perspectival tense indicates that the speaker takes the viewpoint of the referent of a higher subject, or more precisely, the subject of the higher clause in relation to which it is interpreted. Technically, we can think of the possibility that a perspectival tense may be temporally linked to a higher clause and perspectivally linked a higher subject, where the latter is not necessarily the subject of the former. This possibility, which is intuitively quite implausible, can be refuted by considering data like the following:

(25) 2-nen-mae, Ken-wa [[Kanbozia-de   NGO-katudoo-o
      2.years.ago K.-Top   Cambodia-Loc NGO-activity-Acc
      site-i-**ru**]   Yumi-ga kai-ta]   syoosetu-o
      do-Asp-Pres Y.-Nom   write-Past novel-Acc
      syuppan-site-{a. age/b. kure}-ta.
      publish-Ben-Past
      'Two years ago, Ken published the novel that Yumi wrote, who {is/was} working for an NGO in Cambodia (for Yumi's sake).'

The interpretation where the deeply embedded -*ru* is anchored to the time of writing is more predominant for (25b), where -*kureru* indicates that the speaker takes Yumi's viewpoint rather than Ken's. The interpretation where -*ru* is anchored to the time of publishing (and thus the time of writing may be prior to the time when Yumi became an NGO member) is more easily available for (25a), where -*ageru* indicates that the speaker takes Ken's viewpoint or keeps the neutral perspective.

To represent the perspective-sensitivity of the perspectival tense, we need to incorporate the following components in the grammar:

(26) (i)   A formal mechanism to represent the notion of the speaker's perspective.
      (ii) Constraints at the syntax/semantics interface, which allow us

to properly link (through syntactic feature specifications and indexing, for instance) a perspectival tense to a higher subject/predicate.

For (i), we can utilize the theory of linguistic empathy (Kuno and Kaburaki 1977; Kuno 1978, among others) and its model-theoretic implementation along the lines of Oshima (2006, 2007a). I leave details of (ii) open for future studies.

6. Temporal Adverbial Clauses

The independent/relative ambiguity of a tense form is attested in WHEN-clauses as well (at least when the predicate in a WHEN-clause is stative), but not in BEFORE- and AFTER- clauses. BEFORE- and AFTER- clauses allow the relative tense interpretation only.

(27) Ken-wa, Mari-ga benkyoo-site-i-{a. ru/b. ta} toki, terebi-o
      K.-Top M.-Nom study-Asp-Pres/Past   when TV-Acc
      mite-i-ta.
      watch-Asp-Past
      'Ken was watching TV while Mari was studying.'

(28) Ken-wa, Mari-ga kae(t)-{a. ru/b. *ta} mae-ni, ki-ta.
      K.-Top M.-Nom go.home-Pres/Past before come-Past
      'Ken came before Mari went home.'

(29) Ken-wa, Mari-ga kae(t)-{a. *ru/b. ta} ato, ku-ru-daroo.
      K.-Top M.-Nom go.home-Pres/Past after come-Pres-probably
      'Probably Ken will come after Mari goes home.'

Ogihara's (1996) analysis can easily deal with data like (28) and (29); the irregular behavior of a tense under WHEN, however, is a problem for his analysis.

   Furthermore, while a relatively interpreted tense under WHEN is sensitive to the speaker's choice of perspective (on a par with a relatively interpreted tense in a relative clause), there seems to be no reason to believe that a tense under BEFORE or AFTER has this property.

(30) (Intended: 'Ken was quiet while Mari was helping him out.')
      a. Ken$_i$-wa, Mari-ga **zibun**$_i$-o tetudatte-**kurete**-i-{**ru**/?**ta**} toki,
          K.-Top M.-Nom self-Acc help-Ben-Asp-Pres/Past   when
          zutto   damatte-i-ta.
          all.along be.quiet-Asp-Past
      b. Ken$_i$-wa, Mari-ga **kare**$_i$-o tetudatte-**agete**-i-{?**ru**/**ta**} toki,
          K.-Top M.-Nom he-Acc help-Ben-Asp-Pres/Past   when

> zutto   damatte-i-ta.
> all.along   be.quiet-Asp-Past

I propose that tense forms under BEFORE/AFTER are "expletive" (not semantically interpreted; cf. Kratzer 1998). The temporal ordering between the matrix and subordinate events is encoded by the semantics of *mae* 'before' and *ato* 'after'; the present and past forms within BEFORE- and AFTER-clauses are chosen merely due to idiosyncratic selectional conditions enforced by *mae* and *ato*.[6]

7. Conclusion

I argued that the tense forms in Japanese have three distinct uses (putting aside the "expletive" use mentioned in Section 6): (i) the primary indexical use, (ii) the secondary indexical (logophoric) use, and (iii) the perspectival use. The logophoric/perspectival ambiguity is attested in the domain of nominal anaphora too, and thus can be considered an addition to "parallels between tenses and pronouns".

The present study leaves several issues open for future inquiry. First, The precise formulation on syntactic/semantic constraints on the perspectival tense is yet to be developed. Second, questions from the typological view-point, such as "What other languages have perspectival tenses?" are left open, too. Finally, data that involve a fuller range of subordinate clause types (e.g. IF- and BECAUSE- clauses) need to be investigated (cf. Uno and Ikegami 2005).

References

Comrie, B. 1985. *Tense.* Cambridge: Cambridge University Press.

Culy, C. 1997. Logophoric pronouns and point of view. *Linguistics* 35: 845–859.

Hirose, Y. 2000. Siten to tikakukūkan no sōtaika [Point of view and relativization of the cognitive space]. *Kūkanhyōgen to bunpō [Spatial expressions and grammar]*, eds. S. Aoki and K. Takezawa, 143–161. Tokyo: Kurosio Publisher.

Inoue, K. 1989. *Nihongo bunpō syōziten [A small dictionary of the Japanese grammar].* Tokyo: Taishukan.

Kratzer, A. 1998. More structural analogies between pronouns and tenses. *Semantics and Linguistic Theory* 8: 92–110. Cornell: CLC Publications.

Kuno, S. 1978. *Danwa no bunpō [Grammar of discourse].* Tokyo: Taishukan.

Kuno, S. and E. Kaburaki. 1977. Empathy and syntax. *Linguistic Inquiry* 8: 625–672.

Kusumoto, K. 1999. Tense in Embedded Context. Ph.D. thesis, University of Massachusetts.

Levinson, S. C. 2003. *Space in Language and Cognition: Explorations in Cognitive Diversity.* Cambridge: Cambridge University Press.

---

[6] This line of analysis may be applicable to certain irregularities concerning the tense form choice under English *before* and *after* as well (see Ogihara 1996: 184–187).

Ogihara, T. 1996. *Tense, Attitudes, and Scope.* Dordrecht: Kluwer.

Oshima, D. Y. 2004. *Zibun* revisited: Empathy, logophoricity and binding. *Proceedings of the 20th NWLC (University of Washington Working Papers* 23), 175–190. University of Washington.

Oshima, D. Y. 2006. Perspectives in Reported Discourse. Ph.D. thesis, Stanford University.

Oshima, D. Y. 2007a. On empathic and logophoric binding. *Research on Language and Computation* 5(1): 19–35.

Oshima, D. Y. 2007b. Motion deixis, indexicality, and presupposition. *Semantics and Linguistic Theory* 16, 172–189. Cornell: CLC Publications.

Partee, B. 1973. Some structural analogies between tenses and pronouns in English. *Journal of Philosophy* 70: 601–609.

Partee, B. 1984. Nominal and temporal anaphora. *Linguistics and Philosophy* 7: 243–286.

Perry, J. 1997. Indexicals and demonstratives. *A Companion to Philosophy of Language*, eds. C. Wright and B. Hale, 586-612. Oxford: Blackwell.

Pratt, I. and N. Francez. 2001. Temporal prepositions and temporal generalized quantifiers. *Linguistics and Philosophy* 24: 187–221.

Schlenker, P. 2003. A plea for monsters. *Linguistics and Philosophy* 26: 29–120.

Uno, R. and T. Ikegami. 2005. Perspectives and tense in Japanese causal clauses. paper presented at the 9th International Cognitive Linguistics Conference.

Tense and Modality in Japanese Causal Expressions[*]

SANAE TAMURA
Kyoto University

1. Introduction

The Japanese verbal suffix *-ru* is said to be a 'non-past' tense marker. However, in a complex sentence containing the subordinate conjunctive *kara* (because), clauses with *-ru* can refer to past events as in (1).[1,2]

---

[*] I would like to thank Yukinori Takubo, Priya Ananth, Setsuko Arita, Matt Berends, Yurie Hara, Yuka Hayashi, Ikumi Imani, Stefan Kaufmann, Kyung-ae Kim, Eric McCready, Hiroshi Mito, Makoto Ohura, Mariko Otsuka, Sylwia Staniak, Apasara Wungpradit for valuable suggestions and comments. The material in this paper has been presented at Kyoto University, Kyushu University and Northwestern University. I would like to thank the participants of those meetings for their comments and discussions. Thanks are also due to the audience at JK16.

[1] Adjectives and copula have different 'non-past' forms as compared to verbs, for example, *tanosii/tanosikat-ta* ('pleasant': *i*-adjective), *kireida/kireidat-ta* ('beautiful': *na*-adjective) and (*gakusei*) *da/dat-ta* ('be (student)': copula). Some studies use the word '*ru*-form' as a cover term for these 'non-past' forms (Iwasaki 1994, Ka 2001), while others use 'basic form' (Masuoka and Takubo 1992). In the rest of this paper, I will adopt the former term, '*ru*-form', following Iwasaki (1994).

[2] In this paper, the following abbreviations are used: TOP topic marker, NOM nominative case marker, ACC accusative case marker, DAT dative case marker, GEN genitive case marker, PASS passive, NM nominalizer, COP copula.

(1) Ken-wa kinoo takusan tabe-**ru** *kara* onaka-ga itaku
    Ken-TOP *yesterday a.lot* eat-RU *because stomach*-NOM *sore*

    nar-**u** n da.
    become-RU NM COP
    'Because Ken ate a lot yesterday, he had a stomachache.'

In addition, (1) has another interesting property, that is, it has the connotation that the speaker is blaming Ken for his sore stomach.

Neither of the peculiarities exhibited by the above construction has been explained to date. The aim of this paper is to answer the following questions: first, how is it possible that the *ru*-forms in (1) refer to past events? Second, how does (1) get the connotation of 'blaming'? In the following sections, I examine knowledge speaker possess about the world at the time they utter sentences such as (1) and their felicity judgments about these sentences. Subsequently, I will look into the semantic and pragmatic processes involved in communication and interpretation that lead to the meaning yielded by (1).

The structure of the paper is as follows. In Section 2, I review the previous analyses and the basic properties of past *ru* sentences. In Section 3, I show that felicity of past *ru* sentences is affected by changes in the state of speaker's/hearer's knowledge. In Section 4, I propose a new analysis of past *ru* sentences. In Section 5, I explore the pragmatic processes through which past *ru* sentences get their specific blaming connotation. Section 6 summarizes the proposed analysis.

2. Previous Analyses

In this section, I review the previous studies on Japanese tense forms in complex clauses, especially causal sentences.

2.1. Relative Tense Studies

Japanese has two tense morphemes, *-ru* and *-ta*. *-Ru* is regarded as a 'non-past' marker and *-ta* as a 'past' marker.

In simple sentences, when *-ru* attaches to a non-stative verb, the sentence refers to a future event (2).[3]

(2) Boku-wa asita Kyoto-ni ik-**u**. 'I will go to Kyoto tomorrow.'
    I-TOP *tomorrow Kyoto*-to *go*-RU

---

[3] I will limit the discussion to sentences including non-stative predicates, because those with stative predicates show different properties from past *ru* sentences. It may be partly due to the fact that the 'non-past' forms of stative verbs refer to present states and not just to future states. For example:

  (i) a. Watasi-wa koogisitu-ni ir-**u**. 'I am in the lecture room.'
        I-TOP *lecture.room-in be*-RU

     b. Asita-wa kaigi-ga ar-**u**. 'There will be a conference tomorrow.'
        tomorrow-TOP *conference*-NOM *be*-RU

'Verb-*ta*', on the other hand, always refers to a past event.

(3) Kinoo   Kyoto-ni it-**ta**.   'I went to Kyoto yesterday.'
     yesterday Kyoto-to go-TA

However, in embedded clauses, the verbs to which -*ru* attaches can refer to past events as well.

(4) a. Kinoo-wa kaimono-ni ik-**u** *kara*   okane-o   orosi-**ta**.
        yesterday shopping-to go-RU *because money*-ACC *withdraw*-TA
        'Yesterday, I withdrew some money because I would go shopping.'
     b.*Kaimono-ni ik-**u**.
        Intended meaning: 'I went shopping.'

Many of the previous studies analyze examples like (4a) in terms of relative tense (Comrie 1985; Mihara 1991, Yoshimoto 1993, Nakamura 2001, among others). These studies claim that, when -*ru* attaches to the main verb of the embedded clause, the event stated in the main clause is prior to that of the embedded clause.

2.2. Tense forms in *Kara*-Sentences

Shen (1984) points out that, as for sentences containing the causal conjunctive *kara* (henceforth *kara*-sentences), the analyses in terms of relative tense do not always predict the correct interpretation of the time of the events described by the sentence.

Iwasaki (1994) argues that the analysis using the notion of relative tense does not apply to the two types of sentences illustrated in (5) and (1), reiterated here as (6).[4]

(5) Sensei-ga   okor-**u**   *kara,*   gakusei-wa sizukani si-**ta**.
     teacher-NOM *get.angry*-RU *because student*-TOP *quiet*   *do*-TA

                                    (Uno and Ikegami 2006:217 (a)[5])

(6) Ken-wa kinoo   takusan tabe-**ru** *kara*   onaka-ga   itaku
     Ken-TOP *yesterday a.lot*   *eat*-RU *because stomach*-NOM *sore*
     nar-**u**   n   da.
     become-RU NM COP

Although this study is mainly concerned with the latter type of sentences, the former one deserves a look from the viewpoint of Iwasaki's analysis as well. (5) allows both readings in (7).[6]

---

[4] Japanese has another causal conjunctive *node*, which can be used in (5), in the same way as *kara*. However, it is difficult to substitute *kara* with *node* in (6). This fact requires an explanation, but I leave it to further studies.

[5] This example is based on Iwasaki (1994:6 (25)).

[6] In what follows, I will use the notation '$e_1 < e_2$' to mean that 'an event e_1 temporally precedes

(7) a. 'Because the students expected that the teacher would get angry, they went quiet.'
       ^{ok} e$_{quiet}$ < e$_{angry}$ < UT
    b. 'Because the teacher got angry, the students went quiet.'
       ^{ok} e$_{angry}$ < e$_{quiet}$ < UT

The previous studies do not account for the interpretation (7b). If the *ru*-form in the embedded clause is decided by relative tense, getting angry by the teacher should follow getting quiet by the students(= (7a)).

Iwasaki (1994) argues that the sentences of the first type allow the interpretation in (7b) only if the event denoted by the subordinate clause (= e$_{sub}$) is observed from the viewpoint of the main clause's subject, i.e. the interpretation (7b) is available only to sentences that satisfy all the constraints listed in (8). [7]

(8) a. The verb in the *kara*-clause denotes an activity-like event.
    b. The subjects of the *kara*-clause and the main clause are different.
    c. The subject of the main clause is agentive.

On the other hand, this requirement does not apply to the sentences of the second type. Consider the following example. Although (9) does not meet some of the above constraints, it has the (7b)-like reading, i.e. e$_{sub}$ < e$_{main}$.[8]

(9) Anotoki aitu-ni   dea-u   *kara*   matiawase-ni   okure-**ta**
     then   the.person-DAT meet-RU because rendezvous-DAT be.late-TA
     n   da.
     NM COP
     'Because I met him/her at that time, I was late for the appointment.'

I want to point out three properties of causal sentences of (1). First, notice that the *ru*-form may refer to a past event not only in the subordinate clause, but also in the main clause. Moreover, changing either of the *-ru* markers to *-ta* marker does not change the meaning of the sentence. All of the following patterns are possible.

(1)   Ken-wa kinoo takusan tabe-**ru** *kara* onaka-ga itaku nar-**u** n da.

(1') a. Ken-wa kinoo takusan tabe-**ru** *kara* onaka-ga itaku nat-**ta** n da.
     b. Ken-wa kinoo takusan tabe-**ta** *kara* onaka-ga itaku nar-**u** n da.

No major differences have been observed among the three patterns. Thus, I will use the pattern indicated in (1) as a representative for all the three pat-

e$_2$.' 'UT < e$_1$' means 'the utterance time precedes e$_1$.'

[7] We do not go further into (5). For more detailed discussion, see Iwasaki (1994), Ka (2001), Kaminaka (2001) and Otsuka (2005). I wish to thank Mariko Otsuka for drawing my attention to these works.

[8] Example (9) is based on Iwasaki (1994:5 (20)), slightly modified.

terns. In the following, I will use the term 'past *ru-noda* sentences' to refer to sentences like (1).

The second feature is that past *ru-noda* sentences have a special blaming connotation. (1), for example, indicates that the speaker is blaming Ken, while (10) does not. Following Iwasaki (1994), I will call this connotation the Blaming Connotation (BC).

(1)   Ken-wa kinoo takusan tabe-**ru** *kara* onaka-ga itaku na-**ru** n da.
      ↝ Blaming Connotation: Ken should know that he should not eat so much.

(10) Ken-wa kinoo takusan tabe-**ta** *kara* onaka-ga itaku nat-**ta** n da.
      ↛ BC

Native speakers reject past *ru-noda* sentences that describe favorable events, thus I assume BC to be an indispensable feature of past *ru-noda* sentences.

(11) #Yamadasan-wa   sengetu   doroboo-o tukamae-**ru** *kara*
     Mr. Yamada-TOP *last.month thief*-ACC *catch*-RU   *because*
     keisatu-kara kansyazyoo-o   okura-re-**ru**   n   da.
     police-from testimonial-ACC *send*-PASS-RU NM COP
     'Because Mr. Yamada caught a thief last month, the police sent him a testimonial.'

The third property is that past *ru-noda* sentences require *n(o) da* (nominalizer + copula) in the main clauses.

(12) ??Ken-wa   kinoo   takusan tabe-**ru** *kara*   onaka-ga   itaku
     Ken-TOP *yesterday a.lot*   *eat*-RU *because stomach*-NOM *sore*
     nar-**u**.
     become-TA

To summarize, the properties of past *ru-noda* sentences are (i) how verb-*ru* forms can refer to past events (both in main and subordinate clauses) and (ii) why do past *ru-noda* sentences have the Blaming Connotation.

2.3. Previous Analyses of past *ru-noda* sentences

There are only few studies on past *ru-noda* sentences. The analyses presented in them can be divided into two types: the *generic* approach (Shen 1984, Otsuka 2005, Yukimatsu 2006[9]) and the *viewpoint* approach (Uno and Ikegami 2005).

The generic approach assumes that in the past *ru-noda* sentences the temporal features are suppressed by the logical and/or general causal relations. Thus, the past *ru-noda* sentences have been classified in those studies as

---

[9] The details of these analyses differ from each other. Shen (1984) regards *ru*-forms in past *ru-noda* sentences as *detensed*, Otsuka (2005) argues that they have generic or habitual tense, and Yukimatsu (2006) claims that tense forms 'transform' in past *ru-noda* sentences.

generic sentences. This generic meaning allows, according to those studies, the unusual interpretation of the *-ru/-ta* tense markers. However, this approach runs into difficulty with sentences like (1), which include the deictic temporal adverb (*kinoo* 'yesterday', *ototui* 'the day before yesterday', and so on).[10] The generic approach is even more problematic when we examine the felicity conditions of past *ru-noda* sentences. We will discuss this issue in the next section.

For these reasons, the viewpoint approach seems to be more appropriate than the generic approach. However, it is still unclear how the *viewpoint* works and connects *ru*-form with the Blaming Connotation. In my opinion, both approaches have the same flaw, that is, they try to connect the form to the connotation more or less directly. My proposal is to divide the process involved in the interpretation of these sentences into two stages: semantic and pragmatic. In the next section, I will introduce a notion of *foreseeability*, which in my opinion plays an important role in linking these stages.

3. Foreseeability and Felicity

In this section, I will demonstrate that the felicity of past *ru-noda* sentences is affected by the knowledge state. Past *ru-noda* sentences are infelicitous if we cannot foresee the occurrence of the event denoted by B from our knowledge prior to A's occurrence. Suppose the following scenario.

(13) **Snow White—Scenario A**
   1. Snow White dies.
   2. Wondering about the cause of her death, the dwarfs make an investigation.
   3. Then, they find that the apple she had eaten was poisoned.

In this scenario, the utterance (14) is infelicitous.

(14) *Sirayukihime-wa dokuringo-o   tabe-**ru** *kara*   sin-**u**   n
     Snow.White-TOP *poisoned.apple*-ACC *eat*-RU *because die*-RU NM
     da.
     COP
     'Because Snow White had eaten a poisoned apple, she died.'

On the other hand, the utterance of (14) is felicitous in Scenario B.

---

[10] Yukimatsu (2006) herself points out a similar problem.

(15) **Snow White—Scenario B**
1. Snow White buys an apple from a strange woman.
2. The dwarfs examine the apple.
3. They find that the apple was poisoned.
4. They tell Snow White about that.
5. Then, she eats the apple and dies.

What causes the difference in the felicity judgments? What one knows prior to Snow White's eating the apple plays a crucial role in his/her understanding of the sentence.[11] His/her state of knowledge is given in (16).

(16) Our knowledge just before SW's eating the apple
     = {If someone eats a poisoned apple, (s)he will die;
         SW is about to eat the apple; ... }
     ('The apple is poisoned' is *not* in the knowledge.)

Scenario A does not allow the inference indicated in (17). Therefore, the results of eating the apple by Snow White cannot be foreseen.

(17) SW is about to eat the apple.
     $\not\Rightarrow$ SW is about to eat a poisoned apple.

Next, consider Scenario B. The speaker/hearer's state of knowledge in Scenario B is presented in (18).

(18) Our knowledge just before SW's eating the apple
     = {If someone eats a poisoned apple, (s)he will die;
         The apple is poisoned;
         SW is about to eat the apple; ... }

Scenario B allows the inference in (19), hence Snow White's death can be foreseen based on our knowledge prior to her eating the apple.

(19) SW is about to eat the apple.
     $\Rightarrow$ SW is about to eat a poisoned apple.
     $\Rightarrow$ SW will die.

The difference between the felicity judgments of the sentences uttered in various contexts seems to be problematic within the generic approach. In both scenarios above, we know the *general* causal relation between 'eating a poisoned apple' and 'dying' throughout the scenario. Given that, the generic approach does not predict any discrepancy between Scenarios A and B.

Let us next look at the case in which we do not know the causal relation between e_{sub} and e_{main}, prior to the occurrence of e_{sub}.

---

[11] For the sake of simplicity, I limit the discussion to the cases where are no differences between knowledge states of the speaker, the hearer, the people talked about, and the other epistemic agents. If there are any gaps between their knowledge, the situation gets much more complicated.

(20)   Ano kanzya-wa kono kusuri-o painappuru-to issyoni nom-**u**
       That patient-TOP *this pill*-ACC *pineapple-with together drink*-RU

       kara   kaiyoo-ni nar-**u**   n   da.
       because ulcer-to   become-RU NM COP
       'Because the patient took this medicine with pineapple, she got an
       ulcer.'

The utterance in (20) is infelicitous in the following Scenario C, while it is
felicitous in Scenario D.

(21)   **Ulcer—Scenario C**
       1. A patient has a stomach ulcer.
       2. The patient tells the doctor that she took a pill and ate fruit
          cocktail (with apples, peaches and pineapples in it).
       3. The patient gets well soon, but the doctor doesn't know the
          cause.
       4. After one year of research, the doctor finds that the medicine can
          cause an ulcer when taken with pineapple.

(22)   **Ulcer—Scenario D**
       1. A doctor gives a pill to a patient.
       2. The doctor tells the patient not to take it with pineapple, because
          it can cause an ulcer.
       3. Despite doctor's direction, the patient takes the pill with
          pineapple and gets an ulcer.

(23) and (24) describe Scenario C. It is obvious that we *cannot* make the
inference indicated in (24) from our knowledge we have prior to the patient
taking the pill with pineapple (= (23)), because we do not know the causal
relation between taking the pill with pineapple and getting an ulcer.

(23)   Our knowledge just before the patient taking the pill
       = {The patient is about to take the pill with pineapple; ... }
       ('If someone takes the pill with pineapple, (s)he will get an ulcer.' is
       not in the knowledge.)

(24)   The patient is about to take the pill with pineapple.
       $\not\Rightarrow$ The patient will get an ulcer.

   The situation changes in Scenario D. Consider (25) and (26) illustrating
the state of our knowledge. We *can* make the inference in (26) and foresee the
result (getting an ulcer) prior to the patient's taking the pill with pineapple.

(25)   Our knowledge just before the patient's taking the pill
       = {If someone takes the pill with pineapple, (s)he will get an ulcer;
          The patient is about to take the pill with pineapple; ... }

(26) The patient is about to take the pill with pineapple.
   ⇒ The patient will get an ulcer.

In this section, I have shown that past *ru-noda* sentences are infelicitous if we cannot foresee the occurrence of the event denoted by B from our knowledge prior to A's occurrence. In order to account for the felicity condition of past *ru-noda* sentences, it is important to distinguish 'what was known in the past' from 'what is known now'. The viewpoint approach seems to have a simple way to do so, while the *generic* approach does not. In the next section, I will propose the analysis of past *ru-noda* sentences based on the viewpoint approach.

4. Semantics

In this section, I will propose the semantics of past *ru-noda* sentences based on its properties discussed above.

4.1. Foreseeability from a Viewpoint

In order to account for the felicity condition of past *ru-noda* sentences, we need some theoretical devices to handle the changes in the state of knowledge.

We assume that a viewpoint indicates the epistemic perspective.[12] The knowledge that affects interpretation of utterances depends on the person who is interpreting them and the time at which they are interpreted.[13] Hence a viewpoint can be determined by an epistemic agent EA and time t: $\langle EA, t \rangle$. Knowledge at a viewpoint $\langle EA, t \rangle$ can be defined as $K_{\langle EA, t \rangle}$, i.e. the set of propositions the EA knows to be true at the time t.

As I noted in the previous section, foreseeability plays a crucial role in felicity judgment of past *ru-noda* sentences. It is often suggested that a statement about the future is different from the one about the past (or present) by its nature. Statements about the past are usually interpreted according to only one world, that is, the actual world. On the other hand, statements about the future are intrinsically concerned with many worlds, associated with quantification over the worlds.[14]

I propose that *-ru* marks the a course of events that is *foreseeable* from a certain viewpoint, when it attaches to non-stative verbs. Therefore, *ru*-forms

---

[12] The analyses of epistemic modals in terms of points of assessment (Egan et al. 2005, Egan 2007, Stephenson 2005, among others) have much in common with my analysis proposed in this paper. For arguments against them, see von Fintel and Gillies 2006. I would like to thank Eric McCready for drawing my attention to these studies.

[13] Knowledge states may also differ depending on worlds. See (ii).

   (ii) If he had read today's newspaper, he would know about the accident.

However, as far as the purpose of this paper is concerned, worlds play little role, since causal sentences are always factual. For ease of presentation, worlds are suppressed in what follows.

[14] Kaufmann (2005) and Arita (2004) use the notion of *settledness* to grasp this distinction.

can be analyzed in terms of their modality.[15] Following Kratzer (1981, 1991), what is *foreseeable* from a viewpoint $\langle$EA,t$\rangle$ can be defined as follows:

(27) *Foreseeability*: P is *foreseeable* from the viewpoint $\langle$EA,t$\rangle$ iff
in every possible world w such that
    (i) w is compatible with K$_{\langle EA,t \rangle}$ (modal base), and
    (ii) w sufficiently conforms to the natural or planned course of
        events (ordering source),
  $\exists e.[P(e) \;\&\; t < e]$ is true.

Let us first apply (27) to a simple sentence. When a *ru*-form appears in a simple sentence, and functions as the main verb without a modal adverb, the event denoted by the sentence is understood as foreseeable from the speaker's viewpoint, given his/her will, plans, and/or knowledge at the utterance time.[16] For example, consider (2') and (28).

(2') [Boku-wa asita   Kyoto-ni ik-**u**]$_{\langle speaker,UT \rangle}$.
    I-TOP   *tomorrow Kyoto-to go*-RU
    '(According to my current plan,) I will go to Kyoto tomorrow.'

(28) [moosugu ame-ga   hur-**u**]$_{\langle speaker,UT \rangle}$.
    soon   *rain*-NOM *fall*-RU
    '(Based on the knowledge about the current weather,) it will rain
    soon.'

Applying (27) to (2'), we get the interpretation that 'In every world that is compatible with the speaker's knowledge, and conforms enough to the natural/planned course of event, the speaker's going to Kyoto will occur at some time in the future.' It seems to be the correct interpretation. The same applies to (28).

4.2. Shift of the Viewpoint

Let us return to (1). Given the definition of the *foreseeable* event, past *ru-noda* sentences are true only if there is a viewpoint prior to A's occurrence. Therefore, we need to shift the viewpoint from $\langle$speaker,UT$\rangle$ to somewhere else. However, in a main clause, the viewpoint cannot be shifted freely. Then, what shifts the viewpoint in (1)?

Previous studies argue that a viewpoint can be shifted in certain embedded environments.[17] Recall that the past *ru-noda* sentences are less acceptable

---

[15] However, there is some evidence which might prevent us from regarding the suffix *-ru* as a genuine modal element. I will leave the detailed discussion for further study.

[16] In English, the use of a present form in a simple sentence is more restricted than in Japanese (Vetter 1973, Kaufmann 2005, Kaufmann et al. 2006, among others).

[17] For example, in complement clauses of attitude verbs, in *because* clause (Iwasaki 1994, Tenny 2006, Uno and Ikegami 2005, Hara 2006), in relative clauses (Mihara 1991, Hirose 2001, Oshima

without *n(o) da* (nominalizer + copula) attached to the verb in the main clause. It is well-known that certain Japanese predicates of direct experience restrict their subject to first or second person. This person constraint does not apply to complement clauses of *n(o) da* (Kuroda 1973, Tenny 2006). Additionally, the time constraint is also lifted in the complement clauses of *n(o) da* (Higuchi 2001), see (29). Only if it occurs in the complement of *n(o) da*, the verb *waraidasu* (start.laughing) to which *-ru* attaches can refer to a past event.[18]

(29) (Sositara) Yamadasan-ga   kyuuni   waraidas-**u**   *(n da).
     then   Mr.Yamada*-NOM suddenly start.laughing-*RU NM COP
     '(Then,) suddenly Mr.Yamada started laughing.'

Therefore, I assume that *n(o) da* can shift the viewpoint.

4.3. Analysis

As the conjunctive *kara* 'because' plays a crucial role in the past *ru-noda* sentences, it has to be accounted for as well to construct the complete semantics for this sentences. I assume that a causal sentence 'Because P, Q' semantically corresponds to the conditional 'If P, then Q', except that 'Because P, Q' presupposes the truth of P (Sakahara 1985).

Past Reference *A-ru kara B-ru*

The viewpoints occurring in (1) are analyzed as (30).[19]

(30) [Ken-wa [[kinoo   takusan tabe-**ru**] *kara*   [onaka-ga   itaku
     Ken-*TOP yesterday a.lot   eat-*RU   *because* stomach-*NOM sore*
     nar-**u**]]$_{\langle EA,t \rangle}$ n   da]$_{\langle speaker,UT \rangle}$.
     *become-*RU NM COP
     $(t < e_{eat} < e_{stomachache} < UT)$

(30) presupposes that EA can foresee that 'Ken eats a lot' at t, and asserts that EA knows 'If Ken eats a lot, he will have a stomachache' at the time t. Therefore, it is foreseeable for EA that 'Ken has a stomachache'. Because of this presupposition, EA must be an epistemic agent who can foresee 'Ken eats a lot'. Since 'eat' is a volitional verb, Ken is most likely to be the EA. As a result, (1) is interpreted as saying that 'When Ken ate, Ken could foresee that he would have a stomachache'.[20]

2006, among many others), and in complement clauses of evidentials (Tenny 2006, Hara 2006). For general discussion, see Higuchi (2001) and the studies cited there.

[18] Here, we are talking about a case where (29) occurs in the reportive style (Kuroda 1973). The *ru*-form in (29) is regarded as *historical present*.

[19] I assume that EA is an undetermined epistemic agent. EA may be the speaker, the hearer, or some other person.

[20] (iii) and (iv) also have the Blaming Connotation.

   (iii) [Ken-wa [[kinoo takusan tabe-**ru**] kara [onaka-ga itaku nat-**ta**]]$_{\langle EA,t \rangle}$ n da]$_{\langle speaker,UT \rangle}$.

A-ta kara B-ta

As for *A-ta kara B-ta*, we need not shift the viewpoint, since both events are explicitly marked with past tense. The speaker at the UT would be considered to be the viewpoint (as a default).

(31) [Ken-wa [[kinoo takusan tabe-**ta**] kara [onaka-ga itaku nat-**ta**]]
⟨speaker,UT⟩ n da]⟨speaker,UT⟩.
(e$_{eat}$ < e$_{stomachache}$ < UT)

(31) presupposes that at UT, the speaker knows that 'Ken ate a lot', and asserts that at UT, the speaker knows that 'If Ken eats a lot, he will have a stomachache'. In contrast to (30), (31) says nothing about foreseeability of the events.

5. Pragmatics: Invited Inference and the Blaming Connotation

At this point, we have the semantics of past *ru-noda* sentences. Let us turn to the next question: how do we get the Blaming Connotation from this semantics?

According to Sakahara (1985), a causal statement 'Because P, Q' invites the inference that the corresponding counterfactual conditional is true. For example, if one utters (1) or (31), we infer that (32) is also true.

(1) Ken-wa kinoo   takusan tabe-**ru** *kara*   onaka-ga   itaku
     Ken-TOP *yesterday a.lot*   *eat*-RU *because stomach*-NOM *sore*
     nar-**u**   n   da.   (↝ BC)
     become-RU NM COP

(31) Ken-wa kinoo   takusan tabe-**ta** *kara*   onaka-ga   itaku
     Ken-TOP *yesterday a.lot*   *eat*-RU *because stomach*-NOM *sore*
     nat-**ta**   n   da.   (↝̸ BC)
     become-RU NM COP
     'Because Ken ate a lot yesterday, he had a stomachache.'

(32) If Ken had not eaten a lot yesterday, he would not have had a
     stomachache.

It is observed that the events stated in counterfactual conditionals tend to be regarded as desirable. In order to account for this, Akatsuka (1997) proposes the Desirability Hypothesis. In her theory, the DESIRABLE / UNDESIRABLE meaning component plays an important role in understanding conditional reasoning, that is, the desirability of the antecedent and consequent must be the same.

(iv) [Ken-wa [[kinoo takusan tabe-**ta**] kara [onaka-ga itaku nar-**u**]]⟨EA,t⟩ n da]⟨speaker,UT⟩.
The same analysis as in (30) comes along for (iii), but not for (iv), because in (iv) the antecedent is marked by *-ta*. In that case, (iv) does not presuppose that EA can foresee Ken's eating a lot, and that EA might not foresee the consequence. For now, I have no solution to this problem.

Akatsuka's theory is noteworthy, since undesirability and BC seems to be closely related. However, a puzzle remains, namely, in the case of counterfactual conditionals, the antecedent and the consequent can be UNDESIRABLE (33), as well as DESIRABLE (32).

(33) If Naomi had not read that book yesterday, she would have failed the exam.

However, as I have noted above, the antecedent and the consequent cannot be a desirable event in past *ru-noda* sentences.

(34) Naomi-wa   ano hon-o   kinoo   yo-{$^{\#}$**mu** / ^{ok}nda} *kara*
       Naomi-TOP *that book-ACC yesterday read-RU/TA   because*
       siken-ni uka-{$^{\#}$**ru** / ^{ok}tta} n   da.
       exam-at pass-RU/TA   NM COP
       'Because Naomi read that book yesterday, she passed the exam.'

Why do the events have to be undesirable in the past *ru-noda* sentences? Recall that the difference between (1) and (31) is that, in (1), the shifted viewpoint is located at the time prior to the event of the antecedent/consequent. From that viewpoint, the events have not yet occurred, and there are various possible courses of events other than the 'actual' one. This property of (1) may cause BC. However, it is still unclear why (1) is only used to refer to undesirable events.[21]

We shall conclude this section with a tentative analysis of the process in which (1) yields BC.

1. By the semantics of (1), we have (35).
   (35) Ken knew 'if I (= Ken) eat a lot, I will have a stomachache' before he ate a lot.
2. (1) invites the inference that (32) is true.
   (32) If Ken had not eaten a lot yesterday, he would not have had a stomachache.
3. By some pragmatic rule, (32) is understood as desirable.
4. By virtue of 1, Ken can foresee the undesirable result of getting a stomachache prior to eating a lot.
5. ⤳ Ken could have chosen the desirable way.
6. ⤳ Blaming Connotation

---

[21] Fauconnier (1997:14) proposes pragmatic default principle P_1 (egocentric attribution): the speaker's behavior and dispositions in an imaginary situation are construed as desirable. For example, (v) would often entail a criticism of the father, because of P_1.

(v) If I were your father, I would spank you. (Fauconnier ibid.:14)

A similar rule seems to exist and may be responsible for the Blaming Connotation. P_1, however, cannot be directly applied to (1) because (1) says nothing about the speaker.

6. Conclusion

In this paper, I have shown that *foreseeability* affects the felicity of past *ru-noda* sentences. Based on this fact, I propose the following conclusions:

(i) In past *ru-noda* sentences, the viewpoint is shifted to the past. Hence, *ru*-forms may refer to past events.

(ii) Blaming Connotation is obtained in two steps: the semantics of the causal sentences and the pragmatic inferences.

References

Akatsuka, N. 1997. Towards a Theory of Desirability in Conditional Reasoning. *Japanese/Korean Linguistics* 6:41–58. Palo Alto: CSLI.

Arita, S. 2004. (Hu)kanzen Zisei Setu to Nihongo Zyookenbun ((In)complete Tensed Clauses and Conditionals in Japanese). Doctoral Dissertation, Kyoto University.

Comrie, B. 1985. *Tense*. Cambridge: Cambridge University Press.

Egan, A. 2007. Epistemic Modals, Relativism and Assertion. *Philosophical Studies* 133(1):1–22.

Egan, A., J. Hawthorne and B. Weatherson. 2005. Epistemic Modals in Context. *Contextualism in Philosophy : Knowledge, Meaning, and Truth*, eds. Gerhard Preyer and Georg Peter, 131–170. Oxford: Oxford University Press.

Fauconnier, G. 1997. *Mappings in Thought and Language*. Cambridge: Cambridge University Press.

von Fintel, K. and A. S. Gillies. 2006. CIA Leaks. ms, MIT and University of Michigan. (http://mit.edu/fintel/www/cia_leaks.pdf)

Hara, Y. 2006. Grammar of Knowledge Representation: Japanese Discourse Items at Interfaces. Doctoral Dissertation, University of Delaware.

Higuchi, M. 2001. Nihongo no Zisei Hyoogen to Zitai Ninti Siten (Tenses in Japanese, Viewpoint and the Speech Time). *Kyuushuu Koogyoo Daigaku Koogakubu Kiyoo: Ningen Kagaku-hen* 14:53–81.

Iwasaki, T. 1994. *Node*-setu, *Kara*-setsu no Tense ni Tuite (On tense in *node*-clause and *kara*-clause). *Kokugogaku* 179:114–103.

Ka, C. 2001. *Kara/node*-setutyuu no Zyutugo no 'Doozigata *Suru*-kei' (Simultaneous-type *suru*-forms in *kara/node* sentences). *Nihongo to Nihon bungaku* 2:67–84.

Kaminaka, S. *Node*-setu, *Kara*-setu no *Ru*-kei to *Ta*-kei ni Tuite (On *Ru*-forms and *Ta*-forms in *Node*-clause and *Kara*-clause). *Nihongo to Nihon bungaku* 2:31–44.

Kaufmann, S. 2005. Conditional truth and future reference. *Journal of Semantics* 22:231–280.

Kaufmann, S., C. Condoravdi, and V. Harizanov. 2006. Formal approach to modality. *The Expression of Modality*, ed. W. Frawley, 71–106. Berlin: Mouton de Gruyter.

Kratzer, A. 1981. The notional category of modality. *Words, Worlds, and Contexts: New Approaches to Word Semantics*, eds. Eickmeyer, H.-J. and H. Rieser, 163–201. Berlin: Walter de Gruyter.

Kratzer, A. 1991. Modality/Conditionals. *Semantik: Ein Internationales Handbuch der Zeitgenössischen Forschung* (Semantics: An International Handbook of Contemporary Research). 639–650/651–656. Berlin: Walter de Gruyter.

Kuroda, S.-Y. 1973. Where Epistemology, Style, and Grammar Meet: A Case Study from Japanese. *A Festschrift for Morris Halle*, eds. Anderson, S. and P. Kiparsky, 377–391. New York: Holt, Rinehart and Winston.

Masuoka, T. and Y. Takubo. 1992. *Kiso Nihongo Bunpoo* (Basic Japanese Grammar). Tokyo: Kurosio Syuppan.

Mihara, K. 1991. 'Siten no Genri' to Zyuuzokusetu Zisei ('Principle of Perspective' and Tense in Subordinate Clauses). *Nihongogaku* 3: 64–77.

Nakamura, C. 2001. *Nihongo no Zikan Hyoogen* (Temporal Expressions in Japanese). Tokyo: Kurosio Syuppan.

Oshima, D. Y. 2006. Perspective, Logophoricty, and Embedded Tense in Japanese. Presentation at Japanese/Korean Linguistics 16.

Otsuka, M. 2005. Riyuubun no Zisei Kaisyaku to Siten (Interpretation of Tense in Causal Sentences). Kin3 Roundtable handout.

Sakahara, S. 1985. *Nitizyo Gengo no Suiron* (*Inference in Ordinary Language*). Tokyo: University of Tokyo Press.

Shen, M. 1984.Hukugoo Bun no Setuzoku Zyosi de Kukuru Setu no Zyutugo no Tensu: '*Suru ga*' to '*Sita ga*', '*Suru node*' to '*Sita node*' Nado (Tense of Predicate in Subordinate Clause of Complex Sentence: '*Suru ga*' vs. '*Sita ga*', '*Suru node*' vs. '*Sita node*' etc). *Gogaku Kyooiku Kenkyuu Ronsoo* 1:22–122

Stephenson, T. 2005. Assessor Sensitivity: Epistemic Modals and Predicates of Personal Taste. *New Work on Modality: MIT Working Papers in Linguistics 51*, eds. Gajewski, J., V. Hacquard, B. Nickel and S. Yalcin, 179–206.

Tenny, C. L. 2006. Evidentiality, Experiencers, and the Syntax of Sentience in Japanese. *Journal of East Asian Linguistics* 13:245–288

Uno, R. W. and T. Ikegami 2006. Siten to Zikan: *Kara*-setu no Tensu no Bunseki (Perspectives and tense in Japanese causal clauses). *Proceedings of the 6th Annual Meeting of the Japanese Congnitive Linguistics Association* 6:215–223.

Vetter, D. 1973. Someone Solves This Problem Tomorrow. *Linguistic Inquiry* 4:104–108.

Yukimatsu, H. 2006. '*Noda*'-bun ni Okeru Tensu-Asupekuto no Hen'yoo (Transformation of Tense-Aspect Systems in Japanese Sentences Marked by '*NODA*'). *Nihongo Bunpoo* 6(2):79–97.

Yoshimoto, K. 1993. Nihongo-no Bun Kaisoo Koozoo to Syudai, Syooten, Zisei (Topic, Focus, and Tense in Japanese Syntactic Hierarchy). *Gengo Kenkyuu* 103:141–166.

Index

abstract deixis, 266, 269
accessibility to the content of talk, 259
acquisition, 171, 176
actions
  lexical _, 380
  pragmatic _, 380, 381
adjacency pair, 238, 240
adjoined
  _ to the (an) NP, 88, 90, 91
  _ to the following sentence, 88, 89, 98
adjunct, 427, 428, 430
administrative style, 30-34, 36
affected(ness), 423, 424, 427, 430-433
agency, 340, 341
ageru, 319-323, 326
anti-faithfulness, 217, 222-229
apposition, 92, 94-97, 100
argument-licensing, 425

Biànwén [變文], 27–29, 34
bound pronoun, 425

canonical, 324
causal variable, 367, 371, 372, 374
causative (verb), 51-55, 167-170
CCG, 379
characteristic (characterizing) property, 69, 71, 74
child language, 163, 164, 169, 170, 176
Chinese writing system, 26

cleft, 362-367, 374
coherence, 268, 277
cohesion, 266, 269, 274, 276, 277
compensation effects, 179
complementation, 148
compound, 193, 196
conceptual metonymy, 267, 270, 272, 274-276
concrete deixis, 266
condition (C) of the Binding theory, 48, 49, 61
conduit metaphor, 271, 274
continuous prosody, 259
corpus, 319-322, 327
cross-linguistic pattern of the V-to-V coarticulation, 179

definiteness effect, 3-8, 10-15, 17-20, 22, 23
degree abstraction, 412, 414, 417, 418
deletion, 347, 348, 351-355, 357-359
delimiter, 138-140
deontic, 335, 337-340
direct phrasal analysis, 408, 415, 416, 418, 419
direct(ly) translated style, 30-34, 39
Discourse representation theory, 462
double past (Korean), 455
dynamic semantics, 469, 478

epistemic, 335, 340, 342
EPP, 44-46, 49, 50, 53-59, 62
evaluative, 335, 340-342

event, 365-371, 423, 424, 427, 430, 431
existential
_ sentence, 6, 8, 11-13, 17, 19, 23
_ transform, 7, 8, 10-15, 20-23
external possession, 422-425, 428-430, 433

F_0
_-boosting, 440-444
_-compression, 440-445
_-reset, 440, 441, 443, 444
felicity, 497, 501, 502, 504, 508
floating quantifier, 429
focus, 67-69, 71, 363, 365, 367-375
_ intonation prosody (FIP), 438, 440-447
foreseeable (foreseeability), 501, 504-507, 509
formal noun, 330, 332, 333
fragment completion test, 387
fujūbun shūshi (incomplete conclusiveness), 89
function composition, 429

generalized quantifier, 366
generic approach, 500–502
gesture, 166, 176, 265-277
giving, 319, 322-324, 326, 327
grammatical subject (GS), 70, 71, 77
grammaticalization, 285,
grammaticalized, 330, 334, 342
Gǔwén [古文], 26-29, 31, 34, 35, 40

Hànéryányǔ [漢兒言語], 29-36, 39, 40
Hanliwen [漢吏文], 29, 32, 34-40
hata, 165, 168, 169
head-external (HE) existential transform, 10, 11, 13

head-internal (HI)
_ existential transform, 12, 14, 20-22
_ existential transform with a FQ, 12, 20, 21
honorification, 353, 354
HPSG, 379

iconic(ity), 164-167, 169, 172, 174-176
ideophones, 217-223, 225, 226, 228, 229
image schema, 290-292, 294, 302
Imun [吏文], 29, 34, 36-40
inalienable possessive construction, 423
incremental, 379, 380, 383, 384, 390
indeterminate (pronouns), 132, 139
indexical, 484-486, 489, 490
intersective determiners, 4, 5, 14-16, 18, 22, 24
intersubjectification, 112, 280, 285, 286
intervention effect, 371, 372
intonational phrase boundary, 384, 385
Invited inferencing theory, 104, 111-113
island effects, 141-143, 410, 412, 413, 419
Itumun [吏讀文], 28, 36-40

Japanese, 193, 194, 197, 198, 200, 201

kakari musubi (KM), 116-121, 123, 124
-kelita, 165, 168-170
kes-ita, 280-286
Korean, 194, 196-201
koto, 148, 332-336
kotoda, 333-335

Ku-gohō, 126, 128
kureru, 319-323, 326

language of scholarity and literature, 27
language socialization, 236, 238
LFG, 379, 382
light verb construction (Italian), 433
linearization, 355
listener honorifier, 109, 110
locality, 382, 389
logophoric, 484–486, 489, 490
long distance dependency, 381, 382
long form negation, 305

major subject (MS), 70, 71, 74, 78, 79
  _-sentential predicate partition/articulation, 71, 74, 79
metaphorical, 332, 338, 340-342
  _ extension, 111
metonymical, 332, 338, 342
mimetic, 163-176
modal/modality, 329-334, 336-338, 342
mono, 329-342
mon(o)da, 331, 333-341
morau, 319-323, 326
morpho-syntactic and phonological resources, 253
movement (WH-), 143, 144
MSC
  adjunct-type _, 72, 74, 75
  focus-type _, 72
  possessor-type _, 72-75
multi-dominance (MD), 347-353, 355-357, 359
multiple accusative construction, 423

narratives, 456, 458, 461

negation, 146-148, 150-158, 304-307, 310-312, 314-317
negative
  _ interrogative 306-310, 313, 315-317
  _ island, 412, 413
negative polarity item (NPI)
  left peripheral, 377, 384, 386, 388
  right peripheral _, 378
  strongest _, 377, 384
new, 325, 326
  _ information, 467, 468, 475, 478, 479
Nishigauchi, 143
noda, 122, 123, 279-286
nominalized
  _ negation, 305
  _ predicate, 334-338
nominalizers, 116, 117, 121-128
nonconcatenative morphology, 219
nonlinguistic resources, 258, 263
null Q, 143

Okinawan (Ok), 117-128
Old Japanese, 146
omoiyari (empathy), 242
Optimality theory (OT), 217, 223
origo, 265

partial listing, 93-98, 100
participant, 430, 431
  _ external, 113
  _ internal, 113
participation framework, 262, 263
particles, 466, 467, 472–475, 477–480
passive verb, 53, 55-57
passivization, 168
performance, 379, 380
perspective, 487, 489–492

phase, 54, 57
phenomime, 164-166, 172-174
phonological phrase, 193, 194, 196-201
phonomime, 164-166, 172-174
pivot, 79-81
plain sentence, 9-15, 17-19, 21, 23
pluperfect, 455, 458
polite, 235, 240, 241, 245
possessive accusative construction, 423
possessor, 422-434
  _ ascension, 72, 73
pragmatic implicature, 338, 339
prefix, 193, 194, 196-201
presupposition, 154, 157
pro, 426-428, 433, 434
projection of turn, 252
prominent argument, 69, 79-81
pronoun, 489, 490
proposition denial, 154, 155, 158
propositional attitude, 332, 335
prosodic constituency, 357, 359
prosody-scope correspondence (PSC), 438, 441-445
psychomime, 164-166, 171-174
Pusan Korean, 194, 196-200

Q-float, 9,10
Q-particle, 131-134, 137-144

realis, 323, 327
reanalysis, 137-141, 329, 341, 342
reassociation, 424-428, 430, 433
receiving, 319, 322-324, 326, 327
reconstruction, 47
reduced clausal analysis, 408, 418, 419
reference point, 268
relevance, 469–475, 477–479

repetition, 238
request, 238, 239, 243-245
resultative predicate, 429
right node raising (RNR), 347-349, 351, 352, 354, 355, 357-359
ru-form, 496, 497, 499–501, 504–506, 509

scope, 45-47, 49, 59, 62, 146, 147, 150-154, 156-158
scrambling, 44-50, 53-57, 59-63, 372, 373
  local _, 382–384
  long distance _, 382
Sejong Corpus, 104, 389
sentence final, 88, 91
sentential predicate (SP), 70, 71, 80
short form negation, 304
shūshi/rentai distinction, 117
sign
  _-based approach, 305
  _ language, 266
Sino-Korean, 194, 196, 197, 200
sound symbolism, 164, 176
speaker
  _-listener(-oriented honorific)marker, 103, 104, 107, 108, 112
  _-object (honorific) marker, 103, 105, 107, 108
  _'s vantage point, 106
stative predicate, 432
structural underspecification, 381
subject, 49-55, 57
  _ (subjecthood) diagnostics, 76
  _ honorification, 76-81
  _ properties, 65, 66, 76, 77, 79, 81
  _ to object raising (SOR), 77-79
subjectification, 112, 280, 285
  _ theory, 111

subjectivity, 311-317
suru, 164-166, 168-171, 175
syntax/phonology interfaces, 379

Yāyàn [雅言], 27, 30

tasi (again), 427
te, 251
tense
  anaphoric (nature of) _, 457, 458
  deictic (use of) _, 456, 458
  independent interpretation, 486, 487
  relative _, 491, 493
  relative (_) interpretation, 486, 487, 493
textual function, 281, 282, 285, 286
theme, 59, 60, 62
there transform, 6-8,14,15
theta(θ)
  _-Criterion, 425
  _-identification, 429, 430
  _-roles, 424, 425, 431,433
Tōngyǔ [通語], 27, 29, 30
topic, 66-71
  _-comment construction, 334, 336, 339
total listing, 93–97, 100
transitive, 167-169, 174, 175
turn co-construction, 250

unaccusative (verb), 52, 53, 56, 57
unselective binding, 143, 144
Utility theory, 471

verb of contact and impact, 168, 170
viewpoint, 499–501, 504–509
  _ approach, 501, 504
vowel
  _ contrast, 178
  _ harmony, 217, 219, 229
  _ lengthening, 387

Japanese/Korean Linguistics at CSLI Publications

16 volumes of *Japanese/Korean Linguistics* have been published since 1990 with over 400 articles. All volumes remain in print and a cumulative table of contents for the entire series may be found at

http://cslipublications.stanford.edu/ja-ko-contents/jako-collective-toc.html

where articles are grouped by the following subject categories:

Phonetics and Phonology
Syntax and Morphology
Semantics
Pragmatics, Discourse and Conversation
Psycholinguistics and Cognition
L1 and L2 Acquisition
Historical Linguistics, Language Change and Grammaticalization
Sociolinguistics and Language Use

For more information on other volumes in this series, please visit

http://cslipublications.stanford.edu/site/JAKO.html

Recent previous volumes:

Japanese/Korean Linguistics, Vol. 15	Naomi Hanaoka McGloin and Junko Mori, editors
Japanese/Korean Linguistics, Vol. 14	Timothy J. Vance and Kimberly Jones, editors
Japanese/Korean Linguistics, Vol. 13	Mutsuko Endo Hudson, Sun-Ah Jun, Peter Sells, Patricia M. Clancy, Shoichi Iwasaki and Sung-Ock Sohn, editors
Japanese/Korean Linguistics, Vol. 12	William McClure, editor
Japanese/Korean Linguistics, Vol. 11	Patricia M. Clancy, editor
Japanese/Korean Linguistics, Vol. 10	Noriko Akatsuka, Susan Strauss, and Bernard Comrie, editors
Japanese/Korean Linguistics, Vol. 9	Mineharu Nakayama and Charles J. Quinn, Jr., editors
Japanese/Korean Linguistics, Vol. 8	David James Silva, editor
Japanese/Korean Linguistics, Vol. 7	Noriko Akatsuka, Hajime Hoji, Shoichi Iwasaki, Sung-Ock Sohn, and Susan Strauss, editors
Japanese/Korean Linguistics, Vol. 6	Ho-min Sohn and John Haig, editors